Lecture Notes in Computer Science 11821

More information about this series at http://www.springer.com/series/7410

Ron Steinfeld · Tsz Hon Yuen (Eds.)

Provable Security

13th International Conference, ProvSec 2019
Cairns, QLD, Australia, October 1–4, 2019
Proceedings

Editors
Ron Steinfeld (iD)
Monash University
Melbourne, VIC, Australia

Tsz Hon Yuen (iD)
The University of Hong Kong
Pok Fu Lam, Hong Kong

ISSN 0302-9743   ISSN 1611-3349 (electronic)
Lecture Notes in Computer Science
ISBN 978-3-030-31918-2   ISBN 978-3-030-31919-9 (eBook)
https://doi.org/10.1007/978-3-030-31919-9

LNCS Sublibrary: SL4 – Security and Cryptology

This Springer imprint is published by the registered company Springer Nature Switzerland AG
The registered company address is: Gewerbestrasse 11, 6330 Cham, Switzerland

Preface

This volume contains the papers presented at ProvSec 2019: the 13th International Conference on Provable and Practical Security held during October 1–4, 2019, in Cairns, Australia.

There were 51 submissions. Each submission was reviewed by at least two Program Committee members. The committee decided to accept 18 full papers and 6 short papers.

Provable security is an essential tool for analyzing the security of modern cryptographic primitives. The research community has witnessed the great contributions that the provable security methodology made to the analysis of cryptographic schemes and protocols. Today, cryptographic primitives without a rigorous "proof" cannot be regarded as sound. Also, the methodology has been used to discover security flaws in the cryptographic schemes and protocols, which were considered seemingly secure without formal analysis. On the one hand, provable security provides confidence in using cryptographic schemes and protocols for various real-world applications, but on the other hand, schemes with provable security are sometimes not efficient enough to be used in practice, and correctness of the proofs may be difficult to verify.

Therefore, this year we decided to enrich the scope of this conference, by adding "Practical Security" to the theme. The new theme brought together researchers and practitioners to provide a confluence of new practical cyber security technologies, including their applications and their integration with IT systems in various industrial sectors.

We would like to thank the general co-chairs, Joseph K. Liu and Wei Xiang, the publication chair, Jiangshan Yu, and the publicity co-chairs, Xingliang Yuan and Yu Wang, for organizing the conference.

October 2019   Ron Steinfeld
                                                                                Tsz Hon Yuen

Organization

Program Committee

Elena Andreeva	Katholieke Universiteit Leuven, Belgium
Man Ho Au	The Hong Kong Polytechnic University, SAR China
Joonsang Baek	University of Wollongong, Australia
Donghoon Chang	NIST, USA
Jie Chen	East China Normal University, China
Liqun Chen	University of Surrey, UK
Xiaofeng Chen	Xidian University, China
Cheng-Kang Chu	Huawei Singapore, Singapore
Bernardo David	The University of Tokyo, Japan
Keita Emura	National Institute of Information and Communications Technology, Japan
Zekeriya Erkin	Delft University of Technology, The Netherlands
Jinguang Han	Queen's University Belfast, UK
Xinyi Huang	Fujian Normal University, China
Ryo Kikuchi	NTT, Japan
Jongkil Kim	University of Wollongong, Australia
Veronika Kuchta	Monash University, Australia
Jianchang Lai	University of Wollongong, Australia
Hyung Tae Lee	Chonbuk National University, South Korea
Jooyoung Lee	Korea Advanced Institute of Science and Technology, South Korea
Kaitai Liang	University of Surrey, UK
Joseph Liu	Monash University, Australia
Rongxing Lu	University of New Brunswick, Canada
Xiapu Luo	The Hong Kong Polytechnic University, SAR China
Siqi Ma	CSIRO, Australia
Bernardo Magri	Aarhus University, Denmark
Barbara Masucci	University of Salerno, Italy
Bart Mennink	Digital Security Group, Radboud University, Nijmegen, The Netherlands
Chris Mitchell	Royal Holloway, University of London, UK
Kirill Morozov	University of North Texas, USA
Abderrahmane Nitaj	LMNO, Université de Caen, France
Raphael Phan	Monash University, Australia
Josef Pieprzyk	CSIRO, Australia
Kouichi Sakurai	Kyushu University, Japan
Ron Steinfeld	Monash University, Australia
Rainer Steinwandt	Florida Atlantic University, USA

Chunhua Su	University of Aizu, Japan
Shi-Feng Sun	Shanghai Jiao Tong University, China
Willy Susilo	University of Wollongong, Australia
Katsuyuki Takashima	Mitsubishi Electric, Japan
Atsushi Takayasu	The University of Tokyo, Japan
Qiang Tang	New Jersey Institute of Technology, USA
Dongvu Tonien	University of Wollongong, Australia
Damien Vergnaud	Université Pierre et Marie Curie/Institut Universitaire de France, France
Sheng Wen	Swinburne University of Technology, Australia
Qianhong Wu	Beihang University, China
Chung-Huang Yang	National Kaohsiung Normal University, Taiwan
Guomin Yang	University of Wollongong, Australia
Wun-She Yap	Universiti Tunku Abdul Rahman, Malaysia
Xun Yi	RMIT University, Australia
Yong Yu	University of Science and Technology of China, China
Xingliang Yuan	Monash University, Australia
Tsz Hon Yuen	The University of Hong Kong, SAR China
Aaram Yun	University of Minnesota, USA

Additional Reviewers

Anada, Hiroaki	Roy, Arnab
Chen, Haixia	Roy, Dibyendu
Chengjun Lin	Ueshige, Yoshifumi
Datta, Pratish	Wang, Luping
Erson, Oguzhan	Wu, Lei
Ersoy, Oguzhan	Yang, Wenjie
Garg, Surabhi	Zeng, Ming
Hesamifard, Ehsan	Zeng, Yali
Ikematsu, Yasuhiko	Zhao, Hang
Lai, Shangqi	Zhao, Qian
Li, Na	Zhen, Haibin
Liu, Jianghua	Zhu, Fei
Nguyen, Khoa	Zhu, Yan
Ohata, Satsuya	

Contents

Post-quantum Cryptography

Identity-Concealed Authenticated Encryption from Ring Learning with Errors

Chao Liu[1], Zhongxiang Zheng[2], Keting Jia[2(✉)], and Limin Tao[3]

[1] Key Laboratory of Cryptologic Technology and Information Security,
Ministry of Education, Shandong University, Jinan, People's Republic of China
`liu_chao@mail.sdu.edu.cn`
[2] Department of Computer Science and Technology, Tsinghua University,
Beijing, People's Republic of China
`zhengzx13@mails.tsinghua.edu.cn`, `ktjia@mail.tsinghua.edu.cn`
[3] Space Star Technology Co., LTD., Beijing, People's Republic of China

Abstract. *Authenticated encryption* (AE) is very suitable for a resources constrained environment for it needs less computational costs and AE has become one of the important technologies of modern communication security. *Identity concealment* is one of research focuses in design and analysis of current secure transport protocols (such as TLS1.3 and Google's QUIC). In this paper, we present a provably secure identity-concealed authenticated encryption in the public-key setting over ideal lattices, referred to as RLWE-ICAE. Our scheme can be regarded as a parallel extension of higncryption scheme proposed by Zhao (CCS 2016), but in the lattice-based setting. RLWE-ICAE can be viewed as a monolithic integration of public-key encryption, key agreement over ideal lattices, identity concealment and digital signature. The security of RLWE-ICAE is directly relied on the Ring Learning with Errors (RLWE) assumption. Two concrete choices of parameters are provided in the end.

Keywords: Authenticated encryption · RLWE · Lattice-based · Identity-concealed · Provable security

1 Introduction

Authenticated encryption (AE) is a form of encryption that guarantees the confidentiality and authenticity of data at the same time. Because AE can sign and encrypt messages in single step, the computational cost of it is lower than that of traditional signature-then-encryption methods. Some works also shows that AE is functionally equivalent to one-pass authenticated key-exchange [7,11,19]. Since Zheng proposed the first AE scheme [29] in 1997, it has become one of the important technologies of modern communication security.

By *identity concealment*, we mean that the protocol transcript shouldn't leak participants' identity information. ID concealment is relevant for several reasons.

© Springer Nature Switzerland AG 2019
R. Steinfeld and T. H. Yuen (Eds.): ProvSec 2019, LNCS 11821, pp. 3–18, 2019.
https://doi.org/10.1007/978-3-030-31919-9_1

For instance, if the identity is not protected in a wireless device, an attacker can eavesdrop the communications to track the user's location, which leads to attacks directed towards selected users. Identity concealment is mandated or recommended by many standardized and deployed cryptographic protocols like TLS1.3 [22], QUIC [24], EMV [5], etc. Furthermore, we say that a player enjoys *forward ID-privacy* if his ID-privacy preserves even through his static secret-key is compromised. For some famous protocols such as Zheng's signcryption [3,29] and one-pass HMQV (HOMQV) [12,14], the issue of ID-concealment was not considered. In 2016, Zhao [28] introduced that ID-concealment can be integrated with AE to solve the problem of *0-RTT (zero-round trip time) with client authentication*. A *0-RTT option* protocol allows the establishment of a secure connection in "one-shot", which means that cryptographically protected payload data can be sent immediately along with the first single message sent from a sender to a receiver, without the need for a latency-incurring prior handshake protocol. Many large projects have been developed and experimented with 0-RTT protocols, such as Google's QUIC [15], TLS1.3 and Facebook' Zero protocols [13]. But QUIC and TLS1.3 are now only supporting 0-RTT mode *without* client authentication. Zhao proposed higncryption [28] which solved the problem of 0-RTT with client authentication by integrating public-key encryption, entity authentication and ID-concealment into a single primitive.

Some other properties are considered in nowadays public-key settings. A protocol enjoys *"receiver deniability"*, which means that the session transcript, especially the authentication value, can be simulated by a receiver with public parameters and his own secret-key. A protocol enjoys *x-security* [12], which means that the leakage of ephemeral secret does not cause the exposure of sender's static secret or pre-shared secret. For some well-known protocols, Zheng's signcryption [3,29] does not enjoy x-security and is receiver undeniable. Krawczyk's one-pass HMQV (HOMQV) [12] scheme enjoys receiver deniability and x-security, but without forward ID-privacy. Zhao's higncryption [28] has a novel design, and enjoys forward ID-privacy, receiver deniability and x-security.

But above existed authenticated encryptions are mainly based on the classic hard problems, such as the computational/decisional DH problem. It is well known that DH problem is vulnerable to quantum computers [25]. Since the rapid development of quantum computers, searching other counterparts based on problems which are believed to be resistant to quantum attacks is more and more urgent. Naturally we think of such a question: can we come up with an authenticated encryption that can resist quantum attacks and enjoys above several good properties such as ID-concealment, receiver deniability and x-security? Note that lattice-based cryptographic schemes have many advantages such as asymptotic efficiency, conceptual simplicity and worst-case hardness assumption, and it is a perfect choice to build lattice-based authenticated encryption in the public-key settings.

Our Contributions. In this paper, we propose a new authenticated encryption to solve the above motivating questions. We choose Ring Learning With Errors (RLWE), which is as hard as some worst case lattice problems on ideal lattices

[10, 18] to construct our scheme. By utilizing some useful properties of RLWE and discrete Gaussian distributions, we present an approach to combine public/secret key in a manner similar to higncryption [28]. Our scheme not only enjoys many nice properties of higncryption such as identity concealment, 0-RTT option, forward ID-privacy, receiver deniability and x-security, but also enjoys some properties of lattice-based cryptography, such as worst-case hardness assumption, and resistance to quantum computer attacks. We manage to establish a full proof of our scheme' security in the Zhao's strong model [28] by replacing the Diffie-Hellman core of Zhao's model with the lattice-based core. Our scheme may have some other applications. For example we give a direct application of one-pass ID-concealed authenticated key exchange protocol. In the end, we choose the concrete parameters and give the security assessment.

Techniques in Our Scheme. In higncryption, the sender (the encryption party) and the receiver (the decryption party) would compute a same element, which is used in encrypting communication data. Since higncryption works on "nicely-behaved" cyclic groups, which have the property of commutativity, such a "key agreement" can be easily realized. While for lattice-based cryptographic, benefitting from the growth of lattice-based key exchange protocols [4, 8, 21], we can utilize the key agreement technique to construct our scheme. Ding et al. [8] firstly introduced the key reconciliation mechanism to "handling the noises" of RLWE. And Peikert [21] gave an improved version of reconciliation mechanism. We use Peikert's reconciliation mechanism to achieve the key agreement in our scheme. Furthermore, since the perfect randomization properties of cyclic groups, the static key can be "perfectly hidden" in the communication data. While for RLWE based scheme, the goal of perfectly hiding the keys can be realized by using rejection sampling [16]. In the security aspect, secret hidden is necessary, so we apply the rejection sampling technique in our scheme. To prove the security of our scheme, we introduce vPWE assumption, which is a variant of Pairing with Errors (PWE) assumption introduced by Ding et al. [9], and we show that vPWE assumption can be reduced to the RLWE problem. As long as the vPWE assumption is hard, the security of our scheme can be guaranteed.

Related Works. For authenticated protocols from ideal lattices, in 2015, Zhang et al. [27] proposed an authenticated RLWE based key exchange and a one-pass authenticated key exchange over ideal lattices. In 2017, Ding et al. [9] proposed RLWE-based password authenticated key exchange, whose security is proved by using PWE assumption. Yang et al. [26] introduced a RLWE-based two-message key exchange scheme in 2018, and they used Peikert's reconciliation mechanism to construct the scheme.

Roadmap. In Sect. 2, we introduce some backgrounds such as notations, security models, RLWE and some tools used in scheme. Our protocol RLWE-ICAE is introduced in Sect. 3. And in Sect. 4, a theorems is given to guarantee the security of the scheme. The parameters and the security assessment of our scheme are presented in Sect. 5. Finally, we conclude and discuss some further works in Sect. 6.

2 Preliminaries

2.1 Notations

Let n be an integer of the power of 2. Denote the ring of integer polynomials R as $\mathbb{Z}[x]/(x^n + 1)$, and $R_q := \mathbb{Z}_q[x]/(x^n + 1)$ as the ring of integer polynomials modulo $x^n + 1$ with every coefficient is reduced modulo positive integer q. Let the norm of a polynomial be the norm of its coefficients vector. Let $x \xleftarrow{\$} \chi$ denote the coefficients of x are sampled based on the probability distribution χ. For any positive real $\beta \in \mathbb{R}$, and a vector $\mathbf{c} \in \mathbb{R}^m$, let the continuous Gaussian distribution over $\mathbb{R}^m$ with standard deviation β centered at $\mathbf{c}$ be defined by the probability function $\rho_{\beta,\mathbf{c}}(\mathbf{x}) = (\frac{1}{\sqrt{2\pi\beta^2}})^m exp(\frac{-\|\mathbf{x}-\mathbf{v}\|_2^2}{2\beta^2})$. Let $D_{\mathbb{Z}^n,\beta,\mathbf{c}}(\mathbf{x}) = \frac{\rho_{\beta,\mathbf{c}}(\mathbf{x})}{\rho_{\beta,\mathbf{c}}(\mathbb{Z}^m)}$ to indicate the m-dimensional discrete Gaussian distribution. The subscripts β and $\mathbf{c}$ are omitted when they are 1 and $\mathbf{0}$. Usually χ_β denotes Gaussian distribution with standard deviation β and centered at 0.

2.2 Authenticated Encryption with Associated Data

An *authenticated encryption with associated date* (AEAD) scheme transforms a message M and a public packet header, which is usually implicitly determined from the context, into a ciphertext C which provides both privacy (of M) and authenticity (of C and H) [23]. We state the security of AEAD in [28] as follows.

AEAD Security. Let $\prod = (\mathcal{K}, \mathcal{E}, \mathcal{D})$ be a symmetric encryption scheme. The key space $\mathcal{K} = \{0,1\}^\kappa$ is a finite nonempty set of strings. There is a probabilistic polynomial-time algorithm takes a security parameter κ as input and samples a key K from $\mathcal{K}$. The polynomial-time encryption algorithm $\mathcal{E} : \kappa \times \{0,1\}^* \times \{0,1\}^* \rightarrow \{0,1\}^* \cup \{\bot\}$ and the polynomial-time decryption algorithm $\mathcal{D} : \kappa \times \{0,1\}^* \times \{0,1\}^* \rightarrow \{0,1\}^* \cup \{\bot\}$ satisfy:

$$\Pr[K \leftarrow \mathcal{K}; H \in \{0,1\}^*; M \in \{0,1\}^*; C \leftarrow \mathcal{E}_K(H,M) : \mathcal{D}_K(C) \neq M] \leq negl(\kappa),$$

where $negl$ is a negligible function. Generally, we assume the ciphertext C has the associate data H. Let $\mathcal{A}$ be a polynomial-time adversary. A security game for AEAD is described in Table 1. The advantage of $\mathcal{A}$ is defined to be $\text{Adv}_{\prod}^{aead}(\mathcal{A}) = |2 \cdot \Pr[\text{AEAD}_{\prod}^{\mathcal{A}} \text{ returns } \textbf{true}] - 1|$. And we say $\prod$ scheme is AEAD-secure, if for all sufficiently large κ, $\text{Adv}_{\prod}^{\text{AEAD}}(\mathcal{A}) \leq negl(\kappa)$.

2.3 Security Model for ICAE

We recall the security model for identity-concealed authenticated encryption (ICAE) scheme from [28]. An ICAE scheme $\mathcal{IC}$ is specified with four polynomial-time algorithms (**Setup, Keygen, Encrypt, Decrypt**) as follows:

- **Setup**: takes the security parameter κ as input and outputs the system parameter *params* used in the scheme.

Table 1. AEAD security game

main AEAD$_\Pi^\mathcal{A}$:	**procedure Enc**(H, M_0, M_1):	**procedure Dec**(C'):
$K \leftarrow \mathcal{K}$	If $|M_0| \neq |M_1|$, Ret $\perp$	If $\sigma = 1 \wedge C' \notin \mathcal{C}$ then
$\sigma \leftarrow \{0,1\}$	$C_0 \leftarrow \mathcal{E}_K(H, M_0)$	Ret $\mathcal{D}_K(C')$
$\sigma' = \mathcal{A}^{\mathbf{Enc,Dec}}$	$C_1 \leftarrow \mathcal{E}_K(H, M_1)$	else Ret $\perp$
Ret $(\sigma' = \sigma)$	If $C_0 = \perp$ or $C_1 = \perp$, Ret $\perp$	
	$\mathcal{C} \overset{\cup}{\leftarrow} C_\sigma$; Ret C_σ	

- **Keygen**: takes *params* as input and outputs a key pair (pk, sk) used for encryption and decryption.
- **Encrypt**: takes the sender's private key sk_s and public identity information $pid_s = (id_s, pk_s, cert_s)$ where $cert_s$ is issued by a certificate authority, a receiver's public identity information $pid_r = (id_r, pk_r, cert_r)$, message $M \in \{0,1\}^*$, and associated data $H \in \{0,1\}^*$ as input. It returns a ciphertext C or $\perp$ which indicate encrypt failure. We allow $pid_s = (id_s, pk_s, cert_s)$ equal to $pid_r = (id_r, pk_r, cert_r)$, which means that a user encrypts a message to himself. We also assume some *offline-computable* intermediate randomness used in generating C is stored in a variable $\mathcal{ST}_C$.
- **Decrypt**: takes a receiver's private key sk_r, the receiver's public identity information $pid_r = (id_r, pk_r, cert_r)$, a ciphertext C as input. It outputs (pid_s, M) or an error $\perp$.

We say that an ICAE scheme is correctness if for all sufficiently large security parameter κ, key pairs (pk_s, sk_s) and (pk_r, sk_r) which are output by **Keygen**(1^κ), there is

$$\Pr[\mathbf{Decrypt}(sk_r, pid_r, \mathbf{Encrypt}(sk_s, pid_s, pid_r, H, M)) \neq (pid_s, M)] \leq negl(\kappa)$$

where $H, M \in \{0,1\}^*$ such that **Encrypt**$(sk_s, pid_s, pid_r, H, M) \neq \perp$, and *negl* is a negligible function.

Now we present the security model for ICAE. We assume each user possesses a single key pair for encryption and decryption, and each user can encrypt messages to himself. In this model the adversary is allowed to register users adaptively (hence has dishonest users). Let the number of users in the system be N, which is a polynomial in the security parameter κ. We assume all the honest users' key pairs are generated by the challenger according to the key generation algorithm specified in the system. Denote by **HONEST** (reps., **DISHONEST**), the set of public identity information of all the honest (resp., dishonest) users. We denote the public identity information of a user id_i as pid_i $(1 \leq i \leq n)$, the sender's (resp., the receiver's) public identity information as pid_s (resp., pid_r). The adversary's abilities are formalized by providing the adversary with the following oracles:

- **ENO**: takes (pid_s, pid_r, H, M) as inputs, where $pid_r \in$ **HONEST** $\bigcup$ **DISH− ONEST**. If $pid_s \in$ **HONEST**, the oracle returns **Encrypt**$(sk_s, pid_s, pid_r,$

H, M), otherwise return $\perp$. In order to allow for later **Exposure** query against a ciphertext C, some specified offline-computable intermediate randomness to generate C are allowed to be stored into $\mathcal{ST}_C$.

- **DEO**: takes (pid_r, C) as inputs. If $pid_r \in$ **HONEST**, the oracle returns **Decrypt** (sk_r, pid_r, C), otherwise, returns $\perp$.
- **Exposure**: takes $C \neq \perp$ as input. If C is output by an earlier **ENO** query, the oracle returns the offline-computable intermediate randomness (stored in $\mathcal{ST}_C$) used in generating C.
- **Corrupt**: takes $pid_i \in$ **HONEST** as input, $(1 \leq i \leq N)$, and returns user id_i's private key sk_i.

Outsider Unforgeability. Consider the following experiment for $\mathcal{A}^{OU}$:

The encryption experiment Encry-forge$_{\mathcal{A}^{OU}, \mathcal{IC}}(\kappa)$:

- $\mathcal{A}^{OU}$ is given the all the honest users' public keys and can register arbitrary public keys on its own with security parameter κ.
- $\mathcal{A}^{OU}$ is allowed to issue **ENO, DEO, Exposure** and **Corrput** queries. $\mathcal{A}^{OU}$ then outputs (pid_{r*}, C^*) as its output.
- $\mathcal{A}^{OU}$ succeeds if and only if:
  1. **Decrypt**$(sk_{r*}, pid_{r*}, C^*) = (pid_{s*}, M^*)$, where $pid_{s*} \in$ **HONEST**;
  2. $\mathcal{A}^{OU}$ has not issued **Corrupt**(pid_{s*}) or **Corrupt**(pid_{r*}) query, but is allowed to query **Exposure**(C^*) to expose the intermediate randomness in generating C^*.
  3. C^* is not the output of **ENO**$(pid_{s*}, pid_{r*}, H^*, M^*)$ issued by $\mathcal{A}^{OU}$, but $\mathcal{A}^{OU}$ is still allowed to query **ENO**$(pid_{s'}, pid_{r'}, H', M')$ for $(pid_{s'}, pid_{r'}, H', M') \neq (pid_{s*}, pid_{r*}, H^*, M^*)$ and in particular $(pid_{s*}, pid_{r*}, H', M^*)$ for $H' \neq H^*$. $\mathcal{A}^{OU}$ can even query **ENO**$(pid_{s*}, pid_{r*}, H^*, M^*)$ as long as its outputs returned is not C^*. And parts of C^* (the H^*) may appear in previous outputs of **ENO**.
- The experiment returns 1 if $\mathcal{A}^{OU}$ succeeds, otherwise returns 0.

We say that an ICAE scheme $\mathcal{IC}$ has *outside unforgeability*, if for any PPT adversary $\mathcal{A}^{OU}$, there is a negligible function *negl* such that:

$$\Pr[\textbf{Encry-forge}_{\mathcal{A}^{OU}, \mathcal{IC}}(\kappa) = 1] \leq negl(\kappa).$$

Next we introduce the definition of *insider confidentiality*, which is identical to outsider unforgeability, except that **Corrupt**(pid_{r*}) is allowed to the adversary.

Insider Confidentiality. We assume that all the users have equal length public identity information. Consider the following experiment for an adversary $\mathcal{A}^{IC}$:

The encryption experiment Encry-Confident$_{\mathcal{A}^{IC}, \mathcal{IC}}(\kappa)$:

- $\mathcal{A}^{IC}$ is given the all the honest users' public keys and can register arbitrary public keys on its own with security parameter κ.

- $\mathcal{A}^{IC}$ is allowed to issue **ENO**, **DEO**, **Exposure** and **Corrput** queries. $\mathcal{A}^{IC}$ then outputs two equal length messages (M_0, M_1), an associated data H^*, and two pairs of public identity information of equal length $(pid_{s_0^*}, pid_{r^*})$ and $(pid_{s_1^*}, pid_{r^*})$ where $pid_{s_0^*}, pid_{s_1^*}, pid_{r^*} \in$ **HONEST**.
- A uniform bit $\gamma \in \{0, 1\}$ is chosen, and then a ciphertext $C^* =$ **Encrypt** $(sk_{s_\gamma^*}, pid_{s_\gamma^*}, pid_{r^*}, H^*, M_\gamma)$ is computed and given to $\mathcal{A}^{IC}$.
- The adversary $\mathcal{A}^{IC}$ can continue executing the second phase, except asking **DEO**(pid_{r^*}, C^*), **Exposure**(C^*) or **Corrupt**(pid_{r^*}) which will cause $\mathcal{A}^{IC}$ win the game trivially. But the adversary $\mathcal{A}^{IC}$ is allowed to issue **Corrupt**$(pid_{s_0^*})$ and **Corrupt**$(pid_{s_1^*})$, which can capture forward ID-privacy. Eventually, $\mathcal{A}^{IC}$ outputs a bit γ'.
- The output of the experiment is defined to be 1 if $\gamma' = \gamma$, and 0 otherwise. If the output of the experiment is 1, we say that $\mathcal{A}^{IC}$ **succeeds**.

We say that an ICAE scheme $\mathcal{IC}$ has insider confidentiality, if for any PPT adversary $\mathcal{A}^{IC}$ there is a negligible function $negl$ such that:

$$\Pr[\textbf{Encry-Confident}_{\mathcal{A}^{IC}, \mathcal{IC}}(\kappa) = 1] \leq negl(\kappa).$$

Note that the definition of outsider confidentiality is identical to that of insider confidentiality, except that neither **Corrupt**$(pid_{s_0}^*)$ nor **Corrupt**$(pid_{s_1}^*)$.

2.4   Ring Learning with Errors

In 2010, Lyubashevsky, Peikert and Regev [18] proposed the Ring Learning with Erros problems (RLWE), which is based on the Learning with Errors (LWE) in the ring setting. Assume there are uniform random elements $a, s \xleftarrow{\$} R_q$ and an error distribution χ. Let $A_{s,\chi}$ denote the distribution of the RLWE pair $(a, as + e)$, where the error $e \xleftarrow{\$} \chi$. Given polynomial number of samples, the search version of RLWE is to find the secret s, while the decision version of the RLWE problem (DRLWE$_{q,\chi}$) is to distinguish $A_{s,\chi}$ from an uniform distribution pair (a, b) on $R_q \times R_q$. RLWE enjoys a worst case hardness guarantee, which we state here.

Theorem 1 ([18], Theorem 3.6). *Let $R = \mathbb{Z}[x]/(x^n + 1)$ where n is a power of 2, $\delta = \delta(n) < \sqrt{logn/n}$, and $q = 1 \mod 2n$ which is a ploy(n)-bounded prime such that $\delta q \geq \omega(\sqrt{logn})$. Then there exists a ploy(n)-time quantum reduction from $\tilde{O}(\sqrt{n}/\delta)$-SIVP (Short Independent Vectors Problem) on ideal lattices in the ring R to solve DRLWE$_{q,\chi}$ with $l-1$ samples, where $\chi = D_{\mathbb{Z}^n, \varsigma}$ is the discrete Gaussian distribution with parameter $\varsigma = \delta q \cdot (nl/log(nl))^{1/4}/\sqrt{2\pi}$.*

We have the following useful facts.

Lemma 1 ([16], Lemma 4.4). *For any $k > 0$, $\Pr_{x \leftarrow \chi_\beta}(|x| > k\beta) \leq 2e^{-k^2/2}$.*

Note that taking $k = 13$ gives tail probability approximating 2^{-121}.

Lemma 2 ([20]). *Letting real $\beta = \omega(\sqrt{logn})$, constant $\eta > \frac{1}{\sqrt{2\pi}}$, then we have that $Pr_{\mathbf{v} \xleftarrow{\$} D_{\mathbb{Z}^n,\beta}}[\|\mathbf{v}\| > \eta \cdot \beta \sqrt{n}] \leq \frac{1}{2} D^n$, where $D = \eta \sqrt{2\pi e} \cdot e^{-\pi \cdot \eta^2}$. In particular, we have $Pr_{\mathbf{v} \xleftarrow{\$} D_{\mathbb{Z}^n,\beta}}[\|\mathbf{v}\| > \beta \sqrt{n}] \leq 2^{-n+1}$.*

2.5   The Rejection Sampling

Now, we recall the rejection sampling from [17].

Theorem 2 ([17], Theorem 3.4). *Let S be a subset of $\mathbb{Z}^m$, all the elements of S have norms less than T, $\beta = w(T\sqrt{logm})$ be a real, and $\phi : S \rightarrow \mathbb{R}$ be a probability distribution. Then the distribution of the following algorithm $\mathcal{F}$:*

- $\mathbf{c} \xleftarrow{\$} \phi$;
- $\mathbf{z} \xleftarrow{\$} D_{\mathbb{Z}^m,\beta,\mathbf{c}}$;
- *output $(\mathbf{z},\mathbf{c})$ with probability $min\left(\frac{D_{\mathbb{Z}^m,\beta}(\mathbf{z})}{M \cdot D_{\mathbb{Z}^m,\beta,\mathbf{c}}(\mathbf{z})}, 1\right)$.*

is within statistical distance $\frac{2^{-w(logm)}}{M}$ from the distribution of the following algorithm $\mathcal{G}$:

- $\mathbf{c} \xleftarrow{\$} \phi$;
- $\mathbf{z} \xleftarrow{\$} D_{\mathbb{Z}^m,\beta}$;
- *output $(\mathbf{z},\mathbf{c})$ with probability $\frac{1}{M}$.*

where $M = O(1)$ is a constant. Moreover, the probability that $\mathcal{F}$ outputs something is at leat $\frac{1-2^{-w(logm)}}{M}$. More concretely, if $\beta = \eta T$ for any positive η, then $M = e^{12/\eta+1/(2\eta^2)}$ and the output of algorithm $\mathcal{F}$ is within statistical distance $\frac{2^{-100}}{M}$ of the output of $\mathcal{G}$, and the probability that $\mathcal{F}$ outputs something is at leat $\frac{1-2^{-100}}{M}$.

2.6   Reconciliation Mechanism

Firstly, We recall the reconciliation mechanism proposed by Peikert in [21] for transforming approximate agreement to exact agreement. For integer $q > p \geq 2$, we define the modular rounding function $\lfloor \cdot \rceil_p : \mathbb{Z}_q \rightarrow \mathbb{Z}_p$ as $\lfloor x \rceil_p := \lfloor \frac{p}{q} \cdot x \rceil$ and downward-rounded function $\lfloor \cdot \rfloor_p : \mathbb{Z}_q \rightarrow \mathbb{Z}_p$ as $\lfloor x \rfloor_p := \lfloor \frac{p}{q} \cdot x \rfloor$.

Even Modulus. Let the modulus $q \geq 2$ is even, define two disjoint intervals $I_0 := \{0, 1, \ldots, \lfloor \frac{q}{4} \rceil - 1\}$, $I_1 := \{-\lfloor \frac{q}{4} \rceil, \ldots, -1\}$ mod q. Then when $v \in (I_0 + \frac{q}{2}) \cup (I_1 + \frac{q}{2})$, $\lfloor v \rceil_2 = 1$, and when $v \in I_0 \cup I_1$, $\lfloor v \rceil_2 = 0$. Here we define the *cross-rounding* function $\langle \cdot \rangle_2 : \mathbb{Z}_q \rightarrow \mathbb{Z}_2$ as $\langle v \rangle_2 := \lfloor \frac{4}{q} \cdot v \rfloor$ mod 2. Obviously, $\langle v \rangle_2 = b \in \{0,1\}$ such that $v \in I_b \cup (\frac{q}{2} + I_b)$.

Lemma 3 ([21], Claim 3.1). *For $q \geq 2$ is even, if v is uniformly random chosen from $\mathbb{Z}_q$, then given $\langle v \rangle_2$, $\lfloor v \rceil_2$ is uniformly random.*

Define the set $E := [-\frac{q}{8}, \frac{q}{8}) \cap \mathbb{Z}$. Suppose $v, w \in \mathbb{Z}_q$ are sufficiently close, and given w and $\langle v \rangle_2$, we can recover $\lfloor v \rceil_2$ using the reconciliation function rec: $\mathbb{Z}_q \times \mathbb{Z}_2 \to \mathbb{Z}_2$:

$$\mathrm{rec}(w, b) = \begin{cases} 0 & \text{if } w \in I_b + E (\mathrm{mod} q), \\ 1 & \text{otherwise.} \end{cases}$$

Lemma 4 ([21], Claim 3.2). *For $q \geq 2$ is even, if $w = v + e \mod q$ for some $v \in \mathbb{Z}_q$ and $e \in E$, then rec$(w, \langle v \rangle_2)= \lfloor v \rceil_2$.*

Odd Modulus. When q is odd, Peikert proposed a randomized function dbl: $\mathbb{Z}_q \to \mathbb{Z}_{2q}$ to avoid the bias produced in the rounding function. Let $v \in \mathbb{Z}_q$, function dbl is defined to be $\mathrm{dbl}(v) := 2v - \tilde{e} \in \mathbb{Z}_{2q}$ where $\tilde{e} \in \mathbb{Z}$ is independent of v and uniformly random modulo two. Usually we write v with an overbar to means that $\bar{v} \leftarrow \mathrm{dbl}(v)$.

Lemma 5 ([21], Claim 3.3). *For $q > 2$ is odd, if v is uniformly random chosen from $\mathbb{Z}_q$ and $\bar{v} \leftarrow \mathrm{dbl}(v) \in \mathbb{Z}_{2q}$, then $\lfloor \bar{v} \rceil_2$ is uniformly random given $\langle \bar{v} \rangle_2$.*

Define function HelpRec(X): (1) $\overline{X} \leftarrow \mathrm{dbl}(X)$; (2) $W \leftarrow \langle \overline{X} \rangle_2$, $K \leftarrow \lfloor \overline{X} \rceil_2$; (3) return (K, W).

Note that for $w, v \in \mathbb{Z}_q$, we need apply the appropriated rounding function from $\mathbb{Z}_{2q}$ to $\mathbb{Z}_2$, (which means that $\lfloor x \rceil_p = \lfloor \frac{p}{2q} \cdot x \rceil$, $\langle x \rangle_2 = \lfloor \frac{4}{2q} \cdot x \rfloor$), and similar to rec function. Then if $(K, W) \leftarrow \mathrm{HelpRec}(X)$ and $Y = X + e$ with $||e||_\infty < \frac{q}{8}$, then $\mathrm{rec}(2 \cdot Y, W) = K$. By applying coefficient-wise to the coefficients in $\mathbb{Z}_q$ of a ring elements we also can extend these definitions to R_q. That is, for a ring elements $v = (v_0, \ldots, v_{n-1}) \in R_q$, setting $\lfloor v \rceil_2 = (\lfloor v_0 \rceil_2, \ldots, \lfloor v_{n-1} \rceil_2)$; $\langle v \rangle_2 = (\langle v_0 \rangle_2, \ldots, \langle v_{n-1} \rangle_2)$, $\mathrm{HelpRec}(v) = (\mathrm{HelpRec}(v_0), \ldots, \mathrm{HelpRec}(v_{n-1}))$ and for a binary-vector $b = (b_0, \ldots, b_{n-1}) \in \{0, 1\}^n$, setting $\mathrm{rec}(v, b) = (\mathrm{rec}(v_0, b_0), \ldots, \mathrm{rec}(v_{n-1}, b_{n-1}))$.

2.7 A Variant of Pair with Errors Problem

The vPWE Assumption. In [9], Ding et al. propose the Pairing with Errors (PWE) assumption based on Ding's reconciliation mechanism [8]. Here we proposed a variant of their PWE assumption and we call it vPWE assumption. We replace the Ding's reconciliation mechanism with Peikert's reconciliation mechanism. Let χ_β be a Gaussian distribution for fixed $\beta \in \mathbb{R}_+^*$. For any $(X, s) \in R_q \times R_q$, if $(K, W) \leftarrow \mathrm{HelpRec}(X \cdot s)$, then set $\tau(X, s) := K = \lfloor \overline{X \cdot s} \rceil_2$. Let $\mathcal{A}$ be probabilistic, polynomial-time algorithm. $\mathcal{A}$ takes inputs of the form (a, X, Y, W), where $(a, X, Y) \in R_q \times R_q \times R_q$ and $W \in \{0, 1\}^n$, and outputs a list of values in $\{0, 1\}^n$. Given s randomly chosen from χ_β, Y which is a "small additive perturbation" of $a \cdot s$, and $W \leftarrow \langle \overline{X \cdot s} \rangle_2$, $\mathcal{A}$'s objective will be outputting the string $\tau(X, s)$.

To states the hardness of vPWE assumption, We define the decision version of vPWE problem vDPWE as follows. If vDPWE is hard, so is vPWE.

Definition 1 (vDPWE). *Given $(a, X, Y, W, \sigma) \in R_q \times R_q \times R_q \times \{0,1\}^n \times \{0,1\}^n$ where $W = \langle \overline{K} \rangle_2$ for some $K \in R_q$ ($\overline{K} \leftarrow \mathrm{dbl}(K)$), and $\sigma = \mathrm{rec}(2 \cdot K, W)$. The Decision vPWE problem (vDPWE) is to decide whether $K = Xs + e_1$, $Y = as + e_2$ for some s, e_1, e_2 are drawn from χ_β, or (K, Y) are uniformly random in $R_q \times R_q$.*

In order to show the reduction of the vDPWE problem to the RLWE problem, we would like to introduce a definition to what we called the RLWE-DH problem [9] which can be reduced to RLWE problem.

Definition 2 (RLWE-DH). *Let R_q and χ_β be defined as above. Given an input ring element (a, X, Y, K), where (a, X) is uniformly random in R_q^2, The DRLWE-DH problem is to decision if K is $Xs + e_1$ and $Y = as + e_2$ for some $s, e_1, e_2 \xleftarrow{\$} \chi_\beta$ or (K, Y) are uniformly random in $R_q \times R_q$.*

Theorem 3 ([9], Theorem 1). *Let R_q and χ_β be defined as above, then the RLWE-DH problem is hard to solve if RLWE problem is hard.*

Theorem 4. *Let R_q and χ_β be defined as above. The vDPWE problem is hard if the RLWE-DH problem is hard.*

Proof. Suppose there exists an algorithm D which can solve the vDPWE problem on input (a, X, Y, W, σ) where for some $K \in R_q$, $W = \langle \overline{K} \rangle_2$ and $\sigma = \mathrm{rec}(2 \cdot K, W)$ with non-negligible advantage. By using D as a subroutine, we can build a distinguisher D' on input (a', X', Y', K'), solve the RLWE-DH problem:

- Compute $W = \langle \overline{K'} \rangle_2$ and $\sigma = \mathrm{rec}(2 \cdot K', W)$.
- Run D using the input (a', X', Y', W, σ).
  - If D outputs 1 then K' is $X's + e_1$ for some $e_1 \xleftarrow{\$} \chi_\beta$ and $Y' = as + e_2$ for some $s, e_1 \xleftarrow{\$} \chi_\beta$.
  - Else (K', Y') is uniformly random element from $R_q \times R_q$.

Because D solves vDPWE with non-negligible advantage, D' solves RLWE-DH with non-negligible advantage as well, which contradicts RLWE-DH's hardness. □

3   Protocol Construction of Encryption

3.1   The RLWE-ICAE

In this section we present a practical and carefully designed scheme: RLWE-ICAE. The scheme consists of the following four algorithms, **Setup**, **Keygen**, **Encrypt** and **Decrypt**.

Setup: On a security parameter κ, **Setup**(1^κ) returns $params = (n, q, \alpha, \beta, a)$ specifying the underlying ring R_q, Gaussian distribution χ_α, χ_β used in the scheme and public element $a \xleftarrow{\$} R_q$, where n is a power of 2 and q is an odd prime such that $q \bmod 2n = 1$.

Keygen: On the parameters *params*, for each honest user i, $(1 \leq i \leq N)$, **Keygen** samples $s_i, e_i \xleftarrow{\$} \chi_\alpha$, sets $pk_i = a \cdot s_i + e_i$ and $sk_i = s_i$, and outputs the keypair (pk_i, sk_i). The CA issue a certificate $cert_i$ used to authenticated the binding between user identity id_i and public-key pk_i.

Encrypt: Let $\prod = (\mathcal{K}, \mathcal{E}, \mathcal{D})$ be an AEAD scheme. Let $h : \{0,1\}^* \to \chi_\alpha$ be a cryptographic hash function that always outputs invertible elements in R_q, $M \in \{0,1\}^*$ be the message to be encrypted with an associated data H and $KDF : G \times \{0,1\}^* \to \{0,1\}^\kappa$ be a key derivation function. We denote by Alice the sender with public identity information $pid_A = (id_A, pk_A = p_A = a \cdot s_A + e_A \in R_q, cert_A)$, where $s_A, e_A \xleftarrow{\$} \chi_\alpha$, and secret-key $sk_A = s_A$, and by Bob the receiver with possesses public identity information $pid_B = (id_B, pk_B = p_B = a \cdot s_B + e_B \in R_q, cert_B)$, where $s_B, e_B \xleftarrow{\$} \chi_\alpha$, and secret-key $sk_B = s_B$.
$\textbf{Encrypt}(sk_A, pid_A, pid_B, H, M)$ works as follows:

1. Sample $r, f \xleftarrow{\$} \chi_\beta$ and compute $X = a \cdot r + f \in R_q$;
2. Compute $d = h(X, pid_A, pid_B)$, $\hat{r} = r + s_A d$ and $\hat{f} = f + e_A d$;
3. Go to step 4 with probability $\min(\frac{D_{\mathbb{Z}^{2n}, \beta}(\mathbf{v})}{M \cdot D_{\mathbb{Z}^{2n}, \beta, \mathbf{v}_1}(\mathbf{v})}, 1)$, where $\mathbf{v} \in \mathbb{Z}^{2n}$ is the coefficient vector of element $\hat{r}$ concatenated with the coefficient vector of $\hat{f}$, and $\mathbf{v}_1 \in \mathbb{Z}^{2n}$ is the coefficient vector of $s_A d$ concatenated with the coefficient vector of $e_A d$; otherwise go back to step 1;
4. Sample $g \xleftarrow{\$} \chi_\beta$, and compute $\widetilde{X} = p_A \cdot d + X$, $PS_A = p_B \cdot (r + s_A d) + g$;
5. Compute $(PS, w) \leftarrow \text{HelpRec}(PS_A)$;
6. Derive key $K_1 = KDF(PS, \widetilde{X} \| pid_B)$, where $K_1 \in \mathcal{K}$;
7. Compute $C_{AE} \leftarrow \mathcal{E}_{K_1}(H, pid_A \| X \| M)$;
8. Finally, send the ciphertext $C = (H, \widetilde{X}, w, C_{AE})$ to the receiver.

$\textbf{Decrypt}(sk_B, pid_B, C(= (H, \widetilde{X}, w, C_{AE})))$ works as follows:

1. Compute $PS_B = \widetilde{X} \cdot s_B$ and pre-shared secrecy $PS = \text{rec}(2 \cdot PS_B, w)$, and derive the key $K_1 = KDF(PS, \widetilde{X} \| pid_B)$;
2. Run $\mathcal{D}_{K_1}(H, C_{AE})$. If $\mathcal{D}_{K_1}(H, C_{AE})$ returns $\bot$, abort; otherwise get $(pid_A = (id_A, p_A, cert_A), X, M)$;
3. Compute $d = h(X, pid_A, pid_B)$. If $\widetilde{X}$ equals to $p_A \cdot d + X$ and pid_A is valid, accept (pid_A, M); otherwise, abort.

Our scheme is presented in Fig. 1. Note that we use rejection sampling in our scheme, and this technique can protect the secret information $s_A d$ and $e_A d$ from $\widetilde{X} = a \cdot (s_A d + r) + (e_A d + f)$. In our proof of insider confidentiality, such a "secret hidden" is necessary. Reconciliation mechanism is used to compute PS from two approximate values PS_A and PS_B, and this can be regarded to be a key agreement of the sender and the receiver.

pid_A	pid_B
$pk_A : p_A \leftarrow a \cdot s_A + e_A$	$pk_B : p_B \leftarrow a \cdot s_B + e_B$
$sk_A : s_A$	$sk_B : s_B$
where $s_A, e_A \xleftarrow{\$} \chi_\alpha$	where $s_B, e_B \xleftarrow{\$} \chi_\alpha$

$X \leftarrow a \cdot r + f$ where $r, f \xleftarrow{\$} \chi_\beta$

$d \leftarrow h(X, pid_A, pid_B)$

$\widetilde{X} = p_A \cdot d + X$

$PS_A \leftarrow p_B \cdot (r + s_A \cdot d) + g$

where $g \xleftarrow{\$} \chi_\beta$

$(PS, w) \leftarrow \mathrm{HelpRec}(PS_A)$

$K_1 \leftarrow KDF(PS, \widetilde{X} \| pid_B)$

$C_{AE} \leftarrow \mathcal{E}_{K_1}(H, pid_A \| X \| M) \xrightarrow{\quad H, \widetilde{X}, w, C_{AE} \quad} PS_B \leftarrow \widetilde{X} \cdot s_B$

$PS \leftarrow \mathrm{rec}(2 \cdot PS_B, w)$

$K_1 \leftarrow KDF(PS, \widetilde{X} \| pid_B)$

$(pid_A, X, M) \leftarrow \mathcal{D}_{K_1}(H, C_{AE})$

$d \leftarrow h(X, pid_A, pid_B)$

Accept if pid_A valid and $\widetilde{X} = p_A \cdot d + X$

Fig. 1. Protocol structure of RLWE-ICAE.

One-Pass CAKE. In the RLWE-ICAE, there is $K_1 = KDF(PS, \widetilde{X} \| pid_B)$. We can redefine KDF to construct an one-pass CAKE. Define $(K_1, K_2) = KDF(PS, \widetilde{X} \| pid_B)$. Then to cast the RLWE-ICAE scheme into one-pass identity-concealed authenticated key-exchange (CAKE), we need set the session-key to be K_2 which is computationally independent of the key K_1. Hence the exposure of K_1 does not affect the session key security. Note that a similar scheme is Zhang's one-pass key exchange protocol from ideal lattices [27]. Compared Zhang's protocol, our scheme provides identity concealment.

3.2 Correctness

Note that in protocol, if $\lfloor \overline{PS_A} \rceil_2 = \mathrm{rec}(2 \cdot PS_B, w)$, where $\overline{PS_A} \leftarrow \mathrm{dbl}(PS_A)$, the protocols would be correct. By the definition of the reconciliation mechanism and Lemma 4, there needs to $\|PS_A - PS_B\|_\infty < \frac{q}{8}$. We have

$$PS_A = p_B(r + s_A d) + g = (as_B + e_B)(r + s_A d) + g$$
$$= ads_A s_B + e_B s_A d + ars_B + re_B + g,$$
$$PS_B = \widetilde{X} s_B = (p_A d + X)s_B = (as_A d + e_A d + ar + f)s_B$$
$$= ads_A s_B + e_A s_B d + ars_B + f s_B,$$

therefore, we need $\|PS_A - PS_B\|_\infty = \|e_B s_A d + re_B + g - e_A s_B d - f s_B\|_\infty < \frac{q}{8}$ with overwhelming probability.

4   Security for RLWE-ICAE

We assume KDF to be a random oracle.

Theorem 5. *The scheme RLWE-ICAE in Fig. 1 satisfies outsider unforgeability and insider confidentiality in the random oracle model, under the AEAD security and the* vPWE *assumption.*

The proof of Theorem 5 is presented in the full version of this paper in ePrint. We construct a scheme simulator S, which is computationally indistinguishable from that in the real attack game from the view of the adversary and proof that if the adversary can break the outsider unforgeability or insider confidentiality security, vPWE problem can be solved with non-negligible probability.

5   Concrete Parameters

In this section, we present the choices of parameters and give the complexity assessment of RLWE-ICAE.

We use the property for product of two Gaussian distributed random values which are stated in [27]. Let $x, y \in R$ be two polynomials with degree of n. Assume that the coefficients of x and y are distributed according to a discrete Gaussian distribution with parameter β_x, β_y, respectively. Then we have that the individual coefficients of the polynomial xy are approximately normally distributed around zero with parameter $\beta_x \beta_y \sqrt{n}$. Hence for $\|PS_A - PS_B\|_\infty = \|e_B s_A d + r e_B + g - f s_B - e_A s_B d\|_\infty < \frac{q}{8}$, applying Lemma 1 we have that $\|k_A - k_B\|_\infty > 13 \cdot \sqrt{2n\alpha^2\beta^2 + \beta^2 + 2n^2\alpha^6}$ with probability approximating 2^{-121}. We set $13 \cdot \sqrt{2n\alpha^2\beta^2 + \beta^2 + 2n^2\alpha^6} < \frac{q}{8}$ to make sure the correctness of the scheme. Note that since the Theorem 1 of rejection sampling, the distributions of $r + s_A d$ is according to χ_β. We follow a way of parameter choosing in [27]. To choose an appropriate β, we set $\eta = 1/2$ in Lemma 2 such that $\|s_A d\| \leq 1/2n\alpha^2$ with probability at most $2 \cdot 0.943^{-n}$. In order to make the rejection sampling work, we need to set $\beta \geq \zeta \cdot 1/2n\alpha^2$ for some constant ζ. When we set $\zeta = 12$, by Theorem 1, there is an expect number of rejection sampling about $M = 2.72$ and a statistical distance about $\frac{2^{-100}}{M}$.

For the security of our parameters, Alkim et al. [2] analysised RLWE and LWE using two BKZ types attacks: prime attack and dual attack [6]. The thoughts of their approach is to replace the enumeration core-SVP algorithm in BKZ by sieve algorithm, and only evaluate the cost of one call to an SVP oracle in dimension b. For more detail, we refer to [2]. We use their techniques to assess the core-SVP security. But to estimate the security of our scheme more accurately, we follow Albrecht's estimation [1] about the number for the calls to core-SVP oracle. Albrecht estimated it to be $8d$, where d is the dimension of the embedding lattice. We will first compute the core-SVP security, then multiple it with $8d$ to obtain the final security.

Two recommend parameters choices is given in Table 2. Remark that q must be a prime and satisfies $q = 1 \mod 2n$. In the table, we denote classical security

Table 2. Recommend Parameters for RLWE-ICAE

		I	II
n	power of 2	1024	2048
α		2.828	2.828
β	$> \frac{1}{2}n\alpha^2\zeta = \frac{1}{2}n\alpha^2 \cdot 12$	49152	98304
$log_2\beta$		$\approx$15.6	$\approx$16.6
q	$> 104 \cdot \sqrt{2n\alpha^2\beta^2 + \beta^2 + 2n^2\alpha^6}$	231362561	654340097
log_2q		$\approx$27.8	$\approx$29.3
Classical security		120 bits	256 bits
Quantum security		110 bits	234 bits

as the best-known classical attack time complexity, and quantum security as the best-known quantum attack time complexity [2].

6   Conclusion

We proposed the first lattice based identity-concealed authenticated encryption scheme: RLWE-ICAE. The scheme enjoys many nice properties of higncryption such as 0-RTT option, forward ID-privacy, receiver deniability and x-security. Meanwhile since our scheme is based on RLWE, it also enjoys the properties of lattice-based cryptography, such as conceptual simplicity, worst-case hardness assumption, and resistance to quantum computer attacks. Our scheme benefits from Peikert's reconciliation mechanism [21] technique which can help two parties compute a same element from two approximate values. We use the rejection sampling technique to hide the static secret information. To prove the security of our scheme, we introduce vPWE assumption, which is a variant of Pairing with Errors assumption [9] by replacing the reconciliation mechanism in [9] with Peikert's version [21]. For further works, we will consider to construct an identity concealed key exchange from RLWE.

Acknowledgments. This article is supported by The National Key Research and Development Program of China (Grant No. 2017YFA0303903), National Cryptography Development Fund (No. MMJJ20170121), and Zhejiang Province Key R&D Project (No. 2017C01062). Authors thank Aijun Ge for discussions and the anonymous ProvSec'19 reviewers for helpful comments.

References

1. Albrecht, M.R.: On dual lattice attacks against small-secret LWE and parameter choices in HElib and SEAL. In: Coron, J.-S., Nielsen, J.B. (eds.) EUROCRYPT 2017, Part II. LNCS, vol. 10211, pp. 103–129. Springer, Cham (2017). https://doi.org/10.1007/978-3-319-56614-6_4

2. Alkim, E., Ducas, L., Pöppelmann, T., Schwabe, P.: Post-quantum key exchange - a new hope. In: 25th USENIX Security Symposium, USENIX Security 16, Austin, TX, USA, 10–12 August 2016, pp. 327–343 (2016). https://www.usenix.org/conference/usenixsecurity16/technical-sessions/presentation/alkim
3. Baek, J., Steinfeld, R., Zheng, Y.: Formal proofs for the security of signcryption. J. Cryptology **20**(2), 203–235 (2007)
4. Bos, J.W., Costello, C., Naehrig, M., Stebila, D.: Post-quantum key exchange for the TLS protocol from the ring learning with errors problem. In: 2015 IEEE Symposium on Security and Privacy, SP 2015, San Jose, CA, USA, 17–21 May 2015, pp. 553–570 (2015)
5. Brzuska, C., Smart, N.P., Warinschi, B., Watson, G.J.: An analysis of the EMV channel establishment protocol. In: 2013 ACM SIGSAC Conference on Computer and Communications Security, CCS 2013, Berlin, Germany, 4–8 November 2013, pp. 373–386 (2013)
6. Chen, Y., Nguyen, P.Q.: BKZ 2.0: better lattice security estimates. In: Lee, D.H., Wang, X. (eds.) ASIACRYPT 2011. LNCS, vol. 7073, pp. 1–20. Springer, Heidelberg (2011). https://doi.org/10.1007/978-3-642-25385-0_1
7. Dent, A.W.: Hybrid cryptography. IACR Cryptology ePrint Archive 2004, 210 (2004). http://eprint.iacr.org/2004/210
8. Ding, J.: A simple provably secure key exchange scheme based on the learning with errors problem. IACR Cryptology ePrint Archive 2012, 688 (2012). http://eprint.iacr.org/2012/688
9. Ding, J., Alsayigh, S., Lancrenon, J., RV, S., Snook, M.: Provably secure password authenticated key exchange based on RLWE for the post-quantum world. In: Handschuh, H. (ed.) CT-RSA 2017. LNCS, vol. 10159, pp. 183–204. Springer, Cham (2017). https://doi.org/10.1007/978-3-319-52153-4_11
10. Ducas, L., Durmus, A.: Ring-LWE in polynomial rings. In: Fischlin, M., Buchmann, J., Manulis, M. (eds.) PKC 2012. LNCS, vol. 7293, pp. 34–51. Springer, Heidelberg (2012). https://doi.org/10.1007/978-3-642-30057-8_3
11. Gorantla, M.C., Boyd, C., González Nieto, J.M.G.: On the connection between signcryption and one-pass key establishment. In: Galbraith, S.D. (ed.) Cryptography and Coding 2007. LNCS, vol. 4887, pp. 277–301. Springer, Heidelberg (2007). https://doi.org/10.1007/978-3-540-77272-9_17
12. Halevi, S., Krawczyk, H.: One-pass HMQV and asymmetric key-wrapping. In: Catalano, D., Fazio, N., Gennaro, R., Nicolosi, A. (eds.) PKC 2011. LNCS, vol. 6571, pp. 317–334. Springer, Heidelberg (2011). https://doi.org/10.1007/978-3-642-19379-8_20
13. Iyengar, S., Nekritz, K.: Building zero protocol for fast, secure mobile connections (2017). https://code.fb.com/android/building-zero-protocol-for-fast-secure-mobile-connections/
14. Krawczyk, H.: The order of encryption and authentication for protecting communications (or: how secure is SSL?). In: Kilian, J. (ed.) CRYPTO 2001. LNCS, vol. 2139, pp. 310–331. Springer, Heidelberg (2001). https://doi.org/10.1007/3-540-44647-8_19
15. Langley, A., Chang, W.T.: Quic crypto (2014). https://docs.google.com/document/d/1g5nIXAIkN_Y-7XJW5K45IblHd_L2f5LTaDUDwvZ5L6g
16. Lyubashevsky, V.: Lattice signatures without trapdoors. IACR Cryptology ePrint Archive 2011, 537 (2011). http://eprint.iacr.org/2011/537
17. Lyubashevsky, V.: Lattice signatures without trapdoors. In: Pointcheval, D., Johansson, T. (eds.) EUROCRYPT 2012. LNCS, vol. 7237, pp. 738–755. Springer, Heidelberg (2012). https://doi.org/10.1007/978-3-642-29011-4_43

18. Lyubashevsky, V., Peikert, C., Regev, O.: On ideal lattices and learning with errors over rings. In: Gilbert, H. (ed.) EUROCRYPT 2010. LNCS, vol. 6110, pp. 1–23. Springer, Heidelberg (2010). https://doi.org/10.1007/978-3-642-13190-5_1
19. Menezes, A., Qu, M., Vanstone, S.A.: Some new key agreement protocols providing mutual implicit authentication (1995)
20. Micciancio, D., Regev, O.: Worst-case to average-case reductions based on gaussian measures. SIAM J. Comput. **37**(1), 267–302 (2007)
21. Peikert, C.: Lattice cryptography for the internet. In: Mosca, M. (ed.) PQCrypto 2014. LNCS, vol. 8772, pp. 197–219. Springer, Cham (2014). https://doi.org/10.1007/978-3-319-11659-4_12
22. Rescorla, E.: The transport layer security (TLS) protocol version 1.3. RFC 8446, pp. 1–160 (2018)
23. Rogaway, P.: Authenticated-encryption with associated-data. In: Proceedings of the 9th ACM Conference on Computer and Communications Security, CCS 2002, Washington, DC, USA, 18–22 November 2002, pp. 98–107 (2002)
24. Roskind, J.: Quick UDP internet connections: multiplexed stream transport over UDP (2012)
25. Shor, P.W.: Polynomial-time algorithms for prime factorization and discrete logarithms on a quantum computer. SIAM J. Comput. **26**(5), 1484–1509 (1997)
26. Yang, Z., Chen, Y., Luo, S.: Two-message key exchange with strong security from ideal lattices. In: Smart, N.P. (ed.) CT-RSA 2018. LNCS, vol. 10808, pp. 98–115. Springer, Cham (2018). https://doi.org/10.1007/978-3-319-76953-0_6
27. Zhang, J., Zhang, Z., Ding, J., Snook, M., Dagdelen, Ö.: Authenticated key exchange from ideal lattices. In: Oswald, E., Fischlin, M. (eds.) EUROCRYPT 2015, Part II. LNCS, vol. 9057, pp. 719–751. Springer, Heidelberg (2015). https://doi.org/10.1007/978-3-662-46803-6_24
28. Zhao, Y.: Identity-concealed authenticated encryption and key exchange. In: Proceedings of the 2016 ACM SIGSAC Conference on Computer and Communications Security, Vienna, Austria, 24–28 October 2016, pp. 1464–1479 (2016)
29. Zheng, Y.: Digital signcryption or how to achieve cost(signature & encryption) $\ll$ cost(signature) + cost (encryption). In: Kaliski, B.S. (ed.) CRYPTO 1997. LNCS, vol. 1294. Springer, Heidelberg (1997). https://doi.org/10.1007/BFb0052234

Lattice-Based IBE with Equality Test in Standard Model

Dung Hoang Duong$^{(\boxtimes)}$, Huy Quoc Le, Partha Sarathi Roy, and Willy Susilo

Institute of Cybersecurity and Cryptology,
School of Computing and Information Technology, University of Wollongong,
Northfields Avenue, Wollongong, NSW 2522, Australia
{hduong,wsusilo}@uow.edu.au, qhl576@uowmail.edu.au,
royparthasarathi0@gmail.com

Abstract. Public key encryption with equality test (PKEET) allows the testing of equality of underlying messages of two ciphertexts. PKEET is a potential candidate for many practical applications like efficient data management on encrypted databases. Identity-based encryption scheme with equality test (IBEET), which was introduced by Ma (Information Science 2016), can simplify the certificate management of PKEET. Potential applicability of IBEET leads to intensive research from its first instantiation. Ma's IBEET and most of the constructions are proven secure in the random oracle model based on number-theoretic hardness assumptions which are vulnerable in the post-quantum era. Recently, Lee et al. (ePrint 2016) proposed a generic construction of IBEET schemes in the standard model and hence it is possible to yield the first instantiation of IBEET schemes based on lattices. Their method is to use a 3-level hierarchical identity-based encryption (HIBE) scheme together with a one-time signature scheme. In this paper, we propose, for the first time, a concrete construction of an IBEET scheme based on the hardness assumption of lattices in the standard model and compare the data sizes with the instantiation from Lee et al. (ePrint 2016). Further, we have modified our proposed IBEET to make it secure against *insider attack*.

1 Introduction

The concept of IBEET is the combination of PKEET and identity-based encryption (IBE). IBEET can simplify the certificate management of PKEET with all messages encrypted with the receiver's public identity. IBEET is a special kind of IBE featuring equality test between ciphertexts under different as well as the same identity. This property is very useful in various practical applications, such as keyword search on encrypted data, encrypted data partitioning for efficient encrypted data management, personal health record system and spam filtering in encrypted email systems. Due to its numerous practical applications, there have been elegant research outcomes in this direction with the appearance of improved schemes or ones with additional functionalities [8,10,15]. However, they are all proven secure in the random oracle model which does not exist in reality. Therefore it is necessary to construct such a scheme in the standard model. Moreover,

© Springer Nature Switzerland AG 2019
R. Steinfeld and T. H. Yuen (Eds.): ProvSec 2019, LNCS 11821, pp. 19–40, 2019.
https://doi.org/10.1007/978-3-030-31919-9_2

all aforementioned existing schemes base their security on some number-theoretic hardness assumptions which will be efficiently solved in the quantum era [13]. Up to the present, there is only one IBEET scheme secure in the standard model, which was generically constructed by Lee et al. [7]. Their method is to use a 3-level hierarchical identity-based encryption (HIBE) scheme together with a one-time signature scheme. This is the first one with the possibility of yielding a post-quantum instantiation based on lattices, since lattice-based cryptography is the only one among other post-quantum areas up to present offers HIBE primitives, e.g., [1]. Hence it remains a question of either yielding an efficient instantiation or directly constructing an IBEET based on lattices.

On the other hand, supporting equality tests makes the security of IBEET schemes weaken. If the adversary can have a trapdoor for the equality test on the target ciphertext, he can generate a ciphertext of any message by himself and perform equality tests between the target ciphertext and the ciphertext generated by himself. We call this type of attacks as an *insider attack* [15]. IBEET secure against insider attack is proposed by Wu et al. [15]. There is a security flaw which is fixed by Lee et al. [9]. However, the construction is secure in the random oracle model based on number-theoretic hardness assumption. So, it is required to consider the secure construction in standard model based on the hardness assumptions which will remain secure in post-quantum era.

Table 1. Comparison of proposed IBEET with instantiation from [7].

Scheme	Ciphertext	Public key	Master secret key	Secret key
Proposed	$2t + 4m$	$(l + 3)mn + nt$	$2m^2$	$4mt$
Instantiation* from [7]	$8m + 2t + 2mt$	$(l + 3)mn + nt$	$2m^2$	$2mt$

*See Appendix A; **Data sizes are in number of field elements. In case of [7], we do not count the part of ciphertex which is possible to obtain from the public key.

Our Contribution: In this paper, our contribution is twofold:

- According to the best of our knowledge, we propose the first concrete construction of an addaptive secure IBEET scheme secure in the standard model based on the hardness assumption of lattices. From Table 1, it is evident that the proposed construction outperformed the instantiation from [7].
- We have modified the proposed IBEET to make it secure against insider attack. This is also secure in the standard model based on the hardness assumption of lattices, whereas the previous constructions are secure in the random oracle model based on the number-theoretic hardness assumptions.

Our ideas come from the use of the full lattice-based IBE in the standard model by Agrawal et al. [1] and a recent technique by Duong et al. [6] in directly constructing a PKEET based on lattices in the standard model.

Remark 1. *Our proposed schemes achieve only IND-CPA security (defined in Sect. 2), which can be modified to achieve IND-CCA2 security by using the HIBE scheme in [1] through the BCHK's transformation [4]. Hence in definition of security model in Sect. 2, we provide only the definition of CPA-security models, in which the adversary cannot query the decryption oracle.*

2 Preliminaries

2.1 Identity-Based Encryption with Equality Test (IBEET)

Definition 2 (IBEET). *An identity-based encryption with equality test (IBEET) consists of the following polynomial-time algorithms:*

- Setup(λ): *On input a security parameter λ and set of parameters, it outputs a public parameter PP and a master secret key MSK. Note that PP consists of the information of the message space $\mathcal{M}$ and we assume that all other algorithms take PP as an input implicitly without stated.*
- Extract(PP, MSK, ID): *On input PP, MSK and an identity ID, it outputs a user ID's secret key SK_{ID}.*
- Enc(PP, ID, $\mathbf{m}$): *On input PP, an identity ID and a message $\mathbf{m}$, it outputs a ciphertext CT.*
- Dec(PP, SK_{ID}, CT): *On input PP, a user ID's secret key SK and a ciphertext CT, it outputs a message $\mathbf{m}'$ or $\perp$.*
- Td(SK_{ID}): *On input the secret key SK_{ID} for the user ID, it outputs a trapdoor td_{ID}.*
- Test($td_{ID_i}, td_{ID_j}, CT_{ID_i}, CT_{ID_j}$): *On input two trapdoors td_{ID_i}, td_{ID_j} and two ciphertexts CT_{ID_i}, CT_{ID_j} for users ID_i and ID_j respectively, it outputs 1 or 0.*

Correctness. We say that an IBEET scheme is *correct* if the following conditions hold:

(1) For any security parameter λ, any user ID_i and any message $\mathbf{m}$, it holds that

$$\Pr\left[\text{Dec}(PP, SK_{ID}, CT_{ID}) = \mathbf{m} \;\middle|\; \begin{array}{l} SK_{ID} \leftarrow \text{Extract}(PP, MSK, ID) \\ CT_{ID} \leftarrow \text{Enc}(PP, ID, \mathbf{m}) \end{array}\right] = 1.$$

(2) For any security parameter λ, any users ID_i, ID_j and any messages $\mathbf{m}_i, \mathbf{m}_j$, it holds that:

$$\Pr\left[\text{Test}\begin{pmatrix} td_{ID_i} \\ td_{ID_j} \\ CT_{ID_i} \\ CT_{ID_j} \end{pmatrix} = 1 \;\middle|\; \begin{array}{l} SK_{ID_i} \leftarrow \text{Extract}(PP, MSK, ID_i) \\ CT_{ID_i} \leftarrow \text{Enc}(PP, ID_i, \mathbf{m}_i) \\ td_{ID_i} \leftarrow \text{Td}(SK_{ID_i}) \\ SK_{ID_j} \leftarrow \text{Extract}(PP, MSK, ID_j) \\ CT_{ID_j} \leftarrow \text{Enc}(PP, ID_j, \mathbf{m}_j) \\ td_{ID_j} \leftarrow \text{Td}(SK_{ID_j}) \end{array}\right]$$

is 1 if $\mathbf{m}_i = \mathbf{m}_j$ and is negligible in λ for any ciphertexts CT_i, CT_j such that $\text{Dec}(SK_i, CT_i) \neq \text{Dec}(SK_j, CT_j)$, regardless of whether $i = j$.

Security Model of IBEET. For the security model of IBEET, we consider two types of adversaries:

- Type-I adversary: for this type, the adversary can request to issue a trapdoor for the target identity and thus can perform equality tests on the challenge ciphertext. The aim of this type of adversaries is to reveal the message in the challenge ciphertext.
- Type-II adversary: for this type, the adversary cannot request to issue a trapdoor for the target identity and thus cannot perform equality tests on the challenge ciphertext. The aim of this type of adversaries is to distinguish which message is in the challenge ciphertext between two candidates.

The security model of a IBEET scheme against two types of adversaries above is described in the following.

OW-ID-CPA Security Against Type-I Adversaries. We illustrate the game between a challenger $\mathcal{C}$ and a Type-I adversary $\mathcal{A}$ who can have a trapdoor for all ciphertexts of the target identity, say ID^*, that he wants to attack, as follows:

1. **Setup:** The challenger $\mathcal{C}$ runs $\mathsf{Setup}(\lambda)$ to generate the pair $(\mathsf{PP}, \mathsf{MSK})$, and sends the public parameter PP to $\mathcal{A}$.
2. **Phase 1:** The adversary $\mathcal{A}$ may make queries polynomially many times adaptively and in any order to the following oracles:
   - $\mathcal{O}^{\mathsf{Ext}}$: an oracle that on input an identity ID (different from ID^*), returns the ID's secret key $\mathsf{SK}_{\mathsf{ID}}$.
   - $\mathcal{O}^{\mathsf{Td}}$: an oracle that on input an identity ID, return $\mathsf{td}_{\mathsf{ID}}$ by running $\mathsf{td}_{\mathsf{ID}} \leftarrow \mathsf{Td}(\mathsf{SK}_{\mathsf{ID}})$ using the secret key $\mathsf{SK}_{\mathsf{ID}}$ of the identity ID.
3. **Challenge:** $\mathcal{C}$ chooses a random message $\mathbf{m}$ in the message space and run $\mathsf{CT}^*_{\mathsf{ID}^*} \leftarrow \mathsf{Enc}(\mathsf{PP}, \mathsf{ID}^*, \mathbf{m})$, and sends $\mathsf{CT}^*_{\mathsf{ID}^*}$ to $\mathcal{A}$.
4. **Phase 2:** $\mathcal{A}$ can query as in Phase 1 with the constraint that the identity ID^* cannot be queried to the key generation oracle $\mathcal{O}^{\mathsf{Ext}}$.
5. **Guess:** $\mathcal{A}$ output $\mathbf{m}'$.

The adversary $\mathcal{A}$ wins the above game if $\mathbf{m} = \mathbf{m}'$ and the success probability of $\mathcal{A}$ is defined as

$$\mathsf{Adv}^{\mathsf{OW\text{-}ID\text{-}CPA}}_{\mathcal{A}, \mathrm{IBEET}}(\lambda) := \Pr[\mathbf{m} = \mathbf{m}'].$$

Remark 3. *If the message space is polynomial in the security parameter or the min-entropy of the message distribution is much lower than the security parameter then a Type-I adversary $\mathcal{A}$ with a trapdoor for the challenge ciphertext can reveal the message in polynomial-time or small exponential time in the security parameter, by performing the equality tests with the challenge ciphertext and all other ciphertexts of all messages generated by himself. Hence to prevent this attack, we assume that the size of the message space $\mathcal{M}$ is exponential in the security parameter and the min-entropy of the message distribution is sufficiently higher than the security parameter.*

IND-ID-CPA Security Against Type-II Adversaries. We present the game between a challenger $\mathcal{C}$ and a Type-II adversary $\mathcal{A}$ who cannot have a trapdoor for all ciphertexts of the target identity ID^* as follows:

1. **Setup:** The challenger $\mathcal{C}$ runs $\mathsf{Setup}(\lambda)$ to generate $(\mathsf{PP}, \mathsf{MSK})$ and gives the public parameter PP to $\mathcal{A}$.
2. **Phase 1:** The adversary $\mathcal{A}$ may make queries polynomially many times adaptively and in any order to the following oracles:
   - $\mathcal{O}^{\mathsf{Ext}}$: an oracle that on input an identity ID (different from ID^*), returns the ID's secret key $\mathsf{SK}_{\mathsf{ID}}$.
   - $\mathcal{O}^{\mathsf{Td}}$: an oracle that on input an identity ID, return $\mathsf{td}_{\mathsf{ID}}$ by running $\mathsf{td}_{\mathsf{ID}} \leftarrow \mathsf{Td}(\mathsf{SK}_{\mathsf{ID}})$ using the secret key $\mathsf{SK}_{\mathsf{ID}}$ of the identity ID.
3. **Challenge:** $\mathcal{A}$ selects a target user ID^*, which was never queried to the $\mathcal{O}^{\mathsf{Ext}}$ and $\mathcal{O}^{\mathsf{Td}}$ oracles in Phase 1, and two messages $\mathbf{m}_0$ $\mathbf{m}_1$ of same length and pass to $\mathcal{C}$, who then selects a random bit $b \in \{0,1\}$, runs $\mathsf{CT}^*_{\mathsf{ID}^*,b} \leftarrow \mathsf{Enc}(\mathsf{PP}, \mathsf{ID}^*, \mathbf{m}_b)$ and sends $\mathsf{CT}^*_{\mathsf{ID}^*,b}$ to $\mathcal{A}$.
4. **Phase 2:** $\mathcal{A}$ can query as in Phase 1 with the constraint that the target identity ID^* cannot be queried to the secret key extraction oracle $\mathcal{O}^{\mathsf{Ext}}$ and the trapdoor generation oracle $\mathcal{O}^{\mathsf{Td}}$.
5. **Guess:** $\mathcal{A}$ output b'.

The adversary $\mathcal{A}$ wins the above game if $b = b'$ and the advantage of $\mathcal{A}$ is defined as

$$\mathsf{Adv}^{\mathsf{IND}\text{-}\mathsf{ID}\text{-}\mathsf{CPA}}_{\mathcal{A},\mathrm{IBEET}} := \left| \Pr[b = b'] - \frac{1}{2} \right|.$$

2.2   IBEET Against Insider Attack

Definition 4. *An IBEET against insider attack consists of the following polynomial-time algorithms:*

- $\mathsf{Setup}(\lambda)$: *On input a security parameter λ, it outputs a public parameter PP, a master secret key MSK and a master token key MTK.*
- $\mathsf{Extract}(\mathsf{ID}, \mathsf{MSK}, \mathsf{MTK})$: *On input an identity ID, the master secret key MSK and a master token key MTK, it outputs the secret key $\mathsf{SK}_{\mathsf{ID}}$ and token $\mathsf{tok}_{\mathsf{ID}}$ for the identity ID.*
  It is assumed that $\mathsf{SK}_{\mathsf{ID}}$ and $\mathsf{tok}_{\mathsf{ID}}$ are delivered to the user of identity ID and the token $\mathsf{tok}_{\mathsf{ID}}$ is delivered to all group users via secure channel.
- $\mathsf{Enc}(\mathsf{PP}, \mathbf{m}, \mathsf{ID}, \mathsf{tok}_{\mathsf{ID}})$: *On input PP, an identity ID with its token $\mathsf{tok}_{\mathsf{ID}}$ and a message $\mathbf{m}$, it outputs a ciphertext CT.*
- $\mathsf{Dec}(\mathsf{CT}, \mathsf{SK}_{\mathsf{ID}}, \mathsf{tok}_{\mathsf{ID}})$: *On input a ciphertext CT, the secret key $\mathsf{SK}_{\mathsf{ID}}$ and token $\mathsf{tok}_{\mathsf{ID}}$ of the identity ID, it outputs a message $\mathbf{m}'$ or $\bot$.*
- $\mathsf{Test}(\mathsf{CT}_i, \mathsf{CT}_j)$: *On input two ciphertexts CT_i and CT_j, it outputs 1 or 0.*

Correctness. We say that the above IBEET is correct if the following holds:

(1) For any security parameter λ, identity ID and message $\mathbf{m}$, it holds that

$$\Pr[\mathbf{m} \leftarrow \mathsf{Dec}(\mathsf{CT}, \mathsf{SK}_{\mathsf{ID}}, \mathsf{tok}_{\mathsf{ID}})] = 1$$

where $(\mathsf{PP}, \mathsf{MSK}, \mathsf{MTK}) \leftarrow \mathsf{Setup}(\lambda)$, $(\mathsf{SK}_{\mathsf{ID}}, \mathsf{tok}_{\mathsf{ID}}) \leftarrow \mathsf{Extract}(\mathsf{ID}, \mathsf{MSK}, \mathsf{MTK})$ and $\mathsf{CT} \leftarrow \mathsf{Enc}(\mathsf{PP}, \mathbf{m}, \mathsf{ID}, \mathsf{tok}_{\mathsf{ID}})$.

(2) For any security parameter λ, identities $\mathsf{ID}_i, \mathsf{ID}_j$ and messages $\mathbf{m}_i, \mathbf{m}_j$, it holds that

$$\Pr\left[\mathsf{Test}\,(\mathsf{CT}_i, \mathsf{CT}_j) = 1 \,\middle|\, \begin{array}{l} (\mathsf{PP}, \mathsf{MSK}, \mathsf{MTK}) \leftarrow \mathsf{Setup}(\lambda) \\ (\mathsf{SK}_{\mathsf{ID}_i}, \mathsf{tok}_{\mathsf{ID}_i}) \leftarrow \mathsf{Extract}(\mathsf{ID}_i, \mathsf{MSK}, \mathsf{MTK}) \\ (\mathsf{SK}_{\mathsf{ID}_j}, \mathsf{tok}_{\mathsf{ID}_j}) \leftarrow \mathsf{Extract}(\mathsf{ID}_j, \mathsf{MSK}, \mathsf{MTK}) \\ \mathsf{CT}_i \leftarrow \mathsf{Enc}(\mathsf{PP}, \mathbf{m}_i, \mathsf{ID}_i, \mathsf{tok}_{\mathsf{ID}_i}) \\ \mathsf{CT}_j \leftarrow \mathsf{Enc}(\mathsf{PP}, \mathbf{m}_j, \mathsf{ID}_j, \mathsf{tok}_{\mathsf{ID}_j}) \end{array}\right]$$

is 1 if $\mathbf{m}_i = \mathbf{m}_j$ and negligible in the security parameter λ otherwise.

Security Model. The security model of IBEET against insider attack [15] is slightly weaker than the formal security model of traditional IBE. In such a scheme, two messages $\mathbf{m}_0$ and $\mathbf{m}_1$ submitted by the adversary to the challenger should not be queried to the encryption oracle before and after the challenge phase. We call this security model the weak indistinguishability under adaptive identity and chosen message attacks (wIND-ID-CPA). In particular, we present the game between the challenger $\mathcal{C}$ and the adversary $\mathcal{A}$ as the following.

1. **Setup:** The challenger $\mathcal{C}$ runs $\mathsf{Setup}(\lambda)$ to generate $(\mathsf{PP}, \mathsf{MSK}, \mathsf{MTK})$ and gives the public parameter PP to $\mathcal{A}$.
2. **Phase 1:** The adversary $\mathcal{A}$ may make queries polynomially many times adaptively and in any order to the following oracles:
   - $\mathcal{O}^{\mathsf{Ext}}$: an oracle that on input an identity ID, returns the ID's secret key $\mathsf{SK}_{\mathsf{ID}}$, where $(\mathsf{SK}_{\mathsf{ID}}, \mathsf{tok}_{\mathsf{ID}}) \leftarrow \mathsf{Extract}(\mathsf{ID}, \mathsf{MSK}, \mathsf{MTK})$.
   - $\mathcal{O}^{\mathsf{Enc}}$: an oracle that on input a pair of an identity ID and a message $\mathbf{m}$, returns the output of $\mathsf{Enc}(\mathsf{PP}, \mathbf{m}, \mathsf{ID}, \mathsf{tok}_{\mathsf{ID}})$.
3. **Challenge:** $\mathcal{A}$ submits a target identity ID^* and two messages $\mathbf{m}_0, \mathbf{m}_1$ of same length to $\mathcal{C}$, where ID^* was never queried to $\mathcal{O}^{\mathsf{Ext}}$ and $\mathbf{m}_0, \mathbf{m}_1$ were never queried to $\mathcal{O}^{\mathsf{Enc}}$ in Phase 1. Then $\mathcal{C}$ picks a random bit $b \in \{0, 1\}$, runs $\mathsf{CT}^*_{\mathsf{ID}^*, b} \leftarrow \mathsf{Enc}(\mathsf{PP}, \mathbf{m}_b, \mathsf{ID}^*, \mathsf{tok}_{\mathsf{ID}^*})$, and sends $\mathsf{CT}^*_{\mathsf{ID}^*, b}$ to $\mathcal{A}$.
4. **Phase 2:** $\mathcal{A}$ can query as in Phase 1 with the following constraints:
   - The target identity ID^* cannot be queried to $\mathcal{O}^{\mathsf{Ext}}$;
   - The submitted messages $\mathbf{m}_0, \mathbf{m}_1$ cannot be queried to $\mathcal{O}^{\mathsf{Enc}}$;
5. **Guess:** $\mathcal{A}$ outputs a bit b'.

The adversary $\mathcal{A}$ wins the above game if $b = b'$ and the advantage of $\mathcal{A}$ is defined as

$$\mathsf{Adv}^{\mathsf{wIND\text{-}ID\text{-}CPA}}_{\mathcal{A}, \mathsf{IBEET}} := \left| \Pr[b = b'] - \frac{1}{2} \right|.$$

2.3   Lattices

Throughout the paper, we will mainly focus on integer lattices, which are discrete subgroups of $\mathbb{Z}^m$. Specially, a lattice Λ in $\mathbb{Z}^m$ with basis $B = [\mathbf{b}_1, \cdots, \mathbf{b}_n] \in \mathbb{Z}^{m \times n}$, where each $\mathbf{b}_i$ is written in column form, is defined as

$$\Lambda := \left\{ \sum_{i=1}^{n} \mathbf{b}_i x_i | x_i \in \mathbb{Z} \ \forall i = 1, \cdots, n \right\} \subseteq \mathbb{Z}^m.$$

We call n the rank of Λ and if $n = m$ we say that Λ is a full rank lattice. In this paper, we mainly consider full rank lattices containing $q\mathbb{Z}^m$, called q-ary lattices, defined as the following, for a given matrix $A \in \mathbb{Z}^{n \times m}$ and $\mathbf{u} \in \mathbb{Z}_q^n$

$$\Lambda_q(A) := \left\{ \mathbf{e} \in \mathbb{Z}^m \text{ s.t. } \exists \mathbf{s} \in \mathbb{Z}_q^n \text{ where } A^T \mathbf{s} = \mathbf{e} \mod q \right\}$$

$$\Lambda_q^{\perp}(A) := \left\{ \mathbf{e} \in \mathbb{Z}^m \text{ s.t. } A\mathbf{e} = 0 \mod q \right\}$$

$$\Lambda_q^{\mathbf{u}}(A) := \left\{ \mathbf{e} \in \mathbb{Z}^m \text{ s.t. } A\mathbf{e} = \mathbf{u} \mod q \right\}$$

Note that if $\mathbf{t} \in \Lambda_q^{\mathbf{u}}(A)$ then $\Lambda_q^{\mathbf{u}}(A) = \Lambda_q^{\perp}(A) + \mathbf{t}$.

Let $S = \{\mathbf{s}_1, \cdots, \mathbf{s}_k\}$ be a set of vectors in $\mathbb{R}^m$. We denote by $\|S\| := \max_i \|\mathbf{s}_i\|$ for $i = 1, \cdots, k$, the maximum l_2 length of the vectors in S. We also denote $\tilde{S} := \{\tilde{\mathbf{s}}_1, \cdots, \tilde{\mathbf{s}}_k\}$ the Gram-Schmidt orthogonalization of the vectors $\mathbf{s}_1, \cdots, \mathbf{s}_k$ in that order. We refer to $\|\tilde{S}\|$ the Gram-Schmidt norm of S.

Ajtai [2] first proposed how to sample a uniform matrix $A \in \mathbb{Z}_q^{n \times m}$ with an associated basis S_A of $\Lambda_q^{\perp}(A)$ with low Gram-Schmidt norm. It is improved later by Alwen and Peikert [3] in the following Theorem.

Theorem 1. *Let $q \geq 3$ be odd and $m := \lceil 6n \log q \rceil$. There is a probabilistic polynomial-time algorithm $\mathsf{TrapGen}(q, n)$ that outputs a pair $(A \in \mathbb{Z}_q^{n \times m}, S \in \mathbb{Z}^{m \times m})$ such that A is statistically close to a uniform matrix in $\mathbb{Z}_q^{n \times m}$ and S is a basis for $\Lambda_q^{\perp}(A)$ satisfying*

$$\|\tilde{S}\| \leq O(\sqrt{n \log q}) \quad and \quad \|S\| \leq O(n \log q)$$

with all but negligible probability in n.

Definition 1 (Gaussian distribution). *Let $\Lambda \subseteq \mathbb{Z}^m$ be a lattice. For a vector $\mathbf{c} \in \mathbb{R}^m$ and a positive parameter $\sigma \in \mathbb{R}$, define:*

$$\rho_{\sigma, \mathbf{c}}(\mathbf{x}) = \exp\left(\pi \frac{\|\mathbf{x} - \mathbf{c}\|^2}{\sigma^2}\right) \quad and \quad \rho_{\sigma, \mathbf{c}}(\Lambda) = \sum_{\mathbf{x} \in \Lambda} \rho_{\sigma, \mathbf{c}}(\mathbf{x}).$$

The discrete Gaussian distribution over Λ with center $\mathbf{c}$ and parameter σ is

$$\forall \mathbf{y} \in \Lambda \quad, \quad \mathcal{D}_{\Lambda, \sigma, \mathbf{c}}(\mathbf{y}) = \frac{\rho_{\sigma, \mathbf{c}}(\mathbf{y})}{\rho_{\sigma, \mathbf{c}}(\Lambda)}.$$

For convenience, we will denote by ρ_σ and $\mathcal{D}_{\Lambda,\sigma}$ for $\rho_{0,\sigma}$ and $\mathcal{D}_{\Lambda,\sigma,0}$ respectively. When $\sigma = 1$ we will write ρ instead of ρ_1. We recall below in Theorem 2 some useful results. The first one comes from [11, Lemma 4.4]. The second one is from [5] and formulated in [1, Theorem 17] and the last one is from [1, Theorem 19].

Theorem 2. *Let $q > 2$ and let A, B be a matrix in $\mathbb{Z}_q^{n \times m}$ with $m > n$ and B is rank n. Let T_A, T_B be a basis for $\Lambda_q^\perp(A)$ and $\Lambda_q^\perp(B)$ respectively. Then for $c \in \mathbb{R}^m$ and $U \in \mathbb{Z}_q^{n \times t}$:*

1. *Let M be a matrix in $\mathbb{Z}_q^{n \times m_1}$ and $\sigma \geq \|\widetilde{T_A}\|\omega(\sqrt{\log(m + m_1)})$. Then there exists a PPT algorithm $\mathsf{SampleLeft}(A, M, T_A, U, \sigma)$ that outputs a vector $\mathbf{e} \in \mathbb{Z}^{m+m_1}$ distributed statistically close to $\mathcal{D}_{\Lambda_q^{\mathbf{u}}(F_1),\sigma}$ where $F_1 := (A \mid M)$. In particular $\mathbf{e} \in \Lambda_q^U(F_1)$, i.e., $F_1 \cdot \mathbf{e} = U \mod q$.*
2. *Let R be a matrix in $\mathbb{Z}^{k \times m}$ and let $s_R := \sup_{\|\mathbf{x}\|=1} \|R\mathbf{x}\|$. Let $F_2 := (A \mid AR+B)$. Then for $\sigma \geq \|\widetilde{T_B}\| s_R \omega(\sqrt{\log m})$, there exists a PPT algorithm $\mathsf{SampleRight}(A, B, R, T_B, U, \sigma)$ that outputs a vector $\mathbf{e} \in \mathbb{Z}^{m+k}$ distributed statistically close to $\mathcal{D}_{\Lambda_q^U(F_2),\sigma}$. In particular $\mathbf{e} \in \Lambda_q^{\mathbf{u}}(F_2)$, i.e., $F_2 \cdot \mathbf{e} = U \mod q$.*
   Note that when R is a random matrix in $\{-1, 1\}^{m \times m}$ then $s_R < O(\sqrt{m})$ with overwhelming probability (cf. [1, Lemma 15]).

The security of our construction reduces to the LWE (Learning With Errors) problem introduced by Regev [12].

Definition 2 (LWE problem). *Consider publicly a prime q, a positive integer n, and a distribution χ over $\mathbb{Z}_q$. An $(\mathbb{Z}_q, n, \chi)$-LWE problem instance consists of access to an unspecified challenge oracle $\mathcal{O}$, being either a noisy pseudorandom sampler $\mathcal{O}_{\mathbf{s}}$ associated with a secret $\mathbf{s} \in \mathbb{Z}_q^n$, or a truly random sampler $\mathcal{O}_{\$}$ who behaviors are as follows:*

$\mathcal{O}_{\mathbf{s}}$: *samples of the form $(\mathbf{u}_i, v_i) = (\mathbf{u}_i, \mathbf{u}_i^T \mathbf{s} + x_i) \in \mathbb{Z}_q^n \times \mathbb{Z}_q$ where $\mathbf{s} \in \mathbb{Z}_q^n$ is a uniform secret key, $\mathbf{u}_i \in \mathbb{Z}_q^n$ is uniform and $x_i \in \mathbb{Z}_q$ is a noise withdrawn from χ.*
$\mathcal{O}_{\$}$: *samples are uniform pairs in $\mathbb{Z}_q^n \times \mathbb{Z}_q$.*

The $(\mathbb{Z}_q, n, \chi)$-LWE problem allows responds queries to the challenge oracle $\mathcal{O}$. We say that an algorithm $\mathcal{A}$ decides the $(\mathbb{Z}_q, n, \chi)$-LWE problem if

$$\mathsf{Adv}_{\mathcal{A}}^{\mathsf{LWE}} := \left| \Pr[\mathcal{A}^{\mathcal{O}_{\mathbf{s}}} = 1] - \Pr[\mathcal{A}^{\mathcal{O}_{\$}} = 1] \right|$$

is non-negligible for a random $\mathbf{s} \in \mathbb{Z}_q^n$.

Regev [12] showed that (see Theorem 3 below) when χ is the distribution $\overline{\Psi}_\alpha$ of the random variable $\lfloor qX \rceil \mod q$ where $\alpha \in (0, 1)$ and X is a normal random variable with mean 0 and standard deviation $\alpha/\sqrt{2\pi}$ then the LWE problem is hard.

Theorem 3. *If there exists an efficient, possibly quantum, algorithm for decid-ing the $(\mathbb{Z}_q, n, \overline{\Psi}_\alpha)$-LWE problem for $q > 2\sqrt{n}/\alpha$ then there is an efficient quan-tum algorithm for approximating the SIVP and GapSVP problems, to within $\tilde{\mathcal{O}}(n/\alpha)$ factors in the l_2 norm, in the worst case.*

Hence if we assume the hardness of approximating the SIVP and GapSVP problems in lattices of dimension n to within polynomial (in n) factors, then it follows from Theorem 3 that deciding the LWE problem is hard when n/α is a polynomial in n.

3   Proposed Construction: IBEET

3.1   Construction

Setup(λ): On input a security parameter λ, set the parameters q, n, m, σ, α as in Sect. 3.2

1. Use TrapGen(q, n) to generate uniformly random $n \times m$-matrices $A, A' \in \mathbb{Z}_q^{n \times m}$ together with trapdoors T_A and $T_{A'}$ respectively.
2. Select $l + 1$ uniformly random $n \times m$ matrices $A_1, \cdots, A_l, B \in \mathbb{Z}_q^{n \times m}$.
3. Select a uniformly random matrix $U \in \mathbb{Z}_q^{n \times t}$.
4. $H : \{0,1\}^* \rightarrow \{0,1\}^t$ is a hash function.
5. $H' : \{0,1\}^* \rightarrow \{0,1\}^l$ is a hash function.
6. Output the public key and the secret key

$$\mathsf{PK} = (A, A', A_1, \cdots, A_l, B, U) \quad , \quad \mathsf{MSK} = (T_A, T_{A'}).$$

Extract(PP, MSK, ID): On input the public parameter PP, a master secret key MSK and an identity $\mathsf{ID} = (b_1, \cdots, b_l) \in \{-1, 1\}^l$:

1. Let $A_{\mathsf{ID}} = B + \sum_{i+1}^l b_i A_i \in \mathbb{Z}_q^{n \times m}$.
2. Sample $E_{\mathsf{ID}}, E'_{\mathsf{ID}} \in \mathbb{Z}_q^{2m \times t}$ as

$$E_{\mathsf{ID}} \leftarrow \mathsf{SampleLeft}(A, A_{\mathsf{ID}}, T_A, U, \sigma) \quad , \quad E'_{\mathsf{ID}} \leftarrow \mathsf{SampleLeft}(A', A_{\mathsf{ID}}, T_{A'}, U, \sigma).$$

3. Output $\mathsf{SK}_{\mathsf{ID}} := (E_{\mathsf{ID}}, E'_{\mathsf{ID}})$.
Let $F_{\mathsf{ID}} = (A|A_{\mathsf{ID}}), F'_{\mathsf{ID}} = (A'|A_{\mathsf{ID}}) \in \mathbb{Z}_q$ then $F_{\mathsf{ID}} \cdot E_{\mathsf{ID}} = U, F'_{\mathsf{ID}} \cdot E'_{\mathsf{ID}} = U$ in $\mathbb{Z}_q$ and $E_{\mathsf{ID}}, E'_{\mathsf{ID}}$ are distributed as $D_{\Lambda_q^U(F_{\mathsf{ID}}),\sigma}, D_{\Lambda_q^U(F'_{\mathsf{ID}}),\sigma}$ respectively.

Encrypt(PP, ID, m): On input the public parameter PP, an identity ID and a message $\mathbf{m} \in \{0,1\}^t$, do:

1. Let $A_{\mathsf{ID}} = B + \sum_{i+1}^l b_i A_i \in \mathbb{Z}_q^{n \times m}$.
2. Set $F_{\mathsf{ID}} := (A|A_{\mathsf{ID}}), F'_{\mathsf{ID}} := (A'|A_{\mathsf{ID}}) \in \mathbb{Z}_q^{n \times 2m}$
3. Choose uniformly random $\mathbf{s}_1, \mathbf{s}_2 \in \mathbb{Z}_q^n$
4. Choose $\mathbf{x}_1, \mathbf{x}_2 \in \overline{\Psi}_\alpha^t$ and compute

$$\mathsf{CT}_1 = U^T \mathbf{s}_1 + \mathbf{x}_1 + \mathbf{m}\left\lfloor \frac{q}{2} \right\rfloor \quad , \quad \mathsf{CT}_2 = U^T \mathbf{s}_2 + \mathbf{x}_2 + H(\mathbf{m})\left\lfloor \frac{q}{2} \right\rfloor \in \mathbb{Z}_q^t.$$

5. Choose l uniformly random matrices $R_i \in \{-1, 1\}^{m \times m}$ for $i = 1, \cdots, l$ and define $R_{\mathsf{ID}} = \sum_{i=1}^l b_i R_i \in \{-l, \cdots, l\}^{m \times m}$.

6. Choose $\mathbf{y}_1, \mathbf{y}_2 \in \overline{\Psi}_\alpha^m$ and set $\mathbf{z}_1 = R_{\mathsf{ID}}^T \mathbf{y}_1, \mathbf{z}_2 = R_{\mathsf{ID}}^T \mathbf{y}_2 \in \mathbb{Z}_q^m$.
7. Compute

$$CT_3 = F_{\mathsf{ID}}^T \mathbf{s}_1 + \begin{bmatrix} \mathbf{y}_1 \\ \mathbf{z}_1 \end{bmatrix}, CT_4 = (F_{\mathsf{ID}}')^T \mathbf{s}_2 + \begin{bmatrix} \mathbf{y}_2 \\ \mathbf{z}_2 \end{bmatrix} \in \mathbb{Z}_q^{2m}.$$

8. The ciphertext is

$$CT_{\mathsf{ID}} = (CT_1, CT_2, CT_3, CT_4) \in \mathbb{Z}_q^{2t+4m}.$$

Decrypt$(PP, SK_{\mathsf{ID}}, CT)$: On input public parameter PP, private key $SK_{\mathsf{ID}} = (E_{\mathsf{ID}}, E_{\mathsf{ID}}')$ and a ciphertext $CT = (CT_1, CT_2, CT_3, CT_4)$, do:
1. Compute $\mathbf{w} \leftarrow CT_1 - E_{\mathsf{ID}}^T CT_3 \in \mathbb{Z}_q^t$.
2. For each $i = 1, \cdots, t$, compare w_i and $\lfloor \frac{q}{2} \rfloor$. If they are close, output $m_i = 1$ and otherwise output $m_i = 0$. We then obtain the message $\mathbf{m}$.
3. Compute $\mathbf{w}' \leftarrow CT_2 - (E_{\mathsf{ID}}')^T CT_4 \in \mathbb{Z}_q^t$.
4. For each $i = 1, \cdots, t$, compare w_i' and $\lfloor \frac{q}{2} \rfloor$. If they are close, output $h_i = 1$ and otherwise output $h_i = 0$. We then obtain the vector $\mathbf{h}$.
5. If $\mathbf{h} = H(\mathbf{m})$ then output $\mathbf{m}$, otherwise output $\perp$.

Trapdoor(SK_{ID}): On input an identity's secret key $SK_{\mathsf{ID}} = (E_{\mathsf{ID}}, E_{\mathsf{ID}}')$, it outputs a trapdoor $td_i = E_{\mathsf{ID}}'$.

Test$(td_{\mathsf{ID}_i}, td_{\mathsf{ID}_j}, CT_{\mathsf{ID}_i}, CT_{\mathsf{ID}_j})$: On input trapdoors $td_{\mathsf{ID}_i}, td_{\mathsf{ID}_j}$ and ciphertexts $CT_{\mathsf{ID}_i}, CT_{\mathsf{ID}_j}$ for identities $\mathsf{ID}_i, \mathsf{ID}_j$ respectively, computes
1. For each i (resp. j), compute $\mathbf{w}_i \leftarrow CT_{i2} - (E_{\mathsf{ID}_i}')^T CT_{i4} \in \mathbb{Z}_q^t$. For each $k = 1, \cdots, t$, compare each coordinate w_{ik} with $\lfloor \frac{q}{2} \rfloor$ and output $h_{ik} = 1$ if they are close, and 0 otherwise. At the end, we obtain the vector $\mathbf{h}_i$ (resp. $\mathbf{h}_j$).
2. Output 1 if $\mathbf{h}_i = \mathbf{h}_j$ and 0 otherwise.

Theorem 4. *Proposed IBEET construction above is correct if H is a collision-resistant hash function.*

Proof. It is easy to see that if CT is a valid ciphertext of $\mathbf{m}$ then the decryption will always output $\mathbf{m}$. Moreover, if CT_{ID_i} and CT_{ID_j} are valid ciphertext of $\mathbf{m}$ and $\mathbf{m}'$ of identities ID_i and ID_j respectively. Then the Test process checks whether $H(\mathbf{m}) = H(\mathbf{m}')$. If so then it outputs 1, meaning that $\mathbf{m} = \mathbf{m}'$, which is always correct with overwhelming probability since H is collision resistant. Hence, proposed IBEET described above is correct. $\qquad\square$

3.2   Parameters

We follow [1, Sect. 7.3] for choosing parameters for our scheme. Now for the system to work correctly we need to ensure

- the error term in decryption is less than $q/5$ with high probability, i.e., $q = \Omega(\sigma m^{3/2})$ and $\alpha < [\sigma l m \omega(\sqrt{\log m})]^{-1}$,
- that the TrapGen can operate, i.e., $m > 6n \log q$,
- that σ is large enough for SampleLeft and SampleRight, i.e., $\sigma > l m \omega(\sqrt{\log m})$,

– that Regev's reduction applies, i.e., $q > 2\sqrt{n}/\alpha$,
– that our security reduction applies (i.e., $q > 2Q$ where Q is the number of identity queries from the adversary).

Hence the following choice of parameters (q, m, σ, α) from [1] satisfies all of the above conditions, taking n to be the security parameter:

$$m = 6n^{1+\delta} \quad , \quad q = \max(2Q, m^{2.5}\omega(\sqrt{\log n}))$$
$$\sigma = ml\omega(\sqrt{\log n}) \quad , \quad \alpha = [l^2 m^2 \omega(\sqrt{\log n})]^{-1} \tag{1}$$

and round up m to the nearest larger integer and q to the nearest larger prime. Here we assume that δ is such that $n^\delta > \lceil \log q \rceil = O(\log n)$. In [1, Sect. 7.5], it is shown that one can remove the restriction $q > 2Q$ and that $q = m^{2.5}\omega(\sqrt{\log n})$ is sufficient.

3.3   Security Analysis

In this section, we claim that our proposed scheme is OW-ID-CPA secure against Type-I adversaries (cf. Theorem 5) and IND-ID-CPA secure against Type-II adversaries (cf. Theorem 6). The proofs will follow a similar argument of Theorem 8. We omit them in the current version and refer to the full version.

Theorem 5. *The IBEET with parameters $(q, n, m, \sigma, \alpha)$ as in (1) is OW-ID-CPA secure provided that H is a one-way hash function and the $(\mathbb{Z}_q, n, \bar{\Psi}_\alpha)$-LWE assumption holds. In particular, suppose there exists a probabilistic algorithm $\mathcal{A}$ that wins the OW-ID-CPA game with advantage ϵ, then there is a probabilistic algorithm $\mathcal{B}$ that solves the $(\mathbb{Z}_q, n, \bar{\Psi}_\alpha)$-LWE problem with advantage ϵ' such that*

$$\epsilon' \geq \frac{1}{2q}(\epsilon - \epsilon_{H,\text{OW}})$$

where $\epsilon_{H,\text{OW}}$ is the advantage of breaking the one-wayness of H.

Theorem 6. *The IBEET with parameters $(q, n, m, \sigma, \alpha)$ as in (1) is IND-ID-CPA secure provided that H is a one-way hash function and the $(\mathbb{Z}_q, n, \bar{\Psi}_\alpha)$-LWE assumption holds. In particular, suppose there exists a probabilistic algorithm $\mathcal{A}$ that wins the IND-ID-CPA game with advantage ϵ, then there is a probabilistic algorithm $\mathcal{B}$ that solves the $(\mathbb{Z}_q, n, \bar{\Psi}_\alpha)$-LWE problem with advantage ϵ' such that*

$$\epsilon' \geq \frac{1}{4q}(\epsilon - -\epsilon_{H,\text{OW}})$$

where $\epsilon_{H,\text{OW}}$ is the advantage of breaking the one-wayness of H.

4   Proposed Construction: IBEET Against Insider Attack

4.1   Construction

Setup(λ): On input a security parameter λ, set the parameters q, n, m, σ, α as in Sect. 3.2

1. Use $\mathsf{TrapGen}(q, n)$ to generate uniformly random $n \times m$-matrices $A, A' \in \mathbb{Z}_q^{n \times m}$ together with trapdoors T_A and $T_{A'}$ respectively.
2. Select $l + 1$ uniformly random $n \times m$ matrices $A_1, \cdots, A_l, B \in \mathbb{Z}_q^{n \times m}$.
3. Select a uniformly random matrix $U \in \mathbb{Z}_q^{n \times t}$.
4. $H : \{0, 1\}^* \rightarrow \mathbb{Z}_q^m$ is a hash function.
5. Output the public parameter, the master secret key MSK and the master token MTK:

$$\mathsf{PP} = (A, A', A_1, \cdots, A_l, B, U) \quad , \quad \mathsf{MSK} = T_A \quad , \quad \mathsf{MTK} = T_{A'}.$$

Extract(ID, MSK, MTK): On input a master secret key MSK, a master token MTK and an identity $\mathsf{ID} = (b_1, \cdots, b_l) \in \{-1, 1\}^l$:
1. Let $A_{\mathsf{ID}} = B + \sum_{i+1}^l b_i A_i \in \mathbb{Z}_q^{n \times m}$.
2. Sample $E_{\mathsf{ID}} \in \mathbb{Z}_q^{2m \times t}$ as $E_{\mathsf{ID}} \leftarrow \mathsf{SampleLeft}(A, A_{\mathsf{ID}}, T_A, U, \sigma)$.
3. Output $\mathsf{SK}_{\mathsf{ID}} := E_{\mathsf{ID}}$ and $\mathsf{tok}_{\mathsf{ID}} = T_{A'}$.
Let $F_{\mathsf{ID}} = (A | A_{\mathsf{ID}})$ then $F_{\mathsf{ID}} \cdot E_{\mathsf{ID}} = U$ in $\mathbb{Z}_q$ and E_{ID} is distributed as $D_{\Lambda_q^U(F_{\mathsf{ID}}), \sigma}$.

Encrypt(PP, ID, $\mathsf{tok}_{\mathsf{ID}}$, $\mathbf{m}$): On input the public parameter PP, an identity ID with its token $\mathsf{tok}_{\mathsf{ID}}$ and a message $\mathbf{m} \in \{0, 1\}^t$, do:
1. Let $A_{\mathsf{ID}} = B + \sum_{i+1}^l b_i A_i \in \mathbb{Z}_q^{n \times m}$ and set $F_{\mathsf{ID}} := (A | A_{\mathsf{ID}}) \in \mathbb{Z}_q^{n \times 2m}$.
2. Choose uniformly random $\mathbf{s}', \mathbf{s} \in \mathbb{Z}_q^m$.
3. Choose $\mathbf{x} \in \overline{\Psi}_\alpha^t$ and compute

$$\mathsf{CT}_1 = T_{A'} \mathbf{s}'^T + H(\mathbf{m} \| T_{A'}) \in \mathbb{Z}_q^m \quad , \quad \mathsf{CT}_2 = U^T \mathbf{s} + \mathbf{x} + \mathbf{m} \lfloor \frac{q}{2} \rfloor \in \mathbb{Z}_q^t.$$

4. Choose l uniformly random matrices $R_i \in \{-1, 1\}^{m \times m}$ for $i = 1, \cdots, l$ and define $R_{\mathsf{ID}} = \sum_{i=1}^l b_i R_i \in \{-l, \cdots, l\}^{m \times m}$.
5. Choose $\mathbf{y} \in \overline{\Psi}_\alpha^m$ and set $\mathbf{z} = R_{\mathsf{ID}}^T \mathbf{y} \in \mathbb{Z}_q^m$.
6. Compute

$$\mathsf{CT}_3 = F_{\mathsf{ID}}^T \mathbf{s} + \begin{bmatrix} \mathbf{y} \\ \mathbf{z} \end{bmatrix} \in \mathbb{Z}_q^{2m}.$$

7. The ciphertext is

$$\mathsf{CT}_{\mathsf{ID}} = (\mathsf{CT}_1, \mathsf{CT}_2, \mathsf{CT}_3) \in \mathbb{Z}_q^{t+3m}.$$

Decrypt($\mathsf{SK}_{\mathsf{ID}}, \mathsf{tok}_{\mathsf{ID}}, \mathsf{CT}$): On input the private key $\mathsf{SK}_{\mathsf{ID}} = E_{\mathsf{ID}}$, token $\mathsf{tok}_{\mathsf{ID}} = T_{A'}$ and a ciphertext $\mathsf{CT} = (\mathsf{CT}_1, \mathsf{CT}_2, \mathsf{CT}_3)$, do:
1. Compute $\mathbf{w} \leftarrow \mathsf{CT}_2 - E_{\mathsf{ID}}^T \mathsf{CT}_3 \in \mathbb{Z}_q^t$.
2. For each $i = 1, \cdots, t$, compare w_i and $\lfloor \frac{q}{2} \rfloor$. If they are close, output $m_i = 1$ and otherwise output $m_i = 0$. We then obtain the message $\mathbf{m}$.
3. Compute $\mathbf{h} := A' \mathsf{CT}_1 \mod q$.
4. If $\mathbf{h} = A' H(\mathbf{m} \| T_{A'}) \mod q$, then output $\mathbf{m}$, otherwise output $\bot$.

Test($\mathsf{CT}_{\mathsf{ID}_i}, \mathsf{CT}_{\mathsf{ID}_j}$): On input ciphertexts $\mathsf{CT}_{\mathsf{ID}_i}, \mathsf{CT}_{\mathsf{ID}_j}$ for identities $\mathsf{ID}_i, \mathsf{ID}_j$ respectively, if $A' \mathsf{CT}_{i,1} = A' \mathsf{CT}_{j,1}$ then output 1, and 0 otherwise.

Theorem 7. *The above construction is correct if H is a collision-resistant hash function.*

Proof. It is easy to see that if CT is a valid ciphertext of $\mathbf{m}$ then the decryption will always output $\mathbf{m}$. Moreover, if $\mathsf{CT}_{\mathsf{ID}_i}$ and $\mathsf{CT}_{\mathsf{ID}_j}$ are valid ciphertext of $\mathbf{m}$ and $\mathbf{m}'$ of identities ID_i and ID_j respectively. Then the Test process checks whether $H(\mathbf{m}\|T_{A'}) = H(\mathbf{m}'\|T_{A'})$. If so then it outputs 1, meaning that $\mathbf{m} = \mathbf{m}'$, which is always correct with overwhelming probability since H is collision resistant. Hence, proposed construction described above is correct. □

4.2 Security Analysis

In this section, we prove that our IBEET scheme is wIND-ID-CPA secure.

Theorem 8. *The IBEET construction with parameters $(q, n, m, \sigma, \alpha)$ as in (1) is wIND-ID-CPA secure provided that H is a one-way hash function and the $(\mathbb{Z}_q, n, \bar{\Psi}_\alpha)$-LWE assumption holds. In particular, suppose there exists a probabilistic algorithm $\mathcal{A}$ that wins the wIND-ID-CPA game with advantage ϵ, then there is a probabilistic algorithm $\mathcal{B}$ that solves the $(\mathbb{Z}_q, n, \bar{\Psi}_\alpha)$-LWE problem with advantage ϵ' such that*

$$\epsilon' \geq \frac{1}{4q}\left(\epsilon - \epsilon_{H,\mathsf{OW}}\right)$$

where $\epsilon_{H,\mathsf{OW}}$ is the advantage of breaking the one-wayness of H.

Proof. Assume that there is an adversary $\mathcal{A}$ who breaks the wIND-ID-CPA security of the IBEET scheme with non-negligible probability ϵ. We construct an algorithm $\mathcal{B}$ who solves the LWE problem using $\mathcal{A}$. We now describe the behavior of $\mathcal{B}$. Assume that ID^* is the target identity of the adversary $\mathcal{A}$ and the challenge ciphertext is $\mathsf{CT}^*_{\mathsf{ID}^*} = (\mathsf{CT}^*_{\mathsf{ID}^*,1}, \mathsf{CT}^*_{\mathsf{ID}^*,2}, \mathsf{CT}^*_{\mathsf{ID}^*,3})$.

We will proceed the proof in a sequence of games. In game i, let $\mathcal{W}_i$ denote the event that the adversary $\mathcal{A}$ correctly guesses the challenge bit. The adversary's advantage in Game i is $\left|\Pr[\mathcal{W}_i] - \frac{1}{2}\right|$.

Game 0. This is the original wIND-ID-CPA game between the ttacker $\mathcal{A}$ against the scheme and the wIND-ID-CPA challenger.

Game 1. This is similar to Game 0 except the way the challenger $\mathcal{B}$ generates the public key for the identity ID^*, as the following. Let $R_i^* \in \{-1,1\}^{m \times m}$ for $i = 1, \cdots, l$ be the ephemeral random matrices generated for the creation of the ciphertext $\mathsf{CT}^*_{\mathsf{ID}^*}$. In this game, the challenger chooses l matrices R_i^* uniformly random in $\{-1,1\}^{m \times m}$ and chooses l random scalars $h_i \in \mathbb{Z}_q$ for $i = 1, \cdots, l$. Then it generates $A, T_{A'}$ and B as in Game 0 and constructs the matrices A_i for $i = 1, \cdots, l$ as

$$A_i \leftarrow A \cdot R_i^* - h_i \cdot B \in \mathbb{Z}_q^{n \times m}.$$

The remainder of the game is unchanged with R_i^*, $i = 1, \cdots, l$, used to generate the challenge ciphertext. Similar to the proof of [1, Theorem 25] we have that the A_i are close to uniform and hence they are random independent matrices in the view of the adversary as in Game 0. Therefore

$$\Pr[\mathcal{W}_1] = \Pr[\mathcal{W}_0].$$

Game 2. This is similar to Game 1 except that at the challenge phase, $\mathcal{B}$ chooses arbitrary message $\mathbf{m}'$ from the message space and encrypts $\mathbf{m}'$ in $\mathsf{CT}_{\mathsf{ID},1}$. Other steps are similar to Game 1. Here we can not expect the behavior of $\mathcal{A}$. Since A' is public, $\mathcal{A}$ can obtain $A'H(\mathbf{m}'\|T_A')$. At the end if $\mathcal{A}$ outputs $\mathbf{m}'$, call this event E_2, then $\mathcal{A}$ has broken the one-wayness of the hash function H. Therefore we have

$$\Pr[W_1] - \Pr[W_2] \leq \epsilon_{H,\mathsf{OW}}$$

where $\epsilon_{H,\mathsf{OW}}$ is the advantage of $\mathcal{A}$ in breaking the one-wayness of H.

Game 3. This game is similar to Game 2 except that we add an abort that is independent of adversary's view. The challenger behaves as follows:
- The setup phase is identical to Game 2 except that the challenger also chooses random $h_i \in \mathbb{Z}_q$, $i = 1, \cdots, l$ and keeps it to itself.
- In the final guess phase, the adversary outputs a random guess $b' \in \{0, 1\}$ for b. The challenger now does the following:
    1. **Abort check:** for all queries $\mathsf{CT}_{\mathsf{ID}}$ to the decryption oracle $\mathcal{O}^{\mathsf{Dec}}$, the challenger checks whether the identity $\mathsf{ID} = (b_1, \cdots, b_l)$ satisfies $1 + \sum_{i=1}^{h} b_i h_i \neq 0$ and $1 + \sum_{i=1}^{h} b_i^* h_i = 0$. If not then the challenger overwrites b' with a fresh random bit in $\{0, 1\}$ and aborts the game.
    2. **Artificial abort:** the challenger samples a message Γ such that $\Pr[\Gamma = 1]$ is calculated through a function $\mathcal{G}$ (defined as in [1]) evaluated through all the queries of $\mathcal{A}$. If $\Gamma = 1$ the challenger overwrites b' with a fresh random bit and aborts the game (due to artificial abort); see [1] for more details.

It follows from the proof of [1, Theorem 25] that

$$\left| \Pr[\mathcal{W}_3] - \frac{1}{2} \right| \geq \frac{1}{4q} \left| \Pr[\mathcal{W}_2] - \frac{1}{2} \right|.$$

Game 4. We now change the way how A and B are generated in Game 3. In Game 4, A is a random matrix in $\mathbb{Z}_q^{n \times m}$ and B is generated through $\mathsf{TrapGen}(q, n)$ together with an associated trapdoor T_B for $\Lambda_q^{\perp}(B)$. The construction of A_i for $i = 1, \cdots, l$ remains the same as in Game 3, i.e., $A_i = AR_i^* - h_i B$. When $\mathcal{A}$ queries $\mathcal{O}^{\mathsf{Ext}}(\mathsf{ID})$ for the secret key of $\mathsf{ID} = (b_1, \cdots, b_l)$, $\mathcal{B}$ performs as follows:
- $\mathcal{B}$ sets

$$F_{\mathsf{ID}} := (A|B + \sum_{i=1}^{l} A_i) = (A|AR + h_{\mathsf{ID}}B)$$

where

$$R \leftarrow \sum_{i=1}^{l} b_i R_i^* \in \mathbb{Z}_q^{n \times m} \quad \text{and} \quad h_{\mathsf{ID}} \leftarrow 1 + \sum_{i=1}^{l} b_i h_i \in \mathbb{Z}_q. \tag{2}$$

- If $h_{\mathsf{ID}} = 0$ then abort the game and pretend that the adversary outputs a random bit b' as in Game 3.
- Set $E_{\mathsf{ID}} \leftarrow \mathsf{SampleRight}(A, h_{\mathsf{ID}}B, R, T_B, U, \sigma) \in \mathbb{Z}_q^{2m \times t}$. Note that since h_{ID} is non-zero, and so T_B is also a trapdoor for $h_\theta B$. And hence the output E_{ID} satisfies $F_{\mathsf{ID}} \cdot E_{\mathsf{ID}} = U$ in $\mathbb{Z}_q^t$. Moreover, Theorem 2 shows that when $\sigma > \|\widetilde{T_B}\|s_R\omega(\sqrt{m})$ with $s_R := \|R\|$, the generated E_{ID} is distributed close to $\mathcal{D}_{\Lambda_q^U}(F_{\mathsf{ID}})$ as in Game 2.
- Return $\mathsf{SK}_{\mathsf{ID}} := E_{\mathsf{ID}}$.

Game 4 is otherwise the same as Game 3. In particular, in the challenge phase, the challenger checks if $\mathsf{ID}^* = (b_1^*, \cdots, b_l^*)$ satisfies $1 + \sum_{i=1}^l b_i^* h_i = 0$. If not, the challenger aborts the game as in Game 3. Similarly, in Game 4, the challenger also implements an artificial abort in the guess phase. Since Game 3 and Game 2 are identical in the adversary's view, we have that

$$\Pr[\mathcal{W}_4] = \Pr[\mathcal{W}_3].$$

Game 5. Game 5 is identical to Game 4, except that the challenge ciphertext is always chosen randomly. And thus the advantage of $\mathcal{A}$ is always 0.

We now show that Game 4 and Game 5 are computationally indistinguishable. If the abort event happens then the games are clearly indistinguishable. We, therefore, consider only the queries that do not cause an abort.

Suppose now $\mathcal{A}$ has a non-negligible advantage in distinguishing Game 4 and Game 5. We use $\mathcal{A}$ to construct $\mathcal{B}$ to solve the LWE problem as follows.

Setup. First of all, $\mathcal{B}$ requests from $\mathcal{O}$ and receives, for each $j = 1, \cdots, t$ a fresh pair $(\mathbf{a}_i, d_i) \in \mathbb{Z}_q^n \times \mathbb{Z}_q$ and for each $i = 1, \cdots, m$, a fresh pair $(\mathbf{u}_i, v_i) \in \mathbb{Z}_q^n \times \mathbb{Z}_q$. $\mathcal{A}$ announces an identity ID for the target identity. $\mathcal{B}$ constructs the public parameter PP as follows:

1. Assemble the random matrix $A \in \mathbb{Z}_q^{n \times m}$ from m of previously given LWE samples by letting the i-th column of A to be the n-vector $\mathbf{u}_i$ for all $i = 1, \cdots, m$.
2. Assemble the first t unused LWE samples $\mathbf{a}_1, \cdots, \mathbf{a}_t$ to become a public random matrix $U \in \mathbb{Z}_q^{n \times t}$.
3. Run $\mathsf{TrapGen}(q, \sigma)$ to generate uniformly random matrices $A', B \in \mathbb{Z}_q^{n \times m}$ together with their trapdoor $T_{A'}$ and T_B respectively.
4. Choose l random matrices $R_i^* \in \{-1, 1\}^{m \times m}$ for $i = 1, \cdots, l$ and l random scalars $h_i \in \mathbb{Z}_q$ for $i = 1, \cdots, l$. Next it constructs the matrices A_i for $i = 1, \cdots, l$ as
$$A_i \leftarrow AR_i^* - h_iB \in \mathbb{Z}_q^{n \times m}.$$

   Note that it follows from the leftover hash lemma [14, Theorem 8.38] that $A_1, \cdots, A_l$ are statistically close to uniform.
5. Set $\mathsf{PP} := (A, A', A_1, \cdots, A_l, B, U)$ and send to $\mathcal{A}$.

Queries. $\mathcal{B}$ answers the queries as in Game 4, including aborting the game if needed.

Challenge. Now when $\mathcal{A}$ sends $\mathcal{B}$ two messages $\mathbf{m}_0$ and $\mathbf{m}_1$ and a target identity ID^*. $\mathcal{B}$ choose a random bit $b \in \{0,1\}$ and computes the challenge ciphertext $\mathsf{CT}^*_{\mathsf{ID}^*} = (\mathsf{CT}^*_{\mathsf{ID}^*,1}, \mathsf{CT}^*_{\mathsf{ID}^*,2}, \mathsf{CT}^*_{\mathsf{ID}^*,3})$ for $\mathbf{m}_b$ as follows:

1. Choose a random $\mathbf{s}' \in \mathbb{Z}_q^m$ and compute

$$\mathsf{CT}^*_{\mathsf{ID}^*,1} = T_{A'}\mathbf{s}'^T + H(\mathbf{m}_b \| T_{A'}) \in \mathbb{Z}_q^m.$$

2. Assemble $d_1, \cdots, d_t, v_1, \cdots, v_m$ from the entries of the samples to form $\mathbf{d}^* = [d_1, \cdots, d_t]^T \in \mathbb{Z}_q^t$ and $\mathbf{v}^* = [v_1, \cdots, v_m]^T \in \mathbb{Z}_q^m$.
3. Set $\mathsf{CT}^*_{\mathsf{ID}^*,2} \leftarrow \mathbf{d}^* + \mathbf{m}_b \lfloor \frac{q}{2} \rfloor \in \mathbb{Z}_q^t$.
4. Compute $R^*_{\mathsf{ID}^*} := \sum_{i=1}^{l} b_i^* R_i^* \in \{-l, \cdots, l\}^{m \times m}$.
5. Set

$$\mathsf{CT}^*_{\mathsf{ID}^*,3} := \begin{bmatrix} \mathbf{v}^* \\ (R^*_{\mathsf{ID}^*})^T \mathbf{v}^* \end{bmatrix} \in \mathbb{Z}_q^{2m}.$$

Then $\mathcal{B}$ sends $\mathsf{CT}^*_{\mathsf{ID}^*} = (\mathsf{CT}^*_{\mathsf{ID}^*,1}, \mathsf{CT}^*_{\mathsf{ID}^*,2}, \mathsf{CT}^*_{\mathsf{ID}^*,3})$ to $\mathcal{A}$.

Note that in case of no abort, one has $h_{\mathsf{ID}^*} = 0$ and so $F_{\mathsf{ID}^*} = (A | AR^*_{\mathsf{ID}^*})$. When the oracle is pseudorandom, i.e., $\mathcal{O} = \mathcal{O}_s$ then $\mathbf{v}^* = A^T \mathbf{s} + \mathbf{y}$ for some random noise vector $\mathbf{y} \leftarrow \overline{\Psi}_\alpha^m$. Therefore $\mathsf{CT}^*_{\mathsf{ID}^*,3}$ in Step 5 satisfies:

$$\mathsf{CT}^*_{\mathsf{ID}^*,3} := \begin{bmatrix} A^T \mathbf{s} + \mathbf{y} \\ (AR^*_{\mathsf{ID}^*})^T \mathbf{s} + (R^*_{\mathsf{ID}^*})^T \mathbf{y} \end{bmatrix} = (F^*_{\mathsf{ID}})^T \mathbf{s} + \begin{bmatrix} \mathbf{y} \\ (R^*_{\mathsf{ID}^*})^T \mathbf{y} \end{bmatrix}.$$

Moreover, $\mathbf{d}^* = U^T \mathbf{s} + \mathbf{x}$ for some $\mathbf{x} \leftarrow \overline{\Psi}_\alpha^t$ and therefore

$$\mathsf{CT}^*_{\mathsf{ID}^*,2} = U^T \mathbf{s} + \mathbf{x} + \mathbf{m}_b \lfloor \frac{q}{2} \rfloor.$$

Therefore $\mathsf{CT}^*_{\mathsf{ID}^*}$ is a valid ciphertext.

When $\mathcal{O} = \mathcal{O}_{\$}$ we have that $\mathbf{d}^*$ is uniform in $\mathbb{Z}_q^t$ and $\mathbf{v}^*$ is uniform in $\mathbb{Z}_q^m$. Then obviously $\mathsf{CT}^*_{\mathsf{ID}^*,2}$ is uniform. It follows also from the leftover hash lemma (cf. [14, Theorem 8.38]) that $\mathsf{CT}^*_{\mathsf{ID}^*,3}$ is also uniform.

Guess. After Phase 2, $\mathcal{A}$ guesses if it is interacting with a Game 4 or Game 5. The simulator also implements the artificial abort from Game 4 and Game 5 and output the final guess as to the answer to the LWE problem.

We have seen above that when $\mathcal{O} = \mathcal{O}_s$ then the adversary's view is as in Game 4. When $\mathcal{O} = \mathcal{O}_{\$}$ then the view of the adversary is as in Game 5. Hence the advantage ϵ' of $\mathcal{B}$ in solving the LWE problem is the same as the advantage of $\mathcal{A}$ in distinguishing Game 4 and Game 5. Since $\Pr[\mathcal{W}_5] = 0$, we have

$$\Pr[\mathcal{W}_4] = \Pr[\mathcal{W}_4] - \Pr[\mathcal{W}_5] \le \epsilon'.$$

Hence combining the above results yields the desired result. We obtain that

$$\epsilon = \Pr[W_0] \le \epsilon_{H,\mathsf{OW}} + 4q\epsilon'$$

which implies

$$\epsilon' \ge \frac{1}{4q}(\epsilon - \epsilon_{H,\mathsf{OW}})$$

as desired. $\qquad\qquad\qquad\qquad\qquad\qquad\qquad\qquad\qquad\qquad\qquad\qquad\qquad\quad \square$

5   Conclusion

In this paper, we propose a direct construction of IBEET based on the hardness of Learning With Errors problem. Efficiency is the reason to avoid the instantiation of lattice-based IBEET from the generic construction by Lee et al. [7]. In addition, we also modify our scheme to obtain an IBEET against insider attack. We will leave as a future work for improving our schemes to achieve CCA2-security as well as to support flexible authorisation.

Acknowledgement. This work is supported by the Australian Research Council Discovery Project DP180100665. We would like to thank Tsz Hon Yuen and anonymous reviewers for many helpful comments and fruitful discussions.

Appendix A: An Instantiation of Lee et al.'s Construction

In this section, we will present a lattice-based IBEET which is an instantiation of the Lee et al.'s construction [7]. In their generic construction, they need (i) a multi-bit HIBE scheme and (ii) an one-time signature scheme. To instantiate their construction, we modify the lattice based single-bit HIBE of [1] to multi-bit one and use it, along with the signature scheme, to have following construction of lattice based IBEET. Even though one needs only a one-time signature scheme, we choose the full secure signature scheme from [1] to unify the system, since in such case, both signature and HIBE schemes use the same public key. It is required to use multi-bit HIBE and signature scheme to have IBEET from Lee et al.'s [7].

In what follows, we will denote by $[id_1.id_2.id_3]$ the identity of a 3-level HIBE scheme where id_1 is the first level identity, id_2 is the second level identity and id_3 is third level identity. Below, we follow [7] to denote by [ID.0] (resp. [ID.1]) an identity in the second level in which we indicate that ID is the identity of the first level.

A.1 Construction

Setup(λ)

On input security parameter λ, and a maximum hierarchy depth 3, set the parameters $q, n, m, \bar{\sigma}, \bar{\alpha}$. The vector $\bar{\sigma}$ & $\bar{\alpha} \in \mathbb{R}^2$ and we use σ_l and α_l to refer to their l- th coordinate.

1. Use algorithm TrapGen(q, n) to select a uniformly random $n \times m$- matrix $A, A' \in \mathbb{Z}_q^{n \times m}$ with a basis $T_A, T_{A'}$ for $\Lambda_q^\perp(A)$ and $\Lambda_q^\perp(A')$, respectively. Repeat this Step until A and A' have rank n.
2. Select $l + 1$ uniformly random $m \times m$ matrices $A_1, A_2, A_3, \cdots, A_l, B \in \mathbb{Z}_q^{n \times m}$.
3. Select a uniformly random matrix $U \in \mathbb{Z}_q^{n \times t}$.
4. We need some hash functions $H : \{0,1\}^* \to \{0,1\}^t$, $H_1 : \{0,1\}^* \to \{-1,1\}^t$, $H_2 : \{0,1\}^* \to \mathbb{Z}_q^n$ and a full domain difference map $H' : \mathbb{Z}_q^n \to \mathbb{Z}_q^{n \times n}$ as in [1, Sect. 5].

5. Output the public key and the secret key

$$PK = (A, A', A_1, A_2, A_3, \cdots, A_l, B, U) \quad, \quad MSK = T_A, \quad sk_s = T_{A'}$$

Extract(PP, MSK, ID): On input the public parameter PP, a master secret key MSK and an identity $ID(\in \mathbb{Z}_q^n) = (b_1, \cdots, b_l) \in \{-1, 1\}^l$:
1. Let $A_{ID} = A_1 + H'(ID)B \in \mathbb{Z}_q^{n \times m}$.
2. Sample $E \in \mathbb{Z}_q^{2m \times t}$ as

$$E \leftarrow \mathsf{SampleBasisLeft}(A, A_{ID}, T_A, U, \sigma).$$

3. Output $SK_{ID} := E$.
Let $F_{ID} = (A|A_{ID}) \in \mathbb{Z}_q^{n \times 2m}$ then $F_{ID} \cdot E = U$ in $\mathbb{Z}_q$ and E is distributed as $D_{\Lambda_q^U(F_{ID}),\sigma}$.

Enc(PP, ID, m)
On input the public key PK and a message $\mathbf{m} \in \{0, 1\}^t$ do
1. Choose uniformly random $\mathbf{s}_1, \mathbf{s}_2 \in \mathbb{Z}_q^n$.
2. Choose $\mathbf{x}_1, \mathbf{x}_2 \in \overline{\Psi}_\alpha^t$ and compute

$$\mathbf{c}_1 = U^T \mathbf{s}_1 + \mathbf{x}_1 + \mathbf{m} \left\lfloor \frac{q}{2} \right\rfloor \in \mathbb{Z}_q^t,$$

$$\mathbf{c}_2 = U^T \mathbf{s}_2 + \mathbf{x}_2 + H(\mathbf{m}) \left\lfloor \frac{q}{2} \right\rfloor \in \mathbb{Z}_q^t.$$

3. Set $vk_s = A_1 \| \cdots \| A_l$.
4. Set $id := H_2(vk_s) \in \mathbb{Z}_q^n$.
5. Build the following matrices in $\mathbb{Z}_q^{n \times 4m}$:

$$F_{ID.0.vk_s} = (F_{ID}|A_2 + H'(0) \cdot B|A_3 + H'(id) \cdot B),$$
$$F_{ID.1.vk_s} = (F_{ID}|A_2 + H'(1) \cdot B|A_3 + H'(id) \cdot B).$$

6. Choose a uniformly random $n \times 2m$ matrix R in $\{-1, 1\}^{n \times 3m}$.
7. Choose $\mathbf{y}_1, \mathbf{y}_2 \in \overline{\Psi}_\alpha^m$ and set $\mathbf{z}_1 = R^T \mathbf{y}_1, \mathbf{z}_2 = R^T \mathbf{y}_2 \in \mathbb{Z}_q^{3m}$.
8. Compute

$$\mathbf{c}_3 = F_{ID.0.vk_s}^T \mathbf{s}_1 + [\mathbf{y}_1^T | \mathbf{z}_1^T]^T \in \mathbb{Z}_q^{4m},$$

$$\mathbf{c}_4 = F_{ID.1.vk_s}^T \mathbf{s}_2 + [\mathbf{y}_2^T | \mathbf{z}_2^T]^T \in \mathbb{Z}_q^{4m}.$$

9. Let $\mathbf{b} := H_1(\mathbf{c}_1 \| \mathbf{c}_2 \| \mathbf{c}_3 \| \mathbf{c}_4) \in \{-1, 1\}^l$ and define a matrix

$$F = (A'|B + \sum_{i=1}^{l} b_i A_i) \in \mathbb{Z}_q^{n \times 2m}.$$

10. Extract a signature $\mathbf{e} \in \mathbb{Z}^{2m \times t}$ by

$$\mathbf{e} \leftarrow \mathsf{SampleBasisLeft}(A', B + \sum_{i=1}^{l} b_i A_i, T_{A'}, 0, \sigma).$$

Note that $F \cdot \mathbf{e} = 0 \mod q$.

11. Output the ciphertext

$$CT = (vk, \mathbf{c}_1, \mathbf{c}_2, \mathbf{c}_3, \mathbf{c}_4, \mathbf{e}).$$

$\mathsf{Dec}(\mathsf{PP}, \mathsf{SK}_{\mathsf{ID}}, \mathsf{CT})$

On input a secret key $\mathsf{SK}_{\mathsf{ID}}$ and a ciphertext CT, do
1. Parse the ciphertext CT into

$$(vk, \mathbf{c}_1, \mathbf{c}_2, \mathbf{c}_3, \mathbf{c}_4, \mathbf{e}).$$

2. Let $\mathbf{b} := H_1(\mathbf{c}_1 \| \mathbf{c}_2 \| \mathbf{c}_3 \| \mathbf{c}_4) \in \{-1, 1\}^l$ and define a matrix

$$F = (A' | B + \sum_{i=1}^{l} b_i A_i) \in \mathbb{Z}_q^{n \times 2m}.$$

3. If $F \cdot \mathbf{e} = 0$ in $\mathbb{Z}_q$ and $\|\mathbf{e}\| \le \sigma\sqrt{2m}$ then continue to Step 4; otherwise output $\perp$.
4. Set $id := H_2(vk) \in \mathbb{Z}_q^n$ and build the following matrices:

$$F_{\mathsf{ID}.0} = (F_{\mathsf{ID}} | A_2 + H'(0) \cdot B) \in \mathbb{Z}_q^{n \times 3m},$$
$$F_{\mathsf{ID}.1} = (F_{\mathsf{ID}} | A_2 + H'(1) \cdot B) \in \mathbb{Z}_q^{n \times 3m}.$$

$$F_{\mathsf{ID}.0.vk_s} = (F_{\mathsf{ID}} | A_2 + H'(0) \cdot B | A_3 + H'(id) \cdot B) \in \mathbb{Z}_q^{n \times 4m},$$
$$F_{\mathsf{ID}.1.vk_s} = (F_{\mathsf{ID}} | A_2 + H'(1) \cdot B | A_3 + H'(id) \cdot B) \in \mathbb{Z}_q^{n \times 4m}.$$

5. Generate

$$E_{\mathsf{ID}.0} \leftarrow \mathsf{SampleBasisLeft}(F_{\mathsf{ID}}, A_2 + H'(0) \cdot B, E, U, \sigma)$$
$$s.t.\ F_{\mathsf{ID}.0} \cdot E_{\mathsf{ID}.0} = U$$
$$E_{\mathsf{ID}.1} \leftarrow \mathsf{SampleBasisLeft}(F_{\mathsf{ID}}, A_2 + H'(1) \cdot B, E, U, \sigma)$$
$$s.t.\ F_{\mathsf{ID}.1} \cdot E_{\mathsf{ID}.1} = U$$
$$E_{\mathsf{ID}.0.vk_s} \leftarrow \mathsf{SampleBasisLeft}(F_{\mathsf{ID}.0}, A_3 + H'(0) \cdot B, E_{\mathsf{ID}.0}, U, \sigma)$$
$$s.t.\ F_{\mathsf{ID}.0.vk_s} \cdot E_{\mathsf{ID}.0.vk_s} = U$$
$$E_{\mathsf{ID}.1.vk_s} \leftarrow \mathsf{SampleBasisLeft}(F_{\mathsf{ID}.1}, A_3 + H'(1) \cdot B, E_{\mathsf{ID}.1}, U, \sigma)$$
$$s.t.\ F_{\mathsf{ID}.1.vk_s} \cdot E_{\mathsf{ID}.1.vk_s} = U.$$

6. Compute $\mathbf{w} \leftarrow \mathbf{c}_1 - E_{\mathsf{ID}.0.vk_s}^T \mathbf{c}_3 \in \mathbb{Z}_q^t$.
7. For each $i = 1, \cdots, t$, compare w_i and $\lfloor \frac{q}{2} \rfloor$. If they are close, output $m_i = 1$ and otherwise output $m_i = 0$. We then obtain the message $\mathbf{m}$.
8. Compute $\mathbf{w}' \leftarrow \mathbf{c}_2 - E_{\mathsf{ID}.1.vk_s}^T \mathbf{c}_4 \in \mathbb{Z}_q^t$.
9. For each $i = 1, \cdots, t$, compare w'_i and $\lfloor \frac{q}{2} \rfloor$. If they are close, output $h_i = 1$ and otherwise output $h_i = 0$. We then obtain the vector $\mathbf{h}$.
10. If $\mathbf{h} = H(\mathbf{m})$ then output $\mathbf{m}$, otherwise output $\perp$.

Td(SK$_i$)

On input the secret key SK$_i$($= E_i$) of a user U_i, run

$$\text{td}_i \leftarrow \text{SampleBasisLeft}(F_{\text{ID}}, A_2 + H'(1) \cdot B, E_i, U, \sigma).$$

Test(td$_i$, td$_j$, CT$_i$, CT$_j$)

On input trapdoors td$_i$, td$_j$ and ciphertexts CT$_i$, CT$_j$ of users U_i and U_j respectively, for $k = i, j$, do the following

1. Parse CT$_k$ into

$$(vk_k, \mathbf{c}_{k,1}, \mathbf{c}_{k,2}, \mathbf{c}_{k,3}, \mathbf{c}_{k,4}, \mathbf{e}_k).$$

2. Sample $E_{\text{ID}_k.1.vk_s} \in \mathbb{Z}_q^{5m \times t}$ from

$$\text{SampleBasisLeft}(F_{\text{ID}_k.1}, A_{k,3} + H'(1) \cdot B_k, E_{\text{ID}_k.1}, U, \sigma).$$

3. Use $E_{\text{ID}_k.1.vk_s}$ to decrypt $\mathbf{c}_{k,2}$, $\mathbf{c}_{k,4}$ as in Step 8–9 of Dec(SK, CT) above to obtain the hash value $\mathbf{h}_k$.

4. If $\mathbf{h}_i = \mathbf{h}_j$ then ouput 1; otherwise output 0.

Theorem 5 (Correctness). *The above IBEET is correct if the hash function H is collision resistant.*

Proof. Since we employ the multi-bit HIBE and signature scheme from [1], their correctness follow from [1]. The Theorem follows from [7, Theorem 1]. □

A.2 Parameters

We follow [1, Sect. 8.3] for choosing parameters for our scheme. Now for the system to work correctly we need to ensure

- the error term in decryption is less than $q/5$ with high probability, i.e., $q = \Omega(\sigma m^{3/2})$ and $\alpha < [\sigma l m \omega(\sqrt{\log m})]^{-1}$,
- that the TrapGen can operate, i.e., $m > 6n \log q$,
- that σ is large enough for SampleLeft and SampleRight, i.e., $\sigma > l m \omega(\sqrt{\log m})$,
- that Regev's reduction applies, i.e., $q > 2\sqrt{n}/\alpha$,

Hence the following choice of parameters (q, m, σ, α) from [1] satisfies all of the above conditions, taking n to be the security parameter:

$$
\begin{aligned}
m &= 6n^{1+\delta} \quad , \quad q = \max(2Q, m^{2.5}\omega(\sqrt{\log n})) \\
\sigma &= m l \omega(\sqrt{\log n}) \quad , \quad \alpha = [l^2 m^2 \omega(\sqrt{\log n})]
\end{aligned}
\tag{3}
$$

and round up m to the nearest larger integer and q to the nearest larger prime. Here we assume that δ is such that $n^\delta > \lceil \log q \rceil = O(\log n)$.

Theorem 6. *The IBEET constructed in Sect. 5 with paramaters as in (3) is IND-ID-CCA2 secure provided that H_1 is collision resistant.*

Proof. The HIBE is IND-sID-CPA secure by [1, Theorem 33] and the signature is strongly unforgeable by [1, Sect. 7.5]. The result follows from [7, Theorem 5]. □

Theorem 7 ([7, Theorem 3]). *The IBEET with parameters $(q, n, m, \sigma, \alpha)$ as in (3) is OW-ID-CCA2 provided that H is one-way and H_1 is collision resistant.*

Proof. The HIBE is IND-sID-CPA secure by [1, Theorem 33] and the signature is strongly unforgeable by [1, Sect. 7.5]. The result follows from [7, Theorem 6]. □

References

1. Agrawal, S., Boneh, D., Boyen, X.: Efficient lattice (H)IBE in the standard model. In: Gilbert, H. (ed.) EUROCRYPT 2010. LNCS, vol. 6110, pp. 553–572. Springer, Heidelberg (2010). https://doi.org/10.1007/978-3-642-13190-5_28
2. Ajtai, M.: Generating hard instances of the short basis problem. In: Wiedermann, J., van Emde Boas, P., Nielsen, M. (eds.) ICALP 1999. LNCS, vol. 1644, pp. 1–9. Springer, Heidelberg (1999). https://doi.org/10.1007/3-540-48523-6_1
3. Alwen, J., Peikert, C.: Generating shorter bases for hard random lattices. In: Proceedings of the 26th International Symposium on Theoretical Aspects of Computer Science, STACS 2009, Freiburg, Germany, 26–28 February 2009, pp. 75–86 (2009)
4. Boneh, D., Canetti, R., Halevi, S., Katz, J.: Chosen-ciphertext security from identity-based encryption. SIAM J. Comput. **36**(5), 1301–1328 (2007)
5. Cash, D., Hofheinz, D., Kiltz, E., Peikert, C.: Bonsai trees, or how to delegate a lattice basis. In: Gilbert, H. (ed.) EUROCRYPT 2010. LNCS, vol. 6110, pp. 523–552. Springer, Heidelberg (2010). https://doi.org/10.1007/978-3-642-13190-5_27
6. Duong, D.H., Fukushima, K., Kiyomoto, S., Roy, P.S., Susilo, W.: A lattice-based public key encryption with equality test in standard model. In: Jang-Jaccard, J., Guo, F. (eds.) ACISP 2019. LNCS, vol. 11547, pp. 138–155. Springer, Cham (2019). https://doi.org/10.1007/978-3-030-21548-4_8
7. Lee, H.T., Ling, S., Seo, J.H., Wang, H., Youn, T.-Y.: Public key encryption with equality test in the standard model. Cryptology ePrint Archive, Report 2016/1182 (2016)
8. Lee, H.T., Ling, S., Seo, J.H., Wang, H.: Semi-generic construction of public key encryption and identity-based encryption with equality test. Inf. Sci. **373**, 419–440 (2016)
9. Lee, H.T., Wang, H., Zhang, K.: Security analysis and modification of ID-based encryption with equality test from ACISP 2017. In: Susilo, W., Yang, G. (eds.) ACISP 2018. LNCS, vol. 10946, pp. 780–786. Springer, Cham (2018). https://doi.org/10.1007/978-3-319-93638-3_46
10. Ma, S.: Identity-based encryption with outsourced equality test in cloud computing. Inf. Sci. **328**, 389–402 (2016)
11. Micciancio, D., Regev, O.: Worst-case to average-case reductions based on Gaussian measures. In: Proceedings of the 45th Symposium on Foundations of Computer Science (FOCS 2004), Rome, Italy, 17–19 October 2004, pp. 372–381 (2004)
12. Regev, O.: On lattices, learning with errors, random linear codes, and cryptography. In: Proceedings of the 37th Annual ACM Symposium on Theory of Computing, Baltimore, MD, USA, 22–24 May 2005, pp. 84–93 (2005)

13. Shor, P.W.: Polynomial-time algorithms for prime factorization and discrete logarithms on a quantum computer. SIAM J. Comput. **26**(5), 1484–1509 (1997)
14. Shoup, V.: A Computational Introduction to Number Theory and Algebra, 2nd edn. Cambridge University Press, Cambridge (2008)
15. Wu, T., Ma, S., Mu, Y., Zeng, S.: ID-based encryption with equality test against insider attack. In: Pieprzyk, J., Suriadi, S. (eds.) ACISP 2017, Part I. LNCS, vol. 10342, pp. 168–183. Springer, Cham (2017). https://doi.org/10.1007/978-3-319-60055-0_9

Password-Based Authenticated Key Exchange from Standard Isogeny Assumptions

Shintaro Terada and Kazuki Yoneyama$^{(\boxtimes)}$

Ibaraki University, 4-12-1, Nakanarusawa, Hitachi-shi, Ibaraki, Japan
kazuki.yoneyama.sec@vc.ibaraki.ac.jp

Abstract. The isogeny-based cryptosystems are considered as one of post-quantum cryptosystems. Taraskin et al. proposed a password-based authenticated key exchange (PAKE) scheme from isogeny by extending Jao et al.'s supersingular isogeny Diffie-Hellman (SIDH) protocol. In their scheme, a new group action is introduced in addition to SIDH due to non-commutativity of SIDH in order to embed the password to the DH public key. Also, in the security proof, new non-standard assumptions regarding the new group action are necessary. It is not clear if these assumptions are really hard.

In this paper, we propose new PAKE schemes, SIDH-EKE and CSIDH-EKE, which are secure under the standard assumptions (corresponding to the computational DH assumption). Our schemes are obtained by a combination of SIDH (or CSIDH, commutative SIDH) and EKE (encrypted key exchange). We prove security of our schemes under the same standard assumptions as original SIDH and CSIDH in the random oracle model and ideal cipher model. CSIDH-EKE achieves more compact communication overhead than Taraskin et al.'s scheme.

Keywords: Authenticated key exchange ·
Password-based authenticated key exchange ·
Isogeny-based cryposystems

1 Introduction

1.1 Backgrounds

Post-quantum cryptosystems (PQC) are one of hottest research topics in cryptography due to emerging of quantum computers. Though the most studied PQC is lattice-based, other alternatives are also required to risk diversification as NIST's PQC standardization [1]. Isogeny-based cryptosystems are one of candidates of PQC. Given two elliptic curves $E, E'/\mathbb{F}_p$, non-zero homomorphism $\psi : E \to E'$ is called an isogeny. By Vélu's formula [39], given elliptic curve E and point R, we can efficiently compute an isogeny $\psi : E \to E/\langle R \rangle$ with kernel $\langle R \rangle$.

© Springer Nature Switzerland AG 2019
R. Steinfeld and T. H. Yuen (Eds.): ProvSec 2019, LNCS 11821, pp. 41–56, 2019.
https://doi.org/10.1007/978-3-030-31919-9_3

On the other hand, given two isogenous elliptic curves E and E', to find a (compact representation of) isogeny $\psi : E \to E'$ (the isogeny computation problem) is believed to be hard even for quantum computers. Isogeny-based cryptosystems rely on the isogeny computation problem and its derivations. The advantage of isogeny-based cryptosystems against other PQC candidates is compactness of the key size and the ciphertext size.

Couveignes [13] initiated the research of isogeny-based cryptography by formulating the basic notion of *hard homogeneous spaces (HHSs)* which is an abstract form of isogeny graphs and class groups of endomorphism rings of (ordinary) elliptic curves. Rostovtsev and Stolbunov [37] proposed a DH type key exchange scheme from ordinary elliptic curve isogenies. On the other hand, Childs et al. [12] showed that the isogeny computation problem on ordinary elliptic curve isogenies can be analysed in quantum subexponential time. Then, Jao et al. [16, 25] proposed supersingular isogeny-based DH type key exchange (SIDH) scheme because no quantum subexponential time analysis is known for the isogeny computation problem on supersingular elliptic curve isogenies. It is known that j-invariants $j(E) = j(E')$ (where $j(E)$ is deterministically derived from E) iff elliptic curves E and E' are isomorphic. SIDH uses this property to share j-invariants as the common session key between parties. Also, Castryck et al. [11] proposed a new HHS-based key exchange scheme called *CSIDH (commutative SIDH)*, which is constructed from a group action on the set of supersingular elliptic curves defined over a prime field. Since the group action is commutative in CSIDH, we can deal with it as a similar manner to classical DH key exchange. In CSIDH, a common secret curve is obtained between parties resulting from the group action, and the Montgomery coefficient of the curve is shared as the common session key. Moreover, validity of public keys can be efficiently verified while SIDH has no efficient method yet. Hence, CSIDH is very compatible to classical DH.

There is a trade-off between the SIDH system and the CSIDH system. The advantage of SIDH is that computational time is relatively faster than the CSIDH while it is slower than other PQC candidates. For the security level corresponding to 64 bit quantum security and 128 bit classical security (i.e., NIST category 1 [1]), computational time for the SIDH key exchange is about 10 times faster than the CSIDH key exchange. On the other hand, the advantage of CSIDH is that the key size is more compact than SIDH while the key size of SIDH is also more compact than other PQC candidates. For the parameter of NIST category 1, the key size is about one fifth of these of SIDH. Also, another major advantage of CSIDH is efficient puiblic key validation.

Since SIDH and CSIDH are only secure against passive (i.e., just eavesdropping) adversaries, authenticated key exchange (AKE) schemes [18, 19, 33, 34, 40] from isogeny have been recently studied. AKE schemes aim to ensure security against active adversaries such as impersonation resilience, known-key security, and forward secrecy. In AKE, each party has a pre-established static secret key as the credential, and publishes the corresponding static public key. Thus, some public key infrastructure (PKI) is necessary.

On the other hand, in the real world, the most popular authentication mechanism is the password authentication. Hence, password-based authenticated key exchange (PAKE) is important to study in a practical sense. In PAKE, parties shares a human-memorable password in advance, they do not need any PKI. Since passwords are chosen from a small dictionary, we must consider online and off-line dictionary attacks as well as security of AKE. Many PAKE schemes based on the classical DH key exchange have been introduced such as [3,5,9,10,20,21,23,26–30,32,35]. Taraskin et al. [38] introduced the first PAKE scheme (TSJL scheme) from isogeny. The TSJL scheme is an extension of SIDH to password-based. The construction idea is simple: each party encodes the password to SIDH public key, and decodes the received public key with the password. To achieve such an encoding, they proposed a new group action. Also, security of the TSJL scheme is proved in the Bellare-Pointcheval-Rogaway (BPR) model under new assumptions related to the new group action in the random oracle (RO) model. However, in [38], justification of new assumptions is not sufficiently discussed. Thus, it is desirable to construct a PAKE scheme based on a standard isogeny problem.

1.2   Our Contribution

We propose two new PAKE schemes from isogeny, called SIDH-EKE and CSIDH-EKE, which are secure under the standard isogeny assumptions. Our main idea is to compose SIDH (or CSIDH) and encrypted key exchange (EKE) [4]. EKE is a PAKE scheme based on classical DH key exchange, and security is proved in [3] as EKE2. Each party encrypts the DH public key with the password as the key, and decrypts the received ciphertext with the password. The session key is generated by hashing the session key of the classical DH key exchange with session-specific information. In (C)SIDH-EKE, each party encrypts the (C)SIDH public key with the password, and decrypts the received ciphertext with the password. By the same way as (C)SIDH, the key material of the session key can be generated, and the session key is the hashed value of the key material and session-specific information. The computational cost and the communication cost is almost the same as (C)SIDH. We prove that (C)SIDH-EKE is secure in the BPR model under the standard (C)SIDH assumption (i.e., corresponding to the classical computational DH assumption) in the RO model and the ideal cipher (IC) model. The security proof follows the proof of EKE. However, since algebraic structures are different between (C)SIDH-EKE and EKE, we cannot directly use the proof strategy of EKE. Hence, we give the modification of the proof of EKE according to the algebraic structure of (C)SIDH by using the hybrid argument.

The advantage of our SIDH-EKE against the previous PAKE scheme from isogeny (i.e., the TSJL scheme) is that SIDH-EKE can be proved under the standard SIDH assumption while the TSJL scheme is proved under non-standard assumptions. The advantage of our CSIDH-EKE against the TSJL scheme is communication overhead. Though the TSJL scheme (and SIDH-EKE) need 2640 bit overhead for each party, CSIDH-EKE only needs 512 bit overhead for the same security level (NIST category 1)[1] in exchange for the computational cost. The detailed efficiency comparison is given in Table 1.

1.3 Related Work

Many post-quantum key exchange schemes have been studied. Fujioka et al. [17] proposed a generic construction of AKE from KEM, and showed instantiations from lattices and codes. Ding et al. [15] proposed an AKE schemes from the Learning with Errors (LWE) problem and the Ring-LWE (RLWE) problem. Bos et al. [8] proposed an RLWE-based AKE scheme for TLS, and Alkim et al. [2] improved it as NewHope. Also, Bos et al. [7] proposed a LWE-based AKE scheme, Frodo.

On the other hand, there are few post-quantum PAKE schemes. Katz and Vaikuntanathan [31] proposed the first PAKE scheme based on lattices. To remove noise from the shared session key, their scheme uses an error-correcting code; and thus, it needs three moves. Ding et al. [14] proposed RLWE-based PAKE schemes. One guarantees explicit authentication with three moves, and the other needs two moves (not one-round). Generally, isogeny cryptosystem is advantageous to lattice cryptosystem in key sizes. Hence, (C)SIDH-EKE can be implemented by smaller key sizes than these lattice-based PAKE schemes. Also, (C)SIDH-EKE can be executed in one-round (i.e., parties can exchange public keys simultaneously) while known lattice-based PAKE schemes are not.

2 Preliminaries

In this section, we recall SIDH, HHS, CSIDH, EKE and the BPR model.

Throughout this paper we use the following notations. If M is a set, then by $m \in_R M$ we denote that m is sampled randomly from M. If $\mathcal{R}$ is an algorithm, then by $y \leftarrow \mathcal{R}(x; r)$ we denote that y is output by $\mathcal{R}$ on input x and randomness r (if $\mathcal{R}$ is deterministic, r is empty). The security parameter is λ.

2.1 SIDH

Here, we recall the SIDH system [16,25].

For two small primes ℓ_A, ℓ_B (e.g., $\ell_A = 2, \ell_B = 3$), let p be a large prime such that $p \pm 1 = f \cdot \ell_A^{e_A} \ell_B^{e_B}$ for a small f and $\ell_A^{e_A} \approx \ell_B^{e_B} = 2^{\Theta(\lambda)}$. Let E over $\mathbb{F}_{p^2}$ be a random supersingular elliptic curve with $E(\mathbb{F}_{p^2}) \simeq (\mathbb{Z}/(p \pm 1)\mathbb{Z})^2 \supseteq$

---

[1] Very recently, Peikert [36] showed a new quantum security analysis of CSIDH-512, corresponding to NIST category 1, by using the collimation sieve technique, and CSIDH-512 is broken by 40 bit quantum memory and 2^{16} quantum oracle queries (i.e., 56 bit quantum security). Hence, He estimates that the quantum security level of CSIDH-512 is rather weaker than NIST category 1. On the other hand, the quantum circuit for the group operation of CSIDH is very high cost. Thus, by considering such external overheads of circuits in addition to his evaluation, CSIDH-512 still seems safe in reality.

$(\mathbb{Z}/\ell_A^{e_A}\mathbb{Z})^2 \oplus (\mathbb{Z}/\ell_B^{e_B}\mathbb{Z})^2$. For isogenies ψ_A and ψ_B with kernels of orders $\ell_A^{e_A}$ and $\ell_B^{e_B}$, respectively, let $\ker\psi_A = \langle R_A \rangle \subset E[\ell_A^{e_A}]$, $\ker\psi_B = \langle R_B \rangle \subset E[\ell_B^{e_B}]$, $\ker\psi_{BA} = \langle\psi_B(R_A)\rangle \subset E_B[\ell_A^{e_A}]$ and $\ker\psi_{AB} = \langle\psi_A(R_B)\rangle \subset E_A[\ell_B^{e_B}]$. Then, for $\psi_A : E \rightarrow E_A = E/\langle R_A \rangle$ and $\psi_B : E \rightarrow E_B = E/\langle R_B \rangle$, $\psi_{AB} : E_A \rightarrow E/\langle R_A, R_B \rangle$ and $\psi_{BA} : E_B \rightarrow E/\langle R_A, R_B \rangle$ hold. Thus, we can use j-invariants $j(E/\langle R_A, R_B \rangle)$ as the common secret computed by two ways. Please see [16,25] for the detail of the mathematical foundation of the SIDH system.

In the SIDH system, hardness assumptions are defined as classical DH. We recall the computational DH-type assumptions for SIDH defined in [16].

Definition 1 (SI-CDH Problem [16]**).** *For* $a \in_R \mathbb{Z}/\ell_A^{e_A}\mathbb{Z}$, $b \in_R \mathbb{Z}/\ell_B^{e_B}\mathbb{Z}$, $E[\ell_A^{e_A}] = \langle P_A, Q_A \rangle$, $E[\ell_B^{e_B}] = \langle P_B, Q_B \rangle$, $R_A = P_A + aQ_A$, $R_B = P_B + bQ_B$, $\psi_A : E \rightarrow E_A = E/\langle R_A \rangle$ and $\psi_B : E \rightarrow E_B = E/\langle R_B \rangle$, *the advantage of a PPT solver* $\mathcal{S}$ *in the SI-CDH problem for public parameter Param* $= (E, P_A, Q_A, P_B, Q_B)$ *is defined as*

$$\mathsf{Adv}^{\text{si-cdh}}_{E,\ell_A,\ell_B}(\mathcal{S}) =$$
$$\Pr[\mathcal{S}(Param, (E_A, \psi_A(P_B), \psi_A(Q_B)), (E_B, \psi_B(P_A), \psi_B(Q_A))) \rightarrow j(E/\langle R_A, R_B \rangle)].$$

The SI-CDH problem corresponds to the classical computational DH problem.

Protocol of SIDH. Here, we recall the protocol of SIDH [25].

Public Parameters. Let $E[\ell_A^{e_A}] = \langle P_A, Q_A \rangle$ and $E[\ell_B^{e_B}] = \langle P_B, Q_B \rangle$. The public parameters are (E, P_A, Q_A, P_B, Q_B).

Session. Parties A and B executes a key exchange session as follows:

1. Party A chooses $a \in_R \mathbb{Z}/\ell_A^{e_A}\mathbb{Z}$, computes $R_A = P_A + aQ_A$ and $\psi_A : E \rightarrow E_A = E/\langle R_A \rangle$, and sends the public key $\hat{A} = (E_A, \psi_A(P_B), \psi_A(Q_B))$ to party B.
2. Party B chooses $b \in_R \mathbb{Z}/\ell_B^{e_B}\mathbb{Z}$, computes $R_B = P_B + bQ_B$ and $\psi_B : E \rightarrow E_B = E/\langle R_B \rangle$, and sends the public key $\hat{B} = (E_B, \psi_B(P_A), \psi_B(Q_A))$ to party A.
3. On receiving $\hat{B}$, party A computes $R_{BA} = \psi_B(P_A) + a\psi_B(Q_A)$ and generates the session key $SK = j(E_B/\langle R_{BA} \rangle)$.
4. On receiving $\hat{A}$, party B computes $R_{AB} = \psi_A(P_B) + b\psi_A(Q_B)$ and generates the session key $SK = j(E_A/\langle R_{AB} \rangle)$.

Since $E_B/\langle R_{BA} \rangle$ and $E_A/\langle R_{AB} \rangle$ are isomorphic, $j(E_B/\langle R_{BA} \rangle) = j(E_A/\langle R_{AB} \rangle)$ holds.

It is obvious that the session key SK is hard to find for any passive adversary if the SI-CDH problem is hard.

2.2   Hard Homogeneous Space and CSIDH

Here, we recall the definition of HHS [13], and the CSIDH system [11] as an instantiation of HHS.

Definition 2 (Freeness and Transitivity). *X denotes a finite set, and G denotes an abelian group. We say that G acts efficiently on X freely and transitively if there is an efficiently computable map $* : G \times X \to X$ as follows:*

- *for any $x \in X$ and $g, h \in G$, $g * (h * x) = (gh) * x$ holds, and there is an identity element $id \in G$ such that $id * x = x$,*
- *for any $(x, y) \in X \times X$, there is $g \in G$ such that $g * x = y$, and*
- *for any $x \in X$ and $g, h \in G$ such that $g * x = h * x$, $g = h$ holds.*

Definition 3 (Hard Homogeneous Space). *A HHS consists of a finite abelian group G acting freely and transitively on some set X such that the following tasks are efficiently executable:*

- *Computing the group operation on G*
- *Sampling randomly from G with (close to) uniform distribution*
- *Deciding validity and equality of a representation of elements of X*
- *Computing the action of a group element $g \in G$ on some $x \in X$ (i.e., $g * x$)*

The CSIDH system is an instantiation of HHS from $\mathbb{F}_p$-rational supersingular elliptic curves and their $\mathbb{F}_p$-rational isogeny. Let $\mathcal{E}\ell\ell_p(\mathcal{O})$ be the set of elliptic curves over $\mathbb{F}_p$ whose $\mathbb{F}_p$-rational endomorphism ring is some fixed quadratic order $\mathcal{O}$, and $\mathrm{cl}(\mathcal{O})$ be the ideal class group of $\mathcal{O}$. Then, the CSIDH system is regarded as HHS by setting $X = \mathcal{E}\ell\ell_p(\mathcal{O})$ and $G = \mathrm{cl}(\mathcal{O})$ as the parameter of HHS. For curve $E \in X$ and ideal class $[\mathfrak{g}] \in G$, the group action $[\mathfrak{g}] * E$ corresponds to the map $([\mathfrak{g}], E) \longmapsto E/\mathfrak{g}$. Since $E/\mathfrak{g}$ is a supersingular curve, the form of $E/\mathfrak{g}$ is $y^2 = x^3 + cx^2 + x$ for $c \in \mathbb{F}_p$. Then, $[\mathfrak{g}] * E$ can be represented as such Montgomery coefficient c.

Due to commutativity of $\mathrm{cl}(\mathcal{O})$, for $[\mathfrak{g}], [\mathfrak{g}'] \in G$, $E \in X$, $E_{\mathfrak{g}} = E/\mathfrak{g}$ and $E_{\mathfrak{g}'} = E/\mathfrak{g}'$, curves $E_{\mathfrak{g}'}/\mathfrak{g}$ and $E_{\mathfrak{g}}/\mathfrak{g}'$ are identical. Thus, we can use the Montgomery coefficient of $E/\mathfrak{g}\mathfrak{g}'$ (i.e., $([\mathfrak{g}][\mathfrak{g}']) * E$) as the common secret computed by two ways. Please see [11] for the detail of the mathematical foundation of the CSIDH system. In this paper, we use the notation of HHS as the CSIDH system for simplicity.

In the CSIDH system, hardness assumptions are defined as classical DH by using HHS. We recall the computational DH-type assumption for HHS defined in [6].[2]

Definition 4 (CSI-CDH Problem [6]**).** *For $E_0 \in X$, $[\mathfrak{a}], [\mathfrak{b}] \in_R G$, $E_\mathfrak{a} = [\mathfrak{a}] * E_0$ and $E_\mathfrak{b} = [\mathfrak{b}] * E_0$, the advantage of a PPT solver $\mathcal{S}$ in the CSI-CDH problem is defined as*

$$\mathsf{Adv}_{G,X}^{\mathsf{csi\text{-}cdh}}(\mathcal{S}) = \Pr[\mathcal{S}(E_0, E_\mathfrak{a}, E_\mathfrak{b}) \to ([\mathfrak{a}][\mathfrak{b}]) * E_0].$$

---

[2] In [6], assumptions are defined as a generalized form for n-way by using cryptographic invariant maps (CIM). In the case of $n = 1$, CIM is the same as HHS.

The CSI-CDH problem corresponds to the classical computational DH problem.

Protocol of CSIDH. Here, we recall the protocol of CSIDH [11].

Public Parameters. Let $p = (4 \cdot \ell_1 \cdots \ell_{n-1})$ be a large prime where each ℓ_i is a small distinct odd prime. Then, the supersingular elliptic curve $E_0 : y^2 = x^3 + x$ over $\mathbb{F}_p$ with endomorphism ring $\mathcal{O} = \mathbb{Z}[\pi]$ is constructed where π is the Frobenius endomorphism satisfying $\pi^2 = -p$. For the notation of HHS, G is denoted by $\mathrm{cl}(\mathcal{O})$ and X is denoted by $\mathcal{E}\ell\ell_p(\mathcal{O})$; and thus, $E_0 \in X = \mathcal{E}\ell\ell_p(\mathcal{O})$. $[\mathfrak{g}] \in_R G$ means that integers $(e_1, \ldots, e_n)$ are randomly sampled from a range $\{-m, \ldots, m\}$ and $[\mathfrak{g}] = [\mathfrak{l}_1^{e_1} \cdots \mathfrak{l}_n^{e_n}] \in \mathrm{cl}(\mathcal{O})$ where $\mathfrak{l}_i = (\ell_i, \pi - 1)$. $[\mathfrak{g}] * E_0$ is represented by the Montgomery coefficient $c \in \mathbb{F}_p$ of the elliptic curve $[\mathfrak{g}]E_0 : y^2 = x^3 + cx^2 + x$ by applying the action of $[\mathfrak{g}]$ to E_0.

The public parameters are (G, X, E_0).

Session. Parties A and B executes a key exchange session as follows:

1. Party A chooses $[\mathfrak{a}] \in_R G$, and sends the public key $\hat{A} = [\mathfrak{a}] * E_0$ to party B.
2. Party B chooses $[\mathfrak{b}] \in_R G$, and sends the public key $\hat{B} = [\mathfrak{b}] * E_0$ to party A.
3. On receiving $\hat{B}$, party A generates the session key $SK = [\mathfrak{a}] * \hat{B}$.
4. On receiving $\hat{A}$, party B generates the session key $SK = [\mathfrak{b}] * \hat{A}$.

Since G is an abelian group, $[\mathfrak{a}][\mathfrak{b}] = [\mathfrak{b}][\mathfrak{a}]$ holds. Therefore, $[\mathfrak{a}] * \hat{B} = [\mathfrak{a}] * ([\mathfrak{b}] * E_0) = ([\mathfrak{a}][\mathfrak{b}]) * E_0 = ([\mathfrak{b}][\mathfrak{a}]) * E_0 = [\mathfrak{b}] * ([\mathfrak{a}] * E_0) = [\mathfrak{b}] * \hat{A}$ holds from Definition 2.

It is obvious that the session key SK is hard to find for any passive adversary if the CSI-CDH problem is hard.

2.3   EKE

Here, we recall the protocol of EKE [3,4].

Public Parameters. Let p be a λ-bit prime, G' be a cyclic group of order p with a generator g'. Let $H : \{0,1\}^* \to \{0,1\}^\lambda$ be a hash function modelled as a RO. Let $(\mathsf{Enc}, \mathsf{Enc}^{-1})$ be a symmetric key encryption scheme with key size κ bit and input/output size ℓ-bit where $\mathsf{Enc} : \{0,1\}^\kappa \times \{0,1\}^\ell \to \{0,1\}^\ell$ is the encryption algorithm. It is modelled as an IC; that is, for each key k it is equivalent to a random permutation. Then, output a public parameter $params := (p, g', G', H, (\mathsf{Enc}, \mathsf{Enc}^{-1}))$.

Session. Parties A and B having password $pw = pw_{AB}$ executes a key exchange session as follows:

1. Party A chooses $a \in_R \mathbb{Z}_p$, computes $\hat{A} = g'^a$, and sends $\alpha = \mathsf{Enc}_{pw}(\hat{A})$ to party B.
2. Party B chooses $b \in_R \mathbb{Z}_p$, computes $\hat{B} = g'^b$, and sends $\beta = \mathsf{Enc}_{pw}(\hat{B})$ to party A.

3. On receiving β, party A decrypts $\hat{B} = \mathsf{Enc}_{pw}^{-1}(\beta)$ and generates the session key $SK = H(A, B, \hat{A}, \hat{B}, \hat{B}^a)$.
4. On receiving α, party B decrypts $\hat{A} = \mathsf{Enc}_{pw}^{-1}(\alpha)$ and generates the session key $SK = H(A, B, \hat{A}, \hat{B}, \hat{A}^b)$.

We briefly explain why the IC is necessary. In EKE, password pw is used as the key of the symmetric key encryption scheme. However, pw is chosen from dictionary $\mathcal{D}$ which is smaller than the key size. Thus, if we use a concrete symmetric key encryption scheme, security is not guaranteed in the provable way. On the other hand, in the IC model, the adversary must pose query (k, m) to Enc (or query (k, c) to Enc^{-1}) in order to do encryption (or decryption). Also, the IC is guaranteed to be independent random permutations for distinct keys. Hence, the adversary must guess the password and pose query $(pw', \cdot)$ to the IC in order to impersonate a party. Its successful probability is bounded by the number of Send query because the IC guarantees information-theoretic security.

2.4   BPR Model

Here, we recall the BPR model [3] for PAKE.

Protocol Participants and Passwords. A PAKE scheme contains two parties (an initiator and a responder, or a client and a server) who will engage in the protocol. We suppose that the total number of parties in the system is at most N. Let passwords for all pairs of parties be uniformly and independently chosen from a fixed dictionary $\mathcal{D}$. This uniformity requirement is made for simplicity and can be easily removed by adjusting security of an individual password to be the min-entropy of the distribution, instead of $1/|\mathcal{D}|$. Parties P and P' share a password $pw_{PP'}$.

Session. We denote with Π_P^i the ith instance of key exchange sessions that party P runs. Each party can concurrently execute the protocol multiple times with different instances. We suppose that the total number of instances of a party is at most ℓ. The adversary is given oracle access to these instances and may also control some of the instances itself. We remark that unlike the standard notion of an "oracle", in this model instances maintain state which is updated as the protocol progresses. In particular the state of an instance Π_P^i includes the following variables (initialized as null):

- sid_P^i: the session identifier which is the ordered concatenation of all messages sent and received by Π_P^i;
- pid_P^i: the partner identifier whom Π_P^i believes it is interacting ($\mathsf{pid}_P^i \neq P$);
- acc_P^i: a Boolean variable corresponding to whether Π_P^i accepts or rejects at the end of the execution.

We say that two instances Π_P^i and $\Pi_{P'}^j$ are partnered if the following properties hold: $\mathsf{pid}_P^i = P'$ and $\mathsf{pid}_{P'}^j = P$, and $\mathsf{sid}_P^i = \mathsf{sid}_{P'}^j \neq null$ except possibly for the final message.[3] Partnered parties must accept and conclude with the common session key.

Security Definition. An adversary is given total control of the external network connecting parties. This adversarial capability is modeled by giving some oracle accesses[4] as follows:

- Execute(P, i, P', j): This query models passive attacks. The output of this query consists of the messages that were exchanged during the honest execution of the protocol.
- Send(P, i, m): This query models active attacks. The instance Π_P^i runs according to the protocol specification and updates state. The output of this query consists of the message that the party P would generate on receipt of message m. If the input message is empty (say $\bot$), the query means activating the initiator and the output of the query consists of the first move message.
- Reveal(P, i): This query models leakage of session keys by improper erasure of session keys after use or compromise of a host machine. The output of this query consists of the session key SK of Π_P^i if $\mathrm{acc}_P^i = 1$.
- Test(P, i): At the beginning a hidden bit b is chosen. If no session key for instance Π_P^i is defined, then return the undefined symbol $\bot$. Otherwise, return the session key for instance Π_P^i if $b = 1$ or a random key from the same domain if $b = 0$. This query is posed just once.

The adversary is considered successful if it non-trivially guesses b correctly or if it breaks correctness of a session.

Definition 5 (Freshness). *We say that an instance Π_P^i is fresh unless one of the following is true at the conclusion of the experiment:*

- *the adversary poses* Reveal(P, i),
- *the adversary poses* Reveal(P', j) *if Π_P^i and $\Pi_{P'}^j$, are partnered.*

We say that an adversary $\mathcal{A}$ succeeds if either:

- $\mathcal{A}$ poses Test(P, i) for a fresh instance Π_P^i and outputs a bit $b' = b$,
- Π_P^i and $\Pi_{P'}^j$ are partnered, and $\mathrm{acc}_P^i = \mathrm{acc}_{P'}^i = 1$, but session keys are not identical.

The adversary's advantage for protocol Π is formally defined by:

$$\mathsf{Adv}_{\Pi,\mathcal{D}}^{\mathrm{pake}}(\mathcal{A}) = |\Pr[\mathcal{A}\ \text{succeeds}] - 1/2|,$$

where λ is a security parameter.

---

[3] The exception of the final message for matching of sid is needed to rule out a trivial attack that an adversary forwards all messages except the final one.

[4] The model does not contain any explicit corruption oracle access (i.e., to reveal passwords). In the password-only setting, such an oracle is unnecessary because an adversary can internally simulate these oracles by itself. Please see [22, pp.190, footnote 8] for details.

Definition 6 (Security of PAKE). *We say a PAKE protocol is secure if for a dictionary $\mathcal{D}$ and any PPT adversary $\mathcal{A}$ that makes at most q_{Send} queries of* Send *to different instances the advantage* $\mathsf{Adv}_{\Pi,\mathcal{D}}^{\mathrm{pake}}(\mathcal{A})$ *is only negligibly larger than $q_{\mathsf{Send}}/|\mathcal{D}|$ for λ.*

3 (C)SIDH-EKE: PAKE from Isogeny Under (C)SI-CDH Assumption

In this section, we show our new PAKE schemes based on SIDH and CSIDH, named SIDH-EKE and CSIDH-EKE, respectively.

3.1 SIDH-EKE

Our first scheme (SIDH-EKE) is obtained by a combination of SIDH and EKE. SIDH-EKE relies on the RO model and the IC model as EKE. The protocol is basically the same as EKE. Though EKE is based on the classical DH key exchange, SIDH-EKE uses SIDH to share a key material between users. Specifically, each user encrypts the public key of SIDH (i.e., $\hat{A} = (E_A, \psi_A(P_B), \psi_A(Q_B))$ and $\hat{B} = (E_B, \psi_B(P_A), \psi_B(Q_A)))$ with the password as the key for the IC, decrypts the public key of the peer, and computes the session key of SIDH (i.e., $j(E/\langle R_A, R_B\rangle)$) as the key material of our scheme. In the session key generation, public keys are contained in inputs of the hash function as EKE, but j-invariants of a part of public keys are used to reduce the bandwidth.

The protocol of SIDH-EKE is as follows.

Public Parameters. Let (E, P_A, Q_A, P_B, Q_B) be the public parameters of SIDH. Let $H : \{0,1\}^* \to \{0,1\}^\lambda$ be a hash function modelled as a RO. Let $(\mathsf{Enc}, \mathsf{Enc}^{-1})$ be a symmetric key encryption scheme modelled as an IC with key size κ bit $(2^\kappa > |\mathcal{D}|)$ and domain $(\mathbb{F}_{p^2})^2 \times (\mathbb{Z}/\ell_A^{e_A}\mathbb{Z})^2$. Then, output a public parameter $params := (E, P_A, Q_A, P_B, Q_B, H, (\mathsf{Enc}, \mathsf{Enc}^{-1}))$.

Session. Parties A and B having password $pw = pw_{AB}$ executes a key exchange session as follows:

1. Party A chooses $a \in_R \mathbb{Z}/\ell_A^{e_A}\mathbb{Z}$, computes $R_A = P_A + aQ_A$, $\psi_A : E \to E_A = E/\langle R_A\rangle$ and $\hat{A} = (E_A, \psi_A(P_B), \psi_A(Q_B))$, and sends $(A, \alpha = \mathsf{Enc}_{pw}(\hat{A}))$ to party B.
2. Party B chooses $b \in_R \mathbb{Z}/\ell_B^{e_B}\mathbb{Z}$, computes $R_B = P_B + bQ_B$, $\psi_B : E \to E_B = E/\langle R_B\rangle$ and $\hat{B} = (E_B, \psi_B(P_A), \psi_B(Q_A))$, and sends $(B, \beta = \mathsf{Enc}_{pw}(\hat{B}))$ to party A.
3. On receiving (B, β), party A decrypts $\hat{B} = \mathsf{Enc}_{pw}^{-1}(\beta)$, computes $R_{BA} = \psi_B(P_A) + a\psi_B(Q_A)$ and $Z = j(E_B/\langle R_{BA}\rangle)$, and generates the session key $SK = H(A, B, j(E_A), j(E_B), Z)$.
4. On receiving (A, α), party B decrypts $\hat{A} = \mathsf{Enc}_{pw}^{-1}(\alpha)$, computes $R_{AB} = \psi_A(P_B) + b\psi_A(Q_B)$ and $Z = j(E_A/\langle R_{AB}\rangle)$, and generates the session key $SK = H(A, B, j(E_A), j(E_B), Z)$.

Security. Here, we show security of SIDH-EKE in the BPR model. The security proof is slightly different with the security proof of EKE due to the structure of the SIDH system. In EKE, if we set $\hat{A} = g^a \cdot g^\theta$ and $\hat{B} = g^b \cdot g^\phi$, the session key is $SK = H(A, B, \hat{A}, \hat{B}, Z = g^{ab} \cdot g^{a\phi} \cdot g^{b\theta} \cdot g^{\theta\phi})$. Thus, in the EKE proof, in order to change the session key generation in the Execute oracle, the simulator embeds instances of the CDH problem to g^a and g^b, sets public keys as above by choosing θ and ϕ for each session, and finally obtains g^{ab} (i.e., the answer of the CDH problem) from Z. However, in SIDH-EKE, such a simulation does not work because $j(E_A)$ and $j(E_B)$ have no algebraic structure (i.e., j-invariants). Specifically, for $j(E_A) \cdot j(E_\theta)$ and $j(E_B) \cdot j(E_\phi)$, $Z = j(E_A/\langle R_{AB} \rangle) \cdot j(E_A/\langle R_{A\phi} \rangle) \cdot j(E_B/\langle R_{B\theta} \rangle) \cdot j(E_\theta/\langle R_{\theta\phi} \rangle)$ is not guaranteed. Hence, in our proof, we simulate the Execute oracle gradually by using the hybrid argument. Specifically, the output of the Execute query is gradually changed in hybrid experiments, and the simulator sets the public keys of the changed session to be the same as instances of the SI-CDH problem. The simulator directly obtains the answer of the SI-CDH problem as Z for each hybrid experiment. Also, our scheme is secure against off-line dictionary attacks. E_A in the ephemeral public key $\hat{A}$ is an elliptic curve having form $y^2 = x^3 + \alpha x^2 + \beta$ for $\alpha, \beta \in \mathbb{F}_{p^2}$, and $\psi_A(P_B), \psi_A(Q_B) \in \mathbb{Z}/\ell_A^{e_A}\mathbb{Z}$ are some points of E_A. Hence, $\mathsf{Enc}_{pw}(\hat{A})$ is the ciphertext of $(\alpha, \beta, \psi_A(P_B), \psi_A(Q_B))$. The adversary can observe $\mathsf{Enc}_{pw}(\hat{A})$ and try to find pw by posing $(pw', \mathsf{Enc}_{pw}(\hat{A}))$ to Enc^{-1} oracle for guessing password pw'. However, since any information of $(\alpha, \beta, \psi_A(P_B), \psi_A(Q_B))$ is not leaked from $\mathsf{Enc}_{pw}(\hat{A})$ because $(\mathsf{Enc}, \mathsf{Enc}^{-1})$ is the IC, the adversary cannot determine if the guess is valid or not. Thus, our scheme prevents off-line dictionary attacks. Therefore, we can prove security of SIDH-EKE.

Theorem 1. *For the advantage* $\mathsf{Adv}^{\mathsf{si\text{-}cdh}}_{E,\ell_A,\ell_B}(\mathcal{S})$ *of the SI-CDH problem, the advantage* $\mathsf{Adv}^{\mathsf{pake}}_{\mathsf{sidh\text{-}eke},\mathcal{D}}(\mathcal{A})$ *of CSIDH-EKE is as follows in the RO model and the IC model:*

$$\mathsf{Adv}^{\mathsf{pake}}_{\mathsf{sidh\text{-}eke},\mathcal{D}}(\mathcal{A}) \leq \frac{(q_{\mathsf{Send}} + q_{\mathsf{Execute}})^2}{4p^2} + (q_{\mathsf{Execute}} + q_{\mathsf{Send}}) \cdot \mathsf{Adv}^{\mathsf{si\text{-}cdh}}_{E,\ell_A,\ell_B}(\mathcal{S}) + \frac{q_{\mathsf{Send}}}{|\mathcal{D}|}$$

where q_{Send} *and* q_{Execute} *denote the upper bound of* Send *and* Execute *queries, respectively.*

3.2 CSIDH-EKE

Our second scheme (CSIDH-EKE) is obtained by a combination of CSIDH and EKE as SIDH-EKE. Specifically, each user encrypts the public key of CSIDH (i.e., $\hat{A}$ or $\hat{B}$) with the password as the key for the IC, decrypts the public key of the peer, and computes the session key of CSIDH (i.e., $([\mathfrak{a}][\mathfrak{b}]) * E_0$) as the key material of our scheme.

The protocol of CSIDH-EKE is as follows.

Public Parameters. Let (G, X) be an abelian group and a finite set constructing HHS, and $E_0 \in X$ be the supersingular elliptic curve $E_0 : y^2 = x^3 + x$ over $\mathbb{F}_p$. Let $H : \{0,1\}^* \to \{0,1\}^\lambda$ be a hash function modelled as a RO. Let $(\mathsf{Enc}, \mathsf{Enc}^{-1})$ be a symmetric key encryption scheme modelled as an IC with key size κ bit $(2^\kappa > |\mathcal{D}|)$ and domain $\mathbb{F}_p$. Then, output a public parameter $params := (G, X, E_0, H, (\mathsf{Enc}, \mathsf{Enc}^{-1}))$.

Session. Parties A and B having password $pw = pw_{AB}$ executes a key exchange session as follows:

1. Party A chooses $[\mathfrak{a}] \in_R G$, computes $\hat{A} = [\mathfrak{a}] * E_0$, and sends $(A, \alpha = \mathsf{Enc}_{pw}(\hat{A}))$ to party B.
2. Party B chooses $[\mathfrak{b}] \in_R G$, computes $\hat{B} = [\mathfrak{b}] * E_0$, and sends $(B, \beta = \mathsf{Enc}_{pw}(\hat{B}))$ to party A.
3. On receiving (B, β), party A decrypts $\hat{B} = \mathsf{Enc}_{pw}^{-1}(\beta)$ and generates the session key $SK = H(A, B, \hat{A}, \hat{B}, [\mathfrak{a}] * \hat{B})$.
4. On receiving (A, α), party B decrypts $\hat{A} = \mathsf{Enc}_{pw}^{-1}(\alpha)$ and generates the session key $SK = H(A, B, \hat{A}, \hat{B}, [\mathfrak{b}] * \hat{B})$.

Security. Security of CSIDH-EKE can be proved by a similar manner as SIDH-EKE. Here, we discuss security against off-line dictionary attacks. $\hat{A}$ corresponds to the Montgomery coefficient $c \in \mathbb{F}_p$ of the elliptic curve $[\mathfrak{a}]E_0 : y^2 = x^3 + cx^2 + x$ by applying the action of $[\mathfrak{a}]$ to E_0. Hence, $\mathsf{Enc}_{pw}(\hat{A})$ is the ciphertext of c. The adversary can observe $\mathsf{Enc}_{pw}(\hat{A})$ and try to find pw by posing $(pw', \mathsf{Enc}_{pw}(\hat{A}))$ to Enc^{-1} oracle for guessing password pw'. However, since any information of c is not leaked from $\mathsf{Enc}_{pw}(\hat{A})$ because $(\mathsf{Enc}, \mathsf{Enc}^{-1})$ is the IC, the adversary cannot determine if the guess is valid or not. Thus, CSIDH-EKE prevents off-line dictionary attacks.

Theorem 2. *For the advantage* $\mathsf{Adv}_{G,X}^{\mathsf{csi\text{-}cdh}}$ *of the CSI-CDH problem, the advantage* $\mathsf{Adv}_{\mathsf{csidh\text{-}eke}, \mathcal{D}}^{\mathsf{pake}}$ *of CSIDH-EKE is as follows in the RO model and the IC model:*

$$\mathsf{Adv}_{\mathsf{csidh\text{-}eke}, \mathcal{D}}^{\mathsf{pake}}(\mathcal{A}) \leq \frac{(q_{\mathsf{Send}} + q_{\mathsf{Execute}})^2}{2p} + (q_{\mathsf{Execute}} + q_{\mathsf{Send}}) \cdot \mathsf{Adv}_{G,X}^{\mathsf{csi\text{-}cdh}}(\mathcal{S}) + \frac{q_{\mathsf{Send}}}{|\mathcal{D}|}$$

where q_{Send} *and* q_{Execute} *denote the upper bound of* Send *and* Execute *queries, respectively.*

4   Comparison

In this section, we give an efficiency comparison of our schemes and the TSJL scheme [38]. The comparison is shown in Table 1.

Table 1. Comparison among PAKE from isogeny

	Assumption	Communication overhead	Computational time
TJSL scheme [38]	SI-CDH & SI-APC & SI-APD & C-SGA	2640 bit	$\approx 5.0\,\mathrm{ms}$
SIDH-EKE (Sect. 3.1)	SI-CDH	2640 bit	$\approx 5.0\,\mathrm{ms}$
CSIDH-EKE (Sect. 3.2)	CSI-CDH	512 bit	$\approx 80.6\,\mathrm{ms}$

SI-APC, SI-APD and C-SGA mean the supersingular isogeny auxiliary point computation assumption, the supersingular isogeny auxiliary point decision assumption and the computational simultaneous group action assumption, respectively, introduced in [38].

To compare SIDH-based schemes and the CSIDH-based scheme, we use parameters having the same security level (i.e., NIST category 1 [1]) corresponding to the key search on a block cipher with a 128 bit key (i.e., $\kappa = 128$). For SIDH, the parameter corresponding to NIST category 1 is estimated as SIKEp434 in [24]. The public key is an element in $(\mathbb{F}_{p^2})^2 \times (\mathbb{Z}/\ell_A^{e_A}\mathbb{Z})^2$, and the size is estimated as 2640 bit. Computational time of a public key generation and time for a session key generation of SIDH are about 1.9 ms and about 3.1 ms, respectively, based on the performance evaluation of x64-assembly implementation on a 3.4GHz Intel Core i7-6700 (Skylake) processor in [24, Table 2.1]. The TSJL scheme and SIDH-EKE contain an ephemeral public key of SIDH as the message, and computations of a public key generation and a session key generation of SIDH for each party. For CSIDH, the parameter corresponding to NIST category 1 is estimated as CSIDH-512 in [11]. The public key is an element in $\mathbb{F}_p$, and the size is estimated as 512 bit. Computational time of a group action and time for a public key validation of CSIDH are about 40.3 ms and about 1.6 ms, respectively, based on the proof-of-concept implementation on a 3.5GHz Intel Core i5 (Skylake) processor in [11, Table 2]. CSIDH-EKE contains an ephemeral public key of CSIDH as the message, and computations of a public key generation and a session key generation of CSIDH for each party. We simply add these values without any acceleration technique. As shown in Table 1, CSIDH-EKE is more compact than the TSJL scheme, and SIDH-EKE is secure only under the SI-CDH assumption while the TSJL scheme relies on additional assumptions.

5 Conclusion

We introduced two new one-round PAKE schemes, SIDH-EKE and CSIDH-EKE, based on isogeny, which are secure under the standard hardness assumptions. Also, CSIDH-EKE is advantageous in communication overhead though the computational cost is worse. The security proof follows the proof of EKE in the RO and IC model, but there is a technical issue due to the difference between algebraic structures of EKE and (C)SIDH-EKE. Excluding symmetric cryptography operations, the computational cost and communication cost of (C)SIDH-EKE is almost the same as original (C)SIDH.

A remaining problem of further researches is removing idealized building blocks such as ROs and ICs. Otherwise, giving a security proof in the quantum RO (or IC) model is another direction.

References

1. Post-Quantum Cryptography Standardization. National Institute of Standards and Technology (2016)
2. Alkim, E., Ducas, L., Pöppelmann, T., Schwabe, P.: Post-quantum key exchange - a new hope. In: USENIX Security Symposium 2016, pp. 327–343 (2016)
3. Bellare, M., Pointcheval, D., Rogaway, P.: Authenticated key exchange secure against dictionary attacks. In: Preneel, B. (ed.) EUROCRYPT 2000. LNCS, vol. 1807, pp. 139–155. Springer, Heidelberg (2000). https://doi.org/10.1007/3-540-45539-6_11
4. Bellovin, S.M., Merritt, M.: Augmented encrypted key exchange: a password-based protocol secure against dictionary attacks and password file compromise. In: ACM CCS, pp. 244–250 (1993)
5. Ben Hamouda, F., Blazy, O., Chevalier, C., Pointcheval, D., Vergnaud, D.: Efficient UC-secure authenticated key-exchange for algebraic languages. In: Kurosawa, K., Hanaoka, G. (eds.) PKC 2013. LNCS, vol. 7778, pp. 272–291. Springer, Heidelberg (2013). https://doi.org/10.1007/978-3-642-36362-7_18
6. Boneh, D., et al.: Multiparty non-interactive key exchange and more from isogenies on elliptic curves. In: MATHCRYPT 2018 (2018). https://eprint.iacr.org/2018/665
7. Bos, J.W., et al.: Frodo: take off the ring! Practical, quantum-secure key exchange from LWE. In: ACM Conference on Computer and Communications Security 2016, pp. 1006–1018 (2016)
8. Bos, J.W., Costello, C., Naehrig, M., Stebila, D.: Post-quantum key exchange for the TLS protocol from the ring learning with errors problem. In: IEEE Symposium on Security and Privacy 2015, pp. 553–570 (2015)
9. Boyko, V., MacKenzie, P.D., Patel, S.: Provably secure password-authenticated key exchange using Diffie-Hellman. In: Preneel, B. (ed.) EUROCRYPT 2000. LNCS, vol. 1807, pp. 156–171. Springer, Heidelberg (2000). https://doi.org/10.1007/3-540-45539-6_12
10. Canetti, R., Dachman-Soled, D., Vaikuntanathan, V., Wee, H.: Efficient password authenticated key exchange via oblivious transfer. In: Fischlin, M., Buchmann, J., Manulis, M. (eds.) PKC 2012. LNCS, vol. 7293, pp. 449–466. Springer, Heidelberg (2012). https://doi.org/10.1007/978-3-642-30057-8_27
11. Castryck, W., Lange, T., Martindale, C., Panny, L., Renes, J.: CSIDH: an efficient post-quantum commutative group action. In: Peyrin, T., Galbraith, S. (eds.) ASIACRYPT 2018. LNCS, vol. 11274, pp. 395–427. Springer, Cham (2018). https://doi.org/10.1007/978-3-030-03332-3_15
12. Childs, A.M., Jao, D., Soukharev, V.: Constructing elliptic curve isogenies in quantum subexponential time. J. Math. Cryptol. 8(1), 1–29 (2014)
13. Couveignes, J.M.: Hard Homogeneous Spaces. Cryptology ePrint Archive, Report 2006/291 (2006). https://eprint.iacr.org/2006/291
14. Ding, J., Alsayigh, S., Lancrenon, J., RV, S., Snook, M.: Provably secure password authenticated key exchange based on RLWE for the post-quantum world. In: Handschuh, H. (ed.) CT-RSA 2017. LNCS, vol. 10159, pp. 183–204. Springer, Cham (2017). https://doi.org/10.1007/978-3-319-52153-4_11

15. Ding, J., Xie, X., Lin, X.: A simple provably secure key exchange scheme based on the learning with errors problem. IACR Cryptology ePrint Archive 2012/688 (2012). http://eprint.iacr.org/2012/688

16. Feo, L.D., Jao, D., Plût, J.: Towards quantum-resistant cryptosystems from supersingular elliptic curve isogenies. J. Math. Cryptol. **8**(3), 209–247 (2014)

17. Fujioka, A., Suzuki, K., Xagawa, K., Yoneyama, K.: Strongly secure authenticated key exchange from factoring, codes, and lattices. Des. Codes Crypt. **76**(3), 469–504 (2015)

18. Fujioka, A., Takashima, K., Terada, S., Yoneyama, K.: Supersingular isogeny Diffie–Hellman authenticated key exchange. In: Lee, K. (ed.) ICISC 2018. LNCS, vol. 11396, pp. 177–195. Springer, Cham (2019). https://doi.org/10.1007/978-3-030-12146-4_12

19. Galbraith, S.D.: Authenticated key exchange for SIDH. IACR Cryptology ePrint Archive 2018/266 2018 (2018). http://eprint.iacr.org/2018/266

20. Gennaro, R.: Faster and shorter password-authenticated key exchange. In: Canetti, R. (ed.) TCC 2008. LNCS, vol. 4948, pp. 589–606. Springer, Heidelberg (2008). https://doi.org/10.1007/978-3-540-78524-8_32

21. Gennaro, R., Lindell, Y.: A framework for password-based authenticated key exchange. In: Biham, E. (ed.) EUROCRYPT 2003. LNCS, vol. 2656, pp. 524–543. Springer, Heidelberg (2003). https://doi.org/10.1007/3-540-39200-9_33

22. Gennaro, R., Lindell, Y.: A framework for password-based authenticated key exchange. ACM Trans. Inf. Syst. Secur. **9**(2), 181–234 (2006)

23. Groce, A., Katz, J.: A new framework for efficient password-based authenticated key exchange. In: ACM Conference on Computer and Communications Security 2010, pp. 516–525 (2010)

24. Jao, D., et al.: Supersingular Isogeny Key Encapsulation (SIKE). submission to NIST PQC Competition (2017). https://sike.org/

25. Jao, D., De Feo, L.: Towards quantum-resistant cryptosystems from supersingular elliptic curve isogenies. In: Yang, B.-Y. (ed.) PQCrypto 2011. LNCS, vol. 7071, pp. 19–34. Springer, Heidelberg (2011). https://doi.org/10.1007/978-3-642-25405-5_2

26. Jiang, S., Gong, G.: Password based key exchange with mutual authentication. In: Handschuh, H., Hasan, M.A. (eds.) SAC 2004. LNCS, vol. 3357, pp. 267–279. Springer, Heidelberg (2004). https://doi.org/10.1007/978-3-540-30564-4_19

27. Jutla, C., Roy, A.: Relatively-sound NIZKs and password-based key-exchange. In: Fischlin, M., Buchmann, J., Manulis, M. (eds.) PKC 2012. LNCS, vol. 7293, pp. 485–503. Springer, Heidelberg (2012). https://doi.org/10.1007/978-3-642-30057-8_29

28. Katz, J., Ostrovsky, R., Yung, M.: Efficient password-authenticated key exchange using human-memorable passwords. In: Pfitzmann, B. (ed.) EUROCRYPT 2001. LNCS, vol. 2045, pp. 475–494. Springer, Heidelberg (2001). https://doi.org/10.1007/3-540-44987-6_29

29. Katz, J., Ostrovsky, R., Yung, M.: Forward secrecy in password-only key exchange protocols. In: Cimato, S., Persiano, G., Galdi, C. (eds.) SCN 2002. LNCS, vol. 2576, pp. 29–44. Springer, Heidelberg (2003). https://doi.org/10.1007/3-540-36413-7_3

30. Katz, J., Ostrovsky, R., Yung, M.: Efficient and secure authenticated key exchange using weak passwords. J. ACM **57**(1), 1–39 (2009)

31. Katz, J., Vaikuntanathan, V.: Smooth projective hashing and password-based authenticated key exchange from lattices. In: Matsui, M. (ed.) ASIACRYPT 2009. LNCS, vol. 5912, pp. 636–652. Springer, Heidelberg (2009). https://doi.org/10.1007/978-3-642-10366-7_37

32. Katz, J., Vaikuntanathan, V.: Round-optimal password-based authenticated key exchange. In: Ishai, Y. (ed.) TCC 2011. LNCS, vol. 6597, pp. 293–310. Springer, Heidelberg (2011). https://doi.org/10.1007/978-3-642-19571-6_18

33. LeGrow, J., Jao, D., Azarderakhsh, R.: Modeling Quantum-Safe Authenticated Key Establishment, and an Isogeny-Based Protocol. IACR Cryptology ePrint Archive 2018/282 (2018). http://eprint.iacr.org/2018/282

34. Longa, P.: A Note on Post-Quantum Authenticated Key Exchange from Supersingular Isogenies. IACR Cryptology ePrint Archive 2018/267 (2018). http://eprint.iacr.org/2018/267

35. MacKenzie, P., Patel, S., Swaminathan, R.: Password-authenticated key exchange based on RSA. In: Okamoto, T. (ed.) ASIACRYPT 2000. LNCS, vol. 1976, pp. 599–613. Springer, Heidelberg (2000). https://doi.org/10.1007/3-540-44448-3_46

36. Peikert, C.: He Gives C-Sieves on the CSIDH. Cryptology ePrint Archive, Report 2019/725 (2019). https://eprint.iacr.org/2006/291

37. Rostovtsev, A., Stolbunov, A.: Public-Key Cryptosystem Based on Isogenies. Cryptology ePrint Archive, Report 2006/145 (2006). https://eprint.iacr.org/2006/145

38. Taraskin, O., Soukharev, V., Jao, D., LeGrow, J.: An Isogeny-Based Password-Authenticated Key Establishment Protocol. IACR Cryptology ePrint Archive 2018/886 (2018). https://eprint.iacr.org/2018/886

39. Vélu, J.: Isogénies entre courbes elliptiques. Comptes Rendus des Séances de l'Académie des Sciences. Série I. Mathématique **273**, A238–A241 (1971)

40. Xu, X., Xue, H., Wang, K., Tian, S., Liang, B., Yu, W.: Strongly Secure Authenticated Key Exchange from Supersingular Isogeny. IACR Cryptology ePrint Archive 2018/760 (2018)

Signatures

An Efficient Conditional Privacy-Preserving Authentication Scheme for Vehicular Ad Hoc Networks Using Online/Offline Certificateless Aggregate Signature

Kang Li[1,2], Man Ho Au[2(✉)], Wang Hei Ho[3], and Yi Lei Wang[2]

[1] Research Institute for Sustainable Urban Development,
The Hong Kong Polytechnic University, Hung Hom, Hong Kong
`kang.li@connect.polyu.hk`
[2] Department of Computing, The Hong Kong Polytechnic University,
Hung Hom, Hong Kong
{`man-ho-allen.au,yilei.wang`}`@polyu.edu.hk`
[3] Department of Electronic and Information Engineering,
The Hong Kong Polytechnic University, Hung Hom, Hong Kong
`ivanwh.ho@polyu.edu.hk`

Abstract. Vehicular ad hoc networks (VANETs) are fundamental components of building a safe and intelligent transportation system. However, due to its wireless nature, VANETs have serious security and privacy issues that need to be addressed. The conditional privacy-preserving authentication protocol is one important tool to satisfy the security and privacy requirements. Many such schemes employ the certificateless signature, which not only avoids the key management issue of the PKI-based scheme but also solves the key escrow problem of the ID-based signature scheme. However, many schemes have the drawback that the computational expensive bilinear pairing operation or map-to-point hash function are used. In order to enhance the efficiency, certificateless signature schemes for VANETs are usually constructed to support signature aggregation or online/offline computation. In this paper, we propose an efficient conditional privacy-preserving authentication scheme using an online/offline certificateless aggregate signature, which does not require bilinear pairing or map-to-point hash function, to address the security and privacy issues of VANETs. Our proposed scheme is proven to be secure with a rigorous security proof, and it satisfies all the security and privacy requirements with a better performance compared with other related schemes.

1 Introduction

Thanks to the rapid advancement of wireless technologies, the vehicular ad-hoc network (VANET) is introduced to build a safe and intelligent transportation

© Springer Nature Switzerland AG 2019
R. Steinfeld and T. H. Yuen (Eds.): ProvSec 2019, LNCS 11821, pp. 59–76, 2019.
https://doi.org/10.1007/978-3-030-31919-9_4

system in metropolitan cities. In VANET, drivers can get a better awareness of their driving environment and can take early action to respond to an emergent situation to avoid any possible damage or to follow a better route by circumventing traffic bottleneck. However, the transmitted message, which may include sensitive data concerning the drivers' privacy, in DSRC wireless protocol could be easily monitored, altered and forged. For example, a malicious vehicle may broadcast a fake message to cause a traffic accident. For message security, the receiver should verify the legitimacy and integrity of the received message before taking further action. In terms of the privacy issue, anonymity must be provided to prevent the adversaries from extracting private information, such as the real identity, from the transmitted messages. However, privacy protection should be conditional, as traceability should also be guaranteed, which indicates that the TA should be able to reveal the real identity of a malicious vehicle when it is necessary.

Many privacy-preserving authentication schemes based on traditional public key infrastructure (PKI) [11,18] have been proposed to address the security and privacy issues. However, in PKI-based authentication scheme, a certificate is required for every public key of the vehicle and the RSU, which means that a certificate authority needs ma to manage all the certificates and vehicles may have to preload a large number of public/private key pairs together with the corresponding certificates in the local storage. This causes huge storage burden and also makes it difficult for the authority. Due to this drawback, PKI-based scheme is not practical and still infeasible for use in VANETs. In order to remove the burden of certificates, papers such as [3,10], proposed ID-based authentication scheme to enhance the computation and communication efficiency. However, these mechanisms are considered suitable only for private networks, because of the key escrow problem [9]. To solve the key escrow problem of ID-based signature scheme, the concept of certificaletess signature was firstly introduced by Al-Riyami and Paterson [1]. Since then, many authentication schemes using certificateless signatures have been proposed to tackle the security and privacy problems in VANET [5,13,15,25].

Since the OBU only has limited computation capacity and the communication window of VANET is very short, participants in VANETs need to handle a large flow of messages. Hence, aggregate signature is proposed to improve message authentication efficiency in vanet. Signature aggregation means that given n signatures on n distinct messages from n distinct users, it is possible to aggregate all these signatures into a single short signature [4]. This is very useful in the scenario, where RSUs aid the communications in VANET by collecting and aggregating a large set of individual signatures of each vehicle into one signature and broadcasting this aggregated signature to the vehicles, which greatly enhances the efficiency of verification and reduces the communication overhead. Apart from the aggregated signature, an online/offline signature is another approach to further decrease the computation cost. In the offline phase, some heavy computations are executed and the intermediate results are stored in resource-constrained devices. Then in the online phase, on receiving a message, the device can very efficiently compute a signature using the intermediate result from the offline phase.

In this paper, we propose an efficient pairing-free online/offline aggregated certificateless signature scheme with conditional privacy-preserving for VANETs. Our scheme satisfies all the security and privacy requirements for VANETs with a rigorous security proof. In order to further enhance authentication efficiency, our scheme supports online/offline signing, signature aggregation, and batch verification. Moreover, we analyse its computation efficiency, specifically the signing, verifying and aggregated verifying cost and make comparisons with some other similar schemes to demonstrate that the efficiency of our scheme is better than most of other related schemes.

1.1 Related Works

The introduction of the first certificateless signature (CL-PKS) by Al-Riyami and Paterson [1] has inspired a large body of research work on improving the CL-PKS scheme. Yum and Lee [23] described a general method to construct a CL-PKS scheme from any ID-based signature scheme. Later, Li et al. [14] proposed the first CL-PKS scheme using bilinear pairings. Au et al. [2] presented a new security model for CL-PKS schemes, in which a malicious KGC attack is considered. He et al. [7] developed the first CL-PKS without using bilinear pairings. However, in [21], the scheme in [7] is found to be insecure against a strong type II attack. More recently, Yeh et al. [22] proposed a CL-PKS scheme for IoT deployment. However, Jia et al. [12] pointed out that it has security flaws, as any malicious KGC can impersonate the KGC and it cannot resist a public key replacement attack.

The first online/offline signature scheme was introduced by Even, Goldreich and Micali [6]. But, the method is impractical since the size of the signature increases by a quadratic factor [16]. Liu et al. [16] proposed an efficient identity based online/offline signature scheme, but it has the key escrow problem. Recently, Cui et al. [5] proposed an efficient certificateless aggregated signature scheme without pairing for VANETs. However, Kamil et al. [13] found a security flaw in [5].

2 Preliminaries and Background

2.1 Elliptic Curve Cryptosystem and Assumptions

Let F_p be a finite field, which is determined by a λ-bit prime number p. Let a set of elliptic curve points E over F_p be defined by the curve form: $y^2 = x^3 + ax + b$, where $p > 3$, $a, b \in F_p$, and $(4a^3 + 27b^2) \bmod p \neq 0$, and the point at infinity be O. All the points on E including O form an additive group G with order q and generator P. The point addition '+' of element in cyclic group G is defined as follows: Let $P, Q \in G$, l be the line containing P, Q (tangent line to E if $P = Q$), and R is the third point of the intersection of l and E. Let l' be the line connecting R and O. Then P '+' Q is defined as the third point such that l' intersects with E at R and O, which is $-R$. Scalar multiplication over E/F_p can be defined as follows:

$$mP = P + P + P + ... + P \text{ (m times), where } m \in Z_q^*$$

The following complexity assumptions are used in security proof of the proposed scheme. We will use the Discrete Logarithm (DL) assumption and the Computational Diffie-Hellman (CDH) assumption over the additive cyclic group G, which can be defined as follows.

Definition 1 (The DL Assumption). *Discrete Logarithm (DL) Assumption: Given a random point $Q \in G$ on E, it is hard to compute an integer $x \in Z_q^*$ in polynomial time such that $Q = xP$ with non-negligible probability.*

Definition 2 (The CDH Assumption). *Computational Diffie-Hellman (CDH) Assumption: Given two random point $Q, R \in G$ on E, where $Q = xP$, $R = yP$, $x, y \in Z_q^*$, it is hard to compute xyP in polynomial time with non-negligible probability.*

2.2 System Model

Typically, a two-layer vehicular ad hoc network model is suitable for VANETs. Figure 1 shows the typical architecture of VANETs. The lower layer composed of vehicles and roadside units (RSUs) located at the critical points along the road. Each vehicle is equipped with an onboard unit (OBU), which enables vehicles to communicate with other vehicles or RSUs. The communication of Vehicle-to-Everything(V2X), mainly the Vehicle-to-Vehicle (V2V) and Vehicle-to-Infrastructure (V2I), is realized by the dedicated short-range communications (DSRC) protocol, which is identified as IEEE 802.11p. The upper layer of VANET consists of an application server(such as traffic control and analysis

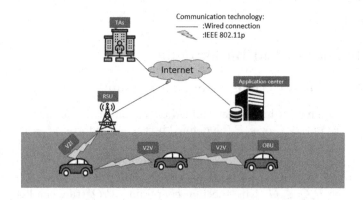

Fig. 1. A typical architecture of VANETs

center), and key generation center (KGC) and trace authority (TRA). The TRA is responsible for RSU and vehicle registration by generating pseudo identities for them and can reveal the real identity of a vehicle from its signed message. The KGC is in charge of generating public and private keys for RSU and vehicles. Besides, we assume that the KGC and TRA are always trusted and cannot be comprised, which is usually assumed in VANET scheme as in [17,24]. The KGC and TRA have sufficient computation power and storage capacity. KGC and TRA are two separate authorities, which can communicate with each other securely using wired networks and secure protocols, such as Transport Layer Security (TLS) protocol. We also assume that each vehicle is equipped with a tamper-proof device, which can prevent the adversary from extracting data from the device. The OBU only has limited computation power, and RSU has greater computation power than OBU. The OBU and RSU are not trusted, and the message sent by them should be authenticated.

3   The Proposed Authentication Scheme

In this section, we present our proposed authentication scheme in detail. First, we define some notations that will be used in the scheme as listed in Table 1.

Table 1. Notations and descriptions

Notation	Description
V_i	The i-th vehicle
psk_i	A partial private key of vehicle V_i
x_{ID_i}	A secret key of vehicle V_i
vpk_{ID_i}	A public key of vehicle V_i
(P_{pub}, α)	The public/private key pair of KGC
(T_{pub}, β)	The public/private key pair of TRA
RID_i	The real identity of a vehicle V_i
PID_i	The pseudo identity of a vehicle V_i
H_1, H_2, H_3	Secure hash functions
T_i	A valid period of the pseudo identity
t_i	A current timestamp
m_i	A traffic-related message
$\oplus$	The exclusive **OR** operation
$\|$	The message concatenation operation

3.1   System Parameter Setup

In this phase, the TRA and KGC will generate the system parameters, such as a finite field, an elliptic curve, public keys, etc.

- Given a security parameter τ, the TAs will generate two large primes p and q, and will choose a non-singular elliptic curve E, which is defined by the equation $y^2 = x^3 + ax + b$, where $p > 3$, $a, b \in F_p$, and $(4a^3 + 27b^2)$ mod p$\neq$ 0.
- The TAs will choose a generator P of the additive group G with the order of q. And it will also choose three secure hash functions which are $H_1 \colon G \times \{0,1\}^* \times \{0,1\}^* \to Z_q^*$, $H_2 \colon \{0,1\}^* \times G \to Z_q^*$, $H_3 \colon \{0,1\}^* \times \{0,1\}^* \times G \times G \times \{0,1\}^* \to Z_q^*$.
- The TRA will randomly choose number $\beta \in Z_q^*$ as its master private key for traceability, and compute $T_{pub} = \beta \cdot P$ as its public key.
- The KGC will randomly choose number $\alpha \in Z_q^*$ as its master private key for partial private key extraction, and compute $P_{pub} = \alpha \cdot P$ as its public key.
- Then, the public parameters are $params = \{P, p, q, E, G, H_1, H_2, H_3, P_{pub}, T_{pub}\}$. Finally,each vehicle pre-loads the public parameters into its temper-proof device and RSU stores $params$ into its local storage.

3.2 Pseudo-Identity-Generation and Partial-Private-Key-Extraction

In this phase, vehicles register with the TRA and KGC to obtain its pseudo identity and partial private key.

- The vehicle choose a random value $k_i \in Z_q^*$, and calculate $PID_{i,1} = k_iP$. Then the vehicle sends its real identity RID_i and $PID_{i,1}$ to the TRA in a secure way.
- Once the TRA receives $(RID_i, PID_{i,1})$ from the vehicle, it first check whether RID_i is valid or not. If RID_i exist in its local database, then TRA computes $PID_{i,2} = RID_i \oplus H_1((\beta \cdot PID_{i,1})\|T_i\|T_{pub})$ and send the $PID_{i,2}$ to the vehicle. Then, the pseudo identity of the vehicle is $PID_i = (PID_{i,1}, PID_{i,2}, T_i)$ where T_i is the valid period of the pseudo identity.
- A vehicle will use its pseudo identity PID_i to communicate with other participants in the VANET. Since only TRA know its master private key β, it has the ability to reveal the real identity of a vehicle by computing $RID_i = PID_{i,2} \oplus H_1((\beta \cdot PID_{i,1})\|T_i\|T_{pub})$ in some situation. Then, the TRA will also send the pseudo identity PID_i to KGC in a secure way.
- After the KGC receives the pseudo identity, it choose a random number $d_i \in Z_q^*$ and compute $Q_{ID_i} = d_iP$. Then it calculates the partial private key as $psk_{ID_i} = d_i + H_2(PID_i\|Q_{ID_i}) \cdot \alpha$ (mod q).
- Then the KGC transmits (Q_{ID_i}, psk_{ID_i}) to the vehicle via a secure channel. Finally the vehicle obtains its pseudo identity PID_i and partial private key psk_{ID_i}. And the vehicle can check the validity of the partial private key using the public parameters by verifying whether the equation $psk_{ID_i} \cdot P = Q_{ID_i} + H_2(PID_i\|Q_{ID_i}) \cdot P_{pub}$ holds or not. If it holds, then the vehicle will store the pseudo identity (PID_i) and partial private key(psk_{ID_i}) in its temper-proof device for further use. Note that the value Q_{ID_i} should be public.

3.3 Vehicle-Key-Generation

In this phase, the vehicle choose a random number $x_{ID_i} \in Z_q^*$ as its secret key and compute $vpk_{ID_i} = x_{ID_i} \cdot P$ as its public key.

3.4 Offline-Sign

In order to maintain the message authentication and integrity, the traffic-related message should be signed before transmitted. Since the computation power of the OBU is limited, we propose to use online-offline signature technique, which allows the vehicles to offline compute some part of the signature when OBU is idle or the traffic density is not high, to enhance the efficiency of generating signatures. The offline signature is generated as follows:

- V_i randomly selects a number $r_i \in Z_q^*$
- V_i computes $R_i = r_i \cdot P$
- V_i stores the offline $\phi_i = (r_i, R_i)$ locally

Generating the offline signature does not require the message, thus a large set of these offline signature pairs could be pre-generated and stored locally for future use.

3.5 Online-Sign

Firstly, it randomly picks a pseudo identity PID_i from its storage and selects the latest timestamp t_i, which is used to prevent the replay message attacks. On input a traffic-related message m_i, it signs the message as the followings steps.

- V_i obtains a fresh offline signature tuple $\phi_i = (r_i, R_i)$ from its storage.
- V_i computes the full private key $sk_i = x_{ID_i} + psk_{ID_i}$
- V_i computes $h_{3i} = H_3(m_i||PID_i||vpk_{ID_i}||R_i||t_i)$.
- V_i computes $s_i = h_{3i} \cdot r_i + sk_i \ (mod q)$
- The output signature is $\sigma_i = (R_i, s_i)$. Finally, the vehicle V_i broadcasts $\{m_i, PID_i, \sigma_i, t_i, vpk_{ID_i}, Q_{ID_i}\}$ to nearby RSUs and vehicles for verification.

3.6 Individual-Verify

In this phase, RSUs or vehicles verify the validity of an individual received message. Once it receives the message $\{m_i, PID_i, \sigma_i, t_i, vpk_{ID_i}, Q_{ID_i}\}$, it checks the validity of the signature as follows.

- Firstly, the verifier will check the freshness of the timestamp t_i. If it is not fresh, then the verifier reject the message and stop the verifying process.
- Then, calculate $h_{3i} = H_3(m_i||PID_i||vpk_{ID_i}||R_i||t_i)$ and $h_{2i} = H_2(PID_i||Q_{ID_i})$
- Then, check whether the equation $s_i \cdot P = h_{3i} \cdot R_i + vpk_{ID_i} + Q_{ID_i} + h_{2i} \cdot P_{pub}$ holds or not. If this equation holds, then the verifier accepts this message, otherwise reject.

Proof of Correctness: Since $h_{3i} = H_3(m_i\|PID_i\|vpk_{ID_i}\|R_i\|t_i)$, $h_{2i} = H_2(PID_i\|Q_{ID_i})$, $sk_i = x_{ID_i} + psk_{ID_i}$, $r_i \cdot P = R_i$, $x_{ID_i} \cdot P = vpk_{ID_i}$, and $psk_{ID_i} \cdot P = Q_{ID_i} + h_{2i} \cdot P_{pub}$, if the signature is generated correctly, then the following equation will hold

$$s_i \cdot P = h_{3i} \cdot r_i \cdot P + x_{ID_i} \cdot P + psk_{ID_i} \cdot P$$
$$= h_{3i} \cdot R_i + vpk_{ID_i} + Q_{ID_i} + h_{2i} \cdot P_{pub}$$

3.7   Aggregate

In some scenarios where the density of transmitted messages is very high, RSUs need to aid the communication by aggregating a collection of certificateless signatures into one. Signature aggregation is the process that on receiving a set of messages $\{m_i, PID_i, \sigma_i, t_i, vpk_{ID_i}, Q_{ID_i}\}$ from n vehicles $\{V_i, V_2, ..., V_n\}$, where $i = 1, 2, 3, ...n$, the RSU aggregate the signature by calculating $S = \sum_{i=1}^{n} s_i$. Then RSUs output $\sigma = (R_1, R_2, R_3...R_n, S)$ as the aggregated signature.

3.8   Aggregate-Verify

This algorithm is assumed to be performed by RSUs or the application centers, such as a traffic control center. Once receiving the aggregated signature $\sigma = (R_1, R_2, R_3...R_n, S)$ from a set of vehicles $\{V_1, V_2, V_3, ..., V_n\}$, with the corresponding parameters $\{m_i, PID_i, t_i, vpk_{ID_i}, Q_{ID_i}\}$, where $i = 1, 2, 3, ...n$, the RSUs or application centers check the validity of the aggregated signature by performing the following steps.

- Firstly, the verifier will check the freshness of the timestamp t_i, for $i = 1, 2, 3, ...n$. If it is not fresh, then the verifier reject the message and stop the verifying process.
- Calculate $h_{3i} = H_3(m_i\|PID_i\|vpk_{ID_i}\|R_i\|t_i)$ and $h_{2i} = H_2(PID_i\|Q_{ID_i})$, for $i = 1, 2, 3, ...n$
- Check whether the following equation holds or not: $S \cdot P = \sum_{i=1}^{n}(h_{3i} \cdot R_i) + \sum_{i=1}^{n} Q_{ID_i} + \sum_{i=1}^{n} vpk_{ID_i} + (\sum_{i=1}^{n} h_{2i}) \cdot P_{pub}$. If this equation holds, the verifier will accept the aggregated signature.

Proof of Correctness: Since we have $h_{3i} = H_3(m_i\|PID_i\|vpk_{ID_i}\|R_i\|t_i)$, $h_{2i} = H_2(PID_i\|Q_{ID_i})$, $sk_i = x_{ID_i} + psk_{ID_i}$, $r_i \cdot P = R_i$, $x_{ID_i} \cdot P = vpk_{ID_i}$, and $psk_{ID_i} \cdot P = Q_{ID_i} + h_{2i} \cdot P_{pub}$, then we can check the correctness as follows:

$$S \cdot P = \sum_{i=1}^{n} s_i \cdot P$$
$$= \sum_{i=1}^{n}(h_{3i} \cdot r_i \cdot P + x_{ID_i} \cdot P + psk_{ID_i} \cdot P)$$
$$= \sum_{i=1}^{n}(h_{3i} \cdot R_i) + \sum_{i=1}^{n} Q_{ID_i} + \sum_{i=1}^{n} vpk_{ID_i} + (\sum_{i=1}^{n} h_{2i}) \cdot P_{pub}$$

3.9   Batch Verification

Sometimes, a participant in VANETs needs to verify multiple signatures in a single instance instead of aggregating them. In this scenario, we need to use the batch verification technique, which allows multiple signatures to be verified at a time. To ensure the non-repudiation of signatures using batch verification, we use the small exponent test technology [10]. On receiving multiple messages $\{m_i, PID_i, \sigma_i, t_i, vpk_{ID_i}, Q_{ID_i}\}$ where $i = 1, 2, 3, ...n$, the verifier checks the signature validity using public parameters. The verification process is presented as follows.

- Firstly, the verifier will check the freshness of the timestamp t_i, for $i = 1, 2, 3, ...n$. If it is not fresh, then the verifier reject the message and stop the verifying process.
- The verifier randomly choose a vector $v = \{v_1, v_2, v_3, ..., v_n\}$,, where v_i is a small random integer in $[1, 2^t]$ and t is a small integer that incurs very little computation head.
- The verifier checks whether the following equation hols, if it holds, it accepts the messages, otherwise rejects the messages.
$(\sum_{i=1}^n s_i \cdot v_i) \cdot P = \sum_{i=1}^n (h_{3i} \cdot R_i \cdot v_i) + \sum_{i=1}^n (vpk_{ID_i} \cdot v_i) + \sum_{i=1}^n (Q_{ID_i} \cdot v_i) + (\sum_{i=1}^n h_{2i} \cdot v_i) \cdot P_{pub}$

Proof of Correctness: The process is similar to that in the aggregated verify. We have $h_{3i} = H_3(m_i\|PID_i\|vpk_{ID_i}\|R_i\|t_i)$, $h_{2i} = H_2(PID_i\|Q_{ID_i})$, $sk_i = x_{ID_i} + psk_{ID_i}$, $r_i \cdot P = R_i$, $x_{ID_i} \cdot P = vpk_{ID_i}$, and $psk_{ID_i} \cdot P = Q_{ID_i} + h_2 \cdot P_{pub}$. We obtain that:

$$(\sum_{i=1}^n s_i \cdot v_i) \cdot P$$
$$= \sum_{i=1}^n ((h_{3i} \cdot r_i + x_{ID_i} + psk_{ID_i}) \cdot v_i) \cdot P$$
$$= \sum_{i=1}^n (h_{3i} \cdot v_i \cdot r_i \cdot P) + \sum_{i=1}^n (v_i \cdot x_{ID_i} \cdot P) + \sum_{i=1}^n (v_i \cdot psk_{ID_i} \cdot P)$$
$$= \sum_{i=1}^n (h_{3i} \cdot R_i \cdot v_i) + \sum_{i=1}^n (psk_{ID_i} \cdot v_i) + \sum_{i=1}^n ((Q_{ID_i} + h_{2i} \cdot P_{pub}) \cdot v_i)$$
$$= \sum_{i=1}^n (h_{3i} \cdot R_i \cdot v_i) + \sum_{i=1}^n (vpk_{ID_i} \cdot v_i) + \sum_{i=1}^n (Q_{ID_i} \cdot v_i) + (\sum_{i=1}^n h_{2i} \cdot v_i) \cdot P_{pub}$$

4   Security Proof

In this section, we give a formal security proof on the proposed certificateless signature scheme. We use a similar approach in [7] to prove the security of the proposed signature scheme. The detailed security proof is shown in the appendix.

5   Discussion

In this section, we first present the security and privacy analysis with respect to the identity privacy-preserving, message authentication, and integrity, traceability, unlinkability and resistance to various attacks. Then we will analyze the performance of the proposed online/offline certificateless signature scheme and compare with some other similar schemes.

5.1   Security Analysis

1. **Identity Privacy Preserving**: Each participant in VANET needs to register with the TRA to obtain a pseudo identity, which is generated by the TRA using its master private key β. The only way for an adversary to reveal the real identity is to compute $RID_i = PID_{i,2} \oplus H_1((\beta \cdot PID_{i,1}) \| T_i \| T_{pub})$, which means that the adversary has to know the master private key β to calculate $\beta \cdot PID_{i,1}$. However, it is infeasible for the adversary to obtain β from $T_{pub} = \beta \cdot P$, as this contradicts the DL assumption. Therefore, our scheme meets the requirement of identity privacy preserving.

2. **Message Authentication and Integrity**: Each transmitted message is signed by a legitimate user before broadcasting in VANET. According to Theorems 1 and 2, there is no polynomial-time adversary can forge a valid signature based on the DL assumption. Hence the verifier can check the validity and integrity of the signature, which guarantees that the message comes from a legitimate user and it is not modified during transmission, by verifying the equation $s_i \cdot P = h_{3i} \cdot R_i + vpk_{ID_i} + Q_{ID_i} + h_{2i} \cdot P_{pub}$. Hence, the proposed scheme ensures the message authentication and integrity.

3. **Traceability**: The pseudo identity is generated using the master private key of the TRA. From the pseudo identity $PID_i = (PID_{i,1}, PID_{i,2}, T_i)$, where $PID_{i,1} = k_i P$, $PID_{i,2} = RID_i \oplus H_1((\beta \cdot PID_{i,1}) \| T_i \| T_{pub})$, the TRA can extract the real identity by computing $RID_i = PID_{i,2} \oplus H_1((\beta \cdot PID_{i,1}) \| T_i \| T_{pub})$. Hence, the traceability is also provided by our scheme.

4. **Unlinkability**: During the pseudo identity generation phase, the OBU choose a random value $k_i \in Z_q^*$ to calculate $PID_{i,1} = k_i P$ and $PID_{i,2} = RID_i \oplus H_1((\beta \cdot PID_{i,1}) \| T_i \| T_{pub})$ which compose the pseudo identity. As for the signature generation, a random value $r_i \in Z_q^*$ is also selected by the vehicle and used to compute the signature. Due to the randomness of k_i and r_i, it is infeasible for the adversary to link two anonymous identities or signatures generated by the same vehicle. Hence, the requirement of unlinkability is also guaranteed by our scheme.

5. **Resistance to Various Attacks**: In this part, we show that our scheme can resist various attacks, including reply attack, modification attack, impersonation attack and stolen verifier table attack.
   - **Reply Attack**: The timestamp t_i inside the message $\{m_i, PID_i, \sigma_i, t_i, vpk_{ID_i}, Q_{ID_i}\}$ is used to resist the reply attack. Before verifying the validity of the signature, the verifier will check the freshness of the timestamp t_i. If it is not a fresh timestamp, the message will be rejected. Hence, the reply attack is avoided in our scheme by using the timestamp.
   - **Message Modification Attact**: Since each message is signed by the sender, any modification of the message will lead to the result that equation $s_i \cdot P = h_{3i} \cdot R_i + vpk_{ID_i} + Q_{ID_i} + h_{2i} \cdot P_{pub}$ does not hold when the verifier checks the validity of the signature. Then the modified message will be disregarded. Hence, our scheme can resist modification attack.
   - **Impersonation Attack**: In order to launch a successful impersonation attack, the adversary should be able to output a message

$\{m_i, PID_i, \sigma_i, t_i, vpk_{ID_i}, Q_{ID_i}\}$ that can pass the verification of the receiver. This means that the adversary should be able to forge a valid signature. However, this is infeasible according to the Theorems 1 and 2. Hence the impersonation attack is impossible for our scheme.

- **Stolen Verifier Table Attack:** In our scheme, OBU and RSU does not maintain a verifier table for message authentication. Therefore, stolen verifier table attack is also impossible for our scheme.

5.2 Performance Evaluation

We adopt a similar approach in [8] to analyze the performance. Below we define the benchmark and security level for comparisons.

For bilinear pairing-based authentication schemes, we use a bilinear pairing $\bar{e} : G_1 \times G_1 \rightarrow G_2$ with the security level of 80-bits, where G_1 is an additive group generated by a point $\bar{P}$ with the order of $\bar{q}$ on the super singular elliptic curve $\bar{E} : y^2 = x^3 + x \bmod \bar{p}$ with the embedding group degree 2, $\bar{p}$ is a 512-bit prime number, $\bar{q}$ is a 160-bit Solinas prime number and the equation $\bar{p}+1 = 12\bar{q}r$ holds. For ECC-based identity-based authentication scheme, we achieve the security level of 80-bits by using an additive group G generated by a point P with the order q on a non-singular elliptic curve E, which is defined by the equation $y^2 = x^3 + ax + b$, where $p > 3$, $a, b \in F_p$, p, q are 160-bit prime number, and $(4a^3 + 27b^2) \bmod p \neq 0$.

5.3 Computation Cost Analysis

We first define some notations about the execution time of the cryptographic operations. The execution time is evaluated using the famous MIRACL cryptographic library. We use the cryptographic operation time directly from [8] to evaluate the performance. Note that some very light operations, such as addition operation in Z_q^* and multiplication operation in Z_q^* are ignored, as the execution time is relatively small.

- T_{bp}: The operation time of a bilinear pairing operation $\bar{e}(P, Q)$, where $\bar{P}, \bar{Q} \in G_1$, 4.2110 ms;
- T_{bp-m}: The operation time of a scalar multiplication $x \cdot \bar{P}$ related to a bilinear pairing, where $\bar{P} \in G_1, x \in Z_{\bar{q}}^*$, 1.7090 ms;
- T_{bp-a}: The operation time of a point addition $\bar{P} + \bar{Q}$ related to a bilinear pairing, where $\bar{P}, \bar{Q} \in G_1$, 0.0071 ms;
- T_{ecc-m}: The operation time of a scalar multiplication $x \cdot P$ related to the ECC, where $P \in G$ and $x \in Z_q^*$, 0.4420 ms;
- T_{ecc-a}: The operation time of a point addition $P + Q$ related to the ECC, where $P, Q \in G$, 0.0018 ms;
- T_H: The execution time of a map-to-point hash function operation, 4.406 ms;
- T_h: The execution time of an ordinary one-way hash function operation, 0.0001 ms.

Table 2. Computation cost comparisons of the proposed scheme with others

Schemes	Sign (ms)	Individual verify (ms)	Total (ms)
[19]	$4T_{bp-m} + 2T_{bp-a} + T_h \approx 6.8503$	$3T_{bp} + 3T_{bp-m} + T_{bp-a} + 2T_h \approx 17.7673$	24.6176
[9]	$2T_{bp-m} + T_{bp-a} + T_h \approx 3.4252$	$3T_{bp} + T_{bp-m} + T_{bp-a} + T_H + T_h \approx 18.7552$	22.1804
[15]	$3T_{bp-m} \approx 5.127$	$3T_{bp} + 2T_H + 2T_{bp-m} \approx 24.863$	29.99
[25]	$3T_{bp-m} \approx 5.127$	$3T_{bp} + T_H + 2T_{bp-m} \approx 20.457$	25.584
[5]	$T_{ecc-m} + T_h + T_{ecc-a} \approx 0.4439$	$3T_{ecc-m} + 2T_{ecc-a} + 2T_h \approx 1.3298$	1.7737
[13]	$3T_{ecc-m} + 3T_h + 2T_{ecc-a} \approx 1.3299$	$2T_{ecc-m} + T_{ecc-a} + T_{h} \approx 0.8859$	2.2158
Our scheme	$T_{ecc-m} + T_h \approx 0.4421$	$3T_{ecc-m} + 3T_{ecc-a} + 2T_h \approx 1.3316$	1.7737

Table 3. Computation cost comparisons of the proposed scheme with others

Schemes	Aggregated verify (ms)
[19]	$3T_{bp} + 3nT_{bp-m} + nT_{bp-a} + 2nT_h$
[9]	$3T_{bp} + nT_{bp-m} + nT_{bp-a} + nT_H + nT_h$
[15]	$3T_{bp} + (n+1)T_H + 2nT_{bp-m}$
[25]	$3T_{bp} + nT_H + 2nT_{bp-m}$
[5]	$(n+2)T_{ecc-m} + 2nT_{ecc-a} + 2nT_h$
[13]	$2T_{ecc-m} + nT_{ecc-a} + nT_h$
Our scheme	$(n+2)T_{ecc-m} + 3nT_{ecc-a} + 2nT_h$

We make comparisons with the recent authentication schemes in VANET [5, 9,13,15,19,25]. The comparisons of computation cost of signing, verifying one message and aggregated verify are given in Tables 2 and 3. From Tables 2 and 3, it is obvious to see that schemes [9,15,19,25] with pairing operation and map-to-point hash functions are much more computationally expensive than schemes based on ECC cryptographic primitives and simple one-way hash functions. Then, comparing to similar schemes [5,13], which also does not require pairing and map-to-point hash function, our scheme also has some advantages. Even through [5] almost has the same computation efficiency as our scheme, it is shown to be insecure under the existing security model in [13]. Kamil et al. [13] proposed an improved scheme after its cryptanalysis of Cui's scheme [5]. Although, the individual verifying phase of our scheme is more expensive than that in [13], the signing cost of our scheme is much lower than that in [13]. And note that, the total cost of signing and verifying a single message is also small than that in [13]. More importantly, our scheme supports online/offline sign, which means that some cryptographic operations can be pre-computed and used directly when signing a message. Hence in our scheme, the signing cost could be lower and only be T_h, as the operation of the relatively expensive scalar multiplication corresponding to T_{ecc-m} can be pre-computed and does not incur computation overhead.

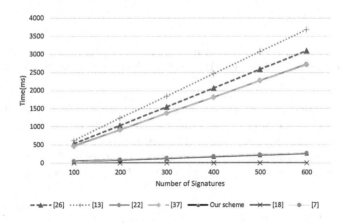

Fig. 2. Aggregated verification time vs. Number of signatures

In Fig. 2, we further investigate the aggregated verification time with respect to the number of signatures. Figure 1 indicates that the aggregated verification time with regards to number of signatures of the schemes, which require bilinear pairings and map-to-point hash functions, increases much faster than that of the schemes without pairings or map-to-point hash functions. The aggregated verification time with regards to the number of signatures of our scheme grows a little faster than that of [13]. However, we argue that typically a RSU is assumed to have much more computation power than the OBU. Hence, in many scenarios, the need to enhance the signing efficiency is more significant than the need to improve the aggregated verification efficiency, which means that the advantage of an efficient sign phase outweight the advantage of an efficient aggregated verification phase. Therefore, our scheme has a slight edge comparing to the scheme [13] in the sense that the signing efficiency is higher than that in [13].

6   Conclusions

In this paper, we propose an efficient conditional privacy-preserving authentication scheme using online/offline certificateless aggregate signature to address the security and privacy issues of VANETs. Our proposed scheme is proven to be secure with a rigorous security proof, and it satisfies all the security and privacy requirements of VANET. The online/offline signature allows some computational expensive operations to be pre-computed offline, thus reducing the computation overhead when signing a message online. Moreover, the proposed scheme does not require the computational expensive bilinear pairing operation and map-to-point hash function, and it supports signature aggregation and batch verification, which are very useful for VANETs scenario. As a result of using these techniques, the proposed scheme has a better computation efficiency compared with many other related schemes.

A   Security Proof

Typically, for a certificateless signature scheme, we define two types of security, namely Type-I security and Type-II security, which corresponds to two types of adversaries $\mathcal{A}_1$ and $\mathcal{A}_2$.

- **Type-I Adversary**: $\mathcal{A}_1$ can launch a public key replacement attack by replacing the public key of any vehicle with a value of its choice. $\mathcal{A}_1$ does not know the master secret key or the partial private key.
- **Type-II Adversary**: $\mathcal{A}_2$ acts as a malicious-but-passive KGC, which knows the master key and the partial private key, but cannot replace any user's public key.

Theorem 1. *The proposed scheme is $(\varepsilon, t, q_c, q_s, q_h)$- secure against the adversary $\mathcal{A}_1$ in the random oracle model, assuming that DL assumption hold in G, where q_c, q_h, q_s are the numbers of **Create**, **Hash** and **Sign** queries that the adversary is allowed to make.*

Proof. Assume there is a probabilistic polynomial-time forger $\mathcal{A}_1$, we construct an algorithm $\mathcal{F}$ that make use of $\mathcal{A}_1$ to solve the discrete logarithm problem(DLP). Suppose $\mathcal{F}$ is given the DLP instance (P, Q) to compute $x \in Z_q^*$ such that $Q = xP$. $\mathcal{F}$ chooses a random identity ID^* as the challenged ID and answers the oracle queries from $\mathcal{A}_1$ as follows:

- **Setup(ID) query**: $\mathcal{F}$ sets $P_{pub} = Q$ and sends the parameters $\{P, p, q, E, G, H_2, H_3, P_{pub}\}$ to $\mathcal{A}_1$.
- **Create(ID) query**: $\mathcal{F}$ maintains a hash list L_c of tuple $(ID, Q_{ID}, vpk_{ID}, psk_{ID}, x_{ID}, h_2)$. When $\mathcal{A}_1$ makes a query on ID, if ID is in L_c, $\mathcal{F}$ responds with $(ID, Q_{ID}, vpk_{ID}, psk_{ID}, x_{ID}, h_2)$. Otherwise, $\mathcal{F}$ will simulate the oracle as follows. It randomly selects three value $a, b, c \in Z_q^*$, and sets $Q_{ID} = a \cdot P_{pub} + b \cdot P$, $vpk_{ID} = c \cdot P$, $psk_{ID} = b$, $x_{ID} = c$, $h_2 = H_2(ID||Q_{ID}) \leftarrow -a(modq)$. Then it responds with $(ID, Q_{ID}, vpk_{ID}, psk_{ID}, x_{ID}, h_2)$, and inserts (ID, Q_{ID}, h_2) to L_{H_2}. Note that the equation $psk_{ID} \cdot P = Q_{ID} + h_2 \cdot P_{pub}$ holds, which means that the partial secret key is valid.
- **H_2 query**: When adversary makes a H_2 query with (ID, Q_{ID}), if ID is already in the hash list L_{H_2}, $\mathcal{F}$ just returns the corresponding h_2. Otherwise, $\mathcal{F}$ runs Create(ID) to get h_2, and send h_2 to $\mathcal{A}_1$.
- **Partial-Private-Key-Extract(ID) query**: If $ID = ID^*$, $\mathcal{F}$ stops the simulation. Otherwise, $\mathcal{F}$ checks the hash list L_c, if ID in the list, then $\mathcal{F}$ response with psk_{ID}. If ID is not in L_c, $\mathcal{F}$ queries Create(ID) to get the psk_{ID}, and sends it to $\mathcal{A}_1$.
- **Public-Key(ID) query**: On receiving the query on ID, if ID is already in L_c, $\mathcal{F}$ response with $pk_{ID} = (Q_{ID}, vpk_{ID})$. Otherwise, $\mathcal{F}$ queries Create(ID) to get the (Q_{ID}, vpk_{ID}), and sends it to $\mathcal{A}_1$.
- **Public-Key-Replacement(ID, pk'_{ID}) query**: $\mathcal{F}$ maintains a hash list L_R of tuple $(ID, d_i, Q_{ID}, x_{ID}, vpk_{ID})$. When $\mathcal{A}_1$ queries with (ID, pk'_{ID}), where $Q'_{ID} = d'_i \cdot P$, $vpk'_{ID} = x'_{ID} \cdot P$ and $pk'_{ID} = (Q'_{ID}, vpk'_{ID})$, $\mathcal{F}$ sets $Q_{ID} = Q'_{ID}$,

$vpk_{ID} = vpk'_{ID}$, $psk_{ID} = \perp$, and $x_{ID} = x'_{ID}$. Then $\mathcal{F}$ updates the list L_R to be $(ID, d'_i, Q'_{ID}, vpk'_{ID}, x'_{ID})$

- **H_3 query:** $\mathcal{F}$ maintains a hash list L_{H_3} of tuple $(m, ID, R, vpk_{ID}, t, h_3)$. If the queries ID is in this list, $\mathcal{F}$ just responds with h_3. Otherwise it chooses a random h_3, sets $h_3 = H_3(m||ID||vpk_{ID}||R||t)$, add it into L_{H_3} and responds with h_3.
- **Sign(ID, m) query:** When $\mathcal{A}_1$ makes a sign query on (ID, m), if ID is in L_R, $\mathcal{F}$ generates random numbers $a, b, c \in Z^*_q$, sets $s = a, R = P, h_3 = H_3(m||ID||vpk_{ID}||R||t) \leftarrow (a - b - c)mod(q)$, inserts $(m, ID, R, vpk_{ID}, t, h_3)$ into L_{H_3}. The output signature is (R, s). If ID is not in L_R, $\mathcal{F}$ acts like the description of the scheme.

Finally, $\mathcal{A}_1$ outputs a forged signature $\sigma = (R, s_{\{1\}})$ on (ID, m), which satisfies the verification process of the verifier. If $ID \neq ID^*$, $\mathcal{F}$ fails and aborts. From the forking lemma in [20], $\mathcal{F}$ rewinds $\mathcal{A}_1$ to the point where it queries H_3, and use a different value. $\mathcal{A}_1$ will output another valid signatures $(R, s_{\{2\}})$ with the same R. Then we have:

$$s_{\{i\}} \cdot P = h_{3_{\{i\}}} \cdot R + vpk_{ID} + Q_{ID} + h_2 \cdot P_{pub}, \text{ where } i = 1, 2$$

From these two linear equations, we can derive the value r by $\frac{s_2 - s_1}{h_{3_{\{2\}}} - h_{3_{\{1\}}}}$. Another rewind on H_2 will allow computation on x.

Probability Analysis: The simulation of Create(ID) oracle fails when the random oracle assignment $H_2(ID||Q_{ID})$ causes inconsistency, which happens with the probability at most q_h/q. The probability of successful simulation of q_c times is at least $(1 - (q_h/q))^{q_c} \geq 1 - (q_h q_c/q)$. Also, the simulation is successful q_h times with the probability at least $(1 - (q_h/q))^{q_h} \geq 1 - (q_h^2/q)$. And $ID = ID^*$ with the probability $1/q_c$. Therefore, the overall successful simulation probability is $(1 - q_h q_c/q)(1 - (q_h^2/q))(1/q_c)\varepsilon$.

The time complexity of the algorithm $\mathcal{F}$ is dominated by the exponentiations performed in the Create and Sign queries, which is equal to $t + O(q_c + q_s)S$, where S is the time of a scalar multiplication operation.

Theorem 2. *The proposed scheme is $(\varepsilon, t, q_c, q_s, q_h)$- secure against the adversary $\mathcal{A}_2$ in the random oracle model, assuming that DL assumption hold in G, where q_c, q_h, q_s are the numbers of **Create, Hash** and **Sign** queries that the adversary is allowed to make.*

Proof. Assume there is a probabilistic polynomial-time forger $\mathcal{A}_2$, we construct an algorithm $\mathcal{F}$ that make use of $\mathcal{A}_2$ to solve the discrete logarithm problem(DLP). Suppose $\mathcal{F}$ is given the DLP instance (P, Q) to compute $y \in Z^*_q$ such that $Q = yP$. $\mathcal{F}$ chooses a random identity ID^* as the challenged ID and answers the oracle queries from $\mathcal{A}_2$ as follows:

- **Setup(ID) query:** $\mathcal{F}$ sets $P_{pub} = x \cdot P, x \in Z^*_q$ and sends the parameters $\{P, p, q, E, G, H_2, H_3, P_{pub}\}$ to $\mathcal{A}_2$.

- **Create(ID) query:** $\mathcal{F}$ maintains a hash list L_c of tuple $(ID, Q_{ID},$ $vpk_{ID}, psk_{ID}, x_{ID}, h_2)$. When $\mathcal{A}_1$ makes a query on ID, if ID is in L_c, $\mathcal{F}$ responds with $(ID, Q_{ID}, vpk_{ID}, psk_{ID}, x_{ID}, h_2)$. If $ID = ID^*$, $\mathcal{F}$ choose $a, b \in Z_q^*$ randomly, sets $Q_{ID} = aP, vpk_{ID} = Q, h_2 = H_2(ID||Q_{ID}) \leftarrow$ $b, psk_{ID} = a + x \cdot h_2, x_{ID} = \perp$. If $ID \neq ID^*$, $\mathcal{F}$ select three random number a, b, c, and sets $Q_{ID} = aP, vpk_{ID} = bP, h_2 = H_2(ID||Q_{ID}) \leftarrow$ $c, psk_{ID} = a + x \cdot h_2, x_{ID} = b$. Finally, $\mathcal{F}$ response the query with $ID, Q_{ID}, vpk_{ID}, psk_{ID}, x_{ID}, h_2$ and add ID, Q_{ID}, h_2 into the hash list L_{H_2}
- **H_2 query:** When adversary makes a H_2 query with (ID, Q_{ID}), if ID is already in the hash list L_{H_2}, $\mathcal{F}$ just returns the corresponding h_2. Otherwise, $\mathcal{F}$ runs Create(ID) to get h_2, and send h_2 to $\mathcal{A}_1$.
- **Partial-Private-Key-Extract(ID) query:** On receiving the query on ID, $\mathcal{F}$ checks the hash list L_c, if ID in the list, then $\mathcal{F}$ response with psk_{ID}. If ID is not in L_c, $\mathcal{F}$ queries Create(ID) to get the psk_{ID}, and sends it to $\mathcal{A}_1$.
- **Public-Key(ID) query:** On receiving the query on ID, if ID is already in L_c, $\mathcal{F}$ response with $pk_{ID} = (Q_{ID}, vpk_{ID})$. Otherwise, $\mathcal{F}$ queries Create(ID) to get the (Q_{ID}, vpk_{ID}), and sends it to $\mathcal{A}_1$.
- **Secrety-Key-Extract(ID) query:** If $ID = ID^*$, $\mathcal{F}$ aborts the simulation. Otherwise, if ID is already in L_c, $\mathcal{F}$ response with x_{ID}. If ID is not already in L_c, $\mathcal{F}$ runs Create(ID) to get $ID, Q_{ID}, vpk_{ID}, psk_{ID}, x_{ID}, h_2$, and sends x_{ID} to the adversary.
- **H_3 query:** $\mathcal{F}$ maintains a hash list L_{H_3} of tuple $(m, ID, R, vpk_{ID}, t, h_3)$. If the quries ID is in this list, $\mathcal{F}$ just responds with h_3. Otherwise it chooses a random h_3, sets $h_3 = H_3(m||ID||vpk_{ID}||R||t)$, add it into L_{H_3} and responds with h_3.
- **Sign(ID, m) query:** If $ID \neq ID^*$, $\mathcal{F}$ acts like the description of the scheme.Otherwise, $\mathcal{F}$ generates random numbers $a, b, f \in Z_q^*$, sets $s = a, h_3 = H_3(m||ID||vpk_{ID}||R||t) \leftarrow f, R = h_3^{-1} \cdot (bP_{pub} - Q)$, and response eith the signature as (R, s). This signature is valid as the equation $s \cdot P = h_3 \cdot R + Q_{ID} + vpk_{ID} + h_2 \cdot P_{pub}$ holds.

Finally, $\mathcal{A}_2$ outputs a forged signature $\sigma = (R, s_{\{1\}})$ on (ID, m), which satisfies the verification process of the verifier. From the forking lemma in [20], $\mathcal{F}$ rewinds $\mathcal{A}_2$ to the point where it queries H_3, and use a different value. $\mathcal{A}_2$ will output another valid signature $(R, s_{\{2\}})$ with the same R. Then we have:

$$s_{\{i\}} \cdot P = h_{3_{\{i\}}} \cdot R + vpk_{ID} + Q_{ID} + h_2 \cdot P_{pub}, \text{ where } i = 1, 2$$
$$s_{\{i\}} = h_{3_{\{i\}}} \cdot r + y + d_i + h_2 x, i = 1, 2$$

Only y, r are unknown. Hence, from these two linear equations, we can derive the two unknown value r, y, and output y as the solution of the DL problem.

Probability Analysis: The simulation of Create(ID) oracle fails when the random oracle assignment $H_2(ID||Q_{ID})$ causes inconsistency, which happens with the probability at most q_h/q. The probability of successful simulation of q_c times is at least $(1 - (q_h/q))^{q_c} \geq 1 - (q_h q_c/q)$. Also, the simulation is successful

q_h times with the probability at least $(1-(q_h/q))^{q_h} \geqq 1-(q_h^2/q)$. And $ID = ID^*$ with the probability $1/q_c$. Therefore, the overall successful simulation probability is $(1 - q_h q_c/q)(1 - (q_h^2/q))(1/q_c)\varepsilon$.

The time complexity of the algorithm $\mathcal{F}$ is dominated by the exponentiations performed in the Create and Sign queries, which is equal to $t + O(q_c + q_s)S$, where S is the time of a scalar multiplication operation.

References

1. Al-Riyami, S.S., Paterson, K.G.: Certificateless public key cryptography. In: Laih, C.-S. (ed.) ASIACRYPT 2003. LNCS, vol. 2894, pp. 452–473. Springer, Heidelberg (2003). https://doi.org/10.1007/978-3-540-40061-5_29
2. Au, M.H., Mu, Y., Chen, J., Wong, D.S., Liu, J.K., Yang, G.: Malicious KGC attacks in certificateless cryptography. In: Proceedings of the 2nd ACM Symposium on Information, Computer and Communications Security, pp. 302–311. ACM (2007)
3. Bayat, M., Barmshoory, M., Rahimi, M., Aref, M.R.: A secure authentication scheme for vanets with batch verification. Wirel. Netw. **21**(5), 1733–1743 (2015)
4. Boneh, D., Gentry, C., Lynn, B., Shacham, H.: Aggregate and verifiably encrypted signatures from bilinear maps. In: Biham, E. (ed.) EUROCRYPT 2003. LNCS, vol. 2656, pp. 416–432. Springer, Heidelberg (2003). https://doi.org/10.1007/3-540-39200-9_26
5. Cui, J., Zhang, J., Zhong, H., Shi, R., Xu, Y.: An efficient certificateless aggregate signature without pairings for vehicular ad hoc networks. Inf. Sci. **451**, 1–15 (2018)
6. Even, S., Goldreich, O., Micali, S.: On-line/off-line digital signatures. In: Brassard, G. (ed.) CRYPTO 1989. LNCS, vol. 435, pp. 263–275. Springer, New York (1990). https://doi.org/10.1007/0-387-34805-0_24
7. He, D., Chen, J., Zhang, R.: An efficient and provably-secure certificateless signature scheme without bilinear pairings. Int. J. Commun Syst **25**(11), 1432–1442 (2012)
8. He, D., Zeadally, S., Xu, B., Huang, X.: An efficient identity-based conditional privacy-preserving authentication scheme for vehicular ad hoc networks. IEEE Trans. Inf. Forensics Secur. **10**(12), 2681–2691 (2015)
9. Horng, S.-J., Tzeng, S.-F., Huang, P.-H., Wang, X., Li, T., Khan, M.K.: An efficient certificateless aggregate signature with conditional privacy-preserving for vehicular sensor networks. Inf. Sci. **317**, 48–66 (2015)
10. Horng, S.-J., et al.: b-SPECS+: batch verification for secure pseudonymous authentication in VANET. IEEE Trans. Inf. Forensics Secur. **8**(11), 1860–1875 (2013)
11. Hubaux, J.-P., Capkun, S., Luo, J.: The security and privacy of smart vehicles. IEEE Secur. Priv. **3**, 49–55 (2004)
12. Jia, X., He, D., Liu, Q., Choo, K.-K.R.: An efficient provably-secure certificateless signature scheme for internet-of-things deployment. Ad Hoc Netw. **71**, 78–87 (2018)
13. Kamil, I.A., Ogundoyin, S.O.: An improved certificateless aggregate signature scheme without bilinear pairings for vehicular ad hoc networks. J. Inf. Secur. Appl. **44**, 184–200 (2019)
14. Li, X.-X., Chen, K.-F., Sun, L.: Certificateless signature and proxy signature schemes from bilinear pairings. Lith. Math. J. **45**(1), 76–83 (2005)
15. Liu, D., Shi, R.-H., Zhang, S., Zhong, H.: Efficient anonymous roaming authentication scheme using certificateless aggregate signature in wireless network. J. Commun. **37**(7), 182–192 (2016)

16. Liu, J.K., Baek, J., Zhou, J., Yang, Y., Wong, J.W.: Efficient online/offline identity-based signature for wireless sensor network. Int. J. Inf. Secur. **9**(4), 287–296 (2010)
17. Lo, N.-W., Tsai, J.-L.: An efficient conditional privacy-preserving authentication scheme for vehicular sensor networks without pairings. IEEE Trans. Intell. Transp. Syst. **17**(5), 1319–1328 (2015)
18. Lu, R., Lin, X., Zhu, H., Ho, P.-H., Shen, X.: ECPP: efficient conditional privacy preservation protocol for secure vehicular communications. In: IEEE INFOCOM 2008-The 27th Conference on Computer Communications, pp. 1229–1237. IEEE (2008)
19. Malhi, A.K., Batra, S.: An efficient certificateless aggregate signature scheme for vehicular ad-hoc networks. Discrete Math. Theor. Comput. Sci. **17**(1), 317–338 (2015)
20. Pointcheval, D., Stern, J.: Security arguments for digital signatures and blind signatures. J. Cryptol. **13**(3), 361–396 (2000)
21. Tsai, J.-L., Lo, N.-W., Wu, T.-C.: Weaknesses and improvements of an efficient certificateless signature scheme without using bilinear pairings. Int. J. Commun Syst **27**(7), 1083–1090 (2014)
22. Yeh, K.-H., Su, C., Choo, K.-K.R., Chiu, W.: A novel certificateless signature scheme for smart objects in the internet-of-things. Sensors **17**(5), 1001 (2017)
23. Yum, D.H., Lee, P.J.: Generic construction of certificateless signature. In: Wang, H., Pieprzyk, J., Varadharajan, V. (eds.) ACISP 2004. LNCS, vol. 3108, pp. 200–211. Springer, Heidelberg (2004). https://doi.org/10.1007/978-3-540-27800-9_18
24. Zhang, C., Lu, R., Lin, X., Ho, P.-H., Shen, X.: An efficient identity-based batch verification scheme for vehicular sensor networks. In: IEEE INFOCOM 2008-The 27th Conference on Computer Communications, pp. 246–250. IEEE (2008)
25. Zhong, H., Han, S., Cui, J., Zhang, J., Xu, Y.: Privacy-preserving authentication scheme with full aggregation in vanet. Inf. Sci. **476**, 211–221 (2019)

History-Free Sequential Aggregate MAC Revisited

Shoichi Hirose[1,2]([✉])[iD] and Junji Shikata[3][iD]

[1] Faculty of Engineering, University of Fukui, Fukui, Japan
hrs_shch@u-fukui.ac.jp
[2] Japan Datacom Co., Ltd., Tokyo, Japan
[3] Graduate School of Environment and Information Sciences,
Yokohama National University, Yokohama, Japan
shikata-junji-rb@ynu.ac.jp

Abstract. Eikemeier et al. introduced and formalized sequential aggregate MAC in 2010. They also constructed a history-free scheme for sequential aggregate MAC using a pseudorandom permutation and a MAC function. In this paper, we reconsider history-free sequential aggregate MAC. We give a definition of its security requirement, which is more general than that of Eikemeier et al. Then, we propose two new schemes for history-free sequential aggregate MAC. The first scheme is constructed with a pseudorandom permutation and a pseudorandom function. The second scheme is constructed only with a pseudorandom function under two keying strategies and without a pseudorandom permutation. We reduce the security of the proposed schemes to the security properties of their underlying primitives. We also discuss an instantiation of the second scheme using a pseudorandom function based on a cryptographic hash function such as HMAC with SHA-2 in some detail.

Keywords: Message authentication · Aggregate MAC · Block cipher · Hash function · Provable security

1 Introduction

Background. Message authentication is one of the important roles of symmetric cryptography. A cryptographic primitive for message authentication is called a MAC function. Let MAC be a MAC function. Two communicating parties, a sender and a receiver, share a secret key SK. The sender sends a message Msg to the receiver together with an authenticator $Tag \leftarrow MAC(SK, Msg)$, which is often called a tag. After receiving (Msg, Tag), the receiver computes $Tag' \leftarrow MAC(SK, Msg)$ and accepts Msg if and only if $Tag' = Tag$.

For authenticated transmission of multiple messages, each message is transmitted with its tag in common cases. Aggregate MAC, which was proposed by Katz and Lindell [17], enables us to aggregate multiple tags into a single tag of

© Springer Nature Switzerland AG 2019
R. Steinfeld and T. H. Yuen (Eds.): ProvSec 2019, LNCS 11821, pp. 77–93, 2019.
https://doi.org/10.1007/978-3-030-31919-9_5

the same length as each of the tags. It is useful for energy-constrained applications such as IoT since a tag makes the amount of transmitted data (more than) double for a very short message.

The Katz-Lindell aggregate MAC scheme aggregates the tags by bitwise modular addition. Thus, it obviously does not reflect the ordering of the messages in the aggregate tag. On the other hand, Eikemeier et al. [11] introduced and formalized sequential aggregate MAC, which enables us to detect any change in the ordering as well as the messages. The scheme proposed by Eikemeier et al. produces a new aggregate tag from a new message and an aggregate-so-far tag without the messages corresponding to the aggregate-so-far tag. Thus, it is called history-free.

Our Contribution. History-free sequential aggregate MAC is reconsidered in this paper. First, its syntax and security requirement are formalized. They are based on those of Eikemeier et al. [11]. The definition of security requirement is, however, more general than theirs in terms of restriction imposed on adversaries. Second, two new schemes are presented. The first scheme is called cipher-based since it requires a pseudorandom permutation and suitable for instantiations using a block cipher such as AES [13]. The second scheme is called hash-based since it requires a pseudorandom function with two keying strategies and suitable for instantiations using a cryptographic hash function such as SHA-2 [12]. The second scheme is just a simple cascade of a pseudorandom function, and it may be interesting in that the scheme presented by Eikemeier et al. [11] requires a pseudorandom permutation as well as the first scheme in the current paper.

Related Work. Inspired by aggregate signatures [8], Katz and Lindell introduced aggregate MAC [17]. They also proposed an aggregate MAC scheme which aggregates tags by bitwise modular addition. The unforgeability of their scheme is reduced to the unforgeability of its underlying MAC function.

Eikemeier et al. [11] gave formal descriptions of sequential aggregate MAC and its security requirement. They also proposed a history-free scheme using a pseudorandom permutation and a MAC function, which was shown to be unforgeable. To aggregate tags, their scheme uses secret keys of the involved users as well as the new schemes proposed in the current paper. Sato, Hirose and Shikata proposed another type of sequential aggregate MAC [20]. Their scheme does not use secret keys of the involved users to aggregate tags.

Aggregate MAC has the following drawbacks: (i) All the messages are required to verify their authenticity with respect to their aggregate tag, and (ii) invalid messages are not identified in the case that the result of authenticity verification is invalid. For the first drawback, aggregate MAC with on-the-fly verification was proposed [9]. For the second drawback, group-testing [10] is applied to aggregate MAC of the Katz-Lindell type [16].

Ma and Tsudik [18] introduced forward-secure sequential aggregate MAC and proposed a scheme using a MAC function and a cryptographic hash function. Ma and Tsudik [19] discussed its application to secure audit log. Hirose and Kuwakado proposed a scheme without cryptographic hash functions [15].

Organization. Notations and definitions are introduced in Sect. 2. Syntax and a security requirement of history-free sequential aggregate MAC are formalized in Sect. 3. Generic constructions using a block cipher and a hash function are presented in Sects. 4 and 5, respectively. Their unforgeability and instantiations are also discussed in these sections. A brief concluding remark is given in Sect. 6.

2 Preliminaries

2.1 Notation

For integers n_1 and n_2 satisfying $n_1 \leq n_2$, let $[n_1, n_2]$ be the set of integers between n_1 and n_2 inclusive.

Selecting an element s uniformly at random from a set $\mathcal{S}$ is denoted by $s \leftarrow \mathcal{S}$. For a set $\mathcal{S}$, let $\mathcal{S}^* \triangleq \bigcup_{i \geq 0} \mathcal{S}^i$ and $\mathcal{S}^+ \triangleq \bigcup_{i \geq 1} \mathcal{S}^i$. For non-negative integers n_1 and n_2 satisfying $n_1 \leq n_2$, let $\mathcal{S}^{[n_1, n_2]} \triangleq \bigcup_{i=n_1}^{n_2} \mathcal{S}^i$.

Let $\Sigma \triangleq \{0, 1\}$. For a non-negative integer l, let Σ^l be the set of all Σ-sequences of length l. Let ε be the Σ-sequence of length 0. For $x \in \Sigma^*$, let $|x|$ be the length of x. For $x, y \in \Sigma^*$, let $x\|y$ be the concatenation of x and y.

Let $\mathcal{F}_{\mathcal{D}, \mathcal{R}}$ be the set of all functions from $\mathcal{D}$ to $\mathcal{R}$. Let $\mathcal{P}_{\mathcal{D}}$ be the set of all permutations over $\mathcal{D}$. For $\mathcal{P}_{\mathcal{D}}$, let id be the identity permutation: $id(x) = x$ for every $x \in \mathcal{D}$.

For a function f, let $\text{time}(f)$ be the amount of time required to compute f.

2.2 Pseudorandom Function and Permutation

A pseudorandom function (PRF) [14] is a keyed function $f \in \mathcal{F}_{\mathcal{K} \times \mathcal{D}, \mathcal{R}}$, where $\mathcal{K}$ is its key space. The security requirement of a PRF is indistinguishability [4, 6, 14]. An adversary **D** against f is given an oracle, which is either f_K or ρ, where $K \leftarrow \mathcal{K}$ and $\rho \leftarrow \mathcal{F}_{\mathcal{D}, \mathcal{R}}$. It makes queries in $\mathcal{D}$ to the oracle adaptively and obtains the corresponding outputs. Finally, it outputs 0 or 1. The prf-advantage of **D** against f is defined by

$$\text{Adv}_f^{\text{prf}}(\mathbf{D}) \triangleq \left| \Pr[\mathbf{D}^{f_K} = 1] - \Pr[\mathbf{D}^\rho = 1] \right|,$$

where **D** is regarded as a random variable. Informally, f is called a secure PRF if any adversary with realistic computational resources can only have negligible prf-advantage against f.

For a pseudorandom permutation (PRP) $p \in \mathcal{F}_{\mathcal{K} \times \mathcal{D}, \mathcal{D}}$, the prp-advantage is defined similarly:

$$\text{Adv}_p^{\text{prp}}(\mathbf{D}) \triangleq \left| \Pr[\mathbf{D}^{p_K} = 1] - \Pr[\mathbf{D}^\varpi = 1] \right|,$$

where $K \leftarrow \mathcal{K}$ and $\varpi \leftarrow \mathcal{P}_{\mathcal{D}}$.

2.3   PRF Under Related-Key Attack

The notion of a PRF under related-key attacks [5] is formalized by Bellare and Kohno. Let $\Phi \subset \mathcal{F}_{\mathcal{K},\mathcal{K}}$ be a set of key-deriving functions. Let $\mathsf{key} \in \mathcal{F}_{\Phi \times \mathcal{K},\mathcal{K}}$ be a function such that $\mathsf{key}(\varphi, K) \triangleq \varphi(K)$. Let $\mathbf{D}$ be an adversary making a Φ-related-key attack (Φ-RKA) against $f \in \mathcal{F}_{\mathcal{K} \times \mathcal{D}, \mathcal{R}}$. $\mathbf{D}$ is given an oracle $g(\mathsf{key}(\cdot, K), \cdot)$, where g is either f or $\rho \twoheadleftarrow \mathcal{F}_{\mathcal{K} \times \mathcal{D}, \mathcal{R}}$, and $K \twoheadleftarrow \mathcal{K}$. For each query $(\varphi, x) \in \Phi \times \mathcal{D}$ made by $\mathbf{D}$, $g(\mathsf{key}(\cdot, K), \cdot)$ returns $g(\varphi(K), x)$. $g(\mathsf{key}(\cdot, K), \cdot)$ is denoted by $g[K]$ for simplicity. The prf-rka-advantage of $\mathbf{D}$ against f is defined by

$$\mathrm{Adv}_{\Phi,f}^{\mathrm{prf\text{-}rka}}(\mathbf{D}) \triangleq \left| \Pr[\mathbf{D}^{f[K]} = 1] - \Pr[\mathbf{D}^{\rho[K]} = 1] \right|.$$

2.4   PRF with Affix

The notion of a PRF with affix is introduced to prove the PRF property of H^2-MAC by Yasuda [21]. The attack scenario of PRF-AX is similar to that of PRF except that an adversary can also obtain information called affix. An adversary $\mathbf{D}$ against $f \in \mathcal{F}_{\mathcal{K} \times \mathcal{D}, \mathcal{R}}$ is given access to a pair of oracles (g, g'), which are either (f_K, f'_K) or (ρ, ρ'), where $K \twoheadleftarrow \mathcal{K}$, $f' \in \mathcal{F}_{\mathcal{K} \times \mathcal{D}', \mathcal{R}'}$, and $(\rho, \rho') \twoheadleftarrow (\mathcal{F}_{\mathcal{D}, \mathcal{R}}, \mathcal{F}_{\mathcal{D}', \mathcal{R}'})$. g' accepts only a single query x' made by $\mathbf{D}$ and returns $g'(x')$ to $\mathbf{D}$. The prf-ax-advantage of $\mathbf{D}$ is defined by

$$\mathrm{Adv}_f^{\mathrm{prf\text{-}ax}^*}(\mathbf{D}) \triangleq \left| \Pr[\mathbf{D}^{(f_K, f'_K)} = 1] - \Pr[\mathbf{D}^{(\rho, \rho')} = 1] \right|.$$

The formalization here is actually slightly different from that of [21], where the query to g' is fixed and cannot be chosen by $\mathbf{D}$. Thus, the notation prf-ax* is used instead of prf-ax of [21].

2.5   Multi-oracle Setting

The prf-advantage can be generalized to the multi-oracle setting. In this setting, an adversary $\mathbf{D}$ against $f \in \mathcal{F}_{\mathcal{K} \times \mathcal{D}, \mathcal{R}}$ is given oracles, which are either $f_{K_1}, f_{K_2}, \ldots, f_{K_m}$ or $\rho_1, \rho_2, \ldots, \rho_m$, where $K_i \twoheadleftarrow \mathcal{K}$ and $\rho_i \twoheadleftarrow \mathcal{F}_{\mathcal{D}, \mathcal{R}}$ for $i \in [1, m]$. The prf-advantage of $\mathbf{D}$ against f is defined by

$$\mathrm{Adv}_f^{m\text{-}\mathrm{prf}}(\mathbf{D}) \triangleq \left| \Pr[\mathbf{D}^{f_{K_1}, \ldots, f_{K_m}} = 1] - \Pr[\mathbf{D}^{\rho_1, \ldots, \rho_m} = 1] \right|.$$

The prf-advantage degrades at most linearly with the number of the oracles:

Lemma 1 (Lemma 3.3 in [3]). *For any adversary $\mathbf{D}_{\mathrm{m}}$ against f with access to m oracles, there exists some adversary $\mathbf{D}_{\mathrm{s}}$ against f such that*

$$\mathrm{Adv}_f^{m\text{-}\mathrm{prf}}(\mathbf{D}_{\mathrm{m}}) \leq m \cdot \mathrm{Adv}_f^{\mathrm{prf}}(\mathbf{D}_{\mathrm{s}}).$$

The run time of $\mathbf{D}_{\mathrm{s}}$ is approximately total of that of $\mathbf{D}_{\mathrm{m}}$ and the time to compute f for the queries made by $\mathbf{D}_{\mathrm{m}}$. The number of the queries made by $\mathbf{D}_{\mathrm{s}}$ is at most $\max\{q_i \mid i \in [1, m]\}$, where q_i is the number of the queries from $\mathbf{D}_{\mathrm{m}}$ to its i-th oracle.

The prp-advantage, the prf-rka-advantage, and the prf-ax-advantage can be generalized to the multi-oracle setting in the similar manner. The similar results to Lemma 1 also hold for these advantages.

2.6   Keyed Merkle-Damgård Iteration

For a keyed function $f : \mathcal{V} \times \mathcal{D} \to \mathcal{V}$ with its key space $\mathcal{V}$, Let $\mathsf{MD}^f : \mathcal{V} \times \mathcal{D}^* \to \mathcal{V}$ be the keyed Merkle-Damgård iteration of f with its key space $\mathcal{V}$. Namely, for $V \in \mathcal{V}$ and an empty sequence $\varepsilon \in \mathcal{D}^0$, $\mathsf{MD}^f(\varepsilon, V) \triangleq V$ and

$$\mathsf{MD}^f((D_1, D_2, \ldots, D_n), V) \triangleq f(D_n, \mathsf{MD}^f((D_1, D_2, \ldots, D_{n-1}), V)),$$

where $D_i \in \mathcal{D}$ for $i \in [1, n]$. $\mathsf{MD}^f(\cdot, V)$ is also denoted by $\mathsf{MD}^f_V(\cdot)$.

2.7   Collision Resistance

Let $\mathcal{H}_{\mathcal{D},\mathcal{R}} \subseteq \mathcal{F}_{\mathcal{D},\mathcal{R}}$ and $|\mathcal{D}| > |\mathcal{R}|$. Let $\mathbf{A}$ be an adversary which takes as input a function in $\mathcal{H}_{\mathcal{D},\mathcal{R}}$ and returns a pair of elements in $\mathcal{D}$. The cr-advantage of $\mathbf{A}$ against $\mathcal{H}_{\mathcal{D},\mathcal{R}}$ is defined by

$$\mathrm{Adv}^{\mathrm{cr}}_{\mathcal{H}_{\mathcal{D},\mathcal{R}}}(\mathbf{A}) \triangleq \Pr[(x, x') \leftarrow \mathbf{A}(h) : x \neq x' \wedge h(x) = h(x')],$$

where $h \twoheadleftarrow \mathcal{H}_{\mathcal{D},\mathcal{R}}$.

3   History-Free Sequential Aggregate MAC

3.1   Syntax

A history-free sequential aggregate MAC (SAM) scheme is defined to consist of the following algorithms:

Key generation $K \leftarrow \mathsf{KG}(1^p)$.
   This algorithm takes as input a security parameter p and produces a secret key K.

Aggregate Tagging $T \leftarrow \mathsf{STag}(K_I, M, I, T')$.
   This algorithm takes as input a pair of a message and an ID (M, I), an aggregate-so-far tag T' and a secret key K_I of the user I, and produces as output a new aggregate tag T.

Verification $d \leftarrow \mathsf{SVer}((K_{I_1}, \ldots, K_{I_n}), ((M_1, I_1), \ldots, (M_n, I_n)), T_n)$.
   This algorithm takes as input a tuple of pairs of a message and an ID $((M_1, I_1), \ldots, (M_n, I_n))$, a tag T_n and secret keys $(K_{I_1}, \ldots, K_{I_n})$ and returns a decision $d \in \{\top, \bot\}$.

   For $((M_1, I_1), \ldots, (M_n, I_n))$, let $T'_i = \mathsf{STag}(K_{I_i}, M_i, I_i, T'_{i-1})$ for $i \in [1, n]$, where T'_0 is a fixed constant. Then, $\mathsf{SVer}((K_{I_1}, \ldots, K_{I_n}), ((M_1, I_1), \ldots, (M_n, I_n)), T_n)$ returns $\top$ if $T_n = T'_n$, and $\bot$ otherwise.
   A sequential aggregate MAC scheme is called history-free if the new aggregate tag depends on the previous messages and IDs only through the aggregate-so-far tag as in the current formalization. A history-free sequential aggregate MAC scheme is simply called a sequential aggregate MAC scheme in the remaining parts of this paper.

3.2   Security Requirement

The security requirement of an SAM scheme SAM $\triangleq$ (KG, STag, SVer) is unforge-ability. An adversary $\mathbf{F}$ against SAM is given access to aggregate tagging, veri-fication and corrupt oracles.

The aggregate tagging oracle receives a pair of a message and an ID (M, I) and an aggregate-so-far tag T' as a query and returns the tag $T \leftarrow \mathsf{STag}(K_I, M, I, T')$. The verification oracle receives pairs of a message and an ID $((M_1, I_1), \ldots, (M_n, I_n))$ and a tag T_n as a query and returns the decision $d \leftarrow \mathsf{SVer}((K_{I_1}, \ldots, K_{I_n}), ((M_1, I_1), \ldots, (M_n, I_n)), T_n)$. The corrupt oracle receives an ID I as a query and returns the corresponding secret key K_I.

$\mathbf{F}$ is allowed to make multiple queries adaptively to the aggregate tagging oracle and the corrupt oracle and finally a query to the verification oracle. Let $\mathsf{Forge}(\mathbf{F})$ be an event that $\mathbf{F}$ succeeds in asking the verification oracle a query $(((M_1, I_1), \ldots, (M_n, I_n)), T_n)$ satisfying the following conditions:

- $\mathsf{SVer}((K_{I_1}, \ldots, K_{I_n}), ((M_1, I_1), \ldots, (M_n, I_n)), T_n) = \top$.
- Let $T_i' = \mathsf{STag}(K_{I_i}, M_i, I_i, T_{i-1}')$ for $i \in [1, n]$. There exists some $j \in [1, n]$ such that $\mathbf{F}$ asks neither (M_j, I_j, T_{j-1}') to the aggregate tagging oracle nor I_j to the corrupt oracle.

Then, the advantage of $\mathbf{F}$ against SAM with respect to unforgeability is defined by

$$\mathsf{Adv}_{\mathsf{SAM}}^{\mathsf{uf}}(\mathbf{F}) \triangleq \Pr[\mathsf{Forge}(\mathbf{F})] \ .$$

SAM is informally said to be unforgeable if $\mathsf{Adv}_{\mathsf{SAM}}^{\mathsf{uf}}(\mathbf{F})$ is negligibly small for any adversary $\mathbf{F}$ with realistic computational resources.

3.3   Discussion

The differences between the formalization of Eikemeier et al. [11] and that of this paper are described below.

In the formalization of unforgeability by Eikemeier et al., an adversary $\mathbf{F}$ works in two phases. In the first phase, $\mathbf{F}$ is allowed to ask queries only to the corrupt oracle. In the second phase, $\mathbf{F}$ is allowed to ask queries only to the sequen-tial aggregate tagging oracle SeqAgg, which receives an aggregate-so-far tag T' and a sequence of pairs of a message and an ID $P \triangleq ((M_1, I_1), \ldots, (M_n, I_n))$ as a query and returns a corresponding tag T as an answer. Let $\mathcal{Q}_{\mathsf{Cor}}$ be the set of ID's $\mathbf{F}$ asks to its corrupt oracle as queries in the first phase. Then, as is mentioned later, it is required that $I_n \notin \mathcal{Q}_{\mathsf{Cor}}$. Let $\mathcal{Q}_{\mathsf{Seq}}$ be the set of pairs of a query by $\mathbf{F}$ to SeqAgg and the corresponding answer $((T', P), T)$. At the end of the second phase, $\mathbf{F}$ outputs a sequence of pairs of a message and an ID and a tag.

To define the successful forgery by $\mathbf{F}$, Eikemeier et al. define the closure of queries made by $\mathbf{F}$. Let

$$\mathsf{Trivial}_{\mathcal{Q}_{\mathsf{Seq}},\mathcal{Q}_{\mathsf{Cor}}}(P',T') \triangleq \{P'\} \cup \bigcup_{((T',P),T)\in\mathcal{Q}_{\mathsf{Seq}}} \mathsf{Trivial}_{\mathcal{Q}_{\mathsf{Seq}},\mathcal{Q}_{\mathsf{Cor}}}(P'\|P,T)$$

$$\cup \bigcup_{\substack{I\in\mathcal{Q}_{\mathsf{Cor}},(M,T)\text{ s.t.}\\ T\leftarrow\mathsf{STag}(K_I,M,I,T')}} \mathsf{Trivial}_{\mathcal{Q}_{\mathsf{Seq}},\mathcal{Q}_{\mathsf{Cor}}}(P'\|(M,I),T)\ .$$

Then, the closure is defined by

$$\mathsf{Closure}(\mathcal{Q}_{\mathsf{Seq}},\mathcal{Q}_{\mathsf{Cor}}) \triangleq \mathsf{Trivial}_{\mathcal{Q}_{\mathsf{Seq}},\mathcal{Q}_{\mathsf{Cor}}}(\varepsilon,\mathsf{cT}),$$

where cT is a constant used as an aggregate-so-far tag for the first message[1].

Suppose that $\mathbf{F}$ outputs the sequence of pairs of a message and an ID and the corresponding tag $(\tilde{P},\tilde{T})$ at the end of the second phase, where $\tilde{P} \triangleq ((\tilde{M}_1,\tilde{I}_1),\ldots,(\tilde{M}_n,\tilde{I}_n))$. Then, $\mathbf{F}$ succeeds in forgery if

$$\mathsf{SVer}((K_{\tilde{I}_1},\ldots,K_{\tilde{I}_n}),((\tilde{M}_1,\tilde{I}_1),\ldots,(\tilde{M}_n,\tilde{I}_n)),\tilde{T}) = \top$$

and $\tilde{P} \notin \mathsf{Closure}(\mathcal{Q}_{\mathsf{Seq}},\mathcal{Q}_{\mathsf{Cor}})$. The security of a sequential aggregate MAC scheme is quantified by the probability of successful forgery. Informally, a sequential aggregate MAC scheme is said to be unforgeable if any adversary with realistic computational resources succeeds in forgery only with a negligible probability.

The security formalization of this paper is more general than that of Eikemeier et al. from the following reason: In the formalization of Eikemeier et al., $\mathbf{F}$ works in two phases and its oracle access is restricted in both of the phases, while such restriction is not assumed in the formalization of this paper.

In the formalization of Eikemeier et al., the oracle SeqAgg receives as a query an aggregate-so-far tag and a sequence of pairs of a message and an ID and returns a corresponding tag. On the other hand, in the formalization of this paper, $\mathbf{F}$ gets a tag for a sequence of pairs of a message and an ID by successive queries to the oracle STag. Thus, $\mathbf{F}$ may not obtain any of the aggregate-so-far tags in the formalization of Eikemeier et al., while it obtain all of the aggregate-so-far tags in the formalization of this paper. In the formalization of Eikemeier et al., from the definition of the closure of queries made by $\mathbf{F}$, $\mathbf{F}$ succeeds in forgery if it can make a correct guess for an aggregate-so-far tag. However, we have to notice the following point.

Let $(((M_1,I_1),\ldots,(M_n,I_n)),T')$ be a query made by $\mathbf{F}$ to SeqAgg. Then, it must hold that $I_n \notin \mathcal{Q}_{\mathsf{Cor}}$. The reason is described below.

In the proof of the unforgeability of the sequential aggregate MAC scheme by Eikemeier et al., it is required that there exists an efficient algorithm to compute T' for given T,K_I,M,I if $T \leftarrow \mathsf{STag}(K_I,M,I,T')$. Then, suppose that $\mathbf{F}$ asks $(((M_1,I_1),\ldots,(M_n,I_n)),\mathsf{cT})$ as a query to SeqAgg and obtains the corresponding tag T_n. In addition, suppose that $\mathcal{Q}_{\mathsf{Cor}} = \{I_n\}$. Then, $\mathbf{F}$ can obtain T_{n-1} from

---

[1] Though the tag for the first message is computed without an aggregate-so-far tag in the formalization of Eikemeier et al., this change is minor.

T_n, K_{I_n}, M_n, I_n. Notice that T_{n-1} is a valid tag for $((M_1, I_1), \ldots, (M_{n-1}, I_{n-1}))$ and $((M_1, I_1), \ldots, (M_{n-1}, I_{n-1}))$ is not included in the closure. Thus, **F** succeeds in forgery by outputting $(((M_1, I_1), \ldots, (M_{n-1}, I_{n-1})), T_{n-1})$.

4   Generic Construction Based on Block Cipher

A SAM scheme is presented, which is constructed from a pseudorandom function and a pseudorandom permutation. Then, it is shown to be unforgeable. Since the scheme uses a pseudorandom permutation, it is suitable for instantiations using a block cipher and is called a cipher-based scheme.

4.1   Scheme

The cipher-based SAM scheme $\mathsf{SAM_c} \triangleq (\mathsf{KG_c}, \mathsf{STag_c}, \mathsf{SVer_c})$ is constructed from a PRF $F : \mathcal{K} \times \mathcal{M} \to \mathcal{L}$ with its key space $\mathcal{K}$ and a PRP $G : \mathcal{L} \times \mathcal{T} \to \mathcal{T}$ with its key space $\mathcal{L}$ as follows:

- $\mathsf{KG_c}$ simply returns $K_I \leftarrow \mathcal{K}$ for a user I.
- $T \leftarrow \mathsf{STag_c}(K_I, M, I, T')$, where $T \triangleq G(F(K_I, M), T')$.
- $\mathsf{SVer_c}((K_{I_1}, \ldots, K_{I_n}), ((M_1, I_1), \ldots, (M_n, I_n)), T_n)$ returns $\top$ if $T_n = T'_n$, and $\bot$ otherwise, where $T'_i = G(F(K_{I_i}, M_i), T'_{i-1})$ for $i \in [1, n]$ and T'_0 is some constant $\mathsf{cT} \in \mathcal{T}$.

The aggregate tagging of $\mathsf{SAM_c}$ is depicted in Fig. 1.

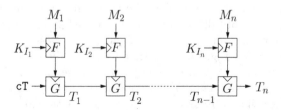

Fig. 1. The aggregate tagging of the proposed scheme $\mathsf{SAM_c}$. The triangle of a box indicates that the corresponding input is a secret key to F or G.

The crucial idea of the proposed scheme is to use the "tag" of a message by F as a secret key of G for aggregate.

4.2   Unforgeability

It is shown that $\mathsf{SAM_c}$ is unforgeable if F is a secure PRF and G is a secure PRP.

Theorem 1. *Suppose that* $\mathsf{SAM_c}$ *has at most u users. For any adversary* **F** *against* $\mathsf{SAM_c}$ *running in time at most s, making at most q_t queries to the aggregate tagging oracle, at most q_c queries to the corrupt oracle and a query of length at most ℓ to the verification oracle, there exist some adversaries* $\mathbf{D}_1$ *and* $\mathbf{D}_2$ *such that*

$$\mathrm{Adv}^{\mathrm{uf}}_{\mathsf{SAM_c}}(\mathbf{F}) \leq u\left(\mathrm{Adv}^{\mathrm{prf}}_F(\mathbf{D}_1) + (q_t + \ell)\,\mathrm{Adv}^{\mathrm{prp}}_G(\mathbf{D}_2) + \frac{\ell}{|\mathcal{T}| - q_t}\right) .$$

$\mathbf{D}_1$ *runs in time at most about* $s + (q_t + \ell)(\mathrm{time}(F) + \mathrm{time}(G)) + uq_c$ *and makes at most $q_t + \ell$ queries to its oracle.* $\mathbf{D}_2$ *runs in time at most about* $s + 2(q_t + \ell)(\mathrm{time}(F) + \mathrm{time}(G)) + uq_c$ *and makes at most $q_t + \ell$ queries to its oracle.*

Proof. Let $\mathcal{I}$ be the set of the users of $\mathsf{SAM_c}$, where $|\mathcal{I}| \leq u$. The adversary $\mathbf{D}_1$ against F works as follows. It first chooses a user $\dot{I} \twoheadleftarrow \mathcal{I}$ and assigns a secret key $K_I \twoheadleftarrow \mathcal{K}$ of F to each user $I \neq \dot{I}$. Then, it runs $\mathbf{F}$. It responds to each oracle query from $\mathbf{F}$ as follows:

- For an aggregate-tagging query (M, I, T'), it returns $G(F(K_I, M), T')$ if $I \neq \dot{I}$, and $G(f(M), T')$ otherwise, where f is the oracle of $\mathbf{D}_1$.
- For a corrupt query I, it returns K_I if $I \neq \dot{I}$, and outputs 0 and aborts otherwise.
- For a verification query $(((M_1, I_1), \ldots, (M_n, I_n)), T_n)$, it evaluates the validity of the query using K_{I_i} for $I_i \neq \dot{I}$ and f for $I_i = \dot{I}$, and returns the result to $\mathbf{F}$. Let $T'_1, T'_2, \ldots, T'_n$ be the intermediate tags obtained during the evaluation. $\mathbf{D}_1$ outputs 1 and terminates if the evaluation result is $\top$ and there exists some $j \in [1, n]$ such that $I_j = \dot{I}$ and $\mathbf{F}$ does not ask (M_j, I_j, T'_{j-1}) to the aggregate tagging oracle before the verification query. (Notice that $\mathbf{D}_1$ aborts as soon as $\mathbf{F}$ asks $\dot{I}$ to the corrupt oracle.) Otherwise, $\mathbf{D}_1$ outputs 0 and terminates.

Then,

$$\Pr[\mathbf{D}_1^{F_K} = 1] \geq \frac{1}{|\mathcal{I}|}\Pr[\mathrm{Forge}(\mathbf{F})] \geq \frac{1}{u}\,\mathrm{Adv}^{\mathrm{uf}}_{\mathsf{SAM_c}}(\mathbf{F}) ,$$

where $K \twoheadleftarrow \mathcal{K}$. Let $\rho \twoheadleftarrow \mathcal{F}_{\mathcal{M},\mathcal{L}}$. Since $\Pr[\mathbf{D}_1^{F_K} = 1] \leq \mathrm{Adv}^{\mathrm{prf}}_F(\mathbf{D}_1) + \Pr[\mathbf{D}_1^{\rho} = 1]$,

$$\mathrm{Adv}^{\mathrm{uf}}_{\mathsf{SAM_c}}(\mathbf{F}) \leq u\,\mathrm{Adv}^{\mathrm{prf}}_F(\mathbf{D}_1) + u\Pr[\mathbf{D}_1^{\rho} = 1].$$

$\mathbf{D}_1$ runs in time at most about $s + (q_t + \ell)(\mathrm{time}(F) + \mathrm{time}(G)) + uq_c$ and makes at most $q_t + \ell$ queries to its oracle.

For $\Pr[\mathbf{D}_1^{\rho} = 1]$, let us consider an adversary $\tilde{\mathbf{D}}_2$ against G. $\tilde{\mathbf{D}}_2$ is given $q \triangleq q_t + \ell$ permutations $g_1, g_2, \ldots, g_q$ in $\mathcal{P}_{\mathcal{T}}$ as its oracles. $\tilde{\mathbf{D}}_2^{g_1, g_2, \ldots, g_q}$ works in the same way as $\mathbf{D}_1^f$ except for the following cases:

- For an aggregate-tagging query $(M, \dot{I}, T')$ made by $\mathbf{F}$, it returns $g_{\mathsf{d}(M)}(T')$.
- For a verification query $(((M_1, I_1), \ldots, (M_n, I_n)), T_n)$ made by $\mathbf{F}$, it evaluates the validity of the query using K_{I_i} for $I_i \neq \dot{I}$ and $g_{\mathsf{d}(M_i)}$ for $I_i = \dot{I}$.

Here, d is a mapping satisfying that $1 \le \mathsf{d}(M) \le q$ and that $\mathsf{d}(M) \ne \mathsf{d}(M')$ if $M \ne M'$. Then,

$$\Pr[\mathbf{D}_1^\rho = 1] = \Pr[\tilde{\mathbf{D}}_2^{G_{L_1}, G_{L_2}, \dots, G_{L_q}} = 1]$$
$$\le \mathrm{Adv}_G^{q\text{-prp}}(\tilde{\mathbf{D}}_2) + \Pr[\tilde{\mathbf{D}}_2^{\varpi_1, \varpi_2, \dots, \varpi_q} = 1],$$

where $L_i \twoheadleftarrow \mathcal{L}$ and $\varpi_i \twoheadleftarrow \mathcal{P}_{\mathcal{T}}$ for $i \in [1, q]$.

Let us consider $\Pr[\tilde{\mathbf{D}}_2^{\varpi_1, \varpi_2, \dots, \varpi_q} = 1]$. For a verification query $(((M_1, I_1), \dots, (M_n, I_n)), T_n)$ made by $\mathbf{F}$, let $T_1', T_2', \dots, T_n'$ be the intermediate tags obtained during the verification of the query. Suppose that $\hat{i}$ is the maximum value of i such that, for any $i' < i$, $I_{i'} \ne \dot{I}$ or $(I_{i'}, M_{i'}, T_{i'-1}')$ is an aggregate-tagging query made by $\mathbf{F}$. Suppose that $\check{i}$ is the minimum value of i such that $T_i'' = G(F(K_{I_{i'}}, M_{i'}), T_{i'-1}'')$ if $I_{i'} \ne \dot{I}$ and $\mathbf{F}$ obtains T_i'' by an aggregate-tagging query $(M_{i'}, I_{i'}, T_{i'-1}'')$ if $I_{i'} = \dot{I}$ for $i < i' \le n$ and $T_n'' = T_n$. Notice that T_i'' is uniquely determined by T_n since G is a keyed permutation and $\varpi_1, \dots, \varpi_q$ are permutations. Let $\mathcal{J} \triangleq \{i \mid I_i = \dot{I} \wedge \hat{i} \le i < \check{i}\}$. Then,

$$\Pr[T_{\check{i}}' = T_{\check{i}}''] = \Pr\Big[(T_{\check{i}}' = T_{\check{i}}'') \wedge \bigvee_{i \in \mathcal{J}} (T_i' = T_i'')\Big] + \Pr\Big[(T_{\check{i}}' = T_{\check{i}}'') \wedge \overline{\bigvee_{i \in \mathcal{J}} (T_i' = T_i'')}\Big]$$
$$\le \Pr\Big[\bigvee_{i \in \mathcal{J}} (T_i' = T_i'')\Big] + \Pr\Big[T_{\check{i}}' = T_{\check{i}}'' \mid \overline{\bigvee_{i \in \mathcal{J}} (T_i' = T_i'')}\Big]$$
$$\le \frac{\ell}{|\mathcal{T}| - q_\mathrm{t}},$$

where the condition $T_i' = T_i''$ is ignored if (M_i, I_i, T_{i-1}') is asked to the aggregate-tagging oracle before the verification query. Thus,

$$\Pr[\tilde{\mathbf{D}}_2^{\varpi_1, \varpi_2, \dots, \varpi_q} = 1] \le \frac{\ell}{|\mathcal{T}| - q_\mathrm{t}}.$$

From the lemma similar to Lemma 1, there exists some adversary $\mathbf{D}_2$ such that

$$\mathrm{Adv}_G^{q\text{-prp}}(\tilde{\mathbf{D}}_2) \le q \cdot \mathrm{Adv}_G^{\mathrm{prp}}(\mathbf{D}_2) .$$

$\mathbf{D}_2$ runs in time at most about $s + 2(q_\mathrm{t} + \ell)(\mathrm{time}(F) + \mathrm{time}(G)) + u q_\mathrm{c}$ and makes at most $q_\mathrm{t} + \ell$ queries to its oracle. $\square$

4.3 Discussion

The proposed scheme SAM_c may not be secure if G is not a keyed permutation. Suppose that G is a secure PRF except that WK is a weak key of G. Suppose that $G(\mathsf{WK}, T) = \mathsf{Tg}$ for any $T \in \mathcal{T}$. Then, the following attack on SAM_c always succeeds in forgery:

1. Ask $\hat{I}$ to the corrupt oracle and obtain $K_{\hat{I}}$.
2. Compute $\hat{M}$ such that $F(K_{\hat{I}}, \hat{M}) = \mathsf{WK}$. Notice that it is possible if, for example, F is a block cipher or a PRF based on CBC-MAC such as CMAC.
3. Ask $(((M, I), (\hat{M}, \hat{I})), \mathsf{Tg})$ to the verification oracle, where $I \ne \hat{I}$.

It is easy to see that $\mathsf{SVer}_\mathrm{c}((K_I, K_{\hat{I}}), ((M, I), (\hat{M}, \hat{I})), \mathsf{Tg}) = \top$ for any (M, I).

5   Generic Construction Based on Hash Function

The other SAM scheme is presented, which is constructed from a pseudorandom function in two keying strategies. Then, it is shown to be unforgeable. As is discussed later, the scheme is suitable for instantiations using a hash function and is called a hash-based scheme.

5.1   Scheme

The hash-based SAM scheme $\mathsf{SAM_h} \triangleq (\mathsf{KG_h}, \mathsf{STag_h}, \mathsf{SVer_h})$ is constructed from a keyed function $H : \mathcal{K} \times \mathcal{M} \times \mathcal{T} \to \mathcal{T}$ as follows:

- $\mathsf{KG_h}$ simply returns $K_I \leftarrow \mathcal{K}$ for a user I.
- $T \triangleq H(K_I, M, T')$, where $T \leftarrow \mathsf{STag_h}(K_I, M, I, T')$.
- $\mathsf{SVer_h}((K_{I_1}, \ldots, K_{I_n}), ((M_1, I_1), \ldots, (M_n, I_n)), T_n)$ returns $\top$ if $T_n = T_n'$, and $\bot$ otherwise, where $T_i' = H(K_{I_i}, M_i, T_{i-1}')$ for $i \in [1, n]$ and T_0' is some constant $\mathsf{cT} \in \mathcal{T}$.

The aggregate tagging $\mathsf{SAM_h}$ is depicted in Fig. 2.

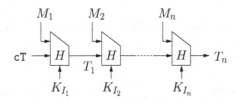

Fig. 2. The aggregate tagging of the proposed scheme $\mathsf{SAM_h}$.

5.2   Unforgeability

It is shown that $\mathsf{SAM_h}$ is unforgeable if H is a secure PRF in two keying strategies. Let H^k and H^t denote the function $H : \mathcal{K} \times \mathcal{M} \times \mathcal{T} \to \mathcal{T}$ with key space $\mathcal{K}$ and $\mathcal{T}$, respectively.

$\mathsf{MD}^{H^t} : (\mathcal{K} \times \mathcal{M})^* \times \mathcal{T} \to \mathcal{T}$ be the keyed Merkle-Damgård iteration of H^t with key space $\mathcal{T}$. MD^{H^t} is a secure PRF against adversaries making only a single query if H^t is a secure PRF:

Lemma 2. *For any adversary* $\mathbf{D}$ *against* MD^{H^t} *making a single query in* $(\mathcal{K} \times \mathcal{M})^{[0,\ell]}$, *there exists some adversary* $\mathbf{D}'$ *against* H^t *such that*

$$\mathrm{Adv}^{\mathrm{prf}}_{\mathsf{MD}^{H^t}}(\mathbf{D}) \leq \ell \cdot \mathrm{Adv}^{\mathrm{prf}}_{H^t}(\mathbf{D}').$$

The run time of $\mathbf{D}'$ *is approximately total of that of* $\mathbf{D}$ *and the time to compute* H^t *for the query made by* $\mathbf{D}$. $\mathbf{D}'$ *makes at most a single query.*

The proof of Lemma 2 is omitted since it follows from the simple and standard hybrid argument.

Theorem 2. *Suppose that* $\mathsf{SAM_h}$ *has at most u users. For any adversary* **F** *against* $\mathsf{SAM_h}$ *running in time at most s, making at most q_t queries to the aggregate tagging oracle, at most q_c queries to the corrupt oracle and a query of length at most ℓ to the verification oracle, there exist some adversaries* $\mathbf{D}_1$ *and* $\mathbf{D}_2$ *such that*

$$\mathrm{Adv}^{\mathrm{uf}}_{\mathsf{SAM_h}}(\mathbf{F}) \leq u \left(\mathrm{Adv}^{\mathrm{prf}}_{H^k}(\mathbf{D}_1) + \ell^2 \, \mathrm{Adv}^{\mathrm{prf}}_{H^t}(\mathbf{D}_2) + \frac{\ell q_t + 1}{|\mathcal{T}|} \right).$$

$\mathbf{D}_1$ *runs in time at most about* $s + (q_t + \ell) \cdot \mathrm{time}(H) + u q_c$ *and makes at most* $q_t + \ell$ *queries to its oracle.* $\mathbf{D}_2$ *runs in time at most about* $s + (q_t + \ell^2 + 2\ell) \cdot \mathrm{time}(H) + u q_c$ *and makes at most a single query to its oracle.*

Proof. At first, the proof is very similar to that of Theorem 1. Let $\mathcal{I}$ be the set of the users of $\mathsf{SAM_h}$, where $|\mathcal{I}| \leq u$. The adversary $\mathbf{D}_1$ against H^k works as follows. It first chooses a user $\dot{I} \twoheadleftarrow \mathcal{I}$ and assigns a secret key $K_I \twoheadleftarrow \mathcal{K}$ of F to each user $I \neq \dot{I}$. Then, it runs **F**. It responds to each oracle query from **F** as follows:

- For an aggregate-tagging query (M, I, T'), it returns $H(K_I, M, T')$ if $I \neq \dot{I}$, and $f(M, T')$ otherwise, where f is the oracle of $\mathbf{D}_1$.
- For a corrupt query I, it returns K_I if $I \neq \dot{I}$, and outputs 0 and aborts otherwise.
- For a verification query $(((M_1, I_1), \ldots, (M_n, I_n)), T_n)$, it evaluates the validity of the query using K_{I_i} for $I_i \neq \dot{I}$ and f for $I_i = \dot{I}$, and returns the result to **F**. Let $T'_1, T'_2, \ldots, T'_n$ be the intermediate tags obtained during the evaluation. $\mathbf{D}_1$ outputs 1 and terminates if the evaluation result is $\top$ and there exists some $j \in [1, n]$ such that $I_j = \dot{I}$ and **F** does not ask (M_j, I_j, T'_{j-1}) to the aggregate tagging oracle before the verification query. (Notice that $\mathbf{D}_1$ aborts as soon as **F** asks $\dot{I}$ to the corrupt oracle.) Otherwise, $\mathbf{D}_1$ outputs 0 and terminates.

Then,

$$\Pr[\mathbf{D}_1^{H^k} = 1] \geq \frac{1}{|\mathcal{I}|} \Pr[\mathsf{Forge}(\mathbf{F})] \geq \frac{1}{u} \mathrm{Adv}^{\mathrm{uf}}_{\mathsf{SAM_h}}(\mathbf{F}),$$

where $K \twoheadleftarrow \mathcal{K}$. Let $\rho \twoheadleftarrow \mathcal{F}_{\mathcal{M} \times \mathcal{T}, \mathcal{T}}$. Since $\Pr[\mathbf{D}_1^{H^k} = 1] \leq \mathrm{Adv}^{\mathrm{prf}}_{H^k}(\mathbf{D}_1) + \Pr[\mathbf{D}_1^{\rho} = 1]$,

$$\mathrm{Adv}^{\mathrm{uf}}_{\mathsf{SAM_h}}(\mathbf{F}) \leq u \, \mathrm{Adv}^{\mathrm{prf}}_{H^k}(\mathbf{D}_1) + u \Pr[\mathbf{D}_1^{\rho} = 1].$$

$\mathbf{D}_1$ runs in time at most about $s + (q_t + \ell) \cdot \mathrm{time}(H) + u q_c$ and makes at most $q_t + \ell$ queries to its oracle.

For $\Pr[\mathbf{D}_1^{\rho} = 1]$, let us consider an adversary $\tilde{\mathbf{D}}_2$ against MD^{H^t}. $\tilde{\mathbf{D}}_2$ has ℓ oracles, which are either $(\mathsf{MD}^{H^t_{S_1}}, \ldots, \mathsf{MD}^{H^t_{S_\ell}})$ or $(\varphi_1, \ldots, \varphi_\ell)$, where $S_i \twoheadleftarrow \mathcal{T}$ and

$\varphi \leftarrow \mathcal{F}_{(\mathcal{K} \times \mathcal{M})^{[0,\ell]}, \mathcal{T}}$ for $i \in [1, \ell]$. $\tilde{\mathbf{D}}_2$ runs $\mathbf{D}_1^\rho$ by simulating ρ with lazy evaluation until $\mathbf{F}$ asks a query to its verification oracle. Let $(((M_1, I_1), \ldots, (M_n, I_n)), T_n)$ be the query made by $\mathbf{F}$ to its verification oracle. Notice that $n \leq \ell$. Suppose that $I_{i_1} = I_{i_2} = \cdots = I_{i_t} = \dot{I}$ for $1 \leq i_1 < i_2 < \cdots < i_t \leq n$ and $I_i \neq \dot{I}$ for $i \in [1, n] \setminus \{i_1, i_2, \ldots, i_t\}$. For $(((M_1, I_1), \ldots, (M_n, I_n)), T_n)$, $\tilde{\mathbf{D}}_2$ computes $T_i' \leftarrow \mathsf{STag}_h(K_{I_i}, M_i, I_i, T_{i-1}')$ for $i = 1, 2, \ldots$, where $T_0' = \mathsf{cT}$, until $\tilde{\mathbf{D}}_2$ finds a new input to ρ. Without loss of generality, suppose that (M_{i_1}, T_{i_1-1}') is the new input. Then, for $j = 1, 2, \ldots, t-1$, $\tilde{\mathbf{D}}_2$ asks $((K_{I_{i_j+1}}, M_{i_j+1}), (K_{I_{i_j+2}}, M_{i_j+2}), \ldots,$ $(K_{I_{i_{j+1}-1}}, M_{i_{j+1}-1}))$ to its i_j-th oracle and gets $T_{i_{j+1}-1}'$ as the answer. If there exists some $j^* \in [2, t]$ such that $(M_{i_{j^*}}, T_{i_{j^*}-1}')$ is not new, then $\tilde{\mathbf{D}}_2$ outputs 1 and aborts. Otherwise, $\tilde{\mathbf{D}}_2$ asks $((K_{I_{i_t+1}}, M_{i_t+1}), (K_{I_{i_t+2}}, M_{i_t+2}), \ldots, (K_n, M_n))$ to its i_t-th oracle and gets T_n' as the answer. $\tilde{\mathbf{D}}_2$ outputs 1 if $T_n' = T_n$ ($\mathbf{F}$ succeeds in forgery) and 0 otherwise. Then,

$$
\begin{aligned}
\Pr[\mathbf{D}_1^\rho = 1] &\leq \Pr[\tilde{\mathbf{D}}_2^{\mathsf{MD}^{H_{S_1}^t}, \ldots, \mathsf{MD}^{H_{S_\ell}^t}} = 1] \\
&\leq \mathrm{Adv}_{\mathsf{MD}^{H^t}}^{\ell\text{-prf}}(\tilde{\mathbf{D}}_2) + \Pr[\tilde{\mathbf{D}}_2^{\varphi_1, \ldots, \varphi_\ell} = 1] \\
&\leq \mathrm{Adv}_{\mathsf{MD}^{H^t}}^{\ell\text{-prf}}(\tilde{\mathbf{D}}_2) + \frac{\ell q_t + 1}{|\mathcal{T}|}.
\end{aligned}
$$

$\tilde{\mathbf{D}}_2$ runs in time at most about $s + (q_t + \ell) \cdot \mathrm{time}(H) + u q_c$ and makes at most a single query to each of its ℓ oracles.

From Lemmas 1 and 2, there exists some adversary $\mathbf{D}_2$ such that

$$
\mathrm{Adv}_{\mathsf{MD}^{H^t}}^{\ell\text{-prf}}(\tilde{\mathbf{D}}_2) \leq \ell^2 \, \mathrm{Adv}_{H^t}^{\mathrm{prf}}(\mathbf{D}_2) \ .
$$

$\mathbf{D}_2$ runs in time at most about $s + (q_t + \ell^2 + 2\ell) \cdot \mathrm{time}(H) + u q_c$ and makes at most a single query to its oracle. □

5.3 Instantiation with HMAC

The case where HMAC using SHA-1 or SHA-2 [12] is used for the aggregate-tagging function H is discussed. HMAC using SHA-1 or SHA-2 will be simply called HMAC.

Let $h : \Sigma^c \times \Sigma^b \to \Sigma^c$ be the compression function of the underlying hash function for HMAC, where $c < b$. For a key K, an aggregate-so-far tag T' and a message M, the aggregate-tagging function $T \leftarrow H(K, M, T')$, which is called EMD^h, is defined in Algorithm 1. Here, $T' \in \Sigma^c$, it is assumed that $K \in \Sigma^b$ and $M \in (\Sigma^b)^+$, and the padding for M is omitted just for simplicity. $\mathsf{IV} \in \Sigma^c$, $\mathsf{ipad}, \mathsf{opad} \in \Sigma^b$ and $\mathsf{pad} \in \Sigma^{b-c}$ are constants. The aggregate-tagging function $\mathsf{EMD}^h(K, M, T')$ is also depicted in Fig. 3.

Since $\mathsf{EMD}^h(K, M, T')$ with its key K is actually HMAC, it is shown to be a PRF under the assumption that h is a PRF with two keying strategies, that is, keyed via chaining variable and keyed via message [1], where the first and

---

Algorithm 1. The aggregate-tagging function $\mathsf{EMD}^h(K, M, T')$ using HMAC

1: **function** $\mathsf{EMD}^h(K, M, T')$ ▷ $K \in \Sigma^b$, $M \in (\Sigma^b)^+$, $T' \in \Sigma^c$
2:     $S \leftarrow h(h(\mathtt{IV}, K \oplus \mathtt{ipad}), T' \| 0^{b-c})$
3:     $V \leftarrow \mathsf{MD}^h(S, M)$
4:     $T \leftarrow h(h(\mathtt{IV}, K \oplus \mathtt{opad}), V \| \mathtt{pad})$
5:     **return** T
6: **end function**

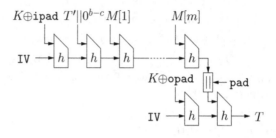

Fig. 3. The aggregate-tagging function EMD^h using HMAC. $M = M[1] \| M[2] \| \cdots \| M[m]$ and $M[i] \in \Sigma^b$ for $i \in [1, m]$.

the second arguments of h are called the chaining variable and the message, respectively.

Here, $\mathsf{EMD}^h(K, M, T')$ with its key T' is shown to be a PRF under reasonable assumptions on h. The proof is similar to the proof for H^2-MAC [21].

For $h : \Sigma^c \times \Sigma^b \to \Sigma^c$, the keyed function h with its key space Σ^c and Σ^b is denoted by h^{m} and h^{cv}, respectively. $h_{\mathtt{IV}}(\cdot) \triangleq h(\mathtt{IV}, \cdot)$.

For EMD^h, let $\mathsf{emd}^h(S, K, M)$ be the function defined by the steps 3, 4 and 5 of Algorithm 1. $\mathsf{EMD}^h(K, M, T') = \mathsf{emd}^h(S, K, M)$ if $S \leftarrow h(h(\mathtt{IV}, K \oplus \mathtt{ipad}), T' \| 0^{b-c})$. $\mathsf{emd}^h(S, K, M)$ is regarded as a keyed function with its key S.

Lemma 3. *For any adversary* $\mathbf{D}$ *against* emd^h *running in time at most* s, *having access to* q *oracles and making at most* q *queries in* $\Sigma^b \times (\Sigma^b)^{[1,l]}$, *there exists some adversary* $\mathbf{D}'$ *against* h^{cv} *having access to* q *oracles such that*

$$\mathrm{Adv}_{\mathsf{emd}^h}^{q\text{-prf}}(\mathbf{D}) \leq (l+1) \cdot \mathrm{Adv}_{h^{\mathrm{cv}}}^{q\text{-prf-ax}^*}(\mathbf{D}').$$

$\mathbf{D}'$ *runs in time at most* $s + (l+2)q \cdot \mathrm{time}(h)$ *and makes at most* q *queries.*

The proof is similar to that of Lemma 3 in [21]. It also uses the multi-oracle-to-multi-oracle reduction in [2].

In the statement of the following theorem, the notation of cr-advantage is abused. Though the compression function h should be chosen uniformly at random from some set of functions, it is not explicit in this subsection.

Theorem 3. *For any adversary* $\mathbf{D}$ *against* EMD^h *running in time at most* s *and making at most* q *queries in* $\Sigma^b \times (\Sigma^b)^{[1,l]}$, *there exist some adversaries* $\mathbf{D}_1$,

$\mathbf{D}_2$ and $\mathbf{D}_3$ such that

$$\mathrm{Adv}^{\mathrm{prf}}_{\mathrm{EMD}^h}(\mathbf{D}) \leq \mathrm{Adv}^{\mathrm{prf}}_{h^{\mathrm{m}}}(\mathbf{D}_1) + (l+1)q \cdot \mathrm{Adv}^{\mathrm{prf\text{-}ax}^*}_{h^{\mathrm{cv}}}(\mathbf{D}_2) + \mathrm{Adv}^{\mathrm{cr}}_{h_{\mathrm{IV}}}(\mathbf{D}_3).$$

$\mathbf{D}_1$ runs in time at most $s + (l+2)q \cdot \mathrm{time}(h)$ and makes at most q queries. $\mathbf{D}_2$ runs in time at most $s + (l+3)q \cdot \mathrm{time}(h)$ and makes at most q queries. $\mathbf{D}_3$ runs in time at most s.

Proof. For any adversary $\mathbf{D}$ against EMD^h,

$$\mathrm{Adv}^{\mathrm{prf}}_{\mathrm{EMD}^h}(\mathbf{D}) = \left| \Pr[\mathbf{D}^{\mathrm{EMD}^h_{T'}} = 1] - \Pr[\mathbf{D}^\rho = 1] \right|,$$

where $T' \leftarrow \Sigma^c$ and $\rho \leftarrow \mathcal{F}_{\Sigma^b \times (\Sigma^b)+, \Sigma^c}$.

Let $\mathbf{D}_1$ be an adversary against h^{m} working as follows. $\mathbf{D}_1$ runs $\mathbf{D}$. For a query (K, M) made by $\mathbf{D}$, $\mathbf{D}_1$ asks its oracle $h(\mathrm{IV}, K \oplus \mathtt{ipad})$ and gets S as an answer. Then, $\mathbf{D}_1$ returns $\mathrm{emd}^h(S, K, M)$ to $\mathbf{D}$. Finally, $\mathbf{D}_1$ outputs the same output as $\mathbf{D}$. Then, $\mathrm{Adv}^{\mathrm{prf}}_{h^{\mathrm{m}}}(\mathbf{D}_1) = \left| \Pr[\mathbf{D}^{h^{\mathrm{m}}_{T'}}_1 = 1] - \Pr[\mathbf{D}^\nu_1 = 1] \right|$, where $T' \leftarrow \Sigma^c$ and $\nu \leftarrow \mathcal{F}_{\Sigma^c, \Sigma^c}$, and $\Pr[\mathbf{D}^{h^{\mathrm{m}}_{T'}}_1 = 1] = \Pr[\mathbf{D}^{\mathrm{EMD}^h_{T'}} = 1]$. $\mathbf{D}_1$ runs in time at most $s + (l+2)q \cdot \mathrm{time}(h)$ and makes at most q queries.

Let $\tilde{\mathbf{D}}_2$ be an adversary against $\mathrm{emd}^h(S, \cdot, \cdot)$ with its key S. $\tilde{\mathbf{D}}_2$ is given q oracles which are either $(\mathrm{emd}^h_{S_1}, \ldots, \mathrm{emd}^h_{S_q})$ or $(\mu_1, \ldots, \mu_q)$, where $S_i \leftarrow \Sigma^c$ and $\mu_i \leftarrow \mathcal{F}_{\Sigma^b \times (\Sigma^b)+, \Sigma^c}$ for $i \in [1, q]$. $\tilde{\mathbf{D}}_2$ runs $\mathbf{D}$. For the i-th query (K, M) made by $\mathbf{D}$, $\tilde{\mathbf{D}}_2$ asks (K, M) to its $\mathsf{d}(i)$-th oracle and returns the answer to $\mathbf{D}$, where $\mathsf{d}(i) \leftarrow \mathsf{d}(i')$ if there exists some $i'(< i)$ such that the i'-th query is (K, M') for some M', and $\mathsf{d}(i) \leftarrow i$ otherwise. Finally, $\tilde{\mathbf{D}}_2$ outputs the same output as $\mathbf{D}$. Then, $\mathbf{D}^\nu_1$ is equivalent to $\tilde{\mathbf{D}}_2^{\mathrm{emd}^h_{S_1}, \ldots, \mathrm{emd}^h_{S_q}}$ as long as $\mathbf{D}$ finds no collision for h_{IV} during the execution of $\tilde{\mathbf{D}}_2^{\mathrm{emd}^h_{S_1}, \ldots, \mathrm{emd}^h_{S_q}}$. Thus, there exists some $\mathbf{D}_3$ such that

$$\left| \Pr[\mathbf{D}^\nu_1 = 1] - \Pr[\tilde{\mathbf{D}}_2^{\mathrm{emd}^h_{S_1}, \ldots, \mathrm{emd}^h_{S_q}} = 1] \right| \leq \mathrm{Adv}^{\mathrm{cr}}_{h_{\mathrm{IV}}}(\mathbf{D}_3) ,$$

and $\mathbf{D}_3$ runs in time at most s. In addition, $\tilde{\mathbf{D}}_2^{\mu_1, \ldots, \mu_q}$ is equivalent to $\mathbf{D}^\rho$ and $\Pr[\tilde{\mathbf{D}}_2^{\mu_1, \ldots, \mu_q}] = \Pr[\mathbf{D}^\rho = 1]$. $\tilde{\mathbf{D}}_2$ runs in time at most s and makes at most q queries.

Putting all things together,

$$\begin{aligned}
\mathrm{Adv}^{\mathrm{prf}}_{\mathrm{EMD}^h}(\mathbf{D}) &= \left| \Pr[\mathbf{D}^{\mathrm{EMD}^h_{T'}} = 1] - \Pr[\mathbf{D}^\rho = 1] \right| \\
&\leq \mathrm{Adv}^{\mathrm{prf}}_{h^{\mathrm{m}}}(\mathbf{D}_1) + \left| \Pr[\mathbf{D}^\nu_1 = 1] - \Pr[\mathbf{D}^\rho = 1] \right| \\
&\leq \mathrm{Adv}^{\mathrm{prf}}_{h^{\mathrm{m}}}(\mathbf{D}_1) + \mathrm{Adv}^{q\text{-}\mathrm{prf}}_{\mathrm{emd}^h}(\tilde{\mathbf{D}}_2) + \mathrm{Adv}^{\mathrm{cr}}_{h_{\mathrm{IV}}}(\mathbf{D}_3) .
\end{aligned}$$

From Lemma 3 and the lemma similar to Lemma 1, there exists some adversary $\mathbf{D}_2$ such that

$$\mathrm{Adv}^{\mathrm{prf}}_{\mathrm{emd}^h}(\tilde{\mathbf{D}}_2) \leq (l+1)q \cdot \mathrm{Adv}^{\mathrm{prf\text{-}ax}^*}_{h^{\mathrm{cv}}}(\mathbf{D}_2) .$$

$\mathbf{D}_2$ runs in time at most $s + (l+3)q \cdot \mathrm{time}(h)$ and makes at most q queries. □

6 Conclusion

This paper has presented two schemes for history-free sequential aggregate MAC. One is suitable for instantiations using a block cipher and the other is suitable for instantiations using a hash function. Future work is to prove the unforgeability of the proposed schemes for adversaries making multiple verification queries.

Acknowledgements. This research was conducted under a contract of Research and Development for Expansion of Radio Wave Resources funded by the Ministry of Internal Affairs and Communications, Japan.

References

1. Bellare, M.: New proofs for NMAC and HMAC: security without collision-resistance. In: Dwork, C. (ed.) CRYPTO 2006. LNCS, vol. 4117, pp. 602–619. Springer, Heidelberg (2006). https://doi.org/10.1007/11818175_36

2. Bellare, M., Bernstein, D.J., Tessaro, S.: Hash-function based PRFs: AMAC and its multi-user security. In: Fischlin, M., Coron, J.-S. (eds.) EUROCRYPT 2016. LNCS, vol. 9665, pp. 566–595. Springer, Heidelberg (2016). https://doi.org/10.1007/978-3-662-49890-3_22

3. Bellare, M., Canetti, R., Krawczyk, H.: Pseudorandom functions revisited: the cascade construction and its concrete security. In: Proceedings of the 37th IEEE Symposium on Foundations of Computer Science, pp. 514–523 (1996)

4. Bellare, M., Kilian, J., Rogaway, P.: The security of cipher block chaining. In: Desmedt, Y.G. (ed.) CRYPTO 1994. LNCS, vol. 839, pp. 341–358. Springer, Heidelberg (1994). https://doi.org/10.1007/3-540-48658-5_32

5. Bellare, M., Kohno, T.: A theoretical treatment of related-key attacks: RKA-PRPs, RKA-PRFs, and applications. In: Biham, E. (ed.) EUROCRYPT 2003. LNCS, vol. 2656, pp. 491–506. Springer, Heidelberg (2003). https://doi.org/10.1007/3-540-39200-9_31

6. Bellare, M., Rogaway, P.: On the construction of variable-input-length ciphers. In: Knudsen, L. (ed.) FSE 1999. LNCS, vol. 1636, pp. 231–244. Springer, Heidelberg (1999). https://doi.org/10.1007/3-540-48519-8_17

7. Biham, E. (ed.): EUROCRYPT 2003. LNCS, vol. 2656. Springer, Heidelberg (2003). https://doi.org/10.1007/3-540-39200-9

8. Boneh, D., Gentry, C., Lynn, B., Shacham, H.: Aggregate and verifiably encrypted signatures from bilinear maps. In: Biham, E. (ed.) EUROCRYPT 2003. LNCS, vol. 2656, pp. 416–432. Springer, Heidelberg (2003). https://doi.org/10.1007/3-540-39200-9_26

9. Chen, Y., Lei, C.: Aggregate message authentication codes (AMACs) with on-the-fly verification. Int. J. Inf. Sec. **12**(6), 495–504 (2013). https://doi.org/10.1007/s10207-013-0202-0

10. Du, D.Z., Hwang, F.K.: Combinatorial Group Testing and Its Applications. Series on Applied Mathematics, 2nd edn, vol. 12, World Scientific, Singapore (2000)

11. Eikemeier, O., et al.: History-free aggregate message authentication codes. In: Garay, J.A., De Prisco, R. (eds.) SCN 2010. LNCS, vol. 6280, pp. 309–328. Springer, Heidelberg (2010). https://doi.org/10.1007/978-3-642-15317-4_20

12. FIPS PUB 180–4: Secure hash standard (SHS), August 2015

13. FIPS PUB 197: Advanced encryption standard (AES) (2001)
14. Goldreich, O., Goldwasser, S., Micali, S.: How to construct random functions. J. ACM **33**(4), 792–807 (1986)
15. Hirose, S., Kuwakado, H.: Forward-secure sequential aggregate message authentication revisited. In: Chow, S.S.M., Liu, J.K., Hui, L.C.K., Yiu, S.M. (eds.) ProvSec 2014. LNCS, vol. 8782, pp. 87–102. Springer, Cham (2014). https://doi.org/10.1007/978-3-319-12475-9_7
16. Hirose, S., Shikata, J.: Non-adaptive group-testing aggregate MAC scheme. In: Su, C., Kikuchi, H. (eds.) ISPEC 2018. LNCS, vol. 11125, pp. 357–372. Springer, Cham (2018). https://doi.org/10.1007/978-3-319-99807-7_22
17. Katz, J., Lindell, A.Y.: Aggregate message authentication codes. In: Malkin, T. (ed.) CT-RSA 2008. LNCS, vol. 4964, pp. 155–169. Springer, Heidelberg (2008). https://doi.org/10.1007/978-3-540-79263-5_10
18. Ma, D., Tsudik, G.: Extended abstract: forward-secure sequential aggregate authentication. In: IEEE Symposium on Security and Privacy, pp. 86–91. IEEE Computer Society (2007). Also published as IACR Cryptology ePrint Archive: Report 2007/052
19. Ma, D., Tsudik, G.: A new approach to secure logging. ACM Trans. Storage **5**(1), 2:1–2:21 (2009)
20. Sato, S., Hirose, S., Shikata, J.: Generic construction of sequential aggregate MACs from any MACs. In: Baek, J., Susilo, W., Kim, J. (eds.) ProvSec 2018. LNCS, vol. 11192, pp. 295–312. Springer, Cham (2018). https://doi.org/10.1007/978-3-030-01446-9_17
21. Yasuda, K.: HMAC without the "Second" Key. In: Samarati, P., Yung, M., Martinelli, F., Ardagna, C.A. (eds.) ISC 2009. LNCS, vol. 5735, pp. 443–458. Springer, Heidelberg (2009). https://doi.org/10.1007/978-3-642-04474-8_35

A Practical Lattice-Based Sequential Aggregate Signature

Zhipeng Wang$^{(\boxtimes)}$ and Qianhong Wu$^{(\boxtimes)}$

School of Cyber Science and Technology, Beihang University, Beijing, China
{ZhipengWang,qianhong.wu}@buaa.edu.cn

Abstract. In this work, we construct a lattice-based efficient Sequential Aggregate Signature (SAS) scheme that is provably secure in standard *ideal cipher model* with some slight changes. This framework is inspired by the scheme of Gentry *et al.* at PKC 2018 which presented trapdoor-permutation-based sequential aggregate signatures. Since to present, there is no known method to construct a lattice-based trapdoor permutation, we use lattice-based trapdoor function instead to design SAS scheme. In particular, our scheme is *history-free*, where the sequentially-executed aggregation operation does not need to take the previous messages in order as one part of its input. We also give software implementation of our SAS scheme using FALCON based trapdoor function, which originates from the provably secure NTRUSign signature scheme proposed by Stehlé and Steinfeld at Eurocrypt 2011. The experiment results show our scheme is efficient and practical.

Keywords: Sequential aggregate signature · Lattice · Trapdoor function · Software implementation

1 Introduction

The concept of Aggregate Signature (AS) is first introduced in [5]. It enables any third party to combine n individual signatures produced by a group of different signers on different messages into a single short signature, while maintaining the same security as n individual signatures. Sequential aggregate signatures (SAS), proposed in [25], differ from the conventional AS schemes by requiring signers to compute the aggregated signature in a sequence and imposing an order-specific generation of aggregate signatures. In particular, one signer uses the output of its predecessor as one part of its input during the signing process. (Sequential) Aggregate signatures are important mechanisms applied to many areas in order to decrease the amount of transmitted data, such as authenticated network routing protocols, sensor data, PKI certification chains, and blockchain protocols. In this paper, we focus on sequential aggregate signatures (SAS). Existing designs of SAS have mostly been dominated by (RSA based) trapdoor permutations [1, 6, 15, 25, 29] and bilinear pairings [3, 10, 21–23].

© Springer Nature Switzerland AG 2019
R. Steinfeld and T. H. Yuen (Eds.): ProvSec 2019, LNCS 11821, pp. 94–109, 2019.
https://doi.org/10.1007/978-3-030-31919-9_6

On the other hand, since the groundbreaking work of Shor [32], the hardness of classical number theoretic assumptions is extremely reduced when faced to an attacker featured with a powerful quantum computer. This induced a lot of research work to replace those affected classical schemes with alternatives of post-quantum security. Due to the features of conjectured security against quantum attacks, algorithmic simplicity and high parallelism, and strong security guarantees from worst-case hardness, lattice-based cryptography is one of the most popular post-quantum cryptography and has been used to construct versatile and powerful cryptographic objects such as encryption schemes, digital signature schemes, identity-based encryption, fully homomorphic encryption and so on. In Post-Quantum Cryptography Standardization of NIST, lattice-based cryptographic schemes account for a large proportion.

However, to the best of our knowledge, there is not much prior work devoted to constructing the lattice-based (sequential) aggregate signature scheme. Hohenberger *et al.* [19] built the first identity-based aggregate signature scheme that admits unrestricted aggregation that is based on leveled multilinear map setting from [12], yet the underlying hardness assumptions are not directly connected to worst-case lattice problems. Inspired by [25,29], Bansarkhani *et al.* [9] first attempted to construct a lattice-based sequential aggregate signature scheme that is secure in the random oracle model. Their SAS scheme can be instantiated by preimage sampleable trapdoor functions and the security model is similar to that in [25,29]. In the design of [9], before operating the signing process, each signer needs to verify the signatures received from the previous signers. This additional check prevents fast aggregate signing. Besides, their SAS scheme is somewhat complex and its security proof is subtle. Lu *et al.* [24] used the "Lattice Intersection Method" proposed in [4] to construct lattice-Based unordered aggregate signature scheme, while in their AS scheme, aggregator needs to solve a linear congruential equation in lattice. This may make the aggregate scheme have a slow computation speed and hard to be implemented in practice. And unfortunately, none of the above schemes considered specific software implementation.

1.1   Our Results and Contribution

In this paper, we provide a practical sequential aggregate signature scheme based on the hardness of lattice-based trapdoor function. Inspired by the work of [15], which used trapdoor permutation and *Ideal Cipher Model* to construct SAS schemes, we replace trapdoor permutation with trapdoor function as so far there is no successful construction of lattice-based trapdoor permutation. To a lattice-based trapdoor function, the sizes of input and output are different. Therefore, we add the encoder-decoder technique proposed in [29] to match the domain and range of trapdoor function with those of ideal cipher. Similar to [15], the security of our scheme is in *Variant Ideal Cipher Model* that has some slight changes compared with *Ideal Cipher Model*.

Our construct is *history-free* [10], which means that the sequentially-executed aggregation algorithm does not need to receive the previous messages in order as one part of its input. Compared to the work of [9], in our SAS the "aggregate-so-far" check is removed, which prompts the improvement of aggregate singing speed and decreases the data of input during the signing process. The main execution that dominates aggregate signing's speed is the preimage sample operation of generate function.

We implement our SAS scheme using the trapdoor generate function in FALCON [11] due to its efficiency and simplicity compared to other lattice-based trapdoor generate functions. The FALCON-based trapdoor function works on ring variant lattice. We experimentally evaluate the performance of our construction. Each aggregate signing and verifying algorithm runs for approximately $1/10$ ms on a modern laptop. The aggregation rate is about 50%.

1.2   Organization

The remainder of this paper is structured as follows. In Sect. 2, we present our notations, models, and preliminary definitions. Section 3 describes our proposed SAS scheme in details. Section 4 gives the security analysis of our proposed scheme. Section 5 presents an analysis of our SAS scheme instantiated with FALCON and RSA. In Sect. 6 we make our conclusion and discuss the future works.

2   Preliminaries

2.1   Notation

If $n \in \mathbb{N}$, then $\{0,1\}^n$ is the set of all n-bit strings, and 0^n is the bit string containing n zeros. $\{0,1\}^*$ is the set of all strings. Let $\mathbf{0}$ denote the empty vector. For an n-bit string x and an integer $0 \leq k \leq n$, $x_{[1,k]}$ denotes the first k bits of x. For two bit strings x and y, $x||y$ denotes these two bit strings are stitched together. If S is a set, and $y \in S$, then $\boldsymbol{x} = (x_1, ..., x_n) \in S^n$ is a n-dimensional vector, $\boldsymbol{x} \cup y$ is the $(n+1)$-dimensional vector $(x_1, ..., x_n, y)$. $|S|$ denotes the number of elements in S. $x \leftarrow U(S)$ denotes the uniform selection of an element from S. If A is an algorithm then $y \leftarrow A(x_1, ..., x_n; r)$ means that we run A on input $(x_1, ..., x_n)$ and coins r and denote y as the output.

2.2   Random Oracle Model

The random oracle is a powerful cryptographic tool introduced by Bellare and Rogaway in [2]. All parties in the random oracle model have oracle access to a function $H : \{0,1\}^* \rightarrow \{0,1\}^*$ where for any $x \in \{0,1\}^*$, $H(x)$ is chosen uniformly at random of some desired output length. Informally speaking, this means that one regards the function H as a black box that responds to a query for the value of $H(x)$ by giving a random value. For each query, the oracle makes an independent random choice, except that it keeps a record of its responses $H(x)$ and repeats the same response if x is queried again. In this paper, a hash function is modeled as a random oracle.

2.3 Ideal Cipher Model

In *ideal cipher model* [31], all parties have oracle access to two functions, π : $\{0,1\}^* \times \{0,1\}^{\geq k} \to \{0,1\}^{\geq k}$ and $\pi^{-1} : \{0,1\}^* \times \{0,1\}^{\geq k} \to \{0,1\}^{\geq k}$, where the first is such that for every $K \in \{0,1\}^*$ and every input length $n \geq k$, $\pi(K,\cdot)$ is an independent random permutation on $\{0,1\}^n$. The second is such that for every $K \in \{0,1\}^*$ and every input length $n \geq k$, $\pi^{-1}(K,\cdot)$ is the inverse of $\pi(K,\cdot)$ on $\{0,1\}^n$. *Ideal cipher model* is mainly used for blockcipher construction and AES can be modeled as an ideal cipher with fixed block length.

In our work, we consider a *variant ideal cipher model* with two functions, $\Pi : \{0,1\}^* \times \{0,1\}^n \to \{0,1\}^k$ and $\Pi^{-1} : \{0,1\}^* \times \{0,1\}^k \to \{0,1\}^n$, where the first is such that for every $K \in \{0,1\}^*$ and every input x with length n, $\Pi(K,x) = \pi(K, x_{[1,k]})$, where $x_{[1,k]}$ is the first k bits of x. The second is such that for every $K \in \{0,1\}^*$ and every input y with length k, $\Pi^{-1}(K,y) = \pi(K,y)\|z$, where z is a bit string chosen from $\{0,1\}^{n-k}$ with $(n \geq k)$.

2.4 Cryptographic Problems on Lattices

Lattices. A lattice Λ is the set of all integer combinations of some linearly independent basis vectors, $\mathbf{B} = \{\boldsymbol{b}_1, .., \boldsymbol{b}_m\} \in \mathbb{R}^{m \times m}$, $\Lambda(\mathbf{B}) = \{\sum_{i=1}^m z_i \boldsymbol{b}_i, z_i \in \mathbb{Z}\}$. An m-dimensional full-rank lattice Λ is a discrete additive subgroup of $\mathbb{R}^m$. The polynomial ring $R = \mathbb{Z}[x]/(x^n + 1)$ is isomorphic to the integer lattice $\mathbb{Z}^n$ where n is a power of 2. A polynomial $f = \sum_{i=1}^{n-1} f_i \cdot x^i$ in R corresponds to the integer vector $(f_0, .., f_{n-1})$ in $\mathbb{Z}^n$. In our instantiation we work with polynomials over R, or $R_q = R/qR = \mathbb{Z}_q[x]/(x^n + 1)$ where q is a prime and $q = 1 \mod 2n$.

Gaussian Distribution. The n-dimensional Gaussian function of center $\boldsymbol{c} \in \mathbb{R}^n$ and width parameter σ is defined as $\rho_{\sigma,c}(\boldsymbol{x}) = exp\left(-\pi \frac{||\boldsymbol{x}-\boldsymbol{c}||^2}{\sigma^2}\right)$, for all $\boldsymbol{x} \in \mathbb{R}^n$. It can be extended to an $n \times n$-matrix $\mathbf{B}$: $\rho_{\mathbf{B},c}(\boldsymbol{x}) = exp\left(-\pi(\boldsymbol{x}-\boldsymbol{c})^T \Sigma^{-1}(\boldsymbol{x}-\boldsymbol{c})\right)$, where $\Sigma = \mathbf{B} \cdot \mathbf{B}^T$. The discrete Gaussian distribution over a lattice Λ is defined as $D_{\Lambda,\sigma,c}(\boldsymbol{x}) = \frac{\rho_{\sigma,c}(\boldsymbol{x})}{\rho_{\sigma,c}(\Lambda)}$.

Ring-SIS/Ring-LWE. We use Ring-SIS and Ring-LWE proposed in [26,30] and [27,33,34], which are proven to be at least as hard as the GapSVP/SIVP problems on ideal lattices.

Definition 1 (R-$SIS_{q,\beta,m}$). *Given a positive real β and m uniformly random elements $a_i \in R_q$, defining a vector $\boldsymbol{a} \in R_q^m$, find a nonzero vector $\boldsymbol{z} \in R^m$ of norm $||\boldsymbol{z}|| \leq \beta$ such that $f_a(\boldsymbol{a}) = \boldsymbol{a}^t \cdot \boldsymbol{z} = \sum_{i=1}^m a_i \cdot z_i = 0 \in R_q$.*

Definition 2 (Decision R-$LWE_{n,q,D_{R,\sigma}}$). *Given m uniformly random elements $a_i \in R_q$, defining a vector $\boldsymbol{a} \in R_q^m$, and $\boldsymbol{b} = \boldsymbol{a} \cdot \boldsymbol{s} + \boldsymbol{e}$, where $s \leftarrow U(R_q)$ and $e \leftarrow D_{R^m,\sigma}$, distinguish $(\boldsymbol{a}, \boldsymbol{b} = \boldsymbol{a} \cdot \boldsymbol{s} + \boldsymbol{e})$ from $(\boldsymbol{a}, \boldsymbol{b})$ drawn from the uniform distribution over $R_q^m \times R_q^m$.*

2.5   Lattice-Based Trapdoor Function

Informally, a trapdoor function is a function that is easy to evaluate and hard to invert on its own, but which can be generated together with some extra "trapdoor" information that makes inversion easy. There are many versions of this basic concept, depending on whether the function in question is injective, surjective, bijective, "lossy," etc.

In lattice cryptography, the trapdoor function is usually presented as a random integer matrix $\mathbf{A} \in \mathbb{Z}_q^{n \times m}$ (with uniform entries modulo q) and a $\mathbf{T}_A$ (typically $\mathbf{T}_A$ is a short basis for the lattice defined by $\mathbf{A}$). The strong trapdoor is used to efficiently "invert" the (Ring) Short Integer Solution (**SIS**) and (Ring) Learning with Errors (**LWE**) functions $f_A = \mathbf{A}x$ and $g_A(s, e) = s^t \mathbf{A} + e^t$ associated to the matrix $\mathbf{A}$. Theoretical solutions to these trapdoor generation and function inversion problems have long been known. There are two distinct but closely related methods to constitute a lattice-based trapdoor function, constructed from short bases [7,16] or gadget [13,20,28]. According to [16], there exists a polynomial-time algorithm $TrapGen$ that on input the security parameter 1^n outputs a public key $\mathbf{A}$ and the corresponding trapdoor $\mathbf{T}_A$ such that the trapdoor function $f_A(\cdot) : B_n \to R_n$ can be inverted by a function $SamplePre(\mathbf{T}_A, \cdot)$ easily with $\mathbf{T}_A$.

We consider the preimage sampleable trapdoor functions that are collision resistant, meaning that it is infeasible to find a collision $f_A(x_1) = f_A(x_2)$ where $x_1, x_2 \in B_n$ and $x_1 \neq x_2$. For a trapdoor-collision-finding algorithm C and $n \in \mathbb{N}$, define its CF-advantage against $TrapGen$ as

$$\mathbf{Adv}_{TrapGen,C}^{cf}(n)$$
$$= \mathbf{Pr}[f_A(x_1) = f_A(x_2) | (f_A, A, T_A) \leftarrow TrapGen(1^n), (x_1, x_2) \leftarrow C(f_A, A)]$$

C is said to (t, ϵ)-breaks a collision-resistant preimage sampleable trapdoor function f_A if it outputs a collision with CF-advantage $\mathbf{Adv}_{TrapGen,C}^{cf}(n)$ at least ϵ and has running time t. Notice that if C find a collision of trapdoor function f_A, it can solve the underlying lattice problem (Ring) Short Integer Solution (**SIS**) or (Ring) Learning with Errors (**LWE**).

2.6   History-Free Sequential Aggregate Signature

A history-free sequential aggregate signature scheme is a tuple ($KeyGen$, $AggSign$, $AggVer$) of algorithms defined as follows.

- $KeyGen$: The key generation algorithm $KeyGen$ on input 1^n outputs a public key pk and matching secret key sk: $(pk, sk) \leftarrow KeyGen(1^n)$.
- $AggSign$: The history-free aggregate signing algorithm $AggSign$ on input secret key sk, message m and aggregate-so-far signature σ^*, outputs a new aggregate signature σ: $\sigma \leftarrow AggSign(sk, m, \sigma^*)$.
- $AggVer$: The aggregate verification algorithm $AggSign$ on input public key pk and messages $(pk_1, m_1), ..., (pk_i, m_i)$ and aggregate signature σ outputs a bit: 1 or $0 \leftarrow AggVer((pk_1, m_1), ..., (pk_i, m_i), \sigma)$.

Security Model. The security notion we use is same to that in [6,15,29]. To a history-free sequential aggregate signature scheme SAS and a forger F, we associate for every $n \in \mathbb{N}$ a SAS unforgeability experiment $Exp_{HF-SAS,F}^{uf}(n)$ that runs in three phases:

- *Setup*: The experiment generates $(pk, sk) \leftarrow KeyGen(1^n)$.
- *Attack*: Then, the experiment runs F on input pk with oracle access to $AggSign(sk, \cdot, \cdot)$ and other random functions.
- *Forgery*: Eventually, F halts with output parsed as $(pk_1, m_1), ..., (pk_n, m_n)$, σ. The experiment outputs 1 iff: (1) $AggVer((pk_1, m_1), ..., (pk_i, m_i), \sigma)$ outputs 1, (2) $pk = pk_{i^*}$ for some $1 \leq i^* \leq n$, (3) F did not make an oracle query of the form $AggSign(sk, m_{i^*}, \cdot)$.

Define the history-free SAS-unforgeability advantage of F as

$$\mathbf{Adv}_{HF-SAS,F}^{uf}(n) = \mathbf{Pr}[Exp_{HF-SAS,F}^{uf}(n) \ outputs \ 1]$$

Aggregation Rate. For a sequential aggregate signature scheme with n signers, we define $size(\sigma_i)$ as the size of the individual signature σ_i for $1 \leq i \leq n$ and $size(\sigma_{SAS})$ as the size of the final aggregate signature σ_{SAS}. The aggregation rate $rate(n)$, which measures the storage savings due to the SAS scheme, is defined as

$$rate(n) = 1 - \frac{size(\sigma_{SAS})}{\sum_{i=0}^{n} size(\sigma_i)}$$

3 Sequential Aggregate Signatures from Lattice-Based Trapdoor Function

The following Algorithms 1 and 2 provide the main steps of our SAS scheme. In our scheme we use the encoder-decoder technique **enc** and **dec** proposed by [29].

$$\mathbf{enc} : \{0,1\}^n \rightarrow \{0,1\}^k \times \{0,1\}^*$$

$$\mathbf{dec} : \{0,1\}^k \times \{0,1\}^* \rightarrow \{0,1\}^n$$

The encoder-decoder technique is originally designed to allow for hiding of additional information to decrease the total data to be sent. In our work, we use it to break and merge the signature in order to map the trapdoor function f's domain space and range space to these of function π. $\mathbf{H_1}$ and $\mathbf{H_2}$ are two functions which hash any bit string down to τ bits: $\mathbf{H_1} : \{0,1\}^* \rightarrow \{0,1\}^\tau, \mathbf{H_2} : \{0,1\}^* \rightarrow \{0,1\}^\tau$.

Theorem 1. *If there exists a forger F that $(t, q_H, q_\Pi, q_S, \epsilon)$-breaks SAS in the ideal cipher model, then there exists a collision-finding algorithm C that (t', ϵ')-breaks the collision-resistant trapdoor function f with*

$$\epsilon' \geq \left(\epsilon - \frac{(q_S + q_H)^2}{2^\tau} - \frac{q_\Pi^2 + q_\Pi}{2^k}\right) \cdot \left(1 - \frac{(q_S + q_H)^2}{2^\tau}\right) \cdot \left(1 - \frac{q_\Pi^2 + q_\Pi}{2^k}\right)$$

$$t' \leq t + (q_H + q_S + q_\Pi) \cdot t_U + (q_S + q_\Pi) \cdot t_f$$

Algorithm 1. AggSign for ith signer in the sequence.

Input: public key f_i, secret key T_i, message m_i, aggregate-so-far signature σ_{i-1};
Output: new aggregate signature σ_i;
1: If $i = 1$, then:
2:      $x_0 \leftarrow 0^n$, $\boldsymbol{\alpha}_0 \leftarrow 0^{n-k}$;
3: Else:
4:      $(x_{i-1}, \boldsymbol{\alpha}_{i-1}) \leftarrow \sigma_{i-1}$;
5:      $K_i \leftarrow f_i \| \mathbf{H}_1(m_i) \| \mathbf{H}_2(\boldsymbol{\alpha}_{i-1})$;
6:      $(z_{i-1}, \alpha_i) \leftarrow \mathbf{enc}(x_{i-1})$;
7:      $y_i \leftarrow \pi^{-1}(K_i, z_{i-1})$;
8:      $x_i \leftarrow SamplePre(T_i, y_i)$;
9:      $\boldsymbol{\alpha}_i \leftarrow \boldsymbol{\alpha}_{i-1} \cup \alpha_i$;
10: $\sigma_i = (x_i, \boldsymbol{\alpha}_i)$
11: **return** σ_i;

Algorithm 2. AggVer

Input: public key and messages $(f_1, m_1), ..., (f_n, m_n)$, aggregate signature σ;
Output: a bit 0 or 1;
1: $(x_n, \boldsymbol{\alpha}_n) \leftarrow \sigma$
2: For $i = n$ down to 1 do:
3:      $y_i \leftarrow f_i(x_i)$;
4:      $K_i \leftarrow f_i \| \mathbf{H}_1(m_i) \| \mathbf{H}_2(\boldsymbol{\alpha}_{i-1})$;
5:      $z_{i-1} \leftarrow \pi(K_i, y_i)$;
6:      $x_{i-1} \leftarrow \mathbf{dec}(z_{i-1}, \alpha_i)$;
7: If $x_0 = 0^n$, then **return** 1;
8: Else **return** 0;

F is said $(t, q_H, q_\Pi, q_S, \epsilon)$-breaks SAS if its SAS-unforgeability advantage $\mathbf{Adv}^{uf}_{HF-SAS,F}(n)$ is at least ϵ with making at most q_Π times Π-queries or Π^{-1}-queries, q_H times H_1-queries or H_2-queries and q_S times sequential signing queries. t_U is the time of each execution of function $U(\cdot)$ and t_f is the time of each execution of function $f(\cdot)$.

4   Security Proof

We first give a *Variant Chain-to-Zero Lemma* originating from [15] that plays a key role in the security analysis of our scheme.

Consider an adversary A has access to the *variant ideal cipher model* where its key K describes a function $f : \{0,1\}^n \rightarrow \{0,1\}^k$ ($n \geq k$) unrelated to the function $\Pi : f \times \{0,1\}^n \rightarrow \{0,1\}^k$ and its inverse $\Pi^{-1} : f \times \{0,1\}^k \rightarrow \{0,1\}^n$. A may submit a Π-query form as $\Pi[f, y]$ to receive a random $x \in \{0,1\}^n$, or a Π^{-1}-query form as $\Pi^{-1}[f, x]$ query to receive a random $y \in \{0,1\}^k$.

We say that Π-table entry $x_i = \Pi[f_{i+1}, y_{i+1}]$ is linked to Π-table entry $x_{i-1} = \Pi[f_i, y_i]$ if $f_i(x_i) = y_i$. We define a Π-table entry $x = \Pi[f, y]$ to be chained to zero if $x = 0^n$ or it is linked to an entry that is chained to zero.

The length of a chain is defined as the number of entries linked in this chain. A Π-table entry $x = \Pi[f, y]$ is a forward query if it is received by making a Π-query and a backward query if it is received by making a Π^{-1}-query.

Lemma 1 (Variant Chain-to-Zero Lemma). *Consider an adversary A makes at most q_Π queries to the variant ideal cipher oracle. Define $\boldsymbol{BAD_\Pi}$ to be the event that some forward query in Π-table is chained to zero. Then $Pr[\boldsymbol{BAD_\Pi}] \leq \frac{q_\Pi^2 + q_\Pi}{2^k}$.*

Proof (Proof of Lemma 1). We give a brief proof of Lemma 1 using the proof method in [15] with some changes.

Consider function $f : \{0,1\}^n \rightarrow \{0,1\}^k$ ($n \geq k$) and q_Π random bit strings $y_1, ..., y_{q_\Pi} \in \{0,1\}^k$. For $1 \leq i \leq q_\Pi$, let Y_i be the random variable giving the size of the pre-image set of $f^{-1}(y_i)$ and let $Y_{max,i}$ be the random variable giving the maximum over i the size of the pre-image set of $f^{-1}(y_i)$. Then we compute

$$\mathbf{E}[Y_i] = \sum_{y_i \in \{0,1\}^k} \frac{1}{2^k} \cdot |f^{-1}(y_i)| = \frac{1}{2^k} \sum_{y_i \in \{0,1\}^k} |f^{-1}(y_i)| = 2^{n-k}$$

$$\mathbf{E}[Y_{max,i}] \leq \sum_{j=1}^{+\infty} j \cdot \mathbf{Pr}[Y_{max,i} = j] = \sum_{j=0}^{+\infty} \mathbf{Pr}[Y_{max,i} > j]$$

$$\leq \sum_{j=0}^{+\infty} \sum_{i=1}^{q_\Pi} \mathbf{Pr}[Y_i > j] = \sum_{i=1}^{q_\Pi} \mathbf{E}[Y_i] = q_\Pi \cdot 2^{n-k}$$

Define **Coll$_1$** to be event that a forward query $x_i = \Pi[f_{i+1}, y_{i+1}]$ is linked to some already existing backward query $x_{i-1} = \Pi[f_i, y_i]$. We say that a forward query collides if satisfies the condition for **Coll$_1$**. Let BQ_{made} denotes the number of backward queries that have been made. Then we have

$$\mathbf{Pr}[\mathbf{Coll_1}] = \sum_{m=1}^{q_\Pi} \mathbf{Pr}[a \; forward \; query \; x = \Pi[f, y] \; collides \; if \; BQ_{made} = m]$$

$$\leq \sum_{m=1}^{q_\Pi} \sum_{j=1}^{\infty} j \cdot \mathbf{Pr}[Y_{max,i} = j, 1 \leq i \leq m] \cdot 2^{-n}$$

$$= \sum_{m=1}^{q_\Pi} \mathbf{E}[Y_{max,i}, 1 \leq i \leq m] \cdot 2^{-n}$$

$$\leq \sum_{m=1}^{q_\Pi} m \cdot 2^{n-k} \cdot 2^{-n}$$

$$\leq \frac{q_\Pi^2}{2^k}$$

Define **Coll$_2$** to be event that a backward query $x_{i-1} = \Pi[f_i, y_i]$ is linked to some already existing query $x_i = \Pi[f_{i+1}, y_{i+1}]$. For an existing query

$x_i = \Pi[f_{i+1}, y_{i+1}]$ and a backward query $x_{i-1} = \Pi[f_i, y_i]$, y_i is chosen randomly and independently while $f_i(x_i)$ is already defined before y_i is chosen. Thus $\mathbf{Pr}[f_i(x_i) = y_i] = 2^{-k}$, which infers

$$\mathbf{Pr}[\mathbf{Coll}_2] \leq \frac{q_\Pi}{2^k}$$

Define $\mathbf{Coll} = \mathbf{Coll}_1 \vee \mathbf{Coll}_2$, then

$$\mathbf{Pr}[\mathbf{Coll}] \leq \mathbf{Pr}[\mathbf{Coll}_2] + \mathbf{Pr}[\mathbf{Coll}_1]$$
$$\leq \frac{q_\Pi^2 + q_\Pi}{2^k}$$

Finally, combine the definitions of $\mathbf{BAD}_{q_\Pi}$ and $\mathbf{Coll}$, we have

$$\mathbf{Pr}[\mathbf{BAD}_{q_\Pi}] \leq \mathbf{Pr}[\mathbf{BAD}_{q_\Pi} \mid \overline{\mathbf{Coll}}] + \mathbf{Pr}[\mathbf{Coll}]$$
$$= 0 + \mathbf{Pr}[\mathbf{Coll}]$$
$$\leq \frac{q_\Pi^2 + q_\Pi}{2^k}$$

*Proof (**Proof of Theorem** 1).* Given the challenge trapdoor function f^*, C runs F on inputing f^* and simulates the environment as follows:

- **Setup:** At the beginning of this game C sets up four empty tables $H_1[\cdot, \cdot]$, $H_2[\cdot, \cdot]$, $\Pi[\cdot, \cdot]$ and $f^*[\cdot, \cdot]$.
- **Response to H_1-query:** When F makes a H_1-query of message m, C draws r uniformly from $\{0, 1\}^\tau$: $r \leftarrow U(\{0, 1\}^\tau)$, records $H_1(m) = r$ in the H_1-table and returns r to F.
- **Response to H_2-query:** When F makes a H_2-query of α, C draws s uniformly from $\{0, 1\}^\tau$: $s \leftarrow U(\{0, 1\}^\tau)$, records $H_2(\alpha) = s$ in the H_2-table and returns s to F.
- **Response to Π-query:** When F makes a Π-query of $f\|r\|s$ and y, C draws x uniformly from $\{0, 1\}^n$: $x \leftarrow U(\{0, 1\}^n)$, records $\Pi[f\|r\|s, y] = x$ in the Π-table and returns x to F.
- **Response to Π^{-1}-query:** When F makes a Π^{-1}-query of $f\|r\|s$ and x, C draws $\hat{x}$ uniformly from $\{0, 1\}^n$: $\hat{x} \leftarrow U(\{0, 1\}^n)$, then computes $f^*(\hat{x}) = y$. Records $\Pi[f\|r\|s, y] = \hat{x}$ in the Π-table and records $f^*(\hat{x}) = y$ in the f^*-table. Finally returns y to F.
- **Response to aggregate signing query:** When F makes a aggregate signing query of m and σ, C draws s and r uniformly from $\{0, 1\}^\tau$: $r \leftarrow U(\{0, 1\}^\tau)$ and $s \leftarrow U(\{0, 1\}^\tau)$.

  If r is in the H_1-table or s is in the H_2-table, then C **aborts**.

  Else C parses σ: $(x_{i-1}, \alpha_{i-1}) \leftarrow \sigma$, draws x_i uniformly from $\{0, 1\}^n$: $x_i \leftarrow U(\{0, 1\}^n)$ and computes $f^*(x_i) = y_i$. Then records $\Pi[f\|r\|s, y_i] = x_i$ in the Π-table and encodes x_{i-1} to obtain (α_i, z_i): $(\alpha_i, z_i) \leftarrow \mathbf{enc}(x_{i-1})$; Appends α_i to α_{i-1}: $\alpha_i \leftarrow \alpha_{i-1} \cup \alpha_i$; Finally returns $\sigma_i = (x_i, \alpha_i)$ to F;

Finally, let $(f_1^*, m_1^*), ..., (f_n^*, m_n^*), \sigma^*$ be the output of forger F. The collision finding algorithm C proceeds as in Algorithm 3 in order to obtain a collision of f^*.

Algorithm 3. Collison-finder of f^*

Input: The output of forger F: $(f_1^*, m_1^*), ..., (f_n^*, m_n^*), \sigma^*$

Output: (x_1, x_2) that satisfy $f^*(x_1) = f^*(x_2)$

   C checks the output of forger F. If there does not exist $1 \leq i^* \leq n$ such that $f_{i^*}^* = f^*$, then C **return** $\perp$;

   If $AggVer((f_1^*, m_1^*), ..., (f_n^*, m_n^*), \sigma^*)$ outputs 0, then C also **return** $\perp$;

   Else C does:

   Parses σ^*: $(x_n^*, \alpha_n^*) \leftarrow \sigma^*$;

   For $i = n$ down to $i^* + 1$ does:

   $y_i^* \leftarrow f_i^*(x_i^*)$;

   $r_i^* \leftarrow \mathbf{H}_1(m_i^*)$;

   $s_i^* \leftarrow \mathbf{H}_2(\alpha_{i-1}^*)$;

   $x_{i-1}^* \leftarrow \Pi[f_i^* || r_i^* || s_i^*, y_i^*]$;

   $y_{i^*}^* \leftarrow f_i^*(x_{i^*}^*)$;

   C looks for $y_{i^*}^*$ in the f^*-table. If $y_{i^*}^*$ is not in f^*-table, then C **return** $\perp$.

   Else let $\hat{x}_{i^*}^*$ be the index of $y_{i^*}^*$ in the f^*-table, C **return** $(x_{i^*}^*, \hat{x}_{i^*}^*)$;

Consider executions of SAS unforgeability experiments with F and of the trapdoor-collision-finding algorithm C over a common set of random coin sequences with the same coins used for common choices across both experiments. In the execution of C in its experiment, let $\mathbf{BAD}_\Pi$ be the event that any forward query is chained to zero. Let $\mathbf{ABORT}$ be the event that C aborts. Let $\mathbf{FORGE}$ be the event that F outputs a valid forgery in its experiment. We claim that

$$\mathbf{Adv}_{TrapGen,C}^{cf}(n) \geq \Pr[\mathbf{FORGE} \wedge \overline{\mathbf{ABORT}} \wedge \overline{\mathbf{BAD}_\Pi}]$$

$$= \Pr[\mathbf{FORGE} \mid \overline{\mathbf{ABORT}} \wedge \overline{\mathbf{BAD}_\Pi}] \cdot \Pr[\overline{\mathbf{ABORT}} \mid \overline{\mathbf{BAD}_\Pi}] \cdot \Pr[\overline{\mathbf{BAD}_\Pi}]$$

$$\geq \Pr[\mathbf{FORGE} \mid \overline{\mathbf{ABORT}} \wedge \overline{\mathbf{BAD}_\Pi}] \cdot \Pr[\overline{\mathbf{ABORT}} \mid \overline{\mathbf{BAD}_\Pi}] \cdot \left(1 - \frac{q_\Pi^2 + q_\Pi}{2^k}\right)$$

The first inequality is because on coin sequences where C does not abort, the execution of F in its experiment and when run by C is equal. Hence, on such coin sequences F also forges in its execution by C. And since F finally produces a valid forgery, it can be inferred that the Π-table entry $x_{i-1}^* = \Pi[f_i^* || m_i^* || s_i^*, y_i^*]$ is chained to zero. Conditioning on $\overline{\mathbf{BAD}_\Pi}$, $x_{i-1}^* = \Pi[f_i^* || m_i^* || s_i^*, y_i^*]$ must be obtained by a backward query. Thus, C can find the index $\hat{x}_{i^*}^*$ of $y_{i^*}^*$ in the f^*-table, which leads to a collision $f^*(\hat{x}_{i^*}) = f^*(x_{i^*})$. The last line is due to the *Variant Chain-to-Zero Lemma 1*.

Next, we prove that

$$\Pr[\overline{\mathbf{ABORT}} \mid \overline{\mathbf{BAD}_\Pi}] \geq 1 - \frac{(q_S + q_H)^2}{2^\tau}$$

On each signing query and hash query, s or r is chosen independently at random. $\mathbf{BAD}_\Pi$ and $\mathbf{ABORT}$ are independent. The probability that $r = H_1(m)$ is already in the H_1-table or $s = H_2(\alpha)$ is already in the H_2-table on a given signing query is at most $\frac{q_S + q_H}{2^\tau}$. Summing over all signing queries we have $\Pr[\mathbf{ABORT} \mid \overline{\mathbf{BAD}_\Pi}] \leq (q_S + q_H)^2 / 2^\tau$.

We finally compute

$$\Pr[\mathbf{FORGE} \mid \overline{\mathbf{ABORT}} \wedge \overline{\mathbf{BAD}_\Pi}]$$

$$= \frac{\Pr[\mathbf{FORGE} \wedge \overline{\mathbf{ABORT}} \wedge \overline{\mathbf{BAD}_\Pi}]}{\Pr[\overline{\mathbf{ABORT}} \wedge \overline{\mathbf{BAD}_\Pi}]}$$

$$= \frac{\Pr[\mathbf{FORGE} \wedge \overline{\mathbf{ABORT} \vee \mathbf{BAD}_\Pi}]}{\Pr[\overline{\mathbf{ABORT}} \wedge \overline{\mathbf{BAD}_\Pi}]}$$

$$= \frac{\Pr[\mathbf{FORGE} - \Pr[\mathbf{FORGE} \mid \mathbf{ABORT} \vee \mathbf{BAD}_\Pi] \cdot \Pr[\mathbf{ABORT} \vee \mathbf{BAD}_\Pi]}{\Pr[\overline{\mathbf{ABORT}} \wedge \overline{\mathbf{BAD}_\Pi}]}$$

$$\geq \Pr[\mathbf{FORGE} - \Pr[\mathbf{ABORT} \vee \mathbf{BAD}_\Pi]$$

$$\geq \Pr[\mathbf{FORGE}] - \Pr[\mathbf{ABORT}] - \Pr[\mathbf{BAD}_\Pi]$$

$$\geq \mathbf{Adv}_{HF-SAS,F}^{uf}(n) - \frac{(q_S + q_H)^2}{2^\tau} - \frac{q_\Pi^2 + q_\Pi}{2^k}$$

Combining all the above, we have

$$\mathbf{Adv}_{TrapGen,C}^{cf}(n)$$

$$\geq \left(\mathbf{Adv}_{HF-SAS,F}^{uf}(n) - \frac{(q_S + q_H)^2}{2^\tau} - \frac{q_\Pi^2}{2^k} \right) \cdot \left(1 - \frac{(q_S + q_H)^2}{2^\tau} \right) \cdot \left(1 - \frac{q_\Pi^2 + q_\Pi}{2^k} \right)$$

We derive an upper bound for the running time of C considering only sample function $U(S)$ which appears in all four types of query, where $S = \{0,1\}^n$ or $S = \{0,1\}^\tau$, and function f, which appears in Π^{-1}-query and aggregate signing query. Therefore, the running time t' is upper bounded by:

$$t' \leq t + (q_H + q_S + q_\Pi) \cdot t_U + (q_S + q_\Pi) \cdot t_f$$

5   Instantiation

In general, any collision-resistant trapdoor function can be used to construct our SAS scheme. In this section we instantiate and analyze our sequential aggregate signature scheme in conjunction with FALCON [11].

FALCON [11] is a candidate cryptographic signature algorithm in the round 2 of NIST Post-Quantum Cryptography Project. It is based on the theoretical framework of lattice-based trapdoor function construction in [16] and is instantiated over NTRU lattices [18], with a trapdoor sampler called "fast Fourier sampling" [8]. The underlying hard problem is the short integer solution problem (**SIS**) over NTRU lattices [33], for which no polynomial time solving algorithm is currently known in the general case, even with the help of quantum computers. Main elements in FALCON are polynomials of degree with integer coefficients. The degree n is normally a power of two(typically 512 or 1024) or a small multiple of a power of two (e.g. 768). Computations are done modulo a monic polynomial of degree n denoted ϕ which is a cyclotomic polynomial in practice.

The public key A is a basis for a lattice of dimension $2n$:

$$A = \left[\begin{array}{c|c} -h & I_n \\ \hline qI_n & O_n \end{array}\right]$$

where I_n is the identity matrix of dimension n, O_n is the zero matrix of dimension n, and h is a polynomial modulo ϕ for an $n \times n$ sub-matrix. q is a specific small prime, and in practice is either $q = 12289$ or $q = 18433$. h's coefficients are integers between 0 and $q - 1$.

The corresponding trapdoor T_A is expressed as:

$$T_A = \left[\begin{array}{c|c} g & -f \\ \hline G & -F \end{array}\right]$$

where f, g, F and G are short integral polynomials modulo ϕ, which satisfy:

$$\begin{cases} h = g/f \mod \phi \mod q \\ fG - gF = q \mod \phi \end{cases}$$

The trapdoor function in our work is:

$$f_A : \mathbb{Z}[x]/(\phi) \times \mathbb{Z}[x]/(\phi) \rightarrow \mathbb{Z}_q[x]/(\phi)$$
$$f_A(s_1, s_2) = s_1 + s_2 \cdot h \mod q$$

where $\|(s_1, s_2)\| \leq \beta$ for a given positive acceptance bound β. The *SamplePre* function is expressed as $SamplePre(T_A, y) = (s_1, s_2) \mod q$, where s_1, s_2 and y satisfy $f_A(s_1, s_2) = y \mod q$.

In our scheme, the aggregate rate is $\tau(n) = 1 - \frac{size(x_n) + \sum_{i=1}^n size(\alpha_i)}{\sum_{i=1}^n size(x_i)}$. If $size(\alpha_i)$ and $size(x_n)$ are not dependent on i, then $\tau(n) \approx 1 - \frac{size(\alpha_i)}{size(x_i)}$. In practical implementation, the input x of f is an array with length 2048, which are integer coefficients of polynomial in $\mathbb{Z}[x]$ and the output y of f is an array with length 1024, which are integer coefficients of polynomial in $\mathbb{Z}_q[x]$. Let $s_1 = x_{[0,1023]}$ and $s_2 = x_{[1024,2047]}$. Function **enc** is simply used to split x into $(x_{[0,1023]}, x_{[1024,2047]})$ and function **dec** merges two arrays with length 1024 to one array with length 2048. We use AES several times to serve as a block cipher and use SHA256 as a hash function. Other parameters we use the recommended values in [11]. We implement our SAS scheme written using language C on tripe-core Intel i5 3.30 GHz CPU with standard CPU benchmarks. Figure 1 shows the efficiency of our AggSign algorithm and AggVer algorithm. In Fig. 1, we add 10 ms to the value of average verify time and 20 ms to the value of average key generate time in order to make a visible difference between the curves of average verify time, average sign time and average key generate time.

We also make an RSA-based trapdoor function construction of our SAS. The public key is (N, d) and the corresponding trapdoor is (N, e), where $N = pq$, p and q are primes, and $ed = 1 \mod \phi(N)$. The trapdoor function f on input $x \in \mathbb{Z}_N^*$ outputs $f(x) = x^e \mod N$ and the *SamplePre* function on input $y \in \mathbb{Z}_N^*$ outputs $SamplePre(y) = y^d \mod N$. In our implementation, the input of trapdoor function is an array with length 244 and the output array is with length 256. Table 1 gives a comparison of aggregate rate and efficiency of SAS based on FALCON trapdoor function and RSA trapdoor function for one signer.

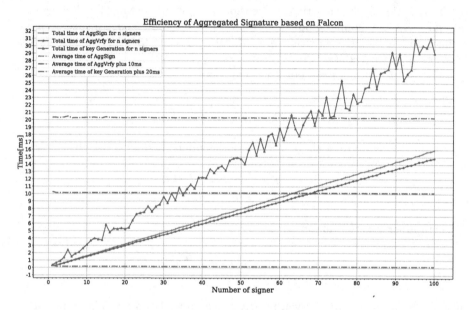

Fig. 1. Efficiency of sequential aggregate signature scheme based on FALCON

Table 1. Comparison of Aggregate rate and Efficiency of SAS based on FALCON trapdoor function and RSA trapdoor function for one signer

Type of trapdoor	rate $\tau(n)$	KeyGen	Sign	Verify
FALCON	$\approx 50\%$	0.302 ms	0.161 ms	0.150 ms
RSA	$\approx 95\%$	≤ 0.001 ms	1.582 ms	0.065 ms

6   Conclusion and Future Works

In this paper we address the problem of constructing lattice-based sequential aggregate signature. We give a practical SAS scheme based on lattice trapdoor function. The scheme is provably secure in *ideal cipher model*. We do a software implementation of SAS using FALCON-based trapdoor and RSA-based trapdoor. The experimental results show that our lattice-based SAS scheme has a high computation speed (approximately 1/10 ms) and can save about 50% storage or transmission costs. Any trapdoor function can be used to construct our SAS, such as the recently improved lattice trapdoor function in [13,14,17], yet our aggregate rate is not optimal as a result of the difference between trapdoor function's sizes of input and output. One interesting open problem is to construct lattice-based trapdoor permutation to improve aggregate rate.

Acknowledgment. This paper is supported by the National Key R&D Program of China through project 2017YFB0802500, by the National Cryptography Development Fund through project MMJJ20170106, by the foundation of Science and Technology on Information Assurance Laboratory through project 61421120305162112006, the Natural Science Foundation of China through projects 61772538, 61672083, 61532021, 61472429, 91646203 and 61402029.

References

1. Bellare, M., Namprempre, C., Neven, G.: Unrestricted aggregate signatures. In: Arge, L., Cachin, C., Jurdziński, T., Tarlecki, A. (eds.) ICALP 2007. LNCS, vol. 4596, pp. 411–422. Springer, Heidelberg (2007). https://doi.org/10.1007/978-3-540-73420-8_37

2. Bellare, M., Rogaway, P.: Random oracles are practical: a paradigm for designing efficient protocols. In: Proceedings of the 1st ACM Conference on Computer and Communications Security, pp. 62–73. ACM (1993)

3. Boldyreva, A., Gentry, C., O'Neill, A., Yum, D.H.: Ordered multisignatures and identity-based sequential aggregate signatures, with applications to secure routing. In: Proceedings of the 14th ACM Conference on Computer and Communications Security, pp. 276–285. ACM (2007)

4. Boneh, D., Freeman, D.M.: Homomorphic signatures for polynomial functions. In: Paterson, K.G. (ed.) EUROCRYPT 2011. LNCS, vol. 6632, pp. 149–168. Springer, Heidelberg (2011). https://doi.org/10.1007/978-3-642-20465-4_10

5. Boneh, D., Gentry, C., Lynn, B., Shacham, H.: Aggregate and verifiably encrypted signatures from bilinear maps. In: Biham, E. (ed.) EUROCRYPT 2003. LNCS, vol. 2656, pp. 416–432. Springer, Heidelberg (2003). https://doi.org/10.1007/3-540-39200-9_26

6. Brogle, K., Goldberg, S., Reyzin, L.: Sequential aggregate signatures with lazy verification from trapdoor permutations. Inf. Comput. **239**, 356–376 (2014)

7. Cash, D., Hofheinz, D., Kiltz, E., Peikert, C.: Bonsai trees, or how to delegate a lattice basis. J. Cryptol. **25**(4), 601–639 (2012)

8. Ducas, L., Prest, T.: Fast fourier orthogonalization. In: Proceedings of the ACM on International Symposium on Symbolic and Algebraic Computation, pp. 191–198. ACM (2016). https://doi.org/10.1145/2930889.2930923

9. El Bansarkhani, R., Buchmann, J.: Towards lattice based aggregate signatures. In: Pointcheval, D., Vergnaud, D. (eds.) AFRICACRYPT 2014. LNCS, vol. 8469, pp. 336–355. Springer, Cham (2014). https://doi.org/10.1007/978-3-319-06734-6_21

10. Fischlin, M., Lehmann, A., Schröder, D.: History-free sequential aggregate signatures. In: Visconti, I., De Prisco, R. (eds.) SCN 2012. LNCS, vol. 7485, pp. 113–130. Springer, Heidelberg (2012). https://doi.org/10.1007/978-3-642-32928-9_7

11. Fouque, P.A., et al.: Falcon: fast-fourier lattice-based compact signatures over NTRU (2018). Accessed 12 June 2019. https://falcon-sign.info/

12. Garg, S., Gentry, C., Halevi, S.: Candidate multilinear maps from ideal lattices. In: Johansson, T., Nguyen, P.Q. (eds.) EUROCRYPT 2013. LNCS, vol. 7881, pp. 1–17. Springer, Heidelberg (2013). https://doi.org/10.1007/978-3-642-38348-9_1

13. Genise, N., Micciancio, D.: Faster Gaussian sampling for trapdoor lattices with arbitrary modulus. In: Nielsen, J.B., Rijmen, V. (eds.) EUROCRYPT 2018. LNCS, vol. 10820, pp. 174–203. Springer, Cham (2018). https://doi.org/10.1007/978-3-319-78381-9_7

14. Genise, N., Micciancio, D., Polyakov, Y.: Building an efficient lattice gadget toolkit: Subgaussian sampling and more. Technical report, Cryptology ePrint Archive, Report 2018/946, 2018 (2018). https://eprint.iacr.org/2018/946.pdf

15. Gentry, C., O'Neill, A., Reyzin, L.: A unified framework for trapdoor-permutation-based sequential aggregate signatures. In: Abdalla, M., Dahab, R. (eds.) PKC 2018. LNCS, vol. 10770, pp. 34–57. Springer, Cham (2018). https://doi.org/10.1007/978-3-319-76581-5_2

16. Gentry, C., Peikert, C., Vaikuntanathan, V.: Trapdoors for hard lattices and new cryptographic constructions. In: Proceedings of the Fortieth Annual ACM Symposium on Theory of Computing, pp. 197–206. ACM (2008)

17. Gür, K.D., Polyakov, Y., Rohloff, K., Ryan, G.W., Savas, E.: Implementation and evaluation of improved Gaussian sampling for lattice trapdoors. In: Proceedings of the 6th Workshop on Encrypted Computing & Applied Homomorphic Cryptography, pp. 61–71. ACM (2018)

18. Hoffstein, J., Howgrave-Graham, N., Pipher, J., Silverman, J.H., Whyte, W.: NTRUSign: digital signatures using the NTRU lattice. In: Joye, M. (ed.) CT-RSA 2003. LNCS, vol. 2612, pp. 122–140. Springer, Heidelberg (2003). https://doi.org/10.1007/3-540-36563-X_9

19. Hohenberger, S., Sahai, A., Waters, B.: Full domain hash from (leveled) multilinear maps and identity-based aggregate signatures. In: Canetti, R., Garay, J.A. (eds.) CRYPTO 2013. LNCS, vol. 8042, pp. 494–512. Springer, Heidelberg (2013). https://doi.org/10.1007/978-3-642-40041-4_27

20. Hu, Y., Jia, H.: A new Gaussian sampling for trapdoor lattices with arbitrary modulus. Des. Codes Crypt. 1–18 (2019). https://doi.org/10.1007/s10623-019-00635-8

21. Lee, K., Lee, D.H., Yung, M.: Sequential aggregate signatures made shorter. In: Jacobson, M., Locasto, M., Mohassel, P., Safavi-Naini, R. (eds.) ACNS 2013. LNCS, vol. 7954, pp. 202–217. Springer, Heidelberg (2013). https://doi.org/10.1007/978-3-642-38980-1_13

22. Lu, S., Ostrovsky, R., Sahai, A., Shacham, H., Waters, B.: Sequential aggregate signatures and multisignatures without random oracles. In: Vaudenay, S. (ed.) EUROCRYPT 2006. LNCS, vol. 4004, pp. 465–485. Springer, Heidelberg (2006). https://doi.org/10.1007/11761679_28

23. Lu, S., Ostrovsky, R., Sahai, A., Shacham, H., Waters, B.: Sequential aggregate signatures, multisignatures, and verifiably encrypted signatures without random oracles. J. Cryptol. 26(2), 340–373 (2013)

24. Lu, X., Yin, W., Wen, Q., Jin, Z., Li, W.: A lattice-based unordered aggregate signature scheme based on the intersection method. IEEE Access 6, 33986–33994 (2018). https://doi.org/10.1109/ACCESS.2018.2847411

25. Lysyanskaya, A., Micali, S., Reyzin, L., Shacham, H.: Sequential aggregate signatures from trapdoor permutations. In: Cachin, C., Camenisch, J.L. (eds.) EUROCRYPT 2004. LNCS, vol. 3027, pp. 74–90. Springer, Heidelberg (2004). https:// doi.org/10.1007/978-3-540-24676-3_5

26. Lyubashevsky, V., Micciancio, D.: Generalized compact knapsacks are collision resistant. In: Bugliesi, M., Preneel, B., Sassone, V., Wegener, I. (eds.) ICALP 2006. LNCS, vol. 4052, pp. 144–155. Springer, Heidelberg (2006). https://doi.org/ 10.1007/11787006_13

27. Lyubashevsky, V., Peikert, C., Regev, O.: On ideal lattices and learning with errors over rings. In: Gilbert, H. (ed.) EUROCRYPT 2010. LNCS, vol. 6110, pp. 1–23. Springer, Heidelberg (2010). https://doi.org/10.1007/978-3-642-13190-5_1

28. Micciancio, D., Peikert, C.: Trapdoors for lattices: simpler, tighter, faster, smaller. In: Pointcheval, D., Johansson, T. (eds.) EUROCRYPT 2012. LNCS, vol. 7237, pp. 700–718. Springer, Heidelberg (2012). https://doi.org/10.1007/978-3-642-29011-4_41

29. Neven, G.: Efficient sequential aggregate signed data. In: Smart, N. (ed.) EUROCRYPT 2008. LNCS, vol. 4965, pp. 52–69. Springer, Heidelberg (2008). https:// doi.org/10.1007/978-3-540-78967-3_4

30. Peikert, C., Rosen, A.: Efficient collision-resistant hashing from worst-case assumptions on cyclic lattices. In: Halevi, S., Rabin, T. (eds.) TCC 2006. LNCS, vol. 3876, pp. 145–166. Springer, Heidelberg (2006). https://doi.org/10.1007/11681878_8

31. Shannon, C.E.: Communication theory of secrecy systems. Bell Syst. Tech. J. **28**(4), 656–715 (1949)

32. Shor, P.W.: Polynomial-time algorithms for prime factorization and discrete logarithms on a quantum computer. SIAM Rev. **41**(2), 303–332 (1999). https://doi. org/10.1137/S0097539795293172

33. Stehlé, D., Steinfeld, R.: Making NTRU as secure as worst-case problems over ideal lattices. In: Paterson, K.G. (ed.) EUROCRYPT 2011. LNCS, vol. 6632, pp. 27–47. Springer, Heidelberg (2011). https://doi.org/10.1007/978-3-642-20465-4_4

34. Stehlé, D., Steinfeld, R., Tanaka, K., Xagawa, K.: Efficient public key encryption based on ideal lattices. In: Matsui, M. (ed.) ASIACRYPT 2009. LNCS, vol. 5912, pp. 617–635. Springer, Heidelberg (2009). https://doi.org/10.1007/978-3-642-10366-7_36

Encryption

Towards Enhanced Security for Certificateless Public-Key Authenticated Encryption with Keyword Search

Xueqiao Liu[1], Hongbo Li[2], Guomin Yang[1(✉)], Willy Susilo[1], Joseph Tonien[1], and Qiong Huang[2]

[1] Institute of Cybersecurity and Cryptology,
School of Computing and Information Technology, University of Wollongong,
Wollongong 2522, Australia
{xl691,gyang,wsusilo,dong}@uow.edu.au
[2] College of Mathematics and Informatics, South China Agricultural University,
Guangzhou 510642, China
hongbo@stu.scau.edu.cn, qhuang@scau.edu.cn

Abstract. Certificateless Public-key Authenticated Encryption with Keyword Search (CLPAEKS) is derived from the Public-key Authenticated Encryption with Keyword Search (PAEKS) and simultaneously combines the features of the Public Key Cryptography (CLPKC). In a CLPAEKS scheme, the ciphertext is designed to meet the need for both confidentiality and authentication, i.e., on one hand, the ciphertext is the encryption of the keyword; on the other hand, adversaries are incapable of generating a valid ciphertext without the owner's private key. He et al. formalized security models for CLPAEKS and proposed a CLPAEKS scheme. However, we find their models are incomplete to capture the security requirements for CLPAEKS and re-formalize the security requirements for CLPAEKS in terms of trapdoor privacy and ciphertext indistinguishability. Besides, we point out that their scheme is vulnerable to the Keyword Guessing Attack (KGA) by a malicious receiver, which is not considered in their security model. Then we modify He et al.'s scheme and prove that the new scheme meets the new security requirements.

Keywords: Public Key Authenticated Encryption with Keyword Search · Keyword Guessing Attack · Certificateless

1 Introduction

Since the widespread of the concept and corresponding applications of the cloud storage, performing search on encrypted data has become a popular research topic. Among all potential solutions, the Public-key Encryption with Keyword Search (PEKS) has attracted considerable attentions from researchers, since it was put forth by Boneh et al. [5]. Due to the properties inherited from the

© Springer Nature Switzerland AG 2019
R. Steinfeld and T. H. Yuen (Eds.): ProvSec 2019, LNCS 11821, pp. 113–129, 2019.
https://doi.org/10.1007/978-3-030-31919-9_7

public key encryption, PEKS not only allows multiple data providers to upload data together with the searchable ciphertext to the server, but permits multiple request users to generate a trapdoor in order to launch a query with underlying keywords of interest as well. A number of PEKS schemes have been presented and proven to be Semantic Secure under Chosen Keyword Attack (SS-CKA).

However, we have to highlight that the security definition of SS-CKA only considers the risk of revealing information from the searchable ciphertext and does not consider the potential leakage from the trapdoor. We take the well-known attack named Keyword Guessing Attack [8,21] as an example. An attacker may collect one trapdoor with the underlying keyword w from the communications between an authorized request user and the server. Then the attacker generates all searchable ciphertexts by exhaustively computing the searchable ciphertext for each keyword in the universal keyword set of limited size. Finally, the attacker matches each searchable ciphertext generated from the underlying keyword w' with the collected trapdoor. Once they match, it means that $w = w'$. In short, some information about the underlying keyword of the trapdoor or query is revealed to the attacker. This attack can be launched in an off-line way on schemes with small keyword space. A considerable number of existing PEKS works are found vulnerable to this attack. On one hand, security model outlining the privacy leakage from trapdoors should be taken into account. On the other hand, generic solution which is naturally immune to this attack should be constructed.

To resist such attacks especially the Inside Keyword Guessing Attack (IKGA) which are launched by the server, PAEKS and its derivation CLPAEKS come into play [12,13]. Both of their ideas are to take the sender's private key as the input of the ciphertext generation algorithm, so that other parties can never impersonate the sender to make a ciphertext. In short, their ciphertexts are supposed to be unforgeable by other parties. Unfortunately, though the scheme in [12] can resist the IKGA from the server, it is vulnerable to KGA launched by other parties, say, the receiver. That is, without the private key of the sender S but with the private key Sk_R of the receiver R, it is possible to modify a real ciphertext $C_{S \to R}(w)$ to a valid ciphertext $C'_{S \to R'}(w)$. Then the malicious receiver R can learn whether the underlying keyword of the current trapdoor $T_{S \to R'}(w')$ sniffed from the communication channel is the same as that of $C'_{S \to R'}(w)$ by running the test algorithm on the new ciphertext and the trapdoor. That is to say, the trapdoor privacy can no more be guaranteed. Furthermore, R can in advance impersonate S and upload $C'_{S \to R'}(w)$ with its own document D to the server, resulting in matching $C'_{S \to R'}(w)$ with the trapdoor $T_{S \to R'}(w)$ and additionally returning D to the innocent receiver R'.

In addition, in an open network environment, there is no fully trusted parties. This is also applicable to the outsourced data storage applications. That is, any party involved in the cloud storage system can be untrusted or even malicious and the forementioned attacks are practical and potential. Thus, a well-defined security model with the ciphertext oracle like [13] is needed. However, the security models of [12] which only consider the searchable ciphertext indistinguishability without accessing the ciphertext oracle cannot accurately capture the security requirements for CLPAEKS.

1.1 Related Work

With the advent of the cloud storage technique, the public are more willing to store their personal data on the cloud after encryption. Even though data encrypted leaks less privacy, direct operations on data such as computations and search are prevented. During the long journey of seeking the solution to enabling search on encrypted data, Public-key Encryption with Keyword Search (PEKS) was proposed [5]. From then on, a large number of PEKS works and its variants [10,15–18] have emerged. However, the security model of the semantic security against chosen keyword attack in [5] only takes the leakage of ciphertext into consideration and does not consider that of trapdoor. That is, schemes do not satisfy the tradoor privacy have the leakage risk against the Keyword Guessing Attack [8,21].

Then some subsequent researches [9,11] focus on designing constructions resisting KGA. As one of the solutions, the Public-key Encryption with Fuzzy Keyword Search (PEFKS) was formalized and a detailed construction was presented which is secure against outside keyword guessing attack in [20]. An alternative solution to KGA prevention is to deploy two servers, assuming the servers never collude [19].

Another creative solution against KGA is the Public-key Authenticated Encryption with Keyword Search (PAEKS) proposed by [13], in which besides computing the searchable ciphertext from each keyword, the data provider also needs to authenticate the searchable ciphertext with her/his secret key. That means the secret key of the data provider is also input of the encryption algorithm. Then the problem naturally comes to defining the security model depicting unforgeability, which is similar to that of signcrpytion [22] to a certain degree.

In order to get rid of unconditional trust in Private Key Generator (PKG), Certificateless Public Key Cryptography (CLPKC) was proposed by Al-Riyami and Paterson [1], keeping users' private key unrevealed to Key Generation Center (KGC) by allowing users to set a secret value themselves. Based on this concept, Certificateless Public Key Encryption (CLPKE) [2,3] and Certificateless Signature (CLS) [1,14] schemes are constructed. Recently, the certificateless public key encryption with keyword search (CLPAEKS) [12] was proposed to avoid the certificate management and the key escrow problem of PAEKS with the help of the certificateless primitive. Similarly, CLPAEKS should also consider unforgeability which is inherited from the security requirements of PAEKS.

1.2 Our Contributions

We outline the contributions of this work as follows:

- We reconsider the security definitions against two types of adversaries and present new security models which better depict the security requirements for CLPAEKS.

- By analyzing the weakness of an existing scheme under our security models, we present a new CLPAEKS scheme.
- We prove that the new scheme is secure under the formalized security models.

2   Preliminaries

2.1   Bilinear Pairing

Let $e : \mathbb{G}_1 \times \mathbb{G}_1 \to \mathbb{G}_2$ be a bilinear pairing, where $\mathbb{G}_1, \mathbb{G}_2$ are cyclic groups of the same prime order q. It satisfies the following [6]:

- For any $x, y \in \mathbb{Z}$, $P, Q \in \mathbb{G}_1$ $e(xP, yQ) = e(P, Q)^{xy}$.
- For any generator $P \in \mathbb{G}_1$, $e(P, P)$ is a generator of $\mathbb{G}_2$.
- For any $P, Q \in \mathbb{G}_1$, $e(P, Q)$ can be computed efficiently.

2.2   Decisional Bilinear Diffie Hellman Problem

Given a generator $P \in \mathbb{G}_1$ and elements $xP, yP, zP \in \mathbb{G}_1$ where x, y, z are randomly chosen from $\mathbb{Z}_q$, distinguish $e(P, P)^{xyz}$ from a random element from $\mathbb{G}_2$ [7].

2.3   Decisional Linear Problem

Given a generator $Q \in \mathbb{G}_1$ and elements $x_1 Q, x_2 Q, x x_1 Q, y x_2 Q \in \mathbb{G}_1$ where x, y, x_1, x_2 are randomly chosen from $\mathbb{Z}_q$, distinguish $(x + y)Q$ from a random element Z from $\mathbb{G}_1$ [4].

3   Certificateless Public-Key Authenticated Encryption with Keyword Search

3.1   Definition

The syntax of CLPAEKS is outlined in [12]: Setup, Extract $-$ partial$-$ private $-$ key, Set $-$ secret $-$ value, Set $-$ private $-$ key, Set $-$ public$-$ key, CLPAEKS, Trapdoor, Test. We omit this session due to limited space.

3.2   Security Models

In this section, we will discuss the security requirements which should be equipped with a CLPAEKS scheme. First of all, CLPAEKS is foremost a PAEKS which should possess trapdoor privacy and ciphertext indistinguishability mentioned in [13]. Then it is a scheme in the form of the certificateless public key cryptography in which given that the scheme has no certificates, a further strengthened security model is taken into account, allowing adversaries to replace the public key of any entity with a value of their choice. In short, the games depicting security requirements for CLPAEKS are designed after taking those of both PAEKS and the certificateless public key cryptography into consideration. As the security requirements of CLPKC, two types adversaries are taken into account in CLPAEKS to depict the outside adversaries (type 1) and the inside adversaries (type 2), respectively [1].

Remark: Type 1 adversary depicts the outside adversary who may be one of the legal system users. That means it can access the secret value and decide the corresponding public key. Thus, type 1 adversary can replace public keys and should designate the public key for replacement at the very beginning. In contrast, type 2 adversary depicts the inside adversary like KGC who can access the master key, but cannot replace public keys.

Trapdoor Privacy. Similar to the security requirement in [13], the adversary should not distinguish two trapdoors given access to responses for a range of queries, including the extract partial private key query, the extract secret value query, the request public key query, the trapdoor query and the ciphertext query which outline the practical capability of the adversary. Besides, the security requirements for the certificateless public key aspect should be taken into consideration. That is, type 1 adversary should be permitted to launch the replace public key query and type 2 adversary should be permitted to access the master key due to the feature of certificateless cryptography [1]. The model is divided into the following two parts correspondingly:

Game 1 (type 1 adversary):

Setup: Given a security parameter λ, the adversary $\mathcal{A}$ chooses the challenge sender's identity ID_S and the new public key Pk'_{ID_S}, the challenge receiver's identity ID_R, the challenger $\mathcal{C}$ generates and sends $(Param, Pk_{ID_R})$ to $\mathcal{A}$.

Query: The adversary $\mathcal{A}$ is allowed to issue the following queries:

- Hash query: $\mathcal{A}$ is allowed to issue queries to all hash oracles.
- Extract partial private key query: Given an identity ID_i, the challenger $\mathcal{C}$ computes the corresponding partial private key d_{ID_i} and returns d_{ID_i} to $\mathcal{A}$. $\mathcal{A}$ is prohibited from querying the partial private key of ID_S.
- Extract secret value query: Given an identity ID_i, the challenger $\mathcal{C}$ computes and returns the corresponding secret value x_{ID_i} to $\mathcal{A}$. $\mathcal{A}$ is prohibited from querying the secret value x_{ID_i} for the identity ID_i s.t. the corresponding public key Pk_i has been replaced by a replace public key query, and the secret value x_{ID_R} for the challenge receiver's identity ID_R .
- Request public key query: Given an identity ID_i, the challenger $\mathcal{C}$ computes the corresponding public key Pk_{ID_i} and returns Pk_{ID_i} to $\mathcal{A}$.
- Replace public key query: Given an identity ID_i, the adversary $\mathcal{A}$ can ask the challenger $\mathcal{C}$ to replace the corresponding public key Pk_{ID_i} with a new public key Pk'_{ID_i}. $\mathcal{A}$ is prohibited from replacing the public key for the challenge receiver's identity ID_R before the challenge phase which would enable $\mathcal{A}$ to receive a challenge trapdoor under a secret value known by $\mathcal{A}$ and trivially win the distinguishing game.

- Trapdoor query: Given a keyword w, $ID_{S'}$ and $ID_{R'}$, the challenger $\mathcal{C}$ computes the corresponding trapdoor T_w with respect to $ID_{S'}$ and $ID_{R'}$, returns T_w to $\mathcal{A}$.
- Ciphertext query: Given a keyword w, $ID_{S'}$ and $ID_{R'}$, the challenger $\mathcal{C}$ computes the corresponding ciphertext C_w with respect to $ID_{S'}$ and $ID_{R'}$, returns C_w to $\mathcal{A}$.

Challenge: $\mathcal{A}$ chooses two keywords w_0, w_1 s.t. $(Pk_{ID_S}, Pk_{ID_R}, w_0)$, $(Pk_{ID_S}, Pk_{ID_R}, w_1)$ have not been queried for trapdoor and ciphertext, sends them to the challenger $\mathcal{C}$. $\mathcal{C}$ randomly chooses $b \in \{0,1\}$, returns T_{w_b} to $\mathcal{A}$.

Query: $\mathcal{A}$ continues launching queries as the above with the same restrictions.

Guess: $\mathcal{A}$ outputs a bit b'. It wins the game if $b' = b$.

Game 2 (type 2 adversary):

The differences of this game from the above game are as follows:

1. the adversary $\mathcal{A}$ chooses the challenge sender's identity ID_S and the challenge receiver's identity ID_R, the challenger $\mathcal{C}$ sends $(Param, Pk_R, Pk_S)$ to $\mathcal{A}$ in the **Setup** phase.
2. the master key s is given to the adversary $\mathcal{A}$ in the **Setup** phase.
3. the adversary $\mathcal{A}$ is prohibited from launching any replace public key queries.
4. the adversary $\mathcal{A}$ is prohibited from launching extract secret value queries on the challenge identities ID_S and ID_R.

Definition 1. *We say that a CLPAEKS satisfies the trapdoor privacy if for any probabilistic polynomial-time (PPT) adversary $\mathcal{A}$, the advantage*

$$Adv^{TP}_{CLPAEKS, \mathcal{A}}(\lambda) = |\Pr[b' = b] - \frac{1}{2}|$$

is negligible.

Ciphertext Indistinguishability. Similar to the security requirement in [13], the adversary should not distinguish two ciphertexts given access to responses for the similar range of queries to that of the trapdoor privacy. Similarly, type 1 adversary should be permitted to launch the replace public key query and type 2 adversary should be permitted to access the master key due to the feature of certificateless [1]. The model is devided into the following two parts correspondingly:

Game 3 (type 1 adversary):

Setup: Given a security parameter λ, the adversary $\mathcal{A}$ chooses the challenge sender's identity ID_S, the challenge receiver's identity ID_R and the public key for replacement Pk'_{ID_R}, the challenger $\mathcal{C}$ generates and sends $(Param, Pk_{ID_S})$ to $\mathcal{A}$.

Query: The adversary $\mathcal{A}$ is allowed to issue similar queries as in Game 1. In the replace public key query, $\mathcal{A}$ is prohibited from replacing ID_S's public key.

Challenge: $\mathcal{A}$ chooses two keywords w_0, w_1 s.t. $(Pk_{ID_S}, Pk_{ID_R}, w_0)$, $(Pk_{ID_S}, Pk_{ID_R}, w_1)$ have not been queried for trapdoor and ciphertext, sends them to the challenger $\mathcal{C}$. $\mathcal{C}$ randomly chooses $b \in \{0,1\}$, returns C_{w_b} to $\mathcal{A}$.

Query: $\mathcal{A}$ continues launching queries as the above with similar restrictions.

Guess: $\mathcal{A}$ outputs a bit b'. It wins the game if $b' = b$.

Game 4 (type 2 adversary):

The differences of this game from the above game is the same to the Game 2 of the trapdoor privacy. For simplicity, we omit the repeated details.

Definition 2. *We say that a CLPAEKS satisfies the ciphertext indistinguishability if for any PPT adversary $\mathcal{A}$, the advantage*

$$Adv^{CI}_{CLPAEKS,\mathcal{A}}(\lambda) = |\Pr[b' = b] - \frac{1}{2}|$$

is negligible.

4   Weakness of He et al.'s Scheme

In this section, we review He et al.'s scheme [12] and point out the scheme is vulnerable to the KGA according to our trapdoor privacy security model.

4.1   He et al.'s Scheme

In this section, we first revisit the CLPAEKS proposed in [12].

1. **Setup** : Given a security parameter l, KGC chooses a cyclic additive group $\mathbb{G}_1$ and a cyclic multiplicative $\mathbb{G}_2$ of the same prime order $q > 2^l$, a generator P of $\mathbb{G}_1$, a bilinear pairing $e : \mathbb{G}_1 \times \mathbb{G}_1 \to \mathbb{G}_2$, a random number $s \in \mathbb{Z}_q^*$ as the master key, computes $P_{pub} = sP$, selects three hash functions: $h_1 : \{0,1\}^* \times \mathbb{G}_1 \to \mathbb{Z}_q^*$, $H_2 : \{0,1\}^* \to \mathbb{G}_1$, $h_3 : \{0,1\}^* \times \mathbb{G}_1 \times \mathbb{G}_1 \times \mathbb{G}_1 \to \mathbb{Z}_q^*$, publishes $Param = \{l, \mathbb{G}_1, \mathbb{G}_2, e, q, P, P_{pub}, h_1, H_2, h_3\}$ and keeps s secret.

2. **Extract** − **partial** − **private** − **key** : Given the sender's identity $ID_S \in \{0,1\}^*$ and the master key s, KGC chooses a random number $r_{ID_S} \in \mathbb{Z}_q^*$, computes $R_{ID_S} = r_{ID_S}P$, $\alpha_{ID_S} = h_1(ID_S, R_{ID_S})$, and $d_{ID_S} = r_{ID_S} + s\alpha_{ID_S} \pmod{q}$. Then KGC returns d_{ID_S} and R_{ID_S} to the sender. d_{ID_R} and R_{ID_R} are computed and returned in the same way as above.

3. **Set** − **secret** − **value** : Given the sender's identity $ID_S \in \{0,1\}^*$ and the receiver's identity $ID_R \in \{0,1\}^*$, the sender chooses a random number $x_{ID_S} \in \mathbb{Z}_q^*$ as its secret value, the receiver chooses a random number $x_{ID_R} \in \mathbb{Z}_q^*$ as its secret value.

4. **Set** − **private** − **key** : Given the sender's secret value x_{ID_S} and the sender's partial private key d_{ID_S}, the sender's private key is set as $SK_{ID_S} = (x_{ID_S}, d_{ID_S})$. Given the receiver's secret value x_{ID_R} and the reciver's partial private key d_{ID_R}, the receiver's private key is set as $SK_{ID_R} = (x_{ID_R}, d_{ID_R})$.

5. $\mathtt{Set - public - key}$: Given the sender's secret value x_{ID_S}, the partial public information R_{ID_S}, the receiver's secret value x_{ID_R}, and the partial public information R_{ID_R}, the sender computes $P_{ID_S} = x_{ID_S}P$, $Pk_{ID_S} = (P_{ID_S}, R_{ID_S})$ is set as the sender's public key, the receiver computes $P_{ID_R} = x_{ID_R}P$, $Pk_{ID_R} = (P_{ID_R}, R_{ID_R})$ is set as the receiver's public key.

6. $\mathtt{CLPAEKS}$: Given the sender's identity ID_S, the receiver's identity ID_R, the sender's secret key SK_{ID_S}, the receiver's public key Pk_{ID_R}, and the keyword w, the sender chooses a random number $r \in \mathbb{Z}_q^*$, computes $\beta_{ID_S} = h_3(ID_S, P_{pub}, P_{ID_S}, R_{ID_S})$, $\beta_{ID_R} = h_3(ID_R, P_{pub}, P_{ID_R}, R_{ID_R})$, $C_1 = (d_{ID_S} + \beta_{ID_S}x_{ID_S})H_2(w) + rP$, $C_2 = r(\beta_{ID_R}P_{ID_R} + R_{ID_R} + \alpha_{ID_R}P_{pub})$, and returns the ciphertext $C_w = (C_1, C_2)$.

7. $\mathtt{Trapdoor}$: Given the sender's identity ID_S, the receiver's identity ID_R, the sender's public key Pk_{ID_S} and the receiver's private key SK_{ID_R}, the receiver computes
$\beta_{ID_S} = h_3(ID_S, P_{pub}, P_{ID_S}, R_{ID_S})$, $\beta_{ID_R} = h_3(ID_R, P_{pub}, P_{ID_R}, R_{ID_R})$ and $T_w = e((d_{ID_R} + \beta_{ID_R}x_{ID_R})H_2(w), \beta_{ID_S}P_{ID_S} + R_{ID_S} + \alpha_{ID_S}P_{pub})$.

8. $\mathtt{Test}$: Given the receiver's identity ID_R and public key Pk_{ID_R}, the trapdoor T_w, and the ciphertext C_w, the server computes $\beta_{ID_R} = h_3(ID_R, P_{pub}, P_{ID_R}, R_{ID_R})$ and checks if $T_w e(C_2, P) = e(C_1, \beta_{ID_R}P_{ID_R} + R_{ID_R} + \alpha_{ID_R}P_{pub})$.

4.2 Weakness of He et al.'s Scheme

We will follow our Game 1 of the trapdoor privacy step by step in order to present the weakness of He et al.'s scheme [12]. The main idea is to make a valid ciphertext C_{w_0} for one of the challenge keywords with respect to the challenge sender ID_S and the challenge receiver ID_R, by processing another ciphertext C'_{w_0} for the same keyword w_0 with respect to ID_S and another receiver $ID_{R'}$ with the private key of $ID_{R'}$ at the beginning, then to run the algorithm $\mathtt{Test}$, given the challenge trapdoor T_{w_b} for the challenge keyword $w_b \in \{w_0, w_1\}$ and C_{w_0} as the inputs.

Query: The adversary $\mathcal{A}$ issues the following queries:

- Extract partial private key query: $\mathcal{A}$ sends a query for an identity $ID_{R'}$, the challenger $\mathcal{C}$ returns the corresponding partial private key $d_{ID_{R'}}$ to $\mathcal{A}$.
- Extract secret value query: The adversary $\mathcal{A}$ sends a query for an identity $ID_{R'}$, the challenger $\mathcal{C}$ returns the corresponding secret value $x_{ID_{R'}}$ to $\mathcal{A}$.
- Request public key query: The adversary $\mathcal{A}$ sends a request public key query for the same identity $ID_{R'}$, the challenger $\mathcal{C}$ returns the corresponding public key $Pk_{ID_{R'}}$ where $PK_{ID_{R'}} = (P_{ID_{R'}}, R_{ID_{R'}})$.
- Ciphertext query: The adversary $\mathcal{A}$ sends a ciphertext query for a keyword w_0 of its choice and the same receiver $ID_{R'}$, the challenger $\mathcal{C}$ returns the corresponding ciphertext C'_w with respect to ID_S and $ID_{R'}$ to $\mathcal{A}$. $C'_{w_0} = (C'_1, C'_2)$ where $C'_1 = (d_{ID_S} + \beta_{ID_S}x_{ID_S})H_2(w_0) + r'P$, $C'_2 = r'(\beta_{ID_{R'}}P_{ID_{R'}} + R_{ID_{R'}} + \alpha_{ID_{R'}}P_{pub})$.

$\mathcal{A}$ firstly computes $\beta_{ID_S} = h_3(ID_S, P_{pub}, P_{ID_S}, R_{ID_S}), \beta_{ID_R} = h_3(ID_R, P_{pub}, P_{ID_R}, R_{ID_R}), \beta_{ID_{R'}} = h_3(ID_{R'}, P_{pub}, P_{ID_{R'}}, R_{ID_{R'}})$, and $r'P = (\beta_{ID_{R'}} x_{ID_{R'}} + d_{ID_{R'}})^{-1}C_2'$, then computes $C_1' - r'P = (d_{ID_S} + \beta_{ID_S} x_{ID_S})H_2(w_0)$.
$\mathcal{A}$ randomly choses $r \in \mathbb{Z}_q^*$ and forges a searchable ciphertext $C_{w_0} = (C_1, C_2)$ for the same keyword w_0 with respect to the challenge identities ID_S and ID_R:
$C_1 = (d_{ID_S} + \beta_{ID_S} x_{ID_S})H_2(w_0) + rP, C_2 = r(\beta_{ID_R} P_{ID_R} + R_{ID_R} + \alpha_{ID_R} P_{pub})$.

Challenge: The adversary $\mathcal{A}$ chooses another keyword w_1, sends w_0, w_1 and the challenge identity ID_R to the challenger $\mathcal{C}$. $\mathcal{C}$ randomly chooses $b \in \{0, 1\}$, computes $T_{w_b} \leftarrow \texttt{Trapdoor}(w_b, Pk_S, Sk_R)$ and returns it to $\mathcal{A}$.

The adversary $\mathcal{A}$ runs $\texttt{Test}(Pk_{ID_R}, T_{w_b}, C_{w_0}) \rightarrow c$.

Guess: If $c = 1$, the adversary $\mathcal{A}$ outputs a bit $b' = 0$; otherwise, $\mathcal{A}$ outputs a bit $b' = 1$. It always wins the game since $b' = b$ holds.

5   Our New CLPAEKS Scheme

In this section, we first present a new CLPAEKS scheme by improving He et al.'s scheme [12] and then prove that it satisfies our security definitions.

5.1   Construction

To obtain our new scheme, we modify their *Setup, CLPAEKS, Trapdoor,* and *Test* algorithms. We only outline the improved four algorithms for simplicity.

1. **Setup** : Given a security parameter l, besides the parameter choice in the original algorithm, KGC additionally chooses a generator Q of $\mathbb{G}_1$.
2. **CLPAEKS** : Given the sender's identity ID_S, the receiver's identity ID_R, the sender's secret key SK_{ID_S}, the receiver's public key Pk_{ID_R}, the keyword w, the sender chooses a random number $r \in \mathbb{Z}_q^*$, computes $\beta_{ID_S}, \beta_{ID_R}, C_2$ as before and $C_1 = (d_{ID_S} + \beta_{ID_S} x_{ID_S})H_2(ID_S, ID_R, w) + rQ$.
3. **Trapdoor** : Given the sender's identity ID_S, the receiver's identity ID_R, the sender's public key Pk_{ID_S} and the receiver's private key SK_{ID_R}, the receiver computes $\beta_{ID_S}, \beta_{ID_R}$ as before and $T_w = e((d_{ID_R} + \beta_{ID_R} x_{ID_R})H_2(ID_S, ID_R, w), \beta_{ID_S} P_{ID_S} + R_{ID_S} + \alpha_{ID_S} P_{pub})$.
4. **Test** : Given the receiver's identity ID_R, the receiver's public key Pk_{ID_R}, the trapdoor T_w, and the ciphertext C_w, the server computes β_{ID_R} as before, and checks if $T_w e(C_2, Q) = e(C_1, \beta_{ID_R} P_{ID_R} + R_{ID_R} + \alpha_{ID_R} P_{pub})$.

5.2   Security Proof

We only provide the proof sketch here. The probability computation is detailed in the full version of this paper[1].

---

[1] Please contact the authors for it.

Theorem 1. *If the adversary $\mathcal{A}$ wins the trapdoor privacy game with advantage ϵ_T, then there exists a probabilistic polynomial time (PPT) adversary $\mathcal{B}$ which can solve the DBDH problem with advantage*

$$\epsilon_{DBDH} \geq min\{\epsilon_T \cdot (1 - \frac{2}{q_{h_1}})^{q_{SV}} \cdot \frac{2}{(q_T + q_C)e}, \epsilon_T \cdot (1 - \frac{1}{q_{h_1}})^{q_{SV} + q_{PPK}} \cdot \frac{2}{(q_T + q_C)e}\}$$

where q_{h_1} is the number of h_1 queries, q_{SV} is the number of extract secret value queries, q_{PPK} is the number of partial private queries, q_T is the number of trapdoor queries and q_C is the number of ciphertext queries.

Proof. Assume that there is a PPT adversary $\mathcal{A}$ which breaks the trapdoor privacy of our CLPAEKS scheme with a non-negligible advantage ϵ_T, we will use it to construct another PPT algorithm $\mathcal{B}$ to solve the DBDH problem.

Game 1 (type 1 adversary):

Setup: The algorithm $\mathcal{B}$ takes a DBDH problem instance as input, i.e., $(\mathbb{G}_1, \mathbb{G}_2, e, q, P, xP, yP, zP, Z)$ where x, y, z are randomly chosen from $\mathbb{Z}_q$. Z is either $e(g, g)^{xyz}$ or a random element of $\mathbb{G}_2$. Let b be a bit such that $b = 0$ if $Z = e(P, P)^{xyz}$, and $b = 1$ if Z is random. $\mathcal{A}$ chooses the challenge sender's identity ID_S and the challenge receiver's identity ID_R. The new public key for the replace public key query with respect to ID_S is P'_{ID_S}. $\mathcal{B}$ randomly chooses $t, \alpha_{ID_S}, \beta_{ID_S} \in \mathbb{Z}_q^*$, $R_{ID_S} \in \mathbb{G}_1$, computes $Q = tP, P_{pub} = \frac{1}{\alpha_{ID_S}}(xP - \beta_{ID_S}P'_{ID_S} - R_{ID_S})$, adds $<ID_S, R_{ID_S}, \alpha_{ID_S}>$ to the L_{h_1} and $<ID_S, R_{ID_S}, \perp, \beta_{ID_S}>$ to L_{E_1}, sets the public parameters as $Param = \{\mathbb{G}_1, \mathbb{G}_2, e, q, P, Q, P_{pub}\}$, the challenge receiver ID_R's public key as $P_{ID_R} = yP$, adds $<ID_R, \perp, P_{ID_R}>$ to the L_{E_2} and sends $(Param, P_{ID_R})$ to the adversary $\mathcal{A}$.

Query: The adversary $\mathcal{A}$ is allowed to issue the following queries:

- h_1 query: $\mathcal{B}$ maintains an L_{h_1} list, which contains tuples $<ID_i, R_{ID_i}, \alpha_i>$. Upon receiving $\mathcal{A}$'s query on (ID_i, R_{ID_i}), if the tuple $<ID_i, R_{ID_i}, \alpha_i>$ is already in the L_{h_1} list, $\mathcal{B}$ returns α_i; otherwise, $\mathcal{B}$ randomly chooses $\alpha_i \in Z_q^*$, adds $<ID_i, R_{ID_i}, \alpha_i>$ to the L_{h_1} list and returns α_i.
- H_2 query: $\mathcal{B}$ maintains an L_{H_2} list, which contains tuples $<w_i, ID_{S'}, ID_{R'}, \mu_i, c_i, H_i>$. Upon receiving $\mathcal{A}$'s query, if the tuple $<w_i, ID_{S'}, ID_{R'}, \mu_i, c_i, H_i>$ is already in the L_{H_2} list, $\mathcal{B}$ returns H_i; otherwise, $\mathcal{B}$ randomly chooses $\mu_i \in Z_q^*$, tosses a coin $c_i \in \{0, 1\}$ so that $Pr[c_i = 0] = \delta$, $\mathcal{B}$ sets $H_i = (1 - c_i)zP + \mu_i P$, adds $<w_i, ID_{S'}, ID_{R'}, \mu_i, c_i, H_i>$ to the L_{H_2} list and returns H_i.
- h_3 query: $\mathcal{B}$ maintains an L_{h_3} list, which contains tuples $<ID_i, P_{ID_i}, R_{ID_i}, \beta_i>$. Upon receiving $\mathcal{A}$'s query on $(ID_i, P_{ID_i}, R_{ID_i})$, if the tuple $<ID_i, P_{ID_i}, R_{ID_i}, \beta_i>$ is already in the L_{h_3} list, $\mathcal{B}$ returns β_i; otherwise, $\mathcal{B}$ randomly chooses $\beta_i \in Z_q^*$, adds $<ID_i, P_{ID_i}, R_{ID_i}, \beta_i>$ to L_{h_3} list and returns β_i.
- Extract partial private key query: $\mathcal{B}$ maintains an L_{E_1} list, which contains tuples $<ID_i, R_{ID_i}, d_{ID_i}, \beta_i>$. Upon receiving $\mathcal{A}$'s query on ID_i, if $<ID_i, R_{ID_i}, d_{ID_i}, \beta_i>$ is already in the L_{E_1} list, $\mathcal{B}$ returns β_i; otherwise,

1. if $ID_i \neq ID_S$, $\mathcal{B}$ randomly chooses $d_{ID_i}, \alpha_i \in Z_q^*$, computes $R_{ID_i} = d_{ID_i}P - \alpha_i P_{pub}$, adds $<ID_i, R_{ID_i}, \alpha_i>$ to the L_{h_1} list and $<ID_i, R_{ID_i}, d_{ID_i}, \beta_i>$ to L_{E_1}.

2. if $ID_i = ID_S$, $\mathcal{B}$ aborts. (This event is denoted by E_4.)

- Extract secret value query: $\mathcal{B}$ maintains an L_{E_2} list, which contains tuples $<ID_i, x_{ID_i}, P_{ID_i}>$. Upon receiving $\mathcal{A}$'s query on ID_i,

   1. if $ID_i \neq ID_R$, $\mathcal{B}$ randomly chooses $x_i \in Z_q^*$, computes $P_{ID_i} = x_{ID_i}P$, adds $<ID_i, x_{ID_i}, P_{ID_i}>$ to the L_{E_2} list and returns x_{ID_i}.

   2. if $ID_i = ID_R$, $\mathcal{B}$ aborts. (This event is denoted by E_1.)

- Request public key query: Upon receiving $\mathcal{A}$'s query on ID_i, $\mathcal{B}$ retrieves the corresponding R_{ID_i}, P_{ID_i} from L_{E_1}, L_{E_2} and returns the public key $Pk_{ID_i} = (R_{ID_i}, P_{ID_i})$ to $\mathcal{A}$.

- Replace public key query: Upon receiving $\mathcal{A}$'s query on $(ID_i, R_{ID_i}, P'_{ID_i})$, $\mathcal{B}$ sets $P_{ID_i} = P'_{ID_i}, d_{ID_i} = \bot, x_{ID_i} = \bot$. $\mathcal{A}$ is prohibited from replacing ID_R's public key, which would enable $\mathcal{A}$ to trivially win the distinguishing game. $\mathcal{A}$ is also prohibited from both replacing the public key for the challenge sender's identity ID_S before the challenge phase and extracting the partial private key for ID_S, which would enable $\mathcal{A}$ to obtain both parts of ID_S's private key.

- Trapdoor query: Upon receiving $\mathcal{A}$'s query, $\mathcal{B}$ retrieves $<w_i, ID_{S'}, ID_{R'}, \mu_i, c_i, H_i>$ from the L_{H_2} list,

   1. if $c_i = 0$, $\mathcal{B}$ aborts. (This event is denoted by E_2.)

   2. otherwise, $\mathcal{B}$ gets $Pk_{ID_{R'}} = (R_{ID_{R'}}, P_{ID_{R'}}), Pk_{ID_{S'}} = (R_{ID_{S'}}, P_{ID_{S'}})$ by launching the *request public key query*, retrieves $\alpha_{ID_{S'}}, \beta_{ID_{S'}}, \alpha_{ID_{R'}}, \beta_{ID_{R'}}$ from the L_{h_1}, L_{h_3} list, computes $T_{w_i} = e(\mu_i(R_{ID_{S'}} + \alpha_{ID_{S'}}P_{pub} + \beta_{ID_{S'}}P_{ID_{S'}}), \beta_{ID_{R'}}P_{ID_{R'}} + R_{ID_{R'}} + \alpha_{ID_{R'}}P_{pub})$, returns T_{w_i} to $\mathcal{A}$.

- Ciphertext query: Upon receiving $\mathcal{A}$'s query, $\mathcal{B}$ retrieves $<w_i, ID_{S'}, ID_{R'}, \mu_i, c_i, H_i>$ from the L_{H_2} list,

   1. if $c_i = 0$, $\mathcal{B}$ aborts. (This event is denoted by E_2.)

   2. otherwise, $\mathcal{B}$ gets $Pk_{ID_{R'}} = (R_{ID_{R'}}, P_{ID_{R'}}), Pk_{ID_{S'}} = (R_{ID_{S'}}, P_{ID_{S'}})$ by launching the request public key query, retrieves $\alpha_{ID_{S'}}, \beta_{ID_{S'}}, \alpha_{ID_{R'}}, \beta_{ID_{R'}}$ from L_{h_1}, L_{h_3}, computes $C_1 = \mu_i(\beta_{ID_{S'}}P_{ID_{S'}} + R_{ID_{S'}} + \alpha_{ID_{S'}}P_{pub}) + rQ, C_2 = r(\beta_{ID_{R'}}P_{ID_{R'}} + R_{ID_{R'}} + \alpha_{ID_{R'}}P_{pub})$, returns $C = (C_1, C_2)$ to $\mathcal{A}$.

Challenge: The adversary $\mathcal{A}$ chooses two keywords w_0, w_1 s.t. $(Pk_{ID_S}, Pk_{ID_R}, w_0), (Pk_{ID_S}, Pk_{ID_R}, w_1)$ have not been queried for trapdoor and ciphertext, sends them to $\mathcal{B}$. $\mathcal{B}$ retrieves $<w_0, ID_S, ID_R, \mu_0, c_0, H_0>, <w_1, ID_S, ID_R, \mu_1, c_1, H_1>$ from L_{H_2}.

1. if $c_0 = c_1 = 1$, $\mathcal{B}$ aborts and outputs a random bit b' as its guess. (This event is denoted by E_3.)

2. otherwise, let $\hat{b}$ be the bit s.t. $c_{\hat{b}} = 0$, $\mathcal{B}$ computes the challenge trapdoor $T_{w_{\hat{b}}}$ as follows and returns it to $\mathcal{A}$.

$$T_{w_{\hat{b}}} = e(zP, xP)^{d_{ID_R}} e(P, xP)^{d_{ID_R}\mu_i} Z^{\beta_{ID_R}} e(yP, xP)^{\beta_{ID_R}\mu_i}.$$

If $Z = e(P, P)^{xyz}$, then we have:

$$T_{w_{\hat{b}}} = e((d_{ID_R} + \beta_{ID_R} x_{ID_R}) H_2(ID_S, ID_R, w_{\hat{b}}), \beta_{ID_S} P_{ID_S} + R_{ID_S} + \alpha_{ID_S} P_{pub}).$$

If Z is a random element from $\mathbb{G}_2$, so is $T_{w_{\hat{b}}}$.

Query: $\mathcal{A}$ continues launching queries with the same restrictions.

Guess: The adversary $\mathcal{A}$ outputs a bit $\hat{b}'$. If $\hat{b}' = \hat{b}$, $\mathcal{B}$ outputs $b' = 0$; otherwise, it outputs $b' = 1$.

Game 2 (type 2 adversary):

Setup: The algorithm $\mathcal{B}$ takes a DBDH problem instance as input, i.e., $(\mathbb{G}_1, \mathbb{G}_2, e, q, P, xP, yP, zP, Z)$ where x, y, z are randomly chosen from $\mathbb{Z}_q$. Z is either $e(P, P)^{xyz}$ or a random element of $\mathbb{G}_2$. Let b be a bit such that $b = 0$ if $Z = e(g, g)^{xyz}$, and $b = 1$ if Z is random. $\mathcal{A}$ chooses the challenge sender's identity ID_S and the challenge receiver's identity ID_R. $\mathcal{B}$ randomly chooses $t, s \in \mathbb{Z}_q^*$, computes $Q = tP, P_{pub} = sP$ and sets the public parameters as $Param = \{\mathbb{G}_1, \mathbb{G}_2, e, q, P, Q, P_{pub}\}$, the challenge sender ID_S's public key as $P_{ID_S} = xP$ and the challenge receiver ID_R's public key as $P_{ID_R} = yP$, adds $<ID_S, \bot, P_{ID_S}>, < ID_R, \bot, P_{ID_R}>$ to the L_{E_2}, and sends $(Param, P_{ID_S}, P_{ID_R})$ to the adversary $\mathcal{A}$.

Query: Here we only detail different answers from that of Game 1:

- Extract partial private key query: $\mathcal{B}$ maintains an L_{E_1} list, which contains tuples $<ID_i, R_{ID_i}, d_{ID_i}, \beta_i>$. Upon receiving $\mathcal{A}$'s query on ID_i, $\mathcal{B}$ randomly chooses $r_{ID_i} \in Z_q^*$ and looks up the L_{h_1} list. If the tuple $<ID_i, R_{ID_i}, \alpha_i>$ is already in the L_{h_1} list, $\mathcal{B}$ retrieves α_i; otherwise, randomly chooses $\alpha_{ID_i} \in Z_q^*$ and adds $<ID_i, R_{ID_i}, \alpha_{ID_i}>$ to the L_{h_1} list. $\mathcal{B}$ computes $d_{ID_i} = r_{ID_i} + s\alpha (\mathrm{mod}\ q), R_{ID_i} = r_{ID_i} P$, adds $<ID_i, R_{ID_i}, d_{ID_i}>$ to the L_{E_1} list and returns R_{ID_i}, d_{ID_i}.
- Extract secret value query: $\mathcal{B}$ maintains an L_{E_2} list, which contains tuples $<ID_i, x_{ID_i}, P_{ID_i}>$. Upon receiving $\mathcal{A}$'s query on ID_i,
  1. if $ID_i \neq ID_S, ID_R$, $\mathcal{B}$ randomly chooses $x_i \in Z_q^*$, computes $P_{ID_i} = x_{ID_i} P$, adds $<ID_i, x_{ID_i}, P_{ID_i}>$ to the L_{E_2} list and returns x_{ID_i}.
  2. if $ID_i = ID_S$, $\mathcal{B}$ aborts. (This event is denoted by E_1.)
  3. if $ID_i = ID_R$, $\mathcal{B}$ aborts. (This event is denoted by E_1.)
- Request public key query: Upon receiving $\mathcal{A}$'s query on ID_i, $\mathcal{B}$ retrieves the corresponding R_{ID_i}, P_{ID_i} from L_{E_1}, L_{E_2} and returns the public key $Pk_{ID_i} = (R_{ID_i}, P_{ID_i})$ to $\mathcal{A}$. replacing the public key for the challenge receiver's identity ID_R before the challenge phase and extracting the partial private key for ID_R in some phase, which would enable $\mathcal{A}$ to receive a challenge trapdoor under a public key for which it could compute the private key.

Challenge: The adversary $\mathcal{A}$ chooses two keywords w_0, w_1 s.t. $(Pk_{ID_S}, Pk_{ID_R}, w_0), (Pk_{ID_S}, Pk_{ID_R}, w_1)$ have not been queried for trapdoor and ciphertext, sends them to $\mathcal{B}$. $\mathcal{B}$ retrieves $<w_0, ID_S, ID_R, \mu_0, c_0, H_0>$, $< w_1, ID_S, ID_R, \mu_1, c_1, H_1>$ from L_{H_2}.

1. if $c_0 = c_1 = 1$, $\mathcal{B}$ aborts and outputs a random bit b' as its guess. (This event is denoted by E_3.)
2. otherwise, let $\hat{b}$ be the bit s.t. $c_{\hat{b}} = 0$, $\mathcal{B}$ computes the challenge trapdoor $T_{w_{\hat{b}}}$ as follows and returns it to $\mathcal{A}$.

$$T_{w_{\hat{b}}} = e(zP, xP)^{d_{ID_R}\beta_{ID_S}} e(P, xP)^{d_{ID_R}\mu_i\beta_{ID_S}} Z^{\beta_{ID_R}\beta_{ID_S}} e(yP, xP)^{\beta_{ID_R}\mu_i\beta_{ID_S}}$$
$$e(zP, R_{ID_S} + \alpha_{ID_S}P_{pub})^{d_{ID_R}} e(P, R_{ID_S} + \alpha_{ID_S}P_{pub})^{d_{ID_R}\mu_i}$$
$$e(yP, zP)^{\beta_{ID_R}d_{ID_S}} e(yP, R_{ID_S} + \alpha_{ID_S}P_{pub}).$$

If $Z = e(P, P)^{xyz}$, then we have:

$$T_{w_{\hat{b}}} = e((d_{ID_R} + \beta_{ID_R}x_{ID_R})H_2(ID_S, ID_R, w_{\hat{b}}), \beta_{ID_S}P_{ID_S} + R_{ID_S} + \alpha_{ID_S}P_{pub}).$$

If Z is a random element from $\mathbb{G}_2$, so is $T_{w_{\hat{b}}}$.

Query: $\mathcal{A}$ continues launching queries with the same restrictions.

Guess: The adversary $\mathcal{A}$ outputs a bit $\hat{b}'$. If $\hat{b}' = \hat{b}$, $\mathcal{B}$ outputs $b' = 0$; otherwise, it outputs $b' = 1$.

Theorem 2. *If the adversary $\mathcal{A}$ wins the ciphertext indistinguishability game with advantage ϵ_C, then there exists a PPT adversary $\mathcal{B}$ which can solve the DLIN problem with advantage*

$$\epsilon_{DLIN} \geq min\{\epsilon_C \cdot (1 - \frac{2}{q_{h_1}})^{q_{SV}} \cdot \frac{2}{(q_T + q_C)e}, \epsilon_C \cdot (1 - \frac{1}{q_{h_1}})^{q_{SV}+q_{PPK}} \cdot \frac{2}{(q_T + q_C)e}\}$$

where q_{h_1} is the number of h_1 queries, q_{SV} is the number of extract secret value queries, q_{PPK} is the number of partial private queries, q_T is the number of trapdoor queries and q_C is the number of ciphertext queries.

Proof. Assume that there is a PPT adversary $\mathcal{A}$ which breaks the ciphertext indistinguishability of our CLPAEKS scheme with a non-negligible advantage ϵ_C, we will use it to construct another PPT algorithm $\mathcal{B}$ to solve the DLIN problem.

Game 3 (type 1 adversary):

Setup: The algorithm $\mathcal{B}$ takes a DLIN problem instance as input, i.e., $(\mathbb{G}_1, e, q, Q, x_1Q, x_2Q, xx_1Q, yx_2Q, Z)$ where x, y, x_1, x_2 are randomly chosen from $\mathbb{Z}_q$. Z is either $(x + y)Q$ or a random element of $\mathbb{G}_1$. Let b be a bit such that $b = 0$ if $Z = (x + y)Q$, and $b = 1$ if Z is random. $\mathcal{A}$ chooses the challenge sender's identity ID_S and the challenge receiver's identity ID_R. The new public key for the replace public key query with respect to ID_R is P'_{ID_R}. $\mathcal{B}$ sets $P = x_1Q$, the challenge sender ID_S's public key as $P_{ID_S} = xP = xx_1Q$, randomly chooses $\alpha_{ID_R}, \beta_{ID_R} \in \mathbb{Z}_q^*$, $R_{ID_R} \in \mathbb{G}_1$, adds $<ID_S, R_{ID_S}, \alpha_{ID_S}>$ to the L_{h_1}, $<ID_S, R_{ID_S}, \perp, \beta_{ID_S}>$ to L_{E_1}, $<ID_S, \perp, P_{ID_S}>$ to the L_{E_2}, sets the master public key as $P_{pub} = \frac{1}{\alpha_{ID_R}}(x_2Q - \beta_{ID_R}P'_{ID_R} - R_{ID_R})$, the public parameters as $Param = \{\mathbb{G}_1, \mathbb{G}_2, e, q, P, Q, P_{pub}\}$, and sends $(Param, P_{ID_S})$ to the adversary $\mathcal{A}$.

Query: Here we only detail different answers from that of Game 1:

- H_2 query: $\mathcal{B}$ maintains an L_{H_2} list, which contains tuples $<w_i, \mu_i, c_i, H_i>$. Upon receiving $\mathcal{A}$'s query on w_i, if the tuple $<w_i, \mu_i, c_i, H_i>$ is already in the L_{H_2} list, $\mathcal{B}$ returns H_i; otherwise, $\mathcal{B}$ randomly chooses $\mu_i \in Z_q^*$, tosses a coin $c_i \in \{0, 1\}$ so that $Pr[c_i = 0] = \delta$, $\mathcal{B}$ sets $H_i = c_i\mu_i P + (1 - c_i)\mu_i Q$, adds $<w_i, \mu_i, c_i, H_i>$ to the L_{H_2} list and returns H_i.
- Extract partial private key query: $\mathcal{B}$ answers queries and denotes event E_4 in the similar way as in Game 1. The only difference is the two cases are divided by checking whether $ID_i = ID_R$ rather than checking $ID_i = ID_S$.
- Extract secret value query: $\mathcal{B}$ answers queries and denotes event E_1 in the similar way as in Game 1. The only difference is the two cases are divided by checking whether $ID_i = ID_S$ rather than checking $ID_i = ID_R$.
- Replace public key query: $\mathcal{B}$ answers queries in the same way as in Game 1. $\mathcal{A}$ is prohibited from replacing ID_S's public key, and both replacing the public key for the challenge receiver's identity ID_R before the challenge phase and extracting the partial private key for ID_R.

Challenge: The adversary $\mathcal{A}$ chooses two keywords w_0, w_1 s.t. $(Pk_{ID_S}, w_0), (Pk_{ID_S}, w_1)$ have not been queried for trapdoor and (Pk_{ID_R}, w_0), (Pk_{ID_R}, w_1) have not been queried for ciphertext, sends them to $\mathcal{B}$. $\mathcal{B}$ retrieves $<w_0, \mu_0, c_0, H_0>, <w_1, \mu_1, c_1, H_1>$ from L_{H_2}.

1. if $c_0 = c_1 = 1$, $\mathcal{B}$ aborts and outputs a random bit b' as its guess. (This event is denoted by E_3.)
2. otherwise, let $\hat{b}$ be the bit s.t. $c_{\hat{b}} = 0$, $\mathcal{B}$ computes the challenge ciphertext $C_{\hat{b}}$ as follows and returns it to $\mathcal{A}$.

$$C_{1,\hat{b}} = d_{ID_S} \cdot \mu_{\hat{b}} Q + \beta_{ID_S} \cdot \mu_{\hat{b}} \cdot (x + y)Q,$$
$$C_{2,\hat{b}} = \beta_{ID_S} \cdot \mu_{\hat{b}} \cdot yx_2 Q.$$

If $Z = (x + y)Q$, then we have:

$$C_{1,\hat{b}} = (d_{ID_S} + \beta_{ID_S} \cdot x_{ID_S})\mu_{\hat{b}} Q + \beta_{ID_S} \cdot \mu_{\hat{b}} \cdot yQ,$$
$$C_{2,\hat{b}} = \beta_{ID_S} \cdot \mu_{\hat{b}} \cdot y(d_{ID_R} P + \beta_{ID_R} P_{ID_R}).$$

If Z is a random element from $\mathbb{G}_2$, so is $C_{1,\hat{b}}$.

Query: $\mathcal{A}$ continues launching queries with the same restrictions.

Guess: The adversary $\mathcal{A}$ outputs a bit $\hat{b}'$. If $\hat{b}' = \hat{b}$, $\mathcal{B}$ outputs $b' = 0$; otherwise, it outputs $b' = 1$.

Game 4 (type 2 adversary):

Setup: The algorithm $\mathcal{B}$ takes a DLIN problem instance as input, i.e., $(\mathbb{G}_1, e, q, Q, x_1 Q, x_2 Q, xx_1 Q, yx_2 Q, Z)$ where x, y, x_1, x_2 are randomly chosen from $\mathbb{Z}_q$. Z is either $(x + y)Q$ or a random element of $\mathbb{G}_1$. Let b be a bit such that $b = 0$ if $Z = (x+y)Q$, and $b = 1$ if Z is random. $\mathcal{A}$ chooses the challenge sender's identity ID_S and the challenge receiver's identity ID_R. $\mathcal{B}$ randomly chooses $s \in \mathbb{Z}_q^*$, computes $P_{pub} = sP$, sets $P = x_1 Q$, the public parameters as $Param = \{\mathbb{G}_1, \mathbb{G}_2, e, q, P, Q, P_{pub}\}$, the challenge sender ID_S's public key as $P_{ID_S} =$

$xP = xx_1Q$. $\mathcal{B}$ randomly chooses $\alpha_{ID_R}, r_{ID_R}, \beta_{ID_R} \in Z_q^*$, computes $d_{ID_R} = r_{ID_R} + s\alpha \pmod{q}$, $R_{ID_R} = r_{ID_R}P$. $\mathcal{B}$ sets the challenge receiver ID_R's public key as $P_{ID_R} = \frac{1}{\beta_{ID_R}}(x_2Q - d_{ID_R} \cdot x_1Q)$, s.t. $(d_{ID_R}P + \beta_{ID_R}P_{ID_R}) = x_2Q$. $\mathcal{B}$ adds $<ID_R, R_{ID_R}, \alpha_{ID_R}>, <ID_R, P_{ID_R}, R_{ID_i}, \beta_{ID_R}>, <ID_R, R_{ID_R}, d_{ID_R}>$ to the $L_{h_1}, L_{h_3}, L_{E_1}$ list, respectively, and sends $(Param, P_{ID_S}, P_{ID_R})$ to the adversary $\mathcal{A}$.

Query: Here we only detail different answers from that of Game 2:

- H_2 query: $\mathcal{B}$ maintains an L_{H_2} list, which contains tuples $<w_i, ID_{S'}, ID_{R'}, \mu_i, c_i, H_i>$. Upon receiving $\mathcal{A}$'s query on w_i, if the tuple $<w_i, ID_{S'}, ID_{R'}, \mu_i, c_i, H_i>$ is already in the L_{H_2} list, $\mathcal{B}$ returns H_i; otherwise, $\mathcal{B}$ randomly chooses $\mu_i \in Z_q^*$, tosses a coin $c_i \in \{0,1\}$ so that $Pr[c_i = 0] = \delta$, $\mathcal{B}$ sets $H_i = c_i\mu_iP + (1 - c_i)\mu_iQ$, adds $<w_i, \mu_i, c_i, H_i>$ to the L_{H_2} and returns H_i.

Challenge: The adversary $\mathcal{A}$ chooses two keywords w_0, w_1 s.t. (Pk_{ID_S}, w_0), (Pk_{ID_S}, w_1) have not been queried for trapdoor and $(Pk_{ID_R}, w_0), (Pk_{ID_R}, w_1)$ have not been queried for ciphertext, sends them to $\mathcal{B}$. $\mathcal{B}$ retrieves $<w_0, \mu_0, c_0, H_0>, <w_1, \mu_1, c_1, H_1>$ from L_{H_2}.

1. if $c_0 = c_1 = 1$, $\mathcal{B}$ aborts and outputs a random bit b' as its guess. (This event is denoted by E_3.)
2. otherwise, let $\hat{b}$ be the bit s.t. $c_{\hat{b}} = 0$, $\mathcal{B}$ computes the challenge ciphertext $C_{\hat{b}}$ as follows and returns it to $\mathcal{A}$.

$$C_{1,\hat{b}} = d_{ID_S} \cdot \mu_{\hat{b}}Q + \beta_{ID_S} \cdot \mu_{\hat{b}} \cdot (x + y)Q,$$
$$C_{2,\hat{b}} = \beta_{ID_S} \cdot \mu_{\hat{b}} \cdot yx_2Q.$$

If $Z = (x + y)Q$, then we have:

$$C_{1,\hat{b}} = (d_{ID_S} + \beta_{ID_S} \cdot x_{ID_S})\mu_{\hat{b}}Q + \beta_{ID_S} \cdot \mu_{\hat{b}} \cdot yQ,$$
$$C_{2,\hat{b}} = \beta_{ID_S} \cdot \mu_{\hat{b}} \cdot y(d_{ID_R}P + \beta_{ID_R}P_{ID_R}).$$

If Z is a random element from $\mathbb{G}_2$, so is $C_{1,\hat{b}}$.

Query: $\mathcal{A}$ continues launching queries with the same restrictions.

Guess: The adversary $\mathcal{A}$ outputs a bit $\hat{b}'$. If $\hat{b}' = \hat{b}$, $\mathcal{B}$ outputs $b' = 0$; otherwise, it outputs $b' = 1$.

6   Conclusion

In this work, we re-formalized the security definitions of CLPAEKS. Under the proposed security models, we pointed out the weakness of an existing scheme and worked out a new scheme by modifying the original one. Finally, we proved the new scheme is secure under the assumptions of DBDH and DLIN.

Acknowledgement. This work is supported by the National Natural Science Foundation of China (Nos. 61872152, 61872409), Guangdong Natural Science Funds for Distinguished Young Scholar (No. 2014A030306021), Guangdong Program for Special Support of Top-notch Young Professionals (No. 2015TQ01X796), and the Graduate Student Overseas Study Program of South China Agricultural University (No. 2018LHPY025).

References

1. Al-Riyami, S.S., Paterson, K.G.: Certificateless public key cryptography. In: Laih, C.-S. (ed.) ASIACRYPT 2003. LNCS, vol. 2894, pp. 452–473. Springer, Heidelberg (2003). https://doi.org/10.1007/978-3-540-40061-5_29
2. Al-Riyami, S.S., Paterson, K.G.: CBE from CL-PKE: a generic construction and efficient schemes. In: Vaudenay, S. (ed.) PKC 2005. LNCS, vol. 3386, pp. 398–415. Springer, Heidelberg (2005). https://doi.org/10.1007/978-3-540-30580-4_27
3. Baek, J., Safavi-Naini, R., Susilo, W.: Certificateless public key encryption without pairing. In: Zhou, J., Lopez, J., Deng, R.H., Bao, F. (eds.) ISC 2005. LNCS, vol. 3650, pp. 134–148. Springer, Heidelberg (2005). https://doi.org/10.1007/11556992_10
4. Boneh, D., Boyen, X., Shacham, H.: Short group signatures. In: Franklin, M. (ed.) CRYPTO 2004. LNCS, vol. 3152, pp. 41–55. Springer, Heidelberg (2004). https://doi.org/10.1007/978-3-540-28628-8_3
5. Boneh, D., Di Crescenzo, G., Ostrovsky, R., Persiano, G.: Public key encryption with keyword search. In: Cachin, C., Camenisch, J.L. (eds.) EUROCRYPT 2004. LNCS, vol. 3027, pp. 506–522. Springer, Heidelberg (2004). https://doi.org/10.1007/978-3-540-24676-3_30
6. Boneh, D., Franklin, M.: Identity-based encryption from the Weil pairing. In: Kilian, J. (ed.) CRYPTO 2001. LNCS, vol. 2139, pp. 213–229. Springer, Heidelberg (2001). https://doi.org/10.1007/3-540-44647-8_13
7. Boyen, X.: The uber-assumption family. In: Galbraith, S.D., Paterson, K.G. (eds.) Pairing 2008. LNCS, vol. 5209, pp. 39–56. Springer, Heidelberg (2008). https://doi.org/10.1007/978-3-540-85538-5_3
8. Byun, J.W., Rhee, H.S., Park, H.-A., Lee, D.H.: Off-line keyword guessing attacks on recent keyword search schemes over encrypted data. In: Jonker, W., Petković, M. (eds.) SDM 2006. LNCS, vol. 4165, pp. 75–83. Springer, Heidelberg (2006). https://doi.org/10.1007/11844662_6
9. Fang, L., Susilo, W., Ge, C., Wang, J.: Public key encryption with keyword search secure against keyword guessing attacks without random oracle. Inf. Sci. **238**, 221–241 (2013)
10. Golle, P., Staddon, J., Waters, B.: Secure conjunctive keyword search over encrypted data. In: Jakobsson, M., Yung, M., Zhou, J. (eds.) ACNS 2004. LNCS, vol. 3089, pp. 31–45. Springer, Heidelberg (2004). https://doi.org/10.1007/978-3-540-24852-1_3
11. Guo, L., Yau, W.C.: Efficient secure-channel free public key encryption with keyword search for EMRs in cloud storage. J. Med. Syst. **39**(2), 11 (2015)
12. He, D., Ma, M., Zeadally, S., Kumar, N., Liang, K.: Certificateless public key authenticated encryption with keyword search for industrial internet of things. IEEE Trans. Ind. Inform. **14**(8), 3618–3627 (2018)
13. Huang, Q., Li, H.: An efficient public-key searchable encryption scheme secure against inside keyword guessing attacks. Inf. Sci. **403**, 1–14 (2017)

14. Huang, X., Susilo, W., Mu, Y., Zhang, F.: On the security of certificateless signature schemes from Asiacrypt 2003. In: Desmedt, Y.G., Wang, H., Mu, Y., Li, Y. (eds.) CANS 2005. LNCS, vol. 3810, pp. 13–25. Springer, Heidelberg (2005). https://doi.org/10.1007/11599371_2

15. Ma, S., Huang, Q., Zhang, M., Yang, B.: Efficient public key encryption with equality test supporting flexible authorization. IEEE Trans. Inf. Forensics Secur. **10**(3), 458–470 (2015)

16. Park, D.J., Kim, K., Lee, P.J.: Public key encryption with conjunctive field keyword search. In: Lim, C.H., Yung, M. (eds.) WISA 2004. LNCS, vol. 3325, pp. 73–86. Springer, Heidelberg (2005). https://doi.org/10.1007/978-3-540-31815-6_7

17. Rhee, H.S., Susilo, W., Kim, H.J.: Secure searchable public key encryption scheme against keyword guessing attacks. IEICE Electron. Express **6**(5), 237–243 (2009)

18. Sun, W., Yu, S., Lou, W., Hou, Y.T., Li, H.: Protecting your right: verifiable attribute-based keyword search with fine-grained owner-enforced search authorization in the cloud. IEEE Trans. Parallel Distrib. Syst. **27**(4), 1187–1198 (2016)

19. Wang, C.H., Tu, T.Y.: Keyword search encryption scheme resistant against keyword-guessing attack by the untrusted server. J. Shanghai Jiaotong Univ. (Sci.) **19**(4), 440–442 (2014)

20. Xu, P., Jin, H., Wu, Q., Wang, W.: Public-key encryption with fuzzy keyword search: a provably secure scheme under keyword guessing attack. IEEE Trans. Comput. **62**(11), 2266–2277 (2013)

21. Yau, W.-C., Heng, S.-H., Goi, B.-M.: Off-line keyword guessing attacks on recent public key encryption with keyword search schemes. In: Rong, C., Jaatun, M.G., Sandnes, F.E., Yang, L.T., Ma, J. (eds.) ATC 2008. LNCS, vol. 5060, pp. 100–105. Springer, Heidelberg (2008). https://doi.org/10.1007/978-3-540-69295-9_10

22. Zheng, Y.: Digital signcryption or how to achieve cost(signature & encryption) << cost(signature)+ cost(encryption). In: Kaliski, B.S. (ed.) CRYPTO 1997. LNCS, vol. 1294, pp. 165–179. Springer, Heidelberg (1997). https://doi.org/10.1007/BFb0052234

Space-Efficient and Secure Substring Searchable Symmetric Encryption Using an Improved DAWG

Hiroaki Yamamoto[1(✉)], Yoshihiro Wachi[2], and Hiroshi Fujiwara[1]

[1] Department of Electrical and Computer Engineering, Shinshu University,
4-17-1 Wakasato, Nagano-shi 380-8553, Japan
{yamamoto,fujiwara}@cs.shinshu-u.ac.jp
[2] NTT COMWARE CORPORATION, Minato-ku, Tokyo, Japan

Abstract. A searchable symmetric encryption (SSE) scheme is a method which searches encrypted data without decrypting it. In this paper, we address the substring search problem such that for a set D of documents and a pattern p, we find all occurrences of p in D. Here a document and a pattern are defined as strings and are encrypted. A directed acyclic word graph (DAWG), which is a deterministic finite automaton, is known for solving a substring search problem on a plaintext. We improve a DAWG so that all transitions of a DAWG have distinct symbols and present a space-efficient and secure substring SSE scheme using an improved DAWG. The novel feature of an improved DAWG is that we can solve the substring search problem using only the labels of transitions. The proposed substring SSE scheme consists of an index with a simple structure and the size is $O(n)$ for the total size n of documents.

1 Introduction

1.1 Backgrounds

In recent years, remote storage services are rapidly spreading in cloud computing. In such a system, there is often a case where a user wants to protect the confidentiality of data on a remote server. In the field of information retrieval, developing a technique for efficiently searching the encrypted data while protecting the confidentiality of data and a query is a major topic. Such a search technique is called searchable encryption, and in particular, a scheme using symmetric key encryption is called *searchable symmetric encryption* (SSE). To securely search data (or documents) with an SSE scheme, the user first generates an encrypted data, including an encrypted index, and stores it on the server. Later, the user interacts with the server to carry out a search on encrypted data. Up to now, researches on SSE schemes have been actively done under such a background [4, 6, 8, 10–13, 16, 17, 19–22, 25].

© Springer Nature Switzerland AG 2019
R. Steinfeld and T. H. Yuen (Eds.): ProvSec 2019, LNCS 11821, pp. 130–148, 2019.
https://doi.org/10.1007/978-3-030-31919-9_8

1.2   Our Contributions

Most of SSE schemes proposed until now support only exact keyword search, and therefore one of the challenging problems for SSE is to develop a secure scheme to efficiently search for all substrings appearing in a document. Here a document is a text string. A trivial technique is that we store all substrings occurring in a document in an index. However, this method generates a huge index because there are $O(n^2)$ substrings in a document of length n. Reducing the size of an index is an important problem. Toward solving this problem, several substring search schemes have been proposed [7,9,13,18,23,26].

A directed acyclic word graph (DAWG) [1,2] for a string w is a deterministic finite automaton (DFA) that accepts all substrings of w and is known as an efficient data structure for representing all substrings. Yamamoto [26] has developed a substring SSE scheme (YA-scheme) using a DAWG by introducing an idea of block words. However YA-scheme needs a large index to enhance the security because the size is in proportion to the size of a block word. Furthermore YA-scheme cannot completely hide the occurrence frequencies of all characters and meets only non-adaptive security.

We will propose a new substring SSE scheme by improving a DAWG. In general, all symbols of transitions of a DAWG are not always distinct. We improve a DAWG by allowing a transition with a string so that all transitions are performed by distinct strings. The improved DAWG is called *an augmented DAWG* (ADAWG) and a string used by a transition of an ADAWG is called *a meta-symbol*. The big advantage of an ADAWG is that we can simulate an ADAWG using only meta-symbols. Therefore we do not need to store transitions of an ADAWG in an index. Furthermore, since all meta-symbols of transitions of an ADAWG are distinct, our scheme can completely hide the occurrence frequencies of characters and the structure of an ADAWG without using dummy data. These features enable us to design a space-efficient and secure substring SSE scheme. The schemes [7,18] need dummy data to hide the tree structure or the occurrence frequencies of characters. The drawback is that the search time get larger a little at the worst case. Let us summarize our scheme below. Here let $D = \{d_0, \cdots, d_{N-1}\}$ be a set of N documents and q be a query of length m. $n_D = \sum_{d_i \in D} |d_i|$ and $D(q)$ is the set of all document ID and position pairs (id, pos) such that q appears at position pos in document d_{id}. A document and a query are defined as a string on an alphabet Σ.

- For any query q of length m, the proposed scheme finds all document ID and position pairs at which q appears. The size of the index is $O(n_D)$ and the search time is $O(m^2 + |D(q)|)$. Our scheme consists of an index with a simpler structure than other substring SSE schemes, and it is possible to make the hidden constant factor of $O(n_D)$ small. The number of rounds of communication between a user and a server is three for a search.
- Adaptive Security: It can be proved that the proposed scheme is adaptively secure under similar leakages as the scheme in [7].

– Frequency and Structure: Our scheme hides frequencies of all characters occurring in a document and a query. If $N \geq 2$ then the number of occurrences of q per a document does not leak out. Furthermore our scheme hides the structure of an ADAWG.

Table 1. Comparison of substring search schemes. Here $k_\sigma = |\Sigma|$ and γ is the length of a block word. The column "# of rounds" denotes the number of rounds of communication between a user and a server for a search. The terms *adapt* and *non-adapt* mean adaptive security and non-adaptive security, respectively. The column "Struct" has "o" if the scheme can hide a data structure underlying an index and $\triangle$ if the scheme requires dummy data. The column "VL" has "o" if the scheme can search for a string of any length. The column "Freq" has "o" if the scheme can hide the occurrence frequency of any character and $\triangle$ if the scheme requires dummy data.

Scheme	# of rounds	Index size	Search time	Security	Struct	Freq	VL
CS-scheme [7]	4	$O(k_\sigma n_D)$	$O(k_\sigma m + |D(q)|)$	Adapt	$\triangle$	o	o
SOR-scheme [24]	3	$O(n_D)$	$O(m^2 + |D(q)|)$	Adapt	×	$\triangle$	o
YA-scheme [26]	3	$O(\gamma n_D)$	$O((m/\gamma)\log n_D + |D(q)|)$	Non-adapt	o	$\triangle$	o
LM-scheme [18]	3	$O(n_D)$	$O(n_D)$	Adapt	o	$\triangle$	$\triangle$
This work	3	$O(n_D)$	$O(m^2 + |D(q)|))$	Adapt	o	o	o

1.3 Related Works

Several substring SSE schemes have been proposed [7,9,13,18,23,26]. To the best of our knowledge, the existing substring SSE schemes can be classified into two types. One is a scheme which uses an advanced data structure which is used in a substring search for a plaintext to achieve sub-linear search time in n_D, and the other is a scheme which does not use such data structure. The schemes of [7,18,23,26] and our scheme belong to the former and the schemes of [9,13] belong to the latter. Faber et al. [9] applied the conjunctive search scheme of [5] to a substring search problem. Their scheme parses a string to k-grams (k consecutive characters) and then searches for the conjunction of the k-grams. The scheme can make a search in one round of communication, but the search time can be $O(n_D)$ because the time depends on the number of occurrences of a k-gram. Hahn [13] proposed a new substring SSE scheme for the existing database, but they use a special encryption scheme called frequency-hiding order-preserving encryption.

The schemes [7,18,23,26] using an advanced data structure aim to achieve search time sublinear in n_D and index size linear in n_D. Since our scheme is also the same type, we compare our scheme with these schemes. Table 1 gives a comparison of these schemes. The search time of the user includes the time to make a trapdoor, but not include the time to decrypt encrypted documents returned from the server. Since we have already discussed YA-scheme, we discuss the other schemes.

Chase and Shen [7] proposed a scheme (CS-scheme) based on a suffix tree which is a data structure constructed from all suffixes of a string. They say that the number of rounds of communication is three in [7]. However, the user gets encrypted IDs from the serve after the third round. Therefore, for the user to get the documents corresponding IDs from the server, the user must send decrypted IDs to the server. Hence CS-scheme needs four rounds. The time and space complexity of CS-scheme depend on $k_\sigma = |\Sigma|$. Therefore CS-scheme runs faster if k_σ is small. However, if $k_\sigma > m$, then the running time is slower than our scheme. Furthermore the size of the index can be drastically large because CS-scheme must insert so many dummy data in the index in order to hide the structure of a suffix tree.

Leontiadis and Li [18] (LM-scheme) have presented a new substring SSE scheme by employing a data structure called FM-index, which is a combination of BWT transformation and a suffix array, for reducing the index size of CS-scheme. The size of the index is $O(n_D)$ and the hidden constant factor is small. LM-scheme regards a k-gram (which is called a bucket) as one symbol and inserts dummy buckets into the original string in order to hide the frequency of buckets. Since the search time depends on the number of occurrences of a bucket, the time becomes $O(n_D)$ in the worst case. Furthermore, for a query such that the length is less than k, LM-scheme does not clearly describe the search procedure. The described search procedure cannot search for such a query or always takes $O(n_D)$ time even if searching for it.

Strizhov and Ray [23,24] proposed a new substring SSE scheme (SOR-scheme) for a space-efficient scheme. SOR-scheme [24] is the revised version of the scheme in [23] and is based on a position heap tree for a string. Their scheme first generates a position heap tree and then builds an encrypted index by encrypting each node of the tree. Hence the structure of the position heap tree is revealed. Furthermore SOR-scheme must compare a query and a document character by character to verify that the query occurs in the document. For that reason, SOR-scheme needs another index made by encrypting a character of documents one by one. This index leaks the frequency of characters. The search takes $O(m^2 + |D(q)|)$ time and needs three rounds of communication.

2   Preliminaries

Throughout this paper, Σ denotes an arbitrary finite alphabet, and a document and a query denote a string (word) in Σ^*. The empty string is denoted by ε. For a string $w \in \Sigma^*$, $|w|$ denotes the length of w. When W is a set, $|W|$ denotes the number of elements of W. For strings $w, x, y, z \in \Sigma^*$, if $w = xyz$, then y is called a substring of w. Let $FACT(w) = \{y \mid y \text{ is a substring of } w\}$ and $FACT(W) = \cup_{w \in W} FACT(w)$. For two strings x and y, $x||y$ denotes the concatenation of x and y.

We consider the following substring search problem. Let $D = \{d_0, \ldots, d_{N-1}\}$ be the set of N documents. We denote by $ID(d)$ the identifier of a document d, which is called a document ID. For a document d_i, $ID(d_i) = i$.

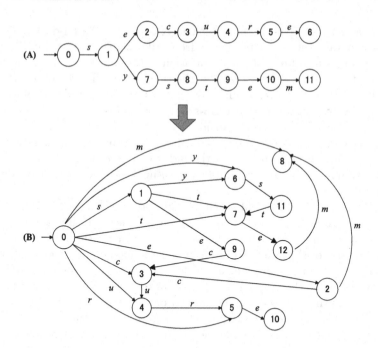

Fig. 1. A DAWG for $\{secure, system\}$

For a document d, we define $n_d = |d|$, $n_D = \sum_{d \in D} n_d$, and $D(q) = \{(i, j) \mid q \text{ appears at position } j \text{ in } d_i\}$. Then the substring search problem is, for a given string q (q is called *a query*), to find $D(q)$. In this paper, we address the substring search problem on encrypted documents using a symmetric encryption scheme. A symmetric encryption scheme consists of three (probabilistic) polynomial time algorithms $\mathsf{SKE} = (\mathsf{KeyGen}, \mathsf{Enc}, \mathsf{Dec})$, where $\mathsf{KeyGen}(1^\lambda)$ takes as an input a security parameter λ and randomly outputs a secret key sk; $\mathsf{Enc}(sk, d)$ takes as inputs a secret key sk and a document d, and returns an encrypted document c; $\mathsf{Dec}(sk, c)$ takes as inputs a key sk and an encrypted document c of d, and returns d if sk is the key that is used to produce c. As seen in [6], we require a symmetric encryption scheme to be secure against pseudorandom chosen-plaintext attacks (PCPA-security). For simplicity, by $\mathsf{Enc}_{sk}(\cdot)$ we denote an encryption function $\mathsf{Enc}(sk, \cdot)$ with a secret key sk. In addition, we use a pseudorandom function $F : \{0, 1\}^\lambda \times \{0, 1\}^{l_1} \to \{0, 1\}^{l_2}$, which is a polynomial-time function that cannot be distinguished from a random function (for example, refer to [15] for the definition). We write $F_{sk}(x)$ for $F(sk, x)$. We define a negligible function for a security definition.

Definition 1. *A function f from natural numbers to positive real numbers is negligible in a security parameter λ if for every positive polynomial $p(\cdot)$ there is an integer λ_0 such that for any $\lambda \geq \lambda_0$ it holds that $f(\lambda) < 1/p(\lambda)$.*

Our SSE scheme consists of two parties, a user and a server. The user is the owner of data and stores data in the server in an encrypted form. The user wants to search encrypted data on the server without revealing the contents of data to the server. We assume that the server is honest but curious. The SSE scheme works as follows.

1. Setup phase: The user constructs a secure index from the set D of documents and encrypts all documents d_i. After that, the user stores them in the server.
2. Search phase: For a query q, the user makes a trapdoor $TRAP(q)$ of q and sends it to the server. The user and the server search for the set $D(q)$ following a search protocol, and the user finally gets $D(q)$ and $\{c_i \mid (i,j) \in D(q)\}$. The user decrypts each c_i and gets the original document d_i.

3   An Augmented Directed Acyclic Word Graph

A directed acyclic word graph (DAWG) is data structure proposed by Blumer, Blumer and Haussler [1] for implementing efficient substring search. In this section, we propose a new data structure called *an augmented DAWG* by improving a DAWG.

3.1   A Directed Acyclic Word Graph

A DAWG for a string $w \in \Sigma^*$ is a deterministic finite automaton (DFA) that accepts $FACT(w)$. Blumer et al. [2] extended a DAWG for a set of strings. We here give definitions and properties of a DAWG. Let $W = \{w_0, \ldots, w_{N-1}\}$ be the set of text strings on Σ. For any string $w = a_1 \cdots a_n \in W$ and $v \in \Sigma^*$, let $end\text{-}set(v, w) = \{i \mid v = a_{i-|v|+1} \cdots a_i\}$. In particular, $end\text{-}set(\varepsilon, w) = \{0, 1, \ldots, n\}$. Then, we define an equivalence class such that strings x and y in Σ^* are equivalent on W if and only if for all $w \in W$, $end\text{-}set(x, w) = end\text{-}set(y, w)$. A DAWG $M(W) = (Q, \Sigma, \delta, init)$ is a DFA such that $M(W)$ accepts $FACT(W)$ and the set Q of states consists of all equivalence classes on W, where δ is the transition function and $init$ is the initial state. Since all states of Q become final states for a DAWG, we omit a set of final states. As with [26], we give a simple algorithm BuildDawg to construct a DAWG $M(W)$ from W in Algorithm 1. The algorithm BuildDawg uses the subset construction method which is the standard method to translate a nondeterministic finite automaton (NFA) into a DFA (for example, see [14]). In a nutshell, we first make a DFA $DF(W)$ which is a trie of W, and then constructs $M(W)$ from $DF(W)$ by setting the initial state of $M(W)$ to the set Q of states. A trie is a data structure for searching a text (for example, see [3]) and can be viewed as a DFA. The algorithm BuildDawg(W) runs in time $O(n_W^2)$, where $n_W = \sum_{w \in W} |w|$. The following proposition is obtained from the results of [1,2].

Algorithm 1. BuildDawg(W)

Input: $W = \{w_1, \ldots, w_k\}$ where w_i is a string on an alphabet Σ

1: make a trie $TR = (V, E)$ for W where V is the set of nodes and E is the set of directed edges. Then TR can be regarded as a DFA $DF(W) = (Q, \Sigma, \delta, p)$ where $Q = \{v \mid v \in V\}$ is a set of state, and the initial state p is the root of TR. Furthermore $\delta(v_1, a) = v_2$ if and only if $(v_1, v_2) \in E$ and the edge is labeled a symbol a.
2: {constructing a DAWG $M(W)$ from $DF(W)$ using the subset construction}
3: let us set the initial state of $M(W)$ to the set Q of states,
4: construct a DAWG $M(W)$ according to $DF(W)$, using the subset construction
5: number states of $M(W)$ from 0, where the initial state is numbered 0
6: **return** $M(W)$

Proposition 1. *(1) The number of states of $M(W)$ is at most $2n_W - 1$, and the number of transitions is at most $3n_W - 4$,*

(2) for any state of $M(W)$, all the incoming transitions of the state have the same symbol,

(3) for any string $x \in \Sigma^*$, $M(W)$ accepts x if and only if there is $w \in W$ such that $x \in FACT(w)$.

We say that for any string x, x is accepted by $M(W)$ at state st if $M(W)$ reaches state st after reading x. For any state st of $M(W)$, let $WORD(st)$ be the set of strings accepted by $M(W)$ at state st. Then note that $WORD(st)$ becomes the equivalence class corresponding to st.

Example 1. Let us give an example of a DAWG in Fig. 1. Given a DFA of (A) for $\{secure, system\}$, the DAWG of (B) is constructed using the subset construction method by setting the initial state of the DAWG to all states of (A). If we regard all states of (B) as the final states, then the DAWG exactly accepts all substrings of *secure* and *system*.

3.2 An Augmented DAWG

To make a secure index, we want to improve a DAWG such that all transitions have a distinct symbol. We achieve this purpose by allowing a DAWG to have a transition by a string. Let $M(W) = (Q, \Sigma, \delta, st_0)$ be the DAWG for a set W of strings. Then we give a new DAWG $\tilde{M}(W) = (Q, \tilde{\Sigma}, \tilde{\delta}, st_0)$ called *an augment DAWG* (ADAWG), which is defined as follows.

1. for any $st_1, st_2 \in Q$, if $\delta(st_1, a) = st_2$ is defined for a symbol $a \in \Sigma$, then we define $\tilde{\delta}(st_1, \sigma a) = st_2$, where σ is the shortest string in $WORD(st_1)$.
2. $\tilde{\Sigma} = \{\sigma \mid \sigma \in FACT(W)$ such that $\exists st_1, st_2 \in Q, \tilde{\delta}(st_1, \sigma) = st_2$ is defined$\}$. We call $\sigma \in \tilde{\Sigma}$ a *meta-symbol*. Note that a meta-symbol is a string over Σ.

Since each state of a DAWG corresponds to an equivalence class, the shortest string in $WORD(st_1)$ is exactly one. Therefore $\tilde{\delta}$ can be defined. We give an

---

Algorithm 2. BuildADawg(W)

Input: $W = \{w_0, \ldots, w_{N-1}\}$
1: make a DAWG $M(W) = (Q, \Sigma, \delta, st_0)$ from W using BuildDawg
2: *State* $\leftarrow \{st_0\}$ and *NEW* $\leftarrow \emptyset$
3: **for all** $st \in Q$ **do**
4:     $st.s \leftarrow \varepsilon$
5: **end for**
6: **while** *State* $\neq \emptyset$ **do**
7:     **for all** $st' \in$ *State* **do**
8:         **for all** transitions $\delta(st', a) = st$ **do**
9:             **if** a transition from st' to st in $\tilde{\delta}$ is not defined **then**
10:                 $\sigma \leftarrow st'.s\|a$, define $\tilde{\delta}(st', \sigma) = st$ and add σ to $\tilde{\Sigma}$,
11:                 **if** $st.s = \varepsilon$ **then**
12:                     $st.s \leftarrow \sigma$ {note that σ is the shortest string reachable to st.}
13:                 **end if**
14:                 *NEW* $\leftarrow$ *NEW* $\cup \{st\}$
15:             **end if**
16:         **end for**
17:     **end for**
18:     *State* $\leftarrow$ *NEW* and *NEW* $\leftarrow \emptyset$
19: **end while**
20: **return** ADAWG $\tilde{M}(W) = (Q, \tilde{\Sigma}, \tilde{\delta}, st_0)$

---

algorithm BuildADawg to construct an ADAWG in Algorithm 2 (Fig. 2). The algorithm BuildADawg(W) runs in time linear in the number of transitions of $M(W)$. An ADAWG $\tilde{M}(W) = (Q, \tilde{\Sigma}, \tilde{\delta}, st_0)$ has the following property.

Proposition 2. *(1) The number of states in $\tilde{M}(W)$ is the same as that of $M(W)$,*

(2) the number of transitions in $\tilde{M}(W)$ is the same as that of $M(W)$,

(3) for any two transitions $\tilde{\delta}(st_1, \sigma_1)$ and $\tilde{\delta}(st_2, \sigma_2)$, $\sigma_1 \neq \sigma_2$.

Proof. Properties (1) and (2) of Proposition 2 are obvious from the definition of an ADAWG. We prove property (3). Since the case $st_1 = st_2$ is obvious, we prove the case $st_1 \neq st_2$. Let us assume that $\sigma_1 = \sigma_2$ and $\sigma_1 = a\sigma$. We note that for any two states st_1 and st_2 in Q, the sets $WORD(st_1)$ and $WORD(st_2)$ are always disjoint because $M(W)$ is a DFA. Therefore, the state reachable by σ on $M(W)$ is exactly one. Hence $st_1 = st_2$ and then the property (3) holds.

Property (3) is a crucial property for security of our scheme because this leads that all transitions of an ADAWG have distinct meta-symbols. $M(W)$ and $\tilde{M}(W)$ have the same structure except for symbols of transitions. Now let q be a string accepted by $M(W)$ at state st and $\tilde{\sigma}_q$ be a sequence of meta-symbols accepted by $\tilde{M}(W)$ at state st. Then there is a one-to-one correspondence between q and $\tilde{\sigma}_q$. We can design an algorithm to translate q into $\tilde{\sigma}_q$. We give the algorithm Translate in Algorithm 3. The following proposition holds for Translate.

Algorithm 3. Translate($q, \tilde{\Sigma}$)

Input: $q = a_1 \cdots a_m$
1: $Used \leftarrow \emptyset$ and $\tilde{\sigma}_q \leftarrow \varepsilon$
2: **if** $a_1 \in \tilde{\Sigma}$ **then**
3:    $\sigma_1 \leftarrow a_1$ and $\tilde{\sigma}_q \leftarrow \tilde{\sigma}_q || \sigma_1$
4: **end if**
5: **for** $i = 2, \ldots, m$ **do**
6:    **for** $j = 1, \ldots, i-1$ **do**
7:       $\sigma_i \leftarrow a_j \cdots a_i$
8:       **if** $\sigma_i \notin Used$ and $\sigma_i \in \tilde{\Sigma}$ **then**
9:          $\tilde{\sigma}_q \leftarrow \tilde{\sigma}_q || \sigma_i$ and $Used \leftarrow Used \cup \{\sigma_i\}$
10:          **break** {go to the next i.}
11:       **end if**
12:    **end for**
13: **end for**
14: **if** $|\tilde{\sigma}_q| = m$ **then**
15:    **return** $\tilde{\sigma}_q$ {this means that $\tilde{\sigma}_q = \sigma_1 \cdots \sigma_m$ has been generated.}
16: **else**
17:    **return** $\emptyset$
18: **end if**

Proposition 3. *Let $q \in \Sigma^*$, $|q| = m$ and let $\tilde{\sigma}_q$ be an output of* Translate$(q, \tilde{\Sigma})$. *Then q is accepted by $M(W)$ at state st if and only if $\tilde{\sigma}_q = \sigma_1 \cdots \sigma_m$ ($\sigma_i \in \tilde{\Sigma}$) and $\tilde{\sigma}_q$ is accepted by $\tilde{M}(W)$ at state st.*

We must note that if we know $\tilde{\Sigma}$ then we can compute $\tilde{\sigma}_q$ from q using Translate. Proposition 3 states that we know $\tilde{\Sigma}$ then we can check if q is accepted by $M(W)$ without simulating $\tilde{M}(W)$ on $\tilde{\sigma}_q$. In other words, if we can make $\tilde{\sigma}_q$ that is not $\emptyset$ from q using Translate then we know that q is accepted by $M(W)$. This fact leads to a secure and space-efficient substring SSE scheme.

3.3   A State-Set Tree

By Proposition 3, we can know whether there is a text string w in W such that w contains a given string x using an ADAWG. However, we cannot know which text string w contains x. We need additional information to identify a text string and a position in which the string x appears. We introduce a state-set tree corresponding to an ADAWG. The state-set tree was originally defined for a DAWG in [1,2]. We use a state-set tree to identify a text string and a position. In Sect. 3.1, we defined an equivalence relation on Σ^* with respect to W using $end\text{-}set(x, w)$. For any $x \in \Sigma^*$, let $[x]_W$ be an equivalence class to which x belongs. As defined in [1,2], we construct a state-tree T_W from equivalence classes as follows.

1. The nodes of T_W consist of equivalence classes.
2. The root of T_W is $[\varepsilon]_W$.

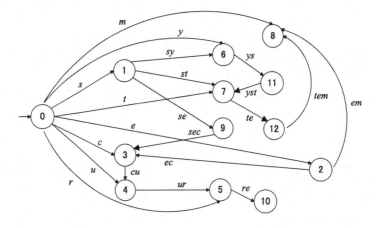

Fig. 2. An augmented DAWG obtained from the DAWG given in Fig. 1.

3. Let $[x]_W$ be any node of T_W and x be the longest string in $[x]_W$. Then, for any $a \in \Sigma$, if $ax \in FACT(W)$, then $[ax]_W$ is a child of $[x]_W$.

It is obvious from the definition of T_W that the following proposition holds.

Proposition 4. *Let $[x_1]_W$ and $[x_2]_W$ be any two nodes of T_W such that $[x_2]_W$ is a descendant of $[x_1]_W$. Then for any strings $s_1 \in [x_1]_W$ and $s_2 \in [x_2]_W$, s_1 is a suffix of s_2.*

Let $M(W)$ be the DAWG for W. Recall that a state of $M(W)$ also corresponds to an equivalence class. Hence there is a one-to-one correspondence between a state of $M(W)$ (that is, a state of $\tilde{M}(W)$) and a node of T_W. Proposition 4 states that if $s \in [x]_W$ for some node $[x]_W$, then s appears in all strings of $[x']_W$ which is a descendant of $[x]_W$. By this property, we assign text string ID and position pairs to a node of T_W as follows. Let $[x]_W$ be any node of T_W and x be a string in $[x]_W$. Furthermore let $(id_1, pos_1), \ldots, (id_l, pos_l)$ be a text string ID and a position (an end position) pairs in which x appears. Then, for any $1 \leq i \leq l$, if (id_i, pos_i) does not appear in a descendant of $[x]_W$, then (id_i, pos_i) is assigned to $[x]_W$; otherwise not assigned. We call a node with text string ID and position pairs *an info-node*. As an example, we give T_W for the DAWG of Fig. 1 in Fig. 3. The nodes of T_W correspond to the states of the DAWG. The info-nodes are 1, 3, 4, 5, 6, 7, 8, 9, 10, 11, and 12. We assign a number to each pair attached to info-nodes of T_W in preorder. In Fig. 3, such a number is attached to the outside of each pair. We use these numbers when constructing indexes. Note that the state-set tree T_W can be constructed together with the corresponding DAWG because a node of T_W corresponds to a state of a DAWG.

Now, by L_v we denote the set of document ID and position pairs assigned to a node v, and by $T_W(v)$ we denote the subtree of T_W rooted by v. Furthermore, let us define $L(T_W(v)) = \cup_{v \in V} L_v$, where V is the set of nodes of $T_W(v)$. Then it follows from Proposition 4 that we obtain the following proposition.

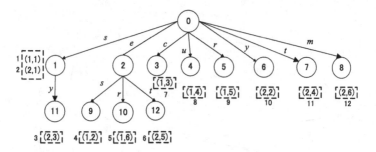

Fig. 3. A state-set tree T_W with (id, pos) for the DAWG given in Fig. 1. The pair (i, j) of numbers in a dotted square denotes the text string ID (document ID) and position. Here $W = \{secure, system\}$ where $ID(secure) = 1$ and $ID(system) = 2$.

Proposition 5. *For any string $x \in \Sigma^*$, let x be accepted by $M(W)$ at state st and let v_{st} be the node of T_W corresponding to st. Then, x occurs in position j of w_i if and only if $(i, j) \in L(T_W(v_{st}))$.*

3.4 Outline of Search Using an ADAWG and a State-Set Tree

Let us explain an outline of a search procedure using an ADAWG and a state-set tree. Given a keyword q, we first make $\tilde{\sigma}_q$ from q by $\mathsf{Translate}(q, \tilde{\Sigma})$. By Proposition 3, if we can make $\tilde{\sigma}_q$ then we know that q appears; otherwise q does not appear. Let st be the state reached after reading $\tilde{\sigma}_q$. We find the node v_{st} corresponding to st and gets $L(T_W(v_{st}))$. In the following section, we describe a substring SSE scheme which securely performs the above mentioned procedure.

4 A Secure Substring SSE Scheme

In the previous section, we used the set W of strings to explain an ADAWG and a state-set tree. Since the set D of documents corresponds to W, we use D instead of W to explain our substring SSE scheme. Our substring SSE scheme $\mathsf{SUB\_SSE} = (\mathsf{KeyGen}, \mathsf{Enc}, \mathsf{Trapdr}, \mathsf{BuildIndex}, \mathsf{Search}, \mathsf{Dec})$ consists of six (probabilistic) polynomial-time algorithms such that

- $\mathsf{KeyGen}(1^\lambda)$ is an probabilistic algorithm that takes as an input a security parameter λ and returns secret keys $SK = (sk_0, sk_1, sk_2, sk_3, sk_4)$,
- $\mathsf{Enc}(sk, d)$ is a probabilistic algorithm that takes as inputs a secret key sk and a document d and returns an encrypted document c, that is, $c = \mathsf{Enc}_{sk}(d)$. In particular, $\mathsf{Enc}_{sk}(D) = \cup_{d \in D} \{\mathsf{Enc}_{sk}(d)\}$,
- $\mathsf{Trapdr}(SK, q)$ is a deterministic algorithm that takes as inputs secret keys SK and a query q, and returns a trapdoor $TRAP(q)$ of q. In our scheme, this consists of $\mathsf{MakeTrap1}$ and $\mathsf{MakeTrap2}$,
- $\mathsf{BuildIndex}(SK, D)$ is a probabilistic algorithm that takes as inputs a secret key SK, a set D of documents and a false positive parameter ν and returns an encrypted index $\Pi = (\mathsf{LSET}, \mathsf{NMAP}, \mathsf{IND})$ and a set of encrypted documents,

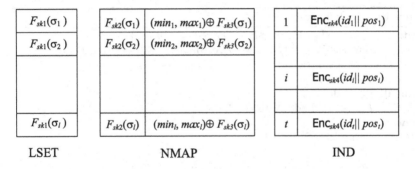

Fig. 4. Index $\Pi = (\mathsf{LSET}, \mathsf{NMAP}, \mathsf{IND})$

- $\mathsf{Search}(q, \Pi)$ is a protocol between the user and the server to search for $D(q)$ using an encrypted index Π. This is described as a search protocol in Sect. 4.2,
- $\mathsf{Dec}(sk, c)$ is a deterministic algorithm that takes as inputs a secret key sk and an encrypted document c and returns the decrypted document d.

In the following, we describe details of Trapdr, $\mathsf{BuildIndex}$, and Search. Our secure indexes are made from an ADAWG and a state-set tree using $\mathsf{SKE} = (\mathsf{KeyGen}, \mathsf{Enc}, \mathsf{Dec})$ and a pseudorandom function F_{sk} for a secret key sk.

4.1 Constructing a Secure Encrypted Index

The encrypted index $\Pi = (\mathsf{LSET}, \mathsf{NMAP}, \mathsf{IND})$ consists of three sub-indexes LSET, NMAP, and IND. The sub-index LSET is the set of encrypted meta-symbols. The sub-index NMAP have information of a state reachable by the last transition of an encrypted ADAWG. The sub-index IND has pairs of document ID and position, and is built from a state-set tree. We will explain these three sub-indexes. We give an algorithm $\mathsf{BuildIndex}$ in Algorithm 4 which constructs an encrypted index Π. Here $\tilde{M}(D) = (Q, \tilde{\Sigma}, \tilde{\delta}, 0)$ is an ADAWG and T_D is state-set tree for the set D of documents. We give an outline of the index Π in Fig. 4, where $\tilde{\Sigma} = \{\sigma_1, \ldots, \sigma_l\}$ and $t = n_D$.

Sub-index LSET. We make LSET so that $\mathsf{LSET} = \{F_{sk_1}(\sigma) \mid \sigma \in \tilde{\Sigma}\}$. Thus LSET consists of encrypted meta-symbols which appears on transitions of $\tilde{M}(D)$.

Sub-index NMAP. We store information of info-nodes corresponding to a state reachable by transitions of $\tilde{M}(D)$ in NMAP for a given query. Let q be a query of length m and $\tilde{\sigma}_q = \sigma_1 \cdots \sigma_m$ be a sequence obtained by $\mathsf{Translate}(q, \tilde{\Sigma})$. Then if a DAWG $M(D)$ reaches a state st by q, then the corresponding ADAWG $\tilde{M}(D)$ also reaches the state st by $\tilde{\sigma}_q$. Then we set $\mathsf{NMAP}[F_{sk_2}(\sigma_m)] = (min, max) \oplus F_{sk_3}(\sigma_m)$. Here min and max is the minimum number and the maximum number among document ID and position pairs attached to info-nodes of the subtree corresponding to a state st. Note that min and max are computed from the state-set tree.

Sub-index IND. The sub-index IND is used to get pairs of a document ID and a position in which a query appears. IND is an array of n_D entries in which

---

Algorithm 4. BuildIndex(SK, D)

Input: $SK = \{sk_0, sk_1, sk_2, sk_3, sk_4\}$, $D = \{d_0, \ldots, d_{N-1}\}$
 1: generate an ADAWG $\tilde{M}(D) = (Q, \tilde{\Sigma}, \tilde{\delta}, 0)$ and a state-set tree T_D
 2: Let $T_D(v)$ be a subtree of T_D rooted by a node v.
 3: {Constructing LSET}
 4: **for all** $\sigma \in \tilde{\Sigma}$ **do**
 5:     $X \leftarrow F_{sk_1}(\sigma)$ and add X to LSET
 6: **end for**
 7: {Constructing NMAP and IND}
 8: **for all** $\sigma \in \tilde{\Sigma}$ **do**
 9:     compute min and max of $T(v_{nst})$ where nst is a state such that $\tilde{\delta}(st, \sigma) = nst$
         for some state st and v_{nst} is the node of T_D corresponding to nst,
10:     compute all (id_i, pos_i) appearing in $T_D(v_{nst})$
11:     NMAP$[F_{sk_2}(\sigma)] \leftarrow (min, max) \oplus F_{sk_3}(\sigma)$
12:     **for all** $min \le i \le max$ **do**
13:         IND$[i] \leftarrow$ Enc$_{sk_4}(id_i \| pos_i)$,
14:     **end for**
15: **end for**
16: **return** $\Pi = ($LSET, NMAP, IND$)$ and $\{c \mid c \in$ Enc$_{sk_0}(D)\}$.

---

document lists are stored. IND is also built from the state-set tree. IND is an array with a document ID and an occurrence position. Each info-node of a state-set tree corresponds to a string occurring in D and has document ID and position pairs in which the string appear. Then, for randomly selected position i, a document ID and position pair (id, pos) is stored in IND$[i]$ in the form Enc$_{sk_4}(id \| pos)$. We have the following theorem from Proposition 2.

Theorem 1. *Let D be a set of documents and let $\Pi = ($LSET, NMAP, IND$)$. Then, the size of Π is $O(n_D)$.*

4.2   A Search Protocol

In our security model, we assume that the server is honest-but-curious. A search protocol is performed in three rounds of communication between a user and a server as follows. For any query q, we first generate $TRAP(q)$ using MakeTrap1(q), which is used to check if q appears in a document. If appears, the user generates (Y, Z) using MakeTrap2(q) in order to gets encrypted pairs of a document ID and a position. Finally the user gets the desired documents. We present the search protocol for a keyword $q = a_1 \cdots a_m$ in the following.

1. **User:** Using MakeTrap1(q), the user makes $TRAP(q) = (\mathcal{X}_1, \ldots, \mathcal{X}_m)$ and sends $TRAP(q)$ to the server.
2. **Server:** Let $EXIST$ be an output of ExistTest($TRAP(q)$, LSET). Then the server sends $EXIST$ to the user.
3. **User:** If $EXIST = \emptyset$ then the search halts. If $EXIST \ne \emptyset$ then the user makes a trapdoor (Y, Z) by MakeTrap2($q, EXIST$). The user sends (Y, Z) to the server.

Algorithm 5. MakeTrap1(q)

Input: $q = a_1 \cdots a_m$
1: $X_1 \leftarrow F_{sk_1}(a_1)$, $\mathcal{X}_1 \leftarrow \{X_1\}$ and $SYM \leftarrow \emptyset$
2: **for** $j = 2, \ldots, m$ **do**
3:      $k \leftarrow 1$
4:      **for** $i = 1, \ldots, j - 1$ **do**
5:          $\sigma \leftarrow a_i \cdots a_j$
6:          **if** $\sigma \notin SYM$ **then**
7:              $X_k \leftarrow F_{sk_1}(\sigma)$, $\mathcal{X}_j \leftarrow \mathcal{X}_j \cup \{X_k\}$, $k + +$, and $SYM \leftarrow SYM \cup \{\sigma\}$
8:          **end if**
9:      **end for**
10: **end for**
11: **return** $TRAP(q) = (\mathcal{X}_1, \ldots, \mathcal{X}_m)$

Algorithm 6. ExistTest($TRAP(q)$, LSET)

Input: $TRAP(q) = (\mathcal{X}_1, \ldots, \mathcal{X}_m)$
1: **for** $j = 1, \ldots, m$ **do**
2:      $Flag \leftarrow false$
3:      **for** $i = 1, \ldots, |\mathcal{X}_j|$ **do**
4:          take X_i from $\mathcal{X}_j$
5:          **if** $X_i \in$ LSET **then**
6:              **if** $j = m$ **then**
7:                  **return** X_i
8:              **end if**
9:              $Flag \leftarrow true$ and **break** {exit this for-loop}
10:         **end if**
11:     **end for**
12:     **if** $Flag = false$ **then**
13:         **return** $\emptyset$
14:     **end if**
15: **end for**

---

4. **Server:** Receiving (Y, Z), the server gets (min, max) by computing NMAP[Y] $\oplus Z$. For all $min \leq i \leq max$, the server sends the value of IND[i] $(= R_i)$ to the user.

5. **User:** Receiving $(R_{min}, \ldots, R_{max})$, the user gets (id_i, pos_i) by decrypting R_i for all $min \leq i \leq max$. The user sends $(id_{min}, \ldots, id_{max})$ to the server.

6. **Server:** Receiving $(id_{min}, \ldots, id_{max})$, the server sends $(c_{id_{min}}, \ldots, c_{id_{max}})$ to the user.

7. **User:** The user decrypts $c_{id_{min}}$ and gets a document $d_{id_{min}}$. If q appears at pos_{min} in $d_{id_{min}}$, then the user knows that q appears in c_{id_i} ($min \leq i \leq max$); otherwise the user knows that q does not appear.

Lemma 1. *For any query q of length m, let EXIST be an output of* ExistTest($TRAP(q)$, LSET). *Then EXIST $\neq \emptyset$ if and only if q appears in documents of D.*

Algorithm 7. MakeTrap2(q, $EXIST$)

Input: $q = a_1 \cdots a_m$
1: **if** $m = 1$ **then**
2:     $X \leftarrow F_{sk_1}(a_1)$
3:     **if** $X = EXIST$ **then**
4:         $Y \leftarrow F_{sk_2}(a_1)$ and $Z \leftarrow F_{sk_3}(a_1)$
5:     **end if**
6: **end if**
7: **if** $m \geq 2$ **then**
8:     **for** $i = 1, \ldots, m - 1$ **do**
9:         $\sigma \leftarrow a_i \cdots a_m$ and $X \leftarrow F_{sk_1}(\sigma)$
10:        **if** $X = EXIST$ **then**
11:            $Y \leftarrow F_{sk_2}(\sigma)$, $Z \leftarrow F_{sk_3}(\sigma)$, and **break**
12:        **end if**
13:    **end for**
14: **end if**
15: **return** (Y, Z)

The lemma is obtained from Proposition 3. That is, ExistTest carries out the same task as that of Translate in an encrypted world. It follows from Lemma 1 and Proposition 5 that the following theorem holds. In the search protocol, the user may get false positive answers with all but negligible probability by collisions of pseudorandom functions. However, the user can filter out these answers by checking just one pair of a document and a position at Step 7.

Theorem 2. *For any query q of length m, the search protocol finds $D(q)$ in $O(m^2 + |D(q)|)$ time and in three rounds of communication.*

5   Security Analysis

We will prove that the proposed scheme meets adaptive security. For the security analysis, we consider a real game **REAL**$_\mathcal{A}$ and a simulation game **SIM**$_{\mathcal{A},\mathcal{S}}$, which are played by three players, a challenger, an adversary and a simulator. As you see below, **REAL**$_\mathcal{A}$ plays using the proposed scheme, while **SIM**$_{\mathcal{A},\mathcal{S}}$ simulates the real scheme using only information that an adversary (that is, a server) can get. Then leakage information **LEAK** for SUB_SSE is listed as follows.

- The length of each document $|d_0|, \cdots, |d_{N-1}|$ and the collection of encrypted documents, the size n_1 of LSET, the size n_2 of NMAP, and the size n_3 of IND.
- (access pattern) For a query q, (min, max) and the set $\{id \mid (id, pos) \in D(q)\}$. Note that a position pos at which q appears does not leak out.
- (search pattern) For a query q, $TRAP(q) = (\mathcal{X}_1, \cdots, \mathcal{X}_m)$ and (Y, Z). In addition, the set $\mathcal{LX} = \mathcal{X} \cap$ LSET, where $\mathcal{X} = \mathcal{X}_1 \cup \cdots \cup \mathcal{X}_m$.
- (prefix pattern) For any query q, the adversary can know whether q is a prefix of the previous queries from the above information leaked.

[adaptive semantic security model]

REAL$_\mathcal{A}(\lambda)$
- The adversary $\mathcal{A}$ chooses D, where $D = \{d_0, \ldots, d_{N-1}\}$ is the set of documents. After that, $\mathcal{A}$ sends them to the challenger $\mathcal{C}$.
- $\mathcal{C}$ generates randomly a secret key $SK = (sk_0, sk_1, sk_2, sk_3, sk_4)$ using KeyGen (1^λ), and builds Π by BuildIndex(SK, D). After that, $\mathcal{C}$ sends $(\Pi, \mathsf{Enc}_{sk_0}(D))$ to $\mathcal{A}$.
- repeat the following polynomially many times.
  1. $\mathcal{A}$ selects a query q and sends q to $\mathcal{C}$.
  2. Perform a search protocol between $\mathcal{A}$ and $\mathcal{C}$, where $\mathcal{A}$ plays as the server and $\mathcal{C}$ plays as the user.
- Finally, $\mathcal{A}$ outputs a bit $b \in \{0, 1\}$.

SIM$_{\mathcal{A},\mathcal{S}}(\lambda)$
- The adversary $\mathcal{A}$ chooses D where $D = \{d_0, \ldots, d_{N-1}\}$ is the set of documents, and then $\mathcal{A}$ sends them to the challenger $\mathcal{C}$.
- $\mathcal{C}$ sends leakage information **LEAK** to the simulator $\mathcal{S}$.
- $\mathcal{S}$ builds an index Π^*, a set $\{c_0^*, \ldots, c_{N-1}^*\}$ of encrypted documents, using **LEAK**. After that, $\mathcal{S}$ sends them to $\mathcal{A}$.
- Repeat the following polynomially many times.
  1. $\mathcal{A}$ selects a query q and sends q to $\mathcal{S}$.
  2. Perform a search protocol between $\mathcal{A}$ and $\mathcal{S}$, where $\mathcal{A}$ plays as the server and $\mathcal{S}$ plays as the user.
- Finally, $\mathcal{A}$ outputs a bit $b \in \{0, 1\}$.

Definition 2. *We say that a substring SSE scheme meets adaptive semantic security if for all probabilistic polynomial time adversaries $\mathcal{A}$, there is a probabilistic polynomial time simulator such that*
$$|Pr(\mathcal{A} \, outputs \, b = 1 \, in \, \mathbf{REAL}_{\mathcal{A}}(\lambda)) - Pr(\mathcal{A} \, outputs \, b = 1 \, in \, \mathbf{SIM}_{\mathcal{A},\mathcal{S}}(\lambda))|$$
is negligible.

Since a symmetric encryption scheme satisfies PCPA-security, the following theorem holds.

Theorem 3. *The proposed scheme* SUB_SSE *meets adaptive semantic security.*

Proof (Sketch). We will describe an outline of the proof. We show a polynomial time simulator $\mathcal{S}$ such that the advantage of any probabilistic polynomial time adversary $\mathcal{A}$ to distinguish between the outputs of $\mathbf{REAL}_{\mathcal{A}}(\lambda)$ and $\mathbf{SIM}_{\mathcal{A},\mathcal{S}}(\lambda)$ is negligible. Let $D = \{d_0, \cdots, d_{N-1}\}$ be a set of documents. $\mathcal{S}$ has three sets $TRAP_x$, $TRAP_y$, and $TRAP_z$ and initially sets them to $\emptyset$.

- Simulating encrypted documents for the document set D. Simulator $\mathcal{S}$ generates a random strings c_i^* of $|d_i|$ bits for a document d_i $(0 \le i \le N-1)$. Since a symmetric encryption scheme is PCPA-secure, c_i and c_i^* is indistinguishable.

– Simulating an encrypted index for the set D of documents.
  The simulator $\mathcal{S}$ builds an index $\Pi^* = (\mathsf{LSET}^*, \mathsf{NMAP}^*, \mathsf{IND}^*)$ using **LEAK**
  as follows.

1. Simulating LSET. The simulator $\mathcal{S}$ knows the size n_1 of LSET from
   LEAK. Then $\mathcal{S}$ generates n_1 random strings $X_1^*, \ldots, X_{n_1}^*$ and builds
   LSET^* as the set $\{X_1^*, \ldots, X_{n_1}^*\}$. We note that all transitions of an
   ADAWG are done by distinct meta-symbols and LSET is built using a
   pseudorandom function. Therefore LSET and LSET^* are indistinguishable with all but negligible probability.
2. Simulating NMAP and IND. The simulator $\mathcal{S}$ knows the size n_2 of NMAP
   and the size n_3 of IND from **LEAK**. $\mathcal{S}$ makes NMAP^* in the following
   way. $\mathcal{S}$ generates n_2 random strings $Y_1^*, \ldots, Y_{n_2}^*$ and n_2 random strings
   $Z_1^*, \ldots, Z_{n_2}^*$, and sets $\mathsf{NMAP}^* = \{(Y_i^*, Z_i^*) \mid 1 \le i \le n_2\}$. Next $\mathcal{S}$ generates
   n_3 random strings $R_1^*, \ldots, R_{n_3}^*$ to build IND and sets $\mathsf{IND}^*[i] = R_i^*$ for
   all $1 \le i \le n_3$. All elements of NMAP are independent of each other
   and are randomized by a pseudorandom function. Therefore NMAP and
   NMAP^* are indistinguishable with all but negligible probability. Similarly,
   since IND is built using a PCPA-secure encryption scheme and all pairs
   of a document ID and a position are distinct, IND and IND^* are also
   indistinguishable with all but negligible probability.

– Simulating a search at time t. Let $q = a_1 \cdots a_m$ be a query at time t. $\mathcal{S}$ knows
  $TRAP(q) = (\mathcal{X}_1, \cdots, \mathcal{X}_m)$, $\mathcal{LX}$, (min, max), and $\{id \mid (id, pos) \in D(q)\}$ from
  LEAK. Given q, $\mathcal{S}$ makes $\mathcal{X}_j^*$ to simulate $\mathcal{X}_j$ by modifying MakeTrap1 as
  follows. Here we note that $\mathcal{S}$ can know a substring of q from which X is made
  for each $X \in \mathcal{X}_j$ because elements of $\mathcal{X}_j$ is sequentially numbered.

1. if $(a_1, X^*) \in TRAP_x$ then add X^* to $\mathcal{X}_1^*$; otherwise if $X \in \mathcal{X}_1$ generating
   from a_1 is in $\mathcal{LX}$ then randomly choose unused X^* from LSET^* and if
   $X \in \mathcal{X}_1$ is not in $\mathcal{LX}$ then generate a random string X^* not in $\mathcal{LX}$. After
   that add X^* to $\mathcal{X}_1^*$ and (a_1, X^*) to $TRAP_x$,
2. for σ at line 5 of MakeTrap1 do the following:
   if $(\sigma, X^*) \in TRAP_x$ then add X^* to $\mathcal{X}_j^*$; otherwise if $X \in \mathcal{X}_j$ generating
   from σ is in $\mathcal{LX}$ then randomly choose unused X^* from LSET^* and if
   $X \in \mathcal{X}_j$ is not in $\mathcal{LX}$ then generate a random string X^* not in LSET^*.
   After that add X^* to $\mathcal{X}_j^*$ and (σ, X^*) to $TRAP_x$.

Clearly $\mathcal{X}_j$ and $\mathcal{X}_j^*$ have the same number of elements. Let $\mathcal{LX}^* = \mathcal{X}^* \cap \mathsf{LSET}^*$
where $\mathcal{X}^* = \mathcal{X}_1^* \cup \cdots \cup \mathcal{X}_m^*$. Then $\mathcal{LX}$ and $\mathcal{LX}^*$ also have the same number
of elements. Since $\mathcal{X}_j$ is randomized by a pseudorandom function, $\mathcal{A}$ cannot
distinguish $\mathcal{X}_j$ and $\mathcal{X}_j^*$ with all but negligible probability. Similarly $\mathcal{A}$ cannot
distinguish $\mathcal{LX}$ and $\mathcal{LX}^*$. Next $\mathcal{S}$ makes a trapdoor (Y^*, Z^*) to simulate
(Y, Z) made by MakeTrap2 as follows. If $(q, Y', Z') \in TRAP_y$ for q then set
$Y^* = Y'$ and $Z^* = Z'$. This case means that q has been used in a search
previously.
Let us consider the case $(q, Y', Z') \notin TRAP_y$ for q. Then $\mathcal{S}$ randomly chooses
an unused position Y' in NMAP^* and sets $Y^* = Y'$. Furthermore $\mathcal{S}$ generates
Z' so that $(min, max) = \mathsf{NMAP}^*[Y'] \oplus Z'$ and sets $Z^* = Z'$. $\mathcal{S}$ adds (q, Y', Z')

to $TRAP_y$. After that, $\mathcal{S}$ sends (Y^*, Z^*) to $\mathcal{A}$. Receiving (Y^*, Z^*), $\mathcal{A}$ sends $\mathsf{IND}^*[i]$ $(min \leq i \leq max)$ to $\mathcal{S}$. Finally, since $\mathcal{S}$ knows all document IDs id such that a document d_{id} contains q, he sends these IDs to $\mathcal{A}$.

By these setting, $\mathcal{S}$ can let $\mathcal{A}$ search for q in a similar way to the real world. Thus $\mathcal{A}$ cannot distinguish $\mathbf{REAL}_{\mathcal{A}}$ and $\mathbf{SIM}_{\mathcal{A},\mathcal{S}}$ with all but negligible probability. Hence the theorem has been proved.

6 Conclusions

We proposed a secure substring SSE scheme by improving a DAWG. Comparing with substring SSE schemes proposed previously, the proposed SSE has a simple structure and is space-efficient, but the search time increases. This is because it takes more time to generate a trapdoor $TRAP(q)$ for a query q. Improving the search time without weakening security is one of future works.

Acknowledgments. This work was supported by JSPS KAKENHI Grant Number JP17K00183.

References

1. Blumer, A., Blumer, J., Haussler, D.: The smallest automaton recognizing the subwords of a text. Theoret. Comput. Sci. **40**, 31–55 (1985)
2. Blumer, A., Blumer, J., Haussler, D., Mcconnell, R.: Complete inverted files for efficient text retrieval and analysis. J. ACM **34**(3), 578–595 (1987)
3. Baeza-Yates, R., Ribeiro-Neto, B.: Modern Information Retrieval (Section 8). ACM Press, Addison-Wesley, New York (1999)
4. Bost, R., Minaud, B., Ohrimenko, O.: Forward and backward private searchable encryption from constrained cryptographic primitives. In: Proceedings of CCS 2017, pp. 1465–1482 (2017)
5. Cash, D., Jarecki, S., Jutla, C., Krawczyk, H., Roşu, M.-C., Steiner, M.: Highly-scalable searchable symmetric encryption with support for Boolean queries. In: Canetti, R., Garay, J.A. (eds.) CRYPTO 2013. LNCS, vol. 8042, pp. 353–373. Springer, Heidelberg (2013). https://doi.org/10.1007/978-3-642-40041-4_20
6. Curtmola, R., Garay, J., Kamara, S., Ostrovsky, R.: Searchable symmetric encryption: improved definitions and efficient constructions. J. Comput. Secur. **19**(5), 895–934 (2011)
7. Chase, M., Shen, E.: Substring-searchable symmetric encryption. In: Proceedings on Privacy Enhancing Technologies 2015, vol. 2015, no. 2, pp. 263–281 (2015)
8. Chamani, J.G., Papadopoulos, D., Papamanthou, C., Jalili, R.: New constructions for forward and backward private symmetric searchable encryption. In: Proceedings of CCS 2018, pp. 1038–1055 (2018)
9. Faber, S., Jarecki, S., Krawczyk, H., Nguyen, Q., Rosu, M., Steiner, M.: Rich queries on encrypted data: beyond exact matches. In: Pernul, G., Ryan, P.Y.A., Weippl, E. (eds.) ESORICS 2015. LNCS, vol. 9327, pp. 123–145. Springer, Cham (2015). https://doi.org/10.1007/978-3-319-24177-7_7

10. Goh, E.-J.: Secure Indexes. Stanford University Technical Report. In: IACR ePrint Cryptography Archive (2003). See http://eprint.iacr.org/2003/216
11. Hacıigümüş, H., Hore, B., Iyer, B., Mehrotra, S.: Search on encrypted data. Adv. Inf. Secur. **33**, 383–425 (2007)
12. Hahn, F., Kerschbaum, F.: Searchable encryption with secure and efficient updates. In: Proceedings of ACM CCS 2014, pp. 310–320 (2014)
13. Hahn, F., Loza, N., Kerschbaum, F.: Practical and secure substring search. In: Proceedings of SIGMOD/PODS 2018, pp. 163–176 (2018)
14. Hopcroft, J.E., Ullman, J.D.: Introduction to Automata Theory Language and Computation. Addison Wesley, Reading (1979)
15. Katz, J., Lindell, Y.: Introduction to Modern Cryptography, Second Edn. CRC Press, Boca Raton (2015)
16. Kurosawa, K., Ohtaki, Y.: UC-secure searchable symmetric encryption. In: Keromytis, A.D. (ed.) FC 2012. LNCS, vol. 7397, pp. 285–298. Springer, Heidelberg (2012). https://doi.org/10.1007/978-3-642-32946-3_21
17. Kamara, S., Papamanthou, C., Roeder, T.: Dynamic searchable symmetric encryption. In: Proceedings of ACM CCS 2012, pp. 965–976 (2012)
18. Leontiadis, I., Li, M.: Storage efficient substring searchable symmetric encryption. In: Proceedings of the 6th International Workshop on Security in Cloud Computing (SCC 2018), pp. 3–14 (2018)
19. Li, J., Wang, Q., Wang, C., Cao, N., Ren, K., Lou, W.: Fuzzy keyword search over encrypted data in cloud computing. In: Proceedings of INFCOM 2010, pp. 441–445 (2010)
20. Miyoshi, R., Yamamoto, H., Fujiwara, H., Miyazaki, T.: Practical and secure searchable symmetric encryption with a small index. In: Lipmaa, H., Mitrokotsa, A., Matulevičius, R. (eds.) NordSec 2017. LNCS, vol. 10674, pp. 53–69. Springer, Cham (2017). https://doi.org/10.1007/978-3-319-70290-2_4
21. Popa, R.A., Redfield, C.M.S., Zeldovich, N., Balakrishnan, H.: CryptDB: processing queries on an encrypted database. Commun. ACM **55**(9), 103–111 (2012)
22. Suga, T., Nishide, T., Sakurai, K.: Secure keyword search using bloom filter with specified character positions. In: Takagi, T., Wang, G., Qin, Z., Jiang, S., Yu, Y. (eds.) ProvSec 2012. LNCS, vol. 7496, pp. 235–252. Springer, Heidelberg (2012). https://doi.org/10.1007/978-3-642-33272-2_15
23. Strizhov, M., Ray, I.: Substring position search over encrypted cloud data using tree-based index. In: Proceedings of IEEE IC2E 2015, pp. 165–174 (2015)
24. Strizhov, M., Osman, Z., Ray, I.: Substring position search over encrypted cloud data supporting efficient multi-user setup. Future Internet **8**(28), 2016 (2016)
25. Song, D.X., Wagner, D., Perrig, A.: Techniques for searchers on encrypted data. In: Proceedings of IEEE Symposium on Security and Privacy, pp. 44–55 (2000)
26. Yamamoto, H.: Secure automata-based substring search scheme on encrypted data. In: Ogawa, K., Yoshioka, K. (eds.) IWSEC 2016. LNCS, vol. 9836, pp. 111–131. Springer, Cham (2016). https://doi.org/10.1007/978-3-319-44524-3_7

Plaintext-Verifiably-Checkable Encryption

Sha Ma[✉], Qiong Huang, Ximing Li, and Meiyan Xiao

College of Mathematics and Informatics, South China Agricultural University,
Guangzhou, Guangdong, China
martin_deng@163.com, {qhuang,liximing,maymayxiao}@scau.edu.cn

Abstract. The notion of plaintext-checkable encryption (PCE) has recently emerged in the application of search on encrypted data only by plaintexts. We observe that existing PCE schemes are not sufficient to guarantee check correctness in the case of a malicious encryptor. To address this concern, we put forth the concept of *plaintext-verifiably-checkable encryption* (PVCE), which captures the basic requirement of output correctness: If M is thought to be the plaintext for a ciphertext ct by the Check algorithm, ct is actually a valid encryption of M. In other words, it does not exist any maliciously generated ciphertext could succeed in plaintext checking. This property guarantees a meaningful notion of correctness and is crucial in several applications. We propose a PVCE construction using pairing-friendly smooth projective hash function with modified language representation and prove it to be unlink-cca security in the standard model. This is the *first* verifiable plaintext-checkable encryption that provides both verifiable checkability and the most desirable security in the standard model. To this end, we show a PVCE instantiation from k-MDDH assumption.

Keywords: Plaintext checkable encryption · Verifiability · Smooth projective hash function · Pairing friendly · k-MDDH assumption

1 Introduction

Encryption technology with functionalities, for example, public/private keyword search or equality test, plays important roles in era of cloud computing, which has been achieved much attraction in recent years. A typical primitive is *public key encryption with keyword searh* (PEKS) [1–5] to search on ciphertexts by a trapdoor from secret key and keyword. Any user owing the trapdoor could infer whether any ciphertext contains the same keyword in the trapdoor without the knowledge of the underlying keyword. Another variant is *public key encryption with equality test* (PKEET) [6–10] to search on ciphertexts by a candidate ciphertext. Any tester (or authorized tester) could know whether two ciphertexts share the same message.

© Springer Nature Switzerland AG 2019
R. Steinfeld and T. H. Yuen (Eds.): ProvSec 2019, LNCS 11821, pp. 149–166, 2019.
https://doi.org/10.1007/978-3-030-31919-9_9

In this paper, we consider the primitive *plaintext-checkable encryption* (PCE) to search on ciphertext *only by plaintext*. It is no surprise that in PCE framework if the check algorithm on a ciphertext and a plaintext returns *true*, the tester could easily obtain the plaintext underlying a ciphertext. Otherwise, the ciphertext should not leak any other knowledge of the plaintext. Compared with PEKS, the trapdoor of PCE is a plaintext without taking any secret information as input while the trapdoor of PEKS is generated only by the data owner using its secret key. Compared with PKEET, PCE provides more simple search way (only by plaintext) without additional encryption of compared plaintext, possibly under different public keys.

We observe that existing PCE schemes are not sufficient to guarantee check correctness. This is essential in the case of a malicious encryptor, where the maliciously generated ciphertext could possibly succeed in plaintext checking. A seemly proper technology is to adopt signature to guarantee the well-formedness of ciphertexts, which is similar to [10] to ensure all unchecked elements in the ciphertexts have not been tampered with. However, this technology is only used in the scenario which implies an assumption that all encryptors are honest. Here we emphasize that **this intention is different from our goal to exclude all invalid ciphertexts which are possibly generated by malicious encryptors.** Next, we use some examples to explain our goal.

- In [11], two PCE constructions in random oracle model do satisfy the verifiable checkability because the test procedure could totally recover the randomness in the encryption procedure and then the verifiability follows.
- In [11], one PCE construction in standard model also satisfies the verifiable checkability, using the pairing property on the check elements in $\mathbb{G}_2$.
- In [12], the ciphertext is $\mathsf{CT} = (W, U, W', V) = (W, \mathsf{ProjHash}_1(\mathsf{hp}_1, W) * M, W', \mathsf{ProjHash}_2(\mathsf{hp}_2, (W, U, W')))$. In the check procedure, W' could be reconstructed and then V is verified by the witness τ of W'. However, U could not be guaranteed to be correct. In other words, a ciphertext without well formedness would pass the check phase. For instance, the adversary could randomly choose $y \in \mathcal{Y}$ and compute the ciphertext $C' = (W, y * M, W', \mathsf{ProjHash}_2(\mathsf{hp}_2, (W, U, W)))$, where $W' = \mathsf{WordGen}(\Gamma(W, y, M))$. Therefore, even if C' is thought to be the encryption of M by the check algorithm, C' is actually not the encryption of M!

Note that although the schemes in [11] satisfy the verifiable checkability, they can not achieve the best desirable unlink-cca security. To the best of our knowledge, we have not seen PCE constructions that have both verifiable checkability and the strongest unlink-cca security in the literature. This is the motivation of our work.

1.1 Related Work

Canard et al. [11] first proposed generic PCE constructions in the random oracle model based on any probabilistic or deterministic encryption and a practical

Scheme	Setting	Model	Join	Aut	Sec$_w$	Sec$_o$	Verif
Yang et al. [6]	public key	RO	full-encrypted	×	–	ow-cca	×
Tang [7]	public key	RO	full-encrypted	√	ow-cca	ind-cca	×
Tang [8]	public key	RO	full-encrypted	√	ow-cca	ind-cca	×
Ma et al. [10]	public key	RO	full-encrypted	√	ow-cca	ind-cca	×
Huang et al. [9]	public key	RO	full-encrypted	√	ow-cca	ind-cca	×
Ma et al. [16]	public key	RO	full-encrypted	√	ow-cca	ind-cca	×
Carbunar et al. [13]	private key	standard	full-encrypted	√	one-way	ind-cpa	×
Furukawa et al. [14]	private key	RO	full-encrypted	√	one-way	ind-cpa	×
Pang et al. [15]	private key	standard	full-encrypted	√	one-way	ind-cpa	√
Canard et al. [11]	public key	RO	semi-encrypted	×	–	unlink	√
Canard et al. [11]	public key	standard	semi-encrypted	×	–	unlink	√
Ma[12]	public key	standard	semi-encrypted	×	–	s-priv-cca	×
This paper	public key	standard	semi-encrypted	×	–	unlink-cca	√

Fig. 1. Comparison with related work.

construction using pairing groups in the standard model, whose security notion is defined as unlink. Recently, Ma et al. [12] proposed a PCE scheme with s-priv1-cca security, which is independent with unlink. As shown in [12], the most desired security of PCE is unlink-cca. In the application, PCE is a useful primitive for private join on encrypted database, where a join attribute is sensitive to be protected and another join attribute is stored in plain. Privacy-preserving join on encrypted database has been received much attention, where most constructions work under the condition that both joined attributes are encrypted. Carbunar and Sion [13] first studied private join on outsourced database in a private key setting, which supports general binary join predicates including range, equality and Hamming distance. Furukawa and Isshiki [14] provided a scheme where the server requires an authorization from the data owner to execute an equijoin. Yang et al. [6] introduced the notion of public key encryption with equality test (PKEET) as a useful primitive for join on two encrypted columns in multiuser setting. Several follow-on [7–10] studies extended PKEET with authorized equality test such that only authorized server can perform equality test on ciphertexts, which is accordance with only authorized server can perform equijoin on encrypted attributes. We show Fig. 1 to summarize the properties of related work according to public/private setting, random oracle/standard model, full/semi-encrypted join, authorization, security with/without authorization and verification, where full-encrypted join denotes join on both two encrypted attributes and semi-encrypted join denotes join on one encrypted attribute and another non-encrypted attribute. We see that only our work has both verifiable checkability and the most desirable security.

2   Pairing-Friendly Smooth Projective Hash Function

2.1   Definition of SPHF

A smooth projective hash function (SPHF) is based on a domain $\mathcal{X}$ and an $\mathcal{NP}$ language $\mathcal{L} \subset \mathcal{X}$. An SPHF system over $\mathcal{L}$ onto a set $\mathcal{Y}$ is defined as follows [17].

- SPHFSetup(k): It takes as input a security parameter k and outputs $(\mathcal{L}, \mathsf{param})$ as the global parameters.
- HashKG($\mathcal{L}, \mathsf{param}$): It generates a hashing key hk.
- ProjKG(hk,($\mathcal{L}$,param),W): It derives the projection key hp from the hashing key hk, possibly depending on the word W.
- Hash(hk,($\mathcal{L}, \mathsf{param}$), W): It outputs the hash value hv $\in \mathcal{Y}$ from the hashing key on any word $W \in \mathcal{X}$.
- ProjHash(hp,($\mathcal{L}$,param),W,w): It outputs the hash value hv$'$ $\in \mathcal{Y}$ from the projection key hp and any word $W \in \mathcal{X}$ with the witness w.

In this paper, we additionally define a WordVF algorithm to verify a word W using a witness w:

- WordVF(($\mathcal{L}, \mathsf{param}$), w, W): It outputs 1 if w is the witness of W, or 0 otherwise.

Correctness. The correctness of SPHF assures that if $W \in \mathcal{L}$ with a witness w, then Hash(hk, ($\mathcal{L}, \mathsf{param}$), W) = ProjHash(hp, ($\mathcal{L}, \mathsf{param}$), W, w).

Smoothness. The *smoothness* of SPHF assures that if $W \in \mathcal{X} \backslash \mathcal{L}$, then the following two distributions are statistically indistinguishable:

$$\{((\mathcal{L}, \mathsf{param}), W, \mathsf{hp}, \mathsf{hv}) | \mathsf{hv} = \mathsf{Hash}(\mathsf{hk}, (\mathcal{L}, \mathsf{param}), W)\},$$

$$\{((\mathcal{L}, \mathsf{param}), W, \mathsf{hp}, \mathsf{hv}) | \mathsf{hv} \xleftarrow{\$} \mathcal{Y}\}.$$

where $(\mathcal{L}, \mathsf{param})$ = SPHFSetup(k), hk = HashKG($\mathcal{L}, \mathsf{param}$) and hp = ProjKG(hk, ($\mathcal{L}, \mathsf{param}$), W).

2-Smoothness. The 2-smoothness of SPHF assures that if $W_1, W_2 \in \mathcal{X} \backslash \mathcal{L} \wedge W_1 \neq W_2$, then the following two distributions are statistically indistinguishable:

$$\{((\mathcal{L}, \mathsf{param}), W_1, W_2, \mathsf{hp}, \mathsf{hv}_1, \mathsf{hv}_2) | \mathsf{hv}_2 = \mathsf{Hash}(\mathsf{hk}, (\mathcal{L}, \mathsf{param}), W_2)\},$$

$$\{((\mathcal{L}, \mathsf{param}), W_1, W_2, \mathsf{hp}, \mathsf{hv}_1, \mathsf{hv}_2) | \mathsf{hv}_2 \xleftarrow{\$} \mathcal{Y}\},$$

where $(\mathcal{L}, \mathsf{param})$ = SPHFSetup(k), hk = HashKG($\mathcal{L}, \mathsf{param}$), hp = ProjKG(hk, ($\mathcal{L}, \mathsf{param}$), W_2) and hv$_1$ = Hash(hk, ($\mathcal{L}, \mathsf{param}$), W_1).

Extended SPHF. An extended SPHF additionally takes an auxiliary element *aux* along with word W as input of Hash and ProjHash algorithm.

2.2 Modified Language Representation

For SPHF, classical language representation has been described in [17–19]. We omit it for brevity. By making modification on classical language representation [17–19], we provide an alternative language representation of a language $\mathcal{L}_{\text{aux}}$. For a language $\mathcal{L}_{\text{aux}}$, there exist two positive integers k and n, a word basis function $\Upsilon : \mathcal{S}et \mapsto \mathbb{G}^{k \times n}$ and a family of functions $\Theta_{\text{aux}} : \mathcal{S}et \mapsto \mathbb{G}^{1 \times n}$, such that for any word $C \in \mathcal{S}et$, $(C \in \mathcal{L}_{\text{aux}}) \Longleftrightarrow (\exists \varphi \in \mathbb{Z}_p^{1 \times k}) \wedge (\exists \delta \in \mathbb{Z}_p^{k \times n})$ such that $\Theta_{\text{aux}}(C) = \varphi \bullet (\delta \bullet \Gamma(C))$, where φ is independent of any word C. In other words, we say that $C \in \mathcal{L}_{\text{aux}}$ if and only if $\widetilde{\Theta}_{\text{aux}}(C)$ is a linear combination of (the exponents in) the rows of some matrix $\delta \bullet \Gamma(C)$. It also requires that a user, who knows a witness w of the membership $C \in \mathcal{L}_{\text{aux}}$, can efficiently compute the above *linear* combination φ. We emphasize that it is difference from the language representation in the literature that **the linear combination φ is required to be independently chosen randomness, while the linear combination λ in the classical language representation possibly includes both the independently chosen randomness and possibly non-independently random elements.** This might be a quite strong requirement but this is actually verified by very expressive language over ciphertexts such as ElGamal, Cramer-Shoup and variants.

We briefly illustrate it on an SPHF for the language of Cramer-Shoup ciphertext encrypting a message $M = \text{aux}$. Words in the language $\mathcal{L}_{\text{aux}}$ is $C = (u_1 = g_1^r, u_2 = g_2^r, e = M \cdot h^r, v = (cd^\xi)^r)$, with $r \in \mathbb{Z}_p$ and $\xi = H(\ell, \boldsymbol{u}, e) \in \mathbb{Z}_p^*$. We choose $k = 2, \text{aux} = M, n = 5$, and the modified language representation on the language of Cramer-Shoup ciphertext is shown as follows.

$$\Gamma = \begin{pmatrix} g_1 & 1 & g_2 & h & c \\ 1 & g_1 & 1 & 1 & d \end{pmatrix} \quad \boldsymbol{\lambda} = (r, r\xi) \quad \begin{aligned} \boldsymbol{\lambda} \bullet \Gamma &= (g_1^r, g_1^{r\xi}, g_2^r, h^r, (cd^\xi)^r) \\ \Theta_M(C) &= (u_1, u_1^\xi, u_2, e/M, v). \end{aligned}$$

$$\Gamma = \begin{pmatrix} g_1 & 1 & g_2 & h & c \\ 1 & g_1 & 1 & 1 & d \end{pmatrix} \quad \boldsymbol{\varphi} = (r, r) \quad \boldsymbol{\delta} = \begin{pmatrix} 1 & 0 \\ 0 & \xi \end{pmatrix} \quad \begin{aligned} \varphi \bullet (\delta \bullet \Gamma) &= (g_1^r, g_1^{r\xi}, g_2^r, h^r, (cd^\xi)^r) \\ \widetilde{\Theta}_M(C) &= (u_1, u_1^\xi, u_2, e/M, v). \end{aligned}$$

2.3 Transformation from SPHF to PF-SPHF

Let PGGen be a probabilistic polynomial time (PPT) algorithm that on input k returns a description $\mathcal{PG} = (P, \widetilde{\mathbb{G}}, \mathbb{G}, \mathbb{G}_T, e, \widetilde{g}, g)$ of asymmetric pairing group, where $\widetilde{\mathbb{G}}$, $\mathbb{G}$ and $\mathbb{G}_T$ are cyclic groups of order p for a k-bit prime p, $\widetilde{g}$ and g are generators of $\widetilde{\mathbb{G}}$ and $\mathbb{G}$, respectively, and $e : \widetilde{\mathbb{G}} \times \mathbb{G}$ is a bilinear map between them.

Notations. We focus here on cyclic group $\mathbb{G}_s$ for $s \in \{1, 2, T\}$ of prime order p and define three operators on the group:

1. $\mathbb{G}_s * \mathbb{G}_s \rightarrow \mathbb{G}_s$. For any $u \in \mathbb{G}_s$ and $v \in \mathbb{G}_s$, $u * v \in \mathbb{G}_s$. Specifically, for any element $u \in \mathbb{G}_s$, we define $u * u^{-1} = 1_{\mathbb{G}_s}$, which is the identity element of $\mathbb{G}_s$. Sometimes we also use $uv = vu \in \mathbb{G}_s$ for $u, v \in \mathbb{G}_s$.

2. $\mathbb{Z}_p \bullet \mathbb{G}_s \to \mathbb{G}_s$ (or $\mathbb{G}_s \bullet \mathbb{Z}_p \to \mathbb{G}_s$). For any $r \in \mathbb{Z}_p$ and $u \in \mathbb{G}_s$, $r \bullet u = u \bullet r = u^r$.
3. $\mathbb{G}_1 \odot \mathbb{G}_2 \to \mathbb{G}_T$ (or $\mathbb{G}_2 \odot \mathbb{G}_1 \to \mathbb{G}_T$). For $u_1 \in \mathbb{G}_1$ and $u_2 \in \mathbb{G}_2$, $u_1 \odot u_2 = u_2 \odot u_1 = e(u_1, u_2)$.

Assume that every pairing-less SPHF has the modified language representation, implying a hash value is represented as $\Theta_{\mathsf{aux}}(C) = \varphi \bullet (\delta \bullet \gamma(C))$. A first naive approach to transform every pairing-less SPHF into PF-SPHF in a bilinear setting is described in the Table 1, where we will always use the implicit notation of elements in $\mathbb{G}_s$, i.e., we let $[u]_{\mathbb{G}_s} = g_s^u$ be an element in $\mathbb{G}_s$. The key idea is to put pairing-less SPHF in a source group $\mathbb{G}$ (resp. $\widetilde{\mathbb{G}}$) of pairing along with an element $\widetilde{g}$ in another source group $\widetilde{\mathbb{G}}$ (resp. $\mathbb{G}$), whose combination contributes to computing a pairing value. Actually, a pairing-friendly SPHF (PF-SPHF) has been used to construct particular SPHFs with the interesting properties, for instance, the structure-preserving SPHF [18] and the trapdoor SPHF [19].

Table 1. Transformation from SPHF to PF-SPHF.

	SPHF	PF-SPHF
Word $C(\Theta(C))$	$[\lambda \bullet \Gamma(C)]_{\mathbb{G}}$	$[\lambda \bullet \Gamma(C)]_{\mathbb{G}}$
Witness w	λ	λ
hk	α	α
hp($\gamma(C)$)	$[\alpha \bullet \Gamma(C)]_{\mathbb{G}}$	$[\alpha \bullet \Gamma(C)]_{\mathbb{G}}$
Hash	$[\alpha \bullet \Theta(C)]_{\mathbb{G}}$	$[\widetilde{g} \odot (\alpha \bullet \Theta(C))]_{\mathbb{G}_T}$
ProjHash	$[\varphi \bullet (\delta \bullet \gamma(C))]_{\mathbb{G}}$	$[(\varphi \bullet \widetilde{g}) \odot (\delta \bullet \gamma(C))]_{\mathbb{G}_T}$
WordVF	—	Check $[\widetilde{g} \odot (\lambda \bullet \Gamma(C))]_{\mathbb{G}_T} \overset{?}{=} [(\lambda \bullet \widetilde{g}) \odot \Gamma(C)]_{\mathbb{G}_T}$

Correctness. Correctness is inherited for word in $\mathcal{L}$ as this reduces to computing the same value but in $\mathbb{G}_T$.

Smoothness. For the words outside the language, the unchanged projection key do not reveal new information, therefore the hash value remain smoothness.

Examples. Two examples of classical SPHF on Diffie-Hellman and Cramer-Shoup encryption of M and their counterparts with PF-SPHF are described in [18]. We omit them for brevity.

2.4   2-Smoothness SPHF

[17] provides an efficient group-theoretic way (See Theorem 3 in [17]) to construct *universal$_2$* projective hash family from *universal* projective hash family. Actually, applying the same technology we can also obtain 2-smoothness extended SPHF directly from smoothness SPHF. Let SPHF = (SPHFSetup, HashKG, ProjKG, Hash, ProjHash) is smooth projective hash function on $\mathcal{X}$ derived from

1. $\mathsf{SPHFSetup}(k)$: It is the same as the SPHFSetup algorithm in SPHF.
2. $\widehat{\mathsf{HashKG}}(\mathcal{L}, \mathsf{param})$: For $i \in \{0, \ldots, n\}$, it generates a hash key $\widehat{\mathsf{hk}} = \{\mathsf{hk}_i = \mathsf{HashKG}(\mathcal{L}, \mathsf{param})\}_{i=0}^{n}$.
3. $\widehat{\mathsf{ProjKG}}(\widehat{\mathsf{hk}}, (\mathcal{L}, \mathsf{param}), W)$: For $i \in \{0, \ldots, n\}$, it derives the projection key $\widehat{\mathsf{hp}}$ from the hashing key $\widehat{\mathsf{hk}}$, possibly depending on the word W: $\widehat{\mathsf{hp}} = \{\mathsf{ProjKG}(\mathsf{hk}_i, (\mathcal{L}, \mathsf{param}), W)\}_{i=0}^{n}$.
4. $\widehat{\mathsf{Hash}}(\widehat{\mathsf{hk}}, (\mathcal{L}, \mathsf{param}), W, aux)$: It outputs the hash value $\widehat{\mathsf{hv}} \in \mathcal{Y}$ from the hash key $\widehat{\mathsf{hk}}$ on any word $W \in \mathcal{X}$ and $aux \in E$ using Hash algorithm:

$$\widehat{\mathsf{hv}} = \mathsf{Hash}(\mathsf{hk}_0, (\mathcal{L}, \mathsf{param}), W) \prod_{i=1}^{n} \mathsf{Hash}(\mathsf{hk}_i, (\mathcal{L}, \mathsf{param}), W)^{\gamma_i},$$

where $(\gamma_1, \cdots, \gamma_n) = \Gamma(W, aux)$.
5. $\widehat{\mathsf{ProjHash}}(\widehat{\mathsf{hp}}, (\mathcal{L}, \mathsf{param}), W, w, aux)$: It outputs the hash value $\mathsf{hv}' \in \mathcal{Y}$ from the projection key $\widehat{\mathsf{hp}}$ and any word $W \in \mathcal{X}$ and $aux \in E$ with the witness w using ProjHash algorithm:

$$\widehat{\mathsf{hv}'} = \mathsf{ProjHash}(\mathsf{hp}_0, (\mathcal{L}, \mathsf{param}), W, w) \prod_{i=1}^{n} \mathsf{ProjHash}(\mathsf{hp}_i, (\mathcal{L}, \mathsf{param}), W, w)^{\gamma_i}$$

where $(\gamma_1, \cdots, \gamma_n) = \Gamma(W, aux)$.

Fig. 2. Constructing 2-Smoothness SPHF from SPHF

$\mathbb{G}$ of order prime p, we define an extended projective hash function $\widehat{\mathsf{SPHF}} = (\widehat{\mathsf{SPHFSetup}}, \widehat{\mathsf{HashKG}}, \widehat{\mathsf{ProjKG}}, \widehat{\mathsf{Hash}}, \widehat{\mathsf{ProjHash}}, \widehat{\mathsf{WordVF}})$ for $(\mathcal{X} \times E, \mathcal{L} \times E)$ based on SPHF as follows and fix an collusion-resistance hash function

$$\Gamma : \mathcal{X} \times E \to \{0, \cdots, p-1\}^n,$$

where n is sufficiently large. The way to construct 2-smoothness SPHF from SPHF is shown in Fig. 2.

3   Definitions

3.1   Plaintext-Verifiably-Checkable Encryption

We define here the notion of plaintext-verifiably-checkable encryption. Let $k \in \mathbb{N}$ be a security parameter. A plaintext-verifiably-checkable encryption (PVCE) is composed of the following five algorithms:

1. $\mathsf{Setup}(k) \to pp$. The setup algorithm takes as input k and outputs a public system parameter pp.
2. $\mathsf{KeyGen}(pp) \to (pk, sk)$. The key generation algorithm takes as input a public system parameter pp and outputs a key pair (pk, sk) of public and secret key, respectively.
3. $\mathsf{Enc}(pk, M) \to \mathsf{ct}$. The encryption algorithm takes as input pk and a plaintext M and outputs a ciphertext ct.
4. $\mathsf{Dec}(sk, \mathsf{ct}) \to M$. The decryption algorithm takes as input sk and a ciphertext ct, and outputs a plaintext M or $\perp$.

5. VerifyCheck(ct, M) → 1/0. The verifiable check algorithm takes as input a ciphertext ct and a plaintext M, and outputs 1 if ct is **indeed generated correctly** for M under the public key pk, and 0 otherwise.

Correctness. The correctness of PCE must verify the following two conditions:

1. Correctness of decryption. For any $k \in \mathbb{N}$ and $m \in \{0,1\}^*$,

$$\Pr[pp \xleftarrow{\$} \mathsf{Setup}(k), (pk, sk) \xleftarrow{\$} \mathsf{KeyGen}(pp), \mathsf{ct} \xleftarrow{\$} \mathsf{Enc}(pk, M) :$$
$$\mathsf{Dec}(sk, \mathsf{ct}) = M] = 1.$$

2. Correctness of plaintext check. For any $k \in \mathbb{N}$ and $m \in \{0,1\}^*$,

$$\Pr[pp \xleftarrow{\$} \mathsf{Setup}(k), (pk, sk) \xleftarrow{\$} \mathsf{KeyGen}(pp), \mathsf{ct} \xleftarrow{\$} \mathsf{Enc}(pk, M) :$$
$$\mathsf{Check}(M, \mathsf{ct}) = 1] = 1.$$

Verifiability. If M is thought to be the plaintext for a ciphertext ct by the Check algorithm, ct is actually a valid encryption of M.

$$\Pr[pp \xleftarrow{\$} \mathsf{Setup}(k), (pk, sk) \xleftarrow{\$} \mathsf{KeyGen}(pp), (\mathsf{ct}, M) \xleftarrow{\$} \mathcal{A}(pp, pk) :$$
$$\mathsf{Check}(\mathsf{ct}, M) = 1 : \exists r \wedge \mathsf{Enc}(pk, M; r) = \mathsf{ct}] = 1.$$

We assume that PCE plaintexts are drawn from a space of *high min-entropy* [11] since the adversary could win the game definitely when PCE plaintexts come from a space without enough entropy. This assumption is reasonable and has existed in many searchable encryptions.

Definition 1 (High min-entropy). *An adversary* $\mathcal{A} = (\mathcal{A}_f, \mathcal{A}_g)$ *is legitimate if there exists a function* $\ell(\cdot)$ *s.t. for all pk and* $m \in [\mathcal{A}_f(1^k, pk)]$ *we have* $|m| = \ell(k)$. *Moreover, we say that an adversary* $\mathcal{A} = (\mathcal{A}_f, \mathcal{A}_g)$ *has min-entropy* μ *if*

$$\forall k \in \mathbb{N} \; \forall pk \; \forall m : \Pr[m' \leftarrow \mathcal{A}_f(1^k, pk) : m' = m] \le 2^{-\mu(k)}.$$

$\mathcal{A}$ *is said to have* high min-entropy *if it has min-entropy* μ *with* $\mu(k) \in \omega(\log k)$.

3.2   Unlink-CCA Security

Informally, the unlink-cca security assures that the adversary $\mathcal{A} = (\mathcal{A}_1, \mathcal{A}_2)$ as a pair of polynomial time algorithms could not get any partial information about the plaintext under the ciphertext even provided the access to a decryption oracle, where $\mathcal{A}_1$ and $\mathcal{A}_2$ **share neither coins nor state.** $\mathcal{A}_1$ takes input pk and returns two plaintexts (M_0, M_1). $\mathcal{A}_2$ takes input pk and a ciphertext ct, and tries to guess b. Note that $\mathcal{A}_2$ does not see M_0 and M_1 as the output of $\mathcal{A}_1$ and hence cannot guess whether ct_b^* is the encryption of M_0 and M_1. The following experiment $\mathbf{Exp}_{\mathsf{PVCE}, \mathcal{A}}^{\mathsf{unlink\text{-}cca}}(k)$ is defined for the adversary $\mathcal{A}$ with high min-entropy against unlink-cca security, which wins with negligible probability.

$\mathrm{Exp}_{\mathsf{PVCE},\mathcal{A}}^{\mathsf{unlink-cca}}(k)$:

1. **Setup Phase.** The challenger runs the $\mathsf{KeyGen}(k)$ algorithm to generate (pk, sk) and sends pk to the adversary $\mathcal{A} = (\mathcal{A}_1, \mathcal{A}_2)$.
2. **Probing Phase I.** The adversary $\mathcal{A}_1$ submits a ciphertext ct to the challenger. The challenger decrypts ct using its secret key sk and returns the plaintext M back to $\mathcal{A}_1$.
3. **Challenge Phase.** The adversary $\mathcal{A}_1$ randomly selects two messages M_0 and M_1, and presents them to the challenger. The challenger selects a random bit $b \in \{0,1\}$ and sends $(\mathsf{ct}_b^*, \mathsf{ct}_1^*) = (\mathsf{Enc}(pk, M_b), \mathsf{Enc}(pk, M_1))$.
4. **Probing Phase II.** For $\mathcal{A}_2$'s submitted ciphertext ct, the challenger responses the same as in the probing phase I with the only constraint that ct is not equal to ct^*.
5. **Guessing Phase.** $\mathcal{A}_2$ outputs a bit b'. The adversary $\mathcal{A}$ is said to win the game if $b' = b$, inducing the output of experiment is 1, and 0 otherwise.

We say PVCE has unlink-cca security if for any polynomial adversary $\mathcal{A}$,

$$\mathbf{Adv}_{\mathsf{PVCE},\mathcal{A}}^{\mathsf{unlink-cca}}(k) = \left| \Pr[b = b'] - \frac{1}{2} \right|,$$

which is negligible on the security parameter k.

4   PVCE Construction

Let the language $\mathcal{L}$ be hard-partitioned subset. Let $\mathsf{SPHF} = (\mathsf{SPHFSetup}, \mathsf{HashKG}, \mathsf{ProjKG}, \mathsf{Hash}, \mathsf{ProjHash})$ be a smooth projective hash function and $\widetilde{\mathsf{SPHF}} = (\widetilde{\mathsf{SPHFSetup}}, \widetilde{\mathsf{HashKG}}, \widetilde{\mathsf{ProjKG}}, \widetilde{\mathsf{Hash}}, \widetilde{\mathsf{ProjHash}})$ be 2-smoothness extended smooth projective hash function, which are both defined on the domain $\mathcal{X}$ for the same language $\mathcal{L}$ under the same security parameter k. Let $\mathsf{PF\text{-}SPHF}$ and $\widehat{\mathsf{PF\text{-}SPHF}}$ be transformed from SPHF and $\widetilde{\mathsf{SPHF}}$ using the technology in Sect. 2.4. We present a construction of $\mathsf{PVCE} = (\mathsf{PVCE.Setup}, \mathsf{PVCE.KeyGen}, \mathsf{PVCE.Enc}, \mathsf{PVCE.Dec}, \mathsf{PVCE.VerifyCheck})$ as follows.

1. **Setup** $\mathsf{PVCE.Setup}(k)$:
   The setup algorithm does the following:
   (a) Taking the security parameter k as input, run the $\mathsf{SPHFSetup}$ algorithm of SPHF to generate the public parameter $(\mathcal{L}, \mathsf{param})$ on $(\mathbb{G}, p)$.
   (b) Define the public parameter $(\mathcal{L}, \mathsf{param}_e = (\widetilde{\mathbb{G}}, \mathbb{G}, \mathbb{G}_T, e, \widetilde{g}, g, p))$ for the transformed $\mathsf{PF\text{-}SPHF}$ in Type 2 paring, which is a type of pairing with the condition $\widetilde{\mathbb{G}} \neq \mathbb{G}$ but there is an efficiently computable homomorphism $\phi : \mathbb{G} \to \widetilde{\mathbb{G}}$.
   (c) Generate a collision-resistant hash functions f defined on: $\mathcal{X} \times \mathbb{G}_T \times \mathbb{G}_T \to \widetilde{\mathbb{G}}$ and $\Gamma : \mathcal{X} \times \mathbb{G}_T \times \widetilde{\mathbb{G}} \to (\mathbb{Z}_p)^n$, n is an integer.
   The public system parameter is $pp = <\mathcal{L}, \mathsf{param}_e, f, \Gamma>$.

2. **KeyGen** PVCE.KeyGen(pp):
   The key generation algorithm does the following:
   (a) Compute the private key:
   $\mathsf{hk} = \mathsf{HashKG}(\mathcal{L}, \mathsf{param})$,
   For $i \in \{0, ..., n\}$, $\mathsf{hk}_i = \mathsf{HashKG}(\mathcal{L}, \mathsf{param})$.
   (b) Compute the public key:
   $\mathsf{hp} = \mathsf{ProjKG}(\mathsf{hk}, (\mathcal{L}, \mathsf{param}))$,
   For $i \in \{0, ..., n\}$, $\mathsf{hp}_i = \mathsf{ProjKG}(\mathsf{hk}_i, (\mathcal{L}, \mathsf{param}))$.
   The public/private key pair (pk, sk) is

$$sk : (\mathsf{hk}, \widehat{\mathsf{hk}}) = (\mathsf{hk}, (\mathsf{hk}_0, \mathsf{hk}_1, \cdots, \mathsf{hk}_n)),$$
$$pk : (\mathsf{hp}, \widehat{\mathsf{hp}}) = (\mathsf{hp}, (\mathsf{hp}_0, \mathsf{hp}_1, \cdots, \mathsf{hp}_n)).$$

3. **Encryption** PVCE.Enc(pk, M) :
   To encrypt a message M, the encryption algorithm does the following:
   (a) Randomly pick a word $W \in \mathcal{L}$ with the witness $w \in \mathbb{Z}_p$.
   (b) Assume $\widehat{\mathsf{ProjHash}}(\widehat{\mathsf{hp}}, (W, X, Y), w)$ is defined as

$$\widehat{\mathsf{ProjHash}}(\widehat{\mathsf{hp}}, (W, X, Y), w) = \mathsf{ProjHash}(\mathsf{hp}_0, W, w) \prod_{i=1}^{n} \mathsf{ProjHash}(\mathsf{hp}_i, W, w)^{\gamma_i},$$

where $(\gamma_1, \cdots, \gamma_n) = \Gamma(W, X, Y) \in (\mathbb{Z}_p)^n$. Compute the encryption of M:

$$X = \mathsf{PF\text{-}ProjHash}(\tilde{g}, \mathsf{ProjHash}(\mathsf{hp}, W, w)) * M,$$
$$Y = (\tilde{g} \bullet w) * f(W, X * M^{-1}, M),$$
$$Z = \mathsf{PF\text{-}\widehat{ProjHash}}(\tilde{g}, \widehat{\mathsf{ProjHash}}(\widehat{\mathsf{hp}}, (W, X, Y), w)).$$

The output of the algorithm is the ciphertext $\mathsf{ct} = (W, X, Y, Z)$.

4. **Dec** PVCE.Dec(sk, CT):
   This algorithm decrypts the ciphertext $\mathsf{ct} = (W, X, Y, Z)$ using the secret key sk in the following way:
   (a) Compute $M \leftarrow X * \mathsf{PF\text{-}Hash}(\tilde{g}, \mathsf{Hash}(\mathsf{hk}, W))^{-1}$.
   (b) Check whether

$$Z = e\left(\tilde{g}, \widehat{\mathsf{Hash}}(\widehat{\mathsf{hk}}, (W, X, Y))\right),$$
$$Z = e\left(Y * f^{-1}(W, X * M^{-1}, M), \widehat{\mathsf{hp}} \bullet (1, \gamma_1, \cdots, \gamma_n)\right).$$

where $(\gamma_1, \cdots, \gamma_n) = \Gamma(W, X, Y)$ and $\widehat{\mathsf{hp}} \bullet (1, \gamma_1, \cdots, \gamma_n)$ is defined as $\mathsf{hp}_0 \mathsf{hp}_1^{\gamma_1} \ldots \mathsf{hp}_n^{\gamma_n}$. If the above equations hold, it outputs the plaintext M for the ciphertext ct. Else it outputs 0.

5. **Check** PVCE.VerifyCheck(M, ct):
   Check whether

$$\mathsf{WordVF}(Y * f^{-1}(W, M), W) = 1,$$
$$X * M^{-1} = e\left(Y * f^{-1}(W, X * M^{-1}, M), \widehat{\mathsf{hp}}\right),$$
$$Z = e\left(Y * f^{-1}(W, X * M^{-1}, M), \widehat{\mathsf{hp}} \bullet (1, \gamma_1, \cdots, \gamma_n)\right).$$

hold or not, where $(\gamma_1, \cdots, \gamma_n) = \Gamma(W, X, Y)$. If the above equations hold, it outputs 1 indicating that M is the plaintext of ct. Else, it outputs 0.

Correctness. We omit the correctness analysis of Dec algorithm and only provide the correctness analysis of Check algorithm as follows. (1) WordVF$(Y * f^{-1}(W, M), W) =$ WordVF$(w \bullet \widetilde{g}, W) = 1$, (2) $XM^{-1} = e(\widetilde{g}, \mathsf{ProjHash}(\mathsf{hp}, W, w)) = e(w \bullet \widetilde{g}, \mathsf{hp}) = e(Y * f^{-1}(W, X * M^{-1}, M), \mathsf{hp})$ and (3) $Z = e(\widetilde{g}, \widehat{\mathsf{ProjHash}}(\widehat{\mathsf{hp}}, (W, X, Y), w)) = e(w \bullet \widetilde{g}, \widehat{\mathsf{hp}} \bullet (1, \gamma_1, \cdots, \gamma_n)) = e(Y * f^{-1}(W, X * M^{-1}, M), \widehat{\mathsf{hp}} \bullet (1, \gamma_1, \cdots, \gamma_n))$. Therefore, if the above equations hold, we say that ct is the encryption of M.

Verifiability. Consider any public key pk, any ciphertext ct and any plaintext M such that VerifyCheck$(pk, \mathsf{ct}, M) = 1$. The key element for verification is $\pi = Y * f^{-1}(W, X * M^{-1}, M) = \widetilde{g}^w$. Because of the property of PF-SPHF, π denoted as $\varphi \odot \widetilde{g}$ in the modified language representation is the witness of both PF-Hash$(\widetilde{g}, \mathsf{Hash}(\mathsf{hk}, W))$ and $\widehat{\mathsf{PF\text{-}Hash}}(\widetilde{g}, \widehat{\mathsf{Hash}}(\widehat{\mathsf{hk}}, (W, X, Y)))$. Meanwhile, it is also the witness of W under the pairing. Therefore, the ciphertext could be correctly verified.

4.1 Security Proof

Theorem 1. PVCE *satisfies* unlink-cca *if it is computationally hard to distinguish any random element* $W^* \in \mathcal{L}$ *from any random element from* $\mathcal{X} \backslash \mathcal{L}$.

Proof. We show that the existence of an adversary $\mathcal{A}$ against unlink-cca security with significant advantage implies the existence of an efficient algorithm $\mathcal{B}$ that decides a random element $W \in \mathcal{L}$ or $W \in \mathcal{X} \backslash \mathcal{L}$. We define the following game between a simulator (as a role of the distinguisher for the hard subset membership problem) and an adversary $\mathcal{A} = (\mathcal{A}_1, \mathcal{A}_2)$ that carries out an unlink-cca attack.

Game$_0$: Game$_0$ is the initial security game.

1. **Setup Phase.** This simulator emulates the initialization of the system as follows. It runs the Setup(k) algorithm by itself to generate the public parameter $pp = <\mathcal{L}, \mathsf{param}_e = (\widetilde{\mathbb{G}}, \mathbb{G}, \mathbb{G}_T, e, \widetilde{g}, g, p), f, \Gamma >$. Then it runs the KeyGen(pp) algorithm to generate a public/secret key pair $(pk, sk) = ((\mathsf{hp}, \widehat{\mathsf{hp}}), (\mathsf{hk}, \widehat{\mathsf{hk}}))$. It gives (pp, pk) to $\mathcal{A}$.
   - Under the alternative language representation in Sect. 2, we define a new function $\widetilde{\Gamma} : Set \mapsto \mathbb{G}^{k \times 1}$. It comes possibly from any column of $\Gamma(W)$ satisfying that $\lambda \bullet \widetilde{\Gamma}(W)$ is completely determined by φ. We denote it by $\widetilde{\Theta}_{\mathsf{aux}}(W) = \lambda \bullet \widetilde{\Gamma}(W)$, which is an element of the vector in $\Theta_{\mathsf{aux}}(W)$. The simulator emulates $\widetilde{g} \in \widetilde{\mathbb{G}}$ in the following special way:

$$\widetilde{g} = \phi((a\lambda) \odot \widetilde{\Gamma}(W)),$$

where a is randomly chosen from $\mathbb{Z}_p$.

2. **Probing Phase I.** For $\mathcal{A}_1$'s submitted ciphertext ct, the simulator returns the plaintext M via the Dec algorithm using its secret key sk.
3. **Challenge Phase.** $\mathcal{A}_1$ presents two random messages M_0 and M_1 to the simulator. The simulator computes the ciphertext $\mathsf{ct}_b^* = (W^*, X^*, Y^*, Z^*)$ of M_b as follows:
   - The simulator chooses a random word $W^* \in \mathcal{L}$, where W^* is the value input to the simulator, and computes

$$
\begin{aligned}
X^* &= \mathsf{PF\text{-}Hash}(\widetilde{g}, \mathsf{Hash}(\mathsf{hk}, W^*)) * M_b \\
Y^* &= \phi((a\lambda) \bullet \widetilde{\Gamma}(W^*)) * f(W^*, X^* * M_b^{-1}, M_b) \\
    &= a \odot \phi(\lambda \bullet \widetilde{\Gamma}(W^*)) * f(W^*, X^* * M_b^{-1}, M_b) \\
    &= a \odot \phi(\widetilde{\Theta}(W^*)) * f(W^*, X^* * M_b^{-1}, M_b) \\
Z^* &= \widehat{\mathsf{PF\text{-}Hash}}(\widetilde{g}, \widehat{\mathsf{Hash}}(\widehat{\mathsf{hk}}, (W^*, X^*, Y^*)))
\end{aligned}
$$

and honestly computes the ciphertext $\mathsf{ct}_1^* = \mathsf{Enc}(pk, M_1)$. Then it returns $(\mathsf{ct}_b^*, \mathsf{ct}_1^*)$ to $\mathcal{A}_2$.
4. **Probing Phase II.** For $\mathcal{A}_2$'s submitted query on the ciphertext ct, the simulator responses the same as in the probing phase I with the only constraint that ct is not equal to ct_b^*.
5. **Guessing Phase.** $\mathcal{A}_2$ outputs its guess b'.

We consider the behaviour of this simulator in two cases:

Case 1: The simulator is given a random element $W^* \in \mathcal{L}$. Let $\mathsf{Yes}^{(1)}$ be the event that the simulator outputs 1 in this case.
Case 2: The simulator is given a random element $W^* \in \mathcal{X} \backslash \mathcal{L}$. Let $\mathsf{No}^{(1)}$ be the event that the simulator outputs 1 in this case.

Let

$$
\mathbf{Adv}^{\mathsf{Dist}}(k) = \left| \Pr[\mathsf{Yes}^{(1)}] - \Pr[\mathsf{No}^{(1)}] \right|, \tag{1}
$$

which is the distinguishing advantage of the simulator. Our goal is to show that $\mathbf{Adv}^{\mathsf{unlink\text{-}cca}}_{\mathsf{PVCE},\mathcal{A}}(k)$ is negligible provided $\mathbf{Adv}^{\mathsf{Dist}}(k)$ is negligible. We now analyze the behaviour of the simulator in these two cases:

Case 1: $W^* \in \mathcal{L}$. In this case, the simulator is perfect. Therefore, we have

$$
\left| \Pr[\mathsf{Yes}^{(1)}] - \frac{1}{2} \right| \geq \mathbf{Adv}^{\mathsf{unlink\text{-}cca}}_{\mathsf{PVCE},\mathcal{A}}(k) \tag{2}
$$

Case 2: $W^* \in \mathcal{X} \backslash \mathcal{L}$. We will use the game-hopping technique for this case.

Game$_1$: Game$_1$ is the same as Game$_0$, so that in addition to rejecting a ciphertext $C = (W, X, Y, Z)$ but $Z = e((a \bullet \phi(\widetilde{\Theta}(W))) * f(W, X * M^{-1}, M)), \widehat{\mathsf{Hash}}(\widehat{\mathsf{hk}}, W, X, Y))$. Let F be the event that $Z = e((a \bullet \phi(\widetilde{\Theta}(W))) *$

$f(W, X * M^{-1}, M)), \widehat{\mathsf{Hash}}(\widehat{\mathsf{hk}}, (W, X, Y)))$. We define the advantage of $\mathcal{A}$ in Game$_1$ as $\mathbf{Adv}_{\mathsf{PVCE}, \mathcal{A}}^{\mathsf{Game}_1}(k)$ and claim that

$$\left| \mathbf{Adv}_{\mathsf{PVCE}, \mathcal{A}}^{\mathsf{Game}_1}(k) - \mathbf{Adv}_{\mathsf{PVCE}, \mathcal{A}}^{\mathsf{Game}_0}(k) \right| \leq \Pr[F] \tag{3}$$

Next, we analyze the probability that the event F happens. For all ciphertxts $C = (W, X, Y, Z) \in \mathcal{X} \times \mathbb{G}_T \times \widetilde{\mathbb{G}} \times \mathbb{G}_T$ with $W \in \mathcal{X} \backslash \mathcal{L}$ submitted to a decryption oracle after the challenge phrase, we divide them into two cases:

1. $(W, X, Y) = (W^*, X^*, Y^*)$. Since Z is uniquely determined by (W, X, Y), the simulator returns $\perp$.
2. $(W, X, Y) \neq (W^*, X^*, Y^*)$. Given W and X, sk is still uniformly distributed with the only constraint that $\mathsf{hp} = \mathsf{ProjKG}(\mathsf{hk})$ and $\widehat{\mathsf{hp}} = \widehat{\mathsf{ProjKG}}(\widehat{\mathsf{hk}})$. Under this condition, we further divide all queried ciphertexts into two cases:
   (a) $(W, X) = (W^*, X^*)$. Since Y is uniquely determined by (W, X), the simulator returns $\perp$.
   (b) $(W, X) \neq (W^*, X^*)$. Due to the 2-smoothness property of PF-SPHF, $\mathsf{PF}\text{-}\widehat{\mathsf{Hash}}(\widehat{\mathsf{hk}}, (W, X, Y))$ is uniformly distributed over $\mathcal{Y}$. Therefore, the probability that the adversary outputs a valid ciphertext $(W, X, Y, \cdot)$ with $W \in \mathcal{X} \backslash \mathcal{L}$ submitted to the decryption oracle is negligible.

Assume that $Q(k)$ denotes the number of decryption queries. From the above analysis, we have

$$\Pr[F] \leq 2\text{-smooth}(k) \cdot Q(k), \tag{4}$$

where $2\text{-smooth}(k)$ denotes the distinguishable probability in the definition of the 2-smoothness property of PF-SPHF. We define $\mathbf{Adv}_{\mathsf{PVCE}, \mathcal{A}}^{\mathsf{Game}_1}(k)$ as the advantage of the adversary $\mathcal{A}$ in **Game**$_1$ and claim that

$$\left| \mathbf{Adv}_{\mathsf{PVCE}, \mathcal{A}}^{\mathsf{Game}_1}(k) - \mathbf{Adv}_{\mathsf{PVCE}, \mathcal{A}}^{\mathsf{Game}_0}(k) \right| \leq 2\text{-smooth}(k) \cdot Q(k), \tag{5}$$

by combining the relations (3) and (4).

Game$_2$: Game$_2$ is the same as **Game**$_1$ except that the simulator sets $X^* = y_1 * M_b$ in stead of computing $X^* = \mathsf{PF}\text{-}\mathsf{Hash}(\widetilde{g}, \mathsf{Hash}(\mathsf{hk}, W^*)) * M_b$ and sets $Z^* = e(a \bullet \phi(\widetilde{\Theta}(W^*)) * f(W^*, y_1, M_b), \widehat{\mathsf{Hash}}(\widehat{\mathsf{hk}}, (W^*, X^*, Y^*))$ in stead of computing $Z^* = e(a \bullet \phi(\widetilde{\Theta}(W^*)) * f(W^*, \mathsf{PF}\text{-}\mathsf{Hash}(\widetilde{g}, \mathsf{Hash}(\mathsf{hk}, W^*)), M_b), \widehat{\mathsf{Hash}}(\widehat{\mathsf{hk}}, (W^*, X^*, Y^*))))$, where $y_1 \in \mathbb{G}_T$ is chosen at random. We define $\mathbf{Adv}_{\mathsf{PVCE}, \mathcal{A}}^{\mathsf{Game}_2}(k)$ as the advantage of the adversary $\mathcal{A}$ in Game$_2$ and claim that

$$\left| \mathbf{Adv}_{\mathsf{PVCE}, \mathcal{A}}^{\mathsf{Game}_2}(k) - \mathbf{Adv}_{\mathsf{PVCE}, \mathcal{A}}^{\mathsf{Game}_1}(k) \right| \leq 2 \cdot \text{smooth}(k), \tag{6}$$

due to the smoothness property of PF-SPHF.

Game₃: **Game₃** is the same as **Game₂** except that the simulator sets $Z^* = y_2 \overset{\$}{\leftarrow} \mathbb{G}_T$ in stead of computing $Z^* = e(a \bullet \phi(\widetilde{\Theta}(W^*)) * f(W^*, y_1, M_b), \widehat{\mathsf{Hash}}(\widehat{\mathsf{hk}}, (W^*, X^*, Y^*)))$. We define the advantage of $\mathcal{A}$ in Game₃ as $\mathbf{Adv}_{\mathsf{PVCE},\mathcal{A}}^{\mathbf{Game_3}}(k)$ be the advantage of the adversary $\mathcal{A}$ in **Game₃** and claim that

$$\left| \mathbf{Adv}_{\mathsf{PVCE},\mathcal{A}}^{\mathbf{Game_3}}(k) - \mathbf{Adv}_{\mathsf{PVCE},\mathcal{A}}^{\mathbf{Game_2}}(k) \right| \leq \mathsf{smooth}(k) \tag{7}$$

due to the smooth property of PF-SPHF. It is evident that the output b' of adversary with high min-entropy in **Game₃** is totally independent of the hidden bit b. Therefore, we have

$$\mathbf{Adv}_{\mathsf{PVCE},\mathcal{A}}^{\mathbf{Game_3}}(k) = \frac{1}{2} + 2^{-\mu(k)}. \tag{8}$$

Combining the relations (5), (6), (7) and (8), we claim that

$$\left| \Pr[\mathsf{No}^{(1)}] - \frac{1}{2} \right| \leq 2\text{-}\mathsf{smooth}(k) \cdot Q(k) + 2 \cdot \mathsf{smooth}(k) + 2^{-\mu(k)}, \tag{9}$$

Combining the relations (2) and (9), we claim that

$$\mathbf{Adv}_{\mathsf{PVCE},\mathcal{A}}^{\mathsf{unlink\text{-}cca}}(k) \leq \mathbf{Adv}^{\mathsf{Dist}}(k) + 2\text{-}\mathsf{smooth}(k) \cdot Q(k) + 3 \cdot \mathsf{smooth}(k) + 2^{-\mu(k)},$$

from which the theorem immediately follows.

5   Instantiated PVCE Construction Under k-MDDH Assumption

In this section, we show a concrete PVCE construction by instantiating SPHF in pairing groups. Because DDH problem is easy on the group $\mathbb{G}$ in the a Type-2 pairing used in the PVCE construction, we can not use the SPHF instances from Diffie-Hellman or Cramer Shoup encryption in [18]. Therefore, we choose Matrix Diffie-Hellman assumption on which to instantiate SPHF for the transformation to PF-SPHF since it is still hard in Type-2 pairing.

Notations. For $s \in \{1, 2, T\}$ and $a \in \mathbb{Z}_p$ we let $[a] = g^a \in \mathbb{G}$ be an element in $\mathbb{G}$ or $[b]_s$ be an element in $\mathbb{G}_s$. More generally, for a matrix $\mathbf{A} = (a_{ij}) \in \mathbb{Z}_p^{n \times m}$ we define $[\mathbf{A}]_s$ as the implicit representation of $\mathbf{A}$ in $\mathbb{G}_s$: $[\mathbf{A}]_s := \begin{pmatrix} g_s^{a_{11}} & \cdots & g_s^{a_{1m}} \\ g_s^{a_{n1}} & \cdots & g_s^{a_{nm}} \end{pmatrix} \in \mathbb{G}_s^{n \times m}$. Given $[a]_1, [b]_2$ one can efficiently compute $[ab]_T$ using the pairing e. For $a, b \in \mathbb{Z}_p^k$ define $e([a]_1, [b]_2) = [a^\top b]_T \in \mathbb{G}_T$.

Definition 2 (Matrix Distribution). *Let $k \in \mathbb{N}$. We call $\mathcal{D}_k$ a matrix distribution if it outputs matrices in $\mathbb{Z}_p^{(k+1) \times k}$ of full rank k in polynomial time.*

Definition 3 *($\mathcal{D}_k$-Matrix Diffie-Hellman $\mathcal{D}_k$-**MDDH**). Let $\mathcal{D}_k$ be a matrix distribution and $s \in \{1, 2, T\}$. We say that the $\mathcal{D}_k$-Matrix Diffie-Hellman ($\mathcal{D}_k$-MDDH) assumption holds relative to PGGen in group $\mathbb{G}_s$ if for all PPT adversaries $\mathcal{D}$,*

$$\mathbf{Adv}_{\mathcal{D}_k}(\mathcal{D}) := \left| \Pr[\mathcal{D}(\mathcal{PG}, [A]_s, [Aw]_s) = 1] - \Pr[\mathcal{D}(\mathcal{PG}, [A]_s, [u]_s) = 1] \right| = negl(k),$$

where the probability is taken over $\mathcal{PG} \overset{\$}{\leftarrow} \mathsf{PGGen}(k)$, $A \overset{\$}{\leftarrow} \mathcal{D}_k$, $w \overset{\$}{\leftarrow} \mathbb{Z}_p^k$, $u \overset{\$}{\leftarrow} \mathbb{Z}_p^{k+1}$.

5.1 Smooth Projective Hash Function on k-MDDH Assumption

Let $\mathcal{D}_k$ be a matrix distribution. We build a smooth hash proof system SPHF = (SPHFSetup, HashKG, ProjKG, Hash, ProjHash, WordVF), whose hard subset membership problem is based on the $\mathcal{D}_k$-Matrix Diffie-Hellman Assumption.

1. SPHFSetup(k): It generates a group $\mathbb{G}$ of prime order p with an underlying matrix assumption using a base matrix $[A] \in \mathbb{G}^{(k+1) \times k}$. Define the language: $\mathcal{L}_{k\text{-MDDH}} = \{[c] = [Ar] \in \mathbb{G}^{k+1} : r \in \mathbb{Z}_p^k\}$. The output of param is $(\mathbb{G}, p, [A])$.
2. HashKG($\mathcal{L}_{k\text{-MDDH}}$, param): It generates a hashing key hk $= x \in \mathbb{Z}_p^{k+1}$.
3. ProjKG(hk, ($\mathcal{L}_{k\text{-MDDH}}$, param)): It derives the projection key hp $= [x^\top A] \in \mathbb{G}^k$.
4. Hash(hk, ($\mathcal{L}_{k\text{-MDDH}}$, param), $[c] \in \mathbb{G}^{k+1}$): It computes the hash value hv $= [x^\top c]$.
5. ProjHash(hp, ($\mathcal{L}_{k\text{-MDDH}}$, param), $[c] \in \mathbb{G}^{k+1}, r$): Using the witness r of $[c]$, it computes the hash value hv$' = [(x^\top A)r]$.
6. WordVF($[c] \in \mathbb{G}^{k+1}, r$): It outputs 1 if $e([1]_{\widetilde{\mathbb{G}}}, [c]) = e([\bar{r}]_{\widetilde{\mathbb{G}}}, [A1]_{\mathbb{G}}) \in \mathbb{G}_T^{k+1}$, where $[1]_{\widetilde{\mathbb{G}}} = (\widetilde{g}, \ldots, \widetilde{g}) \in \widetilde{\mathbb{G}}_p^{k+1}$, $[\bar{r}] = (\widetilde{g}^r, \ldots, \widetilde{g}^r) \in \widetilde{\mathbb{G}}_p^{k+1}$ and $1 = (1, \ldots, 1) \in \mathbb{Z}_p^k$.

5.2 PVCE Instantiation Under k-MDDH Assumption

Based on the above SPHF instantiation from k-MDDH assumption, we immediately obtain a PVCE construction under k-MDDH assumption as follows.

1. Setup(k): It generates the public parameter ($\mathcal{L}_{k\text{-MDDH}}$, param) on $\mathbb{G}$ using the SPHFSetup(k) algorithm of SPHF on k-MDDH assumption and hence the public parameter ($\mathcal{L}_{k\text{-MDDH}}$, param$_e = (\widetilde{\mathbb{G}}, \mathbb{G}, \mathbb{G}_T, e, \widetilde{g}, g, p, A)$) is defined for the transformed PF-SPHF in Type 2 pairing. It chooses a hash $f : \mathbb{G}^{k+1} \times \mathbb{G}_T \times \mathbb{G}_T \to \widetilde{\mathbb{G}}$ and $\Gamma : \mathbb{G}^{k+1} \times \mathbb{G}_T \times \widetilde{\mathbb{G}} \to \mathbb{Z}_p$, where we set $n = 1$ for 2-smoothness $\widehat{\text{SPHF}}$ generation [17]. It sets the public system parameter $pp = <\mathcal{L}_{k\text{-MDDH}}, \text{param}_e, f, \Gamma>$.

2. KeyGen(pp): It outputs the following public/private key pair (pk, sk) for the PVCE scheme.

$$pk : (\mathsf{hp}, \widehat{\mathsf{hp}}) = ([\boldsymbol{A}\boldsymbol{x}], ([\boldsymbol{A}\widehat{\boldsymbol{x}}_1], [\boldsymbol{A}\widehat{\boldsymbol{x}}_2])),$$
$$sk : (\mathsf{hk}, \widehat{\mathsf{hk}}) = (\boldsymbol{x}, (\widehat{\boldsymbol{x}}_1, \widehat{\boldsymbol{x}}_2)).$$

3. Enc(pk, M): It chooses a random number $r \in \mathbb{Z}_p$ and set $\boldsymbol{r} = (r, \dots, r) \in \mathbb{Z}_p^k$ and computes

$$W = [\boldsymbol{c}] = [\boldsymbol{A}\boldsymbol{r}], \quad X = e(\widetilde{g}, [(\boldsymbol{x}^\top \boldsymbol{A})\boldsymbol{r}]) \cdot M,$$
$$Y = \widetilde{g}^r \cdot f(W, XM^{-1}, M), \quad Z = e(\widetilde{g}, [(\widehat{\boldsymbol{x}}_1^\top \boldsymbol{A})\boldsymbol{r}][(\widehat{\boldsymbol{x}}_2^\top \boldsymbol{A})(\gamma \boldsymbol{r})])),$$

where $\gamma = \Gamma(W, X, Y) \in \mathbb{Z}_p$. Finally, it outputs the ciphertext $\mathsf{ct} = (W, X, Y, Z)$ for the plaintext M.

4. Dec(sk, ct): Upon parsing ct as (W, X, Y, Z), it computes $M \leftarrow X \cdot e(\widetilde{g}, [\boldsymbol{x}^\top \boldsymbol{c}])$ and then verifies if

$$Z = e(\widetilde{g}, [\widehat{\boldsymbol{x}}_1^\top \boldsymbol{c}] \cdot [\widehat{\boldsymbol{x}}_2^\top (\gamma \boldsymbol{c})],$$
$$Z = e(Y \cdot f^{-1}(W, XM^{-1}, M), [\widehat{\boldsymbol{x}}_1^\top \boldsymbol{A}\mathbf{1}][\widehat{\boldsymbol{x}}_2^\top \boldsymbol{A}\boldsymbol{\gamma}]),$$

hold or not, where $\mathbf{1} = (1, \cdots, 1) \in \mathbb{Z}_p^k$, $\boldsymbol{\gamma} = (\gamma, \cdots, \gamma) \in \mathbb{Z}_p^k$ and $\gamma = \Gamma(W, X, Y)$. Through this validation, it returns the plaintext M for the ciphertext ct, or $\perp$ otherwise.

5. Check(M, ct): Upon parsing ct as (W, X, Y, Z), we set $[\mathbf{1}]_{\widetilde{\mathbb{G}}} = (\widetilde{g}, \dots, \widetilde{g}) \in \widetilde{\mathbb{G}}_p^{k+1}$, $\boldsymbol{b} = (b, \dots, b) \in \widetilde{\mathbb{G}}_p^{k+1}$ where $b = Y \cdot f^{-1}(W, XM^{-1}, M)$, $\mathbf{1} = (1, \cdots, 1) \in \mathbb{Z}_p^k$ and $\boldsymbol{\gamma} = (\gamma, \cdots, \gamma) \in \mathbb{Z}_p^k$ where $\gamma = \Gamma(W, X, Y)$. Then it checks if

$$e([\mathbf{1}]_{\widetilde{\mathbb{G}}}, [\boldsymbol{c}]) = e(\boldsymbol{b}, [\boldsymbol{A}\mathbf{1}]),$$
$$XM^{-1} = e(\boldsymbol{b}, [\boldsymbol{x}^\top \boldsymbol{A}\mathbf{1}]),$$
$$Z = e(\boldsymbol{b}, [\widehat{\boldsymbol{x}}_1^\top \boldsymbol{A}\mathbf{1}][\widehat{\boldsymbol{x}}_2^\top \boldsymbol{A}\boldsymbol{\gamma}]),$$

hold or not. Through this validation, it returns 1 indicating that M is the plaintext of ct under pk, or 0 otherwise.

6   Conclusion

We provided a notion of plaintext-verifiably-checkable encryption (PVCE) to ensure that any valid ciphertext could be correctly verified in the test procedure, which prevents a maliciously generated ciphertext passing the check algorithm. We proposed a PVCE construction in the standard model, which has unlink-cca security using pairing-friendly smooth projective hash functions (PF-SPHF) as underlying building block. Finally, we obtain a PVCE instantiation from k-MDDH assumption.

Acknowledgement. This work is supported by National Natural Science Foundation of China (No. 61872409, 61872152), Pearl River Nova Program of Guangzhou (No. 201610010037), Guangdong Natural Science Funds for Distinguished Young Scholar (No. 2014A030306021) and Guangdong Program for Special Support of Topnotch Young Professionals (No. 2015TQ01X796).

References

1. Boneh, D., Di Crescenzo, G., Ostrovsky, R., Persiano, G.: Public key encryption with keyword search. In: Cachin, C., Camenisch, J.L. (eds.) EUROCRYPT 2004. LNCS, vol. 3027, pp. 506–522. Springer, Heidelberg (2004). https://doi.org/10. 1007/978-3-540-24676-3_30
2. Park, D.J., Kim, K., Lee, P.J.: Public key encryption with conjunctive field keyword search. In: Lim, C.H., Yung, M. (eds.) WISA 2004. LNCS, vol. 3325, pp. 73–86. Springer, Heidelberg (2005). https://doi.org/10.1007/978-3-540-31815-6_7
3. Di Crescenzo, G., Saraswat, V.: Public key encryption with searchable keywords based on jacobi symbols. In: Srinathan, K., Rangan, C.P., Yung, M. (eds.) INDOCRYPT 2007. LNCS, vol. 4859, pp. 282–296. Springer, Heidelberg (2007). https://doi.org/10.1007/978-3-540-77026-8_21
4. Abdalla, M., Chevalier, C., Pointcheval, D.: Smooth projective hashing for conditionally extractable commitments. In: Halevi, S. (ed.) CRYPTO 2009. LNCS, vol. 5677, pp. 671–689. Springer, Heidelberg (2009). https://doi.org/10.1007/978-3-642-03356-8_39
5. Rhee, H.S., Park, J.H., Susilo, W., Lee, D.H.: Trapdoor security in a searchable public-key encryption scheme with a designated tester. J. Syst. Softw. **83**, 763–771 (2010)
6. Yang, G., Tan, C.H., Huang, Q., Wong, D.S.: Probabilistic public key encryption with equality test. In: Pieprzyk, J. (ed.) CT-RSA 2010. LNCS, vol. 5985, pp. 119–131. Springer, Heidelberg (2010). https://doi.org/10.1007/978-3-642-11925-5_9
7. Tang, Q.: Public key encryption schemes supporting equality test with authorization of different granularity. Int. J. Appl. Cryptogr. **2**(4), 304–321 (2012)
8. Tang, Q.: Public key encryption supporting plaintext equality test and user-specified authorization. Secur. Commun. Netw. **5**(12), 1351–1362 (2012)
9. Huang, K., Tso, R., Chen, Y., Rahman, S., Almogren, A., Alamri, A.: PKE-AET: public key encryption with authorized equality test. Comput. J. **58**(10), 2686–2697 (2015)
10. Ma, S., Huang, Q., Zhang, M., Yang, B.: Efficient public key encryption with equality test supporting flexible authorization. IEEE Trans. Inf. Forensics Secur. **10**(3), 458–470 (2015)
11. Canard, S., Fuchsbauer, G., Gouget, A., Laguillaumie, F.: Plaintext-checkable encryption. In: Dunkelman, O. (ed.) CT-RSA 2012. LNCS, vol. 7178, pp. 332–348. Springer, Heidelberg (2012). https://doi.org/10.1007/978-3-642-27954-6_21
12. Ma, S., Mu, Y., Susilo, W.: A generic scheme of plaintext-checkable database encryption. Inf. Sci. **429**, 88–101 (2018)
13. Carbunar, B., Sion, R.: Toward private joins on outsourced data. IEEE Trans. Knowl. Data Eng. **24**(9), 1699–1710 (2012)
14. Furukawa, J., Isshiki, T.: Controlled joining on encrypted relational database. In: Abdalla, M., Lange, T. (eds.) Pairing 2012. LNCS, vol. 7708, pp. 46–64. Springer, Heidelberg (2013). https://doi.org/10.1007/978-3-642-36334-4_4

15. Hweehwa, P., Xuhua, D.: Privacy-preserving ad-hoc equi-join on outsourced data. ACM Trans. Database Syst. (TODS) **39**(3), 23:1–23:40 (2014)
16. Ma, S.: Authorized equi-join for multiple data contributors in the PKC-based setting. Comput. J. **60**(12), 1822–1838 (2017)
17. Cramer, R., Shoup, V.: Universal hash proofs and a paradigm for adaptive chosen ciphertext secure public-key encryption. In: Knudsen, L.R. (ed.) EUROCRYPT 2002. LNCS, vol. 2332, pp. 45–64. Springer, Heidelberg (2002). https://doi.org/10.1007/3-540-46035-7_4
18. Blazy, O., Chevalier, C.: Structure-preserving smooth projective hashing. In: Cheon, J.H., Takagi, T. (eds.) ASIACRYPT 2016. LNCS, vol. 10032, pp. 339–369. Springer, Heidelberg (2016). https://doi.org/10.1007/978-3-662-53890-6_12
19. Benhamouda, F., Blazy, O., Chevalier, C., Pointcheval, D., Vergnaud, D.: New techniques for SPHFs and efficient one-round PAKE protocols. In: Canetti, R., Garay, J.A. (eds.) CRYPTO 2013. LNCS, vol. 8042, pp. 449–475. Springer, Heidelberg (2013). https://doi.org/10.1007/978-3-642-40041-4_25

Hierarchical Functional Signcryption: Notion and Construction

Dongxue Pan[1,2,3], Bei Liang[4(✉)] ⓘ, Hongda Li[1,2,3], and Peifang Ni[1,2,3]

[1] State Key Lab of Information Security, Institute of Information Engineering, Chinese Academy of Sciences, Beijing, China
{pandongxue,lihongda,nipeifang}@iie.ac.cn
[2] School of Cyber Security, University of Chinese Academy of Sciences, Beijing, China
[3] Data Assurance and Communication Security Research Center, CAS, Beijing, China
[4] Chalmers University of Technology, Gothenburg, Sweden
lbei@chalmers.se

Abstract. With the purpose of achieving fine-grained access control over the signing and decryption capabilities in the context of a traditional digital signcryption scheme, the concept of *functional signcryption* (FSC) is introduced by Datta et al. (ProvSec 2015) to provide the functionalities of both functional encryption (FE) and functional signature (FS) in an integrated paradigm. In this paper, we introduce the notion of hierarchical functional signcryption (HFSC), which augments the standard functional signcryption with hierarchical delegation capabilities on both signcrypting and unsigncrypting, thereby significantly expanding the scope of functional signcryption in hierarchical access-control application. More precisely, our contributions are two-fold: (i) we formalize the syntax of HFSC and its security notion, (ii) we provide a generic construction of HFSC based on cryptographic building blocks including indistinguishability obfuscation (iO) and statistically simulation-sound non-interactive zero-knowledge proof of knowledge (SSS-NIZKPoK) for NP relations, and we formally shows that it satisfies selective message confidentiality and selective ciphertext unforgeability.

Keywords: Hierarchical functional signcryption ·
Indistinguishability obfuscation · Statistically simulation-sound
non-interactive zero-knowledge proof of knowledge

1 Introduction

In order to provide the confidentiality as well as authentication guarantees, *digital signcryption* is introduced by Zheng [13] as a cryptographic primitive that unifies the functionality of both encryption and authentication in an efficient manner. With the purpose of achieving fine-grained access control over the signing and decryption capabilities in the context of a traditional digital signcryption

© Springer Nature Switzerland AG 2019
R. Steinfeld and T. H. Yuen (Eds.): ProvSec 2019, LNCS 11821, pp. 167–185, 2019.
https://doi.org/10.1007/978-3-030-31919-9_10

scheme, the concept of *functional signcryption* (FSC) is introduced by Datta et al. [7] to provide the functionalities of both function encryption (FE) and functional signature (FS) in an integrated paradigm.

In an FSC scheme, in addition to a master secret key that is held by a trusted authority and can be used to signcrypt (unsigncrypt) any message, there are secondary signing keys for some signing functions f (called SK_f), as well as functional decryption keys DK_g for some decryption functions g, both of which are derived from the master secret key. Such a signing key SK_f enables a signcrypter to signcrypt (i.e., encrypt and authenticate simultaneously) any message in the range of f, while a decryption key DK_g allows one to not only verify the authenticity of the ciphertext, but also unsigncrypt the ciphertext (the signcryption of some message m) and retrieve $g(m)$. The notions of security for FSC are message confidentiality and ciphertext unforgeability. The message confidentiality guarantees that anyone holding the decryption key DK_g and a signcryption of any message m, cannot learn any additional information about m from a signcyption, beyond the result $g(m)$, while ciphertext unforgeability assures that given the signing keys for functions $f_1, \ldots, f_s$ of his choice and signcryptions for messages $m_1, \ldots, m_q$ of his choice, any adversary cannot produce a valid signcryption of a message m^* which is not equal to one of the queried messages $m_1, \ldots, m_q$, and if m^* is not in the range of one of the queried functions $f_1, \ldots, f_s$. Based on the existence of indistinguishability obfuscation (iO) for all polynomial-size circuits and statistically simulation-sound non-interactive zero-knowledge proof of knowledge (SSS-NIZKPoK) system for NP relations, Datta et al. [7] proposed a generic construction of FSC from ordinary public key encryption (PKE) and digital signature schemes.

Hierarchical Functional Signcryption (HFSC). Motivated by the applicability of FSC for supporting highly controlled, fine-grained access strategies, in this paper we put forward the new primitive called *hierarchical functional signcryption* (HFSC). The hierarchical notion augments the standard functional signcryption with hierarchical delegation capabilities on both signcrypting and unsigncrypting, significantly expanding the scope of functional signcryption in hierarchical access-control application.

As we know, in an FSC scheme, the trusted authority who holds the master secret key can generate the functional signing key for a signing function f (called SK_f) which allows a signcrypter to produce the signcryption of $f(z)$ for any $z \in D_f$, as well as functional decryption key for a decryption function g (called DK_g) which enables us to unsigncrypt the signcryption of a message m and to retrieve $g(m)$. Here let f and f' be functions with domain D_f and $D_{f'}$ respectively, where the range of f' is a subset of D_f. In an HFSC scheme, the holder of any such functional signing key SK_f can in turn generate a functional signing key $SK_{f \circ f'}$ corresponding to the function $f \circ f'$ for any given function f'. Then, anyone holding the delegated functional signing key $SK_{f \circ f'}$ and any message $z' \in D_{f'}$, can produce the signcryption of $f(f'(z'))$. Furthermore, the holder of the functional decryption key DK_g can in turn generate a functional decryption key $DK_{g' \circ g}$ corresponding to the function $g' \circ g$ for any given function g'. Then, anyone holding the delegated functional decryption key $DK_{g' \circ g}$ and an signcryption of message m, can compute $g'(g(m))$ but cannot learn any additional information about the message m.

It is crucial to notice the conspicuous distinction of the delegation right between functional signing key SK_f and functional decryption key DK_g. The user with SK_f can only delegate his functional signing capability on a function f', the range of which should be a subset of the domain of f, which implies that the capability of delegation is gradually shrinking from the upper level to lower level. It makes sense because in fact the upper-level user with signing key SK_f usually only wants to delegate his signing right on a subset of his domain to a lower-level user, and the upper-level user can choose the function f' such that the range of f' is exactly the subset that he would like to delegate his signing right. Therefore, in the delegation of functional signing key, the successor f' is composed inside the predecessor f. Whereas, the user with functional decryption key DK_g can delegate his functional decryption capability on a function g', the domain of which should cover the range of g, thus, in the delegation of functional decryption key, the successor g' is composed outside the predecessor g.

The significance of considering the hierarchical delegation capability has been recognized by many works, such as the hierarchical augmentation on functional encryption called *hierarchical functional encryption*, which was investigated in [1,4,6], and hierarchical delegation on functional signature called *delegatable functional signature* [2], which realizes the delegation of signing capabilities in a chained manner.

Our Contributions. We begin with formally introducing the syntax of HFSC and formalizing its security notion. We then present a generic construction of this challenging primitive based on cryptographic building blocks including iO and statistically simulation-sound non-interactive zero-knowledge proof of knowledge (SSS-NIZKPoK) for NP relations. Furthermore, we prove that our HFSC proposal achieves selective message confidentiality against chosen plaintext attack (CPA), as well as, selective ciphertext unforgeability against chosen message attack (CMA).

Technical Overview. Formally, an HFSC scheme consists of the standard algorithms of an FSC scheme, with two additional key delegation algorithms, namely, a functional signing key delegation algorithm and a functional decryption key delegation algorithm. Each of delegation algorithms is identical in syntax to the key generation algorithm of FSC, except that it takes a functional signing (or decryption) key SK_f (or DK_g) instead of the master secret key, and the output of the delegation algorithm is a functional signing (or decryption) key $SK_{f \circ f'}$ (or $DK_{g' \circ g}$) corresponding to the composed function $f \circ f'$ (or $g' \circ g$).

Before showing the main idea of our HFSC construction, we recall how the FSC scheme proposed by Datta et al. in [7] (denoted as DDM-FSC) works. In DDM-FSC scheme, the public parameters are set as $MPK = (pk_{PKE}^1, pk_{PKE}^2, vk_0, CRS)$ while the master secret key is set as $MSK = (sk_{PKE}^1, sk_0)$, where (pk_{PKE}^1, sk_{PKE}^1) and (pk_{PKE}^2, sk_{PKE}^2) are PKE key pairs, (vk_0, sk_0) is a signature key pair, and CRS is a common reference string of

SSS-NIZKPoK. Given a function f, the functional signing key is generated as $SK_f = (f, \sigma)$, where σ is the signature (under sk_0) of f. To signcrypt a message z with signing key $SK_f = (f, \sigma)$, the signcrypter computes a ciphertext $CT = (e_1, e_2, \pi)$, where e_1, e_2 are ciphertexts of $f(z)$ under pk^1_{PKE}, pk^2_{PKE} respectively, and π is the proof for the statement that e_1, e_2 are encryptions of $f(z)$ under pk^1_{PKE}, pk^2_{PKE} and σ is a signature of f under sk_0. Given a function g, the functional decryption key is an obfuscation of the program $P^{g, sk^1_{PKE}, MPK}$, which on input the signcryption $CT = (e_1, e_2, \pi)$, first check the validity of the proof and then decrypts e_1 to obtain plaintext m, finally output $g(m)$. The unsigncryption on a ciphertext CT is straightforward by running the obfuscated program on CT.

Our HFSC scheme is come out from the inspiration of DDM-FSC scheme. The public parameters and master secret key (MPK, MSK) are set the same as DDM-FSC scheme. Whereas, our functional signing key is generated as $SK_f = (f, vk_f, \sigma_f, sk_f, \gamma)$, where σ_f is the signature (under sk_0) of the concatenation of a signing function f and a verification key vk_f in a fresh signature key pair (vk_f, sk_f), where (vk_f, sk_f) is generated by the key generation algorithm of a signature scheme using randomness γ. On input $SK_f = (f, vk_f, \sigma_f, sk_f, \gamma)$ and a function f', the functional signing key delegation algorithm outputs a delegated functional signing key as $SK_{f \circ f'} = (f \circ f', vk_f, \sigma_f, vk_{f'}, \sigma_{f'}, sk_{f'}, \gamma')$, where σ_f is the signature (under sk_0) of the concatenation of a signing function f and vk_f, and $\sigma_{f'}$ is the signature (under sk_f) of the concatenation of function f' and $vk_{f'}$ in a fresh signature key pair $(vk_{f'}, sk_{f'})$, where $(vk_{f'}, sk_{f'})$ is generated by the key generation algorithm of a signature scheme using randomness γ'. To signcrypt a message z with $SK_{f_0 \circ \cdots \circ f_i}$, the signcrypter computes a ciphertext $CT = (e_1, e_2, \pi)$, where e_1, e_2 are ciphertexts of $f_0 \circ \cdots \circ f_i(z)$ under pk^1_{PKE}, pk^2_{PKE} respectively, and π proves that e_1, e_2 are produced honestly, each σ_{f_j} $(j \in [0, i])$ is a signature of $f_j \| vk_{f_j}$ (under corresponding verification key vk_0 (if $j = 0$) or $vk_{f_{j-1}}$ (if $j \in [i]$)), and (vk_{f_i}, sk_{f_i}) is a signature key pair.

The decryption key generation algorithm is the same as in DDM-FSC scheme. When considering the delegation algorithm of functional decryption keys, we take advantage of the idea from hierarchical functional encryption scheme proposed by Ananth et al. [1]. Roughly speaking, on input $DK_g = (g, dk_g)$, where dk_g is an obfuscation of the program $P^{g, sk^1_{PKE}, MPK}$, together with a function g', the functional decryption key delegation algorithm outputs a delegated functional decryption key $DK_{g' \circ g}$ consisting of function $g' \circ g$ together with an obfuscation of the program P^{g', dk_g}, where the program P^{g', dk_g} on input a ciphertext $CT = (e_1, e_2, \pi)$, first evaluates the obfuscation dk_g on input CT to obtain $g(m)$, then applies g' on $g(m)$ to obtain $g' \circ g(m)$, which is eventually returned back. The unsigncryption on a ciphertext CT is straightforward by running $DK_{g_i \circ \cdots \circ g_0}$ on a ciphertext CT and output the result.

The notions of security for HFSC that we consider are formalized in the selective security model, namely, message confidentiality (indistinguishability of ciphertexts against chosen plaintext attack) and ciphertext unforgeability (existential unforgeability against chosen message attack). In the selective model, the adversary must declare the challenge messages at the very beginning, before the system parameters are chosen.

Related Works. The significance of considering the hierarchical delegation capability has been recognized by many works, such as the hierarchical augmentation on FE called *hierarchical functional encryption*, and hierarchical delegation on FS called *delegatable functional signature*, which realizes the delegation of decryption and signing capabilities to another party in a chained manner respectively.

Hierarchical Functional Encryption (HFE). Ananth et al. [1] formally introduced the concept of HFE and provided a security notion for HFE schemes. They also briefly showed how to use a general-purpose indistinguishability obfuscator to transform the FE scheme of Garg et al. [8] into an HFE scheme. Their HFE construction can only support hierarchical structures of constant levels. Then, Chandran et al. [6] proposed an adaptively-secure HFE scheme that supports hierarchical structures of any pre-determined polynomial levels by using sub-exponentially-secure iO. Afterwards, Brakerski and Segev [4] present a generic transformation to convert any general-purpose public-key FE scheme into an HFE scheme without relying on iO.

Functional Signature (FS). FS was introduced by Boyle et al. [3] to realized the delegation of the signing capability from a master authority to another party. In an FS scheme, a trusted authority publishes public parameters and holds a master signing key. The master signing key can be used to sign any message, as well as to derive a functional key SK_f, a constrained signing key corresponding to some signing function f. Then the signer with SK_f can sign any message in the range of the function f. Boyle et al. also show how to build an FS scheme with function privacy and succinctness, relying on the succinct non-interactive arguments of knowledge (SNARKS) and (standard) non-interactive zero-knowledge arguments of knowledge (NIZKAoKs) for NP languages.

Delegatable Functional Signatures (DFS). Backes et al. [2] introduced DFS which enables the signer of a message who holds the master signing key to choose an evaluator, specify the ways that the party can modify the signature while keeping its validity, and also allows the evaluator to further delegate its signing capabilities.

Organization. In Sect. 2, we provide the notations and definitions of the building blocks that are used through the paper. In Sect. 3, we propose the notion of hierarchical functional signcryption and show a construction. In Sect. 4, we make a conclusion.

2 Preliminaries

2.1 Notations

We use λ to denote the security parameter. Let $A(\cdot)$ be a probabilistic algorithm and let $A(x)$ be the result of running algorithm A on input x, then we use

$y = A(x)$ (or $y \leftarrow A(x)$) to denote that y is set as $A(x)$. Let $A_r(x)$ be the result of running algorithm A on input x with random value r. For a finite set $\mathcal{S}$, we use $y \in_R \mathcal{S}$ (or $y \leftarrow_R \mathcal{S}$) to denote that y is uniformly selected from $\mathcal{S}$. We use $[l]$ to denote the set $\{1, 2, \cdots, l\}$. We write $negl(\cdot)$ to denote an unspecified negligible function, $poly(\cdot)$ an unspecified polynomial. We denote by $|a|$ the length of string a. We denote by $a\|b$ the concatenation of two bit strings a and b. We use "$X \stackrel{c}{=} Y$" to denote that probabilistic distributions X and Y are computationally indistinguishable. For any language L and any instance $x \in L$, we denote by $\mathcal{R}_L$ the efficiently computable binary NP relation for L and then for any witnesses w of $x \in L$, $\mathcal{R}_L(x, w) = 1$.

2.2   Indistinguishability Obfuscation

Definition 2.1. *Indistinguishability obfuscation (iO)* [8]. *A PPT algorithm iO is called an indistinguishability obfuscator for a circuit ensemble $\{\mathcal{C}_\lambda\}_{\lambda \in N}$ if the following conditions are satisfied:*

- *(functionality) For all security parameters $\lambda \in N$, for all $C \in \mathcal{C}_\lambda$, and for all input x we have that $\Pr[C'(x) = C(x) : C' \leftarrow iO(1^\lambda, C)] = 1$.*
- *(security) For any PPT distinguisher D, there exists a negligible function $negl(\cdot)$ such that the following holds: For all security parameters $\lambda \in N$, for all pairs of same size circuits $C_0, C_1 \in \mathcal{C}_\lambda$, we have that if $C_0(x) = C_1(x)$ for all inputs x, then $\left| \Pr[D(1^\lambda, iO(1^\lambda, C_0)) = 1] - \Pr[D(1^\lambda, iO(1^\lambda, C_1)) = 1] \right| \leq negl(\lambda)$.*

The results [5,8,9,14] on iO support our construction of HFSC.

2.3   Statistically Simulation-Sound Non-interactive Zero-Knowledge Proof of Knowledge

The notion of SSS-NIZKPoK has been introduced and formalized in the full version of [10]. Now we slightly simplify the original definition following [3,7,8].

Definition 2.2. *Statistically Simulation-Sound Non-interactive Zero-Knowledge Proof of Knowledge: SSS-NIZKPoK.* *Let $\mathcal{R} \subset \{0,1\}^* \times \{0,1\}^*$ be an NP (binary) relation. For pairs $(X, W) \in \mathcal{R}$, we call X the statement and W the witness. Let $L \subset \{0,1\}^*$ be the language consisting of statements in $\mathcal{R}$. An SSS-NIZKPoK system for L consists of the following PPT algorithms:*

- ***SSS-NIZKPoK.Setup**(1^λ): The trusted authority takes as input a security parameter 1^λ and publishes a common reference string CRS.*
- ***SSS-NIZKPoK.Prove**(CRS, X, W): Taking as input the common reference string CRS, a statement $X \in L$ along with a witness W, a prover outputs a proof π.*
- ***SSS-NIZKPoK.Verify**(CRS, X, π): On input the common reference string CRS, a statement $X \in \{0,1\}^*$, and a proof π, a verifier outputs 1, if the proof π is acceptable, or 0, otherwise.*

- **SSS-NIZKPoK.SimSetup**$(1^\lambda, X)$: *The simulator takes as input the security parameter 1^λ together with a statement $X \in \{0,1\}^*$. It produces a simulated common reference string CRS along with a trapdoor TR that enables it to simulate a proof for X without access to a witness.*
- **SSS-NIZKPoK.SimProve**(CRS, TR, X): *Taking as input the simulated common reference string CRS, the trapdoor TR, and the statement $X \in \{0,1\}^*$ for which CRS and TR have been generated, the simulator outputs a simulated proof π.*
- **SSS-NIZKPoK.ExtSetup**(1^λ): *The extractor, on input 1^λ, outputs an extraction-enabling common reference string CRS and an extraction trapdoor $\widetilde{TR}$.*
- **SSS-NIZKPoK.Extr**$(CRS, \widetilde{TR}, X, \pi)$: *The extractor takes as input the extraction-enabling common reference string CRS, the extraction trapdoor $\widetilde{TR}$, a statement $X \in \{0,1\}^*$, and a proof π. It outputs a witness W.*

An SSS-NIZKPoK system should have the following properties:

- **Perfect Completeness:** *An SSS-NIZKPoK system is perfectly complete if for all security parameter λ, all $(X, W) \in \mathcal{R}$, all $CRS \leftarrow SSS\text{-}NIZKPoK.Setup(1^\lambda)$, and all $\pi \leftarrow SSS\text{-}NIZKPoK.Prove(CRS, X, W)$:*

$$SSS\text{-}NIZKPoK.Verify(CRS, X, \pi) = 1.$$

- **Statistical Soundness:** *An SSS-NIZKPoK system is statistically sound if for all non-uniform adversaries A there exists a negligible function negl such that for any security parameter λ, we have*

$$\Pr \left[\begin{array}{l} CRS \leftarrow SSS - NIZKPoK.Setup(1^\lambda); (X, \pi) \leftarrow A(CRS) : \\ SSS - NIZKPoK.Verify(CRS, X, \pi) = 1 \land X \notin L \end{array} \right] \leq negl(\lambda).$$

- **Computational Zero-Knowledge:** *We define the SSS-NIZKPoK system to be computationally zero-knowledge if for all non-uniform PPT adversaries A there exists a negligible function negl such that for any security parameter λ, we have for all $X \in L$*

$$\left| \Pr \left[\begin{array}{l} CRS \leftarrow SSS - NIZKPoK.Setup(1^\lambda); \\ \pi \leftarrow SSS - NIZKPoK.Prove(CRS, X, W) : \\ A(CRS, X, \pi) = 1 \end{array} \right] \right.$$
$$\left. -\Pr \left[\begin{array}{l} (CRS, TR) \leftarrow SSS - NIZKPoK.SimSetup(1^\lambda, X); \\ \pi \leftarrow SSS - NIZKPoK.SimProve(CRS, TR, X) : \\ A(CRS, X, \pi) = 1 \end{array} \right] \right| \leq negl(\lambda),$$

where W is a witness corresponding to X.
- **Knowledge Extraction:** *We call an SSS-NIZKPoK system a proof of knowledge for $\mathcal{R}$ if for any security parameter λ the following holds: For all non-uniform adversaries A there exists a negligible function $negl_1$ such that*

$$\left| \Pr \left[\begin{array}{l} CRS \leftarrow SSS - NIZKPoK.Setup(1^\lambda); \\ A(CRS) = 1 \end{array} \right] \right.$$

$$\left. -\Pr \left[\begin{array}{l} (CRS, \widetilde{TR}) \leftarrow SSS - NIZKPoK.ExtSetup(1^\lambda); \\ A(CRS) = 1 \end{array} \right] \right| \leq negl_1(\lambda),$$

and for all non-uniform PPT adversaries A there exists a negligible function $negl_2$ such that

$$\Pr \left[\begin{array}{l} (CRS, \widetilde{TR}) \leftarrow SSS - NIZKPoK.ExtSetup(1^\lambda); \\ (X, \pi) \leftarrow A(CRS); \\ W^* \leftarrow SSS - NIZKPoK.Extr(CRS, \widetilde{TR}, X, \pi) : \\ SSS - NIZKPoK.Verify(CRS, X, \pi) = 1 \wedge (X, w^*) \notin \mathcal{R} \end{array} \right] \leq negl_2(\lambda).$$

- **Statistical Simulation-Soundness:** An SSS-NIZKPoK system is statistically simulation-sound if for all non-uniform adversaries A there exists a negligible function negl such that for any security parameter λ, we have for all statements $X \in \{0,1\}^*$

$$\Pr \left[\begin{array}{l} (CRS, TR) \leftarrow SSS - NIZKPoK.SimSetup(1^\lambda, X); \\ \pi \leftarrow SSS - NIZKPoK.SimProve(CRS, TR, X); \\ (X^*, \pi^*) \leftarrow A(CRS, X, \pi) : \\ X^* \neq X \wedge X^* \notin L \wedge \\ SSS - NIZKPoK.Verify(CRS, X^*, \pi^*) = 1 \end{array} \right] \leq negl(\lambda).$$

There are well-known constructions [11,12] of non-interactive zero-knowledge proof of knowledge (NIZKPoK) for NP relations. Then, based on any NIZKPoK and a non-interactive perfectly binding commitment scheme we can obtain an SSS-NIZKPoK for NP relations follows from the similar technique of [8].

3 Hierarchical Functional Signcryption: Notion and Construction

In this section, we start with presenting the definition of hierarchical functional signcryption (HFSC), which is adapted from the notions of functional signcryption [7] and hierarchical functional encryption [4]. And then we show a construction of HFSC.

3.1 The Notion of Hierarchical Functional Signcryption

Definition 3.1. Hierarchical Functional Signcryption (HFSC). A hierarchical functional signcryption scheme for a message space M, a family of signing functions $F = \{f : D_f \rightarrow M\}$, and a class of decryption functions $G = \{g : M \rightarrow R_g\}$, where D_f and R_g denote the domain of the function f and range of the function g respectively, consists of the following PPT algorithms:

- **HFSC.Setup**(1^λ): *The trusted authority takes as input the security parameter* 1^λ *and publishes the public parameters* MPK, *while keeps the master secret key* MSK *to itself.*
- **HFSC.SKeyGen**(MPK, MSK, f): *Taking as input the public parameters* MPK, *the master secret key* MSK, *and a signing function* $f \in F$ *from a signcrypter, the trusted authority provides a signing key* SK_f *to the signcrypter.*
- **HFSC.SKDelegate**(MPK, SK_f, f'): *Taking as input the public parameters* MPK, *the signing key* SK_f, *and a function* f', *the range of which is a subset of the domain of* f, *the signcrypter provides a signing key* $SK_{f \circ f'}$ *to another signcrypter.*
- **HFSC.Signcrypt**$(MPK, SK_{f_0 \circ \cdots \circ f_i}, z)$: *A signcrypter takes as input the public parameters* MPK, *its signing key* $SK_{f_0 \circ \cdots \circ f_i}$ *corresponding to some signing function* $f_0 \in F$ *and* $\{f_j\}_{j \in [i]}$ *satisfying that the range of* f_j *is a subset of the domain of* f_{j-1}, *and an input* $z \in D_{f_i}$. *It produces a ciphertext* CT *which is a signcryption of* $f_0 \circ \cdots \circ f_i(z) \in M$.
- **HFSC.DKeyGen**(MPK, MSK, g): *On input the public parameters* MPK, *the master secret key* MSK, *and a decryption function* $g \in G$ *from a decrypter, the trusted authority hands the decryption key* DK_g *to the decrypter.*
- **HFSC.DKDelegate**(MPK, DK_g, g'): *Taking as input the public parameters* MPK, *a decryption key* DK_g, *and a function* g' *satisfying that the domain of* g' *contains the range of* g, *the decrypter provides a signing key* $DK_{g' \circ g}$ *to another decrypter.*
- **HFSC.Unsigncrypt**$(MPK, DK_{g_i \circ \cdots \circ g_1 \circ g_0}, CT)$: *A decrypter, on input the public parameters* MPK, *its decryption key* $DK_{g_i \circ \cdots \circ g_1 \circ g_0}$ *associated with some decryption function* $g_0 \in G$ *and* $\{g_j\}_{j \in [i]}$ *satisfying that the domain of* g_j *contains the range of* g_{j-1}, *and a ciphertext* CT *signcrypting a message* $m \in M$, *attempts to unsigncrypt the ciphertext* CT *and outputs* $g_i \circ \cdots \circ g_1 \circ g_0(m)$, *if successful, or a special string* $\perp$ *indicating failure, otherwise.*

An HFSC scheme should possess the following properties:

- **Correctness:** *An HFSC scheme is correct if for all signing function* $f_0 \in F$ *and* $\{f_j\}_{j \in [i_1]}$ *satisfying that the range of* f_j *is a subset of the domain of* f_{j-1}, $z \in D_{f_i}$, *and* $g_0 \in G$ *and* $\{g_j\}_{j \in [i_2]}$ *satisfying that the domain of* g_j *contains the range of* g_{j-1},

$$\text{Pr} \begin{bmatrix} (MPK, MSK) \leftarrow HFSC.Setup(1^\lambda), \\ SK_{f_0} \leftarrow HFSC.SKeyGen(MPK, MSK, f_0), \\ SK_{f_0 \circ \cdots \circ f_j} \leftarrow HFSC.SKDelegate(MPK, \\ \qquad SK_{f_0 \circ \cdots \circ f_{j-1}}, f_j), j \in [i_1], \\ DK_{g_0} \leftarrow HFSC.DKeyGen(MPK, MSK, g_0), \\ DK_{g_j \circ \cdots \circ g_0} \leftarrow HFSC.DKDelegate(MPK, \\ \qquad DK_{g_{j-1} \circ \cdots \circ g_0}, g_j), j \in [i_2] : \\ HFSC.Unsigncrypt\Big(MPK, DK_{g_{i_2} \circ \cdots \circ g_0}, \\ HFSC.Signcrypt(MPK, SK_{f_0 \circ \cdots \circ f_{i_1}}, z)\Big) \\ = g_{i_2} \circ \cdots \circ g_0(f_0 \circ \cdots \circ f_{i_1}(z)) \end{bmatrix} > 1 - negl(\lambda).$$

for some negligible function negl.

- **Selective Security:** *An HFSC scheme has two security requirements, namely, (I) message confidentiality and (II) ciphertext unforgeability which are described below. In the selective model, the adversary must decide the challenge messages up front, before the system parameters are chosen.*

(I) Message Confidentiality: *We define this security notion on indistinguishability of ciphertexts against chosen plaintext attack (CPA) through the following game between a probabilistic adversary A and a probabilistic challenger C.*

Init: *A submits two sequences $(f_{0,0}^*, \cdots, f_{0,i}^*, z_0^*)$, $(f_{1,0}^*, \cdots, f_{1,i}^*, z_1^*)$ of signing function $f_{\alpha,0}^* \in F$ and $\{f_{\alpha,j}^*\}_{j \in [i]}$ satisfying that the range of $f_{\alpha,j}^*$ is a subset of the domain of $f_{\alpha,j-1}^*$ and $z_\alpha^* \in D_{f_{\alpha,i}^*}$ ($\alpha \in \{0,1\}$) that will be used to frame the challenge.*

Setup: *C performs $HFSC.Setup(1^\lambda)$ to obtain (MPK, MSK) and hands MPK to A.*

Query Phase 1: *A may adaptively make any polynomial number of queries which may be of the following types to be answered by C.*

- *Signing key query: Upon receiving a signing key query for a signing function $f_0 \in F$ and $\{f_j\}_{j \in [i_1]}$ satisfying that the range of f_j is a subset of the domain of f_{j-1}, C hands the signing key $SK_{f_0 \circ \cdots \circ f_{i_1}}$ to A, by performing*

$$SK_{f_0} \leftarrow HFSC.SKeyGen(MPK, MSK, f_0)$$
$$SK_{f_0 \circ \cdots \circ f_j} \leftarrow HFSC.SKDelegate(MPK, SK_{f_0 \circ \cdots \circ f_{j-1}}, f_j), j \in [i_1].$$

- *Decryption key query: When A queries a decryption key for a decryption function $g_0 \in G$ and $\{g_j\}_{j \in [i_2]}$ satisfying that the domain of g_j contains the range of g_{j-1} to C subject to the constraint that $\widetilde{g}(f_{0,0}^* \circ \cdots \circ f_{0,i}^*(z_0^*)) = \widetilde{g}(f_{1,0}^* \circ \cdots \circ f_{1,i}^*(z_1^*))$, where $\widetilde{g} = g_{i_2} \circ \cdots \circ g_0$, C provides the decryption key $DK_{\widetilde{g}}$ to A by running*

$$DK_{g_0} \leftarrow HFSC.DKeyGen(MPK, MSK, g_0),$$
$$DK_{g_j \circ \cdots \circ g_0} \leftarrow HFSC.DKDelegate(MPK, DK_{g_{j-1} \circ \cdots \circ g_0}, g_j), j \in [i_2].$$

- *Signcryption query: In response to a signcryption query of A for a signing function $f_0 \in F$ and $\{f_j\}_{j \in [i_3]}$ satisfying that the range of f_j is a subset of the domain of f_{j-1}, and an input $z \in D_{f_{i_3}}$, C hands the ciphertext CT to A, which is a signcryption of $f_0 \circ \cdots \circ f_{i_3}(z)$, by performing*

$$SK_{f_0} \leftarrow HFSC.SKeyGen(MPK, MSK, f_0)$$
$$SK_{f_0 \circ \cdots \circ f_j} \leftarrow HFSC.SKDelegate(MPK, SK_{f_0 \circ \cdots \circ f_{j-1}}, f_j), j \in [i_3],$$
$$CT \leftarrow HFSC.Signcrypt(MPK, SK_{f_0 \circ \cdots \circ f_{i_3}}, z).$$

Challenge: *C flips a random coin $b \leftarrow \{0,1\}$ and generates the challenge ciphertext CT^* by running $SK_{f_{b,0}^*} \leftarrow HFSC.SKeyGen(MPK, MSK, f_{b,0}^*)$,*

$$SK_{f_{b,0}^* \circ \cdots \circ f_{b,j}^*} \leftarrow HFSC.SKDelegate(MPK, SK_{f_{b,0}^* \circ \cdots \circ f_{b,j-1}^*}, f_{b,j}^*), j \in [i],$$
$$CT^* \leftarrow HFSC.Signcrypt(MPK, SK_{f_{b,0}^* \circ \cdots \circ f_{b,i}^*}, z_b^*).$$

Query Phase 2: *A may continue adaptively to make a polynomial number of queries as in **Query Phase 1**, subject to the same restriction as earlier, and C provides the answer to them.*

Guess: *A eventually outputs a guess b' for b and wins the game if $b' = b$.*

An HFSC scheme is defined to be selectively message confidential against CPA if for all PPT adversaries A there exists a negligible function negl such that for any security parameter λ, $Adv_A^{HFSC,s-IND-CPA}(\lambda) = |\Pr[b' = b] - 1/2| < negl(\lambda)$.

(II) Ciphertext Unforgeability: *This notion of security is defined on existential unforgeability against chosen message attack (CMA) through the following game between a probabilistic adversary A and a probabilistic challenger C.*

Init: *A declares a message $m^* \in M$ to C on which the forgery will be outputted.*

Setup: *C runs $HFSC.Setup(1^\lambda)$ to obtain (MPK, MSK) and hands MPK to A.*

Query Phase: *A may adaptively make a polynomial number of queries of the following types to C and C provides the answer to those queries.*

- *Signing key query: Upon receiving a signing key query for a signing function $f_0 \in F$ and $\{f_j\}_{j \in [i_1]}$, satisfying that the range of f_j is a subset of the domain of f_{j-1}, subject to the constraint that there exists no $z \in D_{f_{i_1}}$ such that $f_0 \circ \cdots \circ f_{i_1}(z) = m^*$, C hands the signing key $SK_{f_0 \circ \cdots \circ f_{i_1}}$ to A, by performing*

$$SK_{f_0} \leftarrow HFSC.SKeyGen(MPK, MSK, f_0)$$
$$SK_{f_0 \circ \cdots \circ f_j} \leftarrow HFSC.SKDelegate(MPK, SK_{f_0 \circ \cdots \circ f_{j-1}}, f_j), j \in [i_1].$$

- *Decryption key query: When A queries a decryption key for a decryption function $g_0 \in G$ and $\{g_j\}_{j \in [i_2]}$ satisfying that the domain of g_j contains the range of g_{j-1} to C, C provides the decryption key $DK_{g_{i_2} \circ \cdots \circ g_0}$ to A by running*

$$DK_{g_0} \leftarrow HFSC.DKeyGen(MPK, MSK, g_0),$$
$$DK_{g_j \circ \cdots \circ g_0} \leftarrow HFSC.DKDelegate(MPK, DK_{g_{j-1} \circ \cdots \circ g_0}, g_j), j \in [i_2].$$

– *Signcryption query: In response to a signcryption query of A for a signing function $f_0 \in F$ and $\{f_j\}_{j \in [i_3]}$ satisfying that the range of f_j is a subset of the domain of f_{j-1}, and an input $z \in D_{f_{i_3}}$, C hands the ciphertext CT to A, which is a signcryption of $f_0 \circ \cdots \circ f_{i_3}(z)$, by performing*

$$SK_{f_0} \leftarrow HFSC.SKeyGen(MPK, MSK, f_0)$$
$$SK_{f_0 \circ \cdots \circ f_j} \leftarrow HFSC.SKDelegate(MPK, SK_{f_0 \circ \cdots \circ f_{j-1}}, f_j), j \in [i_3],$$
$$CT \leftarrow HFSC.Signcrypt(MPK, SK_{f_0 \circ \cdots \circ f_{i_3}}, z).$$

– *Unsigncryption query: Upon receiving an unsigncryption query from A for a ciphertext CT under a decryption function $g_0 \in G$ and $\{g_j\}_{j \in [i_4]}$ satisfying that the domain of g_j contains the range of g_{j-1}, C performs algorithms*

$$DK_{g_0} \leftarrow HFSC.DKeyGen(MPK, MSK, g_0),$$
$$DK_{g_0 \circ \cdots \circ g_0} \leftarrow HFSC.DKDelegate(MPK, DK_{g_{j-1} \circ \cdots \circ g_0}, g_j), j \in [i_4],$$
$$HFSC.Unsigncrypt(MPK, DK_{g_{i_4} \circ \cdots \circ g_0}, CT) and sends the result to A.$$

Forgery: *A finally outputs a forgery CT^* on m^*. A wins the game if CT^* is indeed a valid functional signcryption of m^*, i.e., $HFSC.Unsigncrypt(MPK, DK_g, CT^*) = g(m^*)$ for all $g \in G$, and there does not exist any $(f_0, \cdots, f_{i_5}, z)$ sequence such that $(f_0, \cdots, f_{i_5}, z)$ was a signcryption query of A and $m^* = f_0 \circ \cdots \circ f_{i_5}(z)$.*

An HFSC scheme is defined to be selectively ciphertext unforgeable against CMA if for all PPT adversaries A there exists a negligible function negl such that for any security parameter λ, $Adv_A^{HFSC,s-UF-CMA}(\lambda) = \Pr[Awins] < negl(\lambda)$.

3.2   The Construction of Hierarchical Functional Signcryption

In this subsection, we present a generic construction of this challenging primitive, hierarchical functional signcryption, that supports arbitrary polynomial-size signing and decryption functions from known cryptographic building blocks. Let λ be the underlying security parameter. The cryptographic building blocks used in our HFSC construction are the following:

– O: An indistinguishability obfuscator for $P/poly$.
– $PKE = (PKE.KeyGen, PKE.Encrypt, PKE.Decrypt)$: A CPA-secure public key encryption scheme with message space $M \subset \{0,1\}^{n(\lambda)}$, for some polynomial n.
– $SIG = (SIG.KeyGen, SIG.Sign, SIG.Verify)$: An existentially unforgeable signature scheme with message space $\{0,1\}^{n(\lambda)}$, for some polynomial n.
– $SSS\text{-}NIZKPoK = (SSS\text{-}NIZKPoK.Setup, SSS\text{-}NIZKPoK.Prove, SSS\text{-}NIZKPoK.Verify, SSS\text{-}NIZKPoK.SimSetup, SSS\text{-}NIZKPoK.SimProve, SSS\text{-}NIZKPoK.ExtSetup, SSS\text{-}NIZKPoK.Extr)$: An SSS-NIZKPoK system for the NP relation $\mathcal{R}$, with statements of the form

$$X = (pk_{PKE}^1, pk_{PKE}^2, vk_{SIG}, e_1, e_2) \in \{0,1\}^*,$$

witness of the form $W = (m, z, r_1, r_2, f_0, vk_{f_0}, \sigma_{f_0}, \cdots, f_i, vk_{f_i}, \sigma_{f_i}, sk_{f_i}, \gamma^i) \in \{0,1\}^*$, and

$$(X, W) \in \mathcal{R} \Longleftrightarrow \Big(\; e_1 = PKE.Encrypt(pk_{PKE}^1, m; r_1) \; \wedge$$
$$e_2 = PKE.Encrypt(pk_{PKE}^2, m; r_2) \; \wedge$$
$$SIG.Verify(vk_{SIG}, f_0 \| vk_{f_0}, \sigma_{f_0}) = 1 \; \wedge$$
$$SIG.Verify(vk_{f_{j-1}}, f_j \| vk_{f_j}, \sigma_{f_j}) = 1 \text{ for } \forall j \in [i] \; \wedge$$
$$(vk_{f_i}, sk_{f_i}) \leftarrow SIG.KeyGen(1^\lambda; \gamma^i) \; \wedge$$
$$m = f_0 \circ \cdots \circ f_i(z) \Big),$$

for a function family $F = \{f_0 : D_{f_0} \to M\} \subset P/poly$ (with representation in $\{0,1\}^\lambda$).

Then we build an HFSC scheme for message space M, family of signing functions F, and the class of decryption functions $G = \{g : M \to R_g\} \subset P/poly$.

Construction 3.1. (HFSC scheme).

- **HFSC.Setup(1^λ):** The trusted authority takes as input the security parameter 1^λ and proceeds as follows:
  - It generates $(pk_{PKE}^1, sk_{PKE}^1), (pk_{PKE}^2, sk_{PKE}^2) \leftarrow PKE.KeyGen(1^\lambda)$.
  - It obtains $(vk_{SIG}, sk_{SIG}) \leftarrow SIG.KeyGen(1^\lambda)$.
  - It generates $CRS \leftarrow SSS\text{-}NIZKPoK.Setup(1^\lambda)$.
  - It publishes the public parameters $MPK = (pk_{PKE}^1, pk_{PKE}^2, vk_{SIG}, CRS)$, while keeps the master secret key $MSK = (sk_{PKE}^1, sk_{SIG})$ to itself.
- **HFSC.SKeyGen(MPK, MSK, f):** Taking as input the public parameters MPK, the master secret key MSK, and a signing function $f \in F$ from a signcrypter, the trusted authority runs the algorithms $(vk_f, sk_f) \leftarrow SIG.KeyGen(1^\lambda; \gamma)$ with randomness γ and $SIG.Sign(sk_{SIG}, f \| vk_f)$ to obtain a signature σ_f on the concatenation of the signing function f and the verification key vk_f, and then returns the signing key $SK_f = (f, vk_f, \sigma_f, sk_f, \gamma)$ to the signcrypter.
- **HFSC.SKDelegate(MPK, SK_f, f'):** Taking as input the public parameters MPK, the signing key SK_f, and a function f' (from another signcrypter) satisfying that the range of f' is a subset of the domain of f, the signcrypter proceeds as follows:
  - It parses $SK_f = (f, SK_f', sk, \gamma)$.
  - It obtains $(vk_{f'}, sk_{f'}) \leftarrow SIG.KeyGen(1^\lambda; \gamma')$ with randomness γ'.
  - It generates $\sigma_{f'} \leftarrow SIG.Sign(sk, f' \| vk_{f'})$.
  - It returns the signing key $SK_{f \circ f'} = (f \circ f', SK_f', vk_{f'}, \sigma_{f'}, sk_{f'}, \gamma')$ to the signcrypter.
- **HFSC.Signcrypt$(MPK, SK_{f_0 \circ \cdots \circ f_i}, z)$:** A signcrypter takes as input the public parameters MPK, its signing key $SK_{f_0 \circ \cdots \circ f_i}$ corresponding to some signing function $f_0 \in F$ and $\{f_j\}_{j \in [i]}$ satisfying that the range of f_j is a subset of the domain of f_{j-1}, and an input $z \in D_{f_i}$. It prepares the ciphertext as follows:

- It parses $SK_{f_0 \circ \cdots \circ f_i} = (f_0 \circ \cdots \circ f_i, vk_{f_0}, \sigma_{f_0}, \cdots, vk_{f_i}, \sigma_{f_i}, sk_{f_i}, \gamma^i)$.
- It It computes $e_l = PKE.Encrypt(pk_{PKE}^l, f_0 \circ \cdots \circ f_i(z); r_l)$ for $l = 1, 2$, where r_l is the randomness selected for encryption.
- It generates a proof $\pi \leftarrow SSS\text{-}NIZKPoK.Prove(CRS, X, W)$, where $X = (pk_{PKE}^1, pk_{PKE}^2, vk_{SIG}, e_1, e_2)$ is a statement of the NP relation $\mathcal{R}$ and $W = (f_0 \circ \cdots \circ f_i(z), z, r_1, r_2, f_0, vk_{f_0}, \sigma_{f_0}, \cdots, f_i, vk_{f_i}, \sigma_{f_i}, sk_{f_i}, \gamma^i)$ is the corresponding witness.
- It outputs the ciphertext $CT = (e_1, e_2, \pi)$.
- **HFSC.DKeyGen**(MPK, MSK, g): On input the public parameters MPK, the master secret key MSK, and a decryption function $g \in G$ from a decrypter, the trusted authority proceeds as follows:
  - It parses $MSK = (sk_{PKE}^1, sk_{SIG})$.
  - It computes $dk_g \leftarrow O(P^{g, sk_{PKE}^1, MPK})$ using the circuit size $max\{|P_1|, |P_2|\}$, where the programs $P_l = P^{g, sk_{PKE}^l, MPK}$ $(l = 1, 2)$ are defined in Fig. 1.
  - It outputs $DK_g = (g, dk_g)$.
- **HFSC.DKDelegate**(MPK, DK_g, g'): Taking as input the public parameters MPK, a decryption key DK_g, and a function g' (from another decrypter) satisfying that the domain of g' contains the range of g, the decrypter proceeds as follows:
  - It parses $DK_g = (g, dk_g)$.
  - It computes $dk_{g' \circ g} \leftarrow O(P^{g', dk_g})$. The program P^{f', dk_g} on input a ciphertext $CT = (e_1, e_2, \pi)$, first evaluates the obfuscation dk_g on input CT to obtain x. It then evaluates g' on x to obtain $g'(x)$, which it then outputs.
  - It returns the decryption key $DK_{g' \circ g} = (g' \circ g, dk_{g' \circ g})$.
- **HFSC.Unsigncrypt**$(MPK, DK_{g_i \circ \cdots \circ g_0}, CT)$: A decrypter, on input the public parameters MPK, its decryption key $DK_{g_i \circ \cdots \circ g_0}$, and a ciphertext CT signcrypting a message $m \in M$, decrypts the ciphertext as follows:
  - It parses $DK_{g_i \circ \cdots \circ g_0} = (g_i \circ \cdots \circ g_0, dk_{g_i \circ \cdots \circ g_0})$.
  - It computes and outputs $y \leftarrow dk_{g_i \circ \cdots \circ g_0}(CT)$.

$$P_l = P^{g, sk_{PKE}^l, MPK} \ (l = 1, 2)$$

Given input (e_1, e_2, π), the program proceeds as follows:

1. Extract $pk_{PKE}^1, pk_{PKE}^2, vk_{SIG}, CRS$ from MPK.
2. Set $X = (pk_{PKE}^1, pk_{PKE}^2, vk_{SIG}, e_1, e_2)$.
3. If $SSS\text{-}NIZKPoK.Verify(CRS, X, \pi) = 0$, then output $\perp$ and stop. Otherwise, continue to the next step.
4. Output $g(PKE.Decrypt(sk_{PKE}^l, e_l))$.

Fig. 1. Programs P_1 and P_2

Correctness: It is oblivious that the correctness of the proposed scheme follows immediately from the correctness of O, PKE, and SIG, perfect completeness of the $SSS\text{-}NIZKPoK$ system, and the description of the program P_1 in Fig. 1.

3.3   Security Analysis

Theorem 3.1 (Message Confidentiality of HFSC). *Assuming iO O for P/poly, CPA-secure public key encryption PKE, and the statistical simulation-soundness and zero-knowledge properties of the SSS-NIZKPoK system, the HFSC scheme described in Sect. 3.2 is selectively message confidential against CPA as per the definition given in Sect. 3.1.*

Proof. Suppose that at most $q = q(\lambda)$ many decryption key queries are made by any adversary in the selective CPA-message confidentiality game of Definition 3.1. Then for simplicity, we assume the adversary to always make exactly q decryption key queries. We denote $\widetilde{g}_i$ for $i \in [q]$ to be the i-th composite decryption function for which a decryption key query is made. By the rules of the game $\widetilde{g}_i(\widetilde{f}_0^*(z_0^*))$ is constrained to be equal to $\widetilde{g}_i(\widetilde{f}_1^*(z_1^*))$ for $i \in [q]$, where $\widetilde{f}_\alpha^* = f_{\alpha,0}^* \circ \cdots \circ f_{\alpha,i}^*$ for $\alpha \in \{0,1\}$.

We form our proof here into a sequence of hybrids. As in the first hybrid, the challenger signcrypts $\widetilde{f}_0^*(z_0^*)$. And then, we gradually modify the signcryption in multiple hybrid steps into a signcryption of $\widetilde{f}_1^*(z_1^*)$ in the challenge ciphertext. And we show that each hybrid experiment is indistinguishable from the previous one, hence then we can show that our HFSC scheme have selective message confidentiality against CPA.

Sequence of Hybrids:

- Hyb_0: This corresponds to the honest execution of the selective CPA-message confidentiality game introduced in Definition 3.1 when the challenger signcrypts $\widetilde{f}_0^*(z_0^*)$ in the challenge ciphertext $CT^* = (e_1^*, e_2^*, \pi^*)$, i.e. the elements are computed with algorithms $e_l^* = PKE.Encrypt(pk_{PKE}^l, \widetilde{f}_0^*(z_0^*); r_l^*)$ for $l = 1, 2$ and $\pi^* \leftarrow SSS\text{-}NIZKPoK.Prove(CRS, X^*, W^*)$, where the statement $X^* = (pk_{PKE}^1, pk_{PKE}^2, vk_{SIG}, e_1^*, e_2^*)$ and W^* is a valid witness corresponding to X^*.

- $Hyb_{1,i}$ for $i \in [0, q]$: In this sequence of hybrids, we change the form of the decryption keys provided to the adversary in response to its decryption key queries. In hybrid $Hyb_{1,i}$, the first i decryption keys requested by the adversary (with $g_0 \in G$ and $\{g_j\}_{j \in [i_2]}$ satisfying that the domain of g_j contains the range of g_{j-1} to C subject to the constraint that $g_0(\widetilde{f}_0^*(z_0^*)) = g_0(\widetilde{f}_1^*(z_1^*))$) will result in decryption keys generated as $DK_{\widetilde{g}_i} = (\widetilde{g}_i, O(P^{\widetilde{g}_i, sk_{PKE}^1, MPK}))$, where $\widetilde{g}_i = g_{i_2} \circ \cdots \circ g_0$ and $P^{\widetilde{g}_i, sk_{PKE}^1, MPK}$ and $P^{\widetilde{g}_i, sk_{PKE}^2, MPK}$ are depicted in Fig. 1, while the remaining $i + 1$ to q decryption keys are generated by performing

$$DK_{g_0} = (g_0, dk_{g_0}) = (g_0, O(P^{g_0, sk_{PKE}^1, MPK})), \text{ and for } j \in [i_2],$$

$$DK_{g_j \circ \cdots \circ g_0} = (g_j \circ \cdots \circ g_0, dk_{g_j \circ \cdots \circ g_0}) = (g_j \circ \cdots \circ g_0, O(P^{g_j, dk_{g_{j-1} \circ \cdots \circ g_0}})),$$

where $P^{g_j, dk_{g_{j-1} \circ \cdots \circ g_0}}$ on input a ciphertext $CT = (e_1, e_2, \pi)$, first evaluates the obfuscation $dk_{g_{j-1} \circ \cdots \circ g_0}$ on input CT to obtain x. It then evaluates g_j on x to obtain $g_j(x)$. Observe that $Hyb_{1,0}$ is equivalent to Hyb_0.

– Hyb_2: In this hybrid, the common reference string CRS included in the public parameters MPK is generated as

$$(CRS, TR) \leftarrow SSS\text{-}NIZKPoK.SimSetup(1^\lambda, X^*),$$

and the proof π^* included in the challenge ciphertext CT^* is simulated as

$$\pi^* \leftarrow SSS\text{-}NIZKPoK.SimProve(CRS, TR, X^*)$$

where $X^* = (pk_{PKE}^1, pk_{PKE}^2, vk_{SIG}, e_1^*, e_2^*)$. The rest of the experiment continues as in $Hyb_{1,q}$ using the simulated common reference string CRS.

– Hyb_3: This hybrid is the same as the last hybrid except that the challenge ciphertext is computed as

$$e_1^* = PKE.Encrypt(pk_{PKE}^1, \widetilde{f_0^*}(z_0^*); r_1^*),$$
$$e_2^* = PKE.Encrypt(pk_{PKE}^2, \widetilde{f_1^*}(z_1^*); r_2^*),$$
$$\pi^* \leftarrow SSS - NIZKPoK.SimProve(CRS, TR, X^*)$$

where $X^* = (pk_{PKE}^1, pk_{PKE}^2, vk_{SIG}, e_1^*, e_2^*)$.

– $Hyb_{4,i}$ for $i \in [0, q]$: In this sequence of hybrids, we change the form of the decryption keys provided to the adversary in response to its decryption key queries. In $Hyb_{4,i}$, the first i decryption keys requested by the adversary will result in decryption keys generated as $DK_{\widetilde{g}_i} = (\widetilde{g}_i, O(P^{\widetilde{g}_i, sk_{PKE}^2, MPK}))$ while the remaining $i+1$ to q decryption keys are generated as $DK_{\widetilde{g}_i} = (\widetilde{g}_i, O(P^{\widetilde{g}_i, sk_{PKE}^1, MPK}))$ as in Hyb_3, where $P^{\widetilde{g}_i, sk_{PKE}^1, MPK}$ and $P^{\widetilde{g}_i, sk_{PKE}^2, MPK}$ are depicted in Fig. 1. Observe that $Hyb_{4,0}$ is equivalent to Hyb_3.

– Hyb_5: This hybrid is identical to the hybrid $Hyb_{4,q}$ with the exception that the challenge ciphertext is generated as $CT^* = (e_1^*, e_2^*, \pi^*)$ where

$$e_1^* = PKE.Encrypt(pk_{PKE}^1, \widetilde{f_1^*}(z_1^*); r_1^*),$$
$$e_2^* = PKE.Encrypt(pk_{PKE}^2, \widetilde{f_1^*}(z_1^*); r_2^*),$$

and the proof π^* is still simulated.

– $Hyb_{6,i}$ for $i \in [0, q]$: In this sequence of hybrids, we again change the form of the decryption keys provided to the adversary in response to its decryption key queries. In $Hyb_{6,i}$, the first i decryption keys requested by the adversary will result in decryption keys generated as $DK_{\widetilde{g}_i} = (\widetilde{g}_i, O(P^{\widetilde{g}_i, sk_{PKE}^1, MPK}))$ while the remaining $i+1$ to q decryption keys are generated as $DK_{\widetilde{g}_i} = (\widetilde{g}_i, O(P^{\widetilde{g}_i, sk_{PKE}^2, MPK}))$ as in Hyb_5, where $P^{\widetilde{g}_i, sk_{PKE}^1, MPK}$ and $P^{\widetilde{g}_i, sk_{PKE}^2, MPK}$ are depicted in Fig. 1. Observe that $Hyb_{6,0}$ is equivalent to Hyb_5.

– Hyb_7: In this hybrid, the common reference string CRS included in MPK is obtained as

$$CRS \leftarrow SSS\text{-}NIZKPoK.Setup(1^\lambda),$$

and the proof π^* included in the challenge ciphertext CT^* is generated as

$$\pi^* \leftarrow SSS\text{-}NIZKPoK.Prove(CRS, X^*, W^*),$$

where $X^* = (pk^1_{PKE}, pk^2_{PKE}, vk_{SIG}, e_1^*, e_2^*)$ and W^* is a valid witness corresponding to X^*. The remainder of the experiment continues as in $Hyb_{6,q}$ using the honestly generated common reference string CRS.

- $Hyb_{8,i}$ for $i \in [0, q]$: In this sequence of hybrids, we change the form of the decryption keys provided to the adversary in response to its decryption key queries. In hybrid $Hyb_{8,i}$, the first i decryption keys requested by the adversary (with $g_0 \in G$ and $\{g_j\}_{j \in [i_2]}$ satisfying that the domain of g_j contains the range of g_{j-1} to C subject to the constraint that $g_0(\widetilde{f}_0^*(z_0^*)) = g_0(\widetilde{f}_1^*(z_1^*))$) will result in decryption keys $DK_{\widetilde{g}_i}$ $(\widetilde{g}_i = g_{i_2} \circ \cdots \circ g_0)$ generated by performing

$$DK_{g_0} = (g_0, dk_{g_0}) = (g_0, O(P^{g_0, sk^1_{PKE}, MPK})), \ and \ for \ j \in [i_2],$$

$$DK_{g_j \circ \cdots \circ g_0} = (g_j \circ \cdots \circ g_0, dk_{g_j \circ \cdots \circ g_0}) = (g_j \circ \cdots \circ g_0, O(P^{g_j, dk_{g_{j-1} \circ \cdots \circ g_0}})),$$

where $P^{g_j, dk_{g_{j-1} \circ \cdots \circ g_0}}$ on input a ciphertext $CT = (e_1, e_2, \pi)$, first evaluates the obfuscation $dk_{g_{j-1} \circ \cdots \circ g_0}$ on input CT to obtain x. It then evaluates g_j on x to obtain $g_j(x)$. The remaining $i + 1$ to q decryption keys are generated as $DK_{\widetilde{g}_i} = (\widetilde{g}_i, O(P^{\widetilde{g}_i, sk^1_{PKE}, MPK}))$, where $P^{\widetilde{g}_i, sk^1_{PKE}, MPK}$ and $P^{\widetilde{g}_i, sk^2_{PKE}, MPK}$ are depicted in Fig. 1. Observe that $Hyb_{8,0}$ is equivalent to Hyb_7 and that $Hyb_{8,q}$ corresponds to the selective CPA-message confidentiality game when $\widetilde{f}_1^*(z_1^*)$ is signcrypted in the challenge ciphertext.

Proofs of Hybrid Arguments: We now present a sequence of lemmas to show that no PPT adversary can distinguish with non-negligible advantage between any two consecutive hybrids described above, hence then the security in the selective CPA-message confidentiality game follows.

Lemma 1. *Assuming O is an iO for P/poly, no PPT adversary can distinguish with non-negligible advantage between $Hyb_{1,i}$ and $Hyb_{1,i+1}$ for $i \in [0, q-1]$.*

Lemma 2. *Assuming SSS-NIZKPoK system is computationally zero-knowledge, no PPT adversary can distinguish with non-negligible advantage between $Hyb_{1,q}$ and Hyb_2.*

Lemma 3. *Assuming PKE is CPA secure, no PPT adversary can distinguish with non-negligible advantage between the hybrids Hyb_2 and Hyb_3.*

Lemma 4. *Assuming O is an iO for P/poly and SSS-NIZKPoK is statistically simulation-sound, no PPT adversary can distinguish with non-negligible advantage between $Hyb_{4,i}$ and $Hyb_{4,i+1}$ for $i \in [0, q-1]$.*

Lemma 5. *Assuming PKE is CPA secure, no PPT adversary can distinguish with non-negligible advantage between the hybrids $Hyb_{4,q}$ and Hyb_5.*

Lemma 6. *Assuming O is an iO for P/poly and SSS-NIZKPoK is statistically simulation-sound, no PPT adversary can distinguish with non-negligible advantage between $Hyb_{6,i}$ and $Hyb_{6,i+1}$ for $i \in [0, q-1]$.*

Lemma 7. *Assuming   SSS-NIZKPoK system is computationally zero-knowledge, no PPT adversary can distinguish with non-negligible advantage between $Hyb_{6,q}$ and Hyb_7.*

Lemma 8. *Assuming O is an iO for P/poly, no PPT adversary can distinguish with non-negligible advantage between $Hyb_{8,i}$ and $Hyb_{8,i+1}$ for $i \in [0, q-1]$.*

The proofs of Lemmas 1–8 are available in the full version.   □

Theorem 3.2 (Ciphertext Unforgeability of HFSC.) *Under the assumption that SIG is existentially unforgeable against CMA and SSS-NIZKPoK is a proof of knowledge, the HFSC scheme described in Sect. 3.2 is selectively ciphertext unforgeable against CMA as per the definition given in Sect. 3.1.*

The proof of Theorem 3.2 is available in the full version.

4   Conclusion

In this paper, we investigate hierarchical functional signcryption schemes, which augments FSC with delegation capabilities, offering significantly more expressive access control. We first provide formal definition of hierarchical functional signcryption and formulate its security requirements. And then, we present a generic construction of hierarchical functional signcryption from indistinguishability obfuscation and statistically simulation-sound non-interactive zero-knowledge proof of knowledge.

Acknowledgement. This work is supported by National Key R&D Program of China (No. 2017YFB0802500). This work is also partially supported by the Swedish Research Council (Vetenskapsrådet) through the grant PRECIS (621-2014-4845).

References

1. Ananth, P., Boneh, D., Garg, S., Sahai, A., Zhandry, M.: Differing-inputs obfuscation and applications. IACR Cryptology ePrint Archive 2013, 689 (2013)
2. Backes, M., Meiser, S., Schröder, D.: Delegatable functional signatures. In: Cheng, C.-M., Chung, K.-M., Persiano, G., Yang, B.-Y. (eds.) PKC 2016. LNCS, vol. 9614, pp. 357–386. Springer, Heidelberg (2016). https://doi.org/10.1007/978-3-662-49384-7_14
3. Boyle, E., Goldwasser, S., Ivan, I.: Functional signatures and pseudorandom functions. In: Krawczyk, H. (ed.) PKC 2014. LNCS, vol. 8383, pp. 501–519. Springer, Heidelberg (2014). https://doi.org/10.1007/978-3-642-54631-0_29
4. Brakerski, Z., Chandran, N., Goyal, V., Jain, A., Sahai, A., Segev, G.: Hierarchical functional encryption (2017)

5. Brakerski, Z., Dagmi, O.: Shorter circuit obfuscation in challenging security models. In: Zikas, V., De Prisco, R. (eds.) SCN 2016. LNCS, vol. 9841, pp. 551–570. Springer, Cham (2016). https://doi.org/10.1007/978-3-319-44618-9_29
6. Chandran, N., Goyal, V., Jain, A., Sahai, A.: Functional encryption: decentralised and delegatable. IACR Cryptology ePrint Archive 2015, 1017 (2015)
7. Datta, P., Dutta, R., Mukhopadhyay, S.: Functional signcryption: notion, construction, and applications. In: Au, M.-H., Miyaji, A. (eds.) ProvSec 2015. LNCS, vol. 9451, pp. 268–288. Springer, Cham (2015). https://doi.org/10.1007/978-3-319-26059-4_15
8. Garg, S., Gentry, C., Halevi, S., Raykova, M., Sahai, A., Waters, B.: Candidate indistinguishability obfuscation and functional encryption for all circuits. In: IEEE Symposium on Foundations of Computer Science (2013)
9. Garg, S., Miles, E., Mukherjee, P., Sahai, A., Srinivasan, A., Zhandry, M.: Secure obfuscation in a weak multilinear map model. In: Hirt, M., Smith, A. (eds.) TCC 2016. LNCS, vol. 9986, pp. 241–268. Springer, Heidelberg (2016). https://doi.org/10.1007/978-3-662-53644-5_10
10. Groth, J.: Simulation-sound NIZK proofs for a practical language and constant size group signatures. In: Lai, X., Chen, K. (eds.) ASIACRYPT 2006. LNCS, vol. 4284, pp. 444–459. Springer, Heidelberg (2006). https://doi.org/10.1007/11935230_29
11. Groth, J., Ostrovsky, R., Sahai, A.: Perfect non-interactive zero knowledge for NP. In: Vaudenay, S. (ed.) EUROCRYPT 2006. LNCS, vol. 4004, pp. 339–358. Springer, Heidelberg (2006). https://doi.org/10.1007/11761679_21
12. Groth, J., Ostrovsky, R., Sahai, A.: New techniques for noninteractive zero-knowledge. J. ACM 59(3), 1–35 (2012)
13. Zheng, Y.: Digital signcryption or how to achieve cost(signature & encryption) ≪ cost(signature) + cost(encryption). In: Kaliski, B.S. (ed.) CRYPTO 1997. LNCS, vol. 1294, pp. 165–179. Springer, Heidelberg (1997). https://doi.org/10.1007/BFb0052234
14. Zimmerman, J.: How to obfuscate programs directly. In: Oswald, E., Fischlin, M. (eds.) EUROCRYPT 2015. LNCS, vol. 9057, pp. 439–467. Springer, Heidelberg (2015). https://doi.org/10.1007/978-3-662-46803-6_15

Attack

A Critique of Game-Based Definitions of Receipt-Freeness for Voting

Ashley Fraser[1(✉)], Elizabeth A. Quaglia[1], and Ben Smyth[2]

[1] Information Security Group, Royal Holloway, University of London, London, UK
{Ashley.Fraser.2016,Elizabeth.Quaglia}@rhul.ac.uk
[2] Interdisciplinary Centre for Security, Reliability and Trust,
University of Luxembourg, Esch-sur-Alzette, Luxembourg
research@bensmyth.com

Abstract. We analyse three game-based definitions of receipt-freeness; uncovering soundness issues with two of the definitions and completeness issues with all three. Hence, two of the definitions are too weak, i.e., satisfiable by voting schemes that are not intuitively receipt-free. More precisely, those schemes need not even satisfy ballot secrecy. Consequently, the definitions are satisfiable by schemes that reveal how voters vote. Moreover, we find that each definition is limited in scope. Beyond soundness and completeness issues, we show that each definition captures a different attacker model and we examine some of those differences.

1 Introduction

Electronic voting, or e-voting, is the process of voting with the use of electronic aids at some stage in the voting process. We use the term e-voting to refer to remote e-voting that does not require paper at any point in the process and can be accomplished anywhere in the world. E-voting is gaining popularity, both for public office elections and other voting scenarios. In particular, Australia has used iVote [19] for state general elections in New South Wales since 2011 and Estonia has implemented Internet voting in municipal elections since 2005 and in parliamentary elections since 2007 [35]. Moreover, the International Association for Cryptologic Research (IACR) use Helios [1,17] to elect board members [18].

E-voting has created new opportunities, including the introduction of convenience to the voting process, and the potential to automate the process of tallying elections when compared to hand-counting ballots in a traditional paper-based election. It also has the potential to produce *verifiable* elections, one of the main security goals of e-voting.[1] E-voting also creates new challenges. In particular, voter privacy is a concern. This is not new or unique to *electronic* voting but is particularly true for schemes that do not rely on a physical voting booth because

---

[1] Verifiability is typically defined as individual verifiability (any voter can check that their ballot is counted), universal verifiability (anyone can check that the published tally is correct) and eligibility verifiability (only eligible voters voted). The interested reader can consult [11,31,34] for a discussion on the subject of verifiability.

© Springer Nature Switzerland AG 2019
R. Steinfeld and T. H. Yuen (Eds.): ProvSec 2019, LNCS 11821, pp. 189–205, 2019.
https://doi.org/10.1007/978-3-030-31919-9_11

the voter cannot rely upon the privacy afforded by the booth. A step towards overcoming the challenge of ensuring voter privacy is to provide rigorous privacy definitions for e-voting schemes, and then formally prove that a scheme satisfies a given definition.

Privacy for e-voting is often presented as a hierarchy of security properties [13] as follows. First, ballot secrecy, whereby a voter's vote remains secret throughout the election, except when the result of the election reveals the vote, or when partial information about the vote can be deduced from the result. Second, receipt-freeness, the property that a voter cannot prove their vote to anyone. Finally, coercion-resistance, whereby a voter can cast their vote as they intended, even if they are under the control of an attacker for some time during the election.

The relationship between these privacy properties is often considered to be linear [13]. In particular, receipt-freeness strengthens ballot secrecy with additional protection against vote buying. This ensures that potential attackers have no incentive to buy votes, since a voter cannot prove how they voted, and therefore cannot prove that their vote was truly 'bought'. Moreover, coercion-resistance strengthens receipt-freeness by protecting against randomization, abstention and simulation attacks [22]. However, Küesters et al. challenge this hierarchy, showing that increasing the level of ballot secrecy can lead to a decrease in the level of coercion-resistance [24].

Formal ballot secrecy definitions were surveyed in [5,29], where Bernhard et al. and Smyth compared existing ballot secrecy definitions from the literature and presented their own definitions. Similarly, definitions of coercion resistance were surveyed in [32]. Receipt-freeness, on the other hand, has not been surveyed, which motivates this work.

The earliest definitions of receipt-freeness are informal, with the first definition credited to Benaloh and Tuinstra [4]. A general shift towards formal definitions occurred in response to concerns that voting schemes may appear to be receipt-free when they are not [28]. The early formal definitions, with the exception of Moran and Naor's simulation-based definition [27], are formulated in the symbolic model, for example, [2,8,14,15,20,21]. These definitions use a variety of logical languages to capture the intuition of receipt-freeness. In fact, these definitions helped to shape the intuition and determine how to define receipt-freeness. More recently, there has been a movement towards game-based definitions of receipt-freeness, possibly driven by the simplicity of proof techniques in the model. Given that this is a young area of research and, to the best of our knowledge, there is no examination that tests the rigour of these game-based definitions, we revisit existing game-based definitions in the literature and perform a critical analysis.

1.1 Our Contributions

We analyse three game-based definitions of receipt-freeness from the literature: a receipt-freeness definition by Kiayias et al., which we call KZZ [23] (Sect. 3); one by Chaidos et al., which we call CCFG [9] (Sect. 4); and one by Bernhard et al. for schemes that use deniable vote updating, a process that allows a voter to change their vote without detection, which we call DKV [6,7] (Sect. 5). We cast each definition into our syntax (Definition 1) to facilitate analysis and comparison of definitions.

We uncover soundness issues with KZZ and CCFG, and find all three definitions to be incomplete. The soundness issue in KZZ arises because the definition is satisfied by schemes that reveal how voters vote when not all voters vote (Sect. 3.1). An issue arises in CCFG because Chaidos *et al.* do not consider *strong consistency* (Sect. 4.1), a property defined to accompany ballot secrecy definition BPRIV [5], upon which CCFG is based, and is used to detect some attacks against ballot secrecy. The definitions are incomplete because some schemes are out of scope. Schemes that count votes in some particular ways and others that allow voters to submit multiple ballots are out of scope of KZZ (Sect. 3.2). We prove that neither KZZ nor CCFG is satisfiable by JCJ [22] (Sects. 3.2 and 4.2). Finally, DKV limits the class of schemes considered to those that use deniable vote updating.

We discuss the attacker model adopted by each definition, showing that each definition considers a different attacker model. We find that KZZ models a voter that attempts to prove their vote to an attacker, without allowing the voter to interact with the attacker before voting. In particular, the attacker cannot provide instructions to the voter (Sect. 3.3). We demonstrate that the attacker model in CCFG is much stronger, capturing an attacker with some control over the voter (Sect. 4.3). We also comment that DKV does not model a voter who attempts to prove their vote, but only asks whether an attacker can determine whether a voter has updated their vote from the attacker's choice or not. We discuss the consequences of these differing attacker models, questioning whether each definition captures the core intuition of receipt-freeness.

2   Preliminaries

We let $A(y_1, \ldots, y_n; c)$ denote the output of algorithm A on inputs $y_1, \ldots, y_n$ and coins c, and let $A(y_1, \ldots, y_n)$ denote $A(y_1, \ldots, y_n; c)$ for some coins c chosen uniformly at random. Moreover, we let $x \leftarrow M$ denote assignment of M to x.

An e-voting scheme typically consists of the following five phases. First (*Setup*), the election administrator[2] computes and publishes public parameters of the scheme. Secondly (*Register*), the administrator provides eligible voters with a public and private credential and adds the public credential to a list $\mathcal{L}$. Thirdly (*Vote*), each voter selects their vote v. This vote is stored as a ballot b on the ballot box $\mathcal{BB}$. Fourthly (*Tally*), a tallier computes and publishes the result. Finally (*Verification*), voters verify that their ballot is on the ballot box and observers verify that the tally is correct. We now formally introduce the syntax for an e-voting scheme, adapted from [5,9], that follows this structure.

---

[2] For simplicity, we consider each entity to be a single individual but the role of any individual can be distributed.

Definition 1 (E-voting scheme). *An* e-voting scheme Γ *is a tuple of probabilistic polynomial-time algorithms* (Setup, Register, Vote, Append, Tally, Verify) *relative to a result function* $f : \mathbb{V} \to R$ *where* $\mathbb{V}$ *is the set of all possible votes and* R *is the result space such that:*

Setup(1^λ) *On input security parameter* 1^λ, *algorithm* Setup *outputs an election key pair pk and sk, where pk is the public key and sk is the private key.*

Register(1^λ) *On input security parameter* 1^λ, *algorithm* Register *outputs a public/private credential pair upk and usk and updates the list* $\mathcal{L}$ *with upk (i.e.* $\mathcal{L} \leftarrow \mathcal{L} \cup \{upk\}$).

Vote($v, usk, pk, 1^\lambda$) *On input vote* v, *private credential usk, public key pk and security parameter* 1^λ, *algorithm* Vote *outputs a ballot* b.

Append($\mathcal{BB}, b$) *On input ballot box* $\mathcal{BB}$ *and ballot* b, *algorithm* Append *updates* $\mathcal{BB}$ *to include the ballot* b *and outputs the updated ballot box.*

Tally($\mathcal{BB}, \mathcal{L}, sk, 1^\lambda$) *On input ballot box* $\mathcal{BB}$, *list* $\mathcal{L}$, *private key sk and security parameter* 1^λ, *algorithm* Tally *computes the election outcome* r, *and outputs* r *with a tallying proof* ρ *that the tally is correct.*

Verify($\mathcal{BB}, r, \rho, pk, 1^\lambda$) *On input ballot box* $\mathcal{BB}$, *election outcome* r, *proof* ρ, *public key pk and security parameter* 1^λ, *any interested party can check that the outcome of the election was computed correctly. The output of algorithm* Verify *is 1 if the election result verifies and 0 otherwise.*

E-voting schemes must satisfy correctness: let f be a result function,[3] m_b be the maximum number of ballots and m_c be the maximum number of candidates. We say that Γ satisfies correctness with respect to f, m_b and m_c if there exists a negligible function negl such that, for all security parameters λ and choices $v_1, \ldots, v_{n_v} \in \mathbb{V}$ where n_v is an integer such that $n_v \leq m_b \wedge |\mathbb{V}| \leq m_c$, $\Pr\big[(pk, sk) \leftarrow \text{Setup}(1^\lambda); \text{ for } i = 1, \ldots, n_v: \{(upk_i, usk_i) \leftarrow \text{Register}(1^\lambda); b_i \leftarrow \text{Vote}(v_i, usk_i, pk, 1^\lambda); \mathcal{BB} \leftarrow \text{Append}(\mathcal{BB}, b_i)\}; \mathcal{L} \leftarrow \{upk_1, \ldots, upk_{n_v}\}; (r, \rho) \leftarrow \text{Tally}(\mathcal{BB}, \mathcal{L}, sk, 1^\lambda): r = f(v_1, \ldots, v_{n_v})\big] > 1 - \text{negl}(\lambda)$.

Our correctness definition uses ideas from the correctness definitions in [5,34] and considers an experiment in which the outcome is calculated in two ways: (1) the outcome is calculated in the normal way by running Tally, and (2) the outcome is computed by applying a result function f to all the votes input to Vote. Those two ways must compute equivalent outcomes to satisfy the correctness property.

3   Receipt-Freeness by Kiayias, Zacharias and Zhang (KZZ)

In this section, we analyse the receipt-freeness definition by Kiayias *et al.* [23], which we call KZZ. The game captures the following idea: the attacker should be unable to distinguish between a voter who submits a vote and either proves that they submitted that vote, or attempts to prove that they submitted a different vote.

---

[3] Function f must itself be correct, i.e., f must output the election outcome with respect to $v_1, \ldots, v_{n_v}$.

Definition 2 (KZZ). *Let $\Gamma = (\mathsf{Setup}, \mathsf{Register}, \mathsf{Vote}, \mathsf{Append}, \mathsf{Tally}, \mathsf{Verify})$ be an e-voting scheme, $\mathcal{A}$ be an adversary, $\mathcal{S}$ be a simulator,[4] λ be a security parameter, n_v, n_c and t be positive integers and β be a bit. Let $\mathsf{Exp}_{\mathcal{A},\mathcal{S},\Gamma}^{\mathsf{KZZ},\beta}(\lambda, n_v, n_c, t)$ be the game that proceed as follows:*

1. *The challenger initializes $\mathcal{BB}$ as an empty list and inputs $1^\lambda, n_v, n_c$ to adversary $\mathcal{A}$, which outputs a set of eligible voters $\mathcal{I} = \{id_1, \ldots, id_{n_v}\}$ and a set of possible vote choices $\mathbb{V}$ such that $|\mathbb{V}| = n_c$.*
2. *The challenger computes $\mathsf{Setup}(1^\lambda)$ to produce the key pair (pk, sk) and, for each $i \in \{1, \ldots, n_v\}$, computes $\mathsf{Register}(1^\lambda)$ to produce a credential pair (upk, usk). Public credentials are added to the list $\mathcal{L}$, hence, $\mathcal{L} = \{upk_1, \ldots, upk_{n_v}\}$. The challenger inputs pk and $\mathcal{L}$ to $\mathcal{A}$.*
3. *For each $i \in \{1, \ldots, n_v\}$, $\mathcal{A}$ decides whether id_i is corrupt.*
   - *If so, the challenger inputs usk_i to $\mathcal{A}$, which outputs a ballot b.*
   - *Otherwise (id_i is not corrupt), $\mathcal{A}$ outputs votes $v_0, v_1 \in \mathbb{V}$ to the challenger, the challenger computes ballot $b \leftarrow \mathsf{Vote}(v_\beta, usk_i, pk, 1^\lambda)$, and the challenger returns the ballot to $\mathcal{A}$, along with either the view view of the voter during Vote when $\beta = 0$ or $\mathcal{S}(\mathsf{view})$ when $\beta = 1$.[5]*
   Finally, the challenger computes $\mathcal{BB} \leftarrow \mathsf{Append}(\mathcal{BB}, b)$.
4. *The challenger computes $(r, \rho) \leftarrow \mathsf{Tally}(\mathcal{BB}, \mathcal{L}, sk, 1^\lambda)$ and inputs r, ρ and $\mathcal{BB}$ to $\mathcal{A}$, which outputs a bit β'.*
5. *The game outputs 1 if the following conditions are satisfied: (i) $\beta' = \beta$, (ii) the number of corrupted voters is bounded by t, and (iii) $f(\langle v_0 \rangle_{id_i \in \mathcal{V}_h}) = f(\langle v_1 \rangle_{id_i \in \mathcal{V}_h})$, i.e., with respect to uncorrupted voters, denoted by the set $\mathcal{V}_h$, the outcome of the election computed via the result function f is the same, regardless of whether $\beta = 0$ or $\beta = 1$.*

An e-voting scheme Γ satisfies KZZ for n_v voters, n_c candidates and at most t corrupted voters if there exists a probabilistic polynomial-time simulator $\mathcal{S}$ and a negligible function negl such that, for all probabilistic polynomial-time adversaries $\mathcal{A}$ and all security parameters λ, we have

$$\left| \Pr\left[\mathsf{Exp}_{\mathcal{A},\mathcal{S},\Gamma}^{\mathsf{KZZ},0}(\lambda, n_c, n_v, t) = 1\right] - \Pr\left[\mathsf{Exp}_{\mathcal{A},\mathcal{S},\Gamma}^{\mathsf{KZZ},1}(\lambda, n_c, n_v, t) = 1\right] \right| \leq \mathsf{negl}(\lambda).$$

We demonstrate a soundness issue with KZZ, namely, that KZZ guarantees receipt-freeness only if all voters vote (Sect. 3.1). Moreover, KZZ is incomplete because there exists schemes that are receipt-free but do no satisfy KZZ (Sect. 3.2).

3.1 Soundness Issue

KZZ requires that a single ballot is submitted to the ballot box on behalf of each voter. As a result, KZZ declares schemes as receipt-free that reveal how voters

---

[4] Simulator $\mathcal{S}$ models a voter providing fake evidence of a vote they did not submit.
[5] view is defined as the "internal state of the voter" [23]. It refers to any information that the voter inputs to the voting client to produce a ballot, including, but not necessarily limited to, private credentials and the coins input to algorithm Vote.

vote, when not all voters vote. To illustrate this, consider an e-voting scheme for at most n_v voters. If less than n_v voters vote and, hence, $|\mathcal{BB}| \leq n_v - 1$, define algorithm Tally to output an election outcome $r = \{(id_1, v_1), \ldots (id_i, v_i)\}$ where $i \leq n_v - 1$, i.e., it lists each voter that voted and the vote submitted by that voter. Clearly, this scheme is not receipt-free. Indeed, the scheme does not satisfy ballot-secrecy because the result announces the link between voter and vote. However, in the KZZ game, a ballot must be submitted for every voter, so this privacy leakage will not be identified. Therefore, the scheme may satisfy KZZ whilst not being receipt-free. Consequently, a proven secure scheme may leak every voter's vote when a real-world deployment cannot ensure that all voters vote. Hence, there may exist schemes that are proven secure but, in practice, do not offer any degree of privacy for voters.

3.2   Completeness Issues

Schemes with Multiple Ballots Are Out of Scope: KZZ requires the submission of a single ballot on behalf of each voter. Yet, some e-voting schemes require the submission of more than one ballot to achieve receipt-freeness. For instance, e-voting schemes may use fake private credentials (that are indistinguishable from real private credentials). Such schemes require voters to cast dummy ballots using fake credentials and prove the contents of dummy ballots (rather than real ballots) to an attacker. A voter can then cast a ballot for a different vote using their real credential. In these schemes it is necessary that a voter submits two ballots in order to submit a vote but prove that they submitted a different vote. JCJ [22] is an e-voting scheme that achieves receipt-freeness this way, hence, the scheme cannot satisfy KZZ. We obtain the following result, a proof of which appears in the full version of this paper [16].

Proposition 1. JCJ *does not satisfy* KZZ.

KZZ Limits the Set of Result Functions for Which a Scheme Can Be Declared Receipt-Free: We demonstrate this limitation, which exists as a consequence of the condition $f(\langle v_0 \rangle_{id_i \in \mathcal{V}_h}) = f(\langle v_1 \rangle_{id_i \in \mathcal{V}_h})$, by considering an informal argument used by Bernhard *et al.* in [5] to show that ballot-secrecy definition PRIV [3] has the same limitation. Consider an e-voting scheme with two possible candidate choices, namely $\mathbb{V} = \{0, 1\}$, for which f outputs the winning candidate, or '0' in the event of a draw. An adversary against the KZZ game can submit a ballot for '1' on behalf of a corrupted voter and can submit votes on behalf of all other voters such that $\langle v_0 \rangle_{id_i \in \mathcal{V}_h}$ has exactly half entries equal to '0' and half equal to '1', and $\langle v_1 \rangle_{id_i \in \mathcal{V}_h}$ has all entries equal to '0'. Then, $f(\langle v_0 \rangle_{id_i \in \mathcal{V}_h}) = f(\langle v_1 \rangle_{id_i \in \mathcal{V}_h}) = 0$, but the election outcome $r = 1$ (if $\beta = 0$) or 0 (if $\beta = 1$). Thus, the adversary can output $\beta' = \beta$ and the scheme does not satisfy KZZ.

3.3   Further Discussion

KZZ models attack scenarios in which a voter provides evidence of their vote (including their private credential) to the attacker only *after* voting, thereby assuming that honest voters do not reveal their private credentials until they have voted. We illustrate that DEMOS, an e-voting scheme that satisfies KZZ [23, Theorem 5], is no longer receipt-free if an attacker can compel a voter to reveal their credentials before voting, that is, when the assumption does not hold.

DEMOS provides each eligible voter with a voting card (which is a private credential in our terminology). This voting card consists of two parts: the first part contains a list of candidates and a unique vote code associated with each candidate. This is repeated on the second part of the voting card, although the vote codes associated with each candidate are different. To cast a ballot, each voter selects a part of their voting card (part '0' or part '1', which we call the coins, using our terminology) and inputs the selected part and the vote code listed next to their chosen candidate to the voting client. The part of the voting card and the vote code constitute the voter's ballot. The ballot box is updated with the ballot, i.e., algorithm Append outputs $\mathcal{BB} \parallel b$. Intuitively, DEMOS satisfies KZZ because voters can swap vote codes on the voting card, and can make the vote code on their ballot correspond to any candidate they wish. Therefore, the voter can convince the attacker that the submitted vote code corresponds to the attacker's choice of candidate.

However, consider the following scenario: an attacker wants a voter to vote for candidate A but the voter wants to vote for candidate B. The attacker requests to see the voter's voting card *before* voting. Only after seeing the voting card, the attacker requests that the voter cast a ballot for A. In this scenario, the voter may not have switched vote codes for A and B. Thus, the voter cannot vote for A *and* convince the attacker that they voted for B. In contrast, if an attacker does not see the voting card until after voting, the voter can switch the vote codes for A and B. Therefore, DEMOS provides a guarantee of receipt-freeness only if the voting card is revealed after voting.

The scenario above describes an attacker who interacts with a voter before voting, which is outside the scope of KZZ. The question is: should this attack scenario be captured by receipt-freeness, or does it fall under the remit of coercion-resistance? We do not address this in our informal definition of receipt-freeness (Sect. 1) because this is a grey area in the literature. For instance, Delaune *et al.* define receipt-freeness as the property that "a voter does not gain any information (a receipt) which can be used to prove to a coercer that she voted in a certain way" and coercion-resistance as "a voter cannot cooperate with a coercer to prove to him that she voted in a certain way" [14]. This suggests that providing information to an attacker before voting is captured by coercion-resistance, not receipt-freeness. In fact, Delaune *et al.*'s definition of receipt-freeness implies that a voter uses information to prove their vote *after* voting, whereas providing information to an attacker *before* voting is considered cooperation with an attacker. It appears that KZZ captures this intuition. On the other hand, some authors take a different approach. We discuss an approach that leads to a different conclusion in Sect. 4. For now, we note that establishing a boundary between receipt-freeness and coercion-resistance is an open problem.

4   Receipt-Freeness by Chaidos *et al.* (CCFG)

In this section, we consider a definition of receipt-freeness by Chaidos *et al.* [9], which we call CCFG. Chaidos *et al.* consider ballot boxes that contain ballots validated by an algorithm Valid and consider ballot boxes as private, introducing an algorithm Publish that outputs a public view of a ballot box, which we call the bulletin board. Formally, Chaidos *et al.* extend the definition of an e-voting scheme (Definition 1) to include algorithms Valid and Publish such that:

Valid($\mathcal{BB}, b$) On input ballot box $\mathcal{BB}$ and a ballot b, algorithm Valid outputs $\top$, if the ballot is valid, or $\bot$ otherwise.

Publish($\mathcal{BB}$) On input ballot box $\mathcal{BB}$, algorithm Publish outputs bulletin board $\mathcal{PBB}$.

Furthermore, algorithm Verify is redefined to take as input a bulletin board $\mathcal{PBB}$, *rather than* a ballot box $\mathcal{BB}$. All other aspects of Verify remain the same.[6]

In this context, Chaidos *et al.* define CCFG as an extension of the ballot secrecy game BPRIV by Bernhard *et al.* [5]. CCFG captures the idea that the attacker should be unable to determine whether, throughout the game, they are viewing a real or fake election, when the outcome is always computed for the real election. As such, CCFG models two ballot boxes, $\mathcal{BB}_0$ and $\mathcal{BB}_1$, and, respectively, two bulletin boards, $\mathcal{PBB}_0$ and $\mathcal{PBB}_1$. The adversary must determine whether they are viewing $\mathcal{PBB}_0$ or $\mathcal{PBB}_1$, when the outcome is always computed over the contents of $\mathcal{BB}_0$.

CCFG relies on algorithms SimSetup and SimProof, which facilitate the ability to simulate the tallying proof ρ such that the outcome computed over the contents of $\mathcal{BB}_0$ appears to be computed over the contents of $\mathcal{BB}_1$, when $\beta = 1$. Algorithms SimSetup and SimProof are defined as follows:

SimSetup(1^λ) On input security parameter 1^λ, algorithm SimSetup outputs an election key pair pk and sk and auxiliary information aux, which is used to output a simulated proof during the tally phase of the election.

SimProof($\mathcal{BB}, r, aux$) On input ballot box $\mathcal{BB}$, election outcome r and auxiliary information aux, algorithm SimProof outputs a proof ρ that r is the outcome of an election computed over the contents of $\mathcal{BB}$.

Using those algorithms, CCFG is formalized as follows:

Definition 3 (CCFG). *Let* Γ = (Setup, Register, Vote, Valid, Append, Tally, Publish, Verify) *be an e-voting scheme,* $\mathcal{A}$ *be an adversary,* λ *be a security parameter and* β *be a bit. Let* $\mathsf{Exp}_{\mathcal{A},\Gamma}^{\mathsf{CCFG},\beta}(\lambda)$ *be the game that proceeds as follows:*[7] *the*

---

[6] In this section, we use the term e-voting scheme to refer to Definition 1 plus algorithms Valid and Publish.

[7] We omit SimSetup and SimProof as inputs to game $\mathsf{Exp}_{\mathcal{A},\Gamma}^{\mathsf{CCFG},\beta}(\lambda)$ for simplicity.

challenger initializes $\mathcal{BB}_0$ *and* $\mathcal{BB}_1$ *as empty lists and* V_r *and* V_c *as empty sets. Adversary* $\mathcal{A}$ *can then query the oracles defined in Fig. 1, under the constraint that* $\mathcal{O}$setup *must be queried before any other oracles and* $\mathcal{O}$tally *appears only as the final oracle call. The adversary terminates by outputting a bit* β'. *The game outputs 1 if* $\beta' = \beta$.

An e-voting scheme Γ satisfies CCFG *if there exists algorithms* SimSetup *and* SimProof *and a negligible function* negl *such that, for all probabilistic polynomial-time adversaries* $\mathcal{A}$ *and all security parameters* λ, *we have*

$$\left| \Pr\left[\mathsf{Exp}_{\mathcal{A},\Gamma}^{\mathsf{CCFG},0}(\lambda) = 1\right] - \Pr\left[\mathsf{Exp}_{\mathcal{A},\Gamma}^{\mathsf{CCFG},1}(\lambda) = 1\right] \right| \leq \mathsf{negl}(\lambda).$$

We show that CCFG is unsound as it overlooks the needs for strong consistency (Sect. 4.1) and is incomplete, limiting the class of schemes that can be declared receipt-free (Sect. 4.2).

4.1 Soundness Issue

A property called *strong consistency* is introduced in [5] to accompany BPRIV. Strong consistency requires that the outcome output by Tally is consistent with the application of result function f to the votes and is necessary to detect tally policies that may lead to an attack against ballot secrecy. Therefore, as noted in [5, Section IV.D], an e-voting scheme must satisfy BPRIV *and* strong consistency to achieve ballot secrecy. However, Chaidos *et al.* do not consider this property in [9], which results in an unsound definition of receipt-freeness. In fact, there exists schemes satisfying CCFG that are vulnerable to attacks that violate ballot secrecy. We briefly recall an example in [5, Section IV.D], that illustrates this: define an e-voting scheme for two candidates (say, A and B) that outputs a multiset of the submitted votes as the election outcome. Suppose this scheme satisfies CCFG. Now, define a modified scheme such that, if the first voter votes for candidate A, this vote is removed from the election outcome. An adversary against CCFG cannot distinguish games $\mathsf{Exp}_{\mathcal{A},\Gamma}^{\mathsf{CCFG},0}(\lambda)$ and $\mathsf{Exp}_{\mathcal{A},\Gamma}^{\mathsf{CCFG},1}(\lambda)$, where Γ is the modified scheme, because the tally is always computed over the contents of $\mathcal{BB}_0$ and so the election outcome will be the same in both games. However, through removal of the first vote, the tally for this modified scheme allows the adversary to determine whether the first vote is for candidate A or B. Therefore, the modified scheme reveals how the first voter voted. We refer the reader to [5, Section IV.D] for full details of this argument. Unfortunately, CCFG cannot simply adopt the original definition of strong consistency by Bernhard *et al.*, because it is defined over different syntax. In particular, the original definition does not consider algorithm Append. Adapting the original definition to consider this algorithm is a possible direction for future work.

4.2 Completeness Issue

We observe that CCFG is unsatisfiable by schemes for which Append($\mathcal{BB}, b$) outputs $\mathcal{BB} \parallel b$ and Publish($\mathcal{BB}$) outputs $\mathcal{BB}$. That is, Append($\mathcal{BB}, b$) appends ballot

$\mathcal{O}$setup()

if $\beta = 0$ **then**

  $(pk, sk) \leftarrow \mathsf{Setup}(1^\lambda)$

else

  $(pk, sk, aux) \leftarrow \mathsf{SimSetup}(1^\lambda)$

return pk

$\mathcal{O}$register(id)

if $(id, upk, usk) \notin \mathsf{V}_r$ **then**

  $(upk, usk) \leftarrow \mathsf{Register}(1^\lambda)$

  $\mathcal{L} \leftarrow \mathcal{L} \cup \{upk\}$

  $\mathsf{V}_r \leftarrow \mathsf{V}_r \cup \{(id, upk, usk)\}$

return upk

$\mathcal{O}$corrupt(id)

if $(id, upk, usk) \in \mathsf{V}_r$ **then**

  $\mathsf{V}_c \leftarrow \mathsf{V}_c \cup \{(id, upk)\}$

return (upk, usk)

$\mathcal{O}$vote(id, v_0, v_1)

if $v_0, v_1 \in \mathbb{V} \wedge (id, upk, usk) \in \mathsf{V}_r$ **then**

  $b_0 \leftarrow \mathsf{Vote}(v_0, usk, pk, 1^\lambda)$

  $b_1 \leftarrow \mathsf{Vote}(v_1, usk, pk, 1^\lambda)$

  $\mathcal{BB}_0 \leftarrow \mathsf{Append}(\mathcal{BB}_0, b_0)$

  $\mathcal{BB}_1 \leftarrow \mathsf{Append}(\mathcal{BB}_1, b_1)$

$\mathcal{O}$cast(id, b)

if $\mathsf{Valid}(\mathcal{BB}_\beta, b) = \top$ **then**

  $\mathcal{BB}_0 \leftarrow \mathsf{Append}(\mathcal{BB}_0, b)$

  $\mathcal{BB}_1 \leftarrow \mathsf{Append}(\mathcal{BB}_1, b)$

$\mathcal{O}$tally()

if $\beta = 0$ **then**

  $(r, \rho) \leftarrow \mathsf{Tally}(\mathcal{BB}_0, \mathcal{L}, sk, 1^\lambda)$

else

  $(r, \rho') \leftarrow \mathsf{Tally}(\mathcal{BB}_0, \mathcal{L}, sk, 1^\lambda)$

  $\rho \leftarrow \mathsf{SimProof}(\mathcal{BB}_1, r, aux)$

return (r, ρ)

$\mathcal{O}$board()

return $\mathsf{Publish}(\mathcal{BB}_\beta)$

$\mathcal{O}$receipt(id, b_0, b_1)

if $(id, upk) \in \mathsf{V}_c \wedge \mathsf{Valid}(\mathcal{BB}_0, b_0) = \top \wedge \mathsf{Valid}(\mathcal{BB}_1, b_1) = \top$ **then**

  $\mathcal{BB}_0 \leftarrow \mathsf{Append}(\mathcal{BB}_0, b_0)$

  $\mathcal{BB}_1 \leftarrow \mathsf{Append}(\mathcal{BB}_1, b_1)$

Fig. 1. Oracles used in the receipt-freeness game CCFG by Chaidos *et al.* [9]

b to ballot box $\mathcal{BB}$ without processing the ballot in any way and $\mathsf{Publish}(\mathcal{BB})$ outputs $\mathcal{BB}$ such that the ballot that appears on the public view of $\mathcal{BB}$ is identical to the ballot submitted by the voter. Formally, we have the following result.

Proposition 2. *Let* $\Gamma =$ (Setup, Register, Vote, Valid, Append, Tally, Publish, Verify) *be an e-voting scheme for which* $\mathsf{Append}(\mathcal{BB}, b)$ *outputs* $\mathcal{BB} \parallel b$ *and* $\mathsf{Publish}(\mathcal{BB})$ *outputs* $\mathcal{BB}$. *Then* Γ *does not satisfy* CCFG.

Proof. We construct an adversary $\mathcal{A}$ against the CCFG game as follows. $\mathcal{A}$ queries $pk \leftarrow \mathcal{O}\mathsf{setup}()$, $upk \leftarrow \mathcal{O}\mathsf{register}(id)$ and $(upk, usk) \leftarrow \mathcal{O}\mathsf{corrupt}(id)$. Then, $\mathcal{A}$ computes $b_0 \leftarrow \mathsf{Vote}(v_0, usk, pk, 1^\lambda)$ and $b_1 \leftarrow \mathsf{Vote}(v_1, usk, pk, 1^\lambda)$ and queries $\mathcal{O}\mathsf{receipt}(id, b_0, b_1)$, $\mathcal{PBB}_\beta \leftarrow \mathcal{O}\mathsf{board}()$ and $(r, \rho) \leftarrow \mathcal{O}\mathsf{tally}()$. It follows that $\mathcal{PBB}_\beta$ contains the single entry b_0 (if $\beta = 0$) or b_1 (if $\beta = 1$). Therefore, $\mathcal{A}$ can correctly distinguish $\mathsf{Exp}_{\mathcal{A},\Gamma}^{\mathsf{CCFG},0}(\lambda)$ and $\mathsf{Exp}_{\mathcal{A},\Gamma}^{\mathsf{CCFG},1}(\lambda)$ and outputs $\beta' = \beta$. Thus, the e-voting scheme Γ does not satisfy CCFG. □

CCFG is unsatisfiable by these schemes because, in the CCFG game, the adversary submits two ballots to $\mathcal{O}\mathsf{receipt}$. To satisfy CCFG, the adversary must be unable to distinguish a bulletin board that contains ballot b_0 and a bulletin board that contains ballot b_1, where the adversary queries $\mathcal{O}\mathsf{receipt}(id, b_0, b_1)$ in the CCFG game. This requires that ballots are modified in some way before they are appended to $\mathcal{BB}_0$ and $\mathcal{BB}_1$, or before $\mathcal{PBB}_\beta$ is published. Otherwise, the adversary can trivially distinguish as shown in the proof of Proposition 2. Partly, CCFG excludes these schemes by design. Chaidos *et al.* acknowledge that a scheme satisfies CCFG only if it achieves receipt-freeness without the voter relying on some evasion strategy [9]. Generally, schemes that provide voters with an evasion strategy, a procedure that the scheme provides to allow the voter to evade coercion, do not rely on ballot modification but instead on the use of an evasion strategy to achieve receipt-freeness. This means that schemes that rely on evasion strategies to achieve receipt-freeness cannot satisfy CCFG despite the fact that they are receipt-free. For example, JCJ relies on fake credentials, a type of evasion strategy, to achieve receipt-freeness (Sect. 3.2). Thus, we have the following corollary.

Corollary 1. JCJ *does not satisfy* CCFG.

The corollary follows from Proposition 2, since JCJ ballots are not modified before they are appended to the ballot box and $\mathsf{Publish}(\mathcal{BB})$ outputs $\mathcal{BB}$.

4.3 Further Discussion

CCFG captures the scenario in which an honest voter constructs their ballot and gives the attacker the coins used (or possibly uses coins provided by the attacker) to construct their ballot. This allows the attacker to reconstruct the ballot locally and then check whether the ballot appears on the bulletin board. CCFG captures this scenario through the oracle $\mathcal{O}\mathsf{receipt}$, which allows the adversary to construct ballots on behalf of voters and then submit these ballots to $\mathcal{O}\mathsf{receipt}$. The adversary can then view $\mathcal{PBB}_\beta$, and expects to see a ballot corresponding to one of those submitted to $\mathcal{O}\mathsf{receipt}$.

Chaidos *et al.* take a very different approach to the intuition of receipt-freeness than Kiayias *et al.* As mentioned in Sect. 3.3, Delaune *et al.* consider a voter that cooperates with an attacker (e.g. by using coins provided by the attacker) to fall outwith the scope of receipt-freeness. Moreover, Kiayias *et al.* exclude this scenario from the definition of KZZ. However, Chaidos *et al.* consider this to fall within the scope of receipt-freeness although, admittedly, they do refer to CCFG as a definition of *strong* receipt-freeness. Therefore, we see that there is no consensus over the boundary between receipt-freeness and coercion-resistance in the literature and that definitions of receipt-freeness capture varying intuitions.

5   Receipt-Freeness for Deniable Vote Updating by Bernhard, Kulyk and Volkamer (DKV)

In this section, we analyse a definition of receipt-freeness by Bernhard *et al.* [6,7] for schemes that use *deniable vote updating*, which we call DKV. Bernhard *et al.* construct a game-based definition of receipt-freeness for KTV-Helios [25], a variant of the Helios e-voting scheme that uses deniable vote updating whereby a voter casts a ballot, and then changes their vote, without an attacker detecting the change. In [7, Section 4.1] it was recognized that CCFG does not apply to KTV-Helios because deniable vote updating is a type of evasion strategy and the strategy is required to achieve receipt-freeness. Therefore, Bernhard *et al.* introduce a new receipt-freeness definition that modifies CCFG to schemes that use deniable vote updating. We rely on the definition presented in [6] (the technical report associated with the conference version of the paper [7]).

DKV captures the following idea: the attacker should be unable to distinguish a voter who submits a vote and a voter who submits the same vote but then deniably updates their vote, where the adversarial advantage of distinguishing is denoted δ. DKV adopts e-voting syntax (Definition 1) extended with algorithm Valid (Sect. 4) and considers timestamps such that algorithm Vote is redefined to take additional input of a timestamp t, indicating the time at which a ballot is to be cast. DKV relies on algorithms SimSetup and SimProof (Sect. 4) and, additionally, algorithms DenyUpdate and Obfuscate such that:

DenyUpdate$(v_0, v_1, usk, t_u, pk, 1^\lambda)$ On input votes v_0, v_1, private credential usk, timestamp t_u chosen uniformly at random from some probability distribution $\mathbb{P}$, public key pk and security parameter 1^λ, algorithm DenyUpdate outputs a ballot that updates a vote from vote v_0 to vote v_1 at timestamp t_u.

Obfuscate$(\mathcal{BB}, id)$ On input ballot box $\mathcal{BB}$ and voter id, algorithm Obfuscate casts dummy ballots for voter id to hide ballots cast by id in the event that id deniably updates their vote, and outputs the updated ballot box.

Using those algorithms, DKV is formalized as follows:

Definition 4 (DKV). *Let* $\Gamma = $ (Setup, Register, Vote, Valid, Append, Tally, Verify) *be an e-voting scheme with timestamps,* $\mathcal{A}$ *be an adversary,* λ *be a security parameter and* β *be a bit. Let* $\mathsf{Exp}_{\mathcal{A},\Gamma}^{\mathsf{DKV},\beta}(\lambda)$ *be the game that proceeds as follows: the challenger initializes* $\mathcal{BB}_0$ *and* $\mathcal{BB}_1$ *as empty lists. If* $\beta = 0$ *(resp.,* $\beta = 1$*), the challenger computes* Setup(1^λ) *to produce the keypair* (pk, sk) *(resp., computes* SimSetup(1^λ) *to produce the keypair* (pk, sk) *and auxiliary information* aux*) and, for each* $i \in \{1, \ldots, n_v\}$, *computes* Register(1^λ) *to produce a*

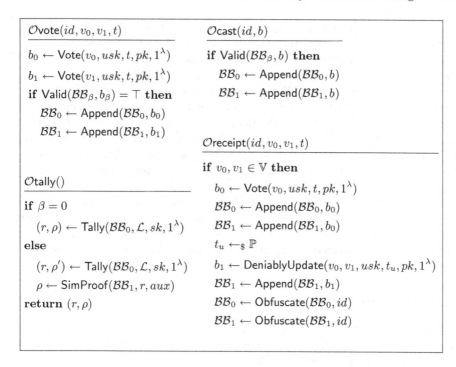

Fig. 2. Oracles used in the receipt-freeness game DKV by Bernhard *et al.* [6]

credential pair (upk, usk). *Public credentials are added to the list* $\mathcal{L}$, *namely*, $\mathcal{L} = \{usk_1, \ldots, usk_{n_v}\}$. *The challenger inputs* pk, $\mathcal{L}$ *and* $\mathcal{BB}_\beta$[8] *to adversary* $\mathcal{A}$. *Adversary* $\mathcal{A}$ *can then query the oracles defined in Fig. 2, under the constraint that* $\mathcal{O}$receipt *can be queried at most once and* $\mathcal{O}$tally *appears only as the final oracle call. The adversary terminates by outputting a bit* β'. *The game outputs* 1 *if* $\beta' = \beta$.

An e-voting scheme Γ *satisfies* DKV *if there exists algorithms* DenyUpdate, Obfuscate, SimSetup *and* SimProof *and a negligible function* negl *such that, for all probabilistic polynomial-time adversaries* $\mathcal{A}$ *and all security parameters* λ, *we have*

$$\left| \Pr\left[\mathsf{Exp}_{\mathcal{A},\Gamma}^{\mathsf{DKV},0}(\lambda) = 1 \right] - \Pr\left[\mathsf{Exp}_{\mathcal{A},\Gamma}^{\mathsf{DKV},1}(\lambda) = 1 \right] - \delta \right| \leq \mathsf{negl}(\lambda).$$

We did not find any soundness issues with DKV. In particular, although DKV uses the same framework as CCFG, DKV does not overlook the need for strong

---

[8] In this game $\mathcal{BB} = \mathcal{PBB}$. Bernhard *et al.* do not mention adversarial access to $\mathcal{BB}_\beta$ in the technical report [6] but do allow the adversary to 'see' $\mathcal{BB}$ in the conference version [7]. We assume that, as DKV is a modification of CCFG, the adversary should have access to $\mathcal{BB}_\beta$. This could be resolved by providing the adversary with access to an oracle $\mathcal{O}$publish as defined for CCFG. This provides the adversary with a view of $\mathcal{BB}_\beta$, which we assume is the intention in this definition.

consistency and defines strong consistency in their syntax in [6]. Clearly, DKV is incomplete because it limits the class of e-voting schemes that can be declared receipt-free to schemes with timestamps that achieve receipt-freeness through the use of deniable vote updating, although this is by design.

Bernhard *et al.* capture a different intuition of receipt-freeness than Kiayias *et al.* and Chaidos *et al.* DKV does not model a voter who interacts with an attacker to prove their vote. In other words, DKV does not model a voter that provides an attacker with any proof of their vote. In particular, there is no mechanism to capture the fact that a voter may try to pass their credentials or coins to an attacker. Certainly, this definition does not pose any issues with respect to whether it captures attack scenarios that should be considered under the heading of coercion-resistance. However, it does raise questions about whether this definition captures receipt-freeness. As there is no mechanism for a voter to attempt to prove their vote, we conclude that receipt-freeness is guaranteed under the assumption that the voter does not pass any proof of their vote to the attacker.

6 Conclusion

We have systematically analysed game-based definitions of receipt-freeness, uncovered completeness and soundness issues, and found that each definition considers a different attacker model.

We proved that KZZ can be satisfied by schemes that leak every voter's vote. Moreover, we found that CCFG does not consider strong consistency, which seems necessary for soundness. By comparison, DKV considers strong consistency, and we believe coupling CCFG with a suitable notion of strong consistency should suffice to achieve soundness, albeit defining such a notion is non-trivial.

We found each definition to be incomplete. KZZ requires that each voter votes, and only once. CCFG is unsatisfiable by a class of schemes that do not process ballots before adding them to the ballot box and for which the bulletin board is identical to the ballot box. Consequently, JCJ does not satisfy KZZ or CCFG. Furthermore, DKV only applies to schemes that use deniable vote updating. Thus, there is no game-based definition of receipt-freeness that can be applied to a wide class of schemes.

Each definition captures a different attacker model: KZZ models a voter that provides evidence of their vote (e.g., coins and credentials) *after* voting. By comparison, CCFG captures scenarios wherein the voter uses coins provided by an attacker. Consequently, KZZ does not capture scenarios where a voter interacts with an attacker before voting (e.g., by providing the attacker with credentials), whereas CCFG does. It is unclear whether a definition of receipt-freeness should capture this scenario, or whether this should be considered beyond the scope of receipt-freeness and be captured by coercion-resistance. The boundary between receipt-freeness and coercion-resistance is unclear and we believe establishing a boundary is an interesting open problem.

We observe that KZZ, CCFG and DKV consider that *all* election authorities are honest, in particular, the election administrator, tallier and ballot box are honest. Moreover, communication channels between voters and/or election authorities are considered to be private. In practice, trust assumptions may be difficult to enforce, or it may not be possible to prove that the assumption holds. Motivated by this, ballot secrecy in the context of a malicious ballot box was considered in [29,30], whereby the adversary controls the contents of the ballot box. We believe that this setting warrants further exploration and that security definitions with minimal trust assumptions are preferable.

A further point of interest is that receipt-freeness (and, more generally, privacy) does not exist in a vacuum and must be considered in the context of other desirable security properties. This has been addressed in recent literature and one notable area of research relates to the relationship between privacy and verifiability. Some results have shown that this relationship is rather intricate: for example, receipt-freeness and universal verifiability are incompatible under certain assumptions on the communication channels and election authorities [10], but are compatible under different assumptions [9,26]. Moreover, Cortier and Lallemand recently showed that ballot secrecy implies individual verifiability [12], assuming the same trust assumptions for both ballot secrecy and individual verifiability, but this result does not hold more generally [33]. We believe that exploring the relationship between privacy and verifiability, particularly with respect to trust assumptions, is an interesting area of future research.

Acknowledgements. This work is partly supported by the EPSRC and the UK government as part of the Centre for Doctoral Training in Cyber Security at Royal Holloway, University of London (EP/P009301/1), and by the Luxembourg National Research Fund (FNR) under the FNR-INTER-VoteVerif project (10415467).

References

1. Adida, B.: Helios: web-based open-audit voting. In: USENIX Security Symposium, vol. 17, pp. 335–348. USENIX (2008)
2. Baskar, A., Ramanujam, R., Suresh, S.P.: Knowledge-based modelling of voting protocols. In: TARK 2007, pp. 62–71. ACM (2007)
3. Benaloh, J.: Verifiable secret-ballot elections. Ph.D. thesis, Yale University (2006)
4. Benaloh, J., Tuinstra, D.: Receipt-free secret-ballot elections. In: STOC 1994, pp. 544–553. ACM (1994)
5. Bernhard, D., Cortier, V., Galindo, D., Pereira, O., Warinschi, B.: SoK: a comprehensive analysis of game-based ballot privacy definitions. In: S&P 2015, pp. 499–516. IEEE (2015)
6. Bernhard, D., Kulyk, O., Volkamer, M.: Security proofs for participation privacy, receipt-freeness, ballot privacy, and verifiability against malicious bulletin board for the Helios voting scheme. IACR ePrint 2016/431
7. Bernhard, D., Kulyk, O., Volkamer, M.: Security proofs for participation privacy, receipt-freeness and ballot privacy for the Helios voting scheme. In: ARES 2017, p. 1. ACM (2017)
8. Braunlich, K., Grimm, R.: Formalization of receipt-freeness in the context of electronic voting. In: ARES 2011, pp. 119–126. IEEE (2011)

9. Chaidos, P., Cortier, V., Fuchsbauer, G., Galindo, D.: BeleniosRF: a noninteractive receipt-free electronic voting scheme. In: CCS 2016, pp. 1614–1625. ACM (2016)
10. Chevallier-Mames, B., Fouque, P.-A., Pointcheval, D., Stern, J., Traoré, J.: On some incompatible properties of voting schemes. Towards Trust. Elect. **6000**, 191–199 (2010)
11. Cortier, V., Galindo, D., Küsters, R., Mueller, J., Truderung, T.: Sok: verifiability notions for e-voting protocols. In: S&P 2016, pp. 779–798. IEEE (2016)
12. Cortier, V., Lallemand, J.: Voting: you can't have privacy without individual verifiability. In: CCS 2018, pp. 53–66. ACM (2018)
13. Delaune, S., Kremer, S., Ryan, M.: Coercion-resistance and receipt-freeness in electronic voting. In: CSFW 2006, pp. 28–42. IEEE (2006)
14. Delaune, S., Kremer, S., Ryan, M.: Verifying privacy-type properties of electronic voting protocols. JCS **17**(4), 435–487 (2009)
15. Dreier, J., Lafourcade, P., Lakhnech, Y.: A formal taxonomy of privacy in voting protocols. In: ICC 2012, pp. 6710–6715. IEEE (2012)
16. Fraser, A., Quaglia, E.A., Smyth, B.: A critique of game-based definitions of receipt-freeness for voting. IACR ePrint 2019/853
17. Helios voting system. https://heliosvoting.org/. Accessed 06 Mar 2018
18. IACR final report of IACR electronic voting committee. www.iacr.org/elections/eVoting/finalReportHelios_2010-09-27.html. Accessed 01 Aug 2017
19. iVote online voting. www.ivote.nsw.gov.au/. Accessed 01 Aug 2017
20. Jonker, H.L., de Vink, E.P.: Formalising receipt-freeness. In: Katsikas, S.K., López, J., Backes, M., Gritzalis, S., Preneel, B. (eds.) ISC 2006. LNCS, vol. 4176, pp. 476–488. Springer, Heidelberg (2006). https://doi.org/10.1007/11836810_34
21. Jonker, H.L., Pieters, W.: Receipt-freeness as a special case of anonymity in epistemic logic. In: IAVoSS Workshop on Trustworthy Elections (WOTE) (2006)
22. Juels, A., Catalano, D., Jakobsson, M.: Coercion-resistant electronic elections. In: WPES 2005, pp. 61–70. ACM (2005)
23. Kiayias, A., Zacharias, T., Zhang, B.: End-to-end verifiable elections in the standard model. In: Oswald, E., Fischlin, M. (eds.) EUROCRYPT 2015. LNCS, vol. 9057, pp. 468–498. Springer, Heidelberg (2015). https://doi.org/10.1007/978-3-662-46803-6_16
24. Küesters, R., Truderung, T., Vogt, A.: Verifiability, privacy, and coercion-resistance: new insights from a case study. In: S&P 2011, pp. 538–553. IEEE (2011)
25. Kulyk, O., Teague, V., Volkamer, M.: Extending Helios towards private eligibility verifiability. In: Haenni, R., Koenig, R.E., Wikström, D. (eds.) VOTELID 2015. LNCS, vol. 9269, pp. 57–73. Springer, Cham (2015). https://doi.org/10.1007/978-3-319-22270-7_4
26. Lee, B., Boyd, C., Dawson, E., Kim, K., Yang, J., Yoo, S.: Providing receipt-freeness in mixnet-based voting protocols. In: Lim, J.-I., Lee, D.-H. (eds.) ICISC 2003. LNCS, vol. 2971, pp. 245–258. Springer, Heidelberg (2004). https://doi.org/10.1007/978-3-540-24691-6_19
27. Moran, T., Naor, M.: Receipt-free universally-verifiable voting with everlasting privacy. In: Dwork, C. (ed.) CRYPTO 2006. LNCS, vol. 4117, pp. 373–392. Springer, Heidelberg (2006). https://doi.org/10.1007/11818175_22
28. Okamoto, T.: Receipt-free electronic voting schemes for large scale elections. In: Christianson, B., Crispo, B., Lomas, M., Roe, M. (eds.) Security Protocols 1997. LNCS, vol. 1361, pp. 25–35. Springer, Heidelberg (1998). https://doi.org/10.1007/BFb0028157

29. Smyth, B.: Ballot secrecy: security definition, sufficient conditions, and analysis of Helios. IACR ePrint 2015/942
30. Smyth, B.: Ballot secrecy with malicious bulletin boards. IACR ePrint 2014/822
31. Smyth, B.: A foundation for secret, verifiable elections. IACR ePrint 2018/225
32. Smyth, B.: Surveying definitions of coercion resistance. IACR ePrint 2019/822
33. Smyth, B.: Verifiability of Helios mixnet. IACR ePrint 2018/017
34. Smyth, B., Frink, S., Clarkson, M.R.: Election verifiability: cryptographic definitions and an analysis of Helios, Helios-C, and JCJ. IACR ePrint 2015/233
35. Springall, D., et al.: Security analysis of the Estonian internet voting system. In: CCS 2014, pp. 703–715. ACM (2014)

Improved Cryptanalysis of the KMOV Elliptic Curve Cryptosystem

Abderrahmane Nitaj[1(✉)], Willy Susilo[2], and Joseph Tonien[2]

[1] LMNO, Université de Caen Normandie, Caen, France
abderrahmane.nitaj@unicaen.fr
[2] Institute of Cybersecurity and Cryptology,
School of Computing and Information Technology, University of Wollongong,
Wollongong, Australia
{willy.susilo,joseph.tonien}@uow.edu.au

Abstract. This paper presents two new improved attacks on the KMOV cryptosystem. KMOV is an encryption algorithm based on elliptic curves over the ring $\mathbb{Z}_N$ where $N = pq$ is a product of two large primes of equal bit size. The first attack uses the properties of the convergents of the continued fraction expansion of a specific value derived from the KMOV public key. The second attack is based on Coppersmith's method for finding small solutions of a multivariate polynomial modular equation. Both attacks improve the existing attacks on the KMOV cryptosystem.

1 Introduction

The RSA cryptosystem [21], invented in 1978 by Rivest, Shamir and Adleman, is the most widely used cryptosystem. The main parameters in RSA are two integers, the RSA modulus $N = pq$ where p and q are large prime numbers, and the public exponent e, which is an integer satisfying $\gcd(e, (p-1)(q-1)) = 1$. The private exponent is the integer d satisfying $ed \equiv 1 \pmod{(p-1)(q-1)}$. In many implementations, the private exponent d is required to be small to ease decryption and signature. Unfortunately, this scenario is dangerous and can be used to break the system [3,6]. In 1990, Wiener [24,25] presented an attack to break the RSA system if the private exponent d satisfies $d < \frac{1}{\sqrt[3]{18}} N^{\frac{1}{4}}$. Since then, Wiener's bound has been extended in many situations, mainly by Boneh and Durfee [2] to $d < N^{0.292}$.

In 1985, Miller [17] and Koblitz [13] independently proposed to use elliptic curves in cryptography. Since then, many cryptosystems have been proposed based on elliptic curves. In the direction of RSA, Koyama, Maurer, Okamoto and Vanstone [14] proposed a cryptosystem, called KMOV, based on the elliptic curve $E_N(0, b)$ where $N = pq$ is an RSA modulus and $E_N(0, b)$ is the set of solutions of the modular equation $y^2 \equiv x^3 + b \pmod{N}$, together with the point at infinity, denoted $\mathcal{O}$. When the prime factors p and q are such that $p \equiv q \equiv 2 \pmod 3$, then any point $P \in E_N(0, b)$ satisfies $(p+1)(q+1)P = \mathcal{O}$. In KMOV, the public key is a pair (N, e) where $N = pq$ with two prime integers satisfying

R. Steinfeld and T. H. Yuen (Eds.): ProvSec 2019, LNCS 11821, pp. 206–221, 2019.
https://doi.org/10.1007/978-3-030-31919-9_12

$p \equiv q \equiv 2 \pmod 3$ and e is an integer satisfying $\gcd(e, (p+1)(q+1)) = 1$. The decryption exponent is the integer d such that $ed \equiv 1 \pmod{(p+1)(q+1)}$.

Notice that the modular equation $ed \equiv 1 \pmod{(p+1)(q+1)}$ is equivalent to the integer key equation $ed - k(p+1)(q+1) = 1$. In 1995, Pinch [20] used the key equation and extended Wiener's attack to KMOV. He showed that one can factor the modulus $N = pq$ if $d < \frac{1}{3}N^{\frac{1}{4}}$. In [11], Ibrahimpasic extended the attack of Pinch by a few bits using an exhaustive search. Both attacks use the convergents of the continued fraction expansion of $\frac{e}{N}$. In [18], Nitaj considered the generalized equation $eu - (p+1)(q+1)v = w$ and showed that one can factor the modulus $N = pq$ if the parameters u, v, w satisfy some specific conditions, especially if $uv < \frac{\sqrt{2}\sqrt{N}}{12}$. The method combines the continued fraction algorithm [4,7] and Coppersmith's method [8] for solving univariate modular equations.

In this paper, we extend the former attacks on KMOV. In the first attack we consider the KMOV key equation $ed - k(p+1)(q+1) = 1$ and instead of using the convergents of $\frac{e}{N}$, we use the convergents of $\dfrac{e}{N+1+\left(1+\frac{3\sqrt{2}}{4}\right)N^{\frac{1}{2}}}$. As a consequence, we show that one can factor the modulus $N = pq$ if the private exponent d is such that $d < 2\sqrt{2}\dfrac{N^{\frac{3}{4}}}{\sqrt{e}}$. This bound improves the former bound $d < \frac{1}{3}N^{\frac{1}{4}}$, especially when the public exponent e is significantly smaller then N.

In the second attack we consider the generalized key equation $eu - (p+1)(q+1)v = w$ and transform it to the modular polynomial equation $v(p+q+1) + Nv + w \equiv 0 \pmod e$. We consider the polynomial $f(x, y, z) = xy + Nx + z$ and apply Coppersmith's method to find the small solutions of the modular polynomial equation $f(x, y, z) \equiv 0 \pmod e$. When $e = N^{\beta}$, $u < N^{\delta}$ and $|w| < N^{\gamma}$, if

$$\delta < \frac{7}{6} - \gamma - \frac{1}{3}\sqrt{6\beta - 6\gamma + 1} - \varepsilon,$$

where ε is a small constant, then Coppersmith's method enables us to find $p + q + 1$, which combined with $N = pq$ gives p and q. We note that in the standard situation of a KMOV instance with $e \approx N$ and $eu - (p+1)(q+1)v = 1$, our new bound is $\delta < 0.284$ which is much larger than the existing bounds.

The rest of this paper is organized as follows. In Sect. 2, we give some preliminaries on Coppersmith's method, continued fractions, elliptic curves and recall the KMOV cryptosystem. In Sect. 3, we present our first attack on KMOV based on continued fractions. In Sect. 4, we present our second attack on KMOV which is based on Coppersmith's method. We conclude the paper in Sect. 5.

2   Preliminaries

In this section, we give some preliminaries on Coppersmith's methods for solving modular polynomial equations, continued fractions and elliptic curves. For completeness, we recall the KMOV cryptosystem.

2.1 Coppersmith's Method

One of the difficult problems in algebra is to solve modular polynomial equations of the form

$$f(x_1, \ldots, x_n) \equiv 0 \pmod{e},$$

where $f(x_1, \ldots, x_n) \in \mathbb{Z}[x_1, \ldots, x_n]$ is multivariate polynomial. In 1996, Coppersmith [8] introduced a rigorous method for finding the small solutions of the univariate polynomial equation $f(x) \equiv 0 \pmod{e}$ and the small roots of the bivariate polynomial equation $f(x, y) = 0$. Coppersmith's method is based on lattice reduction and is useful in cryptography, especially for attacking the RSA cryptosystem (see [1,5,16,19]). Since then, numerous variants of Coppersmith's method have been presented for multivariate polynomial equations assuming certain hypothesis. The following result of Howgrave-Graham [10] is useful for solving the polynomial equations.

Theorem 1 (Howgrave-Graham). *Let e be a positive integer and $h(x, y, z) \in \mathbb{Z}[x, y, z]$ be a polynomial with at most ω monomials. Let m be a positive integer. Suppose that*

$$h(x_0, y_0, z_0) \equiv 0 \pmod{e^m} \quad and$$

$$\|h(xX, yY, zZ)\| = \sqrt{\sum_{i,j,k} a_{i,j,k} x^i y^j z^k} < \frac{e^m}{\sqrt{\omega}},$$

where $|x_0| < X$, $|y_0| < Y$, $|z_0| < Z$. Then $h(x_0, y_0, z_0) = 0$ holds over the integers.

For a multivariate polynomial modular equation $f(x, y, z) \equiv 0 \pmod{e}$, the idea in Coppersmith's method is to build certain modular polynomials equations $h(x, y, z) \equiv 0 \pmod{e^m}$ sharing the modular solution (x_0, y_0, z_0). These polynomials are generally built by applying Jochemz-May [12] method and applying lattice reduction techniques such as the LLL algorithm [15]. The LLL algorithm acts on lattices and the following result is useful (see [12,15,16]).

Theorem 2 (LLL). *Let $\mathcal{L}$ be a lattice spanned by a basis $(u_1, \ldots, u_\omega)$, then the LLL algorithm produces a new basis $(b_1, \ldots, b_\omega)$ satisfying*

$$\|b_1\| \leq \cdots \leq \|b_i\| \leq 2^{\frac{\omega(\omega-1)}{4(\omega+1-i)}} \det(\mathcal{L})^{\frac{1}{\omega+1-i}}, \quad i = 1, \ldots, \omega.$$

To find the root (x_0, y_0, z_0), we use a system with three polynomial equations $h_i(x, y, z) = 0$, $i = 1, 2, 3$. By using Gröbner basis computation or resultant techniques, the system can be solved under the following widely believed assumption.

Assumption 1. *The polynomials $h_1, h_2, h_3 \in \mathbb{Z}[x, y, z]$ that are derived from the reduced basis of the lattice in Coppersmith's method are algebraically independent.*

2.2   Continued Fractions

Let $\xi \neq 0$ be real number. The continued fraction expansion of ξ is an expression of the form

$$\xi = a_0 + \cfrac{1}{a_1 + \cfrac{1}{a_2 + \cfrac{1}{\ddots}}},$$

where a_0 is an integer and for $i \geq 1$, a_i is a positive integer. The integers a_i, $i \geq 0$ are the partial quotients of the continued fraction expansion. The process to compute the integers a_i for $i \geq 0$ is the continued fraction algorithm. The starting term is $x_0 = \xi$ and for $i \geq 0$,

$$a_i = \lfloor x_i \rfloor, \quad x_{i+1} = \frac{1}{x_i - a_i}.$$

When the continued fraction expansion is used with the first $k + 1$ partial quotients, the fraction is a convergent. The following method is very useful for computing the convergents of ξ.

Theorem 3. *The kth convergent can be determined as $[a_0, \dots, a_k] = \frac{p_k}{q_k}$, where the sequences $\{p_n\}$ and $\{q_n\}$ are specified as follows[1]:*

$$p_{-2} = 0, \quad p_{-1} = 1, \quad p_n = a_n p_{n-1} + p_{n-2}, \quad \forall n \geq 0,$$
$$q_{-2} = 1, \quad q_{-1} = 0, \quad q_n = a_n q_{n-1} + q_{n-2}, \quad \forall n \geq 0.$$

There are many properties related to the theory of continued fractions. One of the most important results is Legendre's Theorem (see Theorem 184 of [9]).

Theorem 4. *Let $\xi \neq 0$ be a real number and a, b be two positive integers such that $\frac{a}{b} \notin \mathbb{N}$ and $(a, b) = 1$. If*

$$0 < \left| \xi - \frac{a}{b} \right| < \frac{1}{2b^2}$$

then $\frac{a}{b}$ is a convergent of the continued fraction of ξ.

Note that computing a convergent $\frac{a}{b}$ of ξ with the continued fraction algorithm is done in polynomial time in $\log(b)$.

2.3   Elliptic Curves

Let $p \geq 5$ be a prime number and a and b two integers satisfying $4a^3 + 27b^2 \not\equiv 0 \pmod{p}$. An elliptic curve $E_p(a, b)$ over $\mathbb{F}_p = \mathbb{Z}/p\mathbb{Z}$ is the set of solutions $(x, y) \in \mathbb{F}_p^2$ satisfying the equation

$$E_p(a, b) : \quad y^2 \equiv x^3 + ax + b \pmod{p}, \tag{1}$$

---

[1] The convergents start with $\frac{p_0}{q_0}$, but it is a convention to extend the sequence index to -1 and -2 to allow the recursive formula to hold for $n = 0$ and $n = 1$.

together with a point $\mathcal{O}$, called the point at infinity. If $P_1 = (x_1, y_1)$ and $P_2 = (x_2, y_2)$ are two points, then one have the following properties.

- $P_1 + \mathcal{O} = \mathcal{O} + P_1 = P_1$.
- The opposite of P_1 is $-P_1 = (x_1, -y_1)$.
- If $P_2 = -P_1$, then $P_1 + P_2 = \mathcal{O}$.
- If $P_2 \neq -P_1$, then $P_1 + P_2 = P_3 = (x_3, y_3)$ where

$$x_3 \equiv \lambda^2 - x_1 - x_2 \pmod{p}, \quad y_3 \equiv \lambda(x_1 - x_3) - y_1 \pmod{p},$$

with

$$\lambda = \begin{cases} \dfrac{y_2 - y_1}{x_2 - x_1} & \text{if } x_1 \neq x_2, \\[2ex] \dfrac{3x_1^2 + a}{2y_1} & \text{if } x_1 = x_2. \end{cases}$$

With the former addition law, the set $E_p(a, b)$ is a group of finite order $\#E_p(a, b)$ where $\#E_p(a, b)$ is the number of solutions $(x, y) \in \mathbb{F}_p^2$ of the Eq. (1) together with the point at infinity. According to a famous Theorem of Hasse (see [23], Chap. 5), we have $\#E_p(a, b) = p + 1 - t_p$, with $|t_p| < 2\sqrt{p}$, which is close to $p + 1$, up to a small value t_p.

For specific values of p, $\#E_p(a, b)$ can be explicitly computed as for $p \equiv 2 \pmod{3}$ (see [22]).

Theorem 5. *Let $E_p(0, b)$ be an elliptic curve over $\mathbb{F}_p$ with equation $y^2 \equiv x^3 + b \pmod{p}$. If $p \equiv 2 \pmod{3}$, then number of points on $E_p(0, b)$ is $\#E_p(0, b) = p + 1$.*

Since $\#E_p(a, b)$ is the order of the group $E_p(0, b)$ for the addition law, then $\#E_p(a, b) \cdot P = \mathcal{O}$ for any point $P \in E_p(a, b)$. When $p \equiv 2 \pmod{3}$, then for any point $P \in$, we have $(p + 1)P = \mathcal{O}$. When N is a composite square free integer and a and b are integers satisfying $4a^3 + 27b^2 \not\equiv 0 \pmod{p}$, one can define an elliptic curve $E_N(a, b)$ over the ring $\mathbb{Z}/N\mathbb{Z}$ by the equation

$$E_N(a, b): \quad y^2 \equiv x^3 + ax + b \pmod{N}, \tag{2}$$

together with a point O at infinity. An addition law can be defined over $E_N(a, b)$ by using the same rules as the addition law on $E_p(a, b)$ by replacing modulo p by modulo N. When the division by $x_2 - x_1$ is not possible, this means that $\gcd(x_2 - x_1, n) \neq 1$. Since $0 < |x_2 - x_1| < n$, then $\gcd(x_2 - x_1, n) = p$ or $\gcd(x_2 - x_1, n) = q$. If $N = pq$ is an RSA modulus, this is equivalent to factoring N. Since the integer factorization problem is very hard, especially for RSA moduli, then the scenario that the addition does not exist is unlikely to happen. By the Chinese remainder theorem, every point $P = (x, y) \in E_N(a, b)$ is uniquely represented by a pair of points $(P_p, P_q) \in E_p(a, b) \times E_q(a, b)$ with the convention that O is represented by the pair of points at infinity $(\mathcal{O}_p, \mathcal{O}_q) \in E_p(a, b) \times E_q(a, b)$. It follows that for $p \equiv q \equiv 2 \pmod{3}$ and for any point $P \in E_N(0, b)$, we have

$$(p + 1)(q + 1)P = (p + 1)(q + 1)(P_p, P_q) = (\mathcal{O}_p, \mathcal{O}_q) = \mathcal{O}.$$

2.4   The KMOV Cryptosystem

In 1991, Koyama, Maurer, Okamoto and Vanstone proposed a cryptosystem, called KMOV, based on the elliptic curve $E_N(0, b)$ where $N = pq$ is an RSA modulus. The scheme works as follows.

- **KMOV Key Generation algorithm.**
    1. Choose two distinct prime numbers p and q of similar bit-length with $p \equiv q \equiv 2 \pmod{3}$.
    2. Compute $N = pq$.
    3. Choose e such that $\gcd(e, (p+1)(q+1)) = 1$.
    4. Compute $d = e^{-1} \pmod{(p+1)(q+1)}$.
    5. Keep p, q, d secret, publish N, e.
- **KMOV Encryption algorithm.**
    1. For a message $m = (m_x, m_y) \in \mathbb{Z}_N^2$, compute $b = m_y^2 - m_x^3 \pmod{N}$.
    2. Compute the point $(c_x, c_y) = e(m_x, m_y)$ on the elliptic curve with equation $y^2 \equiv x^3 + b \pmod{N}$. The ciphertext is $c = (c_x, c_y)$.
- **KMOV Decryption algorithm.**
    1. For a ciphertext $c = (c_x, c_y) \in \mathbb{Z}_N^2$, compute $b = c_y^2 - c_x^3 \pmod{N}$.
    2. Compute the point $(m_x, m_y) = d(c_x, c_y)$ on the elliptic curve $y^2 \equiv x^3 + b$ $\pmod{N}$. The plaintext is $m = (m_x, m_y)$.

The complexity of the encryption and decryption algorithms are based on the size of the encryption key e and the size of decryption key d, respectively. In a cryptosystem with a limited resource such as a credit card, it is desirable to have a smaller value of d or e. Unfortunately, when d is too small, Pinch [20] showed that one can factor the RSA modulus $N = pq$ if $d < \frac{1}{3}N^{\frac{1}{4}}$. Using a generalized attack, Nitaj [18] showed that one can factor N when $d \equiv \frac{y}{x} \pmod{(p+1)(q+1)}$ is much larger under some extra conditions on x and y.

3   A New Improved Attack Based on Continued Fractions

In this section, we give an improved attack on KMOV based totally on the continued fraction algorithm.

3.1   The New Attack Based on Continued Fractions

The attacks presented in [20] and [11] take advantage on using the convergents of the continued fraction expansion of $\frac{e}{N}$. Instead of using the convergents of $\frac{e}{N}$, we will use the convergents of $\frac{e}{\phi_0}$ where ϕ_0 is given by $\phi_0 = N + 1 + \left(1 + \frac{3\sqrt{2}}{4}\right)N^{\frac{1}{2}}$. To this end, we will need the following result.

Lemma 1. *For any $N > 10^6$, we have*

$$\frac{\left(\frac{3}{\sqrt{2}} - 2\right)N^{\frac{1}{2}} + 2}{(N + 2N^{\frac{1}{2}})^2} < \frac{1}{8N^{\frac{3}{2}}}$$

Proof. Suppose that

$$\frac{\left(\frac{3}{\sqrt{2}} - 2\right) N^{\frac{1}{2}} + 2}{\left(N + 2N^{\frac{1}{2}}\right)^2} < \frac{1}{8N^{\frac{3}{2}}}.$$

Then, clearing the denominators, we get

$$8N^{\frac{1}{2}} \left(\left(\frac{3}{\sqrt{2}} - 2\right) N^{\frac{1}{2}} + 2\right) < \left(N^{\frac{1}{2}} + 2\right)^2,$$

which is equivalent to

$$\left(12\sqrt{2} - 16\right) N + 16N^{\frac{1}{2}} < N + 4N^{\frac{1}{2}} + 4.$$

This is true if

$$\left(12\sqrt{2} - 16\right) N + 16N^{\frac{1}{2}} < N + 4N^{\frac{1}{2}},$$

or equivalently $12 < \left(17 - 12\sqrt{2}\right) N^{\frac{1}{2}}$. This is valid if

$$N > 10^6 > \left(\frac{12}{17 - 12\sqrt{2}}\right)^2.$$

This terminates the proof.   □

The following lemma is useful for approximating the sizes of the prime factors of an RSA modulus $N = pq$ when p and q are of the same bit-size.

Lemma 2. *Let $N = pq$ be an RSA modulus with $q < p < 2q$. Then*

$$2N^{\frac{1}{2}} < p + q < \frac{3\sqrt{2}}{2} N^{\frac{1}{2}}.$$

Proof. Assume that $q < p < 2q$. Then $1 < \sqrt{\frac{p}{q}} < \sqrt{2}$, so, since the function $f(x) = x + \frac{1}{x}$ is increasing on $[1, +\infty)$, we get

$$2 < \sqrt{\frac{p}{q}} + \sqrt{\frac{q}{p}} < \sqrt{2} + \frac{1}{\sqrt{2}} = \frac{3\sqrt{2}}{2}.$$

If we multiply by $N^{\frac{1}{2}}$, we get

$$2N^{\frac{1}{2}} < p + q < \frac{3\sqrt{2}}{2} N^{\frac{1}{2}}.$$

This terminates the proof.   □

Now, we present our first improved attack on KMOV based on the continued fraction algorithm. The following result shows that the secret information p, q, d in a KMOV cryptosystem can be recovered from public information (e, N).

Theorem 6. *Let (N, e) be a public key in a KMOV cryptosystem with $N = pq > 10^6$, $q < p < 2q$ and $\gcd(e, (p+1)(q+1))$. If $ed \equiv 1 \pmod{(p+1)(q+1)}$ and $d < 2\sqrt{2}\frac{N^{\frac{3}{4}}}{\sqrt{e}}$, then one can factor N in polynomial time in $\log(N)$.*

Proof. Suppose that $N = pq$ with $q < p < 2q$. Then, by Lemma 2, we get

$$N + 1 + 2N^{\frac{1}{2}} < (p+1)(q+1) < N + 1 + \frac{3\sqrt{2}}{2}N^{\frac{1}{2}}.$$

We set $\phi_1 = N + 1 + 2N^{\frac{1}{2}}$ and $\phi_2 = N + 1 + \frac{3\sqrt{2}}{2}N^{\frac{1}{2}}$. Then $(p+1)(q+1) \in]\phi_1, \phi_2[$. Let

$$\phi_0 = N + 1 + \left(1 + \frac{3\sqrt{2}}{4}\right)N^{\frac{1}{2}},$$

be the midpoint of the interval $[\phi_1, \phi_2]$. Since $(p+1)(q+1) \in (\phi_1, \phi_2)$, then

$$|(p+1)(q+1) - \phi_0| \leq \frac{1}{2}(\phi_2 - \phi_1). \tag{3}$$

If $ed \equiv 1 \pmod{(p+1)(q+1)}$, then $ed - k(p+1)(q+1) = 1$, and

$$
\begin{aligned}
\left|\frac{e}{\phi_0} - \frac{k}{d}\right| &= \left|\left(\frac{e}{\phi_0} - \frac{e}{(p+1)(q+1)}\right) + \left(\frac{e}{(p+1)(q+1)} - \frac{k}{d}\right)\right| \\
&= \left|\frac{e((p+1)(q+1) - \phi_0)}{\phi_0(p+1)(q+1)} + \frac{1}{d(p+1)(q+1)}\right| \\
&= \left|\frac{e((p+1)(q+1) - \phi_0)}{\phi_0(p+1)(q+1)} + \frac{e}{(p+1)(q+1)(k(p+1)(q+1) + 1)}\right|.
\end{aligned}
$$

Since $\phi_0(p+1)(q+1) > \phi_1^2$ and $(p+1)(q+1)(k(p+1)(q+1) + 1) > \phi_1^2$, then

$$
\begin{aligned}
\left|\frac{e}{\phi_0} - \frac{k}{d}\right| &< e\frac{\frac{1}{2}(\phi_2 - \phi_1)}{\phi_1^2} + e\frac{1}{\phi_1^2} \\
&= e\frac{\phi_2 - \phi_1 + 2}{2\phi_1^2}.
\end{aligned}
$$

Then, combining (3) and $\phi_1 = N + 1 + 2\sqrt{N} \geq N + 2\sqrt{N}$, we get

$$\left|\frac{e}{\phi_0} - \frac{k}{d}\right| < e\frac{\left(\frac{3\sqrt{2}}{2} - 2\right)\sqrt{N} + 2}{2\left(N + 2\sqrt{N}\right)^2}.$$

Using Lemma 1, for $N > 10^6$, we get

$$\left|\frac{e}{\phi_0} - \frac{k}{d}\right| < \frac{e}{16N^{\frac{3}{2}}}.$$

Now, suppose that $\frac{e}{16N^{\frac{3}{2}}} < \frac{1}{2d^2}$, that is $d < \frac{2\sqrt{2}N^{\frac{3}{4}}}{\sqrt{e}}$, then

$$\left| \frac{e}{\phi_0} - \frac{k}{d} \right| < \frac{1}{2d^2}.$$

It follows by Theorem 4 that $\frac{k}{d}$ is a convergent of $\frac{e}{\phi_0}$ from which we deduce k and d. Using the equation $ed - k(p+1)(q+1) = 1$, we get $p + q = \frac{ed-1}{k} - N - 1$ and combining with $N = pq$, we easily find p and q. This gives to the factorization of $N = pq$. Notice that, since the continued fraction algorithm works in polynomial time, then finding p and q is done in polynomial time.   □

3.2   Comparison with Former Attacks

In [20], Pinch extended Wiener's attack [25] on RSA to KMOV and showed that one can factor the modulus $N = pq$ if the private exponent d satisfies $d < \frac{1}{3}N^{\frac{1}{4}}$. In [11], Ibrahimpasic slightly extended the attack of Pinch by an extra exhaustive research. In both attacks, the bounds do not depend on the size of e. In our new attack, the bound is $d < 2\sqrt{2}\frac{N^{\frac{3}{4}}}{\sqrt{e}}$ and depends on e. In the typical situation where $e \approx N$, our bound becomes $d < 2\sqrt{2}N^{\frac{1}{4}} \approx 2.828N^{\frac{1}{4}}$ while the bound in [20] is $d < \frac{1}{3}N^{\frac{1}{4}} \approx 0.333N^{\frac{1}{4}}$. Observe that our new bound $d < 2\sqrt{2}\frac{N^{\frac{3}{4}}}{\sqrt{e}}$ is more significative for moderately small e.

Let us consider a numerical example. Consider the 1024 bit modulus N

$N = 12807225329156098467573133994262387415557133035180561568147794073786011155320026341140985183132345608858349735519007228389894974636644538941892679949096490221124044712544918169715570671442748362644478109640804487612984437526155152871825794623906498446242687386222945348594999805071603882441098200546624652$7621,

and the 999 bit public exponent.

$e = 2965269350930157104071366860349811896081836896872339304383732609940030086676471766099555068592869575943128645160623336917088658396146737322525219300673462207633313904334714033827193243607557351083333148437728059199194635088486445341236170582989521492255372881221811248133999406005069737107180854644647.

Then, applying the continued fraction algorithm to $\frac{e}{\phi_0}$ and computing the convergents, the 130th convergent is $\frac{k}{d}$ where

$k = 43924611348159354221490725443146132347593190572471054816325792273119943084,$

$d = 18971375900641885458197870183823426822679754287618550012224730563856487159238099$27.

Using this convergent, we get $p + q = \frac{ed-1}{k}$. Then combining with $pq = N$, we get

$$p = 122295652435077729919345520517086986687967509723643022198045090700627888455053960249602784859293184787008459099618173004911179244406300082071971851405178417,$$

$$q = 104723471964426405086080002568566304601367956338101575543737215792893331651240463496547152238295322902114471979717345643807495258326678417021029177829746136.$$

We notice that $\frac{k}{d}$ is not among the convergents of $\frac{e}{N}$ which implies that the methods of Pinch and Ibrahimpasic will not succeed.

4 A New Improved Attack Based on Coppersmith's Method

In this section, we present a new attack on KMOV based on Coppersmith's method.

4.1 The New Attack

Theorem 7. *Let (N, e) be a public key for the KMOV cryptosystem where $N = pq$ is an RSA modulus and $e = N^\beta$. Suppose that e satisfies the equation $eu - (p+1)(q+1)v = w$ with $u < N^\delta$ and $|w| < N^\gamma$. If*

$$\delta < \frac{7}{6} - \gamma - \frac{1}{3}\sqrt{6\beta - 6\gamma + 1} - \varepsilon,$$

for a small positive constant ε, then one can factor N in polynomial time.

Proof. Suppose that $N = pq$ is an RSA modulus and e is a public exponent satisfying $eu - (p+1)(q+1)v = w$. Since $(p+1)(q+1) = N + p + q + 1$, then $v(N+p+q+1)+w \equiv 0 \pmod{e}$, which can be rewritten as $v(p+q+1)+Nv+w \equiv 0 \pmod{e}$. Consider the polynomial $f(x, y, z) = xy + Nx + z$, Then $(x, y, z) = (v, p+q+1, w)$ is a solution of the modular polynomial equation $f(x, y, z) \equiv 0 \pmod{e}$. To find the solution $(v, p+q+1, w)$, we apply Coppersmith's method [8]. Let m and t be two positive integers to be optimized later. We use $f(x, y, z)$ to build the sets of polynomials

$$G_{k,i_1,i_2,i_3}(x, y, z) = x^{i_1-k} z^{i_3} f(x, y, z)^k e^{m-k},$$

$$\text{for} \quad k = 0, \ldots m, \; i_1 = k, \ldots, m, \; i_2 = k, \; i_3 = m - i_1,$$

$$H_{k,i_1,i_2,i_3}(x, y, z) = y^{i_2-k} z^{i_3} f(x, y, z)^k e^{m-k},$$

$$\text{for} \quad k = 0, \ldots m, \; i_1 = k, \; i_2 = k+1, \ldots, i_1 + t, \; i_3 = m - i_1.$$

Let $\mathcal{L}$ denote the lattice spanned by the coefficient vectors of the polynomials $G_{k,i_1,i_2,i_3}(Xx, Yy, Zz)$ and $H_{k,i_1,i_2,i_3}(Xx, Yy, Zz)$. By choosing the increasing ordering following the i_1's, then the i_2's, and the i_3's, one find a left triangular matrix. For $m = 2$ and $t = 1$, the coefficient matrix for $\mathcal{L}$ is presented in Table 1 where the monomials are

$$\{z^3, xz^2, x^2z, x^3, xyz^2, x^2yz, x^3y, x^2y^2z, x^3y^2, x^3y^3, xy^2z^2, x^2y^3z, x^2yz, x^3y^4\}.$$

The non-zero elements are marked with an '⊛' and do not influence the value of the determinant.

Table 1. The coefficient matrix for the case $m = 2$, $t = 1$.

G_{k,i_1,i_2,i_3}	z^3	xz^2	x^2z	x^3	xyz^2	x^2yz	x^3y	x^2y^2z	x^3y^2	x^3y^3
$G_{0,0,0,3}$	Z^3e^3	0	0	0	0	0	0	0	0	0
$G_{0,1,0,2}$	0	XZ^2e^3	0	0	0	0	0	0	0	0
$G_{0,2,0,1}$	0	0	X^2Ze^3	0	0	0	0	0	0	0
$G_{0,3,0,0}$	0	0	0	X^3	0	0	0	0	0	0
$G_{1,1,1,2}$	⊛	0	0	0	XYZ^2e^2	0	0	0	0	0
$G_{1,2,1,1}$	0	⊛	0	0	0	X^2YZe^2	0	0	0	0
$G_{1,3,1,0}$	0	0	⊛	⊛	0	0	X^3Ye^2	0	0	0
$G_{2,2,2,1}$	⊛	⊛	⊛	0	⊛	⊛	0	X^2Y^2Ze	0	0
$G_{2,3,2,0}$	0	⊛	⊛	⊛	0	⊛	⊛	0	X^3Y^2e	0
$G_{3,3,3,0}$	⊛	0	⊛	⊛	⊛	⊛	⊛	⊛	⊛	X^3Y^3
H_{k,i_1,i_2,i_3}										
$H_{0,0,1,3}$	0	0	0	0	⊛	0	0	0	0	⊛
$H_{1,1,2,2}$	0	0	0	0	⊛	⊛	0	⊛	0	0
$H_{2,2,3,1}$	0	0	0	⊛	0	0	⊛	⊛	0	0
$H_{3,3,4,0}$	0	0	0	0	⊛	0	0	⊛	⊛	0

G_{k,i_1,i_2,i_3}	xy^2z^2	x^2y^3z	x^2yz	x^3y^4
$G_{0,0,0,3}$	0	0	0	0
$G_{0,1,0,2}$	0	0	0	0
$G_{0,2,0,1}$	0	0	0	0
$G_{0,3,0,0}$	0	0	0	0
$G_{1,1,1,2}$	0	0	0	0
$G_{1,2,1,1}$	0	0	0	0
$G_{1,3,1,0}$	0	0	0	0
$G_{2,2,2,1}$	0	0	0	0
$G_{2,3,2,0}$	0	0	0	0
$G_{3,3,3,0}$	0	0	0	0
H_{k,i_1,i_2,i_3}				
$H_{0,0,1,3}$	$XY^2Z^2e^2$	0	0	0
$H_{1,1,2,2}$	⊛	X^2Y^3Ze	0	0
$H_{2,2,3,1}$	0	0	X^2YZe	0
$H_{3,3,4,0}$	0	0	0	X^3Y^4

The determinant of the triangular matrix is then the determinant of the lattice $\mathcal{L}$ and can be easily computed as

$$\det(\mathcal{L}) = e^{n_e}X^{n_X}Y^{n_Y}Z^{n_Z}. \tag{4}$$

To find the values of the exponents n_e, n_X, n_Y, n_Z, define the sum $S(a)$ by

$$S(a) = \sum_{k=0}^{m}\sum_{i_1=k}^{m}\sum_{i_2=k}^{k}\sum_{i_3=m-i_1}^{m-i_1} a + \sum_{k=0}^{m}\sum_{i_1=k}^{m}\sum_{i_2=k+1}^{k}\sum_{i_3=m-i_1}^{m-i_1} a.$$

By the construction of the polynomials G and H, we get

$$
\begin{aligned}
n_e &= S(m-k) = \frac{1}{6}m(m+1)(2m+3t+4),\\
n_X &= S(i_1) = \frac{1}{6}m(m+1)(2m+3t+4),\\
n_Y &= S(i_2) = \frac{1}{6}(m+1)\left(m^2+3mt+3t^2+2m+3t\right),\\
n_Z &= S(i_3) = \frac{1}{6}m(m+1)(m+3t+2).
\end{aligned}
\tag{5}
$$

The dimension of the lattice is the number of rows in the matrix. It can be estimated as

$$
\omega = S(1) = \frac{1}{2}(m+1)(m+2t+2).
\tag{6}
$$

If we set $t = \tau m$ for some positive τ, then the dominant terms of the exponents in (5) and 6 are

$$
\begin{aligned}
n_e &\approx \frac{1}{6}(3\tau+2)m^3 + o(m^3),\\
n_X &\approx \frac{1}{6}(3\tau+2)m^3 + o(m^3),\\
n_Y &\approx \frac{1}{6}\left(3\tau^2+3\tau+1\right)m^3 + o(m^3),\\
n_Z &\approx \frac{1}{6}(3\tau+1)m^3 + o(m^3),\\
w &\approx \frac{1}{6}(6\tau+3)m^2 + o(m^2).
\end{aligned}
\tag{7}
$$

Next, we apply the LLL algorithm 2 to the lattice $\mathcal{L}$. We then get a reduced basis where the three first vectors h_i, $i = 1,2,3$ satisfy

$$
\|h_1\| \le \|h_2\| \le \|h_3\| \le 2^{\frac{\omega(\omega-1)}{4(\omega-2)}} \det(\mathcal{L})^{\frac{1}{\omega-2}}.
$$

To apply Howgrave-Graham's Theorem 1 to h_1, h_2 and h_3, we set

$$
2^{\frac{\omega(\omega-1)}{4(\omega-2)}} \det(\mathcal{L})^{\frac{1}{\omega-2}} < \frac{e^m}{\sqrt{\omega}},
$$

from which we deduce

$$
\det(\mathcal{L}) < 2^{-\frac{\omega(\omega-1)}{4}} \frac{1}{\left(\sqrt{\omega}\right)^{\omega-2}} e^{m(\omega-2)}.
$$

Using (4), we get

$$
e^{n_e} X^{n_X} Y^{n_Y} Z^{n_Z} < 2^{-\frac{\omega(\omega-1)}{4}} \frac{1}{\left(\sqrt{\omega}\right)^{\omega-2}} e^{m(\omega-2)}.
\tag{8}
$$

Suppose that $e = N^\beta$, $u < N^\delta$ and $|w| < N^\gamma$. Then, using Lemma 2, we have $p + q + 1 \leq 2p < 2\sqrt{2}\sqrt{N}$. Since $p + q + 1$ is represented by y, we set $Y = \left\lfloor 2\sqrt{2}\sqrt{N} \right\rfloor$. On the other hand, since $(p+1)(q+1) > N$ and $|w| < eu$, we get

$$|v| = \frac{|eu - w|}{(p+1)(q+1)} < \frac{eu + |w|}{(p+1)(q+1)} < \frac{2eu}{N} < 2N^{\beta+\delta-1}. \tag{9}$$

Since v is represented by x, we set $X = \left\lfloor 2N^{\beta+\delta-1} \right\rfloor$. Also, since w is represented by Z, we set $Z = \lfloor N^\gamma \rfloor$. It follows that the solution $(x, y, z) = (v, p+q+1, w)$ satisfies $|x| < X$, $|y| < Y$ and $|z| < Z$ and (8) is satisfied if

$$2^{n_X} \left(2\sqrt{2}\right)^{n_Y} N^{n_e\beta + n_X(\beta+\delta-1) + \frac{n_Y}{2} + n_Z\gamma} < 2^{-\frac{\omega(\omega-1)}{4}} \frac{1}{\left(\sqrt{\omega}\right)^{\omega-2}} N^{m(\omega-2)\beta}. \tag{10}$$

Using the approximations of n_e, n_X, n_Y, n_Z given in (7) and ω given 6, the inequality 8 leads to

$$N^{\left((3\tau+2)\beta + (3\tau+2)(\beta+\delta-1) + \frac{3\tau^2+3\tau+1}{2} + (3\tau+1)\gamma\right)m^3}$$

$$< 2^{-n_X} \left(2\sqrt{2}\right)^{-n_Y} 2^{-\frac{\omega(\omega-1)}{4}} \frac{1}{\left(\sqrt{\omega}\right)^{\omega-2}} N^{-2\beta m} N^{(6\tau+3)\beta m^3}. \tag{11}$$

To homogenize the exponentiation of N, we set

$$2^{-n_X} \left(2\sqrt{2}\right)^{-n_Y} 2^{-\frac{\omega(\omega-1)}{4}} \frac{1}{\left(\sqrt{\omega}\right)^{\omega-2}} N^{-2\beta m} = N^{-\mu m^3},$$

where μ is a small positive constant. Then, taking logarithms and dividing by $m^3 \log N$, we get

$$(3\tau + 2)\beta + (3\tau + 2)(\beta + \delta - 1) + \frac{3\tau^2 + 3\tau + 1}{2} + (3\tau + 1)\gamma - (6\tau + 3)\beta < -\mu.$$

The optimal value for the left hand side is $\tau_0 = \frac{1 - 2\delta - 2\gamma}{2}$, which, plugged in the former inequality leads to

$$-12\delta^2 - 24\delta\gamma - 12\gamma^2 + 8\beta + 28\delta + 20\gamma - 15 < -8\mu,$$

and consequently

$$\delta < \frac{7}{6} - \gamma - \frac{1}{3}\sqrt{6\beta - 6\gamma + 1} - \varepsilon,$$

where ε is a small positive constant that depends on m and N. Within this condition, the reduced lattice has three polynomials $h_1(x, y, z)$, $h_2(x, y, z)$ and $h_2(x, y, z)$ sharing the root $(x_0, y_0, z_0) = (v, p+q+1, w)$. Then, applying Gröbner basis or resultant computations, we get the expected solution (x_0, y_0, z_0) from which we deduce $p + q = y - 1$. Together with the equation $pq = N$, this leads to finding p and q. This terminates the proof.   □

4.2   Comparison with Former Attacks

In [18], Nitaj presented an algorithm for factoring the modulus $N = pq$ when the public exponent e satisfies an equation of the form $eu - (p+1)(q+1)v = w$, where the unknown parameters u, v and w are such that

$$|w| < \frac{(p-q)N^{\frac{1}{4}}v}{3(p+q)}, \quad uv < \frac{\sqrt{2}\sqrt{N}}{12}. \tag{12}$$

The idea in [18] is to compute the convergents of the continued fraction of $\frac{e}{N}$, and for each convergent $\frac{v}{u}$ with $uv < \frac{\sqrt{2}\sqrt{N}}{12}$, to compute U and V with

$$U = \frac{eu}{v} - N - 1, \quad V = \sqrt{|U^2 - 4N|}.$$

Then $\tilde{p} = \frac{1}{2}(U + V)$ is a possible approximation of the prime factor p with error term of at most $2N^{\frac{1}{4}}$. If so, then by applying Coppersmith's method, one can find p, and then factor N.

To compare our new results and the result of [18], suppose that $e = N^\beta$, $u < N^\delta$ and $|w| < N^\gamma$. Then, by (9), we get $|v| < 2N^{\beta+\delta-1}$. Hence, the inequalities (12) are fulfilled if

$$N^\gamma < \frac{2(p-q)N^{\frac{1}{4}}N^{\beta+\delta-1}}{3(p+q)}, \quad 2N^\delta N^{\beta+\delta-1} < \frac{\sqrt{2}\sqrt{N}}{12}.$$

Then, neglecting the constants and assuming that $p - q \approx p + q$, the former two inequalities are true if

$$\gamma < \frac{1}{4} + \beta + \delta - 1, \quad 2\delta + \beta - 1 < \frac{1}{2}.$$

This leads to $\delta < \frac{3}{4} - \frac{1}{2}\beta$, which is to be compared with the new bound

$$\delta < \frac{7}{6} - \gamma - \frac{1}{3}\sqrt{6\beta - 6\gamma + 1} - \varepsilon.$$

Define

$$\delta_0 = \frac{3}{4} - \frac{1}{2}\beta, \quad \delta_1 = \frac{7}{6} - \gamma - \frac{1}{3}\sqrt{6\beta - 6\gamma + 1}.$$

A typical situation is when $e \approx N$, that is $\beta = 1$, and $|w|$ is small, that is $\gamma = 0$. Then the bounds δ_0 and δ_1 are $\delta_0 = 0.25$, $\delta_1 \approx 0.284$. We see that the new method overcome the method of [18] in the most realistic situations of instances of KMOV.

5   Conclusion

We have presented two new attacks on the KMOV cryptosystem which is an RSA type cryptosystem based on elliptic curves. The first attack is based on the continued fraction algorithm and the second is based on Coppersmith's method. Both attacks work when the private key is suitably small and the new results improve the former attacks on the KMOV elliptic curve cryptosystem.

References

1. Boneh, D.: Twenty years of attacks on the RSA cryptosystem. Not. Am. Math. Soc. **46**(2), 203–213 (1999)
2. Boneh, D., Durfee, G.: Cryptanalysis of RSA with private key d less than $N^{0.292}$. IEEE Trans. Inf. Theory **46**, 1339–1349 (2000)
3. Bunder, M., Tonien, J.: A new improved attack on RSA. In: Proceedings of the 5th International Cryptology and Information Security Conference, pp. 101–110 (2016)
4. Bunder, M., Nitaj, A., Susilo, W., Tonien, J.: A new attack on three variants of the RSA cryptosystem. In: Liu, J.K., Steinfeld, R. (eds.) ACISP 2016. LNCS, vol. 9723, pp. 258–268. Springer, Cham (2016). https://doi.org/10.1007/978-3-319-40367-0_16
5. Bunder, M., Nitaj, A., Susilo, W., Tonien, J.: A generalized attack on RSA type cryptosystems. Theor. Comput. Sci. **704**, 74–81 (2017)
6. Bunder, M., Tonien, J.: A new attack on the RSA cryptosystem based on continued fractions. Malays. J. Math. Sci. **11**(S3), 45–57 (2017)
7. Bunder, M., Nitaj, A., Susilo, W., Tonien, J.: Cryptanalysis of RSA-type cryptosystems based on Lucas sequences. Gaussian integers and elliptic curves. J. Inf. Secur. Appl. **40**, 193–198 (2018)
8. Coppersmith, D.: Small solutions to polynomial equations, and low exponent RSA vulnerabilities. J. Cryptol. **10**(4), 233–260 (1997)
9. Hardy, G.H., Wright, E.M.: An Introduction to the Theory of Numbers. Oxford University Press, London (1965)
10. Howgrave-Graham, N.: Finding small roots of univariate modular equations revisited. In: Darnell, M. (ed.) Cryptography and Coding 1997. LNCS, vol. 1355, pp. 131–142. Springer, Heidelberg (1997). https://doi.org/10.1007/BFb0024458
11. Ibrahimpasic, B.: Cryptanalysis of KMOV cryptosystem with short secret exponent. In: Proceedings of Central European Conference on Information and Intelligent Systems (2008)
12. Jochemsz, E., May, A.: A strategy for finding roots of multivariate polynomials with new applications in attacking RSA variants. In: Lai, X., Chen, K. (eds.) ASIACRYPT 2006. LNCS, vol. 4284, pp. 267–282. Springer, Heidelberg (2006). https://doi.org/10.1007/11935230_18
13. Koblitz, N.: Elliptic curve cryptosystems. Math. Comput. **48**, 203–209 (1987)
14. Koyama, K., Maurer, U.M., Okamoto, T., Vanstone, S.A.: New public-key schemes based on elliptic curves over the ring $\mathbb{Z}_n$. In: Feigenbaum, J. (ed.) CRYPTO 1991. LNCS, vol. 576, pp. 252–266. Springer, Heidelberg (1992). https://doi.org/10.1007/3-540-46766-1_20
15. Lenstra, A.K., Lenstra, H.W., Lovász, L.: Factoring polynomials with rational coefficients. Math. Ann. **261**, 513–534 (1982)
16. May, A.: New RSA vulnerabilities using lattics reduction methods. Ph.D. dissertation, University of Paderborn (2003). http://www.cits.rub.de/imperia/md/content/may/paper/bp.ps
17. Miller, V.S.: Use of elliptic curves in cryptography. In: Williams, H.C. (ed.) CRYPTO 1985. LNCS, vol. 218, pp. 417–426. Springer, Heidelberg (1986). https://doi.org/10.1007/3-540-39799-X_31
18. Nitaj, A.: A new attack on the KMOV cryptosystem. Bull. Korean Math. Soc. **51**(5), 1347–1356 (2014)

19. Nitaj, A., Pan, Y., Tonien, J.: A generalized attack on some variants of the RSA cryptosystem. In: Cid, C., Jacobson Jr., M. (eds.) SAC 2018. LNCS, vol. 11349, pp. 421–433. Springer, Cham (2019). https://doi.org/10.1007/978-3-030-10970-7_19
20. Pinch, R.G.E.: Extending the Wiener attack to RSA-type cryptosystems. Electron. Lett. **31**(20), 1736–1738 (1995)
21. Rivest, R., Shamir, A., Adleman, L.: A method for obtaining digital signatures and public-key cryptosystems. Commun. ACM **21**(2), 120–126 (1978)
22. Schmitt, S., Zimmer, H.G.: Elliptic Curves. A Computational Approach. Walter de Gruyter, Berlin (2003)
23. Silverman, J.H.: The Arithmetic of Elliptic Curves. Graduate Texts in Mathematics, vol. 106. Springer, New York (1986). https://doi.org/10.1007/978-1-4757-1920-8
24. Susilo, W., Tonien, J., Yang, G.: The Wiener attack on RSA revisited: a quest for the exact bound. In: Jang-Jaccard, J., Guo, F. (eds.) ACISP 2019. LNCS, vol. 11547, pp. 381–398. Springer, Cham (2019). https://doi.org/10.1007/978-3-030-21548-4_21
25. Wiener, M.: Cryptanalysis of short RSA secret exponents. IEEE Trans. Inf. Theory **36**, 553–558 (1990)

Solving ECDLP via List Decoding

Fangguo Zhang[1,2(✉)] and Shengli Liu[3]

[1] School of Data and Computer Science, Sun Yat-sen University,
Guangzhou 510006, China
`isszhfg@mail.sysu.edu.cn`
[2] Guangdong Key Laboratory of Information Security, Guangzhou 510006, China
[3] Department of Computer Science and Engineering, Shanghai Jiao Tong University,
Shanghai 200240, China

Abstract. We provide a new approach to the elliptic curve discrete logarithm problem (ECDLP). First, we construct Elliptic Codes (EC codes) from the ECDLP. Then we propose an algorithm of finding the minimum weight codewords for algebraic geometry codes, especially for the elliptic code, via list decoding. Finally, with the minimum weight codewords, we show how to solve ECDLP. This work may provide a potential approach to speeding up the computation of ECDLP.

Keywords: Elliptic curves discrete logarithms · Elliptic code · List decoding · Minimum weight codewords

1 Introduction

ECC and ECDLP. In the 1980s, Koblitz [17] and Miller [21] opened the door of elliptic-curve cryptography (ECC). Since the introduction of ECC, the elliptic-curve analogues of cryptographic primitives, like public-key encryption, digital signature, key agreement, etc., were set up and deployed widely in information systems, due to the smaller key sizes and more efficient implementations than their traditional siblings with the same security level. In the last decades, ECC primitives have permeated in cryptographic protocols and deployed in a variety of applications.

The security kernel of ECC is the hardness of the *elliptic curve discrete logarithm problem* (ECDLP). Let $\mathcal{E}$ be an elliptic curve defined over a finite field $\mathbb{F}_q$ and $\mathcal{E}(\mathbb{F}_q)$ be the additive group over $\mathcal{E}$. Let $P \in \mathcal{E}(\mathbb{F}_q)$ be a point of prime order p, and let $\langle P \rangle$ be the subgroup generated by P. If $Q \in \langle P \rangle$, then $Q = sP$ for some integer s $(0 \leq s < p)$, and $s := \log_P Q$ is defined as the discrete logarithm of Q to the base P. The problem of finding s, given P, Q and the parameters of $\mathcal{E}$, is called ECDLP. Up to date, Pollard ρ method [25] with complexity $O(\sqrt{p})$ and its refinements are known as the most efficient solutions to ECDLP, except for some special elliptic curves [7,9,19,26–28]. A good survey of recent works on ECDLP can be found in [8].

R. Steinfeld and T. H. Yuen (Eds.): ProvSec 2019, LNCS 11821, pp. 222–244, 2019.
https://doi.org/10.1007/978-3-030-31919-9_13

ECDLP and Minimum Distance of Elliptic Code. Algebraic geometry codes (AG codes) were introduced in 1977 by V.D. Goppa [11] as a class of linear codes. Elliptic Codes belong to AG codes, and they are constructed from elliptic curve, i.e., algebraic curves of genus $g = 1$. For any $[n, k]$ elliptic code $\mathcal{C}$ constructed from $\mathcal{E}$ over $\mathbb{F}_q$, the minimum distance of $\mathcal{C}$ is either $d = n - k$ or $d = n - k + 1$ [30]. Meanwhile, the minimum distance of $\mathcal{C}$ is closely related to the solution of the ECDLP over $\mathcal{E}$. This connection was first noticed by Driencourt and Michon [5], and rediscovered by Cheng [3]. This brought us a new hope of solving ECDLP: it is possible for us to solve ECDLP over $\mathcal{E}$ if we found a codeword of minimum distance for the elliptic code over $\mathcal{E}$. However, computing the minimum distance of a linear code is one of the fundamental problems in algorithmic coding theory. Vardy [36] showed that it is an NP-hard problem for general linear codes, while Cheng [3] proved that it is still NP-hard (under **RP**-reduction) for elliptic codes. Obviously, the problem of finding Minimum Weight Codewords for a linear code is NP hard as well, since a codeword of minimum weight uniquely determine the minimum distance of this linear code. As a result, it is unlikely for us to design an algorithm of finding codewords of minimum weight in polynomial time, perhaps even not in subexponential time. However, for some NP-hard problems, some algorithms of exponential time do beat the trivial exhaustive search solution.

List Decoding. List decoding is a powerful decoding algorithm for linear error-correction codes. It has a longer history than elliptic-curve cryptography and dates back to the works of Elias [6] and Wozencraft [38] in the 1950s. The breakthroughs of list decoding were due to Goldreich and Levin [10] for the Hadamard code, and to Sudan [33] for the Reed-Solomon(RS) codes. For any $[n, k, d]$ linear code, a well-known fact is that if the number of errors t satisfies $t \leq \lceil (d-1)/2 \rceil$, then there must exist a unique codeword within distance $\lceil (d-1)/2 \rceil$ from the received vector. If $t > (d-1)/2$, however, unique decoding is usually impossible. In 1997, Sudan [33] proposed "List Decoding algorithm" and applied it to Reed-Solomon codes to break the barrier of $t > (d-1)/2$ by allowing the algorithm outputting a list of codewords. Later, Shokrollahi and Wasserman [31] extended Sudan's list decoding algorithm to algebraic-geometry codes. In 1999, Guruswami and Sudan [12] improved the bound of t to $n - \sqrt{nk}$ for both RS and AG codes. Up to now, the list decoding algorithm is one of the most powerful decoding methods for RS and AG codes.

Beyond its application in the field of coding theory, it also led to new developments in complexity theory and cryptography. For instance, it results in new constructions of hardcore predicates from one-way permutations, amplifying hardness of boolean functions, construction of extractors [34], computation of the discrete logarithm over finite fields [4], and constructions of cryptographic schemes [16], etc.

Our Contribution. In this paper, we consider a new approach to the solution of ECDLP, and provide the first try of using list decoding to solve ECDLP. We believe that our work merely scratches the surface of the potential power of list decoding techniques in solving ECDLP, and expect more results on this topic in the near future. Our contributions are listed as follows:

1. We present a general algorithm of finding Minimum Weight Codewords for any linear code that is list decodable. Meanwhile, we show a specific algorithm of finding minimum weight codewords for AG codes using list decoding.
2. We show how to list decode elliptic codes and designed an algorithm of finding minimum distance codewords for elliptic codes.
3. Our work provides the first method of solving ECDLP via list decoding, which is of theoretical significance.

Organization. The rest of our paper is organized as follows. In Sect. 2, we review some preliminaries that will be used in our construction. In Sect. 3, we show how to use List Decoding to find Minimum Weight Codewords of algebraic codes, especially of elliptic codes. In Sect. 4, we present an algorithm of solving ECDLP problems via List Decoding and give the corresponding analysis. Finally, Sect. 5 concludes this paper.

2 Preliminaries

If n is a positive integer, define $[n] := \{1, 2, \ldots, n\}$. Let $\mathcal{S}$ be a set, then $s \leftarrow \mathcal{S}$ denotes choose an element s from $\mathcal{S}$ uniformly at random. If Alg. is an algorithm, then $(b_1, b_2, \ldots, b_i) \leftarrow \mathsf{Alg}.(a_1, a_2, \ldots, a_j)$ means that the algorithm takes $a_1, a_2, \ldots, a_j$ as input and outputs $b_1, b_2, \ldots, b_i$.

2.1 Elliptic Curve and Elliptic Curve Discrete Logarithm Problems

Let $\mathbb{F}_q$ be a finite field of q elements. An elliptic curve $\mathcal{E}$ over $\mathbb{F}_q$ is a cubic curve defined by Weierstrass equation

$$\mathcal{E}:\ y^2 + a_1 xy + a_3 y = x^3 + a_2 x^2 + a_4 x + a_6\ (a_i \in \mathbb{F}_q).$$

The set of $\mathbb{F}_q$-rational points of $\mathcal{E}$ is defined as

$$\mathcal{E}(\mathbb{F}_q) := \{(x, y) \in \mathbb{F}_q \times \mathbb{F}_q : y^2 + a_1 xy + a_3 y = x^3 + a_2 x^2 + a_4 x + a_6\} \cup \{\mathcal{O}\},$$

where $\mathcal{O}$ is the point of infinity,

Equipped with the so-called "chord-and-tangent" rule, $\mathcal{E}(\mathbb{F}_q)$ becomes an abelian group [[29], III.2]. Note that if the characteristic of the finite field is larger than 3, the Weierstrass equation of an elliptic curve $\mathcal{E}$ can be transformed into a short but isomorphic one

$$\mathcal{E}: y^2 = x^3 + ax + b,$$

where $a, b \in \mathbb{F}_q$, $4a^3 + 27b^2 \neq 0 \in \mathbb{F}_q$. For detailed information about elliptic curves, we refer the reader to Silverman's book [29].

Let p be a prime integer which is coprime to q. Let GenG be an elliptic curve group generation algorithm. Taking as input a security parameter 1^κ, GenG outputs q which defines a finite field $\mathbb{F}_q$, an Elliptic Curve $\mathcal{E}$ over $\mathbb{F}_q$, and a point $P \in \mathcal{E}(\mathbb{F}_q)$ of order p. Denote by $\langle P \rangle$ the group of order p generated by P. If $Q \in \langle P \rangle$, it must holds that $Q = sP$ for some integer s, $0 \le s < p$, which is called the logarithm of Q to the base P and denoted by $\log_P Q$. The problem of finding s, given P, Q and the parameters of $\mathcal{E}$, is known as the Elliptic Curve Discrete Logarithm Problem (ECDLP).

The ECDLP problem is a well-known hard problem. It is an essential base for elliptic curve cryptography and pairing-based cryptography, and has been a major research area in computational number theory and cryptography for the last several decades.

2.2   Linear Error Correction Codes

An $[n, k]$ linear error correction code $\mathcal{C}$ over finite field $\mathbb{F}_q$ is a set of codewords, where each codeword contains n elements of $\mathbb{F}_q$ and all codewords constitute a linear space of dimension k over $\mathbb{F}_q$. Therefore, each codeword can be expressed as a vector of length n over $\mathbb{F}_q$. Given a codeword $\boldsymbol{c} = (c_1, c_2, \ldots, c_n) \in \mathbb{F}_q^n$, its Hamming weight, denoted by $\mathsf{wt}(\boldsymbol{c})$, is defined to be the number of non-zero coordinates, i.e.,

$$\mathsf{wt}(\boldsymbol{c}) = |\{i \mid c_i \ne 0, 1 \le i \le n\}|.$$

The distance of two codewords $\boldsymbol{c}_1, \boldsymbol{c}_2$, denoted by $dis(\boldsymbol{c}_1, \boldsymbol{c}_2)$, counts the number of coordinates in which they differ. The minimum distance $d(\mathcal{C})$ of $\mathcal{C}$ is the minimal value of the distances between any two different codewords. In formula,

$$d(\mathcal{C}) := \min_{\boldsymbol{c}_1, \boldsymbol{c}_2 \in \mathcal{C}, \boldsymbol{c}_1 \ne \boldsymbol{c}_2} dis(\boldsymbol{c}_1, \boldsymbol{c}_2).$$

By the linearity of $\mathcal{C}$, we know that $d(\mathcal{C})$ is determined by the minimum Hamming weight among all non-zero codewords in $\mathcal{C}$, i.e.,

$$d(\mathcal{C}) = \min_{c \in \mathcal{C} \setminus \{0\}} \mathsf{wt}(c).$$

If a linear $[n, k]$ code $\mathcal{C}$ has d as the minimum distance, then $\mathcal{C}$ is called a $[n, k, d]$ linear code.

For any linear $[n, k]$ code $\mathcal{C}$ over finite field $\mathbb{F}_q$. Suppose that $\boldsymbol{0} = (0, ..., 0)$ is the transmitted (causal) codeword, and $\boldsymbol{e}$ is a received vector. Define $f(\boldsymbol{e}, t) := |\{\boldsymbol{c} \in \mathcal{C} \setminus \{0\} : |\boldsymbol{e} - \boldsymbol{c}| \le t\}|$ as the number of noncausal codewords within distance t centered around $\boldsymbol{e}$. If $f(\boldsymbol{e}, t) = m$, then $\boldsymbol{e}$ is m-tuply falsely decodable. Define $D(u, t) := \sum_{|e|=u} f(\boldsymbol{e}, t)$ as the total number of falsely decodable words of weight u, counting on all possible received vectors of weight u. By the linearity of $\mathcal{C}$, for any causal codeword $\boldsymbol{c}$ and any error pattern $\boldsymbol{e}$, $f(\boldsymbol{e}, t)$ also denotes the number of noncausal codewords within distance t centered around the received vector $\boldsymbol{r} = \boldsymbol{c} + \boldsymbol{e}$. According to [2,20], we have the following results.

Theorem 1 ([2,20]). *If* $|e| = u$, *then the average number of noncausal code-words in a decoding sphere of radius t over all error patterns of weight u is given by*

$$\bar{L}(u,t) = \frac{D(u,t)}{\binom{n}{u}(q-1)^u}.$$

For an $[n, k, d]$ RS code, Berlekamp and Ramsey proved that $D(u,t) = \binom{d}{t}\binom{n}{d}(q-1)$ if $u + t = d$, hence

$$\bar{L}(u,t) = \frac{1}{(q-1)^{u-1}}\binom{n-u}{t} \quad \text{if } u+t = n-k+1.$$

2.3   Algebraic-Geometry Codes and Elliptic Codes

Algebraic-Geometry (AG) Codes are linear error correction codes defined on algebraic curves. The first AG code was due to Goppa [11] who proposed the so-called "Goppa Code". Algebraic-Geometry Codes can be viewed as generalizations of Reed-Solomon codes. Over the years, AG codes attracted much attention since some AG codes results in linear codes with parameters beating the Gilbert-Varshamov bound [11,32,35].

Let $\mathbb{F}_q$ be a finite field with q elements and $\mathcal{X}$ be an absolutely irreducible curve over $\mathbb{F}_q$ of genus g. Let $\mathbb{F}_q(\mathcal{X})$ denote the function field defined over $\mathcal{X}$.

A divisor D on a curve $\mathcal{X}$ is a formal sum of points $D = \sum_P n_P P$ on the curve $\mathcal{X}$, where $n_P \in \mathbb{Z} \setminus \{0\}$ for a finite number of points on $\mathcal{X}$. Here n_P denotes the multiplicity of the point P on the curve. The degree of a divisor $D = \sum_P n_P P$ is defined as the sum of n_P, i.e., $deg(D) := \sum_P n_P$. The support of a divisor $supp(D)$ is the set of points with nonzero coefficients. A divisor is called *effective* if all coefficients are non-negative.

For each point $P \in \mathcal{X}$ and any $f \in \mathbb{F}_q(\mathcal{X}) \setminus \{0\}$, we can abstract the notion of evaluation of f at P (denoted by $v_P(f)$) by local parameter and discrete valuation function $v_P : \mathbb{F}_q(\mathcal{X}) \to \mathbb{Z} \cup \{\infty\}$. A point P is said to be a zero of multiplicity m if $v_P(f) = m > 0$, a pole of multiplicity $-m$ if $v_P(f) = m < 0$,

Any function $f \in \mathbb{F}_q(\mathcal{X}) \setminus \{0\}$ can be associated with a so-called principal divisor. The principle divisor of $f \in \mathbb{F}_q(\mathcal{X})$ is defined as $div(f) := \sum_P v_P(f)P$. According to [32](Theorem I.4.11), the degree of a principal divisor is always 0, i.e., $deg(div(f)) = 0$.

Let $G = \sum_P n_P P$ be any divisor of degree k on $\mathcal{X}$. Denote by $\mathcal{L}(G)$ all rational functions $f \in \mathbb{F}_q(\mathcal{X})$ such that the divisor $div(f)+G$ is effective, together with the zero function, i.e.,

$$\mathcal{L}(G) := \{f \mid div(f) + G \text{ is effective}\} \cup \{0\}. \tag{1}$$

By the Riemann-Roch theorem, $\mathcal{L}(G)$ is a vector space over $\mathbb{F}_q$ of finite dimension and its dimension is given by $dim(\mathcal{L}(G)) := k - g + 1$, where g is the genus of $\mathcal{X}$.

Given an irreducible curve $\mathcal{X}$ and the function field $\mathbb{F}_q(\mathcal{X})$ defined over $\mathcal{X}$, let $P_1, P_2, ..., P_n$ be distinct rational points on $\mathcal{X}$. The n points determine a divisor $D := P_1 + P_2 + ... + P_n$. Let G be an arbitrary divisor on $\mathcal{X}$ such that $\{P_1, P_2, ..., P_n\} \cap supp(G) = \emptyset$. An AG code $\mathcal{C}(D, G)$ is defined by the following injective mapping $\mathsf{ev} : \mathcal{L}(G) \to \mathbb{F}_q^n$ with

$$\mathsf{ev}(f) := (f(P_1), f(P_2), \ldots, f(P_n))$$

Hence $\mathcal{C}(D, G) = \mathsf{image}(\mathsf{ev})$. If $G = \sum_P n_P P$ is a divisor of degree k, then $\mathcal{C}(D, G)$ is an $[n, k - g + 1, d]$ code over $\mathbb{F}_q$ and $d \geq n - k + 1 - g$. The basic properties of AG codes can be found in [23,32,35].

Elliptic Codes. Elliptic curves can be regarded as a special class of algebraic curves, they are algebraic curves with genus $g = 1$, hence Elliptic Codes are just AG codes constructed from elliptic curve. Let $\mathcal{E}$ be an elliptic curve over $\mathbb{F}_q$ and $\mathbb{F}_q(\mathcal{E})$ be the elliptic function field. Recall that there exists an additive abelian group $\mathcal{E}(\mathbb{F}_q)$ with the group operation defined by the "chord-and-tangent" rule on $\mathcal{E}$. As a result, principal divisors on elliptic curve $\mathcal{E}$ satisfy the following property as shown in the following theorem.

Theorem 2. *[29] Let $\mathcal{E}$ be an elliptic curve over over $\mathbb{F}_q$. Let $D = \sum_{P \in \mathcal{E}(\mathbb{F}_q)} n_P P$ be a divisor of $\mathcal{E}$. Then D is a principal divisor if and only if $\sum_{P \in \mathcal{E}(\mathbb{F}_q)} n_P = 0$ and $\sum_{P \in \mathcal{E}(\mathbb{F}_q)} n_P \cdot P = \mathcal{O}$, where $n_P \cdot P$ denotes the scalar multiplication over the Elliptic Curve group $\mathcal{E}(\mathbb{F}_q)$ and the summation in $\sum_{P \in \mathcal{E}(\mathbb{F}_q)} n_P \cdot P$ is implemented with the addition defined over group $\mathcal{E}(\mathbb{F}_q)$.*

Given an elliptic curve $\mathcal{E}$ defined over $\mathbb{F}_q$, and let $\mathbb{F}_q(\mathcal{E})$ be the elliptic function field. Let $P_1, P_2, \ldots, P_n \in \mathcal{E}(\mathbb{F}_q)$. Define $D := P_1 + P_2 + \ldots + P_n$ be divisors on $\mathcal{E}$. Let G be another divisor on $\mathcal{E}$ such that $0 < deg(G) = k < n$ and $supp(D) \cap supp(G) = \emptyset$. The elliptic code $\mathcal{C}(D, G)$ is defined by G and D with

$$\mathcal{C}(D, G) := \{(f(P_1), \ldots, f(P_n)) \mid f \in \mathcal{L}(G)\} \subseteq \mathbb{F}_q^n,$$

where $\mathcal{L}(G)$ is defined in (1).

The minimum distance of an $[n, k]$ EC code is either $d = n - k$ or $d = n - k + 1$, as shown in [5,30]. If $d = n - k + 1$, the EC code is a Maximum Distance Separable (MDS) code, otherwise it is an Almost MDS(AMDS) code.

An $[n, k]$ EC code $\mathcal{C}(D, G)$ is an AMDS code iff there exists k elements $P_{i_1}, \ldots, P_{i_k} \in Supp(D)$ such that divisor

$$P_{i_1} + \ldots + P_{i_k} - G$$

is a principle divisor according to [30].

2.4   List Decoding of Algebraic-Geometry Codes

In 1999, Guruswami and Sudan [12] proposed a list decoding algorithm for both RS and AG codes. The algorithm is able to efficiently output a list of codewords which lie in the sphere of radius up to $t = n - \sqrt{nk}$ centered around the perturbed (noisy) codeword (i.e., received vector). More precisely, the list decoding algorithm $\mathsf{ListDecode}(\mathcal{C}, r, t)$ takes as input a linear $[n, k]$ code $\mathcal{C}$, a received vector r and a parameter $t \leq n - \sqrt{nk}$, and it outputs a list of codewords whose Hamming distances to r are at most t.

Now we recall the Guruswami-Sudan list coding algorithm $\mathsf{ListDecode}(\mathcal{C}, r, t)$ for an $[n, k, d]$ AG-code $\mathcal{C}_{\mathcal{L}}(D, G)$ [13], where $D = P_1 + P_2 + \ldots + P_n$ and G is a one-point divisor of a curve $\mathcal{X}$ of genus g, i.e., $G = \alpha Q$ and $Q \notin supp(D)$. Assume $\alpha > 2g - 2$, then $dim(\mathcal{L}(\alpha Q)) = k = \alpha - g + 1$ by the Riemann-Roch theorem.

The Guruswami-Sudan list decoding consists of three steps: **initialization**, **interpolation** and **root finding**. We will give a brief (and basic) description of the algorithm. We refer the reader to [12] and [13] for details.

The Guruswami-Sudan List Decoding Algorithm: $\mathsf{ListDecode}(\mathcal{C}, r, t)$.

Input: An AG-code $\mathcal{C}_{\mathcal{L}}(D, G)$ determined by curve $\mathcal{X}$ over $\mathbb{F}_q$ and divisors $G = \alpha Q$ and D, a received vector $r = (r_1, \ldots, r_n)$ and an error bound t, which determines the maximal number of coordinates in which a codeword disagrees with vector r in order for the codeword to be included on the output list.

Output: a list Ω_r of codewords such that $\mathsf{dis}(r, c) \leq t$.

Initialization.
  0.1 $\Omega_r := \emptyset$.
  0.2 Compute list decoding parameters l from n, t and g, where $l \geq \alpha$.
  0.3 Fix a **pole basis** $\{\phi_{j_1} : 1 \leq j_1 \leq l - g + 1\}$ of $\mathcal{L}(lQ)$ such that ϕ_{j_1} has at most $j_1 + g - 1$ poles at Q.
  0.4 For each P_i, $1 \leq i \leq n$, find a **zero basis** $\{\psi_{j_3, P_i} : 1 \leq j_3 \leq l - g + 1\}$ of $\mathcal{L}(lQ)$ such that P_i is a zero of ψ_{j_3, P_i} with multiplicity (or at least) $j_3 - 1$.
  0.5 Compute the set $\{a_{P_i, j_1, j_3} \in \mathbb{F}_q : 1 \leq i \leq n, 1 \leq j_1, j_3 \leq l - g + 1\}$ such that for every i and every j_1, we have $\phi_{j_1} = \sum_{j_3} a_{P_i, j_1, j_3} \psi_{j_3, P_i}$.

Interpolation. Set $s = \frac{l-g}{\alpha}$. Find a nonzero polynomial $H \in \mathcal{L}(lQ)[T]$ of the form

$$H[T] = \sum_{j_2=0}^{s} \sum_{j_1=1}^{l-g+1-\alpha j_2} h_{j_1, j_2} \phi_{j_1} T^{j_2}.$$

Root Finding. Find all roots $h \in \mathcal{L}(\alpha Q)) \subseteq \mathcal{L}(lQ))$ of $H[T]$. For each h, check if $h(P_i) = r_i$ for at least $n - t$ values of $i \in \{1, 2, \ldots, n\}$, and if so, put h in Ω_r.
Return Ω_r.

3 Finding Minimum Weight Codewords Using List Decoding

By means of List Decoding with proper parameters, it is possible for us to find a minimum weight codeword. Beforehand, we introduce two lemmas. The first lemma tells us the property of list decoding when $d = u + t$, where d is the minimum distance of a $[n, k]$ linear code, u is the number of errors in the received vector (i.e., the Hamming distance between the received vector and causal codeword is u) and t is the error bound of list decoding. The second lemma analyzes the average number of falsely decodable (noncausal) codewords when $d = u + t$ and $u \leq t$.

Lemma 1. *For any linear $[n, k, d]$ code $\mathcal{C}$, let $c' = c + e$ be a received vector with causal codeword $c \in \mathcal{C}$ and error vector e with $\mathrm{wt}(e) = u$. Denote the output of the list decoding algorithm $\mathsf{ListDecode}(\mathcal{C}, c', t)$ by set $\Omega_{c'}$.*

1. *If $|\Omega_{c'} \setminus \{c\}| \geq 1$, then for any codewords $c_1 \in \Omega_{c'} \setminus \{c\}$, it holds that $dis(c_1, c) \leq u + t$.*
2. *If $u + t = d$ and $u \leq t$, then either $\Omega_{c'} = \{c\}$ or $|\Omega_{c'}| \geq 2$. If the latter case happens, then for all $c_1 \in \Omega_{c'} \setminus \{c\}$, we have $\hat{c} = c - c_1$ is the minimum weight codeword.*

Proof. 1. List decoding algorithm $\mathsf{ListDec}(\mathcal{C}, c', t)$ will output codewords in the sphere of radius t centered around c'. If $|\Omega_{c'} \setminus \{c\}| \geq 1$, we have that $dis(c_1, c') \leq t$. Together with the fact $dis(c, c') = \mathrm{wt}(e) = u$, we have $dis(c, c_1) \leq u + t$ by the triangle inequality.
2. If $u \leq t$, then $dis(c, c') = u \leq t$. As a result, $c \in \Omega_{c'}$ always holds. The linearity of code $\mathcal{C}$ ensures that $\hat{c} := c - c_1 \in \mathcal{C}$. Hence $\mathrm{wt}(\hat{c}) \geq d$. If $u + t = d$, then $d \leq \mathrm{wt}(\hat{c}) = dis(c, c_1) \leq u + t = d$, which means $\mathrm{wt}(\hat{c}) = d$ and $\hat{c} = c - c_1$ is the minimum weight codeword.

Recall that $\bar{L}(u, t)$ denotes the average number of noncausal codewords in a decoding sphere of radius t over all error patterns of weight u. In [2], Berlekamp and Ramsey presents how to compute $\bar{L}(u, t)$ for RS codes when $u + t = d$ and $u \leq t$ (see Theorem 1). Now we can generalize this result to any $[n, k, d]$ linear code. Specifically, we obtain $\bar{L}(u, t)$ for elliptic codes when $u + t = d$ and $u \leq t$.

Lemma 2. *For any linear $[n, k, d]$ linear code in which the number of minimum weight codewords is μ, the average number of noncausal codewords in a decoding sphere of radius t over all error patterns of weight u satisfies*

$$\bar{L}(u, t) = \frac{\mu \cdot \binom{d}{t}}{\binom{n}{u} (q-1)^u} \quad \text{if } u + t = d \text{ and } u \leq t. \tag{2}$$

Specifically, for an $[n, k]$ Elliptic Code $\mathcal{C}(G, D)$ where G is a divisor of degree k and $D = P_1 + P_2 + \ldots + P_n$. If $u + t = d$ and $u \leq t$, then

$$\bar{L}(u, t) = \begin{cases} \dfrac{1}{(q-1)^{u-1}} \dbinom{n-u}{t} & \text{if } d = n - k + 1; \\[2em] \dfrac{\lambda \cdot \dbinom{u+t}{t}}{\dbinom{n}{u} (q-1)^{u-1}} & \text{if } d = n - k, \end{cases} \tag{3}$$

where λ denotes the number of subsets $\mathcal{J} = \{i_1, i_2, \ldots, i_k\} \subseteq \{1, 2, \ldots, n\}$ such that $G - \sum_{j \in \mathcal{J}} P_j$ is a principal divisor.

Proof. Recall that if $\mathbf{0} = (0, \ldots, 0)$ is the transmitted (causal) codeword, and $\mathbf{e}$ is a received vector, then $f(\mathbf{e}, t) := |\{\mathbf{c} \in \mathcal{C} \setminus \{\mathbf{0}\} : |\mathbf{e} - \mathbf{c}| \le t\}|$ counts the number of noncausal codewords within distance t centered around $\mathbf{e}$. Meanwhile, $\bar{L}(u, t) = \dfrac{\sum_{|\mathbf{e}| = u} f(\mathbf{e}, t)}{\binom{n}{u} (q-1)^u}$ according to [20].

By Lemma 1, if $u + t = d$ and $u \le t$, then either $\Omega_e = \{\mathbf{0}\}$ or $|\Omega_e| \ge 2$. If $|\Omega_e| \ge 2$, then we have the following facts.

- For each $\mathbf{c}_1 \in \Omega_e \setminus \{\mathbf{c}\}$, the codeword $\mathbf{c}_1$ is a noncausal codeword and it must be a codeword of minimum weight d.
- For each $\mathbf{c}_1 \in \Omega_e \setminus \{\mathbf{c}\}$, define $\mathbf{e}' = \mathbf{c}_1 - \mathbf{e}$, then $\mathbf{e}'$ is of weight t. Meanwhile the indices of ones in $\mathbf{e}$ and $\mathbf{e}'$ must be disjoint, i.e., $\{i \mid e_i = 1, i \in [n]\} \cap \{i \mid e'_i = 1, i \in [n]\} = \emptyset$.

There might be many error patterns $\mathbf{e}$ resulting in the same codeword of minimum weight. For each codeword of minimum weight, there are exactly $\binom{d}{t} \left(= \binom{d}{u}\right)$ choices of $\mathbf{e}$ of weight u. If there are totally μ codewords of minimum weight, then there are totally $\mu \cdot \binom{d}{t}$ vector $\mathbf{e}$ of weight u, each of which exactly results in a noncausal codeword in its sphere.

Equation (2) holds since there are totally $\binom{n}{u} (q-1)^u$ vectors of weight u.

For an $[n, k]$ Elliptic Code, the minimal distance d is either $n - k + 1$ or $n - k$. If $d = n - k + 1$, then the Elliptic code is MDS code, the number of the minimal weight codewords is $\binom{n}{d} \cdot (q-1)$. Hence $\bar{L}(u, t) = \dfrac{\binom{d}{t} \cdot \binom{n}{d} \cdot (q-1)}{\binom{n}{u} (q-1)^u} = \dfrac{\binom{n-u}{t}}{(q-1)^{u-1}}$, which is consistent to the result for RS codes in [2].

Now we consider the case of $d = n - k$. Given a subset $\mathcal{J} = \{i_1, i_2, \ldots, i_k\} \subseteq \{1, 2, \ldots, n\}$, define a divisor as $D' = \sum_{j \in \mathcal{J}} P_j - G$. If D' is a principal divisor, then there exists a function $f \in \mathcal{L}(G)$ such that $D' = div(f)$ due to the fact that $D' + G$ is effective. For such an $f \in \mathcal{L}(G)$, we have $f(P_{i_j}) = 0$ with $j \in [k]$. Consequently, the Hamming weight of the codeword $\mathbf{c} = (f(P_{i_1}), f(P_{i_2}), \ldots, f(P_{i_n}))$ is $n - k$, which suggests that $\alpha \cdot \mathbf{c}$ is a codeword of minimum weight for all $\alpha \in \mathbb{F}_q^*$. If there are λ subsets $\mathcal{J} = \{i_1, i_2, \ldots, i_k\} \subseteq \{1, 2, \ldots, n\}$ such that $\sum_{j \in \mathcal{J}} P_j - G$ is a principal divisor, then there are $(q - 1)\lambda$ codewords of minimum weight.

Consequently $\bar{L}(u, t) = \dfrac{\binom{d}{t} \cdot \lambda \cdot (q-1)}{\binom{n}{u} (q-1)^u}$ according to Eq. (2). ∎

Lemma 1 suggests us a way of finding a codeword of minimum weight codeword. If the minimum distance d of $\mathcal{C}$ is known, we can obtain such a codeword of minimum weight, as long as $u + t = d$, $u < t$ and the list decoding algorithm outputs a list of size at least two. According to this idea, we design an algorithm of finding minimum weight codewords for a code $\mathcal{C}$ with unknown minimum distance d, as shown in the next subsection. Lemma 2 helps us to analyze the success probability of the algorithm.

3.1 How to Find Codewords of Minimum Weight

When the minimum distance d is unknown, the intuition is to try a guess d' of the minimum distance. Now we design an algorithm named FindCodeword which takes as input a guess d' of the minimum distance, an error weight u and a bound t_m of the decoding radius of List Decoding for code $\mathcal{C}$. Firstly, randomly choose a codeword c from $\mathcal{C}$ and an random error of weight u. Compute the perturbed vector $c' := c + e$. Then invoke the List Decoding algorithm to decode the perturbed vector c' to output a list $\Omega_{c'}$ of codewords . By linearity, for every $c_i \in \Omega_{c'}$, $c_i - c$ is a codeword of $\mathcal{C}$. We hope that one of $c_i - c$ is a minimum weight codeword. Below we describe the algorithm and then analyze the probability that the algorithm outputs such a minimum weight codeword.

Algorithm FindCodeword$(\mathcal{C}, u, d', t_m)$:

Input: A $[n, k]$ linear code $\mathcal{C}$ which is list-decodable up to t_m errors; two parameters $u, d' \in \mathbb{Z}^+$ with $u < t_m < d'$.
Output: Abort symbol $\perp$ or a codeword $\hat{c} \in \mathcal{C}$.
Procedure: 1. If $d' - u > t_m$, return $\perp$.
    2. Randomly choose a codeword $c \in \mathcal{C}$.
    3. Randomly choose an error pattern e such that $\mathsf{wt}(e) = u$. Compute $c' := c + e$. Set $\Omega_{c'} := \emptyset$.
    4. Invoke $\Omega_{c'} \leftarrow \mathsf{ListDecode}(\mathcal{C}, c', d' - u)$.
    5. If $\Omega_{c'} \setminus \{c\} = \emptyset$, Return$(\perp)$. Otherwise for each codeword $c_i \in \Omega_{c'} \setminus \{c\}$ and compute $\hat{c}_i := c_i - c$, where $i = 1, 2, \ldots, |\Omega_{c'}| - 1$.
    6. Choose $\hat{c}$ of minimal weight from $\{\hat{c}_1, \ldots, \hat{c}_{|\Omega_{c'}|-1}\}$.
    7. Return$(\hat{c})$.

According to [12], the Guruswami-Sudan list decoding algorithm is applicable when $t_m = n - \sqrt{nk}$, and the complexity of ListDecode is $O(\lambda^6 n^3)$ for any AG codes (here λ is the designed list size). The computational complexity of Algorithm FindCodeword$(\mathcal{C}, u, d')$ is dominated by ListDecode, hence is of $O(\lambda^6 n^3)$ as well. There are many works aiming to improve the computational complexity of Guruswami-Sudan list decoding algorithm. For example, Beelen et al. [1] defined a general class of one-point algebraic-geometry codes and proposed a more efficient algorithm for the interpolation step in the Guruswami-Sudan list decoder and the complexity was improved to $O(\lambda^5 n^2 \log^2(\lambda n) \log \log(\lambda n))$.

Suppose that the minimum distance of the $[n, k]$ code $\mathcal{C}$ is d. In the case of $u \le d/2$, $d - u \le t_m$, we analyze the probability that Algorithm FindCodeword$(\mathcal{C}, u, d)$ successfully outputs a codeword of minimum weight.

Theorem 3. *For a* $[n, k, d]$ *linear code* C, *let* μ *be the number of minimum weight codewords. If* $u \leq d/2$ *and* $d - u \leq t_m$, *then*

$$\Pr\left[\hat{c} \leftarrow \textsf{FindCodeword}(C, u, d, t_m) : \textsf{wt}(\hat{c}) = d\right] \approx \frac{\mu \cdot \binom{d}{u}}{\binom{n}{u}(q-1)^u}, \qquad (4)$$

where μ *is the number of minimum weight codewords in* C.

Proof. It directly follows from Lemma 2. ∎

3.2 The Final Algorithm of Finding Minimal Weight Codewords

With a correct guess of d, Algorithm $\textsf{FindCodeword}(C, u, d)$ might be able to output a codeword of minimum weight with some probability (determined by (4)) according to Theorem 3. So we will try to guess the distance with $d' = 3, 4, \ldots, n - k + 1$. Given a specific guess d' of the distance, we will invoke $\textsf{FindCodeword}(C, u, d')$ multiple times. This leads to our final algorithm of finding minimal weight codewords as shown below.

Algorithm MinWeiCodeword(C, Γ, t_m, T_m):

Input: A $[n, k]$ linear code C which is list-decodable with an unknown minimum distance d; A set Γ which is a subset of $\{3, 4, \ldots, n - k + 1\}$. We assume that the elements in Γ is in ascending order. t_m is the bound determined by the list decoding algorithm and T_m is the maximal number of invoking $\textsf{FindCodeword}(C, u, d')$.

Output: Abort symbol $\perp$ or a codeword $\hat{c} \in C$.

$\hat{c} := \perp$; $\textsf{wt}(\hat{c}) := n$

For each $d' \in \Gamma$ (taking d' in ascending order)

    For $u = d' - t_m$ to $\lfloor d'/2 \rfloor$

        For $i = 1$ to T_m

            $\hat{c}' \leftarrow \textsf{FindCodeword}(C, u, d', t_m)$;

            If $\textsf{wt}(\hat{c}') < \textsf{wt}(\hat{c})$ then $\hat{c} := \hat{c}'$.

Return($\hat{c}$)

For an $[n, k, d]$ code C, as long as $d \in \Gamma$, the guess of d' takes the value of d sooner or later. In case of $d' = d$, the probability that Algorithm $\textsf{FindCodeword}(C, u, d)$ outputs a minimum weight codeword is given by (4) according to Theorem 3. In $\textsf{MinWeiCodeword}(C, \Gamma, T_m)$, there are T_m times of invocations of $\textsf{FindCodeword}(C, u, d)$ and u can take values from $d - t_m$ up to $\lfloor d/2 \rfloor$. Therefore, $\textsf{MinWeiCodeword}$ successfully outputs a minimum distance codeword with probability at least

$$\Pr\left[\hat{c} \leftarrow \textsf{MinWeiCodeword}(C, \{d\}, t_m, T_m) : \textsf{wt}(\hat{c}) = d\right]$$

$$\geq 1 - \prod_{u=d-t_m}^{\lfloor d/2 \rfloor} \left(1 - \frac{\mu \cdot \binom{d}{u}}{\binom{n}{u}(q-1)^u}\right)^{T_m}. \qquad (5)$$

If the minimum distance d of $\mathcal{C}$ is known, then we can set $\Gamma = \{d\}$, then MinWeiCodeword successfully outputs a minimum distance codeword with probability at least

$$\Pr\left[\hat{c} \leftarrow \text{MinWeiCodeword}(\mathcal{C}, \{d\}, t_m, T_m) : \text{wt}(\hat{c}) = d\right] \approx 1 - \left(1 - \frac{\mu \cdot \binom{d}{u}}{\binom{n}{u}(q-1)^u}\right)^{T_m}. \quad (6)$$

This approach applies to all list decodable codes. For some linear $[n, k, d]$ codes over $\mathbb{F}_q$, when the choices of n, k, d, q, t_m make (5) noticeable, then it is possible for us to find a codeword of minimum weight in polynomial time with the help of Algorithm MinWeiCodeword$(\mathcal{C}, \Gamma, t_m, T_m)$.

For any list decodable $[n, k, d]$ code, if we already know d or have a correct guess of d, Algorithm FindCodeword$(\mathcal{C}, u, d)$ might be able to output a codeword of minimum weight with some probability (determined by (4)).

Due to the fact that $d = u + t$, given d we can always choose u as small as possible to make the probability in (4) bigger, as long as $t = d - u$ is allowable in the list decoding algorithm. For AG code, The Guruswami-Sudan list decoding algorithm can make t up to be $t_m = \lceil n - \sqrt{nk} \rceil$(This bound is called by GS bound or Johnson bound).

If new development on list decoding makes t_m exceed the current bound of $\lceil n - \sqrt{nk} \rceil$, then Algorithm FindCodeword$(\mathcal{C}, u, d)$ will become more efficient by setting smaller values for u. For example, if we have an efficient list decoding algorithm to correct the maximum fraction of errors, i.e., $t_m = n - k$ (this is called by the Singleton bound) for some codes, then the codeword of minimum weight of these such codes can be efficiently computed using Algorithm FindCodeword$(\mathcal{C}, u, d)$.

There do exist some codes, such as Folded Reed-Solomon Codes or Folded AG codes, that achieve or approach Singleton bound of $t_m = n-k$ for every code rate k/n [14,15,24]. However, it seems impossible for elliptic codes to have effective list decoding algorithm to achieve or approach the Singleton bound, otherwise $\mathcal{P} = \mathcal{NP}$ is proved (due to the fact that the minimum distance problem of elliptic codes is NP-hard under **RP**-reduction [3])! This also means that the problem to show if P=NP can be reduced to the existence of an efficient List decoding algorithm for elliptic codes closing or reaching Singleton bound.

3.3   Instantiation from Elliptic Code $\mathcal{C}[G, D]$

Now we employ MinWeiCodeword$(\mathcal{C}, \Gamma = \{n - k\}, T_m)$ to find minimum weight codewords of an $[n, k, d]$ elliptic code $\mathcal{C}[G, D]$ with $d = n - k$ (recall that it is an easy problem if $d = n - k + 1$). The essential step is the invocation of Guruswami-Sudan list decoding algorithm. Now we show the implementation of Guruswami-Sudan list decoding for one-point elliptic codes (as far as we know, no work is available suggesting the concrete implementations of Guruswami-Sudan list decoding for EC codes).

For an elliptic curve $\mathcal{E}$ defined over $\mathbb{F}_q$, let $G = k\mathcal{O}$ be a divisor of degree k and $D = P_1 + P_2 + \ldots + P_n$ where P_i's are rational points over $\mathcal{E}$. Then $\mathcal{C}(G, D)$ is an elliptic code. The first and important step of the Guruswami-Sudan list decoding algorithm for elliptic codes is finding out two types basis of $\mathcal{L}(l\mathcal{O})$: the **pole basis** and **zero basis**.

It is easy to obtain the **pole basis** of $\mathcal{L}(l\mathcal{O})$, which is $\{\phi_1, \phi_2, ..., \phi_l\} :=$ $\{1, x, y, x^2, xy, x^3, x^2y, .., x^iy^j \mid j = 0 \ or \ 1, \ 2i + 3j = l)\}$.

For each P_i, $1 \leq i \leq n$, we will find a **zero basis** $\{\psi_{j_3, P_i} : 1 \leq j_3 \leq l\}$ of $\mathcal{L}(l\mathcal{O})$ such that P_i is a zero of ψ_{j_3, P_i} with multiplicity (or at least) $j_3 - 1$. Consider the principle divisor

$$div(f_{m,P_i}) = mP_i + (-m \cdot P_i) - (m+1)\mathcal{O}.$$

If $m < l$, then $div(f_{m,P_i}) + l\mathcal{O}$ is effective, hence $div(f_{m,P_i}) \in \mathcal{L}(l\mathcal{O})$. Meanwhile, P_i is a zero of $div(f_{m,P_i})$ with multiplicity m. Set

$$\psi_{1,P_i} = 1, \psi_{2,P_i} = div(f_{1,P_i}), ..., \psi_{l,P_i} = div(f_{l-1,P_i}),$$

then for point P_i, we obtain a **zero basis** of $\mathcal{L}(l\mathcal{O})$. To compute the rational function f_{m,P_i} from the divisor $mP_i + (-m \cdot P_i) - (m+1)\mathcal{O}$, we can use the method described in [22] and Chap. 11 in [37]. Note that $\{\phi_i\}$ and $\{\psi_{j_3, P_i}\}$ are all the bases of vector spaces $\mathcal{L}(l\mathcal{O})$, so it is easy to get the set $\{a_{P_i,j_1,j_3} \in \mathbb{F}_q : 1 \leq i \leq n, 1 \leq j_1, j_3 \leq l\}$ such that for every i and every j_1, $\phi_{j_1} = \sum_{j_3} a_{P_i,j_1,j_3} \psi_{j_3,P_i}$ holds. The **Interpolation** step and the **Root finding** step just follow the the original algorithm shown in Subsect. 2.4.

We show an implementation for an elliptic code via Magma [18]. Here is an example.

The finite field is $\mathbb{F}_{127}$, The elliptic curve (over $\mathbb{F}_{127}$) is $\mathcal{E} : y^2 = x^3 - 3x + 72$. The order of $\mathcal{E}(\mathbb{F}_{127})$ is 137.

Let $P = (44, 65)$ be a random point of $\mathcal{E}$. Obviously $\langle P \rangle = \mathcal{E}(\mathbb{F}_{127})$. Let $\mathcal{O}$ be the infinite point. Then $137P = \mathcal{O}$.

Set divisor $G := 4\mathcal{O}$, and divisor $D := P_1 + P_2 + \ldots + P_{20}$ with $supp(D) =$ $\{P_1 = P, P_2 = (50, 9), P_3 = (49, 90), P_4 = (105, 83), P_5 = (74, 43), P_6 = (114, 94), P_7 = (120, 125), P_8 = (40, 43), P_9 = (112, 60), P_{10} = (36, 97), P_{11} = (10, 91), P_{12} = (126, 70), P_{13} = (108, 126), P_{14} = (2, 57), P_{15} = (14, 19), P_{16} = (46, 49), P_{17} = (90, 87), P_{18} = (7, 93), P_{19} = (54, 23), P_{20} = (36, 30)\}$. We get an $[n, k]$ Algebraic Geometric Code $\mathcal{C}[G, D]$ with $n = 20, k = 4$.

According to [12,13], set $l := 31$ in the Guruswami-Sudan list decoding algorithm for above $[n, k] = [20, 4]$ elliptic codes. It is easy to see that

$$\{\phi_1, \phi_2, ..., \phi_{31}\} = \{1, x, y, x^2, xy, x^3, x^2y, .., x^{15}, x^{14}y\}$$

is a **pole basis** of $\mathcal{L}(31\mathcal{O})$.

For each point P_i, we can obtain a **zero basis** of $\mathcal{L}(l\mathcal{O})$ using follows Magma code:

```
for j:=1 to l do
T, ZB[j+1]:=IsPrincipal(j*Divisor(P_i)+Divisor((-j)P_i)-(j+1)*Divisor(O));
end for;
```

In this way, we obtain 20 zero-bases of of $\mathcal{L}(31\mathcal{O})$. For example, a **zero basis** for $P_{20} = (36, 30)$ is

$\{1,$

$x + 91,$

$y + 94x + 15,$

$80y + 38x^2 + 85x + 29,$

$(41x + 27)y + 88x^2 + 112x + 25,$

$(124x + 91)y + 7x^3 + 62x^2 + 86x + 45,$

$(x^2 + 48x + 75)y + 40x^3 + 74x^2 + 112x + 32,$

$(114x^2 + 26x + 99)y + 34x^4 + 29x^3 + 125x^2 + 107x + 92,$

$(30x^3 + 33x^2 + 86x + 113)y + 33x^4 + 28x^3 + 59x + 61,$

$(30x^3 + 99x^2 + 82x + 24)y + 114x^5 + 121x^4 + 119x^3 + 10x^2 + 89x + 78,$

$(8x^4 + 46x^3 + 41x^2 + 46x + 105)y + 66x^5 + 115x^4 + 122x^3 + 31x^2 + 15x + 11,$

$(35x^4 + 116x^3 + 55x^2 + 29x + 72)y + 91x^6 + 89x^5 + 18x^4 + 31x^3 + 100x^2 + 37x + 38,$

$(55x^5 + 49x^4 + 102x^3 + 72x^2 + 32x + 82)y + 119x^6 + 69x^5 + 55x^4 + 87x^3 + 125x^2 + 3x + 95,$

$(80x^5 + 20x^4 + 51x^3 + 51x^2 + 39x + 48)y + 117x^7 + 57x^6 + 71x^5 + 40x^4 + 90x^3 + 59x^2 + 103x + 73,$

$(106x^6 + 105x^5 + 17x^4 + 85x^3 + 92x^2 + 107x + 13)y + 59x^7 + 126x^6 + 34x^5 + 118x^4 + 5x^3 + 59x^2 + 9x + 83,$

$(83x^6 + 100x^5 + 56x^4 + 99x^3 + 7x^2 + 26x + 11)y + 15x^8 + 53x^7 + 39x^6 + 101x^5 + 80x^4 + 3x^3 + 27x^2 + 95x + 7,$

$(32x^7 + 109x^6 + 91x^5 + 16x^4 + 66x^3 + 32x^2 + 52x + 54)y + 63x^8 + 126x^7 + 26x^6 + 87x^5 + 40x^4 + 42x^3 + 109x^2 + 112x + 40,$

$(119x^7 + 10x^6 + 111x^5 + 45x^4 + x^3 + 40x^2 + 53x + 26)y + 10x^9 + 56x^8 + 108x^7 + 80x^6 + 58x^5 + 56x^4 + 101x^3 + 123x^2 + 43x + 28,$

$(21x^8 + 61x^7 + 78x^6 + 58x^5 + 114x^4 + 28x^3 + 95x^2 + 54x + 45)y + 63x^9 + 111x^8 + 119x^7 + 9x^6 + 88x^5 + 123x^4 + 112x^3 + 44x^2 + 86x + 111,$

$(29x^8 + 21x^7 + 115x^6 + 75x^5 + 98x^4 + 13x^3 + 5x^2 + 21x + 1)y + 46x^{10} + 69x^9 + 80x^8 + 18x^7 + x^6 + 81x^5 + 60x^4 + 100x^3 + 126x^2 + 29,$

$(64x^9 + 106x^8 + 38x^7 + 30x^6 + 20x^5 + 110x^4 + 87x^3 + 61x^2 + 16x + 84)y + 79x^{10} + 15x^9 + 10x^8 + 9x^7 + 123x^6 + 104x^5 + 73x^4 + 73x^3 + 126x^2 + 65x + 103,$

$(57x^9 + 80x^8 + 41x^6 + 52x^5 + 102x^4 + 81x^3 + 5x^2 + 92x + 26)y + 45x^{11} + 86x^{10} + 114x^9 + 103x^8 + 95x^7 + 11x^6 + 58x^5 + 50x^4 + 3x^3 + 116x^2 + 48x + 34,$

$(114x^{10} + 3x^9 + 15x^8 + 117x^7 + 116x^6 + 72x^5 + 16x^4 + 57x^3 + 83x^2 + 31x + 118)y + 2x^{11} + 33x^{10} + 74x^9 + 20x^8 + 112x^7 + x^6 + 83x^5 + 78x^4 + 55x^3 + 69x^2 + 47x + 67,$

$(108x^{10} + 64x^8 + 14x^7 + 95x^6 + 67x^5 + 99x^4 + 113x^3 + 124x^2 + 35x + 101)y + 59x^{12} + 5x^{11} + 34x^{10} + 2x^9 + 33x^8 + 95x^7 + 112x^6 + 65x^5 + 69x^4 + 33x^3 + 119x^2 + 111x + 104,$

$(104x^{11} + 125x^{10} + 109x^9 + 23x^8 + x^7 + 32x^6 + 2x^5 + 90x^4 + 5x^3 + 7x^2 + 44x + 95)y + 7x^{12} + 103x^{11} + 74x^{10} + 88x^9 + 81x^8 + 83x^7 + 124x^6 + 116x^5 + 39x^4 + 91x^3 + 120x^2 + 29x + 39,$

$(25x^{11} + 41x^{10} + 58x^9 + 17x^8 + 77x^7 + 43x^6 + 90x^5 + 99x^4 + 109x^3 + 58x^2 + 30x + 14)y + 80x^{13} + 97x^{12} + 93x^{11} + 126x^{10} + x^9 + 66x^8 + 93x^7 + 60x^6 + 58x^5 + 112x^4 + 60x^3 + 29x^2 + 22x + 27,$

$(19x^{12} + 101x^{11} + 56x^{10} + 94x^9 + 121x^8 + 60x^7 + 88x^6 + 41x^5 + 42x^4 + 71x^3 + 25x^2 + 21x + 35)y + 4x^{13} + 29x^{12} + 101x^{11} + 119x^{10} + 81x^9 + 110x^8 + 122x^7 + 97x^6 + 46x^5 + 121x^4 + 51x^3 + 23x^2 + 15x + 75,$

$(45x^{12} + 34x^{11} + 30x^{10} + 65x^9 + 111x^8 + 11x^7 + 96x^6 + 62x^5 + 123x^4 + 59x^3 + 39x^2 + 82x + 94)y + 117x^{14} + 38x^{13} + 119x^{12} + 123x^{11} + 123x^{10} + 107x^9 + 122x^8 + 80x^7 + 23x^6 + 41x^5 + 112x^4 + 58x^3 + 120x^2 + 25x + 70,$

$(60x^{13} + 45x^{12} + 77x^{11} + 54x^{10} + 49x^9 + 123x^8 + 103x^7 + 51x^6 + 91x^5 + 90x^4 + 37x^3 + 82x^2 + 115x + 119)y + 77x^{14} + 62x^{13} + 20x^{12} + 58x^{11} + 44x^{10} + 24x^9 + 34x^8 + 59x^7 + 77x^6 + 75x^5 + 34x^4 + 99x^3 + 9x^2 + 25x,$

$(10x^{13} + 29x^{12} + +43x^{11} + 120x^{10} + 37x^9 + 114x^8 + 57x^7 + 53x^6 + 112x^5 + 94x^4 + 60x^3 + 47x^2 + 77x + 7)y + 49x^{15} + 40x^{14} + 112x^{13} + 78x^{12} + 30x^{11} + 116x^{10} + 5x^9 + 61x^8 + 39x^7 + 68x^6 + 28x^5 + 5x^4 + 108x^3 + 33x^2 + 62x + 29,$

$(47x^{14} + 16x^{13} + 81x^{12} + 25x^{11} + 36x^{10} + 119x^9 + 107x^8 + 120x^7 + 30x^6 + 72x^5 + 28x^4 + 125x^3 + 95x^2 + 35x + 117)y +$

$60x^{15} + 102x^{14} + x^{13} + 85x^{12} + 113x^{11} + 59x^{10} + x^9 + 53x^8 + 108x^7 + 99x^6 + 13x^5 + 98x^4 + 60x^3 + 27x^2 + 122x + 98,$

$(54x^{14} + 118x^{13} + 10x^{12} + 108x^{11} + 54x^{10} + 120x^9 + 67x^8 + 118x^7 + 6x^6 + 65x^5 + 74x^4 + 16x^3 + 95x^2 + 82x +$

$119)y + 10x^{16} + 20x^{15} + 76x^{14} + x^{13} + 54x^{12} + 88x^{11} + 6x^{10} + 102x^9 + 74x^8 + 96x^7 + 73x^6 + 110x^5 + 76x^4 +$

$62x^3 + 106x^2 + 119x + 15\}$

Now we assume that the received vector is

$$r = (24, 29, 87, 42, 99, 57, 25, 97, 49, 64, 58, 31, 97, 8, 120, 122, 34, 36, 64, 95).$$

Then we can construct a nonzero polynomial $H(T) \in \mathcal{L}(l\mathcal{O})[T]$ using the **pole basis**, all the **zero basis** for each P_i and r, where

$H(T) = (52x^{14} + 56x^{13} + 44x^{12} + 94x^{11} + 107x^{10} + 75x^9 + 96x^8 + 35x^7 + 23x^6 + 77x^5 + 118x^4 + 3x^3 + 61x^2 + 27x +$

$89)y + 112x^{16} + 119x^{15} + 83x^{14} + 102x^{13} + 4x^{12} + 8x^{11} + 111x^{10} + 74x^9 + 13x^8 + 90x^7 + 33x^6 + 110x^5 + 51x^4 + 116x^3 +$

$111x^2 + 18x + 77 + ((43x^{12} + 93x^{11} + 118x^{10} + 92x^9 + 8x^8 + 61x^7 + 25x^6 + 91x^5 + 25x^4 + 88x^3 + 109x^2 + 119x + 82)y +$

$81x^{14} + 47x^{13} + 61x^{12} + 47x^{10} + 27x^9 + 50x^8 + 36x^7 + 55x^6 + x^5 + 31x^4 + 60x^3 + 87x^2 + 65x + 90)T + ((81x^{10} + 82x^9 +$

$90x^8 + 35x^7 + 114x^6 + 62x^5 + 124x^4 + 35x^3 + 29x^2 + 57x + 10)y + 22x^{12} + 115x^{11} + 124x^{10} + 59x^9 + 104x^8 + 27x^7 +$

$112x^6 + 63x^5 + 113x^4 + 71x^3 + 122x^2 + x + 72)T^2 + ((76x^8 + 17x^7 + 78x^6 + 80x^5 + 106x^4 + 123x^3 + 71x^2 + 92x + 23)y +$

$5x^{10} + 24x^9 + 45x^8 + 5x^7 + 46x^6 + 84x^5 + 87x^4 + 13x^3 + 96x^2 + 56x + 19)T^3 + ((125x^6 + 59x^5 + 79x^4 + 80x^3 + 113x^2 +$

$3x + 55)y + 35x^8 + 74x^7 + 100x^6 + 49x^4 + x^3 + 74x^2 + 124x + 88)T^4 + ((37x^4 + 35x^3 + 37x^2 + 74x + 36)y + 119x^6 + 52x^5 +$

$125x^4 + 73x^3 + 119x^2 + 67x + 52)T^5 + ((41x^2 + 49x + 80)y + 61x^4 + 5x^3 + 55x^2 + 44x + 115)T^6 + (59y + 21x^2 + 119x + 53)T^7.$

In the **Root finding** step, we obtain two roots of $H(T)$, which are $68 + 8x + 23y + 66x^2$ and $81 + 102x + 100y + 37x^2$ respectively. Consequently, the decoding results are

$$c_1 := (24, 67, 87, 90, 99, 72, 25, 43, 49, 112, 78, 85, 97, 8, 91, 122, 52, 36, 64, 95)$$

$$c_2 := (24, 29, 46, 42, 38, 57, 91, 97, 49, 64, 58, 31, 97, 37, 120, 81, 34, 97, 84, 95)$$

It is easy to verify that they are both valid codewords, and the distance of c_1 and r is 7, and distance of c_2 and r is 9. Meanwhile,

$$c_1 - c_2 = (0, 38, 41, 48, 61, 15, 61, 73, 0, 48, 20, 54, 0, 98, 98, 41, 18, 66, 107, 0)$$

is a minimum-weight codeword.

4   New Approach to ECDLP

4.1   A Warm-Up

Let us first discuss the relation between ECDLP and minimum-weight codewords of EC code. Let $\mathcal{E}$ be an elliptic curve defined over $\mathbb{F}_q$, $\mathcal{E}(\mathbb{F}_q)$ be the elliptic curve group, $P_1, P_2, \ldots, P_n \in \mathcal{E}(\mathbb{F}_q)$, and G be a divisor of degree k. Let $\mathcal{C}(G, D)$ be the EC code determined by divisors G and $D = P_1 + P_2 + \ldots + P_n$. We know that the minimum distance d of $\mathcal{C}(G, D)$ is either $n - k$ or $n - k + 1$. If $d = n - k + 1$, then the EC code is a MDS code, otherwise the EC code is an *almost* MSD (AMDS) code. Whether $\mathcal{C}(G, D)$ is an MDS code or an AMDS code depends on whether there exist $\{P_{i_1}, P_{i_2}, \ldots, P_{i_k}\} \subseteq (P_1, P_2, \ldots, P_n)$ such that $P_{i_1} + P_{i_2} + \ldots + P_{i_k} - G$ is a principal divisor.

It is easy to find a codeword of minimum weight for a MDS-EC code. As for AMDS-EC code, we show that finding codewords of minimum weight is closely related to solving ECDLP (see the following theorem).

Theorem 4. *Let $\mathcal{E}$ be an elliptic curve over $\mathbb{F}_q$. Let P be a point over group $\mathcal{E}(\mathbb{F}_q)$. Suppose the order of P is a prime p. Let $n = \lceil \log_2 p \rceil$. For any point Q from subgroup $\langle P \rangle$, define an elliptic code $\mathcal{C}(G, D)$ with divisor $G := Q + (k-1)\mathcal{O}$ and divisor $D := P + 2P + \ldots + 2^{n-1}P$. If there exists an algorithm $\mathcal{A}$ who can find a codeword of minimum weight in $\mathcal{C}(G, D)$ with probability ϵ, then another algorithm $\mathcal{B}$ can be constructed to solve the ECDLP $s := \log_P Q$ with probability $\epsilon/(n+1)$.*

Proof. Suppose that $\mathcal{B}$ has an ECDLP instance $(\mathbb{F}_q, \mathcal{E}(\mathbb{F}_q), \ell, Q, P)$ where P is a generator of subgroup $\mathbb{G}$ of prime order p and $Q \in \mathbb{G}$. $\mathcal{B}$ aims to determine $s \in \mathbb{Z}_p$ such that $Q = sP$.

Express $s \in \mathbb{Z}_p$ with binary string $s = (s_1, s_2, \ldots s_n)$ with $n = \lceil \log_2 p \rceil$. $\mathcal{B}$ constructs an EC code to solve the ECDLP as follows.

Algorithm $\mathcal{B}$
Input: $(\mathbb{F}_q, \mathcal{E}(\mathbb{F}_q), p, Q, P)$
Output: s'

(1) $k \leftarrow \{0, 1, \ldots, n\}$.
(2) Define divisor $G = Q + (k-1)\mathcal{O}$ of degree k.
(3) Let $P_i = 2^{i-1}P$ for $i = 1, 2, \ldots, n$;
(4) Define divisor $D = P_1 + P_2 + \ldots + P_n$;
(5) Construct an EC code $\mathcal{C}(G, D)$;
(6) Invoke algorithm $\mathcal{A}$ to find a codeword $c = (c_1, c_2, \ldots, c_n)$ of minimum weight for the EC code $\mathcal{C}(G, D)$.
(7) Suppose the nonzero components in c are $c_{i_1}, c_{i_2}, \ldots, c_{i_k}$. Then compute $s' = \sum_{j=1}^{k} 2^{i_j - 1}$.
(8) Return(s')

Note that k is randomly chosen from $\{0, 1, \ldots, n\}$. Obviously, the probability that $k = \mathsf{wt}(s)$ is $1/(n+1)$.

Now we assume that the event $k = \mathsf{wt}(s)$ happens, or equivalently, the event that $\mathcal{C}(G, D)$ constructed by $\mathcal{B}$ is an AMDS-EC code happens. Since $s = (s_1, s_2, \ldots s_n)$, we have $Q = \sum_{i=1}^{n} s_i P_i$. If $s_{i_1} = s_{i_2} = \ldots = s_{i_k} = 1$ and $s_j = 0$ for $j \notin \{i_1, i_2, \ldots, i_k\}$, then $Q = \sum_{j=1}^{k} s_{i_j} P_{i_j}$.

Define a principal divisor $div(f) := P_{i_1} + P_{i_2} + \ldots + P_{i_k} - Q - (k-1)\mathcal{O}$. It is easy to see that $div(f) \in \mathcal{L}(G)$ since $div(f) + G$ is effective. Consequently, $c := (f(P_1), f(P_2), \ldots, f(P_n))$ is a codeword of $\mathcal{C}(G, D)$, and $f(P_i) = 0$ iff $i \in \{i_1, i_2, \ldots, i_k\}$.

If $\mathcal{A}$ successfully outputs a codeword of minimum weight, then the codeword c must be of weight $n - k$. According to Theorem 2, the principal divisor $div(f)$ suggests that $P_{i_1} + P_{i_2} + \ldots + P_{i_k} - Q - (k-1)\mathcal{O}$ is $\mathcal{O}$ when "+" and "−" are implemented with the elliptic curve group operation. As a result, $Q = P_{i_1} + P_{i_2} + \ldots + P_{i_k}$ holds on the group of $\mathcal{E}(\mathbb{F}_q)$, hence $Q = \sum_{j=1}^{k} 2^{i_j-1} P$.

In this way, $\mathcal{B}$ solves the ECDLP by invoking algorithm $\mathcal{A}$ with probability $\epsilon/(n+1)$.   ∎

Note that in Sect. 3, we construct algorithm MinWeightCode which outputs codewords of minimum weight with probability $1 - \left(1 - \dfrac{\mu \cdot \binom{n-k}{u}}{\binom{n}{u}(q-1)^u}\right)^{T_m}$. Hence we can construct $\mathcal{B}$ to solve the ECDLP with probability

$$\frac{1}{n+1} \cdot \left(1 - \left(1 - \frac{\mu \cdot \binom{n-k}{u}}{\binom{n}{u}(q-1)^u}\right)^{T_m}\right).$$

4.2   The Algorithm of Solving ECDLP

In the proof of the theorem in the previous subsection, algorithm $\mathcal{B}$ wins only if it correctly guesses the Hamming weight of $s(= \log_P Q)$. Hence the security reduction suffers from a security loss of factor $(n+1)$. In this subsection, we try to decrease the security loss factor. We have two observations.

(1) For a random $s \in \mathbb{Z}_p$, the hamming weight of s belongs to $\{0, 1, \ldots, \lceil \log_2 p \rceil)\}$ and it takes the value of $\lceil (\log_2 p + 1)/2 \rceil$ with the maximal probability.

(2) If we increase the number of elements in the support of D and add random elements in the support of divisor D, it is possible for us to improve the probability that $\exists i_1, i_2, \ldots, i_k$ such that $P_{i_1} + P_{i_2} + \ldots + P_{i_k} - G$ is principal divisor. Hence, the probability of $\mathcal{C}(G, D)$ being an AMDS-EC code will be greatly increased.

Based on the above observations, we present a probabilistic algorithm of solving ECDLP by constructing AMDS-EC codes and finding codewords of minimum weight with help of list decoding.

Let P be a point of prime order p in the group $\mathcal{E}(\mathbb{F}_q)$, where $\mathcal{E}$ is an elliptic curve defined over $\mathbb{F}_q$. Given P and $Q(= sP) \in \langle P \rangle$ and the parameter of $\mathcal{E}$, the following algorithm SolveECDLP aims to compute s $(= \log_P Q)$ by invoking MinWeiCodeword which aims to find minimum weight codeword of elliptic codes.

Algorithm SolveECDLP($\mathcal{E}(\mathbb{F}_q), P, Q, p$):

Input: An elliptic curve group $\mathcal{E}(\mathbb{F}_q)$, a generator P of prime order p, and an element $Q \in \langle P \rangle$.

Output: $s \in \mathbb{Z}_p$ (such that $Q = sP$).

1. Define $\theta := \lceil \log_2 p \rceil$, $n := 2\theta$, $k := \lfloor (\theta+1)/2 \rfloor$. If $\mathsf{wt}(p) = k$, then $k := \lfloor (\theta+1)/2 \rfloor + 1$.
2. Define divisor $G := k\mathcal{O}$ and define $P_i := 2^{i-1}P$ for $i = 1, 2, \ldots, \theta$.
3. Randomly choose $r_2, r_3, \ldots, r_{n-\theta}$ from $\mathbb{Z}_p$. Set $r_1 := 1$ and define $P_{\theta+j} := r_j Q$ for $j = 1, 2, \ldots, n-\theta$.
4. Construct an Elliptic code $\mathcal{C}(G, D)$ where divisor $D = P_1 + P_2 + \ldots + P_n$.
5. Set $t_m = n - \sqrt{nk}$ and $T_m = O(poly(n))$.
6. Invoke $c \leftarrow \mathsf{MinWeiCodeword}(\mathcal{C}(G, D), \{n-k\}, t_m, T_m)$;
7. If $c = \bot$, goto Step 3.
8. If $c \neq \bot$, then $\mathsf{wt}(c) = n - k$. Parse $c = (c_1, c_2, \ldots, c_n)$. Suppose the zero components of c are $c_{i_1}, c_{i_2}, \ldots, c_{i_k}$.
9. Suppose $i_{j-1} \leq \theta$ and $i_j > \theta$, then compute $s' :\equiv -(r_{i_j-\theta} + r_{i_{j+1}-\theta} + \ldots + r_{i_k-\theta})^{-1}(2^{i_1-1} + 2^{i_2-1} + \ldots + 2^{i_{j-1}-1}) \mod p$.
10. If $Q = s'P$ then Return(s'); else Return$(\bot)$.

In the above algorithm, it is possible for us to choose the parameters n and k flexibly as to optimize the algorithm.

Take the example in Subsect. 3.3. Let $P = P_1$, $Q = P_9$. Let $r_1 = 1$ and choose $r_2 = 29, r_3 = 93, r_4 = 49, r_5 = 5, r_6 = 98, r_7 = 54, r_8 = 10, r_9 = 103, r_{10} = 59, r_{11} = 15, r_{12} = 108$. Then $P_{10} = 29Q, P_{11} = 93Q, P_{12} = 49Q, P_{13} = 5Q, P_{14} = 98Q, P_{15} = 54Q, P_{16} = 10Q, P_{17} = 103Q, P_{18} = 59Q, P_{19} = 15Q, P_{20} = 108Q$. The output of $\mathsf{MinWeiCodeword}$ is the minimum-weight codeword

$$(0, 38, 41, 48, 61, 15, 61, 73, 0, 48, 20, 54, 0, 98, 98, 41, 18, 66, 107, 0).$$

Therefore, $P_1 + P_9 + P_{13} + P_{20} = \mathcal{O}$, which means $1 + s + 5s + 108s \equiv 0 \mod 137$. This immediately leads to a correct output of $s = 6$ since $Q = 6P$.

4.3   Analysis of Algorithm SolveECDLP

Now we analyze the success probability of Algorithm SolveECDLP via the proof of the following theorem.

Theorem 5. *Let $\mathcal{E}$ be an elliptic curve over $\mathbb{F}_q$. Let P be a point over group $\mathcal{E}(\mathbb{F}_q)$. Suppose the order of P is a prime p. Let $\theta := \lceil \log_2 p \rceil$, $n := 2\theta$, $k := \lfloor (\theta+1)/2 \rfloor$, $u \leq (n-k)/2$ and $u \geq n - k - t_m$. then algorithm SolveECDLP successfully solves the ECDLP problem with probability*

$$\left(1 - \left(1 - \frac{\binom{\theta}{k-1}}{2^\theta}\right)^{n-\theta}\right) \cdot \left(1 - \left(1 - \frac{\lambda \cdot \binom{n-k}{u}}{\binom{n}{u}(q-1)^{u-1}}\right)^{T_m}\right) \cdot \left(1 - \frac{1}{p}\right),$$

where λ denotes the number of subsets $\mathcal{J} = \{i_1, i_2, \ldots, i_k\} \subseteq \{1, 2, \ldots, n\}$ such that $G - \sum_{j \in \mathcal{J}} P_j$ is a principal divisor.

Proof. Note that for $G := k\mathcal{O}$, the Elliptic Code $\mathcal{C}(G, D)$ is an AMDS code iff there exists a principal divisor $div(f) := P_{i_1} + P_{i_2} + \ldots + P_{i_k} - k\mathcal{O} \in \mathcal{L}(G)$. Equivalently, there exist $P_{i_1}, P_{i_2}, \ldots, P_{i_k}$ such that $P_{i_1} + P_{i_2} + \ldots + P_{i_k} + k\mathcal{O} = \mathcal{O}$, i.e,

$$P_{i_1} + P_{i_2} + \ldots + P_{i_k} = \mathcal{O},$$

where the addition is over the elliptic group $\mathcal{E}(\mathbb{F}_q)$. There are three cases all together.

Case I: $i_1 \leq \theta$ and $i_k > \theta$. In this case, suppose that $i_{j-1} \leq \theta$ and $i_j > \theta$, then
$(2^{i_1-1} + 2^{i_2-1} + \ldots + 2^{i_{j-1}-1})P + (r_{i_j-\theta} + r_{i_{j+1}-\theta} + \ldots + r_{i_k-\theta})Q = \mathcal{O}$, that is, $-(r_{i_j-\theta} + r_{i_{j+1}-\theta} + \ldots + r_{i_k-\theta})s \equiv (2^{i_1-1} + 2^{i_2-1} + \ldots + 2^{i_j-1-1}) \mod p$.
Case II: $i_1 > \theta$. In this case, $(r_{i_1-\theta} + r_{i_2-\theta} + \ldots + r_{i_k-\theta})Q = \mathcal{O}$, i.e., $r_{i_1-\theta} + r_{i_2-\theta} + \ldots + r_{i_k-\theta} \equiv 0 \mod p$.
Case III: $i_k \leq \theta$. In this case, $(2^{i_1-1} + 2^{i_2-1} + \ldots + 2^{i_k-1})P = \mathcal{O}$, i.e., $(2^{i_1-1} + 2^{i_2-1} + \ldots + 2^{i_k-1}) \equiv 0 \mod p$. Recall that $\theta := \lceil \log_2 p \rceil$, and $k = \lfloor \theta/2 \rfloor + 1$. Then $(2^{i_1-1} + 2^{i_2-1} + \ldots + 2^{i_k-1}) < 2p$.

Clearly, Case II happens with probability $1/p$ when r_ℓ's are randomly chosen, $\ell \in \{2, 3, \ldots, n - \theta\}$, and Case III never happens since $wt(p) \neq k$.

Now we consider the probability that $\mathcal{C}(G, D)$ is an AMDS code, when $s, r_2, \ldots r_{n-\theta}$ are randomly chosen from $\mathbb{Z}_p$.

$\Pr[\mathcal{C}(G, D) \text{ is AMDS}]$

$= \Pr[\exists i_1, \ldots, i_k \in [n] \text{ s.t. divisor } P_{i_1} + P_{i_2} + \ldots + P_{i_k} - G \text{ is principal}]$

$= \Pr[\exists i_1, \ldots, i_k \in [n] \text{ s.t. } P_{i_1} + P_{i_2} + \ldots + P_{i_k} = \mathcal{O}] \text{ (addition is over } \mathcal{E}(\mathbb{F}_q))$

$= \Pr[\exists i_1, \ldots, i_k \in [n] \text{ s.t. Case I happens}] + \Pr[\exists i_1, \ldots, i_k \in [n] \text{ s.t. Case II happens}]$
$\quad + \Pr[\exists i_1, \ldots, i_k \in [n] \text{ s.t. Case III happens}]$

$= 1/p + \Pr[\exists i_1, \ldots, i_k \in [n] \text{ s.t. Case II happens}] + 0 \qquad (7)$

$\geq \Pr[\exists i_1, \ldots, i_k \text{ s.t. Case II happens}]$

$= \Pr\left[\begin{matrix} \exists i_1, \ldots, i_k \in [n] \\ \exists i_{j-1} \leq \theta, i_j > \theta \end{matrix} : -(r_{i_j-\theta} + \ldots + r_{i_k-\theta})s = (2^{i_1-1} + \ldots + 2^{i_j-1-1}) \mod p\right]$

$\geq \Pr\left[\begin{matrix} \exists i_1, \ldots, i_k \in [n] \\ \exists i_k > \theta \end{matrix} : -r_{i_k-\theta}s = (2^{i_1-1} + \ldots + 2^{i_k-1-1}) \mod p\right]$

$= 1 - \Pr[\nexists i_k, i_k \in [n], i_k > \theta \text{ s.t. } -r_{i_k-\theta}s = (2^{i_1-1} + \ldots + 2^{i_k-1-1}) \mod p]$

$$= 1 - \left(1 - \frac{\binom{\theta}{k-1}}{2^\theta}\right)^{n-\theta}. \qquad (8)$$

Given that $\mathcal{C}(G, D)$ is an AMDS elliptic code, then the minimum distance of $\mathcal{C}(G, D)$ is $d = n - k$. According to (6), $\mathsf{MinWeiCodeword}(\mathcal{C}(G, D), \{n-k\}, t_m, T_m)$ successfully outputs a codeword $c = (c_1, c_2, \ldots, c_n)$ of minimum weight with probability

$$1 - \left(1 - \frac{\lambda \cdot \binom{n-k}{u}}{\binom{n}{u}(q-1)^{u-1}}\right)^{T_m}.$$

Suppose that the zero components of the minimum weight codeword $\boldsymbol{c}$ are given by $c_{i_1}, c_{i_2}, \ldots, c_{i_k}$. Then it must hold that $P_{i_1} + P_{i_2} + \ldots + P_{i_k} = \mathcal{O}$. Similarly, there are three cases: $i_1 \leq \theta$ and $i_k > \theta$; $i_1 > \theta$; $i_k \leq \theta$. As analyzed before, the second case happens with probability $1/p$ and the third case never happens. Therefore, the first case happens with probability $1 - 1/p$. Meanwhile the first case means that $\exists i_{j-1} \leq \theta, i_j > \theta$, so that

$$(2^{i_1-1} + 2^{i_2-1} + \ldots + 2^{i_{j-1}-1})P + (r_{i_j-\theta} + r_{i_{j+1}-\theta} + \ldots + r_{i_k-\theta})Q = \mathcal{O},$$

i.e.,

$$s \equiv -(r_{i_j-\theta} + r_{i_{j+1}-\theta} + \ldots + r_{i_k-\theta})^{-1}(2^{i_1-1} + 2^{i_2-1} + \ldots + 2^{i_{j-1}-1}) \mod p.$$

In this case, Algorithm SolveECDLP successfully solves the ECDLP problem. Consequently,

$$\Pr[\text{SolveECDLP succeeds}] \tag{9}$$
$$= \Pr[\mathcal{C}(G,D) \text{ is AMDS} \wedge \text{MinWeiCodeword succeeds} \wedge \text{Case I happens}] \tag{10}$$
$$= \Pr[\mathcal{C}(G,D) \text{ is AMDS}] \tag{11}$$
$$\cdot \Pr[\text{MinWeiCodeword succeeds} \mid \mathcal{C}(G,D) \text{ is AMDS}] \tag{12}$$
$$\cdot \Pr[\text{Case I happens} \mid \text{MinWeiCodeword succeeds}, \mathcal{C}(G,D) \text{ is AMDS}] \tag{13}$$

$$= \left(1 - \left(1 - \frac{\binom{\theta}{k-1}}{2^\theta}\right)^{n-\theta}\right) \cdot \left(1 - \left(1 - \frac{\lambda \cdot \binom{n-k}{u}}{\binom{n}{u}(q-1)^{u-1}}\right)^{T_m}\right) \cdot (1 - \frac{1}{p}), \tag{14}$$

where λ denotes the number of subsets $\mathcal{J} = \{i_1, i_2, \ldots, i_k\} \subseteq \{1, 2, \ldots, n\}$ such that $G - \sum_{j \in \mathcal{J}} P_j$ is a principal divisor. $\blacksquare$

Remark. The probability of (8) only shows a lower bound of the probability that $\mathcal{C}(G,D)$ is an AMDS code. Even if it is only a lower bound, (8) is already close to 1 (as compared with the loss factor $1/(n+1)$ in the previous subsection). For instance, now we choose the Certicom curve **ECCp-131** over a prime field of 131-bit to construct a EC code, then $\theta = 131, k = 66$. Take $n = 262$, then the probability is at least 0.99992.

Recall that in algorithm MinWeiCodeword($\mathcal{C}(G,D), \{n-k\}, t_m, T_m$), there are T_m times of invocations of FindCodeword($\mathcal{C}(G,D), u, d, t_m$). For each invocation, FindCodeword succeeds in finding a codeword of minimum weight via the Guruswami-Sudan list decoding with probability

$$\Pr[\hat{c} \leftarrow \text{FindCodeword}(\mathcal{C}, u, d, t_m) : \text{wt}(\hat{c}) = d] \approx \frac{\lambda \cdot \binom{d}{u}}{\binom{n}{u}(q-1)^{u-1}}. \tag{15}$$

Therefore, the times T_m of invocations of FindCodeword should be of order

$$\frac{\binom{n}{u}(q-1)^{u-1}}{\lambda \cdot \binom{d}{u}} \tag{16}$$

for MinWeiCodeword to succeed. Algorithm FindCodeword is dominated by the list decoding algorithm. Recall that list decoding algorithms, either the Guruswami-Sudan or Shokrollahi-Wasserman algorithm [31], are polynomial-time algorithms in the codeword length. However, the probability (15) is too small to make T_m a polynomial. Therefore, the algorithm SolveECDLP is not efficient, and it is even not of square-root time algorithm. To decrease the computational complexity of SolveECDLP, a possible way is to increase the error bound t_m of the list decoding. Recall that $u + t = d$ and $t \leq t_m$. A larger t_m implies that we can take a small value of u, so the probability in (15) will be improved which in turn to decrease the computational complexity of SolveECDLP. On the other hand, for a concrete security parameter κ such that $q \approx 2^\kappa$, a more efficient list decoding algorithm will also help us to improve the efficiency of SolveECDLP.

5   Conclusion

We proposed a new method to solve the ECDLP problem. For any ECDLP, we first construct an Elliptic Code, then resort to techniques of List Decoding to find codewords of minimum weight. With such a codeword, we are able to solve the ECDLP problem. Our method of solving ECDLP is still not efficient enough, due to the small probability of finding minimum-weight codeword. Nevertheless, this is a totally new approach and we believe the efficiency can be improved with the new development of List Decoding.

Acknowledgements. This work is supported by the National Natural Science Foundation of China (No. 61672550 and 61672346) and the National Key R&D Program of China(2017YFB0802503).

References

1. Beelen, P., Brander, K.: Efficient list decoding of a class of algebraic-geometrycodes. Adv. Math. Commun. **4**(4), 485–518 (2010)
2. Berlekamp, E.R., McEliece, R.J., van Tilborg, H.C.: On the inherent intractability of certain coding problems. IEEE Trans. Inf. Theory **24**(3), 384–386 (1978)
3. Cheng, Q.: Hard problems of algebraic geometry codes. IEEE Trans. Inf. Theory **54**, 402–406 (2008)
4. Cheng, Q., Wan, D.: On the list and bounded distance decodability of Reed-Solomon codes (extended abstract). In: FOCS, pp. 335–341 (2004)
5. Driencourt, Y., Michon, J.F.: Elliptic codes over fields of characteristics 2. J. Pure Appl. Algebra **45**(1), 15–39 (1987)
6. Elias, P.: List decoding for noisy channels. In: 1957-IRE WESCON Convention Record, pp. 94–104 (1957)
7. Frey, G., Rück, H.: A remark concerning m-divisibility and the discrete logarithm in the divisor class group of curves. Math. Comput. **62**, 865–874 (1994)
8. Galbraith, S.D., Gaudry, P.: Recent progress on the elliptic curve discrete logarithm problem. Des. Codes Cryptogr. **78**(1), 51–72 (2016)
9. Gaudry, P., Hess, F., Smart, N.P.: Constructive and destructive facets of Weil descent on elliptic curves. J. Cryptol. **15**(1), 19–46 (2002)

10. Goldreich, O., Levin, L.A.: A hard-core predicate for all one-way functions. In: Proceedings of the Twenty First Annual ACM Symposium on Theory of Computing, pp. 25–32 (1989)
11. Goppa, V.D.: Codes on algebraic curves. Soviet Math. Dokl. **24**(1), 170–172 (1981)
12. Guruswami, V., Sudan, M.: Improved decoding of reed-solomon and algebraic-geometry codes. IEEE Trans. Inf. Theory **45**(6), 1757–1767 (1999)
13. Guruswami, V., Sudan, M.: On representations of algebraic-geometric codes for list decoding. IEEE Trans. Inf. Theory **47**(4), 1610–1613 (2001)
14. Guruswami, V., Rudra, A.: Explicit codes achieving list decoding capacity: error-correction with optimal redundancy. IEEE Trans. Inf. Theory **54**(1), 135–150 (2008)
15. Guruswami, V., Xing, C.: List decoding reed-solomon, algebraic-geometric, and gabidulin subcodes up to the singleton bound. In: Proceedings of the 45th Annual ACM Symposium on Theory of Computing (STOC), pp. 843–852. ACM (2013)
16. Kiayias, A., Yung, M.: Cryptographic hardness based on the decoding of reed-solomon codes. In: Widmayer, P., Eidenbenz, S., Triguero, F., Morales, R., Conejo, R., Hennessy, M. (eds.) ICALP 2002. LNCS, vol. 2380, pp. 232–243. Springer, Heidelberg (2002). https://doi.org/10.1007/3-540-45465-9_21
17. Koblitz, N.: Elliptic curve cryptosystems. Math. Comput. **48**, 203–209 (1987)
18. MAGMA Computational Algebra System. http://magma.maths.usyd.edu.au/magma/
19. Menezes, A., Okamoto, T., Vanstone, S.: Reducing elliptic curve logarithms to logarithms in a finite field. IEEE Trans. Inf. Theory **39**(2), 1639–1646 (1993)
20. McEliece, R.J.: On the average list size for the Guruswami-Sudan decoder. In: 7th International Symposium on Communications Theory and Applications (ISCTA), July 2003
21. Miller, V.S.: Use of elliptic curves in cryptography. In: Williams, H.C. (ed.) CRYPTO 1985. LNCS, vol. 218, pp. 417–426. Springer, Heidelberg (1986). https://doi.org/10.1007/3-540-39799-X_31
22. Miller, V.: Short programs for functions on curves (1986, unpublished manuscript)
23. Moreno, C.: Algebraic Curves over Finite Fields. Cambridge Tracts in Mathematics, vol. 97. Cambridge University Press, Cambridge (1991)
24. Parvaresh, F., Vardy, A.: Correcting errors beyond the Guruswami-Sudan radius in polynomial time. In: 46th Annual IEEE Symposium on Foundations of Computer Science, pp. 285–294 (2005)
25. Pollard, J.M.: Monte Carlo methods for index computation mod p. Math. Comput. **32**, 918–924 (1978)
26. Semaev, I.A.: Evaluation of discrete logarithms in a group of p-torsion points of an elliptic curve in characteristic p. Math. Comput. **67**(221), 353–356 (1998)
27. Smart, N.P.: The discrete logarithm problem on elliptic curves of trace one. J. Cryptol. **12**(3), 193–196 (1999)
28. Satoh, T., Araki, K.: Fermat quotients and the polynomial time discrete log algorithm for anomalous elliptic curves. Comm. Math. Pauli **47**(1), 81–92 (1998)
29. Silverman, J.H.: The Arithmetic of Elliptic Curves. Springer, New York (1986). https://doi.org/10.1007/978-1-4757-1920-8
30. Shokrollahi, M.A.: Minimum distance of elliptic codes. Adv. Math. **93**, 251–281 (1992)
31. Shokrollahi, M.A., Wasserman, H.: List decoding of algebraic-geometric codes. IEEE Trans. Inf. Theory **45**(2), 432–437 (1999)
32. Stichtenoth, H.: Algebraic Function Field and Codes. Springer, Heidelberg (1993)

33. Sudan, M.: Decoding of reed solomon codes beyond the error-correction bound. J. Complex. **13**, 180–193 (1998)
34. Sudan, M.: List decoding: algorithms and applications. In: van Leeuwen, J., Watanabe, O., Hagiya, M., Mosses, P.D., Ito, T. (eds.) TCS 2000. LNCS, vol. 1872, pp. 25–41. Springer, Heidelberg (2000). https://doi.org/10.1007/3-540-44929-9_3
35. Tsfasman, M.A., Vlădut, S.G.: Algebraic-geometric Codes. Kluwer Academic Publishers (1991)
36. Vardy, A.: The intractability of computing the minimum distance of a code. IEEE Trans. Inf. Theory **43**(6), 1757–1766 (1997)
37. Washington, L.: Elliptic Curves: Number Theory and Cryptography. Chapman and Hall/CRC (2003)
38. Wozencraft, J.M.: List decoding. Quarterly Progress Report, Research Laboratory of Electronics, MIT, vol. 48, pp. 90–95 (1958)

Protocols

Provably Secure Proactive Secret Sharing Without the Adjacent Assumption

Zhe Xia[1], Bo Yang[2(✉)], Yanwei Zhou[2], Mingwu Zhang[3,4], Hua Shen[3], and Yi Mu[5]

[1] School of Computer Science and Technology, Wuhan University of Technology, Wuhan, China
xiazhe@whut.edu.cn
[2] School of Computer Science, Shaanxi Normal University, Xi'an, China
{byang,zyw}@snnu.edu.cn
[3] School of Computers, Hubei University of Technology, Wuhan, China
csmwzhang@gmail.com, cshshen@hbut.edu.cn
[4] State Key Laboratory of Cryptology, Beijing, China
[5] Fujian Provincial Key Laboratory of Network Security and Cryptology, College of Mathematics and Informatics, Fujian Normal University, Fuzhou, China
ymu.ieee@gmail.com

Abstract. In secret sharing (SS), the secret is shared among a number of parties so that only a quorum of these parties can recover the secret, but a smaller set of parties cannot learn any information about the secret. However, the traditional SS technique is insufficient to protect the secret with a long lifetime, because the adversary may gradually compromise enough parties to retrieve the secret over the long time. To solve this issue, proactive secret sharing (PSS) divides the lifetime of the secret into many short time periods and the parties jointly update their secret shares in each time period. The benefit is that if the adversary cannot break into enough parties in a single time period, her compromised shares will become obsolete after the shares being updated.

In the last two decades, many PSS schemes have been proposed and they are widely used in various security protocols. However, the majority of existing PSS schemes require the *adjacent assumption*, i.e. if a party is corrupted during an update phase, it is corrupted in both time periods adjacent to that update phase. Note that this assumption not only hinders the security model to capture the mobile adversary's abilities, but also prevents PSS schemes being used in many real-world applications. In this paper, we revisit the research of PSS, and our work contributes in the following aspects. Firstly, we discuss why some existing schemes (including Herzberg's PSS scheme) cannot maintain their security when the adjacent assumption is removed. Secondly, we use the polynomial truncation method to improve Herzberg's PSS scheme. To the best of our knowledge, our proposed scheme is the first provably secure PSS scheme without the adjacent assumption.

© Springer Nature Switzerland AG 2019
R. Steinfeld and T. H. Yuen (Eds.): ProvSec 2019, LNCS 11821, pp. 247–264, 2019.
https://doi.org/10.1007/978-3-030-31919-9_14

1 Introduction

The secret sharing (SS) technique, first introduced by Shamir [28] and Blakley [5], is an important building block in cryptology to protect secrecy and availability of sensitive information. The secret is divided into a number of shares and each share is held by an individual party. Therefore, if the adversary wants to learn or destroy the secret, she has to break into multiple parties. For example, in a (t, n)-threshold secret sharing, the secret is shared among n parties so that any t parties work together can recover the secret, but less than t parties cannot learn any information of the secret. And the adversary needs to compromise at least $n - t + 1$ parties if her purpose is to destroy the secret. However, the traditional SS technique is not suitable for some cases. For example, it might be insufficient to protect the secret with a long lifetime, e.g. crypto master keys, legal documents, medical records, etc. In these cases, the adversary may gradually compromise enough parties to learn the secret or destroy it, because she breaks into the parties in a monotonic fashion and she has a very long time to mount the attack.

To mitigate the above issue, proactive secret sharing (PSS) has been introduced in which the entire lifetime of the secret is divided into many short time periods and the parties jointly update the shares at the beginning of each time period with the original secret unchanged. The update includes a *share recovery* protocol and a *share refreshment* protocol. In the share recovery protocol, any lost or tampered share is recovered for the corresponding party without disclosing it to the other parties. In the share refreshment phase, the parties interactively compute new shares of the same secret and erase old shares. Because old shares and new ones are independent, if the adversary cannot break into enough parties before the update, any compromised share learned by the adversary will become obsolete after the update. In the case of a (t, n)-threshold PSS, the adversary has to compromise t parties in a single time period in order to learn the secret. This is opposed to compromising t parties over the entire lifetime in traditional SS schemes. For example, suppose some legal document needs to be protected for 10 years. If the shares are updated weekly, then the time slot for the adversary to break into t parties has been dramatically reduced from 10 years to 1 week.

The motivation of PSS is to protect the secret against the *mobile adversary* [23] who can compromise different parties at different time periods. Throughout the entire lifetime of the secret, the mobile adversary may corrupt all parties or break into some parties several times. But the requirement is that she can only compromise less than a quarom of parties in each time period. If a party is no longer corrupted by the mobile adversary, it will be "rebooted" into the safe state immediately.

Informally, proactive security refers to *secrecy* and *robustness* in the presence of the mobile adversary, where secrecy guarantees that the mobile adversary cannot learn any information about the secret in the entire lifetime of the secret, and robustness ensures that the secret can be correctly reconstructed in any time period even in the presence of some corrupted parties. Moreover, a PSS scheme is said to be *optimal resilient* if it is robust against any minority of corrupted parties. Note that this threshold is the maximum number of corrupted parties allowed in SS schemes. In the literature, the threat model widely used in analysing PSS schemes requires the adjacent assumption, i.e. if a party is corrupted during an update phase, it is corrupted in both time periods adjacent to that update phase. In this paper, we investigate the necessity and implications of the adjacent assumption, and explore the design of provably secure PSS schemes without this assumption.

1.1   Related Works

The concept of mobile adversary was first introduced by Ostrovsky and Yung in [23]. The same paper also showed that if there exists pairwise secure communication channels and the parties can erase part of their memory, a lot of secure multiparty computation protocols (e.g. [3, 10, 26]) can be extended to withstand the mobile adversary. However, this idea only works theoretically, because the computation is done by secure distributed circuit evaluations and the communication costs are proportional to the size of circuits. For some specific problems, more efficient solutions are desired. Later, Canetti and Herzberg [9] introduced an efficient method to construct a distributed pseudorandom generator that can be maintained proactively. Canetti et al. [8] also demonstrated how to ensure authenticated and secret communication among parties that is robust against break-ins and key exposures.

Among the research of proactive security, PSS has attracted the most interests. Not only because it is a useful technique to protect secret with a long lifetime, but also it is an important building block for various security protocols, such as proactive threshold cryptosystems [19], proactive secure multiparty computation [2, 30], key management in the ad hoc networks [18, 31], and so on. In PSS, the secret is initially shared among the parties. The tricky part is how to jointly update the shares among the parties. For this task, three approaches have been introduced that achieve the optimal resilience property:

- **Herzberg's approach** [20]: before the update, the secret s is shared among the parties in a (t, n)-threshold fashion using a $t - 1$ degree polynomial $f(x)$ such that $f(0) = s$. To update the shares, the parties jointly generate a random $t - 1$ degree polynomial $\delta(x)$ with $\delta(0) = 0$. After the update, each party holds a new share of the $t - 1$ degree polynomial $f'(x) = f(x) + \delta(x)$. Because $f'(0) = f(0) + \delta(0) = s$, the shares have been updated without changing the original secret s.
- **Frankel's approach** [12]: before the update, the secret is also shared among the parties in a (t, n)-threshold fashion. To update the shares, the parties first jointly transform the (t, n) polynomial sharing of the secret into an (n, n) additive sharing of the secret. To achieve optimal resilience, each share of the (n, n) additive sharing is further shared among the parties in the (t, n)-threshold fashion. Then, the parties jointly transform the (n, n) additive sharing of the secret back to a (t, n) polynomial sharing of the secret. Note that in both transformations, the secret is not revealed to any individual party, and after

the update, the polynomial used to share the secret is independent from the one before the update.

- **Rabin's approach** [25]: before the update, the secret is additively shared among the parties. To achieve optimal resilience, each of the old share is further shared among the parties in the (t, n)-threshold fashion. To update the shares, each party first shares her old share among the parties using another (n, n) additive sharing. In this process, each party will receive a share of the old share, called *fragement*, from every other party. Then, each party sums the received fragements, obtaining the new share of the secret. For optimal resilience, each party also needs to further share this new share among the parties in the (t, n)-threshold fashion. Now, the new shares form an independent (n, n) additive sharing of the original secret.

Based on the above PSS schemes, a lot of further investigations have been carried out in proactive security in the last two decades. For example, Stinson and Wei [29] have proposed an unconditionally secure PSS scheme using symmetric bivariate functions, in which both the secrecy and robustness properties are unconditionally protected. Canetti [7], followed by Frankel [14] and Almansa [1], have introduced the methods to extend PSS to withstand adaptive adversaries who can choose which parties to corrupt at any time during the run of the protocol. Cachin [6] and Zhou [32] have introduced PSS that is secure in the asynchronous communication model. Schultz et al. [27] have introduced a mobile PSS scheme that allows on-the-fly reconfiguration of the threshold, so that the scheme is able to accommodate more changes in the environment.

1.2   Our Contributions

In this paper, we revisit the research of provably secure and optimal resilient PSS, and we contribute in the following aspects:

- Firstly, although the adjacent assumption is widely used in existing PSS schemes, it not only hinders the security model to capture the mobile adversary's abilities, but also prevents PSS schemes from being used in many real-world applications. However, if this assumption is removed, we show that some existing schemes (including Herzberg's PSS scheme) will become insecure.
- Secondly, we use the polynomial truncation method to improve Herzberg's PSS scheme, resulting a provably secure PSS scheme without the adjacent assumption. To the best of our knowledge, it is the first PSS scheme satisfying this feature.

1.3   Organisation of the Paper

The rest of the paper is organised as follows: Sect. 2 outlines some preliminaries, including a new threat model without the adjacent assumption and some cryptographic building blocks. In Sect. 3, we show that the secrecy property in Herzberg's PSS scheme might be violated by the mobile adversary in our threat model. In Sect. 4, we use the polynomial truncation method to modify Herzberg's scheme, making it secure in our threat model. Finally, we conclude in Sect. 5.

2   Preliminaries

2.1   Models and Definitions

The Players. The players in our environment are n parties $P_1, P_2, \ldots, P_n$ and the mobile adversary $\mathcal{A}$. We assume that all these players can be modelled as probabilistic polynomial time (PPT) Turing machines [17]. Moreover, we assume that the system is synchronised, the parties can access to some common global clock, and each party has a local source of randomness. In this paper, we denote $n = 2t - 1$, where t is the threshold.

Time Periods. The entire lifetime of the secret is divided into many short time periods (e.g. a day, a week, etc.) which are determined by the common global clock. At the beginning of the first time period, there is a share distribution phase in which the secret is shared among the parties either by a trusted party or in a distributed fashion [16]. For all the other time periods, there is an update phase at the beginning of each time period. After the update, the lost or tampered shares are recovered and the parties hold new shares of the secret while the old shares are erased.

The Mobile Adversary. Following the description in [23], the mobile adversary can be envisioned as follows: it has $t - 1$ pebbles, and at the beginning of each time period, she places the pebbles on any $t - 1$ parties. If the pebble is placed on a party, this party is corrupted by the mobile adversary. Corrupting a party means learning this party's private information, changing its intended behaviour, disconnecting it, and so on. When the pebble is removed from a party, this party will be "rebooted" to the safe state at the beginning of the next time period, and her share will be jointly recovered by the parties. After each time period, the mobile adversary can move pebbles from a set of parties to a different set of parties. Therefore, the mobile adversary has more power than the ordinary adversary in traditional SS schemes, because the mobile adversary may corrupt all parties or break into some parties multiple times throughout the lifetime of the secret. However, it is assumed that the mobile adversary corrupts less than t parties in each time period.

The Communication Channel. We assume that all players are connected to a common authenticated broadcast channel $\mathcal{C}$, such that any message sent through $\mathcal{C}$ can be heard by the other players. The mobile adversary cannot modify messages send by an uncorrupted party through $\mathcal{C}$, nor she can prevent an uncorrupted party from receiving messages from $\mathcal{C}$. Moreover, we assume that there are pairwise secure communication channels among the parties, and the mobile adversary is unable to tamper or intercept the messages send through these secure channels. With these assumptions, we can focus our discussions on the proactive secret sharing schemes without considering the low level technical details. We note that both the authenticated broadcast channel and the pairwise secure channels can be implemented using standard techniques such as encryption and signature functions.

In the majority of existing PSS schemes (e.g. [1,12–15,20,21,27]), there is an assumption that if a party is corrupted during an update phase, it is corrupted during both time periods adjacent to that update phase. In comparison, our threat model does not require this assumption. We only assume that if a party is corrupted during an update phase, it is corrupted in the same time period but not in the preceeding time period. We show that this gives the adversary more power and such an adversary better mimics the mobile adversary. To simplify the description, considering the case that the entire lifetime of the secret has been divided into two time periods (as shown in Fig. 1). In the existing works, the adversary who corrupts $t-1$ parties during the update phase will corrupt the same parties throughtout the lifetime of the secret. In this case, the mobile adversary does not have more power than the ordinary adversary in traditional SS schemes. But in our threat model, the mobile adversary can corrupt some parties in time period 1 and then move to corrupt some other parties in time period 2. Therefore, the mobile adversary in our threat model has more power and our model better captures the ability of the mobile adversary. Moreover, the adjacent assumption will prevent the PSS schemes being used in many real-world applications. For example, PSS schemes were suggested to be used in Ad Hoc networks to safeguard the crypto keys in the distributed fashion [18,31]. But since the topology structure of the networks may change dynamically, and nodes may join or leave any time, the existing PSS schemes with the adjacent assumption are not suitable for these circumstances.

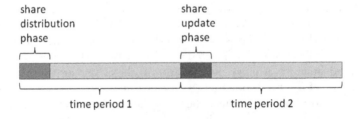

Fig. 1. A demonstration of the time periods

In order to provide rigorous security analysis for our proposed PSS scheme, we use the following security definitions:

Definition 1 (Robustness:) *A proactive secret sharing scheme is robust if in the presence of the mobile adversary, the secret can be correctly recovered in any time period throughout the entire lifetime of the secret.*

Definition 2 (Secrecy:) *A proactive secret sharing scheme is secret if after polynomially many updates, the mobile adversary still cannot learn any information of the secret.*

Definition 3 (Optimal resilience:) *A proactive secret sharing scheme is optimal resilient if it is robust against the mobile adversary who has the ability to corrupt any minority of the parties.*

2.2   Cryptographic Building Blocks

Shamir's Secret Sharing   [28]. Denote p as a large prime such that $p > n$. In the rest of this paper, we assume that all computations are modulo p unless otherwise stated. To share the secret $s \in \mathbb{Z}_p$, the dealer first generates a polynomial $f(x) = a_0 + a_1 x + \cdots + a_{t-1} x^{t-1}$ over $\mathbb{Z}_p$ with degree $t - 1$ such that $a_0 = s$. Then the dealer evaluates the polynomial $f(x)$ at different public and pre-defined values x_i for $i \in \{1, 2, \ldots, n\}$, and she sends the share $s_i = f(x_i)$ to the party P_i through the secure channel. If any t parties work together, they can recover the secret using polynomial interpolation as $s = \sum_{i=1}^{t} s_i \cdot L_i$, where $L_i = \prod_{j=1, j \neq i}^{t} x_j / (x_j - x_i)$ is the Lagrange coefficient. It is obvious that Shamir's SS is correct. To see why any $t - 1$ colluding parties cannot learn any information of the secret, the $t - 1$ points $(x_1, s_1), \ldots, (x_{t-1}, s_{t-1})$ are known by these parties. But for each possible value $s' \in \mathbb{Z}_p$, the point $(0, s')$ can be used to interpolate a unique polynomial, and the probability of these polynomials is equal. However, Shamir's SS is not robust: the cheating parties may release fake shares when recovering the secret. To solve this issue, either of the following verifiable secret sharing (VSS) techniques can be used.

Feldman's VSS   [11]. Let p be a large prime and g is a generator of a subgroup of $\mathbb{Z}_p^*$ in which the discrete logarithm cannot be solved in polynomial time. To share the secret $s \in \mathbb{Z}_p$, the dealer first generates a $t - 1$ degree polynomial $f(x) = a_0 + a_1 x + \cdots + a_{t-1} x^{t-1}$ over $\mathbb{Z}_p$ such that $a_0 = s$. Then, the dealer computes $A_i = g^{a_i}$ for $i \in \{0, 1, \ldots, t - 1\}$, and makes these values public. Finally, the dealer computs and sends the share $s_i = f(x_i)$ to each party. Once receiving the share, the party can verify its validity by

$$g^{s_i} = \prod_{j=0}^{t-1} A_j^{x_i^j}$$

When recovering the secret, anyone can also use the above equation to verify that the parties have revealed the correct shares.

Pedersen's VSS   [24]. Let p, q be two large primes such that $q | p - 1$, and G is a subgroup of $\mathbb{Z}_p^*$ with order q. Both g and h are elements of G, but nobody knows the value $\log_g h$[1]. To share the secret $s \in \mathbb{Z}_q$, the dealer generates two random polynomials $f(x)$ and $f'(x)$ over $\mathbb{Z}_q$ with degree $t - 1$:

$$f(x) = a_0 + a_1 x + \cdots + a_{t-1} x^{t-1} \quad f'(x) = b_0 + b_1 x + \cdots + b_{t-1} x^{t-1}$$

---

[1] It is crucial that nobody knows the value $\log_g h$. To generate g and h, we first select g in the group G. Then, a distributed coin flipping protocol [3] can be used to generate a random value $r \in \mathbb{Z}_p^*$. Finally, h can be computed as $h = r^{(p-1)/q}$. In case if $h = 1$, we can go back to select another random value $r \in \mathbb{Z}_p^*$ until $h \neq 1$.

where $a_0 = s$. Then the dealer publishes $C_i = g^{a_i} h^{b_i}$ for $i \in \{0, 1, \ldots, t - 1\}$. Finally, the dealer computes and sends the share $s_i = f(x_i)$ and $s_i' = f'(x_i)$ to each party. Once receiving the share, the party can verify its validity by

$$g^{s_i} h^{s_i'} = \prod_{j=0}^{t-1} C_j^{x_i^j}$$

When recovering the secret, anyone can also use the above equation to verify that the parties have revealed the correct shares.

3   Analysis of Herzberg's PSS Scheme

In this section, we first briefly review Herzberg's PSS scheme [20]. We then show that the secrecy property of Herzberg's scheme might be violated by the mobile adversary in our threat model. We also discuss the impact of this vulnerability with respect to some other PSS schemes.

3.1   Review of Herzberg's PSS Scheme

Denote p as some large prime, and $\{x_1, x_2, \ldots, x_n\}$ be the public index values associated with each party, respectively. In the k-th time period, the secret $s \in \mathbb{Z}_p$ is shared among the parties through the $t - 1$ degree polynomial $f^{(k)}(x) = a_0 + a_1 x + \cdots + a_{t-1} x^{t-1}$ over $\mathbb{Z}_p$ such that $a_0 = s$. The party P_i holds the share $s_i^{(k)} = f^{(k)}(x_i)$. At the beginning of the $(k+1)$-th time period, the parties will jointly update these shares. And the update phase includes a share recovery protocol followed by a share refreshment protocol.

Share Recovery. The set of parties in Λ, where $|\Lambda| \geq t$, jointly recover the lost share $s_r^{(k)}$ for the party P_r as follows:

1. P_i picks a random $t-1$ degree polynomial $\delta_i(x) = \delta_{i,0} + \delta_{i,1} x + \cdots + \delta_{i,t-1} x^{t-1}$ over $\mathbb{Z}_p$ such that $\delta_i(x_r) = 0$. For example, P_i can first randomly pick the coefficients $\{\delta_{i,j}\}_{j \in \{1,\ldots,t-1\}}$ from $\mathbb{Z}_p$, and then computes $\delta_{i,0} = -\sum_{j=1}^{t-1} \delta_{i,j} x_r^j$.
2. P_i computes $u_{i,j} = \delta_i(x_j)$ and sends it to each other party P_j using the secure channel.
3. P_i computes $s_i' = s_i^{(k)} + \sum_{j \in \Lambda} u_{j,i}$ and sends this value to P_r using the secure channel.
4. Finally, P_r uses the received values to interpolate a polynomial $g(x) = f^{(k)}(x) + \sum_{i \in \Lambda} \delta_i(x)$, obtaining $s_r^{(k)} = g(x_r)$.

Because each of the polynomial $\delta_i(x)$ is randomly chosen, P_r cannot learn the polynomial $f^{(k)}(x)$. Hence, P_r cannot learn the secret. And the share $s_r^{(k)}$ is recovered for P_r without being disclosed to the other parties.

Share Refreshment. Each party P_i, $i \in \{1, 2, \ldots, n\}$, performs the share refreshment protocol as follows:

1. P_i picks random values $\{\lambda_{i,j}\}_{j \in \{1,2,\ldots,t-1\}}$ from $\mathbb{Z}_p$. These values define the polynomial $\lambda_i(x) = \lambda_{i,1} x + \cdots + \lambda_{i,t-1} x^{t-1}$ over $\mathbb{Z}_p$ such that $\lambda_i(0) = 0$.
2. P_i computes $w_{i,j} = \lambda_i(x_j)$ and sends it to each other party P_j using the secure channel.
3. P_i computes its new share $s_i^{(k+1)} = s_i^{(k)} + \sum_{j=1}^n w_{j,i}$, and erases the old share $s_i^{(k)}$ as well as all the intermediate values. Now, the same secret is shared among the parties through the $t - 1$ degree polynomial $f^{(k+1)}(x) = f^{(k)}(x) + \sum_{i=1}^n \lambda_i(x)$.

To achieve the robustness property, Feldman's VSS is used both in the share recovery and in the share refreshment, ensuring that the parties have generated and shared the polynomial properly.

3.2   Threat Analysis of Herzberg's Scheme in Our Threat Model

The security of Herzberg's PSS scheme have been proved in [21]. However, the proof relies on the adjacent assumption. Now, we show that if this assumption is removed, as in our threat model, the secrecy property of Herzberg's scheme may be violated by the mobile adversary.

To simplify the description, considering the case that the entire lifetime of the secret is divided into two time periods, as shown in Fig. 1. We allow the mobile adversary to corrupt some parties in time period 1 and then move on to corrupt some other parties in time period 2. Without loss of generality, we assume that the parties $\{P_1, P_3, P_4 \ldots, P_t\}$ are corrupted in time period 1, and the parties $\{P_2, P_3, P_4, \ldots, P_t\}$ are corrupted in time period 2. Because the mobile adversary can learn the corrupted parties' private information, for each polynomial $\lambda_i(x)$ in the share refreshment protocol, the mobile adversary knows that $t - 1$ points $(x_2, w_{i,2}), (x_3, w_{i,3}), \ldots, (x_t, w_{i,t})$ will pass this polynomial. In addition, the mobile adversary also knows that the point $(0,0)$ will pass this polynomial. Therefore, these t points allows the mobile adversary to interpolate the polynomial $\lambda_i(x)$. With the knowledge of all these polynomials $\lambda_i(x)$ for $i \in \{1, 2, \ldots, n\}$, the old shares and the new shares are no longer independent. In other words, the mobile adversary knows how a given share in time period 1 has been updated into time period 2. Therefore, the mobile adversary can combine P_1's share in time period 1 with the $t - 1$ shares of $P_2, P_3, \ldots, P_t$ in time period 2 to recover the secret[2].

Note that in the share recovery protocol, the mobile adversary may also find out all polynomials $\delta_i(x)$ for $i \in \Lambda$, because she knows $t - 1$ points held by the corrupted parties and an additional point $(x_r, 0)$. Hence, these t points can be used to interpolate each of these polynomials. However, since these polynomials

---

[2] Note that a similar problem has been independently discovered by Nikov and Nikova in [22]. But its consequences were not elaborated and no solution of this problem was proposed in that work.

are only used privately by the party P_r, the knowledge of these polynomials does not affect the secrecy property in Herzberg's scheme.

3.3   Some Other PSS Schemes in Our Threat Model

In the literature, several other proactive secret sharing schemes are suffering similar vulnerabilities. A common feature of these schemes is that they all use $t - 1$ degree polynomials to update the shares. For example, in [21], Jarecki has introduced a scheme that replaces Feldman's VSS with Pedersen's VSS, while the other technical details remain the same as in Herzberg's scheme. In [29], Stinson et al. have introduced an unconditional secure proactive secret sharing scheme, in which a $t-1$ degree symmetric bivariate function is used to refresh the shares. In [27], Schultz et al. have introduced a PSS scheme that allows on-the-fly reconfiguration of the threshold. In Schultz's scheme, the share recovery protocol is combined with the share refreshment protocol, and $t - 1$ degree polynomials are used to refresh the shares. Therefore, the secrecy property in these scheme also might be violated by the mobile adversary in our threat model.

The above discussions may give the readers a false intuition that any PSS scheme using $t - 1$ degree polynomials to update the shares is vulnerable in our threat model. A counterexample is that although Ostrovsky and Yung [23] also have used $t - 1$ degree polynomials to update the shares, the above threat analysis does not apply to it. Because Ostrovsky's scheme has used two layers of SS, while the other vulnerable schemes only use one layer of SS. For similar reasons, this threat analysis is not directly applicable with Frankel's scheme [12] or Rabin's scheme [25]. However, we note that these schemes are not specially designed to withstand the mentioned attack, and it is still unknown whether their security can be formally proved in our new threat model.

4   Modification of Herzberg's PSS Scheme

In this section, we modify Herzberg's PSS scheme, making it secure against the mobile adversary in our threat model. Because the share recovery protocol in Herzberg's scheme does not suffer the vulnerability discussed in the previous section, we focus our description on the share refreshment protocol.

As a high level overview, we use $2t - 1$ degree random polynomials with 0 in the constant coefficient to refresh the shares. Hence, the mobile adversary who corrupts $t - 1$ parties cannot learn any information of these polynomials. However, after adding these $2t - 1$ degree random polynomials with the original $t - 1$ degree polynomial that shares the secret, the result polynomial will have a degree $2t-1$ rather than $t-1$. But this implies that the secret cannot be recovered by any t parties, violating the optimal resilience property. To further address this issue, the parties need to jointly truncate the $2t - 1$ degree polynomial into a $t - 1$ degree polynomial with the constant coefficient unchanged.

4.1 Jointly Polynomial Truncation

In [3], Ben-Or et al. have introduced a novel technique to jointly truncate polynomials. We adapt this method in our proposed scheme with two necessary changes. Firstly, in Ben-Or's scheme, a $2t$ degree polynomial is truncated into a t degree polynomial with the first $t + 1$ coefficients unchanged. While in our proposed scheme, a $2t - 1$ degree polynomial is truncated into a $t - 1$ degree polynomial with only the constant coefficient unchanged. In other words, we truncate the polynomial in a randomised fashion instead of a fixed one. And we show later that this change is crucial for the security of our proposed scheme. Secondly, to ensure the robustness property, error correction codes are used in Ben-Or's scheme, but we use VSS instead in order to achieve the optimal resilience property.

Lemma 1. *For $i \in \{1, 2, \ldots, n\}$, suppose a_i is some public constant and z_i is the private input of the party P_i, then the linear function $F(z_1, z_2, \ldots, z_n) = a_1 z_1 + a_2 z_2 + \cdots + a_n z_n$ can be computed by the parties in a secure and distributed fashion.*

Proof. (Sketch) Firstly, each party P_i shares its private input z_i among the parties using (t, n)-threshold verifiable secret sharing. Denote $s_{i,j}$ as the share of z_i held by the party P_j. Then $a_1 s_{1,j} + a_2 s_{2,j} + \cdots + a_n s_{n,j}$ will be the corresponding share of $a_1 z_1 + a_2 z_2 + \cdots + a_n z_n$ held by P_j, thanks to the homomorphic property of secret sharing [4]. If the result is supposed to be made public, each party broadcasts its computed share and anyone can retrieve the result by polynomial interpolation. And if the result is supposed to be known by some certain party, then each party sends its computed share to this party using the secure channel. Therefore, the function $F(z_1, z_2, \ldots, z_n)$ can be computed in a secure and distributed fashion. Here, the word "secure" implies both correctness and secrecy. Correctness means that if the private inputs are properly shared, the correct result can always be computed even in the presence of any minority of cheating parties, and this property can be ensured using VSS. Secrecy means that apart from the final result, the adversary who corrupts any minority of parties learns no additional information.

Lemma 2. *Suppose M is a public $n \times n$ matrix. For $i \in \{1, 2, \ldots, n\}$, z_i is the private input of the party P_i. Denote Z as a vector $[z_1, z_2, \ldots, z_n]$ and Y as another vector $[y_1, y_2, \ldots, y_n]$. Then $Y = Z \cdot \mathsf{M}$ can be computed in a secure and distributed fashion, such that by the end of the computation, each party P_i obtains the value y_i without leaking any other information.*

Proof. Since y_i is the vector Z times the i-th column of the matrix M. It can be computed in a secure and distributed fashion by Lemma 1. By the end of the computation, each party sends its computed share to the party P_i using the secure channels. Hence, only P_i knows the value y_i. If this process is repeated for $i \in \{1, 2, \ldots, n\}$, the desired computation can be carried out in a secure and distributed fashion.

Theorem 1. *Suppose $h(x) = h_0 + h_1 x + h_2 x^2 + \cdots + h_{2t-1} x^{2t-1}$ is a polynomial with degree $2t - 1$, and each party P_i holds a share of $h(x)$ as $s_i = h(x_i)$. Then, these parties can jointly truncate $h(x)$ into a $t - 1$ degree polynomial $k(x) = k_0 + k_1 x + \cdots + k_{t-1} x^{t-1}$ in a secure and distributed fashion with the constant coefficient unchanged, i.e. $h_0 = k_0$. By the end of the computation, each party holds a share of $k(x)$ as $r_i = k(x_i)$.*

Proof. (Sketch) Denote B as an $n \times n$ Vandermonde matrix

$$
\mathsf{B} = \begin{pmatrix}
1 & 1 & \cdots & 1 \\
x_1 & x_2 & \cdots & x_n \\
\vdots & \vdots & \ddots & \vdots \\
x_1^{n-1} & x_2^{n-1} & \cdots & x_n^{n-1}
\end{pmatrix}
$$

$H = [h_0, h_1, \ldots h_{2t-1}, \ldots, 0]$ is an n-vector that represents the coefficients of $h(x)$; $K = [k_0, k_1, \ldots k_{t-1}, 0, \ldots, 0]$ is an n-vector that represents the coefficient of $k(x)$; the $n \times n$ projection matrix P satisfies $H \cdot P = K$ (i.e. the first column is a vector led by 1 and followed by 0s, the second column till the t-th column are random vectors generated in a distributed fashion and shared among the parties [16], and the other columns are all zero vectors); $S = [s_1, s_2, \ldots, s_n]$ is an n-vector that represents the shares of $h(x)$; $R = [r_1, r_2, \ldots, r_n]$ is an n-vector that represents the shares of $k(x)$. Hence, we have $H \cdot \mathsf{B} = S$ and $K \cdot \mathsf{B} = R$. Moreover, because B is a Vandermonde matrix, it is always reversible as its determinant cannot be 0. Therefore, we have $S \cdot (\mathsf{B}^{-1} \cdot \mathsf{P} \cdot \mathsf{B}) = R$. Denote $\mathsf{T} = \mathsf{B}^{-1} \cdot \mathsf{P} \cdot \mathsf{B}$, we have $S \cdot \mathsf{T} = R$, where T can be jointly computed in a secure and distributed fashion. By Lemma 2, the $2t - 1$ degree polynomial $h(x)$ can be truncated into a $t - 1$ degree $k(x)$ in a secure and distributed fashion with the constant coefficient unchanged.

4.2   Our Proposed Scheme

Our proposed scheme works as follows: denote p as a large prime and g is a generator of a subgroup of $\mathbb{Z}_p^*$ in which the discrete logarithm cannot be solved in polynomial time. Suppose in the k-th time period, the secret $s \in \mathbb{Z}_p$ is shared among the parties $P_1, P_2, \ldots, P_n$ using a $t - 1$ degree polynomial $f^{(k)}(x) = a_0 + a_1 x + \cdots + a_{t-1} x^{t-1}$ over $\mathbb{Z}_p$ such that $s = a_0$, and the commitments $A_i = g^{a_i}$ for $i \in \{0, 1, \ldots, t-1\}$ are made public. Each party P_i's secret share is $s_i^{(k)} = f^{(k)}(x_i)$, and P_i can verify the validity of its share by

$$
g^{s_i^{(k)}} = \prod_{j=0}^{t-1} A_j^{x_i^j}
$$

In the share refreshment, each party P_i, for $i \in \{1, 2, \ldots, n\}$, performs as follows:

1. P_i generates a random $2t - 1$ degree polynomial as $\lambda_i(x) = \lambda_{i,1} x + \lambda_{i,2} x^2 + \cdots + \lambda_{i,2t-1} x^{2t-1}$ over $\mathbb{Z}_p$ such that $\lambda_i(0) = 0$. P_i also broadcasts $B_{i,j} = g^{\lambda_{i,j}}$ for $j \in \{1, 2, \ldots, 2t - 1\}$.

2. P_i computes $w_{i,j} = \lambda_i(x_j)$ and sends it to each other parties P_j using the secure channel. P_i can verify whether its received share $w_{j,i}$ from each other party is valid by

$$g^{w_{j,i}} = \prod_{k=1}^{2t-1} B_{j,k}^{x_i^k}$$

3. In order to achieve the optimal resilience property, once receiving the value $w_{j,i}$, P_i needs to further share this value among the parties in a (t, n)-threshold fashion. If some parties are found faulty in Step 2 or in Step 3, they will be disqualified from the protocol and their polynomials will be excluded. At this moment, the set of the remaining parties is denoted as Λ.

4. P_i computes $s_i = s_i^{(k)} + \sum_{j \in \Lambda} w_{j,i}$, and this value is a share of the $2t-1$ degree polynomial

$$h(x) = f^{(k)}(x) + \sum_{j \in \Lambda} \lambda_j(x) = h_0 + h_1 x + \cdots + h_{2t-1} x^{2t-1}$$

The commitments of $h(x)$ can be publicly computed as $C_i = g^{h_i} = A_i \cdot \prod_{j \in \Lambda} B_{j,i}$ for $i \in \{0, 1, \ldots, t-1\}$ and $C_I = g^{h_I} = \prod_{j \in \Lambda} B_{j,I}$ for $I \in \{t, t+1, \ldots, 2t-1\}$.

5. Finally, the parties jointly truncate the $2t-1$ degree polynomial $h(x)$ into a $t-1$ degree polynomial $k(x)$ with the constant coefficient unchanged. Denote $S = [s_1, s_2, \ldots, s_n]$ as the n-vector that represents the shares of $h(x)$, and $R = [r_1, r_2, \ldots, r_n]$ as the n-vector that represents the shares of $k(x)$, the truncation is done by $S \cdot T = R$, where T can be computed in a secure and distributed fashion as shown in Theorem 1. Now, $k(x)$ is the updated polynomial that will be used in the $(k+1)$-th time period as $f^{(k+1)}(x)$, and each party P_i holds a share $s_i^{(k+1)} = r_i$. Note that if any party P_i is found cheating in this step, the corresponding share s_i will be recovered by the uncorrupted parties. And this ensures that this step will always finish successfully.

4.3   Security Analysis

Theorem 2. *Our proposed PSS scheme is robust and secret in the presence of the mobile adversary who has the ability to corrupt any minority of the parties.*

Proof. We prove this theorem using the inductive method. Firstly, we assume that at initialisation of the protocol, the secret is properly shared among the parties through (t, n)-threshold secret sharing. Furthermore, we assume that in each time period $1, 2, \ldots, k$, the above theorem holds. And we prove that in the time period $k+1$, the adversary who has the ability to corrupt any minority of the parties can neither prevent the secret from being recovered nor learn any information of the secret.

Robustness: In each time period, the validity of the shares can be verified using the public commitments. Without loss of generality, we assume that the shares $s_1^{(k+1)}, s_2^{(k+1)}, \ldots, s_t^{(k+1)}$ are valid and they will be used to recover the secret. Denote $L_i = \prod_{j=1, j \neq i}^{t} x_j/(x_j - x_i)$ as the Lagrange coefficients for $i \in \{1, 2, \ldots, t\}$. Then we have

$$\sum_{i=1}^{t} s_i^{(k+1)} \cdot L_i = f^{(k+1)}(0) = f^{(k)}(0) + \sum_{j \in \Lambda} \lambda_j'(0) = s$$

where $\lambda_j'(x) = \lambda_{i,1}' x + \lambda_{i,2}' x^2 + \cdots + \lambda_{i,t-1}' x^{t-1}$. Although the polynomials $\lambda_j'(x)$ and $\lambda_j(x)$ are independent because of the randomised truncation, the equation $\lambda_j'(0) = \lambda_j(0) = 0$ always holds for all $j \in \Lambda$. Therefore, based on the assumption that the mobile adversary cannot corrupt more than $t - 1$ parties in time period $k + 1$, there exists at least t uncorrupted parties and the secret can be correctly recovered.

Secrecy: To prove that the proposed scheme achieves the secrecy property. We prove that there exists a PPT simulator $\mathcal{SIM}$ who can simulate the mobile adversary's view in share refreshment, and the simulated view is indistinguishable from the one in the real run of the protocol. Without loss of generality, we assume that the parties $P_1, P_2, \ldots, P_{t-1}$ are corrupted and the mobile adversary knows their shares $s_1^{(k)}, s_2^{(k)}, \ldots, s_{t-1}^{(k)}$. The simulator $\mathcal{SIM}$ works as follows:

1. Each party P_i generates a random $2t - 1$ degree polynomial as $\widetilde{\lambda}_i(x) = \widetilde{\lambda_{i,1}} x + \widetilde{\lambda_{i,2}} x^2 + \cdots + \widetilde{\lambda_{i,2t-1}} x^{2t-1}$ over $\mathbb{Z}_p$ such that $\widetilde{\lambda}_i(0) = 0$. P_i also broadcasts $\widetilde{B_{i,j}} = g^{\widetilde{\lambda_{i,j}}}$ for $j \in \{1, 2, \ldots, 2t - 1\}$.
2. P_i computes $\widetilde{w_{i,j}} = \widetilde{\lambda}_i(x_j)$ and sends it to each other party P_j using the secure channel. P_i can verify the validity of $\widetilde{w_{j,i}}$ using the public commitments $\widetilde{B_{j,k}}$ for $k \in \{1, 2, \ldots, 2t - 1\}$. Those values received by the corrupted parties are forwarded to the mobile adversary.
3. Once receiving the value $\widetilde{w_{j,i}}$, P_i further shares this value among the parties using (t, n)-threshold verifiable secret sharing. Similarly, any cheating party will be disqualified, and the set of the remaining parties is denoted as Λ.
4. In this step, the simulator $\mathcal{SIM}$ computes $s_i = s_i^{(k)} + \sum_{j \in \Lambda} \widetilde{w_{j,i}}$ for $i \in \{1, 2, \ldots, t - 1\}$, and it sends these values to the mobile adversary.
5. In order to truncate the $2t - 1$ degree polynomial $h(x)$ into a $t - 1$ degree polynomial $k(x)$ with the constant coefficient unchanged, each party P_i needs to share its value s_i among the parties in a (t, n)-threshold fashion. For those corrupted parties, the simulator $\mathcal{SIM}$ can share their values in the normal way. However, $\mathcal{SIM}$ does not know the values $s_t, s_{t+1}, \ldots, s_n$. To simulate the (t, n)-threshold secret sharing of these values, the simulator $\mathcal{SIM}$ computes

$$g^{s_i} = g^{s_i^{(k)}} \cdot \prod_{l \in \Lambda} g^{\widetilde{w_{l,i}}} = \prod_{j=0}^{t-1} A_j^{x_i^j} \cdot \prod_{l \in \Lambda} g^{\widetilde{w_{l,i}}}$$

for $i \in \{t, t + 1, \ldots, n\}$. Then, for each of the value $\{g^{s_i}\}_{i \in \{t, t+1, \ldots, n\}}$, $\mathcal{SIM}$ selects $t - 1$ random values $\{\epsilon_i\}_{i \in \{1, 2, \ldots, t-1\}}$ and sends these values to the $t - 1$ corrupted parties respectively. Denote $\mathcal{M}$ as the following $t \times t$ matrix

$$M = \begin{pmatrix} 1 & 0 & 0 & \ldots & 0 \\ 1 & x_1 & x_1^2 & \ldots & x_1^{t-1} \\ 1 & x_2 & x_2^2 & \ldots & x_2^{t-1} \\ & & \vdots & & \\ 1 & x_{t-1} & x_{t-1}^2 & \ldots & x_{t-1}^{t-1} \end{pmatrix}$$

and $\sigma_{i,j}$ is the (i,j)-th entry of M^{-1}. Now, $\mathcal{SIM}$ broadcasts the commitments $\{D_i\}_{i\in\{0,1,\ldots,t-1\}}$, where $D_0 = g^{s_i}$ and $D_j = (g^{s_i})^{\sigma_{j,1}} \cdot \prod_{l=1}^{t-1}(g^{\epsilon_l})^{\sigma_{j,l+1}}$ for $j \in \{1,2,\ldots,t-1\}$. Note that these commitments ensures that the mobile adversary will accept the values $\{\epsilon_i\}_{i\in\{1,2,\ldots,t-1\}}$ as the shares of s_i. As follows, the parties jointly trancate the polynomial $h(x)$ into $k(x)$.

It is obvious that the above simulation can finish in polynomial time. Now, we show that the mobile adversary cannot distinguish the above simulated conversation from a real run of the protocol.

- **Indistinguishability of information in Step 1 and 2:** the $2t - 1$ degree polynomials $\{\lambda_i(x)\}$ and $\{\widetilde{\lambda}_i(x)\}$ for $i \in \{1,2,\ldots,n\}$ are randomly selected both in the real protocol and in the simulation. Hence, they are indistinguishable.
- **Indistinguishability of information in Step 3:** both the real protocol and the simulation share the values $w_{j,i}$ and $\widetilde{w_{j,i}}$ among the parties using a random $t - 1$ degree polynomial. Hence, they are indistinguishable.
- **Indistinguishability of information in Step 4:** the s_i values hold by the corrupted parties are randomly distributed in $\mathbb{Z}_p$ both in the real protocol and in the simulation. Hence, they are indistinguishable.
- **Indistinguishability of information in Step 5:** the mobile adversary's view of sharing the values $\{s_i\}_{i\in\{1,2,\ldots,n\}}$ is consistent both in the real protocol and in the simulation. Moreover, by Theorem 1, the joint polynomial truncation can be done in a secure and distributed fashion. Hence, the real protocol and the simulation in this step is also indistinguishable.

Therefore, the simulated view cannot be distinguished from the one in the real run of the protocol. In other words, the mobile adversary cannot learn any information of the secret in time period $k + 1$.

4.4   Some Discussions

Once the reason is clear why Herzberg's PSS scheme fails to maintain its security in our new threat model, it is quite natural to come up with the idea of using polynomials with higher degrees to update the shares in the share refreshment and then truncating the resulting polynomial to the desirable degree. However, we show that if one uses Ben-Or's polynomial truncation method directly, the construction still suffers the same problem as in Herzberg's PSS scheme.

Ben-Or's original method is also capable of truncating a $2t-1$ degree polynomial into a $t-1$ degree polynomial. But it keeps the first t coefficients unchanged rather than just keeping the constant coefficient unchanged as in our proposed scheme. Recall that $\lambda(x)$ is the polynomial used to refresh the shares, $h(x)$ is the polynomial before truncation and $k(x)$ is the polynomial after the truncation. Their shares are w_i, s_i, r_i, respectively. Denote $p(x)$ as a polynomial with degree $t-1$ containing the first t coefficients of the polynomial $\lambda(x)$. The relationship $h(x)-k(x) = \lambda(x)-p(x)$ always holds if Ben-Or's polynomial truncation method is used directly. Thanks to the homomorphic property of SS, the value $w_i+r_i-s_i$ represents a share for the polynomial $p(x)$. Therefore, if the mobile adversary $\mathcal{A}$ is assumed to corrupt $t-1$ parties, $\mathcal{A}$ can obtain $t-1$ shares of $p(x)$. And this implies that $\mathcal{A}$ is able to launch the same attack as shown in Sect. 3.2. This is why we have adapted a variant of Ben-Or's method in our proposed scheme so that the truncation is performed in the randomised fashion instead of a fixed one.

5 Conclusion

In this paper, we revisited the research of provably secure and optimal resilient PSS. We discussed the negative aspects caused by the adjacent assumption which is widely used in the existing PSS schemes. And this motivates us to consider whether this assumption can be removed from the threat model in PSS schemes. However, we showed that if it is removed, many existing schemes will become insecure. We then used the polynomial truncation method to improve Herzberg's PSS scheme, making it secure without the adjacent assumption. To the best of our knowledge, this is the first PSS scheme satisfying this feature.

Acknowledgement. This work was partially supported by the National Natural Science Foundation of China (Grant No. 61572303, 61772326, 61822202, 61672010, 61702168, 61872087). We are very grateful to the anonymous reviewers for pointing out an error in a previous version of this paper as well as many valuable comments.

References

1. Almansa, J.F., Damgård, I., Nielsen, J.B.: Simplified threshold RSA with adaptive and proactive security. In: Vaudenay, S. (ed.) EUROCRYPT 2006. LNCS, vol. 4004, pp. 593–611. Springer, Heidelberg (2006). https://doi.org/10.1007/11761679_35
2. Baron, J., Defrawy, K., Lampkins, J., Ostrovsky, R.: How to withstand mobile virus attacks, revisited. In: ACM Symposium on Principles of Distributed Computing (PODC 2014), pp. 293–302 (2014)
3. Ben-Or, M., Goldwasser, S., Wigderson, A.: Completeness theorems for non-cryptographic fault-tolerant distributed computation. In: Proceedings of the 20th ACM Symposium on Theory of Computing (STOC 1988), pp. 1–10 (1988)
4. Benaloh, J.C.: Secret sharing homomorphisms: keeping shares of a secret secret (extended abstract). In: Odlyzko, A.M. (ed.) CRYPTO 1986. LNCS, vol. 263, pp. 251–260. Springer, Heidelberg (1987). https://doi.org/10.1007/3-540-47721-7_19

5. Blakley, R.: Safeguarding cryptographic keys. In: Proceedings of the National Computer Conference, vol. 48, pp. 313–317 (1979)
6. Cachin, C., Kursawe, K., Lysyanskaya, A., Strobl, R.: Asynchronous verifiable secret sharing and proactive cryptosystems. In: 9th ACM Conference on Computer and Communication Security (CCS 2002), pp. 88–97 (2002)
7. Canetti, R., Gennaro, R., Jarecki, S., Krawczyk, H., Rabin, T.: Adaptive security for threshold cryptosystems. In: Wiener, M. (ed.) CRYPTO 1999. LNCS, vol. 1666, pp. 98–116. Springer, Heidelberg (1999). https://doi.org/10.1007/3-540-48405-1_7
8. Canetti, R., Halevi, S., Herzberg, A.: Maintaining authenticated communication in the presence of break-ins. In: Proceedings of the 16th ACM Symposium on Principles of Distributed Computing (PODC 1997), pp. 15–24 (1997)
9. Canetti, R., Herzberg, A.: Maintaining security in the presence of transient faults. In: Desmedt, Y.G. (ed.) CRYPTO 1994. LNCS, vol. 839, pp. 425–438. Springer, Heidelberg (1994). https://doi.org/10.1007/3-540-48658-5_38
10. Chaum, D., Crépeau, C., Damgård, I.: Multiparty unconditionally secure protocols. In: Proceedings of the 20th ACM Symposium on Theory of Computing (STOC 1988), pp. 11–19 (1988)
11. Feldman, P.: A practical scheme for non-interactive verifiable secret sharing. In: Proceedings of the 28th IEEE Symposium on Foundation of Computer Science (FOCS 1987), pp. 427–437 (1987)
12. Frankel, Y., Gemmell, P., MacKenzie, P., Yung, M.: Optimal-resilience proactive public-key cryptosystems. In: Proceedings of the 38th IEEE Symposium on the Foundations of Computer Science (FOCS 1997), pp. 384–393 (1997)
13. Frankel, Y., Gemmell, P., MacKenzie, P.D., Yung, M.: Proactive RSA. In: Kaliski, B.S. (ed.) CRYPTO 1997. LNCS, vol. 1294, pp. 440–454. Springer, Heidelberg (1997). https://doi.org/10.1007/BFb0052254
14. Frankel, Y., MacKenzie, P., Yung, M.: Adaptively-secure optimal-resilience proactive RSA. In: Lam, K.-Y., Okamoto, E., Xing, C. (eds.) ASIACRYPT 1999. LNCS, vol. 1716, pp. 180–194. Springer, Heidelberg (1999). https://doi.org/10.1007/978-3-540-48000-6_15
15. Frankel, Y., MacKenzie, P.D., Yung, M.: Adaptive security for the additive-sharing based proactive RSA. In: Kim, K. (ed.) PKC 2001. LNCS, vol. 1992, pp. 240–263. Springer, Heidelberg (2001). https://doi.org/10.1007/3-540-44586-2_18
16. Gennaro, R., Jarecki, S., Krawczyk, H., Rabin, T.: Secure distributed key generation for discrete-log based cryptosystems. J. Cryptol. 1, 51–83 (2007)
17. Goldreich, O., Micali, S., Wigderson, A.: How to play any mental game, or a completeness theorem for protocols with honest majority. In: Proceedings of the 19th ACM Symposium on Theory of Computing (STOC 1987), pp. 218–229 (1987)
18. Hegland, A., Winjum, E., Mjolsnes, S., Rong, C., Kure, O., Spilling, P.: A survey of key management in ad hoc networks. IEEE Commun. 8(3), 48–66 (2006)
19. Herzberg, A., Jakobsson, M., Jarecki, S., Krawczyk, H., Yung, M.: Proactive public key and signature systems. In: 4th ACM Conference on Computer and Communication Security (CCS 1997), pp. 100–110 (1997)
20. Herzberg, A., Jarecki, S., Krawczyk, H., Yung, M.: Proactive secret sharing or: how to cope with perpetual leakage. In: Coppersmith, D. (ed.) CRYPTO 1995. LNCS, vol. 963, pp. 339–352. Springer, Heidelberg (1995). https://doi.org/10.1007/3-540-44750-4_27
21. Jarecki, S.: Proactive secret sharing and public key cryptosystems. Master's thesis, Department of Electrical Engineering and Computer Science, MIT (1995)

22. Nikov, V., Nikova, S.: On proactive secret sharing schemes. In: Handschuh, H., Hasan, M.A. (eds.) SAC 2004. LNCS, vol. 3357, pp. 308–325. Springer, Heidelberg (2004). https://doi.org/10.1007/978-3-540-30564-4_22
23. Ostrovsky, R., Yung, M.: How to withstand mobile virus attacks. In: Proceedings of the 10th ACM Symposium on the Principle of Distributed Computing (PODC 1991), pp. 51–61 (1991)
24. Pedersen, T.P.: Non-interactive and information-theoretic secure verifiable secret sharing. In: Feigenbaum, J. (ed.) CRYPTO 1991. LNCS, vol. 576, pp. 129–140. Springer, Heidelberg (1992). https://doi.org/10.1007/3-540-46766-1_9
25. Rabin, T.: A simplified approach to threshold and proactive RSA. In: Krawczyk, H. (ed.) CRYPTO 1998. LNCS, vol. 1462, pp. 89–104. Springer, Heidelberg (1998). https://doi.org/10.1007/BFb0055722
26. Rabin, T., Ben-Or, M.: Verifiable secret sharing and multiparty protocols with honest majority. In: Proceedings of the 21st ACM Symposium on Theory of Computing (STOC 1989), pp. 73–85 (1989)
27. Schultz, D., Liskov, B., Liskov, M.: MPSS: mobile proactive secret sharing. ACM Trans. Inf. Syst. Secur. **13**(4), 34 (2010)
28. Shamir, A.: How to share a secret. In: Proceedings of 22nd Communication of ACM, pp. 612–613 (1979)
29. Stinson, D.R., Wei, R.: Unconditionally secure proactive secret sharing scheme with combinatorial structures. In: Heys, H., Adams, C. (eds.) SAC 1999. LNCS, vol. 1758, pp. 200–214. Springer, Heidelberg (2000). https://doi.org/10.1007/3-540-46513-8_15
30. Yung, M.: The "mobile adversary" paradigm in distributed computation and systems. In: ACM Symposium on Principles of Distributed Computing (PODC 2015), pp. 171–172 (2015)
31. Zhou, L., Haas, Z.: Securing ad hoc networks. IEEE Netw. **13**, 24–30 (1999)
32. Zhou, L., Schneider, F., Renesse, R.: APSS: proactive secret sharing in asynchronous systems. ACM Trans. Inf. Syst. Secur. **8**(3), 259–286 (2005)

A Coin-Free Oracle-Based Augmented Black Box Framework

Kyosuke Yamashita[1]($\boxtimes$), Mehdi Tibouchi[1,2], and Masayuki Abe[1,2]

[1] Graduate School of Informatics, Kyoto University, Kyoto, Japan
yamashita.kyousuke.75w@st.kyoto-u.ac.jp, abe.masayuki.7a@kyoto-u.ac.jp
[2] Secure Platform Laboratories, NTT Corporation, Tokyo, Japan
tibouchi.mehdi@lab.ntt.co.jp

Abstract. After the work of Impagliazzo and Rudich (STOC, 1989), the black box framework has become one of the main research domain of cryptography. However black box techniques say nothing about non-black box techniques such as making use of zero-knowledge proofs. Brakerski *et al.* introduced a new black box framework named *augmented* black box framework, in which they gave a zero-knowledge proof oracle in addition to a base primitive oracle (TCC, 2011). They showed a construction of a non-interactive zero knowledge proof system based on a witness indistinguishable proof system oracle. They presented augmented black box construction of chosen ciphertext secure public key encryption scheme based on chosen plaintext secure public key encryption scheme and augmented black box separation between one-way function and key agreement.

In this paper we simplify the work of Brakerski *et al.* by introducing a proof system oracle without witness indistinguishability, named *coin-free* proof system oracle, that aims to give the same construction and separation results of previous work. As a result, the augmented black box framework becomes easier to handle. Since our oracle is not witness indistinguishable, our result encompasses the result of previous work.

Keywords: Black box construction · Zero-knowledge proof · NIZK · Witness indistinguishability

1 Introduction

Investigating the relationships between cryptographic primitives is one of the most important task in theoretical cryptography. After the work of Impagliazzo and Rudich [6], the black box framework has become one of the main research domain of cryptography. Non-black box techniques are also extensively studied, whereas black box techniques say nothing about them. A widely known non-black box construction result is the work of Naor and Yung [8], which makes use of a zero-knowledge (ZK) proof [5] to construct a chosen ciphertext secure public key encryption scheme (CCA-PKE) based on a chosen plaintext secure public key encryption scheme (CPA-PKE).

© Springer Nature Switzerland AG 2019
R. Steinfeld and T. H. Yuen (Eds.): ProvSec 2019, LNCS 11821, pp. 265–272, 2019.
https://doi.org/10.1007/978-3-030-31919-9_15

·Although black box and non-black box techniques are developed independently each other, a new framework that combines them came into existence. Brakerski *et al.* [2] introduced the *augmented* black box framework, which makes use of a ZK oracle in addition to a cryptographic primitive oracle. They presented an oracle that instantiates a witness indistinguishable (WI) proof system [4] and showed that they could construct a non-interactive zero-knowledge proof (NIZK) based on the oracle in a black box manner. They demonstrated the power of the framework by showing construction and separation results; the Naor-Yung construction [8], and the separation between one-way function (OWF) and key agreement (KA) [3] in their model respectively.

Here we explain the motivation of our work. In the black box research, making an oracle that implements a base primitive simpler is an important direction. Introducing a simplified oracle helps to handle the oracle. Moreover it may make security proofs simpler. One of the major black box technique is relativizing reduction [9], which assures that a black box construction/reduction result holds relative to any oracle that implements a base primitive. In the beginning of the line of the black box task, researchers treated simple oracles such as implementing OWF [8]. However as more sophisticated primitives appeared, researchers had to deal with oracles that implement these primitives in the black box framework. For instance they began to handle oracles implementing trapdoor permutation [1,12], which led more advanced security proof. Moreover in [2], the augmented black box framework was accompanied by further complicated oracle that implements a NIZK. Although the augmented black box framework is an elegant framework, security proofs in this framework might become cumbersome task due to the high complexity of the oracle. Thus it it fruitful to simplify the oracle in the augmented black box framework.

In this paper we simplify the work of [2] by introducing a simpler proof system oracle without witness indistinguishability that aims to give the same construction and separation results of previous work. More concrete we simplify the interface of the proof system oracle and show the construction of a WI proof system from the simplified oracle. Then our result encompasses the results of [2], as the new oracle implements a general proof system.

2   Preliminaries

We follow the terminologies in [2]. Throughout this paper $n \in \mathbb{N}$ denotes the security parameter. We denote polynomial functions and negligible functions by poly and negl respectively. An oracle machine is a Turing machine which is allowed to make queries to an oracle. We write M^O an oracle machine M with oracle access to an oracle O. For any $\mathcal{L} \in \mathtt{NP}^O$, we let $R_{\mathcal{L}}$ denote an NP-relationship associated with $\mathcal{L}$. For an oracle O, we say that a primitive P *exists* relative to O if there exists a secure implementation f^O of P.

Definition 1. *A tuple of Turing machines* (Crs, Prv, Vrf, CrsSim, PrvSim) *that work as follows is a* non-interactive zero-knowledge proof system *for a language* $\mathcal{L}$ *where* Vrf *is deterministic and others are probabilistic:*

Crs: $crs \leftarrow \mathsf{Crs}(1^n)$ takes 1^n, and outputs crs.

Prv: $\pi \leftarrow \mathsf{Prv}(crs, x, w)$ takes crs, an instance x and a witness w, and outputs a proof π or $\perp$.

Vrf: $b \leftarrow \mathsf{Vrf}(crs, x, \pi)$ takes crs, an instance x and a proof π, and outputs $b \in \{0, 1\}$.

CrsSim: $(crs, \tau) \leftarrow \mathsf{CrsSim}(1^n)$ takes 1^n, and outputs τ and crs.

PrvSim: $\pi \leftarrow \mathsf{PrvSim}(crs, x, \tau)$ takes crs, an instance x and τ, and outputs π.

Definition 2. *A NIZK* $(\mathsf{Crs}, \mathsf{Prv}, \mathsf{Vrf}, \mathsf{CrsSim}, \mathsf{PrvSim})$ *for a language* $\mathcal{L}$ *is a NIZK with* perfect complete, statistical sound *and* adaptive black box zero-knowledge *properties if it has the following properties;*

perfect completeness: *for any* $n \in \mathbb{N}$, *for any* $(x, w) \in R_{\mathcal{L}}$ *and any* $crs \in \{0, 1\}^{poly(n)}$, $\mathsf{Vrf}(crs, x, \mathsf{Prv}(crs, x, w)) = 1$;

statistical soundness: *for any* $n \in \mathbb{N}$, *for any* $x \notin \mathcal{L}$ *and any* $\pi \in \{0, 1\}^{poly(n)}$, $\Pr_{crs \leftarrow \mathsf{Crs}(1^n)} \mathsf{Vrf}(crs, x, \pi) = 1 \leq negl$; *and*

adaptive black box zero-knowledge: *for any adversary* $\mathcal{A}$, *the following is negligible;*

$$
\left| \Pr \begin{bmatrix} crs \leftarrow \mathsf{Crs}(1^n); \\ (x, w) \leftarrow \mathcal{A}(crs); & : \mathcal{A}(\pi) = 1 \\ \pi \leftarrow \mathsf{Prv}(crs, x, w) & \wedge (x, w) \in R_{\mathcal{L}} \end{bmatrix} \right.
$$
$$
\left. - \Pr \begin{bmatrix} (crs, \tau) \leftarrow \mathsf{CrsSim}(1^n); \\ (x, w) \leftarrow \mathcal{A}(crs); & : \mathcal{A}(\pi) = 1 \\ \pi \leftarrow \mathsf{PrvSim}(crs, x, \tau) & \wedge (x, w) \in R_{\mathcal{L}} \end{bmatrix} \right|.
$$

We simply denote a NIZK $(\mathsf{Crs}, \mathsf{Prv}, \mathsf{Vrf}, \mathsf{CrsSim}, \mathsf{PrvSim})$ with perfect complete, statistical sound and adaptive black box zero-knowledge properties by a NIZK.

3   WI Proof System Oracle

In this section we review [2]. They introduced an instantiation of a WI proof system oracle and presented a construction of a NIZK based on the oracle. Moreover they defined the augmented black box framework and demonstrated the power of the framework by showing the construction and separation results.

Definition 3. *A pair* (P, V) *of machines that works as follows is a* proof system *for a language* $\mathcal{L}$;

P: $\pi \leftarrow \mathsf{P}(x, w, r)$ takes an instance x, a witness w and a random coin r, and outputs a proof π, and

V: $b \leftarrow \mathsf{V}(x, \pi)$ takes an instance x and a proof π, and outputs a bit b, where V accepts π if $b = 1$ and V rejects otherwise.

Definition 4. *A proof system* (P, V) *for a language* $\mathcal{L}$ *is a* proof system with perfect complete *and* statistical sound *properties if it has the following properties;*

perfect completeness: *for any* $n \in \mathbb{N}$, *for any* $(x, w) \in R_{\mathcal{L}}$, *and any random coin* $r \in \{0, 1\}^n$, $\mathsf{V}(x, \mathsf{P}(x, w, r)) = 1$;
perfect soundness: *for any* $n \in \mathbb{N}$, *any* $x \notin \mathcal{L}$, *and any* $\pi \in \{0, 1\}^{\mathrm{poly}(n)}$, $\mathsf{V}(x, \mathsf{P}(x, w, r)) = 0$.

We simply say a proof system with perfect complete and perfect sound properties a proof system.

Definition 5. *A proof system* $\mathsf{WI} = (\mathsf{P}, \mathsf{V})$ *for a language* $\mathcal{L}$ *is a* witness indistinguishable *proof system, if for any adversary* $\mathcal{A}$ *the advantage* $|\Pr[\mathtt{ExptWI}_{\mathcal{A}}(n) = 1] - \frac{1}{2}|$ *of the following experiment* $\mathtt{ExptWI}_{\mathcal{A}}(n)$ *is negligible;*

$$
\begin{aligned}
&(x, w_0, w_1) \leftarrow \mathcal{A}^{\mathsf{WI}}(1^n); \\
&b \leftarrow \{0, 1\}; \ r \leftarrow \{0, 1\}^n; && \text{if } (x, w_0), (x, w_1) \in R_{\mathcal{L}} \\
&\pi \leftarrow \mathsf{P}(x, w_b, r); && : && \text{output 1 iff } b' = b \\
&b' = \mathcal{A}^{\mathsf{WI}}(1^n, \pi) && \text{else output a random bit.}
\end{aligned}
$$

Instantiation of a WI Proof System Oracle

For the reminder of this paper, we set $\mathcal{L} = \mathsf{CIRCUIT\text{-}SAT}^O$ where O is an oracle that implements a primitive. The WI proof system oracle $\mathsf{WI} = (\mathsf{P}, \mathsf{V})$ is defined as follows;

prover oracle: The prover oracle P is a random function s.t. $\mathsf{P} : \{0, 1\}^{3n} \to \{0, 1\}^{7n}$. The input is parsed as tuples $(x, w, r) \in \{0, 1\}^n \times \{0, 1\}^n \times \{0, 1\}^n$. Note that P does not check if $(x, w) \in R_{\mathcal{L}}$.
verifier oracle: The verifier oracle V is a function s.t. $\mathsf{V} : \{0, 1\}^{8n} \to \{0, 1\}$. The input is parsed as pairs $(x, \pi) \in \{0, 1\}^n \times \{0, 1\}^{7n}$. V is defines as

$$
\mathsf{V}(x, \pi) = \begin{cases} 1 & \text{if } \exists w, r \text{ s.t. } \pi = \mathsf{P}(x, w, r) \wedge (x, w) \in R_{\mathcal{L}} \\ 0 & \text{otherwise.} \end{cases}
$$

They showed that WI is a WI proof system oracle.

Theorem 1. *Let* O *be an oracle s.t. there exists a OWF* f^O *relative to* O, *and* WI *be a WI proof system oracle. Then* f^O *is one-way relative to* O *and* WI.

Theorem 2. *There exists a construction of a NIZK with perfect complete, statistical sound and adaptive black box zero-knowledge properties, based on* WI.

Definition 6. *There exists an (fully) augmented black box construction of a primitive* Q *based on a primitive* P *if there are PPTs* G *and* S *s.t.*

- *for any oracle* O *and WI proof system oracle* WI *for* NP^O *where* O *implements* P, *the oracle machine* $G^{O,\mathsf{WI}}$ *implements* Q; *and*
- *for any oracle* O, *WI proof system oracle* WI *for* NP^O *and adversary* $\mathcal{A}$ *that breaks* $G^{O,\mathsf{WI}}$, *the adversary* $S^{\mathcal{A},O,\mathsf{WI}}$ *breaks* O *or breaks witness indistinguishability of* WI.

Theorem 3. *There is an augmented black box construction of a CCA-PKE based on a CPA-PKE.*

Theorem 4. *There is no augmented black box construction of KA based on OWF.*

4   Simplified Proof System Oracle

4.1   Coin-Free Proof System Oracle

In this section we introduce a more simplified proof system oracle. In [2], they constructed a NIZK by making use of witness indistinguishability of WI proof system oracle defined in Sect. 3. However as the prover oracle is a random function, we observe that we can omit the random coin r from its interface, resulting a simpler prover oracle. We first introduce such simplified proof system oracle. Then we present that we can construct a WI proof system based on the simplified oracle in the black box manner.

Definition 7. *A pair* (P, V) *of oracles is a* coin-free proof system oracle *for a language* $\mathcal{L}$ *if it works as following;*

prover oracle: *The prover oracle* P *is a random function* $\mathsf{P} : \{0,1\}^{2n} \to \{0,1\}^{6n}$. *The input is parsed as pairs of the form* $(x, w) \in \{0,1\}^n \times \{0,1\}^n$. *Note that* P *does not check if* $(x, w) \in R_{\mathcal{L}}$.

verifier oracle: *The verifier oracle* V *is* $\mathsf{V} : \{0,1\}^{7n} \to \{0,1\}$. *The input is parsed as pairs of the form* $(x, \pi) \in \{0,1\}^n \times \{0,1\}^{6n}$. V *is defined as*

$$
\mathsf{V}(x, \pi) = \begin{cases} 1 & \text{if } \exists w \text{ s.t. } \pi = \mathsf{P}_n(x, w) \ \wedge \ (x, w) \in R_{\mathcal{L}} \\ 0 & \text{otherwise.} \end{cases}
$$

It is clear that (P, V) constitutes a proof system. We denote a coin-free proof system oracle by $\mathsf{CF} = (\mathsf{P}, \mathsf{V})$. We remark that CF is no longer witness indistinguishable, since an adversary, given a proof π, can decide which of witness w_0 or w_1 was used to generate π by making queries $\mathsf{P}(x, w_0)$ and $\mathsf{P}(x, w_1)$.

Construction of WI Proof System

We show the construction of a WI proof system based on a coin-free proof system oracle. Our construction is similar to the construction of the NIZK in [2]. The key difference is an "extended" language. We introduce a language that includes randomness, and this randomness yields the witness indistinguishability. However it does not work simply adding a randomness in the new language (if so, the WI prover have to send the randomness itself to prove her knowledge about it). Thus we include a OWF in the new language and let the WI prover to prove her knowledge about the output of OWF. A OWF f is ϵ-OWF or has ϵ-*security* if for any PPT $\mathcal{A}$, $\Pr[\mathcal{A}(f(x)) \in f^{-1}(f(x))] \leq \mathsf{negl}$.

Let O be an oracle and $\mathsf{CF} = (\mathsf{P}, \mathsf{V})$ be a coin-free proof system oracle for $\mathcal{L}$ s.t. there exists an ϵ-OWF $f^O : \{0,1\}^n \to \{0,1\}^{2n}$ relative to O and CF. We can argue this due to Theorem 1 and the fact that a WI proof system implies a proof system generally. We define $\mathcal{L}' := \{(x, c) \mid \exists \ w, r \text{ s.t. } c = f^O(r) \wedge (x, w) \in R_{\mathcal{L}}\}$.

We construct a WI proof system $(\mathsf{Prv}, \mathsf{Vrf})$ as follows:

Prv: $\hat{\pi} \leftarrow \mathsf{Prv}(x, w)$
   Given $x, w \in \{0,1\}^n$. Choose $r \leftarrow \{0,1\}^n$, and compute $c = f^O(r)$. Let $x' := (x, c)$ and $w' := (w, r)$. Note that if $(x, w) \in R_{\mathcal{L}}$ then $(x', w') \in R_{\mathcal{L}'}$.

Apply Levin reduction to $(x', w') \in R_{\mathcal{L}'}$ to obtain $(\hat{x}, \hat{w}) \in R_{\mathcal{L}}$. Compute $\pi = \mathsf{P}(\hat{x}, \hat{w})$, and output $\hat{\pi} := (c, \pi)$.

Vrf: $b \leftarrow \mathsf{Vrf}(x, \hat{\pi})$

Given $x \in \{0,1\}^n$ and $\hat{\pi} = (c, \pi) \in \{0,1\}^n \times \{0,1\}^{6n}$. Let $x' := (x, c)$. Apply Levin reduction to $x' \in \mathcal{L}'$ to obtain $\hat{x} \in \mathcal{L}$. Output $b = \mathsf{V}(\hat{x}, \pi)$.

Lemma 1. *The above* $(\mathsf{Crs}, \mathsf{Prv})$ *is a WI proof system for* $\mathcal{L} \in \mathsf{NP}^O$.

Proof. The perfect completeness property is immediate. We show that $(\mathsf{Prv}, \mathsf{Vrf})$ is perfectly sound. Considering the definition of $\mathcal{L}'$, we can apply Karp reduction [7] to an instance of $\mathcal{L}$ to obtain an instance of $\mathcal{L}'$. Thus if there exists an instance $(x, c) \notin \mathcal{L}'$ but applying Levin reduction results in an instance $\hat{x} \in \mathcal{L}$, then we can break the perfect soundness of CF.

We show the witness indistinguishability of $(\mathsf{Prv}, \mathsf{Vrf})$ following the idea of the proof of Theorem 3 in [2]. Let $\mathcal{A}$ be an adversary and q be a polynomial upper bound on the number of queries that $\mathcal{A}$ can make. We note that an adversary in the experiment $\mathtt{ExptWI}$ has oracle access to O and CF. We abuse notation to write $\mathcal{A}$ to denote $\mathcal{A}^{O, \mathsf{CF}}$. Without loss of generality, we assume that $\mathcal{A}$ outputs values (x, w_0, w_1) with $(x, w_0), (x, w_1) \in R_{\mathcal{L}}$. Then $\mathcal{A}$ is given a proof $\hat{\pi} = (c, \pi)$ for the instance (x, w_b) where $b \in \{0, 1\}$ and tries to decide whether w_0 or w_1 was used to generate $\hat{\pi}$. In the following we first define an bad event s.t. $\mathcal{A}$ breaks the witness indistinguishability by accident and prove that such an event occurs only with negligible probability. Then we show that, assuming such event never happens, if $\mathcal{A}$ breaks the witness indistinguishability of $(\mathsf{Prv}, \mathsf{Vrf})$, then there exists an adversary that breaks the ϵ-security of f^O.

Let $\mathtt{Spoof}$ be the event that $\mathcal{A}$ makes a query $\mathsf{V}(x^*, \pi^*)$ returning 1, yet no query $\mathsf{P}(x^*, w^*)$ with $(x^*, w^*) \in R_{\mathcal{L}}$ was made previously. We prove that the probability $\mathtt{Spoof}$ occurs is negligible. At most 2^{2n} elements are uniformly distributed in the domain of P, and the size of the range is 2^{6n}. Although making a P-query reveals one point in the range, it tells nothing about other points since P is a random function. Thus the probability that $\mathcal{A}$ makes a query $\mathsf{V}(x^*, \pi^*)$ returning 1 yet π^* was not output by P previously is at most 2^{-4n}. Taking a union bound, the probability that $\mathtt{Spoof}$ occurs is at most $q \cdot 2^{-4n}$.

We prove that, assuming $\mathtt{Spoof}$ never occurs, if $(\mathsf{Prv}, \mathsf{Vrf})$ is not witness indistinguishable then there exists an adversary $\mathcal{A}'$ that breaks the ϵ-security of f^O. Since P is a random function, the adversary $\mathcal{A}$ that breaks the witness indistinguishability of $(\mathsf{Prv}, \mathsf{Vrf})$ makes the P-query resulting in $\hat{\pi}$. In the course of such computation, $\mathcal{A}$ has to find the pre-image of c as c is independent of the witness w_b. Thus an adversary $\mathcal{A}'$, given c, simulates $\mathcal{A}$ and outputs the pre-image of c, which contradicts the ϵ-security of f^O. Summing the above discussion, the probability that an adversary breaks witness indistinguishability of $(\mathsf{Prv}, \mathsf{Vrf})$ is at most $q \cdot 2^{-4n} + \epsilon$, which is negligible.

Corollary 1. *Let O be an oracle that implements a primitive Q, WI be a WI proof system oracle and CF be a coin-free proof system oracle. If there exists an augmented black box construction of a primitive P based on O and CF, then there exists an augmented black box construction of P based on O and WI.*

We say an augmented black box construction that making use of a coin-free proof system oracle a *simplified* augmented black box construction.

4.2 Construction

We show that we can construct a CCA-PKE based on a CPA-PKE in the simplified augmented black box model. If we can construct a NIZK, then we can construct a CCA-PKE by following the Naor-Yung construction [8]. Due to the construction of the NIZK in Theorem 3 and Lemma 1, we can construct a NIZK based on a coin-free proof system oracle. Thus we can construct a CCA-PKE based on a CPA-PKE in the simplified augmented black box model.

Let O be an oracle that implements a CPA-PKE $(\mathsf{G}, \mathsf{E}, \mathsf{D})$ and $\mathsf{CF} = (\mathsf{P}, \mathsf{V})$ be a coin-free proof system oracle. As shown in the previous discussion, we can construct a NIZK $(\mathsf{Crs}, \mathsf{Prv}, \mathsf{Vrf}, \mathsf{CrsSim}, \mathsf{PrvSim})$ in the simplified augmented black box model. Moreover we can translate $(\mathsf{Prv}, \mathsf{Vrf})$ into a *simulation sound* NIZK [10] $(\mathsf{Prv}_{ssZK}, \mathsf{Vrf}_{ssZK})$ for a language
$$\mathcal{L}' = \{(c_0, c_1, pk_0, pk_1) \mid \exists\, m, r_0, r_1 \text{ s.t.} c_0 = \mathsf{E}^O_{pk_0}(m, r_0) \ \wedge \ c_1 = \mathsf{E}^O_{pk_1}(m, r_1)\}.$$

Lemma 2. *Let O be an oracle that implements a CPA-PKE and CF be a coin-free proof system oracle. We can construct a CCA-PKE based on O and CF.*

4.3 Separation

As stated in Sect. 1, one of the motivation of our work is to simplify security proofs in the augmented black box framework. However, in the separation proof of [2], they did not make use of the witness indistinguishability (i.e., the random coin r) of the proof system oracle, resulting the same proof logic in the simplified augmented black box framework. (We omit the construction of the adversary because of space limitation, and describe the adversary in the full version of this paper [11].) Thus, we can construct the same adversary by simply replacing a WI proof system oracle with a coin-free proof system oracle. To sum up the above, we obtain the following lemma:

Lemma 3. *Let O be a random oracle and CF be a coin-free proof system oracle s.t. a OWF f exists relative to O and CF. There is no simplified augmented black box construction of KA with perfect completeness based on f.*

5 Conclusion

In this paper we introduced coin-free proof system oracle, a more simplified one, and showed the same construction and separation results as in [2]. Thus when we apply the augmented black box framework to some black box work, we become to be able to prove it in more simplified and general condition.

There are open questions still remain. One of such question is to show other construction or separation results in the simplified black box model (especially to known black box separation results). Focusing on specific topic, the construction of the NIZK is based on a proof system oracle for NP-complete language, which seems too strong. It is still debatable whether we can construct a NIZK based on a proof system oracle for more restricted language.

References

1. Boneh, D., Papakonstantinou, P., Rackoff, C., Vahlis, Y., Waters, B.: On the impossibility of basing identity based encryption on trapdoor permutations. In: Proceedings of the 2008 49th Annual IEEE Symposium on Foundations of Computer Science, FOCS 2008, pp. 283–292. IEEE Computer Society, Washington, DC, USA (2008). https://doi.org/10.1109/FOCS.2008.67
2. Brakerski, Z., Katz, J., Segev, G., Yerukhimovich, A.: Limits on the power of zero-knowledge proofs in cryptographic constructions. In: Ishai, Y. (ed.) TCC 2011. LNCS, vol. 6597, pp. 559–578. Springer, Heidelberg (2011). https://doi.org/10.1007/978-3-642-19571-6_34
3. Diffie, W., Hellman, M.: New directions in cryptography. IEEE Trans. Inf. Theory **22**, 644–654 (1976). https://doi.org/10.1109/TIT.1976.1055638
4. Feige, U., Shamir, A.: Witness indistinguishable and witness hiding protocols. In: Proceedings of the Twenty-second Annual ACM Symposium on Theory of Computing, STOC 1990. pp. 416–426. ACM, New York (1990). https://doi.org/10.1145/100216.100272
5. Goldwasser, S., Micali, S., Rackoff, C.: The knowledge complexity of interactive proof-systems. In: Proceedings of the Seventeenth Annual ACM Symposium on Theory of Computing, STOC 1985, pp. 291–304. ACM, New York (1985). https://doi.org/10.1145/22145.22178
6. Impagliazzo, R., Rudich, S.: Limits on the provable consequences of one-way permutations. In: Proceedings of the Twenty-first Annual ACM Symposium on Theory of Computing, STOC 1989, pp. 44–61. ACM, New York (1989). https://doi.org/10.1145/73007.73012
7. Karp, R.M.: Reducibility among Combinatorial Problems. In: Miller, R.E., Thatcher, J.W., Bohlinger, J.D. (eds.) Complexity of Computer Computations. The IBM Research Symposia Series, pp. 85–103. Springer, Boston (1972). https://doi.org/10.1007/978-1-4684-2001-2_9
8. Naor, M., Yung, M.: Public-key cryptosystems provably secure against chosen ciphertext attacks. In: Proceedings of the Twenty-Second Annual ACM Symposium on Theory of Computing, STOC 1990. pp. 427–437. ACM, New York (1990). https://doi.org/10.1145/100216.100273
9. Reingold, O., Trevisan, L., Vadhan, S.: Notions of reducibility between cryptographic primitives. In: Naor, M. (ed.) TCC 2004. LNCS, vol. 2951, pp. 1–20. Springer, Heidelberg (2004). https://doi.org/10.1007/978-3-540-24638-1_1
10. Sahai, A.: Non-malleable non-interactive zero knowledge and adaptive chosen-ciphertext security. In: Proceedings of the 40th Annual Symposium on Foundations of Computer Science. FOCS 1999, p. 543. IEEE Computer Society, Washington, DC (1999)
11. Yamashita, K., Tibouchi, M., Abe, M.: A coin-free oracle-based augmented black box framework. Cryptology ePrint Archive, Report 2019/859 (2019). https://eprint.iacr.org/2019/859
12. Yao, A.C.: Theory and application of trapdoor functions. In: Proceedings of the 23rd Annual Symposium on Foundations of Computer Science, SFCS 1982, pp. 80–91. IEEE Computer Society, Washington, DC (1982). https://doi.org/10.1109/SFCS.1982.95

Blockchain

A Lattice-Based Anonymous Distributed E-Cash from Bitcoin

Zeming Lu[1], Zoe L. Jiang[1,2(✉)] ⓘ, Yulin Wu[1] ⓘ, Xuan Wang[1,2] ⓘ,
and Yantao Zhong[3]

[1] Harbin Institute of Technology, Shenzhen, China
zoeljiang@hit.edu.cn
[2] Cyberspace Security Research Center, Peng Cheng Laboratory, Shenzhen, China
[3] Shenzhen Network Security Testing Technology Co. Ltd, Shenzhen, China

Abstract. Although Bitcoin was the first widely adopted cryptographic currency system, it provides a limited form of anonymity and privacy. To protect the anonymity and privacy of Bitcoin transactions, many Bitcoin-based cryptocurrency extensions were proposed. However, most of the systems with anonymity and privacy are based on traditional cryptographic algorithms, which may become insecure in the next decades due to the attack of quantum computing. In this paper, we propose a lattice-based distributed e-cash scheme protecting payer's anonymity, which is built upon the framework of Zerocoin and lattice-based zero-knowledge argument. Firstly, payer who owes a transaction redeems it to a newly-minted coin. Secondly, to pay for the next transaction, he/she collects a set of such coins to hide his owns, which can further hide his/her identity. Thirdly, to prove that the payer has one of the coins and no attempts to double-spend have occurred, we adapt a zero-knowledge argument of membership based on a lattice-based accumulator and a commitment protocol. Finally, the security proof of the scheme are given.

Keywords: Bitcoin · Anonymity · Lattice-based cryptocurrency · Zero-knowledge argument

1 Introduction

Bitcoin has become the most popular cryptographic currency in the last few years. While Bitcoin offers new ways for transaction, it has serious anonymity problems. Bitcoin relies on pseudonyms (addresses) for providing anonymity, which was initially thought to be powerful enough. However, it soon became clear that as blockchain makes all information about Bitcoin transactions public, it can sometimes track the flow of money among pseudonyms, which could conclude that pseudonyms can be controlled by the same person [7]. In order to solve the anonymity problem, some schemes have been designed and some new cryptographic currencies based on Bitcoin have been developed. Yet no proposed Bitcoin system with anonymity and privacy can resists attacks by quantum computers.

ⓒ Springer Nature Switzerland AG 2019
R. Steinfeld and T. H. Yuen (Eds.): ProvSec 2019, LNCS 11821, pp. 275–287, 2019.
https://doi.org/10.1007/978-3-030-31919-9_16

With the emergence of quantum computers, the concept of security in most cryptographic applications will change. Shor pointed out in his breakthrough work that quantum computers can effectively attack secure encryption schemes based on the hardness assumed by number theory [15]. Since then, many efforts have been made to find alternatives to meet this challenge. Lattice-based cryptography is a promising option.

Over the past years, a number of highly efficient cryptographic systems have emerged whose security is based on the hardness of the well-studied lattice problem. Unlike RSA and other classical structures, there is no subaxial time attack for lattice problem that are relevant for practice. All known attacks run in exponential time and thus provide a solid argument for a transition to lattice-based cryptosystems.

Our Idea. Our high-level idea to design the scheme is as follows. In Bitcoin system, each transaction tx clearly shows the pseudonyms of payer and payee, as well as the value. When payee intends to initiate a new transaction and changes his/her identity to *payer*, he/she should generate a trapdoor skc and mint a coin **d** using skc which is actually a commitment to **I**, followed by generate the signature of tx and **d** using his/her secret key. By doing so, transaction tx is redeemed to coin **d** and **d** belongs to the *payer*. To spend the coin, payer randomly collects a set of coins **C** in condition that $\mathbf{d} \in \mathbf{C}$, then provides proof that (1) he/she owns one of the coins in **C** and (2) the coin has never been spent before. It is achieved by using accumulator and zero-knowledge argument of membership, as well as the commitment mentioned above. Note that transaction-specific information is also included in the proof by adapting Fiat-Shamir heuristic [18].

The rest of this paper proceeds as follows: Sect. 2 discusses the existing Bitcoin anonymity schemes, Sect. 3 formally defines the notion of decentralized e-cash scheme of Zerocoin [13], and reviews the lattice-based accumulator and zero-knowledge argument [9]. Then describe the newly-designed lattice-based E-cash scheme in Sect. 4 and analyze the security in Sect. 5. Section 6 concludes the paper with some future work.

2   Related Work

Bitcoin Anonymity. To provide anonymity in Bitcoin, users can create new pseudonyms (addresses) at any time, which, was argued, can provide anonymity early. However due to the public nature of blockchain, it quickly became clear that sometimes it is possible to trace the transaction between pseudonyms [7]. Hence, many Bitcoin's cryptocurrency extensions extend the protocol to allow completely anonymous currency transactions.

In Mixcoin [3], Bonneau et. al proposed coinjoin technique, which can provide a third-party mix system to users. Blindcoin [17] extended Mixcoin. However, both of them have obvious shortcomings: the correlation between addresses can still be analyzed by asymmetric change address amount as they do not use cryptography, and they are not a distributed system.

Zerocoin [13] used zero-knowledge proof to provide anonymity: a prover (payer) sets a sublist of all available coins including his/her own coin. Using RSA-based zero-knowledge proof, others can check if his coin is included in without knowing which one the coin is. In doing so, payer's anonymity is achieved.

Zerocash [14] is an even stronger scheme than Zerocoin, which is based on ZK-SNARKs [19]. Neither payer and payee's identities nor the transaction amount will be exposed to others are hidden. However, it is very difficult to detect vulnerabilities or problems in its trusted setup.

CryptoNote used ring signatures, and Monero further improved the protocol by using a variant of linkable ring signature [10], and named it as Ring Confidential Transactions (RingCT). RingCT 2.0 [16] targeted to improve RingCT protocol by reducing the size.

3   Preliminaries

In this section, firstly, we introduce the decentralized e-cash scheme of Zerocoin, followed by reviewing the lattice-based accumulator and zero-knowledge proof using the concept and notation of [9].

3.1   Zerocoin

Bitcoin defines a cryptocurrency as a chain of digital signatures. Each owner (payer) of the cryptocurrency spends it to others by adding the digital signature of the hash of the previous transaction ptx and the next owner (payee)'s public key pk to the end of the cryptocurrency. The payee can prove that it is the payer of the chain by verifying the digital signature. As shown in Fig. 1, user1 has a previous transaction ptx_{0-1} (indicating that the transaction is given to user1 by user0). User1 uses ptx_{0-1} and the public key (address) pk_2 to HASH($ptx_{0-1}\|pk_2$) and outputs h_{1-2}, then signs h_{1-2} with user1's private key sk_1. The above

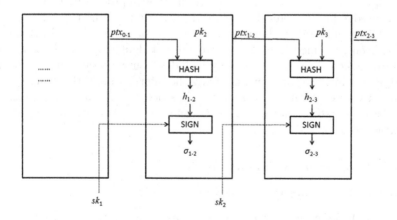

Fig. 1. Transaction on Bitcoin

transaction is named $ptx_{1-2} = (ptx_{0-1}, pk_2, \sigma_{1-2})$. The miners on the blockchain verify ptx_{1-2} using user1's public key pk_1. If $\mathsf{Verify}(ptx_{1-2}, pk_1) = 1$, then user2 owns the transaction ptx_{1-2}, which means user2 owns the corresponding Bitcoin of ptx_{1-2}. User2 can transfer ptx_{1-2} to user3 as follows.

In Bitcoin system, user's public key is used as a pseudonym to ensure the user's privacy of both sides of transaction, which is not secure enough as discussed above.

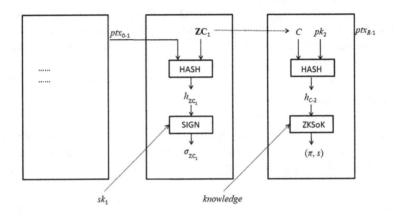

Fig. 2. Transaction on Zerocoin

Hence, Zerocoin was proposed, which can protect the anonymity of transactions. The idea is as follows: randomly create digital coins which do not have value or owner, then assign them value and owner by combining it with transactions. After passing miners' verification on blockchain, they become to valid Zerocoins (**ZC**). When user1(payer) spends **ZC**, he/she randomly selects a number of **ZC**s of equal denomination from all valid **ZC**s on blockchain as a set $C = \mathbf{ZC}_i | i = 1, \cdots, n$. Then create a zero-knowledge proof π by non-interactive zero-knowledge proof protocol, which can prove that (1) the payer has one **ZC** in C, while it is unable to know which one it is (anonymity); and (2) this **ZC** has not been redeemed into Bitcoin (to prevent double spending). π is also a signature of the message m (m mainly includes transaction information such as C and pk_2), which can prevent modifying the information of this transaction.

The proposed scheme is similar to the scheme above instead of adapting lattice-based cryptography to construct, and has the correctness and security properties as [13].

3.2 Cryptographic Accumulator

An accumulator scheme was designed by [4] as follows:

- $\mathsf{TSetup}(n)$: Take security parameter n as input, output pp as the public parameter.

- TAcc_{pp}: Take a set $R = \{\mathbf{d}_i | i = \{0, 1, \cdots, N - 1\}\}$ as input, output an accumulator value $\mathbf{u}$ with constant size.
- $\mathsf{TWitness}_{pp}$: Take R and a value $\mathbf{d}_i$ as input. If $\mathbf{d}_i \in R$, output w for $\mathbf{d}_i$ as a witness that $\mathbf{d}_i$ is accumulated in $\mathsf{TAcc}(R)$. Otherwise, output $\bot$.
- $\mathsf{TVerify}_{pp}$: take $\mathbf{u}$, $\mathbf{d}_i$, and $\mathbf{d}_i's$ witness w as input. The algorithm outputs 1 if $(\mathbf{d}_i, w)$ is valid for the accumulator $\mathbf{u}$. Otherwise, output 0.

3.3 Lattice-Based Merkle-Tree Accumulator

One of the techniques used in our scheme is Merkle hash tree constructed by a lattice-based hash function, whose security relies on Small Integer Solution (SIS) problem, which is modified by the hash functions considered in [1,6,12]. Thus, we introduce the SIS problem first [2,5]:

Definition 1. $\mathsf{SIS}^\infty_{n,m,q,\beta}$ *problem is defined as follows: Given uniformly random matrix* $\mathbf{A} \in \mathbb{Z}_q^{n \times m}$ *find a non-zero vector* $\mathbf{x} \in \mathbb{Z}^m$ *such that* $\|\mathbf{x}\|_\infty \leq \beta$ *and* $\mathbf{A} \cdot \mathbf{x} = \mathbf{0} \bmod q$.

If $m, \beta = \mathsf{poly}(n)$, and $q > \beta \cdot \widetilde{\mathcal{O}}(\sqrt{n})$, then the $\mathsf{SIS}^\infty_{n,m,q,\beta}$ problem is at least as hard as the worst-case lattice problem SIVP_γ for some $\gamma = \beta \cdot \widetilde{\mathcal{O}}(\sqrt{nm})$ ([5]). Specifically, when $\beta = 1, q = \widetilde{\mathcal{O}}(n), m = 2n\lceil \log q \rceil$, the $\mathsf{SIS}^\infty_{n,m,q,1}$ problem is at least as hard as $\mathsf{SIVP}_{\widetilde{\mathcal{O}}(n)}$.

Then define a kind of matrix:

$$\mathbf{G} = \begin{bmatrix} 1\ 2\ 4\ \ldots\ 2^{k-1} & & & \\ & 1\ 2\ 4\ \ldots\ 2^{k-1} & & \\ & & \ldots & \\ & & & 1\ 2\ 4\ \ldots\ 2^{k-1} \end{bmatrix} \in \mathbb{Z}_q^{n \times nk}.$$

Then $\mathsf{bin}(\mathbf{v}) \in \{0,1\}^{nk}$ denotes the binary representation of $\mathbf{v}$ such that $\mathbf{v} = \mathbf{G} \cdot \mathsf{bin}(\mathbf{v})$ for every $\mathbf{v} \in \mathbb{Z}_q^n$.

Definition 2. *The function family* $\mathcal{H}$ *mapping* $\{0,1\}^{nk} \times \{0,1\}^{nk}$ *to* $\{0,1\}^{nk}$ *is defined as* $\mathcal{H} = \{h_\mathbf{A} | \mathbf{A} \in \mathbb{Z}_q^{n \times m}\}$, *where for* $\mathbf{A} = [\mathbf{A}_0 | \mathbf{A}_1]$ *with* $\mathbf{A}_0, \mathbf{A}_1 \in \mathbb{Z}_q^{n \times nk}$, *and for any* $(\mathbf{u}_0, \mathbf{u}_1) \in \{0,1\}^{nk} \times \{0,1\}^{nk}$, *we have:*

$$h_\mathbf{A}(\mathbf{u}_0, \mathbf{u}_1) = \mathsf{bin}(\mathbf{A}_0 \cdot \mathbf{u}_0 + \mathbf{A}_1 \cdot \mathbf{u}_1 \bmod q) \in \{0,1\}^{nk}.$$

This function is collision-resistant according to Lemma 1 [9].

Basing on the hash function $\mathcal{H}$ defined above, a Merkle tree accumulator can be constructed as follows, the definition of this accumulator is a litte different from above:

$\mathsf{TSetup}(n)$: Randomly select a matrix $\mathbf{A} \in \mathbb{Z}_q^{n \times m}$, output $\mathbf{A}$ as public parameter pp.

$\mathsf{TAcc}_\mathbf{A}(R = \{\mathbf{d}_0, \ldots, \mathbf{d}_{N-1}\})$: Let $\mathbf{d}_j = \mathbf{u}_{j_1, \ldots, j_\ell}$, note that $(j_1, \ldots, j_\ell)$ is the binary form of j. the algorithm works as follows:

If the depth $i \neq 0$, the node $\mathbf{u}_{b_1,\ldots,b_i} = h_\mathbf{A}(\mathbf{u}_{b_1,\ldots,b_i,0}, \mathbf{u}_{b_1,\ldots,b_i,1})$. $(b_1,\ldots,b_i) \in \{0,1\}^i$ is the binary string.

If the depth $i = 0$, the root $\mathbf{u} = h_\mathbf{A}(\mathbf{u}_0, \mathbf{u}_1)$. Then output the root value $\mathbf{u}$.

TWitness$_\mathbf{A}(R, \mathbf{d})$: If $\mathbf{d}$ is not a member of R, return $\perp$. Otherwise, output the witness $w = ((j_1,\ldots,j_\ell), (\mathbf{u}_{j_1,\ldots,j_{\ell-1},\bar{j}_\ell}, \ldots, \mathbf{u}_{j_1,\bar{j}_2}, \mathbf{u}_{\bar{j}_1})) \in \{0,1\}^\ell \times (\{0,1\}^{nk})^\ell$, as $\mathbf{d} = \mathbf{d_j}$ in the tree.

TVerify$_\mathbf{A}(\mathbf{u}, \mathbf{d}, w)$: On input values $(\mathbf{u}, \mathbf{d}, w)$ and public parameter $\mathbf{A}$, the algorithm computes the path $\mathbf{v}_\ell, \mathbf{v}_{\ell-1}, \ldots, \mathbf{v}_1, \mathbf{v}_0 \in \{0,1\}^{nk}$ as follows: let $\mathbf{v}_\ell = \mathbf{d}$ and

$$\forall i \in \{\ell-1,\ldots,1,0\} : \mathbf{v}_i = \begin{cases} h_\mathbf{A}(\mathbf{v}_{i+1}, \mathbf{w}_{i+1}), & \text{if } j_{i+1} = 0; \\ h_\mathbf{A}(\mathbf{w}_{i+1}, \mathbf{v}_{i+1}), & \text{if } j_{i+1} = 1. \end{cases}$$

Returns 1 if $\mathbf{v}_0 = $ the root value $\mathbf{u}$. Otherwise, returns 0.

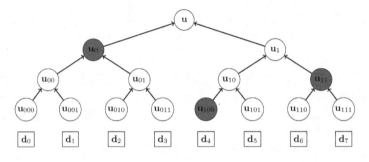

Fig. 3. A Merkle tree accumulator with 8 leaves

The accumulator above is secure if the SIVP$_{\widetilde{O}(n)}$ problem is hard [9].

Further, a zero-knowledge argument system can be constructed. It supports prover $\mathcal{P}$ to convince verifier $\mathcal{V}$ to accept a statement: prover $\mathcal{P}$ knows a secret value $(\mathbf{d})$ is accumulated into the root which computed by the accumulator described above.

To describe the zero-knowledge argument system, firstly, several supporting notations and techniques must be introduced as defined in [9]: B_m^{nk}, $\mathcal{S}_m$, $\mathsf{ext}(b, \mathbf{v})$, $F_{b,\pi}$. As defined above, and the accumulator computes path as follows:

$$\forall i \in \{\ell-1,\ldots,1,0\} : \mathbf{v}_i = \begin{cases} h_\mathbf{A}(\mathbf{v}_{i+1}, \mathbf{w}_{i+1}), & \text{if } j_{i+1} = 0; \\ h_\mathbf{A}(\mathbf{w}_{i+1}, \mathbf{v}_{i+1}), & \text{if } j_{i+1} = 1. \end{cases} \tag{2}$$

Equation (2) then can be interpreted as:

$$\mathbf{A} \cdot \mathsf{ext}(j_{i+1}, \mathbf{v}_{i+1}) + \mathbf{A} \cdot \mathsf{ext}(\bar{j}_{i+1}, \mathbf{w}_{i+1}) = \mathbf{G} \cdot \mathbf{v}_i \bmod q. \tag{3}$$

$\mathcal{P}$ has to convince $\mathcal{V}$ in ZK that $\mathcal{P}$ knows $(\mathbf{d}, w)$($\mathcal{V}$ can not get them) satisfying

$$\begin{cases} \mathbf{A} \cdot \mathsf{ext}(j_1, \mathbf{v}_1) + \mathbf{A} \cdot \mathsf{ext}(\bar{j}_1, \mathbf{w}_1) = \mathbf{G} \cdot \mathbf{u} \bmod q; \\ \forall i \in [\ell-1] : \mathbf{A} \cdot \mathsf{ext}(j_{i+1}, \mathbf{v}_{i+1}) + \mathbf{A} \cdot \mathsf{ext}(\bar{j}_{i+1}, \mathbf{w}_{i+1}) = \mathbf{G} \cdot \mathbf{v}_i \bmod q \end{cases} \tag{4}$$

(4) can be rewritten by $\mathbf{z}_i = \mathsf{ext}(j_i, \mathbf{v}_i^*)$ and $\mathbf{y}_i = \mathsf{ext}(\bar{j}_i, \mathbf{w}_i^*)$, and names the new equation (5).

The argument system can develop by a Stern-type protocol [8], first, Extend matrix and vectors as in [9] and get $\mathbf{A}^*, \mathbf{G}^*, \mathbf{v}_1^*, \ldots, \mathbf{v}_\ell^*, \mathbf{w}_1^*, \ldots, \mathbf{w}_\ell^*$.

$\mathcal{P}$ wants to prove in ZK that (1): $\mathbf{v}_i^*, \mathbf{w}_i^* \in \mathsf{B}_m^{nk}$, $\mathbf{z}_i = \mathsf{ext}(j_i, \mathbf{v}_i^*)$, $\mathbf{y}_i = \mathsf{ext}(\bar{j}_i, \mathbf{w}_i^*)$ for all $i \in [\ell]$; (2): equation (5) holds. $\mathcal{P}$ works as follows:

1. For each $i \in [\ell]$, $\mathcal{P}$ samples $\pi_i, \phi_i \xleftarrow{\$} \mathcal{S}_m$ and $b_i \xleftarrow{\$} \{0, 1\}$, then shows $\mathcal{V}$ that: $\pi_i(\mathbf{v}_i^*) \in \mathsf{B}_m^{nk}$, $\phi_i(\mathbf{w}_i^*) \in \mathsf{B}_m^{nk}$, and $F_{b_i, \pi_i}(\mathbf{z}_i) = \mathsf{ext}(j_i \oplus b_i, \pi_i(\mathbf{v}_i^*))$, $F_{\bar{b}_i, \pi_i}(\mathbf{y}_i) = \mathsf{ext}(\bar{j}_i \oplus b_i, \phi_i(\mathbf{w}_i^*))$. Because of the randomness of π_i, ϕ_i and b_i, $\mathcal{V}$ can convince the facts $\mathcal{P}$ wants to prove, but learning nothing useful.

2. $\mathcal{P}$ samples vectors $\mathbf{r}_\mathbf{v}^{(1)}, \ldots, \mathbf{r}_\mathbf{v}^{(\ell-1)} \xleftarrow{\$} \mathbb{Z}_q^m; \mathbf{r}_\mathbf{z}^{(1)}, \ldots, \mathbf{r}_\mathbf{z}^{(\ell)}, \mathbf{r}_\mathbf{y}^{(1)}, \ldots, \mathbf{r}_\mathbf{y}^{(\ell)} \xleftarrow{\$} \mathbb{Z}_q^{2m}$ in uniform random way, and then it shows $\mathcal{V}$ that equation (5) holds in ZK.

The detail of the interaction between prover $\mathcal{P}$ and verifier $\mathcal{V}$ above is in [9].

Further, the interaction above can be used to construct a ring signature [9]. In the ring signature scheme, let $\mathsf{bin}(\mathbf{A} \cdot \mathbf{x} \bmod q) = \mathbf{d}$, and $sk = \mathbf{x}, pk = \mathbf{d}$. $\mathcal{P}$ has to convince $\mathcal{V}$ one more thing that he knows a vector $\mathbf{x}$ such that $\mathsf{bin}(\mathbf{A} \cdot \mathbf{x} \bmod q) = \mathbf{d}$. We modify it in our scheme and show details in next section.

4   Lattice-Based Distributed E-Cash Scheme

We now describe our lattice-based distributed E-cash scheme used on Bitcoin, which is based on the lattice-based accumulator [9]. It includes 4 algorithms as defined in [13]:

- **Setup**$(n) \rightarrow params$: On input a security parameter n, then sample the matrix $\mathbf{A}$ and $\mathbf{B}$ such that $\mathbf{A}, \mathbf{B} \in \mathbb{Z}_q^{n \times m}$ as $q = \tilde{\mathcal{O}}(n), m = 2n\lceil \log q \rceil$. Output params as $(\mathbf{A}, \mathbf{B}, n, m, q)$.

- **Mint**$(params) \rightarrow (\mathbf{d}, skc)$. Select $\mathbf{I}, \mathbf{x} \in \{0, 1\}^m$ and compute $\mathbf{A} \cdot \mathbf{x} + \mathbf{B} \cdot \mathbf{I} = \mathbf{G} \cdot \mathbf{d} \bmod q$. Set $skc = (\mathbf{I}, \mathbf{x})$ and output $(\mathbf{d}, skc)$.

- **Spend**$(params, \mathbf{d}, skc, M, \mathbf{C}) \rightarrow (\Pi, S)$. If $\mathbf{d} \notin \mathbf{C}$ output $\bot$. Otherwise compute $\mathsf{TAcc}_\mathbf{A}(\mathbf{C})$ to build the Merkle tree accumulator, and obtain the root $\mathbf{u}$. Run $\mathsf{TWitness}(\mathbf{C}, \mathbf{d})$ to get a witness ω. Output $(\Pi, \mathbf{S})$ where Π comprises the following zero-knowledge argument of knowledge:

$$\Pi = \mathbf{ZKAoK}[M]\{(\mathbf{d}, w, \mathbf{x}) : \mathbf{TVerify}(u, \mathbf{d}, w) = 1 \wedge (\mathbf{A} \cdot \mathbf{x} + \mathbf{B} \cdot \mathbf{I} = \mathbf{G} \cdot \mathbf{d} \bmod q\}$$

Specially, we should consider how to compute Π with the ring signature. On input $(\mathbf{x}, \mathbf{d}, w)$, repeat the protocol in Fig. 4 $\kappa = \omega(\log n)$ times. The next challenge is how to make non-interactive, this is done via the Fiat-Shamir heuristic: compute $\Pi = (\{\mathrm{CMT}_i\}_{i=1}^\kappa, \mathrm{CH}, \{\mathrm{RSP}\}_{i=1}^\kappa)$, where

$$\mathrm{CH} = \mathcal{H}_{\mathsf{FS}}\big(M, \{\mathrm{CMT}_i\}_{i=1}^\kappa, \mathbf{A}, \mathbf{B}, \mathbf{u}, \mathbf{C}\big) \in \{1, 2, 3\}^\kappa.$$

1. Commitment. $\mathcal{P}$ samples randomness ρ_1, ρ_2, ρ_3 for COM and

$$\begin{cases} b_1, \ldots, b_\ell \xleftarrow{\$} \{0,1\}; \pi_1, \ldots, \pi_\ell, \phi_1, \ldots, \phi_\ell \xleftarrow{\$} \mathcal{S}_m; \tau \xleftarrow{\$} \mathcal{S}_{2m}; \\ \mathbf{r_v}^{(1)}, \ldots, \mathbf{r_v}^{(\ell-1)} \xleftarrow{\$} \mathbb{Z}_q^m; \mathbf{r_z}^{(1)}, \ldots, \mathbf{r_z}^{(\ell)}, \mathbf{r_y}^{(1)}, \ldots, \mathbf{r_y}^{(\ell)}, \mathbf{r_x} \xleftarrow{\$} \mathbb{Z}_q^{2m}. \end{cases}$$

It then sends $\mathcal{V}$ commitment $CMT = (C_1, C_2, C_3)$, where

$$\begin{cases} C_1 = \mathsf{COM}\big(\{b_i; \pi_i; \phi_i\}_{i=1}^\ell; \tau; \mathbf{A}^* \cdot \mathbf{r_z}^{(1)} + \mathbf{A}^* \cdot \mathbf{r_y}^{(1)}; \widehat{\mathbf{A}} \cdot \mathbf{r_x} - \mathbf{G}^* \cdot \mathbf{r_v}^{(l)}; \\ \qquad \{\mathbf{A}^* \cdot \mathbf{r_z}^{(i+1)} + \mathbf{A}^* \cdot \mathbf{r_y}^{(i+1)} - \mathbf{G}^* \cdot \mathbf{r_v}^{(i)}\}_{i=1}^{\ell-1}; \rho_1\big) \\ C_2 = \mathsf{COM}\big(\{\pi_i(\mathbf{r_v}^{(i)}); F_{b_i, \pi_i}(\mathbf{r_z}^{(i)}); F_{\bar{b}_i, \phi_i}(\mathbf{r_y}^{(i)})\}_{i=1}^\ell; \tau(\mathbf{r_x}); \rho_2\big) \\ C_3 = \mathsf{COM}\big(\{\pi_i(\mathbf{v}_i^* + \mathbf{r_v}^{(i)}); F_{b_i, \pi_i}(\mathbf{z}_i + \mathbf{r_z}^{(i)}); F_{\bar{b}_i, \phi_i}(\mathbf{y}_i + \mathbf{r_y}^{(i)})\}_{i=1}^\ell; \\ \qquad \tau(\mathbf{x}^* + \mathbf{r_x}); \rho_3\big) \end{cases}$$

2. Challenge. $\mathcal{V}$ sends challenge $Ch \xleftarrow{\$} \{1,2,3\}$ to $\mathcal{P}$ after received CMT.

3. Response. $\mathcal{P}$ checks Ch and sends the response RSP as follows:

- Case $Ch = 1$: Let $\mathbf{s_x} = \tau(\mathbf{x}^*)$; $t_x = \tau(\mathbf{r_x})$ and for each $i \in [\ell]$, let:

$$a_i = j_i \oplus b_i; \mathbf{s_v}^{(i)} = \pi_i(\mathbf{v}_i^*); \mathbf{s_w}^{(i)} = \phi_i(\mathbf{w}_i^*);$$

$$\mathbf{t_v}^{(i)} = \pi_i(\mathbf{r_v}^{(i)}); \mathbf{t_z}^{(i)} = F_{b_i, \pi_i}(\mathbf{r_z}^{(i)}); \mathbf{t_y}^{(i)} = F_{\bar{b}_i, \pi_i}(\mathbf{r_y}^{(i)})$$

Then let $RSP_1 = \big(\{a_i; \mathbf{s_v}^{(i)}; \mathbf{t_z}^{(i)}; \mathbf{t_v}^{(i)}; \mathbf{s_w}^{(i)}; \mathbf{t_y}^{(i)}\}_{i=1}^\ell; \mathbf{s_x}; t_x; \rho_2; \rho_3\big)$

- Case $Ch = 2$: Let $\widehat{\tau} = \tau$, $\mathbf{e_x} = \mathbf{x}^* + \mathbf{r_x}$ and for each $i \in [\ell]$, let:

$$c_i = b_i; \widehat{\pi}_i = \pi_i; \widehat{\phi}_i = \phi_i; \mathbf{e_v}^{(i)} = \mathbf{v}_i^* + \mathbf{r_v}^{(i)}; \mathbf{e_z}^{(i)} = \mathbf{z}_i + \mathbf{r_z}^{(i)}; \mathbf{e_y}^{(i)} = \mathbf{y}_i + \mathbf{r_y}^{(i)};$$

Then let $RSP_2 = \big(\{c_i; \widehat{\pi}_i; \widehat{\phi}_i; \mathbf{e_v}^{(i)}; \mathbf{e_z}^{(i)}; \mathbf{e_y}^{(i)}\}_{i=1}^\ell; \widehat{\tau}; \mathbf{e_x}; \rho_1; \rho_3\big)$

- Case $Ch = 3$: Let $\widetilde{\tau} = \tau$, $\mathbf{p_x} = \mathbf{r_x}$ and for each $i \in [\ell]$, let:

$$d_i = b_i; \widetilde{\pi}_i = \pi_i; \widetilde{\phi}_i = \phi_i; \mathbf{p_v}^{(i)} = \mathbf{r_v}^{(i)}; \mathbf{p_z}^{(i)} = \mathbf{r_z}^{(i)}; \mathbf{p_y}^{(i)} = \mathbf{r_y}^{(i)};$$

Then let $RSP_3 = \big(\{d_i; \widetilde{\pi}_i; \widetilde{\phi}_i; \mathbf{p_v}^{(i)}; \mathbf{p_z}^{(i)}; \mathbf{p_y}^{(i)}\}_{i=1}^\ell; \widetilde{\tau}; \mathbf{p_x}; \rho_1; \rho_2\big)$

Verification. Receiving RSP, $\mathcal{V}$ proceeds as follows.

- Case $Ch = 1$: Parse RSP_1. Check that $\mathbf{s_x} \in \mathsf{B}_{2m}^m$, and $\mathbf{s_v}^{(i)}, \mathbf{s_w}^{(i)} \in \mathsf{B}_m^{nk}$ for all $i \in [\ell]$. Next, for each $i \in [\ell]$, let $\mathbf{s_z}^{(i)} = \mathsf{ext}(a_i, \mathbf{s_v}^{(i)})$ and $\mathbf{s_y}^{(i)} = \mathsf{ext}(a_i, \mathbf{s_w}^{(i)})$. Then check that:

$$\begin{cases} C_2 = \mathsf{COM}\big(\{\mathbf{t_v}^{(i)}; \mathbf{t_z}^{(i)}; \mathbf{t_y}^{(i)}\}_{i=1}^\ell; t_x; \rho_2\big) \\ C_3 = \mathsf{COM}\big(\{\mathbf{s_v}^{(i)} + \mathbf{t_v}^{(i)}; \mathbf{s_z}^{(i)} + \mathbf{t_z}^{(i)}; \mathbf{s_y}^{(i)} + \mathbf{t_y}^{(i)};\}_{i=1}^\ell; \mathbf{s_x} + t_x; \rho_3\big) \end{cases}$$

- Case $Ch = 2$: Parse RSP_2 and check that:

Fig. 4. A modified zero-knowledge argument of knowledge

$$\begin{cases} C_1 = \mathsf{COM}\big(\{c_i; \widehat{\pi}_i; \widehat{\phi}_i\}_{i=1}^{\ell}; \widehat{\tau}; \mathbf{A}^* \cdot \mathbf{e}_{\mathbf{z}}^{(1)} + \mathbf{A}^* \cdot \mathbf{e}_{\mathbf{y}}^{(1)} - \mathbf{G} \cdot \mathbf{u}; \widehat{\mathbf{A}} \cdot \mathbf{e}_{\mathbf{x}} - \\ \qquad \mathbf{G}^* \cdot \mathbf{e}_{\mathbf{v}}^{(\ell)} + \mathbf{B} \cdot \mathbf{I}; \{\mathbf{A}^* \cdot \mathbf{e}_{\mathbf{z}}^{(i+1)} + \mathbf{A}^* \cdot \mathbf{e}_{\mathbf{y}}^{(i+1)} - \mathbf{G}^* \cdot \mathbf{e}_{\mathbf{v}}^{(i)}\}_{i=1}^{\ell-1}; \rho_1\big) \\ C_3 = \mathsf{COM}\big(\{\widehat{\pi}_i(\mathbf{e}_{\mathbf{v}}^{(i)}); F_{c_i,\widehat{\pi}_i}(\mathbf{e}_{\mathbf{z}}^{(i)}); F_{\widehat{c}_i,\widehat{\phi}_i}(\mathbf{e}_{\mathbf{y}}^{(i)})\}_{i=1}^{\ell}; \widehat{\tau}(\mathbf{e}_{\mathbf{x}}); \rho_3\big) \end{cases}$$

- Case $Ch = 3$: Parse RSP_3 and check that:

$$\begin{cases} C_1 = \mathsf{COM}\big(\{d_i; \widetilde{\pi}_i; \widetilde{\phi}_i\}_{i=1}^{\ell}; \widetilde{\tau}; \mathbf{A}^* \cdot \mathbf{p}_{\mathbf{z}}^{(1)} + \mathbf{A}^* \cdot \mathbf{p}_{\mathbf{y}}^{(1)}; \mathbf{A}^* \cdot \mathbf{p}_{\mathbf{x}} - \mathbf{G}^* \cdot \mathbf{p}_{\mathbf{v}}^{(\ell)}; \\ \qquad \{\mathbf{A}^* \cdot \mathbf{p}_{\mathbf{z}}^{(i+1)} + \mathbf{A}^* \cdot \mathbf{p}_{\mathbf{y}}^{(i+1)} - \mathbf{G}^* \cdot \mathbf{p}_{\mathbf{v}}^{(i)}\}_{i=1}^{\ell-1}; \rho_1\big) \\ C_2 = \mathsf{COM}\big(\{\widetilde{\pi}_i(\mathbf{p}_{\mathbf{v}}^{(i)}); F_{d_i,\widetilde{\pi}_i}(\mathbf{p}_{\mathbf{z}}^{(i)}); F_{\widetilde{d}_i,\widetilde{\phi}_i}(\mathbf{p}_{\mathbf{y}}^{(i)})\}_{i=1}^{\ell}; \widetilde{\tau}(\mathbf{p}_{\mathbf{x}}); \rho_2\big) \end{cases}$$

In each case, $\mathcal{V}$ outputs 1 if all the conditions hold. Otherwise outputs 0.

Fig. 4. (continued)

- **Verify**$(params, \Pi, I, M, \mathbf{C}) \rightarrow \{0, 1\}$. On input these values, this algorithm proceeds as follows:
  1. Compute the root $\mathbf{u}$ of $\mathbf{C}$ by $\mathsf{TAcc_A}(\mathbf{C})$;
  2. If $\mathrm{CH} \neq \mathcal{H}_{\mathsf{FS}}(...)$ defined above, return 0;
  3. For each $i = 1, 2, ..., \kappa$, run the verification phase of the protocol from Fig. 4. If any of the conditions is not valid, return 0;
  4. If $\mathbf{I}$ is not a new serial number, return 0. Otherwise, return 1.

5   Security Analysis

The proposed scheme is also required the correctness and security properties as in [13]. The proof of the correctness is straightforward and omitted. Now we mainly discuss how to prove the security.

Anonymity and Balance games were used to define the security of a decentralized e-cash scheme [13].

Theorem 1. *If the zero-knowledge argument of knowledge is statistically zero-knowledge in the random oracle model, then the scheme satisfies Anonymity property.*

Proof. The simulation is shown as follows: first, the parameters are generated, and uniformly samples two vectors $\mathbf{d}_0, \mathbf{d}_1$ from the set of $\{0, 1\}^m$ as two coins. $\mathcal{A}_1$ inputs these values. Then outputs a set $\mathbf{C}$ and an information string $\mathbf{M}$ whatever scheme it uses. Next, runs $\mathcal{A}_2$ with the input including a simulated Π and a random number $\mathbf{I}$. Note that if Π is at least statistical zero-knowledge, from the perspective of $\mathcal{A}$, the simulation works as in the real world with negligible probability, which means $\mathcal{A}$'s advantage in this game is negligible.

Theorem 2. *If the signature proof Π is sound in the random oracle model, the* SIVP_γ *problem is hard, then the scheme* (**Setup, Mint, Spend, Verify**) *satisfies the Balance property.*

Proof. Suppose $\mathcal{A}$ is an adversary who wins the Balance game with non-negligible advantage ϵ. The simulation first constructs an algorithm $\mathcal{B}$ that takes input as defined above:$(\mathbf{A}, \mathbf{B}, n, m, q)$, and outputs a solution of SIVP_γ problems for some $\gamma = \beta \cdot \widetilde{\mathcal{O}}(\sqrt{nm})$. $\mathcal{B}$ works as follows:

On input public values, setup parameters. For $i = 1$, mint coins by running $(\mathbf{d}_i, skc_i) \leftarrow \mathbf{Mint}(params)$, store $(\mathbf{I}_i, x_i)$ as skc_i, and run $\mathcal{A}(params, \mathbf{d}_1, \ldots, \mathbf{d}_K)$. Use secret values to answer $\mathcal{A}$'s queries to $\mathcal{O}_{spend}$. Let $(I_1, R_1),$ $\ldots, (I_l, R_l)$ be the set of values as the oracle records.

1. If the extractor can not extract the values, abort and label this event as EVENT$_{\mathrm{EXT}}$.
2. If $\mathbf{d}_j^* \notin \mathbf{C}_j'$, abort and label this event as EVENT$_{\mathrm{ACC}}$.
3. If $\mathbf{d}_j^* \in \{\mathbf{d}_1, \ldots, \mathbf{d}_K\}$:
   (a) If $(\mathbf{I}_j', \mathbf{x}_j^*) = (\mathbf{I}_i, \mathbf{x}_i)$ and $R_j' \neq R_i$ for some i, abort and label this event as EVENT$_{\mathrm{FORGE}}$.
   (b) Otherwise if $(\mathbf{I}_j', \mathbf{x}_j^*) = (\mathbf{I}_i, \mathbf{x}_i)$ for some i, abort and label this event as EVENT$_{\mathrm{COL}}$.
   (c) Otherwise set $(a, b) = (\mathbf{I}_i, \mathbf{x}_i)$.
   (d) If $\mathbf{d}_j^* = \mathbf{d}_i^*$ for some i, set $(a, b) = (\mathbf{I}_i', \mathbf{x}_i^*)$.

If the simulation is successful, we now get $(\mathbf{d}_j^*, \mathbf{x}_j^*, \mathbf{I}_j', a, b)$ and have the equation: $\mathbf{d}_j^* \equiv [\mathbf{A}, \mathbf{B}] \begin{pmatrix} \mathbf{x}_j^* \\ \mathbf{I}_j' \end{pmatrix} \equiv [\mathbf{A}, \mathbf{B}] \begin{pmatrix} a \\ b \end{pmatrix}$. Output a nonzero solusion $\mathbf{z} = \begin{pmatrix} \mathbf{x}_j^* - a \\ \mathbf{I}_j' - b \end{pmatrix}$ for $[\mathbf{A}, \mathbf{B}] \, \mathbf{z} = \mathbf{0}$.

The analysis of this simulation is similar to [13]. Briefly, when the simulation does not abort, $\mathcal{A}$ wins this game by two ways: 1) $\mathcal{A}$ has spent one coin that does not belong to him by providing a new serial number for it; or 2) $\mathcal{A}$ has double spent the same coin. Both of them means that we get a solusion of SIVP_γ problems.

Abort probability

1. Apparently, the probability of the extractor fails is negligible. Let $\nu_1(\lambda)$ be the negligible probability(same as $\nu_2(\lambda)$, $\nu_3(\lambda)$ below), $\mathbf{Pr}[\mathrm{EVENT}_{\mathrm{EXT}}] \leq (M + 1)\nu_1(\lambda)$.

2. The EVENT$_{\mathrm{COL}}$ implies that for some i, $\mathcal{A}$ has produced a pair $\begin{pmatrix} \mathbf{x}_j^* \\ \mathbf{I}_j' \end{pmatrix} = \begin{pmatrix} \mathbf{x}_i \\ \mathbf{I}_i \end{pmatrix}$ where $\mathbf{I}_j'$ has not been produced by $\mathcal{O}_{spend}$.

Theorem 3. *([11], Theorem 8) For any matrix* $\mathbf{A} \in \mathbb{Z}_q^{n \times m}$ *and a uniformly random* $\mathbf{x} \in \{0, 1\}^m$, *the probability that there exists another* $\mathbf{x}' \in \{0, 1\}^m \backslash \{\mathbf{x}\}$ *such that* $\mathbf{A} \cdot \mathbf{x} = \mathbf{A} \cdot \mathbf{x}' \bmod q$ *is at least* $1 - 2^{n \cdot \log q - m}$.

According to the theorem 3, there are $l(l \geq 2)$ distinct vectors satisfy $\mathbf{d}_j^* \equiv$ $[\mathbf{A}, \mathbf{B}] \begin{pmatrix} \mathbf{x} \\ \mathbf{I} \end{pmatrix}$ with overwhelming probability, and they are independent in $\mathcal{A}'s$ view. Thus $\mathbf{Pr}[\text{EVENT}_{\text{COL}}] \leq 1/l$.

3. If the $\text{SIVP}_{\widetilde{\mathcal{O}}(n)}$ problem is hard to solve, then $\mathbf{Pr}[\text{EVENT}_{\text{ACC}}] \leq \nu_2(\lambda)$.

This proof is similar to those used by [9] Appendix C. In the nutshell, let $\mathcal{A}'$ be an adversary who induces $\text{EVENT}_{\text{ACC}}$ with non-negligible probability ϵ' in the simulation above. An algorithm $\mathcal{B}'$ can break the security of the accumulator with non-negligible probability by the support of $\mathcal{A}'$: $\mathcal{B}'$ defines the public parameters. It generates $(\mathbf{d}_1, \ldots, \mathbf{d}_K)$, then runs $\mathcal{A}'$. To induce $\text{EVENT}_{\text{ACC}}$, $\mathcal{A}'$ produces valid output $(\Pi', \mathbf{C}')$ and a $c^* \notin \mathbf{C}'$. $\mathcal{B}'$ now extracts ω^* from Π' which means breaking the security of the accumulator, makes the $\text{SIVP}_{\widetilde{\mathcal{O}}(n)}$ problem is not hard.

4. Observe that our scheme uses the modification of the ring signature scheme, thus it satisfies the same property according to theorem 4 and clearly that $\mathbf{Pr}[\text{EVENT}_{\text{FORGE}}] \leq \nu_3(\lambda)$:

Theorem 4. *([9], Theorem 4) The scheme provides unforgeability w.r.t. insider corruption in the random oracle model if the $\text{SIVP}_{\widetilde{\mathcal{O}}(n)}$ problem is hard.*

To summarize, if $\mathcal{A}$ wins the Balance game with non-negligible advantage ϵ, then $\mathcal{B}$ succeeds with probability $= \epsilon[(1 - (M + 1)\nu_1(\lambda)) \times (1 - \nu_2(\lambda)) \times (1 - \nu_3(\lambda)) \times (1 - 1/l))]$.

6   Concluding Remarks and Future Work

We propose a latticed-based distributed e-cash scheme based on Zerocoin's framework, which can protect payer's anonymity and resist quantum computer's attacks. We modify a ring signature based on a zero-knowledge argument scheme to achieve this goal, and show the security proof of this scheme. In future work, it is worthy considering replace [9] with more efficient lattice-based accumulator or ring signature [20, 21].

Acknowledgements. This work is supported in part National Natural Science Foundation of China (No. 61872109), Guangdong Key R&D Program (No. 2019B010136001), Key Technology Program of Shenzhen, China, (No. JSGG20170824163239586).

References

1. Ajtai, M.: Generating hard instances of the short basis problem. In: Wiedermann, J., van Emde Boas, P., Nielsen, M. (eds.) ICALP 1999. LNCS, vol. 1644, pp. 1–9. Springer, Heidelberg (1999). https://doi.org/10.1007/3-540-48523-6_1
2. Ajtai, M.: Generating hard instances of lattice problems (extended abstract). In: Miller, G.L. (ed.) STOC, pp. 99–108. ACM (1996)

3. Bonneau, J., Narayanan, A., Miller, A., Clark, J., Kroll, J.A., Felten, E.W.: Mixcoin: anonymity for bitcoin with accountable mixes. In: Christin, N., Safavi-Naini, R. (eds.) FC 2014. LNCS, vol. 8437, pp. 486–504. Springer, Heidelberg (2014). https://doi.org/10.1007/978-3-662-45472-5_31
4. Camenisch, J., Lysyanskaya, A.: Dynamic accumulators and application to efficient revocation of anonymous credentials. In: Yung, M. (ed.) CRYPTO 2002. LNCS, vol. 2442, pp. 61–76. Springer, Heidelberg (2002). https://doi.org/10.1007/3-540-45708-9_5
5. Gentry, C., Peikert, C., Vaikuntanathan, V.: Trapdoors for hard lattices and new cryptographic constructions. In: Proceedings of the 40th Annual ACM Symposium on Theory of Computing, pp. 197–206. ACM (2008)
6. Goldreich, O., Goldwasser, S., Halevi, S.: Collision-free hashing from lattice problems. In: Goldreich, O. (ed.) Studies in Complexity and Cryptography. Miscellanea on the Interplay between Randomness and Computation. LNCS, vol. 6650, pp. 30–39. Springer, Heidelberg (2011). https://doi.org/10.1007/978-3-642-22670-0_5
7. Herrera-Joancomartí, J.: Research and challenges on bitcoin anonymity. In: Garcia-Alfaro, J., et al. (eds.) DPM/QASA/SETOP -2014. LNCS, vol. 8872, pp. 3–16. Springer, Cham (2015). https://doi.org/10.1007/978-3-319-17016-9_1
8. Kawachi, A., Tanaka, K., Xagawa, K.: Concurrently secure identification schemes based on the worst-case hardness of lattice problems. In: Pieprzyk, J. (ed.) ASIACRYPT 2008. LNCS, vol. 5350, pp. 372–389. Springer, Heidelberg (2008). https://doi.org/10.1007/978-3-540-89255-7_23
9. Libert, B., Ling, S., Nguyen, K., Wang, H.: Zero-knowledge arguments for lattice-based accumulators: logarithmic-size ring signatures and group signatures without trapdoors. In: Fischlin, M., Coron, J.-S. (eds.) EUROCRYPT 2016. LNCS, vol. 9666, pp. 1–31. Springer, Heidelberg (2016). https://doi.org/10.1007/978-3-662-49896-5_1
10. Liu, J.K., Wei, V.K., Wong, D.S.: Linkable spontaneous anonymous group signature for Ad Hoc groups. In: Wang, H., Pieprzyk, J., Varadharajan, V. (eds.) ACISP 2004. LNCS, vol. 3108, pp. 325–335. Springer, Heidelberg (2004). https://doi.org/10.1007/978-3-540-27800-9_28
11. Lyubashevsky, V.: Lattice-based identification schemes secure under active attacks. In: Cramer, R. (ed.) PKC 2008. LNCS, vol. 4939, pp. 162–179. Springer, Heidelberg (2008). https://doi.org/10.1007/978-3-540-78440-1_10
12. Micciancio, D., Regev, O.: Worst-case to average-case reductions based on Gaussian measures. In: 45th Annual IEEE Symposium on Foundations of Computer Science, pp. 372–381. IEEE (2004)
13. Miers, I., Garman, C., Green, M., Rubin, A.D.: Zerocoin: anonymous distributed e-cash from bitcoin. In: 2013 IEEE Symposium on Security and Privacy, pp. 397–411. IEEE (2013)
14. Sasson, E.B., et al.: Zerocash: decentralized anonymous payments from bitcoin. In: 2014 IEEE Symposium on Security and Privacy, pp. 459–474 (2014). https://doi.org/10.1109/SP.2014.36
15. Shor, J.S., Bemis, L., Kurtz, A.D., Grimberg, I., Weiss, B.Z., Macmillian, M.F., Choyke, W.J.: Characterization of nanocrystallites in porous p-type 6H-SiC. J. Appl. Phys. 76(7), 4045–4049 (1994)
16. Sun, S.-F., Au, M.H., Liu, J.K., Yuen, T.H.: RingCT 2.0: a compact accumulator-based (linkable ring signature) protocol for blockchain cryptocurrency monero. In: Foley, S.N., Gollmann, D., Snekkenes, E. (eds.) ESORICS 2017. LNCS, vol. 10493, pp. 456–474. Springer, Cham (2017). https://doi.org/10.1007/978-3-319-66399-9_25

17. Valenta, L., Rowan, B.: Blindcoin: blinded, accountable mixes for bitcoin. In: Brenner, M., Christin, N., Johnson, B., Rohloff, K. (eds.) FC 2015. LNCS, vol. 8976, pp. 112–126. Springer, Heidelberg (2015). https://doi.org/10.1007/978-3-662-48051-9_9

18. Fiat, A., Shamir, A.: How to prove yourself: practical solutions to identification and signature problems. In: Odlyzko, A.M. (ed.) CRYPTO 1986. LNCS, vol. 263, pp. 186–194. Springer, Heidelberg (1987). https://doi.org/10.1007/3-540-47721-7_12

19. Ben-Sasson, E., Chiesa, A., Genkin, D., Tromer, E., Virza, M.: SNARKs for C: verifying program executions succinctly and in zero knowledge. In: Canetti, R., Garay, J.A. (eds.) CRYPTO 2013. LNCS, vol. 8043, pp. 90–108. Springer, Heidelberg (2013). https://doi.org/10.1007/978-3-642-40084-1_6

20. Lu, X., Au, M.H., Zhang, Z.: Raptor: a practical lattice-based (linkable) ring signature. In: Deng, R.H., Gauthier-Umaña, V., Ochoa, M., Yung, M. (eds.) ACNS 2019. LNCS, vol. 11464, pp. 110–130. Springer, Cham (2019). https://doi.org/10.1007/978-3-030-21568-2_6

21. Yang, R., Au, M.H., Zhang, Z., Xu, Q., Yu, Z., Whyte, W.: Efficient lattice-based zero-knowledge arguments with standard soundness: construction and applications. In: Boldyreva, A., Micciancio, D. (eds.) CRYPTO 2019. LNCS, vol. 11692, pp. 147–175. Springer, Cham (2019). https://doi.org/10.1007/978-3-030-26948-7_6

A Centralized Digital Currency System with Rich Functions

Haibo Tian$^{(\boxtimes)}$, Peiran Luo, and Yinxue Su

Guangdong Key Laboratory of Information Security,
School of Data and Computer Science, Sun Yat-Sen University,
Guangzhou 510275, Guangdong, People's Republic of China
tianhb@mail.sysu.edu.cn

Abstract. The developments of cryptocurrencies push central banks of many countries to consider their own digital fiat currencies. As banks are usually taken as a trusted third party, it is unnecessary to rebuild a blockchain system to rebuild trust. However, cryptocurrencies provide many interesting features except the basic financial functions. It is naturally to absorb the interesting parts of cryptocurrencies to the centralized bank system. We here extract a stateful authentication mechanism from the practice of Ethereum and show how to run puzzle and payment channel templates in a centralized system, based on which we may build a fiat currency lighting network to support direct exchanges of users.

Keywords: Digital fiat currency · Stateful authentication · Payment channel · Lighting network

1 Introduction

Digital fiat currency is a new concept. Bordo and Levin [8] define a digital currency as an asset stored in electronic form as physical currency. Bitcoin [10] and Ether [21] could be viewed as kinds of digital currency if they could be viewed as assets. Meaning et al. [5] define a central bank digital currency as an electronic, fiat liability of a central bank that can be used to settle payments or as a store of value. RSCoin [3] could be viewed as fiat coin since it relies on a central bank to issue coins. Yao [22] describes fiat currency as a credit and algorithm based smart currency supported by cryptographic techniques. So a main difference about fiat currency and non-fiat currency is the issuer of coins. Note that the fiat currency here is not similar to the traditional e-cash concept [24] since there are no digital coins to be really transferred between users.

As a new form of coin, digital fiat currency has attracted the attention of many central banks. The Bank of England has published a serial of staff working papers to discuss topics about fiat currency [13]. The work of Meaning et al. [5] is just one of their achieved papers. The RSCoin system is also inspired by their research agenda [3]. The Bank of Canada [12] has also published a serial of staff working papers and a Jasper project is in progressing to settle interbank

© Springer Nature Switzerland AG 2019
R. Steinfeld and T. H. Yuen (Eds.): ProvSec 2019, LNCS 11821, pp. 288–302, 2019.
https://doi.org/10.1007/978-3-030-31919-9_17

payments. The European Central Bank [23], the Sveriges Riksbank [15] and the People's Bank of China [22] also give research works and experimental projects to study the digital fiat currency.

Among the experimental projects, the RSCoin [3] system is designed for a central bank. It uses the Bitcoin transaction formats so that the coins are embedded in unspent transaction outputs (UTXOs). The UTXOs are divided into shards by transaction identities and each shard is managed by a few mintettes. When some coins are to be spent, a user has to find endorsements from the mintettes managed the coins, and to register new coins to responsible mintettes, which is the essence of their two-phase commitment consensus. The changes of managed coins are recorded by mintettes locally and are submitted to a central bank to form a public ledger. New coins could be poured into the system by the central bank with a blank input. Han et al. [4] gave a user friendly RSCoin system to improve the efficiency of user's client.

Corda [9] system is also designed for financial services. It heavily developed the script abilities of Bitcoin. A transaction is used as a contract of involved participants. Notaries are trusted entities in the system to track the status of transaction outputs. There is no global ledger but notaries may run some consensus algorithm to maintain a permissioned ledger. Quorum [14] system also maintains a permissioned ledger. Smart contracts are used to ensure that only known parties can join the network. For private transactions, only hashes of the transactions are maintained in the permissioned ledger. The plain transaction is kept locally by related nodes.

Tian et al. [19] proposed an AFCoin framework with basic financial functions. Their framework is designed for the central bank and commercial bank binary architecture. It includes a central bank, some commercial banks and a lot of users. The central bank issues fiat currencies to commercial banks, manages a public ledger and a private database for all users and commercial banks. A commercial bank manages fiat currency and normal bank accounts with real identities for users in the bank. A commercial bank submits blocks to the central bank, which includes only hash values of transactions. The AFCoin system is scalable, supports regulations, provides enough privacy for users and could be deployed step by step.

1.1 Related Works

The templates in our paper work in a similar way to smart contracts in the Ethereum and function similar to payment channels in Bitcoin. We here give a short survey about smart contracts and payment channels.

It is generally believed that smart contracts are Nick Szabo's idea [16]. The Ethereum platform makes the concept practical. Delmolino et al. [2] show their experiences to develop a secure smart contract on Ethereum. They revealed a serial of problems including transaction order dependence (TOD), stack size, logic errors and privacy protection. Luu et al. [7] identifies four problems of smart contracts including the time stamp dependence problem. They propose to improve the Ethereum platform to solve problems like TOD. The basic idea is to rely on user's predication to judge whether the starting point of a transaction is correct. They also propose an automatic detection tool "Oyente" which found out about 45% problematic smart contracts at that time. Recently, some new tools emerge like MAINA [11], Mythril [17], Securify [20] and so on.

The payment channel technique is developed to solve the scalability problem of Bitcoin. Poon and Dryja [6] proposed the Bitcoin lighting network. A payment channel of the lighting network is maintained by two users. They should establish a fund transaction and two initial commitment transactions. The fund transaction is published after the initial commitment transactions are exchanged. Users should exchange remedy transaction to falsify the previous commitment transactions and establish new commitment transactions reflecting the new balances of users in the channel. The Raiden network [18] has a similar goal as the Bitcoin lighting network. They provide smart contracts to open, fund, withdraw and close a channel. Users of a channel exchange balance proofs to confirm new status of the channel.

1.2 Contributions

We extract a stateful authentication mechanism from the practice of Ethereum. And we give templates and procedures using the stateful authentication mechanism to enable lighting network in a centralized system. For simplicity, we show a commercial bank could provide smart functions such as puzzle prize or payment channel. Our payment channel template is different to the Bitcoin payment channel or Ethereum Raiden contract. We technically fuses the Raiden and lighting networks. We use counters to differentiate new and old commitments that is similar to the Raiden network. And we require two signatures to open or settle a channel that is similar to the lighting network. The fused templates and procedures are more compact.

2   Stateful Authentication

In Ethereum, a user has an account in the global state maintained by each honest Ethereum node independently. When a user sends a transaction to Ethereum nodes, the user needs to read a counter in its local wallet as T_n. A transaction looks like

$$T = (T_n, \ldots, T_\omega, T_r, T_s)$$

where (T_ω, T_r, T_s) is the signature of the user. The user then increase the counter by one. The Ethereum nodes will verify the signature. If the signature is correct, it checks whether $T_n = \sigma[S(T)]_n$ where $S(T)$ is the user's account address, σ is the global state of Ethereum, and $\sigma[S(T)]_n$ is the counter of the user in the global state. If they are not equivalent, the transaction is dropped. Otherwise, the counter will be increased by one in the global state.

Boyd et al. [1] defined a general stateful authentication scheme. We adapt it to the signature case.

Definition 1. *A stateful authentication scheme Π for a message space $\mathcal{M}$, a key space $\mathcal{K}$, and an output space $\mathcal{C}$ is a tuple of algorithms:*

- $Kgn(1^\lambda) \rightarrow_\$ (sk, pk)$: *A probabilistic key generation algorithm that outputs a signing key sk and a verification key pk where λ is a security parameter.*
- $Snd(sk, m) \rightarrow_\$ c$: *A probabilistic authentication algorithm that takes as input a key $sk \in \mathcal{K}$, a message $m \in \mathcal{M}$, and outputs a message signature pair $c \in \mathcal{C}$.*
- $Rcv(pk, c) \rightarrow \alpha$: *A deterministic verification algorithm that takes as input a verification key $pk \in \mathcal{K}$, a message signature pair $c \in \mathcal{C}$, and outputs a bit $\alpha \in \{0, 1\}$.*

Correctness is that for all $m \in \mathcal{M}$, all $(sk, pk) \leftarrow Kgn(1^\lambda)$, all c such that $c \leftarrow Snd(sk, m)$, we have that $Rcv(pk, c) = 1$.

The security of a stateful authentication scheme of the level 4 in [1] is adapted as follows.

Definition 2. *Let Π be a stateful authentication scheme and let $\mathcal{A}$ be an adversary algorithm. The stateful authentication experiment for Π is given by $Exp_\Pi^{auth}(\mathcal{A})$. The advantage of adversary is defined as*

$$Adv_\Pi^{auth}(\mathcal{A}) := Pr\left[Exp_\Pi^{auth}(\mathcal{A}) = 1\right].$$

The experiment is defined as follows:

$$Exp_\Pi^{auth}(\mathcal{A}) := \begin{pmatrix} (sk, pk) \leftarrow Kgn(1^\lambda) \\ u \leftarrow 0, v \leftarrow 0 \\ r \leftarrow 0 \\ \mathcal{A}^{Send(\cdot), Recv(\cdot)}() \\ return\ r \end{pmatrix}$$

where the $Send(\cdot)$ and $Recv(\cdot)$ oracles are defined as follows:

$$Send(m) := \begin{pmatrix} u \leftarrow u + 1 \\ sent_u \leftarrow Snd(sk, m) \\ return\ sent_u\ to\ \mathcal{A} \end{pmatrix}$$

$$Recv(c) := \begin{pmatrix} v \leftarrow v + 1 \\ rcvd_v \leftarrow c \\ \alpha \leftarrow Rcv(pk, c) \\ if\ (\alpha = 1) \wedge ((u < v) \vee (c \neq sent_v))\ then \\ \quad r \leftarrow 1 \\ return\ r\ to\ \mathcal{A} \end{pmatrix}$$

According to the Ethereum rules, define $c := (m, T_w, T_r, T_s)$ where $T_n \in m$, and pk could be recovered from (T_w, T_r, T_s). That is, the Snd function uses the ECDSA algorithm to sign a message such that signer's public key could be recovered. $Rcv(pk, c)$ in the Ethereum has an explicit counter check step, that is $T_n = \sigma[S(T)]_n$. If $T_n \neq \sigma[S(T)]_n$, a transaction will be dropped, which means $\alpha \neq 1$.

Theorem 1. *Let $c := (m, T_\omega, T_r, T_s)$ where $T_n \in m$, and assume that the Rcv function includes an explicit counter check step. If there is an adversary that could win the $Exp_\Pi^{auth}(\mathcal{A})$ experiment with an advantage ϵ, then the adversary could forge an ECDSA signature with the same advantage.*

Proof. Note that if an adversary wins the game, it outputs 1. There are only two conditions for the adversary to request the *Rcv* oracle to set r as 1. The first condition is that $\alpha = 1$ and $u < v$. $u < v$ means that the *Snd* function has not produced the v-th signature and the *Rcv* function receives the v-th signature. Since $\alpha = 1$, the counter and signature of the v-th signature is correct, which means a successful ECDSA forgery. The second condition is that $\alpha = 1$ and $c \neq sent_v$. By assumption, *Rcv* function includes an explicit counter check step. If $\alpha = 1$, it means the counter in m is equivalent to v so that $c = sent_v$. So the second condition is always false. This means that the advantage of the adversary against the $Exp_\Pi^{auth}(\mathcal{A})$ experiment is the same as the advantage of an adversary against an ECDSA signature scheme.

The above theorem shows that the Ethereum implies a stateful authentication scheme. According to the level 4 definition in [1], the stateful authentication scheme is secure against forgeries, replays, reordering of messages, and dropped messages.

3   A Smart Commercial Bank

A smart commercial bank could provide many services that is unavailable traditionally. However, to enable these services, a user should have an address account. The AFCoin framework provides an "Open Account" method to fulfil this task. But the normal account number of a user and the password of the account is plain. We here use the stateful authentication method to allow a user to open account with privacy. Since there is money transfer in the procedure, we call this operation as "Load".

3.1   Load

A user in a CMB has a normal bank account with real identity of the user. On request of the user, the CMB could set an address account for the user. By the *Snd* function of the stateful authentication, the user sets

$$m_{Load} = (Load, \{NAN, PWD, SN\}_{pk_{CMB}}, v_n, Nonce_A, TS_A)$$

where $Load$ is the identifier of the message, NAN is the normal bank account number of the user, PWD is the password of the normal account, SN is a sequence number for stateful authentication, $\{NAN, PWD, SN\}_{pk_{CMB}}$ denotes a ciphertext encrypted by the public key of the commercial bank CMB, v_n is the initial value transferred from the normal bank account to the address account, and TS_A is the user's timestamp. Then the user produces a key pair by

$(sk, vk) \leftarrow Kgn(1^\lambda)$, computes $c \leftarrow Snd(sk, m_{load})$. The user establishes a TLS channel to the CMB and submits c to the CMB through the channel. Initially, $Nonce_A$ and SN are zeros.

The CMB extracts pk from c and uses $Rcv(pk, c)$ to receive user's message. If $\alpha = 1$ and $Nonce_A = 0$, a new account should be opened. CMB decrypts the ciphertext $\{NAN, PWD, SN\}_{pk_{CMB}}$. It verifies that (NAN, PW) is valid and the SN is zero. Then CMB computes an address account $addr_A = h(pk)$ where $h(\cdot)$ is a hash function. CMB stores $(NAN, 0, addr_A)$ in its private database. CMB then verifies the balance of the NAN and the value v_n. If the balance of NAN is less than v_n, it returns

$$R_{Load} = (h(c), addr_A, 0, TS_{CMB}, \delta_{CMB})$$

where 0 indicates the address account has no money, TS_{CMB} is the bank's timestamp and δ_{CMB} is a signature of the CMB. If the balance of NAN is not less than v_n, it reduces the balance in the NAN by subtracting v_n. CMB then returns

$$R_{Load} = (h(c), addr_A, v_n, TS_{CMB}, \delta_{CMB})$$

to the user. The state of the address account $addr_A$ is updated as $(UA, v_n, 1)$ where UA means that the address account is a user account, v_n is the balance of the account, 1 is the nonce value of $addr_A$.

Next, if $\alpha = 1$ and $Nonce_A \neq 0$, CMB decrypts the ciphertext

$$\{NAN, PWD, SN\}_{pk_{CMB}}.$$

It verifies that (NAN, PW) is valid and the SN is equivalent to one plus the sequence number stored in the bank's private database. Then CMB updates $(NAN, SN, addr_A)$ in its private database. It then verifies the balance of the NAN and the value v_n as before, and returns R_{Load} to the user. The state of the address account $addr_A$ is updated as $(UA, v + v_n, 1)$ where v is the balance of the address account before the "Load" operation.

No matter which value $Nonce_A$ is, CMB puts $(h(c), h(R_{Load}))$ to its local block template and stores $(h(c), c), (h(R_{Load}), R_{Load})$ to its local private database. When the number of hashes in the block template exceeds a threshold or a timeout event happens, a block is produced by the CMB.

Note that we use twice the stateful authentication mechanism. One is about the usage of user's normal bank account. The other is about the state update of an address account.

3.2   Puzzle Prize Template

After a user has an address account, the user could transfer or deposit coins as specified by the AFCoin framework. Further, a commercial bank may develop various conditional transfer templates to enable their users to transfer their money under some conditions. For example, Alice may want to pay fiat coins to anybody who could solve a hash puzzle.

We here define a puzzle prize template. Some symbols in the template will be explained later.

- Name: PuzzlePrize
- Inputs: A puzzle string s, a prize integer v_n and a withdraw time t.
- Execution:
  1. Timeout Event: If the local time is greater than the state variable t of the template address, it checks the state variable v_n of the template address. If the value is greater than zero, it transfers the value to the creator address account, clears the template address account, and returns false. When the amount of the template address is zero, it directly clears the template address account, and returns false.
  2. Prize Event: If the local time is not greater than the state variable t of the template address, it checks state variables of an answer a' and a beneficial address. If they are invalid or empty, it returns true and stops. If the two state variables are valid, it verifies whether $h(a') = s$. If the equation holds, it transfers v_n value to the beneficial address, clears the template address account, and returns false.
- Outputs: A boolean value that indicates the existence of the template address.

To understand the template, we give a user case as follows. Suppose the commercial bank is CMB. It provides the "PuzzlePrize" template. Now a user Alice with an address account in the CMB wants to set a puzzle.

- Alice selects an answer a at random and computes $s = h(a)$. She sets the prize v and the deadline of the puzzle t. Then an m_{Open} message is created, and is wrapped by the Snd function. The output c of the Snd function is sent to CMB.

$$m_{Open} = (Open, PuzzlePrize, s, t, v_n, TS_A)$$

where (s, t, v_n) is the inputs arguments of the $PuzzlePrize$ template.
- CMB uses the Rcv function to receive c. If $\alpha = 1$, CMB checks the $Open$ and $PuzzlePrize$ identifiers in the message m_{Open}. If the two identifiers exist, CMB creates a template address as

$$addr_{A1} = h(pk_A, Nonce_A, PuzzlePrize)$$

where pk_A and $Nonce_A$ are extracted from the message c. CMB updates the state of the $addr_{A1}$ as

$$(TA, v_n, 0, s, t, TS_A, addr_A)$$

where TA denotes a template account, v is the balance of the account, 0 is the nonce value of the account, s and t are the puzzle string and withdraw time, TS_A is the timestamp of Alice, $addr_A$ is the creator address account. The state of $addr_A$ is updated as

$$(UA, v - v_n, Nonce_A + 1).$$

CMB returns $addr_{A1}$ to Alice as part of a R_{Open} message.

Now Alice publishes $addr_{A1}$ with deadline t and the challenge s. Suppose a user Bob gets an answer a' of s. Bob creates an answer message as

$$m_{Answer} = (Answer, addr_{A1}, a', TS_B)$$

and wraps the message by the Snd function. The output c of the Snd functions is sent to the CMB in a secure channel.

CMB uses the Rcv function to receive c. If $\alpha = 1$, CMB checks the identifier. If it is $Answer$, CMB checks whether $addr_{A1}$ exist. If the template address exists, CMB updates the state of the $addr_{A1}$ by adding the answer a' and a beneficial address $addr_B$. CMB then runs the template.

In summary, a puzzle prize template could be opened to have an independent address account storing its long term variables. The variables are the data to be operated by the code in a template. When a template is executed, the address account could be updated or removed.

3.3   Payment Channel Template

Payment channel is an important technique to enable off the chain payment in the fields of cryptocurrencies. As a centralised system, a CMB could also provide a payment channel template to function similarly.

- Name: PaymentChannel
- Inputs: An address $addr_A$, a value v_A, an address $addr_B$, a value v_B, and a timeout parameter t.
- Execution:
  1. Timeout Event: If the local time is greater than state variable t of the template address, it checks the state variables v_A and v_B of the template address. If $v_A \neq 0$ or $v_B \neq 0$, it transfers the non-zero values to their corresponding accounts, separately. And then clears the template address account, and returns false. Otherwise, it clears the template address account, and returns false.
  2. Channel Settlement: If the local time is not greater than state variable t of the template address, it checks the sum of state variables sv_A and sv_B. It the sum is not equal to $v_A + v_B$, it returns true and stops. Else it checks whether the state variable sn is less than the state variable nsn. If the check fails, it returns true and stops. Else it sets $sn \leftarrow nsn$, $v_A \leftarrow sv_A$, $v_B \leftarrow sv_B$, $t \leftarrow nt$ where nt is a state variable, and returns true.
- Outputs: A boolean value that indicates the existence of the template address.

Now suppose a commercial bank CMB provides the $PaymentChannel$ template. User Alice and user Bob want to establish a payment channel.

- Alice negotiates with Bob the channel parameters about address accounts $addr_A$ and $addr_B$, values v_A and v_B and the time parameter t.

– Alice signs the negotiated parameters $m_A = (addr_A, v_A, addr_B, v_B, t, TS_A)$ with the private key of $addr_A$ to get a signature δ_A. Alice sends (m_A, δ_A) to Bob.

– Bob creates an m_{Open} message as

$$m_{Open} = (Open, PaymentChannel, m_A, \delta_A, 0, TS_B)$$

where 0 is the initial sequence number of the payment channel. Bob uses Snd function to wrap the m_{Open} message and sends the output c to CMB.

– CMB uses Rcv function to receive c. If $\alpha = 1$, CMB checks that the identifiers are $Open$ and $PaymentChannel$. If the identifiers are correct, it then checks the timestamp in m_A and verifies the message signature pair (m_A, δ_A). If all verifications passed, it creates a template address as

$$addr_{B1} = h(pk_B, Nonce_B, PaymentChannel).$$

CMB sets the state of $addr_{B1}$ as

$$(TA, v_A + v_B, 0, v_A, addr_A, v_B, addr_B, t, TS_A, TS_B)$$

where $v_A + v_B$ denotes the balance of the template address account, 0 is the last sequence number of the payment channel as the state variable sn, TS_A and TS_B are timestamps in the message c, other state variables are the input arguments of a payment channel template. CMB updates the balance of $addr_A$ as $v - v_A$ and the balance of $addr_B$ as $v' - v_B$ where v and v' are the original balances of the address accounts, respectively. CMB returns $addr_{B1}$ to Bob in a R_{Open} message.

Bob sends the template address $addr_{B1}$ to Alice. Alice could check the state of the address for confirmations from the CMB. Then with this channel, Alice and Bob could exchange values without the help of a bank.

– If Alice wants to pay v_A^1 value to Bob, she signs a message

$$m_A^1 = (addr_{B1}, addr_A, v_A - v_A^1, addr_B, v_B + v_A^1, t^1, 1, TS_A^1)$$

where $v_A - v_A^1$ and $v_B + v_A^1$ are the new balances of the two addresses $addr_A$ and $addr_B$ in the channel, t^1 is a new timeout parameter, 1 is the new sequence number of the channel, TS_A^1 is a timestamp. Alice signs m_A^1 to get a signature δ_A^1. Alice sends the message signature pair to Bob.

– Bob checks whether the new sequence number in m_A^1 is equivalent to its local current sequence number plus one, and whether the timeout parameter is greater than its local stored timeout value, and checks the validity of balances, addresses, and the timestamp in m_A^1. If these parameters are valid, Bob updates its local sequence number and new balances of the channel. Bob could create a commitment message m_C^1 to update the channel state now. m_C^1 is defined as

$$m_C^1 = (m_A^1, \delta_A^1, TS_B^1, \delta_B^1).$$

Bob sends back Alice values similarly. When Alice and Bob could create a commitment message with a higher sequence number, the older messages with smaller sequence numbers could be deleted.

Alice or Bob has the ability to update a payment channel with a commitment message.

- If Alice or Bob wants to update a payment channel, it submits a commitment transaction by the Snd function. Suppose Alice produces an update message as

$$m_{Update} = (Update, m_C^i, TS_A)$$

  where m_C^i is the i-th commitment message. m_{Update} is wrapped in the Snd function to produce a message c that is sent to the CMB.
- CMB runs Rcv function to verify the received c. If $\alpha = 1$ and the identifier is $Update$, CMB finds the address parameter $addr_{B1}$. If the address account is not exist, CMB stops. Otherwise, CMB checks the timestamps and signatures in m_C^i. For example, the two timestamps should be close enough. CMB checks the addresses in m_C^i are the same as the addresses in the state of $addr_{B1}$. If all the checks are correct, CMB updates the state of the address by adding new state variables $sv_A \leftarrow v_A - v_A^i$ and $sv_B \leftarrow v_B + v_A^i$, $nt \leftarrow t^i$, and $nsn \leftarrow i$. CMB then executes the payment channel template.

Remark 1. Note that only the timeout event of the payment channel may remove a payment channel template account. So for payment channel users, before the timeout of a payment channel, they should check the sequence number in the template address account and the sequence number in their local storage. If Alice or Bob does have a higher sequence number commitment message, they should certainly submit the new commitment message to update the payment channel. In this way, the impact of an older commitment message could be removed.

In summary, we build a payment channel template. Users could establish a bidirectional payment channel, change the status of the channel, and close the channel. Especially, the status changing operations are executed without the help of a bank.

3.4   Hashed Time Lock Contract

The hashed time lock contract (HTLC) technique is critical to change payment channels to payment network. It is easy to support HTLC in a centralized system. The *PaymentChannel* template keeps unchanged. When Alice or Bob exchange values in the channel, an extra hash value h_v and a hash preimage h_p are added.

- If Alice wants to pay v_A^1 value to Bob conditioned on that Bob provides the hash preimage of h_v, she signs a message

$$m_A^1 = (addr_{B1}, addr_A, v_A - v_A^1, addr_B, v_B + v_A^1, t^1, h_v, 1, TS_A^1)$$

  where the only change is to add a parameter h_v.

– Bob checks m_A^1 as before. Now if Bob knows the hash preimage h_p such that $h_v = hash(h_p)$, it could create a commitment message m_C^1 to update the channel state, where

$$m_C^1 = (m_A^1, \delta_A^1, h_p, TS_B^1, \delta_B^1).$$

When the new type of commitment message are sent to a CMB, the CMB adds a verification to check that $h_v = hash(h_p)$.

– The m_{Update} has not changed.
– CMB now checks whether $h_v = h(h_p)$. If all the checks are correct, CMB operates as before.

3.5 Payment Network

With the HTLC ability, users with payment channels could establish a payment network without a bank similarly to the Bitcoin lighting network.

Suppose there are three users Alice, Bob and Charlie. Alice has established a payment channel with Bob at address $addr_{B1}$, and Bob has established a payment channel with Charlie at address $addr_{C1}$. Now, Alice wants to transfer one fiat coin to Charlie with the help of Bob.

– Alice contacts Charlie to obtain a hash value h_v.
– Alice signs a message

$$m_A^i = (addr_{B1}, addr_A, v_A - 1, addr_B, v_B + 1, t^i, h_v, i, TS_A^i)$$

where i is the new payment channel sequence number of Alice and Bob. Alice sends this message and its signature to Bob with the identity of Charlie.
– Bob signs a message

$$m_B^j = (addr_{C1}, addr_B, v_B - 1, addr_C, v_c + 1, t^j, h_v, j, TS_B^j)$$

where j is the new payment channel sequence number of Bob and Charlie. Bob sends this message and its signature to Charlie.
– Charlie signs a commitment message

$$m_C^j = (m_B^j, \delta_B^j, h_p, TS_C^j, \delta_C^j).$$

Charlie sends back this message and its signature to Bob.
– Bob signs a commitment message

$$m_C^i = (m_A^i, \delta_A^i, h_p, TS_B^i, \delta_B^i).$$

Bob sends back this message and its signature to Alice.

Now the channel states of the two channels are changed without the help of a bank. Alice sends one fiat coin to Bob and Bob transfers one fiat coin to Charlie. It is natural for Bob to set a transferring fee for this service. Then a profitable payment network without a bank could be established.

Remark 2. In the above example, after Bob sends values to Charlie, Charlie should send back the corresponding commitment message. If Charlie does not send back such a commitment message, Bob could update the payment channel of Bob and Charlie with a commitment message containing an older sequence number. So Bob should have the last commitment message before Bob transfers new coins to Charlie.

4 Security Analysis

4.1 Regulations of Commercial Banks

We have shown that CMB could provide new services for users with an address account. It seems that a user has to totally trust its CMB. However, in the framework of AFCoin, this problem is alleviated.

In the AFCoin framework, each CMB should have a valid certificate from the trustable central bank CB. That is, a CMB registers its public key pk_{CMB} to the CB through a register interface provided by CB. They may follow a registration routine in a certificate authority. The CB only communicates with registered CMBs. Each registered CMB stores a certificate of CB.

CMB should pack the hashes of transactions and responses into a block. The block head includes a Merkel tree root whose leaves are hash pairs, a Merkle Patricia tree root about the global state of the bank, and a previous block head hash value to form a chain. Note that all blocks in a chain are produced by the same CMB. CMB are expected to submit its blocks, related transactions, responses, a list of states and templates to the CB. CB may use some blind test policies to check the validity of blocks. For valid blocks, CB put them in a distributed database. CB sets a public read right so that anybody could check the blocks in the database.

So in the AFCoin system, the public ledger is simply a distributed database with public read rights and private write rights. A block chain is produced by a CMB. Different CMBs have different block chains. Except block heads, the only useful information in the public ledger is hash values. Hash values are useful for a user to confirm their transactions. If a user receives a response from their CMB, and the user could not find the hashes of the transaction and response from the public ledger after a reasonable waiting time, the user could complain the CMB through an interface provided by the CB. The CB should take some actions to punish a careless CMB if a complain is confirmed.

The AFCoin system also provides an idea to alleviate the burden of CB. CB may produce a list of CMBs in the public ledger. Periodically, CB may put a random number in the public ledger too. Then a CMB could use the last random number in the ledger to select two random audit CMBs. Then the CMB submits a new block with its related transactions, responses and templates to the audit CMBs. For correct blocks, an audit CMB should produce a list of states to be updated by the block with their signature. Then the CMB could submit blocks with the extra two valid signatures and a list of states to CB. For a block with three signatures, CB could skip the verification steps and update the states according to the list.

So a CMB is regulated by users, random audit CMBs and the CB. A user could put their trust on the whole system instead of a single CMB.

4.2 Templates Security

Note that templates in our design are provided by banks. It is impossible for a user to develop a hostile template and wish it to be invoked by a bank. These templates should be checked carefully to remove logic errors and other common errors such as memory overflow before they serve users. Then there left a transaction order dependence problem and a time stamp dependence problem.

If our templates are deployed as smart contracts on the Ethereum, they suffer from the two problems. If the "PuzzlePrize" template serves as a smart contract, the transaction order dependence problem is obvious. Suppose two users send their valid answers at almost the same time. A miner could select one of them as the lucky one to get the prize. Or a miner could create their own transaction with the right answer, and put the transaction before other transactions. The time stamp dependence problem also exists since we use timestamps in the templates.

However, in the AFCoin framework, the above problems are weakened. Note that a CMB should give a response to a transaction. The timestamps on the responses and transactions could be used as evidences in the regulation phase if CMB executes a transaction in a wrong order. Additionally, a CMB has a certificate from CB. It is not a random node in the Ethereum. If a CMB behaves dishonestly, it may be revoked from the financial system, which is a cost higher than obtaining some benefits from their users. Finally, it is more easy for a regulated system to establish a trusted time mechanism than the totally distributed system like Ethereum. Time stamps could be used in the templates and protocols.

5   Conclusion

We show that a centralized system could provide templates to provide smart services like other cryptocurrencies. In fact, banks should select some typical services of the cryptocurrencies, build well-tested templates for their users. For simplicity, we here do not consider the inter-bank cases of the smart functions. We notice that the AFCoin framework provides an inter-bank transfer procedure, which may be used here to enable smart functions serving inter-bank users.

Acknowledgment. This work is supported by the National Key R&D Program of China (2017YFB0802500), Guangxi Key Laboratory of Cryptography and Information Security (No. GCIS201711), Natural Science Foundation of China (61672550), Fundamental Research Funds for the Central Universities (No. 17lgjc45). Natural Science Foundation of Guangdong Province of China (2018A0303 130133).

References

1. Boyd, C., Hale, B., Mjølsnes, S.F., Stebila, D.: From stateless to stateful: generic authentication and authenticated encryption constructions with application to TLS. In: Sako, K. (ed.) CT-RSA 2016. LNCS, vol. 9610, pp. 55–71. Springer, Cham (2016). https://doi.org/10.1007/978-3-319-29485-8_4
2. Delmolino, K., Arnett, M., Kosba, A., Miller, A., Shi, E.: Step by step towards creating a safe smart contract: lessons and insights from a cryptocurrency lab. In: Clark, J., Meiklejohn, S., Ryan, P.Y.A., Wallach, D., Brenner, M., Rohloff, K. (eds.) FC 2016. LNCS, vol. 9604, pp. 79–94. Springer, Heidelberg (2016). https://doi.org/10.1007/978-3-662-53357-4_6
3. Danezis, G., Meiklejohn, S.: Centrally banked cryptocurrencies. In: Network and Distributed System Security Symposium 2016, NDSS 2016, pp. 1–14. ACM (2016)
4. Han, X., Liu, Y., Xu, H.: A user-friendly centrally banked cryptocurrency. In: Liu, J.K., Samarati, P. (eds.) ISPEC 2017. LNCS, vol. 10701, pp. 25–42. Springer, Cham (2017). https://doi.org/10.1007/978-3-319-72359-4_2
5. Meaning, J., Dyson, B., Barker, J., Clayton, E.: Broadening narrow money: monetary policy with a central bank digital currency (2018). https://www.bankofengland.co.uk/working-paper/2018/. Accessed 12 Aug 2018
6. Poon, J., Dryja, T.: The bitcoin lightning network: scalable off-chain instant payments (2016). http://lightning.network/lightning-network-paper.pdf
7. Luu, L., Chu, D.-H., Olickel, H., Saxena, P., Hobor, A.: Making smart contracts smarter. In: Proceedings of the 2016 ACM SIGSAC Conference on Computer and Communications Security, CCS 2016, New York, NY, USA, pp. 254–269. ACM (2016)
8. Bordo, M.D., Levin, A.T.: Central bank digital currency and the future of monetary policy (2017). https://www.hoover.org/sites/default/files/bordo-levin_bullets_for_hoover_may2017.pdf. Accessed 12 Aug 2018
9. Hearn, M.: Corda: a distributed ledger (2016)
10. Nakamoto, S.: Bitcoin: a peer-to-peer electronic cash system (2008). https://bitcoin.org/bitcoin.pdf. Accessed 4 Aug 2017
11. Nikolic, I., Kolluri, A., Sergey, I., Saxena, P., Hobor, A.: Finding the greedy, prodigal, and suicidal contracts at scale (2018). https://arxiv.org/abs/1802.06038. Accessed 1 July 2019
12. Bank of Canada: Staff working papers (2018). https://www.bankofcanada.ca/research/browse/?content_type[]=31. Accessed 12 Aug 2018
13. Bank of England: Staff working papers (2018). https://www.bankofengland.co.uk/news/publications. Accessed 12 Aug 2018
14. Quorum: Welcome to the quorum wiki! (2016). https://github.com/jpmorganchase/quorum/wiki. Accessed 12 Aug 2018
15. Riksbank, S.: The Riksbank's e-krona project (2018). https://www.riksbank.se/globalassets/media/rapporter/e-krona/2017/handlingsplan_ekrona_171221_eng.pdf. Accessed 12 Aug 2018
16. Szabo, N.: Formalizing and securing relationships on public networks. First Monday 2(9), 1 (1997)
17. M. Team. Mythril (2018). https://github.com/ConsenSys/mythril. Accessed 1 July 2019
18. R. N. Team: Raiden network 0.100.3 documentation (2019). https://raiden-network.readthedocs.io/en/latest

19. Tian, H., Chen, X., Ding, Y., Zhu, X., Zhang, F.: AFCoin: a framework for digital fiat currency of central banks based on account model. In: Guo, F., Huang, X., Yung, M. (eds.) Inscrypt 2018. LNCS, vol. 11449, pp. 70–85. Springer, Cham (2019). https://doi.org/10.1007/978-3-030-14234-6_4

20. Tsankov, P.: Security analysis of smart contracts in datalog. In: Margaria, T., Steffen, B. (eds.) ISoLA 2018. LNCS, vol. 11247, pp. 316–322. Springer, Cham (2018). https://doi.org/10.1007/978-3-030-03427-6_24

21. Wood, D.G.: Ethereum: a secure decentralised generalised transaction ledger homestead (2014). http://gavwood.com/paper.pdf. Accessed 4 Aug 2017

22. Yao, Q.: A systematic framework to understand central bank digital currency. Sci. China Inf. Sci. **61**(3), 033101 (2018)

23. Mersch, Y.: Digital base money: an assessment from the ECB's perspective (2017). http://www.ecb.europa.eu/press/key/date/2017/html/sp170116.en.html. Accessed 12 Aug 2018

24. Zhang, F., Zhang, F., Wang, Y.: Fair electronic cash systems with multiple banks. In: Qing, S., Eloff, J.H.P. (eds.) SEC 2000. ITIFIP, vol. 47, pp. 461–470. Springer, Boston, MA (2000). https://doi.org/10.1007/978-0-387-35515-3_47

Chameleon Hash Time-Lock Contract for Privacy Preserving Payment Channel Networks

Bin Yu[1,2], Shabnam Kasra Kermanshahi[1,2(✉)], Amin Sakzad[1],
and Surya Nepal[2]

[1] Monash University, Melbourne, VIC 3800, Australia
{bin.yu,shabnam.kasra,amin.sakzad}@monash.edu
[2] CSIRO Data 61, Melbourne, VIC 3008, Australia
Surya.Nepal@data61.csiro.au

Abstract. Payment channel networks (PCNs) have been proposed to address the low transaction throughput of the permissionless blockchain protocols. Though the PCNs allow users to have the unlimited number of transactions in the channel without interacting with blockchain, it leaks the entire payment paths to the public. To address the payment path leakage issue, we propose a Chameleon-hash based payment protocol, called Chameleon Hash Time-Lock Contract (CHTLC). Using Chameleon-hash function in a multi-layer fashion guarantees that no user can recover the payment path if at least one intermediate payment node is honest. For the same payment path, compared with Multi-hop Hash Time-Lock Contract (MHTLC) protocol of Malavolta et al. [1], CHTLC is 5 times faster in the payment data initialisation, and the communication bandwidth is reduced significantly from $17,000\,\mathrm{KB}$ to just $7.7\,\mathrm{KB}$.

Keywords: Blockchain · Payment channel networks · Payment privacy

1 Introduction

Bitcoin [2] and Ethereum [3] are two largest cryptocurrencies in the world. Instead of storing the transactions on a centralised ledger, these transactions are stored on different participants in an immutable chain structure database. However, due to the scalability nature, it is difficult to have all the nodes to achieve consistency in a relatively short time which results in the low transaction throughput. On average, Bitcoin can only handle 7 transactions per second [4], while Visa can handle 2000 transactions per second [4].

To address the low transaction throughput issue, Bitcoin proposes a new payment scheme called "lightning network" [5] which supports off-chain transactions to avoid the transaction confirmation time. In a nutshell, a pair of users open a payment channel by locking their bitcoins in the smart contract as deposits. After that, off-chain payment transactions can be placed by agreeing on the new distribution of the deposits. The payment channel is closed by publishing the

R. Steinfeld and T. H. Yuen (Eds.): ProvSec 2019, LNCS 11821, pp. 303–318, 2019.
https://doi.org/10.1007/978-3-030-31919-9_18

allocation of the final deposit on the blockchain by any party. Though the transaction throughput is increased by avoiding putting all the transactions on the blockchain, it limits the payment to be settled between two direct users. It is a great convenience if the existing payment channels can forward the payment for the users who has no direct payment channels. To address this issue, payment channel networks (PCNs) are proposed and instantiated by some popular protocols [6–9]. However, there exists a serious payment privacy leakage in the PCNs [10–12]. If some/all the intermediate nodes who are involved in the payment path put the transaction on the chain as the closing transaction, anyone can recover the partial/full payment path. Additionally, intermediate nodes can collude with each other to identify part/all of the nodes that are involved in a given payment path.

For all the PCNs, all the payment protocols should ensure that the payment is secured which means none of the participants loses their money if the payment channel is terminated unexpectedly. Additionally, to make the PCNs more attractive to privacy-sensitive users, the system should prevent others from knowing who is paying whom. PriPay [13] leverages the trusted hardware to encrypt the PCNs data at the server and uses oblivious algorithms to hide the access patterns. Nevertheless, PrivPay suffers from the low scalability and single point failure. TumbleBit [14] employs a trusted intermediary to achieve the privacy of the payment path, however, all the participants should trust the intermediary. SlientWhisper [12] employs the long-term keys and temporary keys schemes to ensure that the payment between each intermediate nodes are signed by different keys, thus, no one can link the transactions in a payment. However, the participants need to run a complicated key management process. MHTLC [1] avoids the complicated key management and can work in a trust-free environment. Our protocol aims to prevent the blockchain observer from knowing the payment value between the sender and the receiver. In our framework, unless all the intermediate nodes collude with each other, none can recover the payment path between the sender and the receiver. Compared with MHTLC, for each intermediate node, we reduce the communication size from 1650 KB to 0.32 KB; additionally, we avoid the time-consuming zero-knowledge proof generation process, which consumes 309 ms in MHTLC. Hence the contributions of our work are as follows:

- We propose a new payment protocol called Chameleon Hash Time-Lock Contract (CHTLC), which hides the payment path from the view of payment participants and the observer who analyses the blocks that are committed on the chain. We also prove the security of CHTLC and show that CHTLC achieves the same level of security as MHTLC.
- Our protocol is efficient in both time and space. Our experimental results indicate that in comparison with MHTLC protocol [1], our protocol is much more efficient in payment forwarding. That is, MHTLC spends 309 ms per user to generate the zero-knowledge proof required for the payment, whereas such procedure is avoided in our protocol. For each intermediate node, MHTLC needs to transmit 1, 650 KB data between each node, while it is reduced to only 0.96 KB data in our CHTLC protocol.

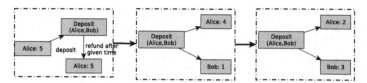

Opening Transaction   Intermediate Transaction   Closing Transaction

(a) Off-chain payment.

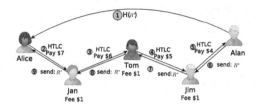

(b) HTLC payment channel networks.

Fig. 1. PCNs.

2   Background

We first present the preliminaries required for understanding this paper. For the sake of readability, the notations which are used frequently are presented in Table 1.

2.1   Payment Channel

A payment channel [15–17] establishes a private peer-to-peer medium, ruled by a set of pre-set instructions, e.g., smart contract. The payment channel allows the involved participants to consent to the state updates unanimously by exchanging authenticated state transitions off-chain [18]. Figure 1a demonstrates how the payment channel is established between two entities. Before the payment is placed, they need to agree on a transaction known as the opening transaction to be put on the blockchain. In the opening transaction, two parties make the deposit to the "joint-account" of which the signatures from both parties are required to spend the money. Both parties can have the transactions off the chain once the channel is opened. Any party can close the channel by putting the latest transaction known as the closing transaction on the blockchain which

Table 1. Notations

Notation	Definition
B	Blockchain
t	Expiration time
f	fee
v	Channel capacity
$c_{\langle u,u' \rangle}$	A unique channel identifier between users u and u'
$\mathcal{F}$	Ideal functionality
$\mathcal{L}$	List of the off-chain payments
$\mathcal{C}$	List of the closed channels
$|B| = t$	Time corresponds to the number of entries of the blockchain
h	Entry identifier in $\mathcal{L}$
u	A user
$H_i(x, r)$	Chameleon hash using public key of u_i with input x and randomness r

shows how the money in the "joint account" is distributed back to them. To avoid any party publish the historical transaction unilaterally as the closing transaction of his favor to invalid the rest of the transactions[1], asymmetric revocable commitment schemes are employed [19]. Payment channels can be further extended with a special type of smart contract (e.g., Hash Time-Locked Contracts (HTLC) [15,20], Global Preimage [11]) that allows the participants to commit funds to a redeemable secret with an expiration time [19]. HTLS has already been integrated with Bitcoin Lightning network [16] and DMCs [15]. We assume the sender Alice wants to pay Bob, x dollars, with the expectation y, the hash function Hash and the locked time t, the **HTLC** looks like the following [16]:

> **HTLC**(Alice, Bob, x, y, t) **If** B can provide the condition R^* such that Hash(R^*) = y before t seconds, Alice pays Bob, x dollars.
> **Else** if t seconds elapsed, Alice will be fully refund.

2.2   Payment Channel Network

The design of having the established channel firstly before having the transactions disadvantages discourages some parties who may not be willing to make a deposit to the one they do not have the transactions frequently. To address this issue, **HTLC** based PCNs are proposed to avoid setting up the payment

---

[1] For instance, the sender pays the receiver 10 times through the channel, however, the sender may put the first transaction on the chain to invalid the rest of the transactions.

channels while preserving the high transaction throughput. In PCNs, the sender involves the nodes in the network to help them relay the payment by offering transaction fees as the award for forwarding the payment. Figure 1b demonstrates how Alice as a sender pays \$4 to Alan as a receiver through the payment network (we assume the transaction fees for all the intermediate nodes are set to \$1). Firstly, Alan sends hash value of a random secret R^* to Alice. In the second step, Alice creates a payment with Jan asking her to forward the payment to Tom. In the payment, "Alice is committing 7 of her channel balance to be paid to Jan if Jan releases the secret R^* in 10 s, or the money is refunded back to Alice if 10 s elapsed". On receiving this payment, Jan knows that Tom can show her the secret R^* and helps her to get the money that Alice committed to her. She deducts \$1 from the payment amount as the transaction fee and creates a similar payment between herself and Tom. Finally, in step 5, Alan receives this \$4 payment commitment, as he is the one who has the secret R^*, thus revealing R^* to Jim to redeem the money from Jim's commitment. Since Jim can only redeem the payment from Tom by revealing the R^*, Jim sends the R^* to Tom and claims the money. In this way, the payment between Alice and Alan is settled without having a payment channel established directly.

In **HTLC**, every participant is assigned with a maximum time frame that they can pull the money from the sender to avoid any part suspends the channel by refusing forwarding the payment. Though **HTLC** is compatible with Bitcoin, it leads to serious privacy leakages. First, for any colluded nodes, by exchanging the Hash(R^*) they received and sent, they can tell whether they are involved in the same payment. Additionally, if they are the nodes that linked directly with the sender and receiver, they can release the identities of the sender and receiver. Second, if the **HTLC** commitments are broadcast on the blockchain, observers who are not involved in the payment can recover the payment path by identifying the transactions on the blockchain with the same Hash(R^*).

Syntax of PCN. We define the payment channel as a directed graph $\mathbb{G} := (\mathbb{V}, \mathbb{E})$ where $\mathbb{V}$ is the set of Bitcoin accounts and $\mathbb{E}$ is the set of currently open payment channels. A PCN consists of following algorithms [1].

- OpenChannel(u_i, u_j, β, t, f) $\rightarrow$ $\{0, 1\}$: This algorithm admits two Bitcoin addresses $u_i, u_j \in \mathbb{V}$, an initial channel capacity β, a timeout t, and a fee value f, if the operation is authorized by u_i, and u_i owns at least β bitcoins. Then, it creates a new payment channel $\left(c_{\langle u_i, u_j \rangle}, \beta, f, t \right) \in \mathbb{E}$, where $c_{\langle u_i, u_j \rangle}$ is a fresh channel identifier. Then this channel identifier is uploaded to B and returns 1. Otherwise, it returns 0.
- CloseChannel($c_{\langle u_i, u_j \rangle}, v$) $\rightarrow$ $\{0, 1\}$: This algorithm gets a channel identifier $c_{\langle u_i, u_j \rangle}$ and a balance v as inputs. If the operation is authorized by both users, CloseChannel removes the corresponding channel from $\mathbb{G}$, includes the balance v in B, and finally returns 1. Otherwise, it returns 0.
- Pay($\left(c_{\langle u_1, u_2 \rangle}, \dots, c_{\langle u_{n-1}, u_n \rangle} \right), v$) $\rightarrow$ $\{1, 0\}$: This algorithm inputs a list of channel identifiers $\left(c_{\langle u_1, u_2 \rangle}, \dots, c_{\langle u_{n-1}, u_n \rangle} \right)$ which form a path from the

sender u_1 to the receiver u_n and a payment value v. If each payment channel $c_{\langle u_i, u_{i+1} \rangle}$ in the path has at least a current balance $\gamma_i \geq v_i'$, with $v_i' = v - \sum_{j=1}^{i-1} \text{fee} u_j)$, the Pay operation decreases the current balance for each payment channel $c_{\langle u_i, u_{i+1} \rangle}$ by v_i' and returns 1. Otherwise, none of the balances at the payment channels is modified and the Pay operation returns 0.

PCN Security and Privacy Goals. The security and privacy goals of our PCNs system are summarised as follows:

- Balance security: It guarantees that any honest user involved in a payment does not lose money even when the other involving participants are corrupted.
- Serializability: We require that the executions of PCN are serializable. That is, for every concurrent execution of Pay operation, there exists an equivalent sequential execution.
- (Off-path) Value Privacy: This ensures that for a Pay operation involving only honest users, corrupted users outside the payment path learn no information about the payment value.
- (On-path) Relationship Anonymity: Given two simultaneous successful Pay operations of the form $\left\{ \mathsf{Pay}_i \left(\left(c_{\langle s_i, u_1 \rangle}, \ldots, c_{\langle u_n, r_i \rangle} \right), v \right) \right\}_{i \in [0,1]}$ with at least one honest intermediate user $u_{j \in [1,n]}$ corrupted intermediate users cannot determine the pair (s_i, r_i) for a given Pay_i with probability better than $1/2$.

Ideal World Functionality. To satisfy the security and privacy of our construction, we apply the ideal functionality as defined in [1]. This model captures Balance security, Serializability, Value privacy, and Relationship anonymity (see [1] for detailed discussions). The ideal world functionality $\mathcal{F}$ for PCNs consists of three main algorithms: OpenChannel, CloseChannel, and Pay. This is a trusted functionality, which interacts with the users and maintains the blockchain B using two lists $\mathcal{L}$ and $\mathcal{C}$. The adversary $\mathscr{A}$ is a probabilistic polynomial-time machine which is capable of adding users to the system and corrupt them at any time to gain the internal state of the users and all of incoming/outgoing communications.

- OpenChannel: This algorithm inputs $\left(\text{Open}, c_{\langle u, u' \rangle}, v, u', t, f \right)$ from a user u. The ideal functionality $\mathcal{F}$ checks $c_{\langle u, u' \rangle}$ for valid identifiers and not being duplicated, then sends $\left(c_{\langle u, u' \rangle}, v, t, f \right)$ to u'. If u' authorizes the operation, $\mathcal{F}$ appends $\left(c_{\langle u, u' \rangle}, v, t, f \right)$ to B and $\left(c_{\langle u, u' \rangle}, v, t, h \right)$ to $\mathcal{L}$, for some random h. $\mathcal{F}$ returns h to u and u'.
- CloseChannel: This algorithm inputs $\left(\text{Close}, c_{\langle u, u' \rangle}, h \right)$ from u or u'. In this framework, $\mathcal{F}$ checks B for $\left(c_{\langle u, u' \rangle}, v, t, f \right)$ and $\mathcal{L}$ for $\left(c_{\langle u, u' \rangle}, v, t, h \right)$ where $h \neq \perp$. If $(c_{\langle u, u' \rangle} \in \mathcal{C}$ or $t > |\mathsf{B}|$ or $t' > |\mathsf{B}|)$ the functionality aborts. Otherwise, the ideal functionality $\mathcal{F}$ adds $\left(c_{\langle u, u' \rangle}, u', v', t' \right)$ to B and adds $c_{\langle u, u' \rangle}$ to $\mathcal{C}$. Then, $\mathcal{F}$ notifies both users involved with a message $\left(c_{\langle u, u' \rangle}, \perp, h \right)$.
- Pay: Given $\left(\text{Pay}, v, \left(c_{\langle u_1, u_2 \rangle}, \ldots, c_{\langle u_{n-1}, u_n \rangle} \right), (t_0, \ldots, t_n) \right)$ from u_1, the ideal functionality $\mathcal{F}$ performs the interactive payment protocol as presented in Algorithm 1.

As defined in Algorithm 1, $\mathcal{F}$ first ensures that the channel has enough capacity. Then, each user decides to accept or reject a payment. At the end, $\mathcal{F}$ updates the $\mathcal{L}$ and notifies the involving users.

Algorithm 1. Payment protocol in Ideal world

Input: $\left(\text{Pay}, v, \left(c_{\langle u_1, u_2 \rangle}, \ldots, c_{\langle u_{n-1}, u_n \rangle}\right), (t_0, \ldots, t_n)\right)$

Output: updated $\mathcal{L}$

1: **for** $i = 2, \ldots, n$ **do**
2:     Sample h_i at random
3:     **if** $\left(c_{\langle u_{i-1}, u_i' \rangle}, v_i, t_i', f_i\right) \in \mathrm{B}$ **then**
4:         Send $\left(h_i, h_{i+1}, c_{\langle u_{i-1}, u_i \rangle}, c_{\langle u_i, u_{i+1} \rangle}, v - \sum_{j=i}^n f_j, t_{i-1}, t_i\right)$ to $u_{i \neq n}$ via private channel
5:         Send $\left(h_{n+1}, c_{\langle u_{n-1}, u_n \rangle}, v, t_n\right)$ to the receiver
6:         **for** $\left(c_{\langle u_{i-1}, u_i \rangle}, v_i', \cdot\right) \in \mathcal{L}$ **do**
7:             **if** $v_i' \geq \left(v - \sum_{j=i}^n f_j\right)$ & $t_{i-1} \geq t_i$ **then**
8:                 Add $d_i = \left(c_{\langle u_{i-1}, u_i \rangle}, \left(v_i' - \left(v - \sum_{j=i}^n f_j\right)\right), t_i, \bot\right)$ to $\mathcal{L}$
9:             **else**
10:                 Delete all d_i added in this phase to $\mathcal{L}$ and abort.
11:     **else**
12:         Abort
13: **for** $i = n, \ldots, 1$ **do**
14:     Query u_i with (h_i, h_{i+1}) via private channel
15:     **if** $\exists u_j$ return $\bot$ s.t. all u_i returned $\top$ $(i > j)$ **then**
16:         $j = 0$
17: **for** $i = j + 1, \ldots, n$ **do**
18:     Update $d_i \in \mathcal{L}$ to $(-, -, -, h_i)$
19:     Send (success, h_i, h_{i+1}) to u_i
20: **for** $i = 1 \ldots, j$ where $j \neq 0$ **do**
21:     Remove d_i from $\mathcal{L}$
22:     Send $(\bot, h_i, h_{i+1})$
23: **return** updated $\mathcal{L}$

2.3 Routing in PCNs

For an effective routing protocol, it should work out the payment path from the sender to the receiver with a short time delay. It is also important that the routing protocol can be applied in the dynamic PCNs, in which nodes may join/leave the network frequently. Since it is impossible for the sender to store all the payment paths in the network, landmark routing technique [21] is proposed to maintain a set of paths between the sender and the receiver. The key idea is to provide a path from the sender to the receiver through an intermediate node called landmark node. However, the landmark nodes may not contain all the possible paths which may result in a payment path with low success probability [10,13]. Flare [22] asks all the participants to maintain some of the path information of the neighbors. This design discourages the client which has limited computation source (e.g., smart phone payers), additionally, it cannot guarantee that the provided payment path has the relatively low transaction fee. SpeedyMurmurs [23] is another routing algorithm for PCNs which provides formal privacy guarantees in fully distributed settings. However, because of the overhead in privacy guarantees, it is not that effective in a dynamic PCNs.

2.4   Chameleon-Hash Functions

Chameleon-hash functions [24] also known as trapdoor-hash functions are the hash functions which have a trapdoor allowing one to find arbitrary collisions in the domain of the functions. However, as long as the trapdoor is not known, Chameleon-hash functions are collision resistant. A chameleon-hash function **CH** consists of the following algorithms:

- CHSetup: This algorithm first chooses two large prime numbers p and q such that $p = kq + 1$ for an integer k. Then, selects g of order q in $\mathbb{Z}_p^*$. Finally, it outputs $\xi \in \mathbb{Z}_q^*$ as the private key sk and $y = g^\xi \mod p$ as the public key pk.
- CHash: On an input value x, this algorithm chooses a random value $r \in \mathbb{Z}_q^*$ and outputs $H_{\mathrm{pk}}(x, r) = g^x y^r \mod p$.
- Trapdoor collision: Given $x, x', r \in \mathbb{Z}_q^*$ as input, this algorithm outputs r' such that $H_{\mathrm{pk}}(x, r) = H_{\mathrm{pk}}(x', r')$. This is done by solving for r' in $x + \xi r = x' + \xi r' \mod q$.

Definition 1. (Indistinguishability). *For all pairs of message x and x', the probability distribution of the random value $H_{\mathrm{pk}}(x, r)$ and $H_{\mathrm{pk}}(x', r)$ are computationally indistinguishable.*

Definition 2. (Collision-Resistance). *Without the knowledge of trapdoor key sk, there exists no efficient algorithm that, on input x, x', and a random string r, outputs a string r' that satisfy $H_{\mathrm{pk}}(x, r) = H_{\mathrm{pk}}(x', r')$, with non-negligible probability.*

3   CHTLC Construction Overview

We consider the following assumptions and research scope regards to our CHTLC.

- The underlying blockchain system which PCNs interacts with is secure and free from attacks. The security issues related with blockchain itself is beyond the scope of this paper.
- We focus on design of the CHTLC protocol, the efficiency of the routing protocols in PCNs is beyond our research scope. We applied the routing protocol proposed in Flare [22] in our CHTLC.
- All the intermediate nodes in the PCNs are reasonable nodes. That is, they are motivated by collecting transaction fees to forward the transactions unless they are corrupted. Reasonable nodes will not disclose their secret key for encrypted communication between other nodes or any message they received through private channels to the public.

- Some intermediate nodes might collude, while it is impossible for all the nodes that include in a payment path to collude with each other.
- The communication between each pair of nodes in the network is encrypted.
- The network is bounded by a weak synchronous communication [25]. This indicates that the participants in the network can achieve the same status within a suitable time t. This assumption can be achieved by applying a loosely synchronised clock among the users in PCN [26].
- The security of the individual node is beyond our research scope. The system cannot prevent the compromised nodes from paying other nodes through PCNs.

We now present a brief overview of CHTLC through an example. To make the discussion concise, we take as an example the payment between u_A and u_D with no direct payment channel to demonstrate the functionally of our protocol. To make the illustration simple we avoid the details of the messages (e.g., the payment value, the time for lock the deposit) that exchanged between two nodes and assume there exists a payment path of 4 nodes shown in Fig. 2. We define u_A as the $\overset{\circ}{S}dr$ and u_D as the $\overset{\circ}{R}cv$, the intermediate nodes are u_B, u_C and u_D. Firstly, u_A receives the random value x from u_D and calculates $\mu_D = H_D(x, r_D)$, $\mu_C = H_C(\mu_D, r_C)$, $\mu_B = H_B(\mu_C, r_B)$, and $\mu_A = H_A(\mu_B, r_A)$ with the public key of each node retrieved from B. Second, u_A sends (μ_B, r_A), (μ_C, r_B) to u_B and u_C respectively through the private channels. Now, the payment can be carried out as u_A makes a commitment to u_B saying if u_B can provide a value (p_B, r_A) such that $H_A(H_B(p_B), r_A)$ collides with μ_A given seconds[2], u_A pays u_B. User u_B firstly checks that the μ_B on the blockchain satisfies the condition that $\mu_A == H_A(\mu_B, r_A)$, otherwise aborts the payment. Since u_B does not know the input μ'_B, r_B such that $\mu_B = H_B(\mu'_B, r_B)$, u_B makes a commitment with u_C saying that if u_C can provide (p_C, r_B) such that $\mu_B == H_B(H_C(p_C), r_B)$, node u_B will pay u_C the promised money. Finally, u_D with its secret key and secret value x, generates the collision against $H_d(x, r_D)$ with (x', r') and sends $p = (x', r', r_C)$ to u_C. Similarly, u_C generates p_C that satisfy $H_B(H_C(p'), r_B)$ collides with μ_B and forwards (p_C, r_B) to u_B. Finally, all the nodes are paid with the promised amount of money.

3.1   CHTLC Construction

In this section, we discuss the details of the following operations:

OpenChannel(u_i, u_j, β, t, f): This operation establishes a direct channel between u_i and u_j. f indicates the transaction fee charged by u_i if u_i helps other users to forward the transaction to u_j. β indicates the total amount of money that u_i can transfer to u_j. To open a channel, u_i needs to create an opening transaction in which the input is β from u_i's wallet and the output is the joint-wallet in which the money need both u_i's and u_j's permission to be

---

[2] The money is locked within this time slot, if u_B fails to satisfy u_A, the money is refunded to u_A.

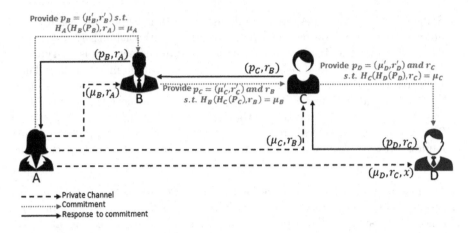

Fig. 2. CHTLC diagram.

spent. To avoid the scenario that u_j's does not cooperate and β is locked in the contract, the money in the join-wallet will refund to u_i if has not been spent within a given time. After u_i puts the opening transaction and path information $c_{ij} = (e_{ij}, f_{ij}, \beta, t)$ on B, this payment channel is accepted by PCNs.

CloseChannel($c_{\langle u_i, u_j \rangle}, v$): When node u_i wants to terminate the channel with node u_j, it needs to create a closing transaction. The input of the closing transaction is the joint wallet and the output of the transaction is the u_i's private wallet and u_j's private wallet. Let v as the balance in the joint wallet, v_i, v_j as the money that paid to node u_i and u_j respectively. The close commitment is invalid if $v \neq v_i + v_j$. u_i and u_j sign on the closing transaction and any node upload the close commitment on the B to finalize the close channel operation.

Pay$\left(\left(c_{\langle u_1, u_2 \rangle}, \ldots, c_{\langle u_{n-1}, u_n \rangle} \right), v \right)$:The function pay pays v dollars from the u_1 to u_n (as the sender and receiver, respectively). The sender initiates the payment protocol by running the setup algorithm shown in Algorithm 2.

We assume that there exists a payment path denoted as $\mathbb{P} = \{u_1, u_2, \ldots, u_n\}$ where u_1 is the payer and u_n is the receiver. u_n samples a random value denoted as x and sends it to u_1 in a private channel. Sender u_1 retrieves the public key of all the nodes from B to generate the commitment value μ for each intermediate nodes.

We denote the cost of sending v dollars from u_1 to u_n as v_1 which is $v_1 = v + \sum_{i=2}^{n-1} fee(u_i)$. If u_1 does not have enough money to pay all the transaction fees, it aborts the process.

The detailed algorithm is shown in Algorithm 3 (pay sender). u_1 finds out the length of the payment path, works out the path and locked time for each intermediate node. It forwards (μ_i, r_{i-1}) and path $c_{\langle u_i, u_{i+1} \rangle}$ to the intermediate nodes (line 9 in **Sender node** section Algorithm 3). Then, it creates a HTLC commitment with u_2 saying that if u_2 can provide a pair (p_2, r_1) within t seconds such that $H_1(H_2(p_2), r_1) = \mu_1$, user u_1 pays v_1 dollars to u_2 (line 10 in **Sender** node section Algorithm 3). Finally, u_1 sends message m_n to the receiver u_n to enable u_n claim the money from u_{n-1}.

For the intermediate node u_i, when it receives the payment commitment from the node u_{i-1}, it verifies that 1. it has enough money to fulfill the payment. 2. The correctness of the contract lock time t_{i+1}. 3. whether node u_{i-1} provides the valid commitment (line 2 in **Intermediate node** Algorithm 3). Then it makes the HTLC commitment with the successor node u_{i+1}. Finally, u_i waits for u_{i+1} to send back $m* = (p_{i+1}, r_i)$ to claim the money from u_i (line 7 in **Intermediate node** Algorithm 3). With the help of p_{i+1}, node u_i generate (p_i) (line 9,10 in **Intermediate node** Algorithm 3) and sends (p_i, r_{i-1}) to node u_{i-1} and claims the money (line 11 in **Intermediate node** Algorithm 3).

For the receiver u_n, once it receives the commitment μ_{n-1} from the previous node, it verifies the validity of the commitment and whether it can meet the condition within the time tn (line 1 in **Receiver** Algorithm 3). Then it applies (x, r) with its secret key to generate p_n and send (p_n, r_{n-1}) to u_{i-1} to claim the money.

Since every intermediate node redeems the money by generating the collision with the parameter it received from the successor nodes, it has to wait for the successor node to redeem the money firstly. Finally, all the nodes are paid with the promised money.

Algorithm 2. *Setup*

1: **function** *Setup*$(\mathbb{P}, x, n)$
2:     **for** $u_i \in \mathbb{P}$ **do**
3:         $\mu_i \leftarrow GenMsg(x, u_i, n)$
4:     **Return** μ_i
5: **function** *GenMsg*(x, u_i, n)
6:     **for** $i = n, ..., 1$ **do**
7:         Choose a random value $r_i \in Z_q^*$
8:         **if** $i = n$ **then**
9:             $\mu_i = H_i(x, r_i)$
10:        **else**
11:            $\mu_i = H_i\left(GenMsg(x, \mu_{i+1}, n)\right), r_i)$
12:        $i \leftarrow i - 1$
13:    **Return** μ_i

3.2   Security Discussion

The proposed construction provides the same level of the security as [1] without requiring zero knowledge proofs. The security of CHTLC follows the security model introduced by [1] according to the universal composable (UC) security paradigm [27]. Let $\text{EXEC}_{\pi, \mathscr{A}, \mathcal{E}}$ be the ensemble of the outputs of the environment $\mathcal{E}$ when interacting with the adversary $\mathscr{A}$ and parties running the protocol π. The UC-Security is defined as follows.

Algorithm 3. Payment Protocol

Sender node:

1: $v_1 = v + \sum_{i=2}^{n-1} fee(u_i)$
2: if $v_1 \leq \mathrm{cap}(c_{\langle u_1, u_2 \rangle})$ then
3:     $\mathrm{cap}(c_{\langle u_1, u_2 \rangle}) := \mathrm{cap}\left(c_{\langle u_1, u_2 \rangle}\right) - v_1$
4:     $t_0 := t_{\mathrm{now}} + \Delta \cdot n$
5:     for $1 < i < n$ do
6:         $v_i := v_1 - \sum_{j=1}^{i-1} fee\,(u_j)$
7:         $t_i := t_{i-1} - \Delta$
8:         $\mu_i \leftarrow Setup(\mathbb{P}, x, n)$
9:         Send $m_i = (c_{\langle u_{i-1}, u_i \rangle}, c_{\langle u_i, u_{i+1} \rangle},$
       $v_{i+1}, t_i, t_{i+1}, \mu_i, r_{i-1})$ to u_i
10:    **HTLC**$(u_1, u_2, v_1, \mu_1, t_1)$
11:    Send $m_n = (c_{\langle u_{n-1}, u_n \rangle}, v_n, t_n, \mu_n,$
       $r_{n-1}, r_n)$ to u_n
12: else
13:    Abort

Receiver node (m_n):

1: if $H_n(x, r_n) = \mu_n$ and $t_n > t_{now} + \Delta$ then
2:    Select x' and compute r' s.t. $H_n(x', r')$
   collides with μ_n
3:        $p_n \leftarrow (x', r')$

4:        Send (p_n, r_{n-1}) to u_{n-1}
5: else
6:        Abort

Intermediate node (m_i):

1: Read μ_{i-1} from B
2: if $v_{i+1} \leq \mathrm{cap}(c_{\langle u_i, u_{i+1} \rangle})$ and $t_{i+1} = t_i - \Delta$
   and $H_{i-1}(\mu_i, r_{i-1}) = \mu_{i-1}$ then
3:    $\mathrm{cap}(c_{\langle u_i, u_{i+1} \rangle}) := \mathrm{cap}\left(c_{\langle u_i, u_{i+1} \rangle}\right) - v_{i+1}$
4:        **HTLC**$(u_i, u_{i+1}, v_{i+1}, \mu_i, t_{i+1})$
5: else
6:        Abort
7: if receive $m^* = (p_{i+1} = (\mu'_{i+1}, r'_{i+1}), r_i)$
   from u_{i+1} then
8:    if $H_i(H_{i+1}(p_{i+1}), r_i) = \mu_i$ then
9:        Select μ'_i and compute r'_i s.t.
       $H_i(\mu'_i, r'_i)$ collides with μ_i
10:        $p_i \leftarrow (\mu'_i, r'_i)$
11:        Send (p_i, r_{i-1}) to u_{-1}
12:    else
13:        Abort
14: else
15:    Abort

Definition 3. *A protocol π UC-realizes an ideal functionality $\mathcal{F}$ if for any adversary $\mathcal{A}$ there exists a simulator $\mathcal{S}$ such that for any environment $\mathcal{E}$, the ensembles $\mathrm{EXEC}_{\pi, \mathcal{A}, \mathcal{E}}$ and $\mathrm{EXEC}_{\mathcal{F}, \mathcal{S}, \mathcal{E}}$ are computationally indistinguishable.*

Theorem 1. *Let $H : \{0,1\}^* \rightarrow \{0,1\}^\lambda$ be a Chameleon hash function modelled as a random oracle, then CHTLC UC-realizes the ideal functionality $\mathcal{F}$ (as defined in Sect. 2.2).*

Proof. We define the simulator $\mathcal{S}$ which simulates the real world execution protocol while interacting with the ideal functionality $\mathcal{F}$ as defined in Sect. 2.2. It also handles users corrupted by the adversary $\mathcal{A}$ and impersonates them until the environment $\mathcal{E}$ makes a corruption query on one of the users. Upon such query, $\mathcal{S}$ hands over to $\mathcal{A}$ the internal state of the target user and routes all of the subsequent communications to $\mathcal{A}$, who can reply arbitrarily. $\mathcal{E}$ does not expect any interaction with $\mathcal{S}$ regarding the operations exclusively among corrupted users. Moreover, $\mathcal{A}$ does not learn anything about communication between honest users that happened through secure channels. $\mathcal{S}$ simulates the random oracle H via lazy-sampling. The operations to be simulated for a PCN are described in the following.

OpenChannel $\left(c_{\langle u_1, u_2 \rangle}, \beta, t, f\right)$: Let u_1 be the user that initiates the request, the are two possible cases as follows:

– *Corrupted u_1:* $\mathcal{A}$ sends a request $\left(c_{\langle u_1, u_2 \rangle}, \beta, t, f\right)$ on behalf of u_1 to $\mathcal{S}$ who in turn initiates a two-user agreement protocol with $\mathcal{A}$ to convey upon a local fresh channel identifier $c_{\langle u_1,u_2\rangle}$. If the protocol successfully terminates, $\mathcal{S}$ sends $(open, c_{\langle u_1,u_2\rangle}, \beta, t, f)$ to $\mathcal{F}$, which eventually returns $(c_{\langle u_1,u_2\rangle}, h)$.

- *Corrupted u_2*: $\mathcal{S}$ receives a message $(c_{\langle u_1,u_2\rangle}, v, t, f)$ from $\mathcal{F}$ engages $\mathcal{A}$ in a two-user agreement protocol on behalf of u_1 for the opening of the channel. If the execution is successful, $\mathcal{S}$ sends an accepting message to $\mathcal{F}$ which returns $(c_{\langle u_1,u_2\rangle}, h)$, otherwise it outputs $\perp$.

If the opening was successful the simulator initializes an empty list $\mathcal{L}_{c_{\langle u_1,u_2\rangle}}$ and appends the value $(h, v, \perp, \perp)$.

CloseChannel$(c_{\langle u_1,u_2\rangle}, v)$: similar to Open Channel, there are two cases that might happen as follows (assuming u_1 is an initiator):

- *Corrupted u_1*: $\mathcal{A}$ sends a closing request on behalf of u_1 to $\mathcal{S}$ who fetches $\mathcal{L}_{c_{\langle u_1,u_2\rangle}}$ for some value (h, v, x, y). If such a value does not exist then it aborts. Otherwise it sends $(close, c_{\langle u_1,u_2\rangle}, h)$ to $\mathcal{F}$.
- *Corrupted u_2*: $\mathcal{S}$ receives $(c_{\langle u_1,u_2\rangle}, h, \perp)$ from $\mathcal{F}$ and simply notifies $\mathcal{A}$ of the closing of the channel $c_{\langle u_1,u_2\rangle}$.

Pay$\big((c_{\langle u_1,u_2\rangle}, \dots, c_{\langle u_{n-1},u_n\rangle}), v\big)$: the users acting differently according to their role in the protocol, thus we consider the cases separately.

Sender: In order to initiate a payment, $\mathcal{A}$ must provide each honest user u_i with $m_i = (c_{\langle u_{i-1},u_i\rangle}, c_{\langle u_i,u_{i+1}\rangle}, v_{i+1}, t_i, t_{i+1}, \mu_i, r_{i-1})$ and notifies the receiver with $(c_{\langle u_n,u_{n+1}\rangle}, v_n, t_n, \mu_n, r_{n-1}, r_n)$.

If $t_i \geq t_{i+1}$ then $\mathcal{S}$ sends $(\mathsf{Pay}, v_i, (c_{\langle u_{i-1},u_i\rangle}, c_{\langle u_i,u_{i+1}\rangle}), t_{i-1}, t_i)$ to $\mathcal{F}$ and sends $(\mathsf{Pay}, v, c_{\langle u_{n-1},u_n\rangle}, t_n)$ to the receiver, otherwise it aborts. For each intermediate user u_i the simulator confirms the payment only when receives from the user u_{i+1} a pair (p_{i+1}, r_i) such that $H_i(H_{i+1}(p_{i+1}), r_i)$ collides with μ_i. If the receiver is honest then $\mathcal{S}$ confirms the payment if the amount v corresponds to what agreed with the sender and if $H_n(p_n, r_{n-1}) = \mu_n$. If the payment is confirmed the entry $(h_i, v^* - v_i, \mu_i)$ is added to $\mathcal{L}_{c_{\langle u_{i-1},u_i\rangle}}$, where $(h_i^*, v^*, \cdot, \cdot)$ is the entry of $\mathcal{L}_{c_{\langle u_{i-1},u_i\rangle}}$ with the lowest v^*, and the same happens for the receiver.

Receiver: $\mathcal{S}$ receives some $(h, c_{\langle u_{n-1},u_n\rangle}, v, t_n)$ from $\mathcal{F}$, then it samples two random $x, r \in \{0,1\}^\lambda$ and returns $p_n = (x, r)$ to $\mathcal{A}$ the tuple $(p_n, H_n(p_n, r_{n-1}), v)$. If $\mathcal{A}$ returns $p^* = p_n$, then $\mathcal{S}$ returns $\top$ to $\mathcal{F}$, otherwise it sends $\perp$.

Intermediate user: $\mathcal{S}$ is notified that a corrupted user is involved in a payment with a message of the form $(h_i, h_{i+1}, c_{\langle u_{i-1},u_i\rangle}, c_{\langle u_i,u_{i+1}\rangle}, v, t_{i-1}, t_i)$ by $\mathcal{F}$.

$\mathcal{S}$ samples three random values $r, x', r' \in \{0,1\}^\lambda$, sets $p' = (x', r')$ then sends the tuple $(c_{\langle u_{i-1},u_i\rangle}, c_{\langle u_i,u_{i-1}\rangle}, \mu_i = H_i(H_{i+1}(p'), r), \mu_{i+1} = H_{i+1}(p'),$ $p', v, t_{i-1}, t_i)$ to $\mathcal{A}$. If $\mathcal{A}$ outputs r^* such that $H_i(H_{i+1}(p'), r^*)$ collides with μ_i, then $\mathcal{S}$ aborts. At some point of the execution the simulator is queried again on (h_i, h_{i+1}), then it sends r to $\mathcal{A}$ on behalf of u_{i+1}. If $\mathcal{A}$ outputs $\mu_i' = H_i(H_{i+1}(p'), r)$ which collides with μ_i, the simulator sends $\top$ to $\mathcal{F}$ and appends $(h_i, v^* - v, \mu_i', H_{i+1}(p'))$ to $\mathcal{L}_{c_{\langle u_{i-1},u_i\rangle}}$, where $(h_i^*, v^*, \cdot, \cdot)$ is the entry of $\mathcal{L}_{c_{\langle u_{i-1},u_i\rangle}}$ with the lowest v^*, otherwise it sends $\perp$.

The OpenChannel and CloseChannel algorithms are exactly the same as [1] and the indistinguishability argument is trivial. Thus, we exclude further discussion about them. For the payment, the sender provides the values to the user via private channel which mimics exactly the real-world protocol. Each user u_i confirms the transaction to $\mathcal{F}$ only once it receives the values p_{i+1} and r_i such that $H_i(H_{i+1}(p_{i+1}), r_i)$ collides with μ_i. The payment chain does not stop at a honest node (excluding the sender), thus the simulation does not aborts. The simulation aborts if adversary aim to interrupt the payment by outputting r^* such that $H_i(H_{i+1}(p_{i+1}), r^*)$ collides with μ_i without getting r from the simulator. According to *Indistinguishability* and *Collision-Resistance* properties of Chameleon hash function as defined in Sect. 2.4, the probability that $\mathscr{A}$ be able to output p^* in such a way is negligible, hence $Pr[abort] \leq negl(\lambda)$.

4   Experimental Results

To evaluate the CHTLC protocol, we implement it in Golang language. We deploy our experiment on the server equipped with i7-4770k CPU and 32 GB memory. We set the chameleon-hash key size as 2048 bits and the output of the hash function is 2048 bits. According to our observation, 90% of the payment can be finished within 10 nodes, thus we set our evaluation in the payment path consists of 10 nodes. We compare the size of data transmitted and the protocol time consumption in CHTLC with MHTLC proposed in [1].

Table 2. Performance comparison

Scheme	Performance			
	Key pair generation	Generate message	Verify message	Redeem payment
Multi-Hop HTLC	NA	309 ms	130 ms	Not provided
CHTLC	8 ms	55 ms	20 ms	8 ms

Data Size. In CHTLC, the sender needs to forward the secret value to each of the intermediate nodes which accounts for 2048 bits (256 Bytes). For the path that consists of 10 nodes, the total number of data sent by the sender is roughly 2.56 KB. However, according to the experiment demonstrated in [1], the sender needs to forward about 17 MB data. In MHTLC protocol, the communication between the intermediate nodes is required to ensure the correctness of the received data from the sender while it is not necessary for our scenario. In conclusion, the data needed to be transmitted in much smaller than the MHTLC approach.

Time Consumption. We evaluate the time consumption in CHTLC and make the comparison with MHTLC protocol in Table 2. For CHTLC, we need each node to generate the chameleon hash key pairs which takes about 8 ms. In MHTLC, since it is based on a general hash function, this step is not needed(As it is shown as not available in Table 2). It takes 55 ms (for the first intermediate node, it take 10 ms while the last node it takes 100 ms) on average to generate the message which sent to each intermediate node. However, in MHTLC, it takes 309 ms. To verify the correctness of the message(proof in MHTLC), CHTLC needs 20 ms while MHTLC consumes 130 ms. To redeem the commitment from the previous node, our protocol needs 8 ms to generate the collision of the committed hash value, while in [1], this evaluation is not addressed by the authors (As it is shown as not discussed in Table 2).

In conclusion, the data transferred in our protocol is much small than that transferred in MHTLC. Our protocol also has a great advantage in the time consumption of generating/verifying the message (proof). It takes 8 ms to redeem the money from the commitment which is totally accepted by most of the scenarios.

5   Conclusion

In this paper, we propose a new payment protocol called CHTLC to address the payment path privacy issue in PCNs. With the help of chameleon hash function, no one can recover the payment path by analysing the payment commitment made by the payment participants. It is demonstrated by the evaluation that compared with MHTLC, our protocol consumes less bandwidth while much faster in transaction processing.

References

1. Malavolta, G., Moreno-Sanchez, P., Kate, A., Maffei, M., Ravi, S.: Concurrency and privacy with payment-channel networks. In: Proceedings of the 2017 ACM SIGSAC Conference on Computer and Communications Security, pp. 455–471. ACM (2017)
2. Nakamoto, S., et al.: Bitcoin: a peer-to-peer electronic cash system (2008)
3. Wood, G., et al.: Ethereum: a secure decentralised generalised transaction ledger. Ethereum Proj. Yellow Pap. **151**, 1–32 (2014)
4. Bitcoin transaction throughput. https://en.wikipedia.org/wiki/Bitcoin_scalability_problem. Accessed on 14 Feb
5. Bitcoin lightning network. https://en.wikipedia.org/wiki/Lightning_network. Accessed on 14 Feb 2018
6. Ghosh, A., Mahdian, M., Reeves, D.M., Pennock, D.M., Fugger, R.: Mechanism design on trust networks. In: Deng, X., Graham, F.C. (eds.) WINE 2007. LNCS, vol. 4858, pp. 257–268. Springer, Heidelberg (2007). https://doi.org/10.1007/978-3-540-77105-0_25
7. Stellar protocol. www.stellar.org. Accessed on 14 Feb 2018
8. Ripple network. https://ripple.com/. Accessed on 14 Feb 2018

9. Fugger, R.: Money as IOUs in social trust networks & a proposal for a decentralized currency network protocol. Hypertext document, vol. 106 (2004). http://ripple.sourceforge.net

10. Viswanath, B., Mondal, M., Gummadi, K.P., Mislove, A., Post, A.: Canal: scaling social network-based sybil tolerance schemes. In: Proceedings of the 7th ACM European Conference on Computer Systems, pp. 309–322. ACM (2012)

11. Miller, A., Bentov, I., Kumaresan, R., McCorry, P.: Sprites: payment channels that go faster than lightning. arXiv preprint arXiv:1702.05812 (2017)

12. Malavolta, G., Moreno-Sanchez, P., Kate, A., Maffei, M.: SilentWhispers: enforcing security and privacy in credit networks. In: 24th Annual Network and Distributed System Security Symposium, NDSS (2017)

13. Moreno-Sanchez, P., Kate, A., Maffei, M., Pecina, K.: Privacy preserving payments in credit networks. In: Network and Distributed Security Symposium (2015)

14. Heilman, E., Alshenibr, L., Baldimtsi, F., Scafuro, A., Goldberg, S.: TumbleBit: an untrusted bitcoin-compatible anonymous payment hub. In: Network and Distributed System Security Symposium (2017)

15. Decker, C., Wattenhofer, R.: A fast and scalable payment network with bitcoin duplex micropayment channels. In: Pelc, A., Schwarzmann, A.A. (eds.) SSS 2015. LNCS, vol. 9212, pp. 3–18. Springer, Cham (2015). https://doi.org/10.1007/978-3-319-21741-3_1

16. Poon, J., Dryja, T.: The bitcoin lightning network: scalable off-chain instant payments (2016)

17. McCorry, P., Möser, M., Shahandasti, S.F., Hao, F.: Towards bitcoin payment networks. In: Liu, J.K.K., Steinfeld, R. (eds.) ACISP 2016. LNCS, vol. 9722, pp. 57–76. Springer, Cham (2016). https://doi.org/10.1007/978-3-319-40253-6_4

18. Gudgeon, L., Moreno-Sanchez, P., Roos, S., McCorry, P., Gervais, A.: SoK: off the chain transactions. Cryptology ePrint Archive, Report 2019/360 (2019). https://eprint.iacr.org/2019/360

19. Antonopoulos, A.M.: Mastering Bitcoin: Unlocking Digital Cryptocurrencies. O'Reilly Media Inc., Sebastopol (2014)

20. Hashed timelock contracts. https://en.bitcoin.it/wiki/Hashed_Timelock_Contracts. Accessed 14 Feb 2018

21. Tsuchiya, P.F.: The landmark hierarchy: a new hierarchy for routing in very large networks. In: ACM SIGCOMM Computer Communication Review, vol. 18, no. 4, pp. 35–42. ACM (1988)

22. Prihodko, P., Zhigulin, S., Sahno, M., Ostrovskiy, A., Osuntokun, O.: Flare: an approach to routing in lightning network. White Paper (2016)

23. Roos, S., Moreno-Sanchez, P., Kate, A., Goldberg, I.: Settling payments fast and private: efficient decentralized routing for path-based transactions. arXiv preprint arXiv:1709.05748 (2017)

24. Krawczyk, H., Rabin, T.: Chameleon hashing and signatures. IACR Cryptol. ePrint Arch. **1998**, 10 (1998)

25. Attiya, H., Welch, J.: Distributed Computing: Fundamentals, Simulations, and Advanced Topics, vol. 19. Wiley, Hoboken (2004)

26. Cristian, F., Aghili, H., Strong, R.: Approximate clock synchronization despite omission and performance failures and processor joins. In: Proceedings of the 16th International Symposium on Fault-Tolerant Computing, pp. 218–223 (1986)

27. Canetti, R.: Universally composable security: a new paradigm for cryptographic protocols. In: Proceedings 2001 IEEE International Conference on Cluster Computing, pp. 136–145. IEEE (2001)

Short Papers

On-demand Privacy Preservation for Cost-Efficient Edge Intelligence Model Training

Zhi Zhou$^{(\boxtimes)}$ⓘ and Xu Chenⓘ

School of Data and Computer Science, Sun Yat-sen University,
Guangzhou 51006, China
{zhouzhi9,chenxu35}@mail.sysu.edu.cn

Abstract. With the advancement of Internet-of-Things (IoT), enormous IoT data are generated at the network edge, incurring an urgent need to push the frontiers of artificial intelligence (AI) to network edge so as to fully unleash the potential of the IoT big data. To match this trend, edge intelligence—an emerging paradigm that hosts AI applications at the network edge—is being recognized as a promising solution. While pilot efforts on edge intelligence have mostly focused on facilitating efficient model inference at the network edge, the training of edge intelligence model has been greatly overlooked. To bridge this gap, in this paper, we investigate how to coordinate the edge and the cloud to train edge intelligence model, with the goal of simultaneously optimizing the resource cost and preserving data privacy in an on-demand manner. Leveraging Lyapunov optimization theory, we design and analyze a cost-efficient optimization framework to make online decisions on training data scheduling to balance the tradeoff between cost efficiency and privacy preservation. With rigorous theoretical analysis, we verify the efficacy of the presented framework.

1 Introduction

As a key driver that boosts development of artificial intelligence (AI), big data is undergoing a radical shift of data source from the mega-scale cloud datacenters to the increasingly widespread mobile devices and IoT devices. Pushing the AI frontier to the IoT ecosystem that resides at the last mile of the Internet, however, is highly non-trivial, due to the concerns on performance, cost and privacy. To address these challenges, edge computing [1] has recently been proposed. With edge computing, resources and services are pushed from the centralized clouds to the network edges that are in closer proximity to IoT devices and data sources, promising benefits on performance, cost-efficiency and privacy protection [1]. Indeed, the marriage of edge computing and AI has given rise to a new research area, namely 'edge intelligence' or 'edge AI' [2].

Research and practice on edge intelligence is still in its infancy. In particular, a majority of existing efforts focus on optimizing the inference phase of

© Springer Nature Switzerland AG 2019
R. Steinfeld and T. H. Yuen (Eds.): ProvSec 2019, LNCS 11821, pp. 321–329, 2019.
https://doi.org/10.1007/978-3-030-31919-9_19

edge intelligence, i.e., reducing the latency and/or energy consumption of model (e.g., deep learning model) inference on resource- and energy-constrained IoT devices [3–6]. Instead, the training of edge intelligence model has been greatly overlooked. This is due to the fact that compared to model inference, model training is far more data- and resource-intensive, and delay-tolerant. Therefore, the current de-facto standard for edge intelligence is to train the model at the cloud and then distribute the trained model to the IoT devices for local inference. Undoubtedly however, with the burgeoning of data volumes, training IoT data fully at the vulnerable cloud is increasingly insecure and susceptible to attacks due to the high concentration of information of a big pile of users [1,7,8].

To address the above challenge, in this paper we advocate a privacy-preserving and cost-efficient optimization framework for edge intelligence model training. The basic intuition is to coordinate the edge and the cloud to train the model in a cloud-edge synergic manner, and thus to simultaneously embrace the cost-efficiency advantage of the cloud and the privacy-preserving benefit of the edge. To strike a new balance between the above dual goals, we propose to minimize the resource cost over the long run, under the constraint of a long-term privacy preservation requirement (in terms of percentage of the training data outsourced to the cloud) that can be pre-defined by the system operator in an on-demand manner. With cloud-edge synergy, the delay-tolerance of model training further enables us to exploit the resource price which typically show both spatial (edge v.s. cloud) and temporal diversities. That is, by temporally buffering the training data in a data queue, and deferring data training to the near future when the resource price of the edge or the cloud falls down, the resource cost for model training can be greatly reduced.

With the presence of time-varying and bursty data arrivals that are typically unpredictable, optimizing the performance-cost tradeoff in the long run is by no means trivial, since the on-demand privacy preservation constraint and the queuing dynamics of the training data couple the control decisions across time slots. In response, we leverage Lyapunov optimization theory to rigorously design a cost-efficient and online optimization framework. Our framework is able to effectively incorporate the long-term privacy preservation requirement into a series of on-shot optimization problems, and thus to make simple and effective decision on dynamic training data scheduling, without requiring any future information as a priori. The upshot of our new online framework is that it is rigorously proved to facilitate a delicate $[O(1/V), O(V)]$ cost-privacy tradeoff that can be flexibly adjusted by a tunable control parameter V, which represents how much we emphasize the cost minimization compared to privacy preservation.

2   System Model and Problem Formulation

2.1   System Overview

As illustrated in Fig. 1, we consider an edge computing service provider running an AI-based intelligent services as exemplified by video surveillance, smart driving and industrial internet-of-things (IIoT). This intelligent service continuously senses large volumes of edge big data (e.g., video, picture and audio) from the widespread and intelligent end-devices, ranging from smartphone and video cameras to internet-of-vehicles (IoV) [1].

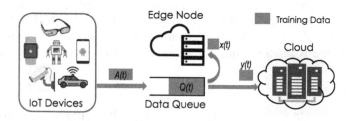

Fig. 1. A cloud-edge synergic system for edge intelligence model training, in which the training data are buffered in the data queue before scheduled to the edge or the cloud for processing.

In line with the recent modeling work on edge computing [9], we adopt a discrete time-slotted model to fully characterize and leverage the system dynamics (e.g., time-varying data arrival and resource cost), each time slot $t = (0, 1, 2, ...)$ matches the time scale at which the control decisions are updated. At each time slot t, the arrival of the training data of the intelligent service is denoted as a random variable $A(t)$. Without loss of generality, a deterministic peak level of training data arrival $A_i^{\max}$ is assumed, such that $\{A(t) \leq A_{\max}, \forall t\}$. However, since the data arrivals in the edge computing environment are usually time-varying and unpredictable (e.g., due to the mobility of end-devices), our model does not assume any priori knowledge of the statistics of $A(t), \forall t$.

2.2 Data Training Model

Unlike EI inference task that is mission critical and requires low delay, EI model training task is typically delay-tolerant, i.e., the data can be deferred to be trained at some time in the future. This flexibility provides great optimization opportunities for cost reduction of the model training, by temporally shifting workload to exploit the time-varying resource prices of the edge node and the cloud. To this end, the arrived training data with an amount of $A(t)$ is first buffered in a data queue at the edge node, and then scheduled to processed when the resource price falls down. Since the training data of the EI model can be processed in both the edge node and the remote cloud, we use $x(t)$ to denote the amount of buffered training data processed at the edge, and $y(t)$ to denote the amount of buffered training data transmitted to and processed in the cloud, at time slot t. Since the edge node is resource-limited, then $x(t)$ satisfies the resource capacity constraint $\{x(t) \leq C(t), \forall t\}$, where $C(t)$ is the amount of available resource of the edge node at time slot t. Considering the limited bandwidth of the wide-area-network (WAN) link between the edge node and the cloud, $y(t)$ follows the bandwidth constraint $\{y(t) \leq B(t), \forall t\}$, where $B(t)$ is the available WAN bandwidth at time slot t.

For the queue that temporally buffers the training data, its departure rate at each time slot t is given by $x(t)+y(t)$. Besides, recall that the arrival rate of newly generated training data to the queue at each time slot t is $A(t)$. Then if we further use backlog $Q(t)$ to denote the total amount of buffered training data in the queue, it evolves according to the dynamics: $Q(t+1) = Q(t) - x(t) - y(t) + A(t)$, here the constraint $x(t)+y(t) \leq Q(t)$ ensures that the amount data to be trained at each time slot is no more than the amount of data buffered in the queue.

2.3   Cost Model

For the edge intelligence model training system, its primary objectives is to minimize the cost of the cloud and edge resource usage when training the edge intelligence model. For modern computing systems ranging from edge servers to cloud datacenters, it is widely recognized that the energy cost consists the majority of the operational expenditure (OpEX). While in real-time electricity markets where the edge servers and cloud datacenters participate in, the electricity prices are determined dynamically and thus fluctuate over time. Therefore, achieving this goal of cost saving requires us to carefully exploit both spatial (i.e., cloud v.s. edge) and temporal heterogeneities of the resource usage price. Here we use $P_E(t)$ and $P_C(t)$ to denote the resource price of training one unit data at the edge and at the cloud, respectively. Clearly, both $P_E(t)$ and $P_C(t)$ can be time-varying in practice. Then, at each time slot t, the resource cost of the edge intelligence training system can be denoted as $Cost(t) = P_E(t)x(t) + P_C(t)y(t)$. Due to the delay-tolerance and deferability of the training data, optimizing the training cost at each individual time slot t does not necessarily minimize the training cost over the long-term. Intuitively, to optimize the long-term training cost, the time-average $\lim_{T\to\infty} \frac{1}{T}\sum_{t=0}^{T-1} \mathbb{E}\{Cost(t)\}$ over the long-term is expected to be minimized.

2.4   On-Demand Privacy Preservation Model for Training Data

Fully preserving privacy for edge intelligence training requires that no training data would be offloaded to the cloud. However, this is neither cost-efficient nor scalable since the computing capability of the edge node is expensive and limited. For better cost-efficiency and scalability, we propose to preserve the privacy for edge intelligence model training in an on-demand manner. Specifically, we first quantify the degree of privacy preservation with the ratio of the total amount of data processed in the cloud to the total amount of data arrival over the long-term, i.e., $\lim_{T\to\infty} \frac{\sum_{t=0}^{T-1} y(t)}{\sum_{t=0}^{T-1} A(t)}$. Clearly, a smaller ratio indicates that less data is offloaded to the cloud, and the privacy is better preserved. In this paper, we realize training data privacy preservation via enforcing the above ratio within a tolerable level as follows: $\lim_{T\to\infty} \frac{\sum_{t=0}^{T-1} y(t)}{\sum_{t=0}^{T-1} A(t)} \leq K$. Here K is a tunable parameter representing the maximum tolerable degree of training data privacy pre-defined by the system. By tuning K, the system is able to flexibly adjust the degree of training data privacy in an on-demand manner.

2.5 Queue Stability Model

Recall that when computing the resource cost $Cost(t)$, we account for the processed training data rather than the arrived and buffered training data. In this case, the system would aggressively defer the training and buffer them in the data queue to jointly reduce the resource cost and preserve the data privacy. To prevent from this dilemma, we introduce the queue stability model to ensure that all the arrived training data would be processed within finite deadline. Formally, queue stability refers to the situation that as the data arrives persistently over time, the time-averaged backlog of the edge queues and cloud queues are deterministically bounded as follows: $\overline{Q} = \lim_{T \to \infty} \frac{1}{T} \sum_{t=0}^{T-1} \mathbb{E}\{Q(t)\} < \infty$. Note that the queue stability constraint implies finite time-averaged queue backlog, and hence, finite average delay for the arrived training data according to the celebrated Little's law [10].

2.6 Problem Formulation

Having formulated the resource cost model, the on-demand privacy preservation model and the queue stability model, we are now ready to minimize the long-term time-averaged cost under the privacy preserving and queue stability constraint.

$$\min \ \lim_{T \to \infty} \frac{1}{T} \sum_{t=0}^{T-1} \mathbb{E}\{Cost(t)\} \tag{1}$$

$$\text{s.t.} \ \lim_{T \to \infty} \frac{\sum_{t=0}^{T-1} y(t)}{\sum_{t=0}^{T-1} A(t)} \leq K \tag{2}$$

$$\overline{Q} = \lim_{T \to \infty} \frac{1}{T} \sum_{t=0}^{T-1} \mathbb{E}\{Q(t)\} < \infty \tag{3}$$

$$Q(t+1) = Q(t) - x(t) - y(t) + A(t), \tag{4}$$

$$x(t) + y(t) \leq Q(t), \tag{5}$$

$$0 \leq x(t) \leq C(t), 0 \leq y(t) \leq B(t). \tag{6}$$

For this problem, since the privacy preservation constraint captured in Eq. (2) and the queue stability constraint captured in Eq. (3) temporally couple the control decisions across time slots, therefore decisions at current slot can have a non-negligible impact on the decisions in the future. Therefore, it is unpractical to solve the problem in an offline manner. Instead, an online approach that does require any future information as a priori is highly desirable.

3   An Online Optimization Framework

3.1   Problem Transformation with Lyapunov Optimization

We first transform the long-term privacy preservation constraint in Eq. (2) into a well-studied queue stability problem. To this end, we introduce a virtual queue $H(t)$ for the system. Initially, we let the virtual queue to be empty, i.e. $H(0) = 0$. Then, we update the virtual queue at each time slot $t + 1$ according to $H(t + 1) = \max\{H(t) + y(t) - KA(t), 0\}$. Intuitively, for this virtual queue $H(t)$, $y(t)$ can be viewed as its arrival rate, while the term $KA(t)$ can be viewed its service rate. Then, maintaining the privacy preservation constraint can be interpreted as enforcing that the long-term total arrivals $\sum_{t=0}^{T-1} y(t)$ is no larger than the long-term service rate $\sum_{t=0}^{T-1} KA(t)$ of the virtual queue. Interestingly, the length of the virtual queue $H(t)$ actually acts as the historical measurement of the accumulated difference between the total arrivals $\sum_{t=0}^{T-1} y(t)$ and the total service rate $\sum_{t=0}^{T-1} KA(t)$ during the interval $[0, t - 1]$. Motivated by these insights, a straightforward approach to satisfying the on-demand privacy preservation constraint is to enforce the stability of the virtual queue $H(t)$, as suggested by the following Theorem 1.

Theorem 1. *If the virtual queue $H(t)$ is stable over time, i.e., $\lim_{T\to\infty} \frac{\mathbb{E}\{H(T)\}}{T} = 0$, the on-demand privacy preservation constraint in Eq. (2) is satisfied.*

Theorem 1 indicates that by introducing the virtual queue $H(t)$, we can transform the original privacy preserving constraint into a well-studied queue stability control problem. Towards ensuring finite upper bounds for $Q(t)$ and $H(t)$ to maintaining the stability of both real and virtual queues, we resort to Lyapunov optimization which is a powerful tool to control and stabilize queuing systems in control theory. For our problem in specific, we let we let $\Theta(t) = [Q(t), H(t)]$ be a concatenated vector of all the real and virtual queues. We also define a widely adopted quadratic Lyapunov function [10] as $L(\Theta(t)) = \frac{1}{2}[Q^2(t) + H^2(t)]$. Intuitively, by persistently pushing the Lyapunov function towards a lower congestion state, we can keep the real and virtual queues strongly stable, i.e., with finite upper bounds. To this end, we further introduce $\Delta(\Theta(t))$ as the one-step conditional Lyapunov drift $\Delta(\Theta(t)) = \mathbb{E}\{L(\Theta(t + 1)) - L(\Theta(t))|\Theta(t)\}$. The drift $\Delta(\Theta(t))$ measures the change of the Lyapunov function between two consecutive slots. Clearly, by minimizing the drift per slot to restrain the Lyapunov function, we can prevent the queue backlogs of the real and virtual queues from unbounded growth, and thus maintain the system stability.

In the sense of Lyapunov control, our underlying two-fold objectives of minimizing the time-averaged cost while still maintaining the stability of the queue system, is now transformed to minimize the drift-plus-cost at each time slot t: $\Delta(\Theta(t)) + V\mathbb{E}\{Cost(t)|\Theta(t)\}$. Here the control parameter $V(\geq 0)$ represents a design knob of the stability-cost tradeoff, i.e., how much we shall emphasize minimizing the unified cost compared to relieving the congestion of the queues.

3.2 An Online Optimization Algorithm

So far, we have transformed the original long-term problem to a set of one-shot drift-plus-cost minimization subproblems over each time slot $t \in \{0, 1, 2, \cdots, T\}$. However, directly minimizing the drift-plus-cost $\Delta(\Theta(t)) + V\mathbb{E}\{Cost(t)|\Theta(t)\}$ requires to handle the implicit $\max[*]$ terms. In response, we seek to design an online algorithm to minimize the supremum derived by the following Theorem.

Theorem 2. *For any queue backlogs $\Theta(t)$ at each time slot t, the drift-plus-cost $\Delta(\Theta(t)) + V\mathbb{E}\{Cost(t)|\Theta(t)\}$ of the edge intelligence model training system under any data training decision satisfies the following inequality, where $\Phi \triangleq \frac{1}{2}[(C_{\max} + B_{\max})^2 + B_{\max}^2 + (1 + K^2)A_{\max}^2]$ is a finite constant.*

$$\Delta(\Theta(t)) + V\mathbb{E}\{Cost(t)|\Theta(t)\} \leq \Phi + V\mathbb{E}\{Cost(t)|\Theta(t)\}$$
$$-\mathbb{E}\{Q(t)[x(t) + y(t) - A(t)]|\Theta(t)\} - \mathbb{E}\{H(t)[KA(t) - y(t)]|\Theta(t)\} \quad (7)$$

Theorem 2 derives a supremum of drift-plus-cost $\Delta(\Theta(t)) + V\mathbb{E}\{Cost(t)|\Theta(t)\}$ at each time slot t, which only involves the current information and resource provisioning decision. By omitting the constant terms $Q(t)A(t)$ and $KH(t)A(t)$ in the right-hand-side of Eq. (7), we obtain the following real-time and deterministic optimization problem which minimizes the supremum of the drift-plus-cost expression at each time slot t.

$$V \times Cost(t) - Q(t)[x(t) + y(t)] + H(t)y(t) \quad (8)$$

For this weighted linear programming, we propose a price-based greedy scheme for resource allocation to the training data, as elaborated in the following cases.

- **Case 1:** $VP_E(t) - Q(t) \geq 0$ and $VP_C(t) - Q(t) + H(t) \geq 0$, then the objective in Eq. (8) is increasing on both $x(t)$ and $y(t)$. Therefore leading to the "full data deferring" optimal solution that aggressively defers the buffer training without provisioning any resource to it, i.e., $x^*(t) = y^*(t) = 0$.
- **Case 2:** $VP_E(t) - Q(t) \geq 0$ while $VP_C(t) - Q(t) + H(t) \leq 0$, then the objective in Eq. (8) is increasing on $x(t)$ but decreasing on $y(t)$. Therefore leading to the "training in the cloud" optimal solution that trains as more data in the cloud as possible, i.e., $x^*(t) = 0, y^*(t) = \min\{B(t), Q(t)\}$.
- **Case 3:** $VP_E(t) - Q(t) \leq 0$ while $VP_C(t) - Q(t) + H(t) \geq 0$, then the objective in Eq. (8) is decreasing on $x(t)$ but increasing on $y(t)$. Therefore leading to the "training at the edge" optimal solution that trains as more data at the edge as possible, i.e., $x^*(t) = \min\{C(t), Q(t)\}, y^*(t) = 0$.
- **Case 4:** $VP_E(t) - Q(t) \leq VP_C(t) - Q(t) + H(t) \leq 0$, then the objective in Eq. (8) is increasing on $x(t)$ and $y(t)$. Since the net price of the edge resource is more cheaper, it leads to the "edge prioritized hybrid training" optimal solution that trains as more data at the edge as possible, and further trains data in the cloud if the capacity of the edge node is not enough, i.e., $x^*(t) = \min\{C(t), Q(t)\}, y^*(t) = \min\{Q(t) - x^*(t), B(t)\}$.

– **Case 5:** $VP_C(t) - Q(t) + H(t) \leq VP_E(t) - Q(t) \leq 0$, then the objective in Eq. (8) is increasing on $x(t)$ and $y(t)$. Since the net price of the cloud resource is more cheaper, it leads to the "cloud prioritized hybrid training" optimal solution that trains as more data in the cloud as possible, and further trains data at the edge if the bandwidth of the WAN is not enough, i.e., $x^*(t) = \min\{C(t), Q(t) - y^*(t)\}, y^*(t) = \min\{Q(t), B(t)\}$.

Theorem 3. *For any control parameter $V > 0$, the presented online optimization algorithm guarantees that all the real and virtual queues are strongly stable over time slots:*

$$Q(t) \leq VP_{\max} + A_{\max}, \tag{9}$$
$$H(t) \leq 2VP_{\max} + A_{\max}, \tag{10}$$

where $P_{max} = \max_t \max\{P_E(t), P_C(t)\}$, $A_{\max} = \max_t A(t)$. Furthermore, the gap between the achieved time-averaged unified cost and the offline optimal solution $Cost^{opt}$ is within Φ/V, where Φ is a constant defined in Theorem 1.

$$\lim_{T \to \infty} \frac{1}{T} \sum_{t=0}^{T-1} \mathbb{E}\{Cost(t)\} \leq Cost^{opt} + \frac{\Phi}{V} \tag{11}$$

4   Conclusion

In response to the burgeoning IoT data originated at the network edge, this paper designs and analyzes a cost-efficient and privacy-preserving online control framework of edge intelligence model training. To address the challenge of time-varying and unpredictable data arrivals, our framework leverages Lyapunov optimization theory to make online control decisions on scheduling of the training data. The upshot of our new online framework is that it can approach a long-term resource cost that is arbitrarily close to the offline optimum, yet preserving the training data privacy which can be pre-defined in an on-demand manner, without requiring any future information as a priori. Rigorous theoretical analysis verifies the efficacy of our proposed framework.

References

1. Shi, W., Cao, J., Zhang, Q., Li, Y., Xu, L.: Edge computing: vision and challenges. IEEE IoT J. **3**(5), 637–646 (2016)
2. Zhou, Z., Chen, X., Li, E., Zeng, L., Luo, K., Zhang, J.: Edge intelligence: paving the last mile of artificial intelligence with edge computing. Proc. IEEE (2019)
3. Li, E., Zhou, Z., Chen, X.: Edge intelligence: on-demand deep learning model co-inference with device-edge synergy. In: Proceedings of ACM MECOMM (2018)
4. Kang, Y., et al.: Neurosurgeon: collaborative intelligence between the cloud and mobile edge. In: Proceedings of ACM ASPLOS (2017)
5. Liu, S., Lin, Y., Zhou, Z., Nan, K., Liu, H., Du, J.: On-demand deep model compression for mobile devices: a usage-driven model selection framework. In: Proceedings of ACM Mobisys (2018)

6. Guo, P., Hu, B., Li, R., Hu, W.: FoggyCache: cross-device approximate computation reuse. In: Proceedings of ACM Mobicom (2018)
7. Mao, Y., You, C., Zhang, J., Huang, K., Letaief, K.B.: A survey on mobile edge computing: the communication perspective. IEEE Commun. Surv. Tutor. **19**, 2322–2358 (2017)
8. Abbas, N., Zhang, Y., Taherkordi, A., Skeie, T.: Mobile edge computing: a survey. IEEE IoT J. **5**, 450–465 (2017)
9. Zhou, Z., Wu, Q., Chen, X.: Online orchestration of cross-edge service function chaining for cost-efficient edge computing. IEEE J. Sel. Areas Commun. **37**, 1866–1880 (2019)
10. Neely, M.J.: Stochastic Network Optimization with Application to Communication and Queueing Systems. Morgan & Claypool, San Rafael (2010)

One-Round Authenticated Group Key Exchange from Isogenies

Atsushi Fujioka[1], Katsuyuki Takashima[2], and Kazuki Yoneyama[3(✉)]

[1] Kanagawa University, Yokohama, Japan
[2] Mitsubishi Electric, Kamakura, Japan
[3] Ibaraki University, Hitachi, Japan
kazuki.yoneyama.sec@vc.ibaraki.ac.jp

Abstract. This paper proposes two one-round authenticated group key exchange protocols from newly employed *cryptographic invariant maps* (CIMs): one is secure in the quantum random oracle model and the other resists against maximum exposure where a non-trivial combination of secret keys is revealed. The security of the former (resp. latter) is proved under the n-way decisional (resp. n-way gap) Diffie–Hellman assumption on the CIMs in the quantum random (resp. random) oracle model.

We instantiate the proposed protocols on the *hard homogeneous spaces* with limitation where the number of the user group is two. In particular, the protocols instantiated by using the *CSIDH, commutative supersingular isogeny Diffie–Hellman*, key exchange are currently more realistic than the general n-party CIM-based ones due to its realizability. Our two-party one-round protocols are secure against quantum adversaries.

Keywords: One-round authenticated group key exchange ·
Cryptographic invariant maps · Hard homogeneous spaces ·
Commutative supersingular isogeny Diffie–Hellman · G-CK model ·
G-CK$^+$ model · Quantum adversary

1 Introduction

1.1 Background

Recently, National Institute of Standards and Technology (NIST) has initiated a process to standardize quantum-resistant public-key cryptographic algorithms [17], so, to study quantum-resistant cryptosystems is a hot research area. A wide range of quantum-resistant primitives (i.e., mathematical foundations) have been scrutinized by experts on cryptography and mathematics over the world. They include lattice-based, code-based, and multivariate cryptography. We treat with one (relatively) newly entered quantum-resistant primitive, which is called isogeny-based cryptography.

Key establishing over insecure channels is one of important cryptographic techniques. Recent researches on this have led to *authenticated key exchange*

© Springer Nature Switzerland AG 2019
R. Steinfeld and T. H. Yuen (Eds.): ProvSec 2019, LNCS 11821, pp. 330–338, 2019.
https://doi.org/10.1007/978-3-030-31919-9_20

(AKE) and its multiparty extension, that is, *authenticated group key exchange* (AGKE). We then propose quantum-resistant AKE and AGKE schemes from isogenies on elliptic curves. In fact, we establish them on some abstract notions obtained from isogenies called *cryptographic invariant maps* (CIMs) and *hard homogeneous spaces* (HHSs).

HHS, CIM and CSIDH Key Exchange. In an unpublished but seminal paper [3], Couveignes initiated the research of isogeny-based cryptography where he formulated the basic notion of HHSs which is an abstract form of isogeny graphs and class groups of endomorphism rings of (ordinary) elliptic curves.

Independently, Rostovtsev and Stolbunov [18] proposed a Diffie–Hellman type key exchange from ordinary elliptic curve isogenies, which is now called RS key exchange and intensively studied very recently in [4]. While the RS key exchange uses ordinary curves, De Feo et al. employed supersingular isogenies for a practical key exchange protocol called supersingular isogeny Diffie–Hellman (SIDH) key exchange since ordinary isogeny problems suffer from subexponential quantum attacks. Jao et al. submitted an isogeny-based encryption scheme called SIKE (supersingular isogeny key encapsulation) to the NIST post-quantum cryptography competition, and the scheme is an enhanced form of the SIDH key exchange.

Castryck et al. [2] put forward a new HHS-based cryptographic construction called CSIDH (commutative SIDH) key exchange, which is constructed from a group action on the set of *supersingular elliptic curves defined over a prime field*. This ingenious key exchange opened a new research avenue in isogeny cryptography. As another new proposal, Boneh et al. [1] initiated to study a candidate multiparty non-interactive key exchange on CIMs, whose underlying structure is given by a HHS, (X, G), where X is a finite set and G is a finite abelian group, and the invariant map is defined on the n-th product X^n equipped with nice homomorphic (or equivariant) properties. As in the traditional Diffie–Hellman and pairing primitives, we can consider n-way computational, decisional, and gap Diffie–Hellman problems and assumptions on CIMs.

The notions of HHS and CIM give very concise conceptualizations of the above wonderful recent developments. We propose a generic conversion method from these key exchanges to authenticated ones.

We omit definitions, proofs and discussions because of page limitation. See [6] in details.

1.2   Our Contributions

One-Round AGKE from CIM. We propose two one-round AGKE protocols on the CIMs. One is called n-UM (n-Unified Model) which satisfies the G-CK security. The security of n-UM is proved under the n-way DDH assumption in the *quantum* random oracle model. The other is called BC n-DH (biclique n-Diffie–Hellman) which satisfies the G-CK$^+$ security. The security of BC n-DH is proved under the n-way GDH assumption in the random oracle model. The

Table 1. Comparison of one-round AGKE protocols.

	#parties	Assumption	Model	Post-quantum	Proof
[10]	n	KEM, PRF	weak G-CK[a]	Based on ingredients	StdM
[16]	3	gap-BDH	G-eCK	No	ROM
[19]	3	DBDH	G-CK$^+$	No	StdM
[14]	n	MLMs	G-eCK	No	StdM
[12]	n	iO	G-CK	No	StdM
n-UM	n	n-DDH	G-CK	Yes	QROM
BC n-DH	n	n-GDH	G-CK$^+$	Yes	ROM

[a]The model does not capture weak perfect forward secrecy (wPFS).

BC n-DH protocol requires that the number of the user group is bounded by logarithm of the security parameter. Comparison with existing one-round AGKE protocols is shown in Table 1.

Instantiating One-Round Two-Party AKE from HHS. We instantiate the proposed protocols on the HHS with limitation where the number of the user group is two. In particular, the CSIDH-based protocols are currently more realistic than the general n-party CIM-based ones due to its realizability. Our two-party one-round protocols are secure against quantum adversaries.

Compared to the previous SIDH-based one-round (two-party) AKE protocols [5,7], the proposed protocols have several merits. While Galbraith et al. [8] proposed an active attack on the SIDH protocol by using the auxiliary points exchanged between users, the attack cannot be applied to our CSIDH-based ones since they include no auxiliary points. In [9], one attack scenario for the

Table 2. Comparison of isogeny-based AKE protocols.

	Assumption	Model	#rounds	Proof
SIDH TS2 [7]	SI-CDH	CK	1[a]	ROM
AKE-SIDH-SIKE [15]	SI-DDH	CK$^+$	2	ROM
LJA [13]	SI-DDH	qCK	2	QROM
AKE$_{\text{SIDH-2}}$ [20]	SI-DDH	CK$^+$	2	ROM
SIDH UM [5]	SI-DDH	CK	1	QROM
biclique SIDH [5]	di-SI-GDH	CK$^+$	1	ROM
HKSU [11]	IND-CPA PKE	modified CK	2	QROM
HHS-UM	2-DDH	CK	1	QROM
HHS-BC	2-GDH	CK$^+$	1	ROM

[a]Galbraith claims that the protocol is one-round however the description shows that it is two-round as the responder generates the response after receiving the first message [7].

gap Diffie–Hellman (GDH) problem on the SIDH protocol is given since the degrees of isogenies used are fixed by public parameters as $\ell_i^{e_i}$ for small primes ℓ_i, e.g., $\ell_1 = 2, \ell_2 = 3$. As the CSIDH protocol uses random multiples consisting of several primes ℓ_i $(i = 1, \ldots, n)$ for the degrees and they are not fixed by public parameters, the attack cannot be applied to the CSIDH setting. Thus, the GDH assumption on CSIDH has no effective attacks at present, and we have a strong confidence on the security of our CSIDH-based BC protocol, which is reduced from the CSIDH GDH assumption. Comparison with existing isogeny-based AKE protocols is shown in Table 2.

2 n-UM: G-CK Secure n-Party Authenticated Group Key Exchange

2.1 Protocol

Public Parameters. We set $\Pi = \mathsf{nUM}$. Let λ be a security parameter. Let MapGen be a generation algorithm of a cryptographic invariant map, and $(X, S, G, e) \leftarrow_R \mathsf{MapGen}(1^\lambda)$ and $x \leftarrow_R X$ are chosen. Let $H : \{0,1\}^* \to \{0,1\}^\lambda$ be a hash function modeled as a quantum random oracle. Public parameters are (Π, X, S, G, e, x, H).

Static Secret and Public Keys. Party U_i chooses $t_i \in G$ as the SSK. Then, U_i computes $T_i = t_i * x$ as the SPK.

Key Exchange. W.l.o.g, we suppose a session executed by $\mathbf{U} = (U_1, \ldots, U_n) \subseteq \mathcal{U}$.

1. U_i chooses $r_i \leftarrow_R G$ as the ESK, and computes $R_i = r_i * x$ as the EPK. Then, U_i broadcasts $(\Pi, \mathsf{role}_{i'}, U_i, R_i)$ to $\mathbf{U} \setminus U_i$.
2. On receiving $(\Pi, \mathsf{role}_{j'}, U_j, R_j)$ for all $j \neq i$, U_i computes $Z_1 = e_{n-1}(T_1, \ldots, T_{i-1}, t_i * T_{i+1}, \ldots, T_n)$ and $Z_2 = e_{n-1}(R_1, \ldots, R_{i-1}, r_i * R_{i+1}, \ldots, R_n)$.[1] Then, U_i generates the session key $SK = H(\Pi, U_1, \ldots, U_n, R_1, \ldots, R_n, Z_1, Z_2)$, and completes the session (Fig. 1).

$$
\begin{array}{ccccc}
T_1 = t_1 * x & \cdots & T_i = t_i * x & \cdots & T_n = t_n * x \\
\hline
R_1 = r_1 * x & \cdots & R_i = r_i * x & \cdots & R_n = r_n * x \\
\xrightarrow{R_1} \cdots & \xleftarrow{R_i} & & \xrightarrow{R_i} \cdots & \xleftarrow{R_n}
\end{array}
$$

$$
\begin{array}{c}
\hline
Z_1 = e_{n-1}(T_1, \ldots, T_{i-1}, t_i * T_{i+1}, T_{i+2}, \ldots, T_n) \\
Z_2 = e_{n-1}(R_1, \ldots, R_{i-1}, r_i * R_{i+1}, R_{i+2}, \ldots, R_n) \\
SK = H(\Pi, U_1, \ldots, U_n, R_1, \ldots, R_n, Z_1, Z_2)
\end{array}
$$

Fig. 1. Outline of n-UM protocol.

---

[1] T_i and R_i are indexed in the cyclic manner in modulo n. For example, when $i = n$, then $Z_1 = e_{n-1}(t_n * T_1, \ldots, T_n)$ and $Z_2 = e_{n-1}(r_n * R_1, \ldots, R_n)$.

2.2 Security

Theorem 2.1. *Suppose that H is modeled as a quantum random oracle and that the n-DDH assumption holds. Then the n-UM protocol is a post-quantum G-CK-secure n-party authenticated group key exchange protocol in the quantum random oracle model.*

In particular, for any quantum adversary $\mathcal{A}$ against the n-UM protocol that runs in time at most t, involves at most n_u honest parties and activates at most n_s sessions, and makes at most n_h queries to the quantum random oracle and n_q SessionReveal queries, there exists a n-DDH quantum solver $\mathcal{S}$ such that

$$\mathbf{Adv}_{\mathcal{S}}^{n\text{-DDH}}(\lambda) \geq \frac{2\mathbf{Adv}_{n\mathrm{UM},\mathcal{A}}^{\mathrm{g\text{-}ck}}(\lambda)^2}{n_u^2 n_s^2 (8n_h n_q + 3(n_h + n_q + 1)^4)},$$

where $\mathcal{S}$ runs in time t plus time to perform $\mathcal{O}\big((n_u + n_s)\lambda\big)$ group action operations.

3 Biclique n-DH : G-CK$^+$ Secure n-Party Authenticated Group Key Exchange

3.1 Protocol

Public Parameters. We set $\Pi = \mathsf{BCnDH}$. Let λ be a security parameter. Let MapGen be a generation algorithm of a cryptographic invariant map, and $(X, S, G, e) \leftarrow_R \mathsf{MapGen}(1^\lambda)$ and $x \leftarrow_R X$ are chosen. Let $H : \{0,1\}^* \rightarrow \{0,1\}^\lambda$ be a hash function modeled as a random oracle. Public parameters are (Π, X, S, G, e, x, H).

Static Secret and Public Keys. Party U_i chooses $t_i \in G$ as the SSK. Then, U_i computes $T_i = t_i * x$ as the SPK.

Key Exchange. As in Sect. 2, we suppose a session executed by $\mathbf{U} = (U_1, \ldots, U_n) \subseteq \mathcal{U}$.

1. U_i chooses $r_i \leftarrow_R G$ as the ESK, and computes $R_i = r_i * x$ as the EPK. Then, U_i broadcasts $(\Pi, \mathrm{role}_{i'}, U_i, R_i)$ to $\mathbf{U} \setminus U_i$.
2. On receiving $(\Pi, \mathrm{role}_{j'}, U_j, R_1, \ldots, R_n)$, U_i computes $Z_\emptyset = e_{n-1}(T_1, \ldots, T_{i-1}, t_i * T_{i+1}, T_{i+2}, \ldots, T_n), \ldots, Z_I = e_{n-1}(R_1, \ldots, R_{i-1}, r_i * R_{i+1}, R_{i+2}, \ldots, R_n)$ as follows:[2] for all $P \in \mathcal{P}(I)$,
   - if $i \in P$, then $v_i = r_i$, and else if $i \notin P$, then $v_i = t_i$,
   - for all $k \in I$ $(k \neq i)$, if $k \in P$, then $V_k = R_k$, and else if $k \notin P$, then $V_k = T_k$, and
   - U_i computes Z_P as $Z_P = e_{n-1}(V_1, \ldots, V_{i-1}, v_i * V_{i+1}, V_{i+2}, \ldots, V_n)$.
   Then, U_i generates the session key $SK = H(\Pi, U_1, \ldots, U_n, R_1, \ldots, R_n, Z_\emptyset, \ldots, Z_I)$, and completes the session (Fig. 2).

---

[2] T_i and R_i are indexed in the cyclic manner in modulo n.

$$
\begin{array}{ccccc}
T_1 = t_1 * x & \cdots & T_i = t_i * x & \cdots & T_n = t_n * x \\
\hline
R_1 = r_1 * x & \cdots & R_i = r_i * x & \cdots & R_n = r_n * x
\end{array}
$$

$$\xrightarrow{R_1} \cdots \xleftarrow{R_i} \qquad \xrightarrow{R_i} \cdots \xleftarrow{R_n}$$

$$Z_\emptyset = e_{n-1}(T_1, \ldots, T_{i-1}, t_i * T_{i+1}, T_{i+2}, \ldots, T_n)$$

$$\vdots$$

$$Z_I = e_{n-1}(R_1, \ldots, R_{i-1}, r_i * R_{i+1}, R_{i+2}, \ldots, R_n)$$
$$SK = H(\Pi, U_1, \ldots, U_n, R_1, \ldots, R_n, Z_\emptyset, \ldots, Z_I)$$

Fig. 2. Outline of biclique n-DH protocol.

It is worth to note here that we need to assume that the number of the user group is bounded by logarithm of the security parameter, λ.

Otherwise, we need exponential computations in λ as the number of the shared values is 2^n.

3.2 Security

Theorem 3.1. *Suppose that H is modeled as a random oracle and that the n-way GDH assumption holds for S. Then the biclique n-DH protocol is a post-quantum G-CK$^+$ secure n-party authenticated group key exchange protocol in the random oracle model.*

In particular, for any AGKE quantum adversary A against the biclique n-DH protocol that runs in time at most t, involves at most n_u honest parties and activate at most n_s sessions, and makes at most n_h queries to the random oracle, there exists a n-way GDH quantum solver S such that

$$\mathbf{Adv}_S^{n\text{-GDH}}(\lambda) \geq \min\left\{\frac{1}{n_u^n}, \frac{1}{n_u^{n-1}n_s}, \ldots, \frac{1}{n_u n_s^{n-1}}, \frac{1}{n_s^n}\right\} \cdot \mathbf{Adv}_{\mathrm{BCnDH}, A}^{\mathrm{g\text{-}ck+}}(\lambda),$$

where S runs in time t plus time to perform $\mathcal{O}\big((n_u + n_s)\lambda\big)$ group action operations and make $\mathcal{O}(n_h + n_s)$ queries to the n-DDH oracle.

4 Two-Party Authenticated Key Exchanges from Hard Homogeneous Spaces

4.1 G-CK Secure AKE Protocol (from HHS)

We give our HHS-based UM protocol. Public parameters are $pp = (X, G)$. We set $\Pi = $ HHS-UM, that is, the protocol ID is "HHS-UM." The secret-key space for initiators and responders is given by the group G.

User U_1 has static public key, $T_1 = t_1 * x$, where $t_1 \leftarrow_R G$, and t_1 is U_1's static secret key. User U_2 has static public key, $T_2 = t_2 * x$, where $t_2 \leftarrow_R G$, and t_2 is U_2's static secret key. Here, ephemeral secret keys for U_1 and U_2 are given as $r_1 \leftarrow_R G$, and $r_2 \leftarrow_R G$, respectively. U_1 sends a ephemeral public key R_1

$$T_1 = t_1 * x \qquad\qquad T_2 = t_2 * x$$
$$R_1 = r_1 * x \xrightarrow{\quad R_1 \quad} R_2 = r_2 * x$$
$$\xleftarrow{\quad R_2 \quad}$$

| $T_1 = t_1 * x$ | | $T_2 = t_2 * x$ | | $Z_1 = t_1 * T_2$ | $Z_1 = t_2 * T_1$ |

$T_1 = t_1 * x \qquad\qquad T_2 = t_2 * x$

$R_1 = r_1 * x \xrightarrow{\quad R_1 \quad} R_2 = r_2 * x$
$\xleftarrow{\quad R_2 \quad}$

$Z_1 = t_1 * T_2 \qquad\qquad Z_1 = t_2 * T_1$ $Z_1 = t_1 * T_2 \qquad Z_1 = t_2 * T_1$

$Z_2 = r_1 * R_2 \qquad\qquad Z_2 = r_2 * R_1$ $Z_2 = r_1 * T_2 \qquad Z_2 = t_2 * R_1$

$SK = H(\Pi, U_1, U_2, R_1, R_2, Z_1, Z_2)$ $Z_3 = t_1 * R_2 \qquad Z_3 = r_2 * T_1$

$Z_4 = r_1 * R_2 \qquad Z_4 = r_2 * R_1$

$SK = H(\Pi, U_1, U_2, R_1, R_2, Z_1, Z_2, Z_3, Z_4)$

Fig. 3. Outline of HHS UM protocol.   **Fig. 4.** Outline of HHS biclique protocol.

as $R_1 = r_1 * x$ to U_2, U_2 sends back a ephemeral public key R_2 as $R_2 = r_2 * x$ to U_1.

U_1 computes $Z_1 = t_1 * T_2$, and $Z_2 = r_1 * R_2$, and then, obtains the session key SK as $SK = H(\Pi, U_1, U_2, R_1, R_2, Z_1, Z_2)$, where H is a hash function.

U_2 can computes the session key SK as $SK = H(\Pi, U_1, U_2, R_1, R_2, Z_1, Z_2)$ from $Z_1 = t_2 * T_1$, and $Z_2 = r_2 * R_1$ (Fig. 3).

It is clear that the session keys of both parties are equal.

The security of this scheme is given as a corollary of Theorem 2.1.

Corollary 4.1. *Suppose that H is modeled as a quantum random oracle and that the 2-DDH assumption holds on the HHS (X, G). Then the 2-UM protocol is a post-quantum G-CK-secure 2-party authenticated key exchange protocol in the quantum random oracle model.*

4.2   G-CK$^+$ Secure AKE Protocol (from HHS)

We give our HHS-based biclique protocol. Public parameters are $pp = (X, G)$. We set $\Pi = $ HHS-BC, that is, the protocol ID is "HHS-BC." Static and ephemeral keys are the same as our HHS UM protocol. The secret-key space for initiators and responders is given by the group G.

User U_1 has static public key, $T_1 = t_1 * x$, where $t_1 \leftarrow_R G$, and t_1 is U_1's static secret key. User U_2, also, has static public key, $B = t_2 * x$, where $t_2 \leftarrow_R G$, and t_2 is U_2's static secret key. Here, ephemeral secret keys for U_1 and U_2 are given as $r_1 \leftarrow_R G$, and $r_2 \leftarrow_R G$, respectively. U_1 sends an ephemeral public key R_1 as $R_1 = r_1 * x$ to U_2, U_2 sends back an ephemeral public key R_2 as $R_2 = r_2 * x$ to U_1.

U_1 computes the non-trivial combinations of the ephemeral and static public keys as $Z_1 = t_1 * T_2$, $Z_2 = r_1 * T_2$, $Z_3 = t_1 * R_2$, and $Z_4 = r_1 * R_2$, and then, obtains the session key SK as $SK = H(\Pi, U_1, U_2, R_1, R_2, Z_1, Z_2, Z_3, Z_4)$, where H is a hash function.

U_2 can computes the session key SK as $SK = H(\Pi, U_1, U_2, R_1, R_2, Z_1, Z_2, Z_3, Z_4)$ from $Z_1 = t_2 * T_1$, $Z_2 = t_2 * R_1$, $Z_3 = r_2 * T_1$, and $Z_4 = r_2 * R_1$ (Fig. 4).

It is clear that the session keys of both parties are equal.

The security of this scheme is given as a corollary of Theorem 3.1.

Corollary 4.2. *Suppose that H is modeled as a random oracle and that the 2-way GDH assumption holds on the HHS (X, G). Then the biclique 2-DH protocol is a post-quantum G-CK$^+$ secure authenticated key exchange protocol in the random oracle model.*

References

1. Boneh, D., et al.: Multiparty non-interactive key exchange and more from isogenies on elliptic curves. In: MATHCRYPT 2018 (2018). https://eprint.iacr.org/2018/665
2. Castryck, W., Lange, T., Martindale, C., Panny, L., Renes, J.: CSIDH: an efficient post-quantum commutative group action. In: Peyrin, T., Galbraith, S. (eds.) ASIACRYPT 2018, Part III. LNCS, vol. 11274, pp. 395–427. Springer, Cham (2018). https://doi.org/10.1007/978-3-030-03332-3_15
3. Couveignes, J.M.: Hard homogeneous spaces. IACR Cryptology ePrint Archive 2006, 291 (2006). http://eprint.iacr.org/2006/291
4. De Feo, L., Kieffer, J., Smith, B.: Towards practical key exchange from ordinary isogeny graphs. In: Peyrin, T., Galbraith, S. (eds.) ASIACRYPT 2018, Part III. LNCS, vol. 11274, pp. 365–394. Springer, Cham (2018). https://doi.org/10.1007/978-3-030-03332-3_14
5. Fujioka, A., Takashima, K., Terada, S., Yoneyama, K.: Supersingular isogeny Diffie–Hellman authenticated key exchange. In: Lee, K. (ed.) ICISC 2018. LNCS, vol. 11396, pp. 177–195. Springer, Cham (2019). https://doi.org/10.1007/978-3-030-12146-4_12
6. Fujioka, A., Takashima, K., Yoneyama, K.: One-round authenticated group key exchange from isogenies. IACR Cryptology ePrint Archive 2018, 1033 (2018). http://eprint.iacr.org/2018/1033
7. Galbraith, S.D.: Authenticated key exchange for SIDH. IACR Cryptology ePrint Archive 2018, 266 (2018). http://eprint.iacr.org/2018/266
8. Galbraith, S.D., Petit, C., Shani, B., Ti, Y.B.: On the security of supersingular isogeny cryptosystems. In: Cheon, J.H., Takagi, T. (eds.) ASIACRYPT 2016, Part I. LNCS, vol. 10031, pp. 63–91. Springer, Heidelberg (2016). https://doi.org/10.1007/978-3-662-53887-6_3
9. Galbraith, S.D., Vercauteren, F.: Computational problems in supersingular elliptic curve isogenies. IACR Cryptology ePrint Archive 2017, 774 (2017). http://eprint.iacr.org/2017/774
10. Gorantla, M.C., Boyd, C., González Nieto, J.M., Manulis, M.: Generic one round group key exchange in the standard model. In: Lee, D., Hong, S. (eds.) ICISC 2009. LNCS, vol. 5984, pp. 1–15. Springer, Heidelberg (2010). https://doi.org/10.1007/978-3-642-14423-3_1
11. Hövelmanns, K., Kiltz, E., Schäge, S., Unruh, D.: Generic authenticated key exchange in the quantum random oracle model. IACR Cryptology ePrint Archive 2018, 928 (2018). http://eprint.iacr.org/2018/276
12. Lan, X., Xu, J., Guo, H., Zhang, Z.: One-round cross-domain group key exchange protocol in the standard model. In: Chen, K., Lin, D., Yung, M. (eds.) Inscrypt 2016. LNCS, vol. 10143, pp. 386–400. Springer, Cham (2017). https://doi.org/10.1007/978-3-319-54705-3_24
13. LeGrow, J., Jao, D., Azarderakhsh, R.: Modeling quantum-safe authenticated key establishment, and an isogeny-based protocol. IACR Cryptology ePrint Archive 2018, 282 (2018). http://eprint.iacr.org/2018/282

14. Li, Y., Yang, Z.: Strongly secure one-round group authenticated key exchange in the standard model. In: Abdalla, M., Nita-Rotaru, C., Dahab, R. (eds.) CANS 2013. LNCS, vol. 8257, pp. 122–138. Springer, Cham (2013). https://doi.org/10.1007/978-3-319-02937-5_7

15. Longa, P.: A note on post-quantum authenticated key exchange from supersingular isogenies. IACR Cryptology ePrint Archive 2018, 267 (2018). http://eprint.iacr.org/2018/267

16. Manulis, M., Suzuki, K., Ustaoglu, B.: Modeling leakage of ephemeral secrets in tripartite/group key exchange. IEICE Trans. **96-A**(1), 101–110 (2013)

17. National Institute of Standards and Technology: Post-Quantum crypto standardization: Call for Proposals Announcement, December 2016. http://csrc.nist.gov/groups/ST/post-quantum-crypto/cfp-announce-dec2016.html

18. Rostovtsev, A., Stolbunov, A.: Public-key cryptosystem based on isogenies. IACR Cryptology ePrint Archive 2006, 145 (2006). http://eprint.iacr.org/2006/145

19. Suzuki, K., Yoneyama, K.: Exposure-resilient one-round tripartite key exchange without random oracles. In: ACNS 2013, pp. 458–474 (2013)

20. Xu, X., Xue, H., Wang, K., Tian, S., Liang, B., Yu, W.: Strongly secure authenticated key exchange from supersingular isogeny. IACR Cryptology ePrint Archive 2018, 760 (2018). http://eprint.iacr.org/2018/760

TumbleBit++: A Comprehensive Privacy Protocol Providing Anonymity and Amount-Invisibility

Yi Liu[1,2], Zhen Liu[1(✉)], Yu Long[1(✉)], Zhiqiang Liu[1(✉)], Dawu Gu[1(✉)], Fei Huan[1(✉)], and Yanxue Jia[1]

[1] School of Electronic Information and Electrical Engineering,
Shanghai Jiao Tong University, Shanghai, China
{1780790324,liuzhen,longyu,ilu_zq,dwgu,huanfei,jiayanxue}@sjtu.edu.cn
[2] Shanghai Viewsource Information Science and Technology Co., Ltd.,
Shanghai, China

Abstract. Since the advent of bitcoin, the privacy of bitcoin has become a hot issue. Many coin mixing protocols guarantee the anonymity and unlinkability of the payer and payee of a transaction. However, due to the publicity of blockchain, the confidentiality of transaction amounts has not been provided. Everyone has the chance to get the amount of a transaction, which poses a challenge to the privacy of users.

To overcome the problem, we propose an improved mixing protocol based on TumbleBit, which is named TumbleBit++. TumbleBit++ combines confidential transactions with centralized untrusted anonymous payment hub, and achieves the protection of transaction amounts without undermining the anonymity of TumbleBit. TumbleBit++ allows multiple payers to trade in different transaction amounts, and Tumbler, as an untrusted third party, does not know the exact amount of each transaction and the flow of funds between the payer and payee of one transaction.

Keywords: TumbleBit · Confidential transactions · Bitcoin

1 Introduction

The most important aspect of bitcoin's privacy is the hiding of transaction information, such as transaction address and transaction amount. In order to achieve the anonymity of bitcoin, the technology of coin mixing [1,2,9] has been adopted to separate the relationship between the input and output addresses. TumbleBit [2], as a centralized mixing protocol, uses an untrusted third party, Tumbler, to offer mixing service with transaction flow invisible to the third party. However, an attacker can still get information about the flow of transactions by the increasing or decreasing amount of money [2]. Confidential transactions [3] realized the protection of transaction amounts on blockchain, but with no concern of anonymity.

© Springer Nature Switzerland AG 2019
R. Steinfeld and T. H. Yuen (Eds.): ProvSec 2019, LNCS 11821, pp. 339–346, 2019.
https://doi.org/10.1007/978-3-030-31919-9_21

Several currencies have contributed to the protection of amounts. Monero is a cryptocurrency based on the CryptoNote protocol [4], which provides unlinkability and untraceability by ring signature, stealth address and Pedersen commitment [11]. However, the ring signature requires space and verification overheads on blockchain and makes it difficult for clients to distinguish the spent transaction outputs for pruning [5]. Zerocoin [6] is a zero-knowledge-proof-based currency. Users can mint bitcoin into zerocoin with hidden addresses for trading. Zerocash [7] uses the non-interactive zero-knowledge proof technology which is zk-SNARK to achieve privacy and anonymity and to support arbitrary denomination transactions. Because of the need for complex mathematical calculation, the cost of Zerocoin and Zerocash is high. Besides, the dependence on trusted setup and the non-falsifiable cryptographic assumptions [8] makes it have low acceptance. Valueshuffle [10] based on Coinshuffle++ [9], aims at hiding the amounts of transactions by combining confidential transactions and stealth address. In Valueshuffle, DiceMix protocol is run to mix output triples, which consist of output addresses, value commitments and range proofs. However, since the range proof is quite large, Valueshuffle splits the output triple into chunks to mix and recombines the messages after mixing. This arrangement demands high computation costs and more redundance. Inheriting the features of Coinshuffle++, the scheme can not resist DoS attacks and Sybil attacks.

Our Contribution: TumbleBit++. In this paper, we present TumbleBit++, a complete privacy protection protocol that combines confidential transactions with centralized coin mixing protocol, TumbleBit. TumbleBit++ provides the invisibility of amounts on the basis of anonymity, which makes the amounts and flow of transactions invisible to not only users but also the third party.

TumbleBit++ modifies the 2-of-2 escrow smart contract of TumbleBit, and allows multiple bitcoins to be packaged in one transaction without revealing the value. Verification, blinding and zero-knowledge proof steps are applied to prevent theft and provide anonymity.

2   Preliminaries

TumbleBit. TumbleBit [2] is a centralized coin mixing scheme with an untrusted anonymous payment hub, which is compatible with bitcoin. TumbleBit uses RSA encryption algorithm [13] and ECDSA [14] to ensure the anonymity and unforgeability of transactions. TumbleBit uses off-chain puzzle payments to replace on-chain payments, which also improves the efficiency of coin mixing.

Puzzle-promise protocol and RSA-puzzle-solver protocol are two important sub-protocols of TumbleBit, which turn bitcoin payments into off-chain puzzle payments. Puzzle-promise protocol generates puzzle pairs for off-chain payments between Tumbler and the payee. RSA-puzzle-solver protocol provides the solution to the specific puzzle through interactions between the payer and Tumbler.

The anonymity of TumbleBit is achieved by blinding. The payee B uses the blind factor r, which is only visible to B, to blind the puzzle z. So that the third party T cannot link the blinded puzzle $\bar{z}$ from the payer A to the original puzzle z, which splits the relationship between A and B. In TumbleBit, the blinding of puzzle z is based on RSA encryption process. For a blind factor r, the blinding of puzzle z is $\bar{z} = r^e z \bmod N$.

Pedersen Commitment. Pedersen commitment [11] is a scheme which allows the user to commit to a secret value without revealing it. Besides, the value can be revealed later and the user can prove the revealed value to be correct [15]. Pedersen commitment is applied in confidential transactions to hide the amounts of transactions.

Pedersen commitment is a homomorphic commitment, which means that the commitment of sum equals the sum of commitments. For example, the commitment of value x_1 is $com_1 = com(x_1, r_1)$, while the commitment of value x_2 is $com_2 = com(x_2, r_2)$. r_1 and r_2 are random values for encryption. The homomorphic property makes it that the commitment of value $(x_1 + x_2)$ is $com(x_1 + x_2, r_1 + r_2) = com_1 \oplus com_2 = com(x_1, r_1) \oplus com(x_2, r_2)$. Therefore, homomorphic commitment makes it convenient and effective to verify the balance of transaction amounts.

3   TumbleBit++

3.1   System Entities and Overview

The system entities of TumbleBit++ are similar to that of TumbleBit. The payer is Alice A, and the payee is Bob B. Tumbler T is an untrusted third party.

In TumbleBit++, the amounts of all on-chain transactions, which are the four transactions in Fig. 1, are hidden in commitments. For example, the transaction

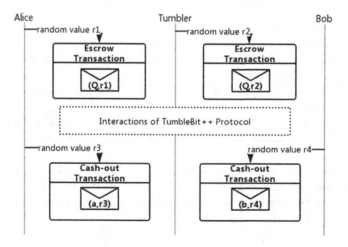

Fig. 1. System entities of TumbleBit++, in which the values in four transactions are hidden. In theory, values a and b should be equal.

amount in the escrow transaction between A and T, which is the upper limit Q of one round, is committed with the random value $r1$ of A; The transaction amount in the escrow transaction between T and B, which is also the upper limit Q, is committed with the random value $r2$ of T. In cash-out transactions which are used to activate the escrow transactions, the amounts a and b are committed with random values of A and B separately.

Before the interactions, A escrows Q BTCs on chain and T also escrows Q BTCs on chain. Through the interactions of TumbleBit++ protocol, a BTCs in escrow transaction flow from A to T, and b BTCs flow from T to B. In one payment, a and b should be equal. Meanwhile, T does not know the relationship between A and B and the transaction amounts which are a and b. After one round of payments, which includes multiple transactions, unspent bitcoins in escrow transactions will be withdrawn.

The interactions of TumbleBit++ protocol involve interactions between T and B through puzzle-promise protocol, interactions between A and T through RSA-puzzle-solver protocol, and interactions between A and B for parameter values. The details are described in Sect. 3.2.

In the enhanced 2-of-2 escrow smart contract of TumbleBit++, we stipulate that the transaction value in $T_{fulfill}$ [2] is a commitment of the actual amount of transaction between A and B, and the amount that $T_{fulfill}$ can take from T_{escrow} is exactly the amount committed in $T_{fulfill}$, rather than the fixed 1 BTC in TumbleBit.

3.2   Concrete Protocol

As Fig. 2 shows, TumbleBit++ has three phases.

Escrow Phase. In this phase, there are three steps.

– On-chain escrow transactions.
  A and T escrow Q BTCs in commitments in escrow transactions separately on chain. The detailed output addresses are described in TumbleBit.
– Puzzle-promise protocol.
  If B aims to get b BTCs from T, B and T generate a puzzle pair (c, z) through puzzle-promise protocol. Different from TumbleBit, the signature σ of T to the cash-out transaction is committed in $comm(\sigma, r_c)$ and r_c is a random value of T. The commitment is encrypted by puzzle solution ε.
– Blinding.
  Besides the blinding of puzzle z, the commitment of value b, which is c_B is also blinded by blinding factor r_B of B. However, the blinding of puzzle z is based on RSA encryption algorithm which can be found in Sect. 2, while the blinding of c_B is based as follows.

For a commitment $c = comm(v, r) = v \cdot H + r \cdot G$, the random blind factor r_1 is selected and the commitment is blinded to $\bar{c} = c + r_1 \cdot G$.

After blinding, Δr_1 is calculated by B at the same time. $\bar{z}$, $\bar{c}_B$ and Δr_1 are prepared to send to A for verification and puzzle solution.

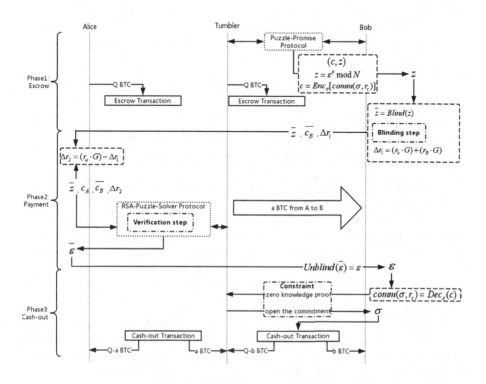

Fig. 2. TumbleBit++ protocol.

Payment Phase. Compared to TumbleBit, the most important step in this phase is verification. Since multiple bitcoins are packaged into one transaction, it is necessary for third-party Tumbler to ensure the balance of revenue and expenditure of one transaction. In commitments, the value of a is committed in $c_A = comm(a, r_a)$, and the value of b is committed in $c_B = comm(b, r_b)$. The additive homomorphism of Pedersen commitment [11] ensures verifiability.

The phase has two steps.

– Off-chain puzzle payment.
  A makes a payment to B for a blinded puzzle $\bar{z}$, $\bar{c}_B$ and Δr_1. For the later verification, A calculates Δr_2 for prepare.

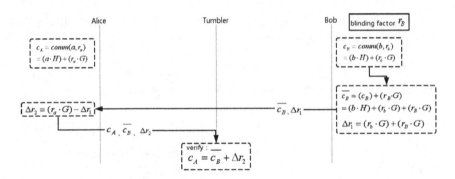

Fig. 3. Verification of TumbleBit++.

– RSA-puzzle-solver protocol and verification.
  In the RSA-puzzle-solver protocol, it is necessary for T to verify $c_A = \bar{c}_B + \Delta r_2$. The correctness of the verification can be verified in Fig. 3.

  If the verification is proved, A obtains the solution $\bar{\varepsilon}$ of $\bar{z}$ through RSA-puzzle-solver protocol with T and sends it to B.

Cash-Out Phase. In order to prevent A and B from cheating T with wrong verification information, constraint using zero-knowledge proof is added in this phase.

  Three steps are involved in the cash-out phase.

– Unblinding.
  After receiving $\bar{\varepsilon}$ from A, B unblinds it by the blind factor r_B and gets the solution ε. As mentioned in the escrow phase, in puzzle-promise protocol of TumbleBit++, the signature σ of $T_{cash(T,B)}$ from T, are protected by commitment. The information B gets by decrypting after getting ε is $comm(\sigma, r_c)$ rather than the signature σ.
– Constraint.
  In order to open the commitment to get σ, B is supposed to provide T with a zero-knowledge proof, which can proof that the blinded value $\bar{c}_B$ of c_B is included in a set of $\bar{c}_B$ maintained by T and T doesn't know exactly which $\bar{c}_B$ is the value. Obviously, T knows a set of $\bar{c}_B$ from all previous interactions with A.
  In this scheme, if A generates $\bar{c}_B$ and Δr_2 at will, the set of $\bar{c}_B$ will not include the corresponding commitment of c_B, so that B cannot get σ, which has no benefit to A.

  After the verification of zero-knowledge proof, T opens the commitment to B and B obtains the signature σ to complete the cash-out transaction.
– On-chain cash-out transactions.
  Finally, B claims bitcoins from T's escrow transaction by on-chain cash-out transaction. Unspent bitcoins in escrow transactions will be withdrawn.

Since TumbleBit++ is an enhancement of TumbleBit protocol, some details such as cut and choose scheme and smart contract can be found in TumbleBit [2].

4   Security Analysis

TumbleBit++ has several security properties. Due to the limitation of space, we conclude the properties briefly.

- Anonymity.
  Inherited from TumbleBit, anonymity is provided by blinding scheme, which includes blinding of puzzle and blinding of commitments.
- Amounts invisibility.
  Invisibility of amounts is realized by Pedersen commitments of confidential transactions. In addition, TumbleBit++ can mix transactions with different amounts, which means that it is more efficient and flexible than the traditional fixed-value transactions in TumbleBit.
- Tumbler untrustworthiness.
  Inherited from TumbleBit, Tumbler is unable to know the amount and flow information in the transaction, which is realized by commitments and blinding.
- Theft prevention.
  The verification step and constraint based on zero-knowledge proof prevent theft from payers and payees effectively. Besides, the authority of generating commitments avoids Tumbler modifying values of commitments.
- DoS resistance.
  Inherited from TumbleBit, since the independence between users of coin mixing transactions, even if some network resources are occupied, it does not affect the process of mixing.
- Sybils resistance.
  Sybil attack [12] is a form of attack in peer-to-peer networks. The property is also inherited from TumbleBit.

5   Conclusion

In the privacy protection of bitcoin, many mixing schemes can provide anonymity reasonably, but there is no systematic mechanism for the amounts concealment. Confidential transaction is a scheme that hides the amounts of transactions with Pedersen commitments.

In this paper, based on TumbleBit protocol and CT scheme, TumbleBit++ protects the amounts, and inherits the anonymity and the third party's untrustworthiness of TumbleBit, which is realized by blinding on commitments, verification, and constraint based on zero-knowledge proof. In summary, we get a comprehensive privacy protocol, TumbleBit++, which provides anonymity and amount-invisibility.

Acknowledgement. The authors are supported by the National Natural Science Foundation of China (Grant No. 61672347, 61572318, 61672339, 61872142), the National Cryptography Development Fund (No. MMJJ20170111) and Minhang Technology Innovation Program for SMEs, a finance business platform based on blockchain technology (2018MH110).

References

1. Ruffling, T., Moreno-Sanchez, P., Kate, A.: Coinshuffle: practical decentralized coin mixing for bitcoin. In: Kutylowski, M., Vaudya, J. (eds.) ESORICS 2014. LNCS, vol. 8713, pp. 345–364. Springer, Cham (2014)
2. Heilman, E., AlShenibr, L., Baldimtsi, F., Scafuro, A., Goldberg, S.: TumbleBit: an untrusted Bitcoin-compatible anonymous payment hub. In: NDSS 2017 (2017)
3. Maxwell, G.: Confidential transactions (2015). https://people.xiph.org/~greg/confidential_values.txt
4. Noether, S.: Review of CryptoNote white paper. https://downloads.getmonero.org/whitepaper_review.pdf
5. OmegaStarScream: Bitcoin Core & pruning mode. Bitcoin Forum. https://bitcointalk.org/index.php?topic=1599458.0
6. Miers, I., Garman, C., Green, M., Rubin, A.D.: Zerocoin: anonymous distributed e-cash from Bitcoin. In: S&P 2013 (2013)
7. Ben-Sasson, E., et al.: Zerocash: decentralized anonymous payments from Bitcoin. In: S&P 2014 (2014)
8. Gentry, C., Wiches, D.: Separating succinct non-interactive arguments from all falsifiable assumptions. In: STOC 2011 (2011)
9. Ruffling, T., Moreno-Sanchez, P., Kate, A.: P2P mixing and unlinkable Bitcoin transactions. In: NDSS 2017 (2017)
10. Ruffing, T., Moreno-Sanchez, P.: ValueShuffle: mixing confidential transactions for comprehensive transaction privacy in bitcoin. In: Brenner, M., et al. (eds.) FC 2017. LNCS, vol. 10323, pp. 133–154. Springer, Cham (2017). https://doi.org/10.1007/978-3-319-70278-0_8
11. Pedersen, T.P.: Non-interactive and information-theoretic secure verifiable secret sharing. In: Feigenbaum, J. (ed.) CRYPTO 1991. LNCS, vol. 576, pp. 129–140. Springer, Heidelberg (1992). https://doi.org/10.1007/3-540-46766-1_9
12. Douceur, J.R.: The sybil attack. In: Druschel, P., Kaashoek, F., Rowstron, A. (eds.) IPTPS 2002. LNCS, vol. 2429, pp. 251–260. Springer, Heidelberg (2002). https://doi.org/10.1007/3-540-45748-8_24
13. Rivest, R.L., Shamir, A., Adleman, L.: A method for obtaining digital signatures and public-key cryptosystems. Commun. ACM **21**(2), 120–126 (1978)
14. Johnson, D., Menezes, A., Vanstone, S.: The elliptic curve digital signature algorithm (ECDSA). Int. J. Inf. Secur. **1**, 36–63 (2001)
15. Damgård, I.: Commitment schemes and zero-knowledge protocols. In: Damgård, I.B. (ed.) EEF School 1998. LNCS, vol. 1561, pp. 63–86. Springer, Heidelberg (1999). https://doi.org/10.1007/3-540-48969-X_3

Secure Online/Offline Attribute-Based Encryption for IoT Users in Cloud Computing

Xiang Li[1], Hui Tian[1(✉)], and Jianting Ning[2]

[1] College of Computer Science and Technology, National Huaqiao University,
Xiamen, People's Republic of China
xlics@stu.hqu.edu.cn, cshtian@126.com
[2] School of Computing, National University of Singapore, Singapore, Singapore
jtning88@gmail.com

Abstract. To ensure the security of mass data sharing in the Internet of Things, the cloud computing platform is supposed to provide data-storage services. The ciphertext-policy attribute-based encryption (CP-ABE) schemes has attracted wide-scale attention since users can access the cloud platform in a fine-grained manner. However, there are still some problems in the existing CP-ABE schemes when directly applied in the Internet of Things environment. The problem of simultaneously achieves large computational cost in the encryption and decryption. Moreover, the privacy of access control policy actually still remains unresolved. To fill the gap of the existing schemes, this paper proposes a suitable data sharing scheme for IoT devices which can't always be online. We use the online/offline CP-ABE technology with privacy, while hiding the access control structure and reducing the computational cost of the devices when they are online. The asymptotic complexity comparison also shows that our scheme achieves high computation efficiency.

Keywords: Internet of Things · Cloud computing · Online/offline encryption · Privacy protection · Hidden access structure

1 Introduction

Nowadays, the Internet of Things (IoT) has attracted the attention of researchers in academia and industry. With the development of Internet of Things technology continuously, it is widely used in some areas, such as aviation, rail transit, safe city, industrial manufacturing, logistics management, medical and health, and smart home, etc. However, the computing and storage resources of IoT devices are often limited, which greatly limit the application of the Internet of Things in various fields. Cloud computing provides an on-demand service that provides users with useful and convenient network access. Therefore, cloud computing services can solve the problems, which include technically limited of IoT devices, and satisfy the exchange and sharing requirements of large data volume that the Internet of Things requires. However, cloud computing service providers are not completely trusted. When the data owner stores the data on the cloud server, it loses absolute control over the data. Cloud service providers (CSP) may privately share data to unauthorized users when they are tempted by

© Springer Nature Switzerland AG 2019
R. Steinfeld and T. H. Yuen (Eds.): ProvSec 2019, LNCS 11821, pp. 347–354, 2019.
https://doi.org/10.1007/978-3-030-31919-9_22

interests. Cloud service providers may also receive internal and external attacks, resulting in authorization exceptions and data leakage for their users and roles. In the IoT environment, sensor devices are characterized by massiveness, device differentiation and security and privacy protection difficulty. Thus, Internet of Things users have higher requirements for data security and privacy protection.

Attributes-based encryption (ABE) can well meet the needs of data confidentiality and fine-grained access control in the Internet of Things. We divide ABE into two categories: KP-ABE [1] and CP-ABE [2]. In the CP-ABE scheme, the access policy is related to the ciphertext, while the key is connected to the attribute. KP-ABE scheme is the opposite. For reducing equipment burden, some selectively efficient ABE schemes [3–6] were proposed, such as outsource data to third parties which can save local storage and computing resources. At the same time, some efficient online/offline encryption solutions [7–10] have proposed.

In the above solution, the data provider needs to be online in real-time while the ciphertext is related to the access control policy, which resulting in increasing the encrypting computational overhead. In addition, during the decryption phase, the cloud service provider needs to send the access control policy to data users along with the ciphertext, while the access policy may contain some sensitive information. If the access control policy for this data is compromised, it may be illegal. Therefore, how to reduce the encryption computing overhead while realizing the hiding of access policies has become one of the urgent problems in the cloud computing environment.

In this paper, we proposed a secure online/offline attribute-based encryption for IoT users in cloud computing. Our scheme mainly uses the online/offline ABE technology to solve the problem of large computing cost in ABE that the most expensive encrypt operations have been executed in the offline phase. What's more, in order to protect the security of access control structure. When the user uploads and downloads the ciphertext, the access control structure will be hiding.

2 Related Work

Currently, the attribute-based encryption (ABE) system has been widely used. Its main dependency is to use a set of attributes that describe the user's identity to represent the identity of the user. The data user's key is generated by the authorization center according to each user's attribute set, which is a set of characteristic information of the data user. Matching relationship between the user attribute set and the access structure, the decryption capability of the user is determined by realizing the control of the ciphertext. The data provider does not need to distribute the corresponding key for each data consumer. They only need to manage the attributes of the corresponding file by modifying the access control structure, which greatly increases the flexibility of access control. Considering the computational burden of the IoT device during the encryption and decryption phase, it is mainly to delegate the complex calculation by constrained IoT devices to the enough computing power nodes at present. In 2010, to address the burden of key distribution and data management, Yu et al. [3] strengthened the attribute-based access strategy, while allowing data owners to put most of their computing tasks on the cloud server. Hur et al. proposed an attribute-based access control method [4] using CP-ABE to enforce access control policies with efficient attribute and user revocation capability. This fine-grained access control method is implemented by the ABE and the double encryption mechanism of the selective group key distribution method in each attribute group. For the ABE outsourcing decryption scheme, in the literature [5], they adopt the bilinear pairing method to realize the outsource decryption, that is, the calculate operation in the resource-constrained client is outsourced to the semi-trusted third party. However, in the above scheme, the user still needs to operate the index and multiplication operations multiple times. Green et al. [6] proposed an outsourced decryption scheme based on LSSS matrix, which allows the cloud to convert ciphertexts satisfying user attributes into ciphertext of constant size, while the cloud cannot read any part of the user's message.

Meanwhile, IoT devices include not only sensor devices with weak underlying computing capabilities, but also devices with strong computing power. These devices are sufficient to perform encryption and decryption work, but there is no guarantee that resources will be online in real time. Online/offline cryptography is an effective tool for improving encryption efficiency. The complex encryption operations are preprocessed by using high-performance devices that makes lightweight devices only need to perform a small amount of simple operations. Hohenberg [7] first proposed constructing an online/offline ABE encryption scheme in which the computational work is divided into two phases: the offline phase (preparation process) and the online phase. In 2015, Datta [8] combines searchable encryption and access control with security proof. Later, Cui [9] uses outsourced ABE technology to place most of the decryption work on the cloud server while implementing keyword search, which greatly reduces the user's computational cost. Considering resources with limited resources, Liu [10] quickly performs keyword encryption or token generation by consuming costs to the offline phase, while the mobile device is powered without consuming battery. However, the above operations do not consider the operation of the multi-authority ABE. We know that the computing power of sensor devices is limited. Before sending the sensitive message to users, we must encrypt these messages for protecting the privacy. This is a great challenge for the IoT sensor devices. Consequently, it would be much better to do a part of encrypt operation in the free time.

3   System Design

3.1   System Model and Design Goals

As shown in Fig. 1, the system architecture of our proposed scheme consists of four entities: a cloud service provider (CSP), an attribute authority (AA), data owners (DOs) and data users (DUs).

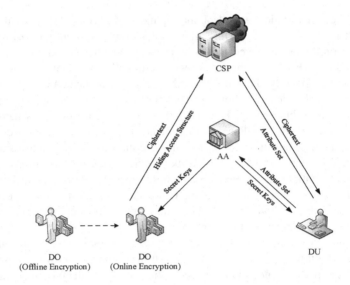

Fig. 1. System architecture of the scheme in cloud model

- CSP is responsible for storing a large amount of data generated in the Internet of Things which is composed of multiple servers. It has strong computing power, which is honest and curious.
- AA is an independent attribute authority that can generate a public key and a master secret key for DO by executing an *AuthoritySetup* algorithm. After receiving the attribute set from the user, it returns the attribute private key generating by *SecretKeyGen* algorithm.
- DO is the owner of the data. In the IoT environment, the data owner is a resource-constrained entity. It cannot guarantee that its computing resources are always online. Since most of costly computations can evaluated by running *Offline.Encrypt* algorithm, the efficiency of encryption can be greatly improved because *Online. Encrypt* algorithm only incurs little computation costs.
- DU refers to the actual user of the actual data in the Internet of Things. The entity can obtain a plaintext message through the *Decrypt* algorithm.

In our scheme, we prescribe some security assumptions to meet the real IoT environment's needs. we assume AA is fully trusted while does not reveal user data and collude with users. The CSP is semi-trusted (honest-but-curious) entity which can honestly save user-uploaded data and perform user's tasks. But it may be curious about the data content. Meanwhile, users are not completely trusted. Malicious users may hide their identity to obtain sensitive information.

3.2 Proposed Scheme

This section is dedicated to proposing our scheme, which has six algorithms: *GlobalSetup, AuthoritySetup, SecretKeyGen, Offline.Encrypt, Online.Encrypt, Decrypt.*

System Initialization. Similar to the scheme [11], this phase is required to initialization the public parameter and to generation public keys and secret keys.

GlobalSetup(1^k) → (PP) This algorithm inputs a security parameter 1^k, and then outputs public parameter

$$PP = \{g, h, e, p, \mathbb{G}, \mathbb{G}_T, H\}.$$

The algorithm chooses two random generators g, h from $\mathbb{G}$. And selects two bilinear groups $\mathbb{G} \times \mathbb{G} \to \mathbb{G}_T$ of prime order e, p. Furthermore, we employ a strong collision-resistant hash function $H : \{0, 1\} \to \mathbb{G}$.

AuthoritySetup(PP) → (PK, MSK). Taking as input the system public parameters PP, the authority chooses α, β, γ randomly from $\mathbb{Z}_p$. Then, AA picks random generators u from $\mathbb{G}$. AA publishes the public key and the master secret key

$$PK = \left\{ e(g, g)^{\alpha}, h^{\beta}, g^{\gamma}, u \right\}, MSK = \{PK, \alpha\}.$$

Secret Key Generation. In this phase, the attribute authority issues a key extract algorithm with hidden access structure, which not get any information about user's identifier and attributes to protect user's privacy.

SecretKeyGen($PP, \text{GID}_U, PK, U, De_{ID}, CM_{ID}$) → ($SK_U$). Firstly, data user execute commitment algorithm Commit(PP, GID_U) → (CM_{ID}, De_{ID}) and send (CM_{ID}, De_{ID}) to attribute authority. Then AA take public parameters PP, an attribute set $U = \{A_1, A_2, \ldots, A_n\}$, the public key PK and commitment (CM_{ID}, De_{ID}) as input. Then if Decommit algorithm output the right sight, it computes $K_1 = g^{\beta}$, and for i = 1 to n, it computes $K_{i,1} = (u^{A_i} h^{\beta})^{t_i}, K_{i,2} = g^{t_i}$. Otherwise, it outputs the error messages and the *SecretKeyGen* algorithm is terminated. The algorithm outputs

$$SK_U = \left\{ K_1, \left\{ K_{i,1}, K_{i,2} \right\}_{i \in [1,n]} \right\}$$

which authority picks $t_1, t_2, \ldots, t_n \in \mathbb{Z}_p$.

Encryption. This phase is divided into the offline data creation and online data creation. Data owner who is resource-limited generates offline ciphertexts by running *Offline.Encrypt* and generates the final ciphertext by running *Online.Encrypt*.

Offline.Encrypt(PP, PK) → $\left(CT_{Off} \right)$. The offline encryption algorithm takes in the public parameters only. The algorithm randomly picks s, $\lambda \in \mathbb{Z}_p$ and computes $C_0 = g^s$. Next it chooses random $\tau_j, x_j \in \mathbb{Z}_p$ for each $j \in [1, n]$ The algorithm sets key = $e(g, g)^{\alpha s}, C_{j,1} = g^{-\tau_j}, C_{j,2} = \left(u^{x_j} h^{\beta} \right)^{\tau_j}, C_{j,3} = h^{x_j}$. The algorithm outputs

$$CT_{Off} = \left\{ key, C_0, \{C_{j,1}, C_{j,2}, C_{j,3}, x_j, \tau_j\}_{j \in [1,n]} \right\}.$$

Online.Encrypt$\left(PP, U, CT_{Off}, PK \right)$ → (CT). The online encryption algorithm takes as input the public parameters PP, the data owner's attribute U, an offline ciphertext CT_{Off} and the public key PK. The owner computes $P_j = e\left(h^{\beta}, H(U_j) \right)$ for each

$j \in [1, Y]$, where U_j denotes attribute of access policy T and Y is the number of attributes in T. Next, the access policy T is converted to LSSS access control structure (M, ρ), while we use P_j to replace the attribute U_j in the access policy. The structure control matrix M is an $l \times n$ matrix and $1 \le P$. It set the vector $\mathbf{y} = (s, y_2, \ldots, y_n)^T$ in which $y_2, \ldots, y_n \in \mathbb{Z}_p$ is random where T denotes the transpose of the matrix. Then it computes a vector of shares of s as $(\lambda_1, \lambda_2, \ldots, \lambda_l)^T = M\mathbf{y}$. The algorithm computes $C_{j,4} = \lambda_j - x_j, C_{j,5} = \tau_j(A_j - x_j)$. Eventually, the algorithm sets the ciphertext as

$$CT = \left\{ (M, \rho), C_0, C_1, \left\{ C_{j,1}, C_{j,2}, C_{j,3}, C_{j,4}, C_{j,5} \right\}_{j \in [1,P]} \right\}.$$

Decryption. In this phase, data user downloads a ciphertext CT from CSP, and performs the following algorithm Decrypt based on secret key SK_u to recover the consequent message.

Decrypt(SK, CT) $\rightarrow$ key. It takes a secure private key $SK_U = \left\{ K_1, \left\{ K_{i,1}, K_{i,2} \right\}_{i \in [1,n]} \right\}$ from *SecretKeyGen* algorithm and a ciphertext $CT = \left\{ (M, \rho), C_0, C_1, \left\{ C_{j,1}, C_{j,2}, C_{j,3}, C_{j,4}, C_{j,5} \right\}_{j \in [1,P]} \right\}$ for hiding access structure (M, ρ). If SK_U does not satisfy the hiding structure, then the algorithm outputs an error message. Or else, the algorithm computes constants $\sum_{i \in I} w_i \lambda_i = s$ for making $w_i \in \mathbb{Z}_p, I \subseteq \{1, 2, \ldots, l\}$ and setting λ_i is the result of the secret s share. The cloud computes

$$e(g, g)^{\alpha s} = \frac{e(K_0, C_0)}{e(h^{\sum_{i \in I} w_i \cdot C_{j,4}}, K_1) \cdot \prod_{i \in I} \left(e(K_{i,1}, C_{j,1}) \right) \cdot e(K_{i,2}, C_{j,2} \cdot u^{C_{j,5}}) \cdot e(K_1, C_{j,3}) \right)^{w_i}}$$

where j is the index of the attribute A_i in S (it depends on i).

4 Performance Evaluation

Table 1. Computation cost comparisons of online/offline attribute-based encryption schemes

Schemes	Offline encryption	Online encryption	Decryption (user side)
OOABE [7]	$(3N + 3)E + N\cdot M$	$(|A| + 1)M$	$3kP + 2kE + 3km$
DCP-ABKS-CKDO [11]	$2M + (5M + G)$	$E + M + 2(M + G)$	$2kE + 2km$
ABDS [12]	$3E$	$4P + (2k + 2)E + (3k + 2)M + H$	$3kP + 2kE + 3km$
OOABKS [9]	$G + 4E + N\cdot M$	$(|A| + 1)M + G$	$kP + kE$
Ours	$3E + 2N\cdot M$	$E + H + (|A| + 1)M$	$3kP + kE + 3km$

In this section, we provide estimate on the performance of the comparison results in Table 1, which compare the proposed scheme with some existing schemes in the efficient respects. The comparison results are summarized in Table 1, where **A**, **G**, **P**, **E** and **M** represent the number of attributes, the size of an element in $\mathbb{Z}_p$, a pairing operation, an exponentiation operation and a multiplication operation in bilinear groups, respectively. And the complexity of the access structure is denoted by k. The symbol **H** is a chameleon hash operation. The symbol **N** means the size of offline ciphertext pool and it is determined by the size of the attribute universe (Table 2).

Table 2. Function compare between our scheme and other scheme

Schemes	Access structure	Hidden policy	Protect GID privacy	Online/Offline encryption
OOABE [7]	LSSS	No	No	Yes
DCP-ABKS-CKDO [11]	LSSS	No	No	Yes
ABDS [12]	LSSS	No	No	Yes
OOABKS [9]	LSSS	No	No	Yes
CSCD [13]	$(AND/OR)_m$	Yes	Yes	No
HCPABE [14]	AND	Yes	No	No
Ours	LSSS	Yes	Yes	Yes

We compare the proposed scheme with the state-of-the-art schemes with regard to the generation cost of the offline encryption cost, the online encryption cost and the decryption cost. In the online phase, our scheme reduces nearly half of cost compared with ABDS [12] while it less than other schemes. Because in our scheme, we only complete the encryption of using the access control policy in this phase. Our scheme incurs more computation costs than ABDS [12] in the offline phase, but the total workload of the user can be significantly reduced, which is suitable for the resource-limited users. Thus, the proposed scheme is efficient with respect to the computation costs on the user side and achieves security goals. Consider the function of our proposed scheme and several related schemes, we can observe that our scheme is superior to other schemes. All the online/offline schemes are allowed LSSS ciphertext policies.

5   Conclusion

In this paper, aiming at tackling the computation efficiency and weak data security issues, we proposed a secure online/offline attribute-based encryption for IoT users in cloud computing. Different from existing CP-ABE schemes, our scheme realizes efficient data encryption and privacy protection while heavy encryption computations are performed during the offline phase making the whole encryption phase faster and more efficient than existing schemes. For protect the access control, we hide the access structure in online phase and protect the data user key in secret key generation phase. Theoretical analysis indicate that the proposed data sharing scheme is extremely suitable for IoT users who have enough computing power but not real-time online. The security of our scheme is proven secure in the proposed selective chosen attribute set. The performance analysis show that our solution can be used to control access for shared data in an internet of things environment.

Acknowledgements. This research is supported by the National Natural Science Foundation of China under Grant Nos. U1536115 and U1405254, the Natural Science Foundation of Fujian Province of China under Grant No. 2018J01093, and the Subsidized Project for Postgraduates' Innovative Fund in Scientific Research of Huaqiao University No. 18013083012.

References

1. Goyal, V., Pandey, O., Sahai, A., Waters, B.: Attribute-based encryption for fine-grained access control of encrypted data. In: Proceedings of the 13th ACM Conference on Computer and Communications Security - CCS 2006, Alexandria, Virginia, USA, pp. 89–98. ACM Press (2006)
2. Bethencourt, J., Sahai, A., Waters, B.: Ciphertext-policy attribute-based encryption. In: 2007 IEEE Symposium on Security and Privacy (SP 2007), pp. 321–334 (2007)
3. Yu, S., Wang, C., Ren, K., Lou, W.: Achieving secure, scalable, and fine-grained data access control in cloud computing. In: 2010 Proceedings IEEE INFOCOM, pp. 1–9 (2010)
4. Hur, J., Noh, D.K.: Attribute-based access control with efficient revocation in data outsourcing systems. IEEE Trans. Parallel Distrib. Syst. **22**, 1214–1221 (2011)
5. Tsang, P.P., Chow, S.S.M., Smith, S.W.: Batch pairing delegation. In: Miyaji, A., Kikuchi, H., Rannenberg, K. (eds.) IWSEC 2007. LNCS, vol. 4752, pp. 74–90. Springer, Heidelberg (2007). https://doi.org/10.1007/978-3-540-75651-4_6
6. Green, M., Hohenberger, S., Waters, B.: Outsourcing the decryption of ABE ciphertexts, 16
7. Hohenberger, S., Waters, B.: Online/offline attribute-based encryption. In: Krawczyk, H. (ed.) PKC 2014. LNCS, vol. 8383, pp. 293–310. Springer, Heidelberg (2014). https://doi.org/10.1007/978-3-642-54631-0_17
8. Datta, P., Dutta, R., Mukhopadhyay, S.: Fully secure online/offline predicate and attribute-based encryption. In: Lopez, J., Wu, Y. (eds.) ISPEC 2015. LNCS, vol. 9065, pp. 331–345. Springer, Cham (2015). https://doi.org/10.1007/978-3-319-17533-1_23
9. Cui, J., Zhou, H., Xu, Y., Zhong, H.: OOABKS: online/offline attribute-based encryption for keyword search in mobile cloud. Inf. Sci. **489**, 63–77 (2019)
10. Liu, Z., Jiang, Z.L., Wang, X., Huang, X., Yiu, S.M., Sadakane, K.: Offline/online attribute-based encryption with verifiable outsourced decryption. Concurr. Comput. Pract. Exper. **29**, e3915 (2017)
11. Xu, Q., Tan, C., Zhu, W., Xiao, Y., Fan, Z., Cheng, F.: Decentralized attribute-based conjunctive keyword search scheme with online/offline encryption and outsource decryption for cloud computing. Future Gener. Comput. Syst. **97**, 306–326 (2019)
12. Li, J., Zhang, Y., Chen, X., Xiang, Y.: Secure attribute-based data sharing for resource-limited users in cloud computing. Comput. Secur. **72**, 1–12 (2018)
13. Zhang, Y., Li, J., Yan, H.: Constant size ciphertext distributed CP-ABE scheme with privacy protection and fully hiding access structure. IEEE Access **7**, 47982–47990 (2019)
14. Phuong, T.V.X., Yang, G., Susilo, W.: Hidden ciphertext policy attribute-based encryption under standard assumptions. IEEE Trans. Inf. Forensics Secur. **11**, 35–45 (2016)

FSPVDsse: A Forward Secure Publicly Verifiable Dynamic SSE Scheme

Laltu Sardar[2(✉)] and Sushmita Ruj[1,2]

[1] CSIRO Data61, Marsfield, NSW, Australia
[2] Indian Statistical institute, Kolkata, India
laltuisical@gmail.com, sushmita.ruj@csiro.au

Abstract. A symmetric searchable encryption (SSE) scheme allows a client (data owner) to search on encrypted data outsourced to an untrusted cloud server. The search may either be a single keyword search or a complex query search like conjunctive or Boolean keyword search. Information leakage is quite high for dynamic SSE, where data might be updated. It has been proven that to avoid this information leakage an SSE scheme with dynamic data must be *forward private*. A dynamic SSE scheme is said to be forward private, if adding a keyword-document pair does not reveal any information about the previous search result with that keyword.

In SSE setting, the data owner has very low computation and storage power. In this setting, though some schemes achieve forward privacy with honest-but-curious cloud, it becomes difficult to achieve forward privacy when the server is malicious, meaning that it can alter the data. Verifiable dynamic SSE requires the server to give a proof of the result of the search query. The data owner can verify this proof efficiently. In this paper, we have proposed a generic publicly verifiable dynamic SSE (DSSE) scheme that makes any forward private DSSE scheme verifiable without losing forward privacy. The proposed scheme does not require any extra storage at owner-side and requires minimal computational cost as well for the owner. Moreover, we have compared our scheme with the existing results and show that our scheme is practical.

Keywords: Searchable encryption · Forward privacy · Verifiability · BLS signature · Cloud computing

1 Introduction

Data stored in untrusted servers is prone to attacks by the server itself. In order to protect confidential information, clients store encrypted data. This makes searching on data quite challenging. A searchable symmetric encryption (SSE) scheme enables a client or data owner to store its data in a cloud server without loosing the ability to search over them. When an SSE scheme supports update, it is called a dynamic SSE (DSSE) scheme.

© Springer Nature Switzerland AG 2019
R. Steinfeld and T. H. Yuen (Eds.): ProvSec 2019, LNCS 11821, pp. 355–371, 2019.
https://doi.org/10.1007/978-3-030-31919-9_23

There are plenty of works on SSE as well as DSSE. Most of them considers the cloud server to be honest-but-curious. An honest-but-curious server follows the protocol but wants to extract information about the plaintext data and the queries. However, if the cloud itself is malicious, it does not follow the protocol correctly. In the context of search, it can return only a subset of results, instead of all the records of the search. So, there is need to verify the results returned by the cloud to the Yoneyamaquerier. An SSE scheme for static data where the query results are verifiable is called Verifiable SSE (VSSE). Similarly, if the data is dynamic the scheme is said to be a verifiable dynamic SSE (VDSSE).

There are single keyword search VSSE schemes which are either new constructions supporting verifiability or design techniques to achieve verifiability on the existing SSE schemes by proposing generic algorithm. VSSE with single keyword search has been studied in [5,7,13]. In [20,21] etc., VSSE scheme with conjunctive query has been studied. Moreover, there are also works that gives VDSSE scheme for both single keyword search [14] as well as complex query search including fuzzy keyword search [26] and Boolean query [9]. However, Most of them are *privately verifiable*. A VSSE or VDSSE scheme is said to be privately verifiable if only querier, who receive search result, can verify it. On the other hand, a VSSE or VDSSE scheme is said to be *publicly verifiable* if any third party, including the database owner, can verify the search result without knowing the content of it.

There is also literature on public verifiability. Soleimanian and Khazaei [18] and Zhang et al. [24] have presented SSE schemes which are publicly verifiable. VSSE with Boolean range queries has been studied by Xu et al. [22]. Though, their verification method is public, since the verification is based over blockchain databases, it has extra monetary cost. Besides, Azraoui et al. [1] presented a conjunctive search scheme that is publicly verifiable. In case of dynamic database, publicly verifiable scheme by Jiang et al. [9] supports Boolean Query and that by Miao et al. [14] supports single keyword search.

However, file-injection attack [25], in which the client encrypts and stores files sent by the server, recovers keywords from future queries, has forced researchers to think about dynamic SSE schemes to be forward private where adding a keyword-document pair does not reveal any information about the previous search result with that keyword. In addition, in presence of malicious cloud server, the owner can outsource the verifiabilty to a third party auditor to reduce its computational overhead. The only forward private single keyword search VSSE scheme is proposed by Yoneyama and Kimura [23]. However, the scheme is privately verifiable and the owner requires significant amount of computation for verification.

1.1   Our Contribution

In this paper, we have contributed the followings in the literature of VSSE.

1. We have formally define a verifiable dynamic SSE scheme. Then, we have proposed a generic publicly verifiable dynamic SSE scheme (Ψ_f) which is very efficient and easy to integrate.

2. Our proposed scheme is forward private. This property is necessary to protect a DSSE scheme from file injection attack. However, no previous publicly verifiable scheme is forward private. In fact, only forward private scheme [23] is privately verifiable.
3. We present formal security proof for this scheme and show that it is adaptively secure in random oracle model.

The scheme does not use any extra storage, at owner side, than the embedded schemes. Thus, for a resource constrained client, the scheme is very effective and efficient.

In Table 1, we have compared our proposed scheme with existing ones.

Table 1. Different verifiable SSE and DSSE schemes

Data type	Static				Dynamic			
Query type	Single		Complex		Single		Complex	
Verification	Private	Public	Private	Public	Private	Public	Private	Public
Schemes	[5], [7], [16], [13],	[18]	[21], [11], [22]	[18]	[23], [3]	[14], Ψ_f	[26]	[9]
Forward private	Not applicable				[23], Ψ_f			

1.2 Organization

We have briefly described the works related to verifiable SSE in Sect. 2. We have discussed the required preliminary topics in Sect. 3. In Sect. 4, we present our proposed generic construction of publicly verifiable DSSE scheme in details. We have compared its complexity with similar publicly verifiable schemes in Sect. 5. Finally, we summaries our work in Sect. 6 with possible future direction of research.

2 Related Works

The term *Searchable Symmetric Encryption* is first introduced by Curtmola et al. [8] where they have given formal definition of keyword search schemes over encrypted data. Later, Chase et al. [6] and Liesdonk et al. [12] presented single keyword search SSE for static database. Thereafter, as the importance of database updating is increased, the work has been started on dynamic SSE. SSE deals with set of documents where each contains some keywords. There are works considering graph data where queries are shortest distance query, link prediction query [17], neighbor query [6] etc.

Kamara et al. [10] first have introduced a dynamic single keyword search scheme based on encrypted inverted index. There are remarkable works on single keyword search on dynamic database. However, file-injection attack, by Zhang et al. [25] have forced the researchers to think about dynamic SSE schemes to be forward private. It is easy to achieve forward privacy with ORAM. However, due to large cost of communication, computation and storage, ORAM based schemes are almost impractical.

In 2016 Bost [2] has presented a non-ORAM based forward private dynamic SSE scheme. Later, few more forward private schemes have been proposed. Though, the works [4], [19] etc. provide backward privacy, now we are not bother about it since there is no formal attack on non-backward private DSSE schemes. Though, till now there are no formal attack on non-backward private DSSE schemes, there are works [4] and [19] that provide backward privacy. In most of the above mentioned schemes, the cloud service providers are considered to be honest-but-curious. However, the schemes fails to provide security in presence of malicious cloud server.

Chai and Gong [5] have introduced the first VSSE scheme. They stores the set of document identifiers in a trie like data structure where each node corresponding to some keyword stores identifiers containing it. Secure indistinguishability obfuscation based VSSE scheme, proposed by Cheng et al. [7], supports Boolean queries and provides publicly verifiability on the return result. Ogata and Kurosawa [16] have presented a no-dictionary generic private verifiable SSE scheme using cuckoo hash table. With multi-owner setting, Liu et al. [13] have presented a VSSE with aggregate keys. However, all of the above schemes were for static database and are privately verifiable where the VSSE schemes by Soleimanian and Khazaei [18] and Zhang et al. [24] are publicly verifiable.

The above works are only for static data. There are few works also that deals with complex queries when the data is static. Conjunctive query on static data has been studied by Sun et al. [20], Miao et al. [15], Wang et al. [21], Li et al. [11] etc. These schemes have private verifiability. Boolean range queries on SSE has been studied by Xu et al. [22]. Though, their verification method is public, since the verification is based over blockchain databases it has good monetary cost.

Dynamic verifiable SSE with complex queries also has been studied. Zhu et al. [26] presented a dynamic fuzzy keyword search scheme which is privately verifiable and Jiang et al. [9] has studied Publicly Verifiable Boolean Query on dynamic database. Moreover, single keyword search scheme on dynamic data is described by Yoneyama and Kimura [23], Bost et al. [3] etc.

A publicly verifiable SSE scheme is recently also proposed by Miao et al. [14]. Yoneyama and Kimura [23] presented a scheme based on Algebraic PRF which is verifiable as well as forward private that performs single keyword search. However, the scheme is privately verifiable and the owner requires significant amount of computation for verification.

Our proposed scheme Ψ_f is generic forward private verifiable scheme which is compatible with any existing forward private DSSE scheme. Our scheme also do not use any extra owner-storage for verifiability and has minimal search time computation for the owner.

3   Preliminaries

3.1   Cryptographic Tools

Bilinear Map. Let $\mathbb{G}$ and $\mathbb{G}_T$ be two (multiplicative) cyclic groups of prime order q. Let $\mathbb{G} = <g>$. A map $\hat{e} : \mathbb{G} \times \mathbb{G} \to \mathbb{G}_T$ is said to be an *admissible non-degenerate bilinear map* if – (a) $\hat{e}(u^a, v^b) = \hat{e}(u, v)^{ab}$, $\forall u, v \in \mathbb{G}$ and $\forall a, b \in \mathbb{Z}$ (bilinearity) (b) $\hat{e}(g, g) \neq 1$ (non-degeneracy) (c) $\hat{e}$ can be computed efficiently.

Bilinear Hash. Given a bilinear map $\hat{e} : \mathbb{G} \times \mathbb{G} \to \mathbb{G}_T$ and a generator g, a bilinear hash $\mathcal{H} : \{0, 1\}^* \to \mathbb{G}$ maps every random string to an element of $\mathbb{G}$. The map is defined as $\mathcal{H}(m) = g^m$, $\forall m \in \{0, 1\}^*$.

Bilinear Signature (BLS). Let $\hat{e} : \mathbb{G} \times \mathbb{G} \to \mathbb{G}_T$ be a bilinear map where $|\mathbb{G}| = |\mathbb{G}_T| = q$, a prime and $\mathbb{G} =< g >$. A bilinear signature (BLS) scheme $\mathcal{S}=(\texttt{Gen}, \texttt{Sign}, \texttt{Verify})$ is a tuple of three algorithms as follows.

- $(sk, pk) \leftarrow \texttt{Gen}$: It selects $\alpha \xleftarrow{\$} [0, q-1]$. It keeps the private key $sk = \alpha$. publishes the public key $pk = g^\alpha$.
- $\sigma \leftarrow \texttt{Sign}(sk, m)$: Given $sk = \alpha$, and some message m, it outputs the signature $\sigma = (\mathcal{H}(m))^\alpha = (g^m)^\alpha$ where $\mathcal{H} : \{0, 1\}^* \to \mathbb{G}$ is a bilinear hash.
- $\{0/1\} \leftarrow \texttt{Verify}(pk, m, \sigma)$: Return whether $\hat{e}(\sigma, g) = \hat{e}(\mathcal{H}(m), g^\alpha)$.

3.2   System Model

In this section, we briefly describe the system model considered in this paper. In our model of verifiable dynamic SSE, there are three entities–Owner, Auditor and Cloud. The system model is shown in the Fig. 1. We briefly describe them as follows.

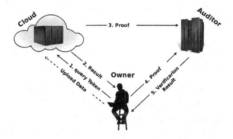

Fig. 1. The system model

1. **Owner:** Owner is the owner as well as user of the database. It is considered to be *trusted*. It builds an secure index, encrypts the data and then outsources both to the cloud. Later, it sends encrypted query to the cloud for searching. Therefore, it is the querier as well. It is the client who requires the service.

2. **Cloud:** Cloud or the cloud server is the storage and computation service provider. It stores the encrypted data sent from the owner and gives result of the query requested by it. The cloud is assumed to be *malicious*. It can deviate from protocol by not only computing on, or not storing the data but also making the querier fool by returning incorrect result.

3. **Auditor:** Auditor is an *honest-but-curious* authority which does not collude with the cloud. Its main role is to verify whether the cloud executes the protocol honestly. It tells the querier whether the returned result is correct or not.

3.3   Design Goals

Assuming the above system model, we aim to provide solution of the verifiability problem of existing forward private schemes. In our design, we take care to achieve the following objectives.

1. **Confidentiality:** The cloud servers should not get any information about the uploaded data. On the other hand, queries should not leak any information about the database. Otherwise the cloud may get knowledge about the plaintext information.

2. **Efficiency:** In our model, the cloud has a large amount of computational power as well as good storage. The owner is weak. So, in the scheme the owner should require significantly small amount of computation and storage cost while performing verifiability.

3. **Scalability:** Since, the owner have to pay for the service provided by the cloud, it is desirable to outsource as much data as possible. The owner should capable to outsource large amount of data to the cloud. On the other hand, the cloud should answer the queries fast using less computation power.

4. **Forward privacy:** It is observed previously that a DSSE scheme without forward privacy is vulnerable to even honest-but-curious adversary. So, our target is to make a publicly verifiable DSSE scheme without loosing its forward privacy property.

3.4   Definitions

Let $\mathcal{W}$ be a set of keywords. $\mathcal{D}$ be the space of document identifiers and $\mathcal{DB}$ be the set of documents to be outsourced. Thus, $\mathcal{DB} \subseteq \mathcal{D}$. For each keyword $w \in \mathcal{W}$, the set of document identifiers that includes w is denoted by $DB(w) = \{id_1^w, id_1^w, \ldots, id_{c_w}^w\}$, where $c_w = |DB(w)|$ and $id_i^w \in \mathcal{DB}$. Thus, $\bigcup\limits_{w \in \mathcal{W}} DB(w) \subseteq \mathcal{DB}$. Let $\overline{DB} = \{c_{id} : id \in \mathcal{D}\}$ where c_{id} denotes the encrypted document that has identifier id.

We assume that there is a one-way function H' that maps each identifier id to certain random numbers. These random numbers is used as document name corresponding to the identifier. The function is can be computed by both the owner and cloud. However, from a document name, the identifier can not be recovered. Throughout, we use identifiers. However, when we say cloud returns documents to the owner, we assume the cloud performs the function on every identifiers before returning them.

Let, $H : \{0,1\}^* \to \{0,1\}^\lambda$ be a cryptographic hash function, $\mathcal{H}$ be a bilinear hash, $R : \{0,1\}^* \to \{0,1\}^*$ be a PRNG and $F : \{0,1\}^\lambda \times \{0,1\}^* \to \{0,1\}^\lambda$ be a HMAC. A *stateful algorithm* stores its previous states and use them to compute the current state.

3.5 Verifiable Dynamic Searchable Symmetric Encryption (VDSSE)

An SSE scheme allows a client to outsource a dataset it owns to a cloud service provider in encrypted form without loosing the ability to perform query over the data. The most popular query is the keyword search where the dataset is a collection of documents. The client can retrieve partial encrypted data without revealing any meaningful information to the cloud. Throughout we take query as single keyword search query.

A *dynamic SSE* (DSSE) scheme is a SSE scheme that supports updates. A *Verifiable DSSE* (VDSSE) scheme is a DSSE scheme together with verifiability. The verification can be done either by an external auditor or the owner. The primary reason to bring a auditor is to reduce computational costs of verifiability at owner-side. This allows an owner to be lightweight.

Though a VDSSE scheme supports update, we do not verify whether the cloud updates the database correctly or not. We only want to get the correct result with respect to current state of the database. If cloud updates the database incorrectly, it can not give the actual result. Due to verifiability, it will be failed in verification process to the auditor. We define a verifiable DSSE scheme formally as follows.

Definition 1 (Verifiable Dynamic SSE.) A verifiable dynamic SSE (VDSSE) scheme Ψ is a tuple (VKeyGen, VBuild, VSearchToken, VSearch, VUpdateToken, VUpdate) of algorithms defined as follows.

- $K \leftarrow$ VKeyGen(1^λ): It is a probabilistic polynomial-time (PPT) algorithm run by the owner. Given security parameter λ it outputs a key K.
- $(\overline{DB}, \gamma) \leftarrow$ VBuild($K, \mathcal{DB}$): The owner run this PPT algorithm. Given a key K and a set of documents $\mathcal{DB}$, it outputs the encrypted set of documents $\overline{DB}$ and an encrypted index γ.
- $\tau_s \leftarrow$ VSearchToken(K, w): On input a keyword w and the key K, the owner runs this PPT algorithm to output a search token τ_s.
- $(R_w, \nu_w) \leftarrow$ VSearch(t_s, γ): It is a PPT algorithm run by the cloud and the auditor collaboratively that returns a set of document identifiers result R_w to the owner with verification bit ν_w.
- $\tau_u \leftarrow$ VUpdateToken(K, id): It is a owner-side PPT algorithm that takes the key K and a document identifier id and outputs a update token τ_u.
- $(\overline{DB}', \gamma') \leftarrow$ VUpdate($\tau_u, op, \gamma, \overline{DB}$): It is a PPT algorithm run by the cloud. It takes an update token τ_u, operation bit op, the encrypted document set $\overline{DB}$ and the index γ and outputs updated $(\overline{DB}', \gamma')$.

Computational Correctness. A VDSSE scheme Ψ is said to be *correct* if $\forall \lambda \in \mathbb{N}$, $\forall K$ generated using $\mathtt{KeyGen}(1^{\lambda})$ and all sequences of search and update operations on γ, every search outputs the correct set of identifiers, except with a negligible probability.

Verifiability. Note that, when we are saying a scheme is verifiable, it means that it verifies whether the search result is from the currently updated state of the database according to the owner. Verification does not include update of the database at cloud side. For example, let an owner added a document with some keywords and the cloud does not update the database. Later, if the owner searches with some keywords present in the document and it should get the identifier of the document in the result set. Then, the result can be taken as verified.

3.6 Security Definitions

We follow security definition of [18]. There are two parts in the definition – confidentiality and soundness. We define security in adaptive adversary model where the adversary can send query depending on the previous results. Typically, most of the dynamic SSE schemes define its security in this model.

A DSSE, that does not consider verifiability, considers honest-but-curious (HbC) cloud server. In these cases, The owner of the database allows some leakage on every query made. However, it guarantees that no meaningful information about the database are revealed other than the allowed leakages. Soundness definition ensures that the results received form the cloud server are correct.

Confidentiality. Confidentiality ensures that a scheme does not give any meaningful information other than it is allowed. In our model, we have considered the cloud to be malicious. However, the auditor is HbC. Since, verifiability has some monetary cost for the owner, it wants verifiability only when it is required. Also the auditor does not have the database and search ability. Given the proof, it only verifies the result. Thus, if the scheme is secure from cloud, it is so from auditor. Again, we have assumed that the cloud and the auditor do not collude. Hence, we do not consider the auditor in our definition of confidentiality.

Definition 2 (CKA2-Confidentiality.)
Let $\Psi = (\mathtt{VKeyGen}, \mathtt{VBuild}, \mathtt{VSearchToken}, \mathtt{VSearch}, \mathtt{VUpdateToken})$ be a verifiable DSSE scheme. Let $\mathcal{A}$, $\mathcal{C}$ and $\mathcal{S}$ be a stateful adversary, a challenger and a stateful simulator respectively. Let $\mathcal{L} = (\mathcal{L}_{bld}, \mathcal{L}_{srch}, \mathcal{L}_{updt})$ be a stateful leakage algorithm. Let us consider the following two games.

***Real*$_{\mathcal{A}}(\lambda)$:**

1. The challenger $\mathcal{C}$ generates a key $K \leftarrow \mathtt{VKeyGen}(1^{\lambda})$.
2. $\mathcal{A}$ generates and sends $\mathcal{DB}$ to $\mathcal{C}$.
3. $\mathcal{C}$ builds $(\overline{\mathcal{DB}}, \gamma) \leftarrow \mathtt{VBuild}(K, \mathcal{DB})$ and sends $(\overline{\mathcal{DB}}, \gamma)$ it to $\mathcal{A}$.

4. $\mathcal{A}$ makes a polynomial number of adaptive queries. In each of them, it sends either a search query for a keyword w or an update query for a keyword-document pair (w, id) and operation bit op to $\mathcal{C}$.
5. $\mathcal{C}$ returns either a search token $\tau_s \leftarrow$ VSearchToken(K, w) or an update token $\tau_u \leftarrow$ VUpdateToken(K, id) to $\mathcal{A}$ depending on the query.
6. Finally $\mathcal{A}$ returns a bit b that is output by the experiment.

$Ideal_{\mathcal{A},\mathcal{S}}(\lambda)$:

1. $\mathcal{A}$ generates a set $\mathcal{DB}$ of documents and gives it to $\mathcal{S}$ together with $\mathcal{L}_{bld}(\mathcal{DB})$.
2. $\mathcal{S}$ generates $(\overline{DB}, \gamma)$ and sends it to $\mathcal{A}$
3. $\mathcal{A}$ makes a polynomial number of adaptive queries q. For each query, $\mathcal{S}$ is given either $\mathcal{L}_{srch}(w, \mathcal{DB})$ or $\mathcal{L}_{updt}(op, w, id)$ depending on the query.
4. $\mathcal{S}$ returns, depending on the query q, to $\mathcal{A}$ either search token τ_s or update token τ_u.
5. Finally $\mathcal{A}$ returns a bit b' that is output by the experiment.

We say Ψ is $\mathcal{L}$-secure against adaptive dynamic chosen-keyword attacks if $\forall$ PPT adversary $\mathcal{A}$, $\exists$ a simulator $\mathcal{S}$ such that

$$|Pr[\textbf{Real}_{\mathcal{A}}(\lambda) = 1] - Pr[\textbf{Ideal}_{\mathcal{A},\mathcal{S}}(\lambda) = 1]| \leq \mu(\lambda) \tag{1}$$

where $\mu(\lambda)$ is negligible in λ.

Soundness. The soundness property ensures that if a malicious cloud tries to make the owner fool by returning incorrect result it will be caught to the auditor. We define game-based definition of soundness as follows.

Definition 3. *Let Ψ be a verifiable DSSE scheme with $\Psi =$ (VKeyGen, VBuild, VSearchToken, VSearch, VUpdateToken). Let us consider the following game.*

$sound_{\mathcal{A},\Psi}(\lambda)$:

1. *The challenger $\mathcal{C}$ generates a key $K \leftarrow$ VKeyGen(1^λ).*
2. *$\mathcal{A}$ generates and sends $\mathcal{DB}$ to $\mathcal{C}$.*
3. *$\mathcal{C}$ computes $(\overline{DB}, \gamma) \leftarrow$ VBuild$(K, \mathcal{DB})$ and sends $(\overline{DB}, \gamma)$ to $\mathcal{A}$.*
4. *$\mathcal{A}$ makes a polynomial number of adaptive queries. In each of them, it sends either a search query for a keyword w or an update query for a keyword-document pair (w, id) and operation bit op to $\mathcal{C}$.*
5. *$\mathcal{C}$ returns either a search token $\tau_s \leftarrow$ VSearchToken(K, w) or an update token $\tau_u \leftarrow$ VUpdateToken(K, id) to $\mathcal{A}$ depending on the query.*
6. *After making polynomial number of queries, $\mathcal{A}$ chooses a target keyword w and send search query to $\mathcal{C}$.*
7. *$\mathcal{C}$ returns a search token τ_s. $\mathcal{A}$ executes and gets (R_w, ν_w) where $\nu_w = accept$ is verification bit from $\mathcal{C}$.*
8. *$\mathcal{A}$ generates pair (R_w^*) for a keyword w and gets verification bit $\nu_w^* = accept$.*
9. *If $\nu_w^* = accept$ even when $R_w^* \neq DB(w)$, $\mathcal{A}$ returns 1 as output of the game, otherwise returns 0.*

We say that Ψ is sound if $\forall$ PPT adversaries $\mathcal{A}$, $Pr[sound_{\mathcal{A},\Psi}(\lambda) = 1] \leq \mu(\lambda)$.

4   Our Proposed FSPVDsse Scheme

In this section, we propose a simple generic dynamic SSE scheme which is forward secure as well as verifiable. Let Σ_f = (KeyGen, Build, Search, SearchToken, Update, UpdateToken) be a result revealing forward secure dynamic SSE scheme.

It is to be noted that any forward private SSE scheme stores the present state of the database at client side. Corresponding to each keyword, most of them stores the number of documents containing it. Let $C = \{c_w : w \in \mathcal{W}\}$ be the list of such numbers.

Since, it considers any forward secure scheme Σ_f, it only adds an additional encrypted data structure to make the scheme verifiable. The algorithms of Our proposed scheme are given in Fig. 2. They are divided into three phases– initialization, search and update.

Initialization Phase: In this phase, secret and public keys are generated by the owner and thereafter the encrypted searchable structure is built. During key generation, three types of keys are generated – K_{Σ_f} for the Σ_f; (sk, pk) for the bilinear signature scheme; and two random strings K_s, K_t for seed and tag generation respectively.

Thereafter, a signature table T_{sig} is generated, before building the secure index γ and encrypted database $\overline{DB}$, to store the signature corresponding to each keyword-document pair. For each pair (w, id_i^w), the position $pos_i^w = F(tag_w, id_i^w \| i)$ is generated with a HMAC F. The position is actually act as key of a key-value pair for a dictionary. The document identifier is bounded with pos_i^w together with $tag_w = F(K_t, w)$. The tag_w is fixed for a keyword and is given to the server to find pos_i^w. The signature σ_i^w for the same pair is also bounded with random number r_i^w which can only be generated from PRG R with the seed s_w. Then (σ_i^w, pos_i^w) pair is added in the table T_{sig} as key-value pair. After the building process, the owner outsources γ, $\overline{DB}$ and T_{sig} to the cloud.

Search Phase: In this phase, the owner first generates a search token τ_{Σ_f} to search on Σ_f. Then, it regenerates the tag_w and the seed s_w and then, sends them to the cloud.

The cloud performs search operation according to Σ_f and use the result identifiers $\{id_1, id_2, \ldots id_{c'_w}\}$ to gets the position in T_{sig} corresponding to each pair. It is not able to generate the positions if it does not search for the document identifiers. It collects the signatures stored in those positions, multiplies them and sends multiplication result to the auditor as its part pf_c of the proof. It sends the search result to the owner.

The owner first generates random numbers $\{r_1, r_2, \ldots r_{c'_w}\}$ and regenerates aggregate message $m = \sum_{i=1}^{i=c'_w} r_i.id_i^w \mod q$ of the identifiers and sends m to the auditor as pf_o, owner's part of the proof. After receiving pf_c and pf_o, the auditor only computes $\mathcal{S}.\text{Verify}(pk, m, \sigma')$. It outputs accept if signature verification returns *success*. We can see that the no information about the search results is leaked to the auditor during verification.

$\underline{\Psi_f.\mathsf{VKeyGen}(1^\lambda)}$

1. $K_{\Sigma_f} \leftarrow \Sigma_f.\mathsf{KeyGen}(1^\lambda)$
2. $(sk, pk) \leftarrow \mathcal{S}.\mathsf{Setup}(1^\lambda)$
3. $K_s \leftarrow \{0,1\}^\lambda$
4. $K_t \leftarrow \{0,1\}^\lambda$
5. Return $K_{\Psi_f} = (K_t, K_s, sk, pk, K_{\Sigma_f})$

$\underline{\Psi_f.\mathsf{VBuild}(\mathcal{DB}, K_{\Psi_f})}$

1. $T_{sig} \leftarrow$ empty list of size $|\mathcal{W}|$
2. **for** $w \in \mathcal{W}$
   (a) $s_w \leftarrow F(K_s, w);\ tag_w \leftarrow F(K_t, w)$
   (b) **for** $i = 1$ **to** $c_w (= |DB(w)|)$
      i. $r_i^w \leftarrow R(s_w||i)$;
      ii. $m_i^w \leftarrow r_i^w.id_i^w \mod q$
      iii. $\sigma_i^w \leftarrow \mathcal{S}.\mathsf{Sign}(sk, m_i^w)$
      iv. $pos_i^w \leftarrow F(tag_w, id_i^w||i)$
      v. $T_{sig}[pos_i^w] \leftarrow \sigma_i^w$
3. $(\gamma, \overline{DB}) \leftarrow \Sigma_f.\mathsf{Build}(\mathcal{DB}, K_{\Sigma_f})$
4. Return $(\gamma, \overline{DB}, T_{sig})$ to the cloud

$\underline{\Psi_f.\mathsf{VSearchToken}(w, K_{\Psi_f})}$

1. $(K_t, K_s, sk, pk, K_{\Sigma_f}) \leftarrow K_{\Psi_f}$
2. $\tau_{\Sigma_f} \leftarrow \Sigma_f.\mathsf{SearchToken}(w, K_{\Sigma_f})$
3. $tag_w \leftarrow F(K_t, w)$;
4. $\tau_s^{\Psi_f} \leftarrow (\tau_{\Sigma_f}, tag_w)$
5. Return $\tau_s^{\Psi_f}$ to cloud

$\underline{\Psi_f.\mathsf{VSearch}(\gamma, \tau_s^{\Psi_f})}$

Cloud:

1. Receive $\tau_{\Psi_f} = (\tau_{\Sigma_f}, tag_w)$ from Owner
2. $\{id_1'^w, \ldots, id_{c_w'}'^w\} \leftarrow \Sigma_f.\mathsf{Search}(\gamma, \tau_{\Sigma_f})$
3. **for** $i = 1$ **to** c_w'
   (a) $pos_i^w \leftarrow F(tag_w, id_i'^w||i)$
   (b) $\sigma_i' \leftarrow T_{sig}[pos_i^w]$;
4. $\sigma' \leftarrow \prod_{i=1}^{c_w'} \sigma_i'$
5. $R_w \leftarrow \{id_1'^w, id_2'^w, \ldots, id_{c_w'}'^w\}$
6. $pf_c \leftarrow \sigma'$
7. Return pf_c to auditor and R_w to Owner

Owner:

1. Receives R_w
2. $c_w \leftarrow C[w]$
3. If $c_w \neq c_w'$ **Return** reject bit.
4. $s_w \leftarrow F(K_s, w)$
5. **for** $i = 1$ **to** c_w **do**
   (a) $r_i^w \leftarrow R(s_w||i)$
   (b) $m_i^w \leftarrow id_i'^w.r_i^w \mod q$
6. $m = \sum_{i=1}^{c_w} m_i^w \mod q$
7. Send $pf_o = m$ to the auditor

Auditor:

1. Receives $pf_o = m$ from owner and $pf_c = \sigma'$ from cloud
2. $b_v \leftarrow \mathcal{S}.\mathsf{Verify}(pk, m, \sigma')$
3. If $b_v = failure$, **Return** $reject$

$\underline{\Psi_f.\mathsf{VUpdateToken}(K_{\Psi_f}, w, id)}$

1. $\tau_u \leftarrow \Sigma_f.\mathsf{UpdateToken}(K_{\Sigma_f}, w, id)$
2. Return τ_u

$\underline{\Psi_f.\mathsf{VUpdate}(T_{tag}, \gamma, \tau_u)}$

Owner:

1. $\{w_1, w_2, \ldots, w_{n_{id}}\} \in id$
2. **for** $i = 1$ **to** n_{id}
   (a) $\tau_u \leftarrow \Psi_f.\mathsf{VUpdateToken}(K_{\Psi_f}, w_i, id)$ $\forall i \in [c_w]$
   (b) $b_v \leftarrow \Sigma_f.\mathsf{Update}(\gamma, \tau_u)$
   (c) **if** $b_v \neq succsess$ Return
3. **for** $i = 1$ **to** n_{id}
   (a) $tag_{w_i} \leftarrow F(K_t, w_i)$
   (b) $c_{w_i} \leftarrow C[w_i]$
   (c) $s_w \leftarrow F(K_s, w)$;
   (d) $r \leftarrow R(s_w||(c_{w_i}+1))$
   (e) $m \leftarrow id.r \mod q$
   (f) $\sigma_i \leftarrow \mathcal{S}.\mathsf{Sign}(sk, m)$
   (g) $pos_i \leftarrow F(tag_{w_i}, id||(c_{w_i}+1))$
   (h) $C[w] = C[w] + 1$
4. $pos \leftarrow \{pos_1, pos_2, \ldots, pos_{n_{id}}\}$
5. $\sigma \leftarrow \{\sigma_1, \sigma_2, \ldots, \sigma_{n_{id}}\}$
6. send $\tau_u^{\Psi_f} = (pos, \sigma)$ to cloud

Cloud:

1. $\{pos_1, pos_2, \ldots, pos_{n_{id}}\} \leftarrow pos$
2. $\{\sigma_1, \sigma_2, \ldots, \sigma_{n_{id}}\} \leftarrow \sigma$
3. $T_{sig}[pos_i] \leftarrow \sigma_i$, $\forall i \in [n_{id}]$

Fig. 2. Generic verifiable dynamic SSE scheme Ψ_f without extra client storage

Update Phase: In our scheme, while adding a document, instead of being updated only a keyword-document pair, we assume that all such pairs corresponding to the document is added. To add a document with identifier id and keyword set $\{w_1, w_2, \ldots, w_{n_{id}}\}$, the owner generates the position and the corresponding signature for each containing keyword. The cloud gets them from the owner and adds them in the table T_{sig}.

Correctness. For correctness it is enough to check the following.

$$\hat{e}(\mathcal{H}(m), pk) = \hat{e}(g^m, g^\alpha) = \hat{e}(g^{\alpha \sum m_i}, g) = \hat{e}(\prod g^{\alpha m_i}, g) = \hat{e}(\prod \sigma_i, g) = \hat{e}(\sigma, g)$$

Cost for Verifiability. We achieve, forward privacy as well as public verifiability without client storage in Ψ_f. This increases the cloud-storage by $O(N)$, where N is the number of document-keyword pairs. The proof has two parts one from the client and another from the owner. For a keyword w, the sizes of them are one group element and one random λ-bit string only. Thus Auditor receives one element from both. The owner has to compute R_w integer multiplication and addition, and then has to send one element.

Forward Privacy. We can see that while adding a document, it only adds some keyword-document pair, in the form of key-value pairs. So, During addition, the cloud server is adding key-value pairs in the dictionary. From these pairs, it can not guess the keywords present in it. Again, when it perform searches, it gets about the key (i.e., position on the table) only when it gets the identifiers. The one possibility to get the newly added key-value pair linked with the previous is if the added document gives the identifier of it. Since, the one-way function H' gives the document-name of the adding document, the cloud server can not linked it with the previously searched keywords.

4.1   Security

The security of the scheme is shown in two parts – confidentiality and soundness.

Soundness. The cloud server can cheat the owner in three ways by sending

1. Incorrect number of identifiers – but it is not possible as the owner keeps the number of identifiers.
2. Same size result of other keywords – m is generated with a random numbers which can be generated only with the searched keyword and signatures are bound with that. So, the signature verification will be failed.
3. Result with some altered identifiers – since signatures are bounded with keywords and the random number, altering any will change m and similarly the signature verification will be failed.

Thus the owner always will get the correct set of document identifiers.

Confidentiality. Let $\mathcal{L}^{\Sigma_f} = (\mathcal{L}_{bld}^{\Sigma_f}, \mathcal{L}_{srch}^{\Sigma_f}, \mathcal{L}_{updt}^{\Sigma_f})$ the leakage function of Σ_f. Let $\mathcal{L}^{\Psi_f} = (\mathcal{L}_{bld}^{\Psi_f}, \mathcal{L}_{srch}^{\Psi_f}, \mathcal{L}_{updt}^{\Psi_f})$ be the leakage function of Ψ_f, given as follows.

$$\mathcal{L}_{bld}^{\Psi_f}(\mathcal{DB}) = \{\mathcal{L}_{bld}^{\Sigma_f}(\mathcal{DB}), |T_{sig}|\}$$
$$\mathcal{L}_{srch}^{\Psi_f}(w) = \{\mathcal{L}_{srch}^{\Sigma_f}(w), \{(id_i^w, pos_i^w, \sigma_i^w) : i = 1, 2, \ldots, c_w\}\}$$
$$\mathcal{L}_{updt}^{\Psi_f}(f) = \{id, \{(\mathcal{L}_{updt}^{\Sigma_f}(w_i, id), pos^{w_i}, \sigma^{w_i}) : i = 1, 2, \ldots, n_{id}\}\}$$

We show that Ψ is $\mathcal{L}^{\Psi_f}$-secure against adaptive dynamic chosen-keyword attacks in the random oracle model, in the following theorem.

Theorem 1. *If F is a PRF, R is a PRG and Σ_f is $\mathcal{L}^{\Sigma_f}$-secure, then Ψ_f is $\mathcal{L}^{\Psi_f}$-secure against adaptive dynamic chosen-keyword attacks.*

Simulating F We simulate R with a table RO. Given $\overline{(x, y)}$, If $RO[(x, y)] = \perp$, then do $RO[(x, y)] \leftarrow \{0, 1\}^\lambda$ and return $RO[(x, y)]$, else return the existing value $RO[(x, y)]$.

Simulating Build Leakage function is given by $\mathcal{L}_{bld}^{\Psi_f}(\mathcal{DB}) = \{\mathcal{L}_{bld}^{\Sigma_f}(\mathcal{DB}), |T_{sig}|\}$. Let S_{bld} be returned by the simulator Sim_{Σ_f}. Let us consider a table $\widetilde{T}_{tag}$. For each keyword w it stores a random λ-bit string. On input w, it returns $\widetilde{tag}_w \leftarrow \widetilde{T}_{tag}(w)$. Sim_{Ψ_f} keeps an extra table $\widetilde{T}'_{sig}$ such that it indicates whether the entry is queried or not. The simulation is done as follows.

1. Take empty tables $\widetilde{T}_{sig}$ and $\widetilde{T}'_{sig}$
2. For each $i = 1$ to $i = |T_{sig}|$ do
   (a) $pos_i \xleftarrow{\$} \{0, 1\}^\lambda; r'_i \xleftarrow{\$} \{0, 1\}^\lambda$
   (b) $val_i \xleftarrow{\$} g^{r_i}$
   (c) $\widetilde{T}_{sig}[pos_i] \leftarrow val_i$
   (d) $\widetilde{T}'_{sig}[pos_i] \leftarrow 0$
3. Simulate Σ_f with $S_{bld} \leftarrow \text{Sim}_{\Sigma_f}(\mathcal{DB})(\mathcal{L}_{bld}^{\Sigma_f}(\mathcal{DB}))$
4. return $(S_{bld}, \widetilde{T}_{sig})$ and keeps $\widetilde{T}'_{sig}$

Simulating Search token Leakage function for a queried keyword w is given by $\mathcal{L}_{srch}^{\Psi_f}(w) = \{\mathcal{L}_{srch}^{\Sigma_f}(w), \{(id_i^w) : i = 1, 2, \ldots, c_w\}\}$.

We keep a table RO where $(\widetilde{tag}_w, id, i)$ is the key and pos is the value. Given search leakage corresponding to the keyword w, Sim_{Ψ_f} does the following things.

1. If $\widetilde{T}_{tag}[w]$ is null, i.e, the keyword is searched first time
   (a) $\widetilde{tag}_w \xleftarrow{\$} \{0, 1\}^\lambda$
   (b) $\widetilde{T}_{tag}[w] \leftarrow \widetilde{tag}_w$
   Else
   (a) $\widetilde{tag}_w \leftarrow \widetilde{T}_{tag}[w]$

2. If $RO[(\widetilde{tag}_w, id_i^w, i)]$ is not null,
   (a) $pos_i \leftarrow RO[(\widetilde{tag}_w, id_i^w, i)]$
   Else
   (a) $pos_i \leftarrow$ a random pos_i such that $\widetilde{T}'_{sig}[pos_i] = 0$
   (b) $RO[(\widetilde{tag}_w, id_i^w, i)] \leftarrow pos_i$
   (c) $\widetilde{T}'_{sig}[pos_i] \leftarrow 1$
3. Simulate Σ_f with $\widetilde{\tau}_{\Sigma_f} \leftarrow \text{Sim}_{\Sigma_f}(\mathcal{L}_{srch}^{\Sigma_f}(w))$
4. return $\widetilde{\tau}_s^{\Psi_f} = (\widetilde{\tau}_{\Sigma_f}, \widetilde{tag}_w)$

Simulating Update token Leakage function to add a document f with identifier id containing keyword set $\{w_1, w_2, \ldots, w_{n_w}\}$ is given by $\mathcal{L}_{updt}^{\Psi_f}(f) = \{H'(id), \{(\mathcal{L}_{updt}^{\Sigma_f}(w_i, id)) : i = 1, 2, \ldots, n_{id}\}\}$.

1. For each keyword $w_i \in f$
   (a) $\widetilde{\tau}_u^i \leftarrow \text{Sim}_{\Sigma_f}(\mathcal{L}_{updt}^{\Sigma_f}(w, id))$
   (b) If $\widetilde{T}_{tag}[w_i]$ is null, i.e, the keyword is searched first time
      i. $\widetilde{tag}_{w_i} \xleftarrow{\$} \{0, 1\}^\lambda$
      ii. $\widetilde{T}_{tag}[w_i] \leftarrow \widetilde{tag}_w$
      Else
      i. $\widetilde{tag}_{w_i} \leftarrow \widetilde{T}_{tag}[w_i]$
   (c) $c_{w_i} \leftarrow C[w_i] + 1$
   (d) If $RO[(\widetilde{tag}_{w_i}, id, (c_{w_i} + 1))]$ is not null
      i. $\widetilde{pos}_i \leftarrow RO[(\widetilde{tag}_{w_i}, id, (c_v + 1))]$
      Else
      i. $\widetilde{pos}_i \leftarrow$ a random pos_i such that $\widetilde{T}_{sig}[pos_i]$ is null
      ii. $RO[(\widetilde{tag}_{w_i}, id, (c_{w_i} + 1))] \leftarrow \widetilde{pos}_i$
      iii. $\widetilde{T}'_{sig}[pos_i] \leftarrow 1$
   (e) $\widetilde{\sigma}_i \xleftarrow{\$} \mathbb{G}$
2. $\widetilde{pos} \leftarrow \{\widetilde{pos}_1, \widetilde{pos}_2, \ldots, \widetilde{pos}_{n_{id}}\}$
3. $\widetilde{\sigma} \leftarrow \{\widetilde{\sigma}_1, \widetilde{\sigma}_2, \ldots, \widetilde{\sigma}_{n_{id}}\}$
4. Return $\widetilde{\tau}_u^{\Psi_f} = (\widetilde{pos}, \widetilde{\sigma})$

Fig. 3. Simulation of build, search token and update token

Proof. To prove the above theorem, it is sufficient to show that there exists a simulator Sim_{Σ_f} such that $\forall$ PPT adversary $\mathcal{A}$, the output of $\textbf{Real}_{\mathcal{A}}(\lambda)$ and $\textbf{Ideal}_{\mathcal{A},\text{Sim}_{\Sigma_f}}(\lambda)$ are computationally indistinguishable.

We construct such a simulator Sim_{Σ_f} which adaptively simulates the extra data structure T_{sig} and query tokens. Let Sim_{Σ_f} be the simulator of the Σ_f. We simulate the algorithms in Fig. 3.

Since, in each entry, the signature generated in T_{sig} is of the form $g^{\alpha m r}$ and corresponding entry in $\widetilde{T}_{sig}$ is of the form $g^{\alpha r'}$, where r is pseudo-random (as R is so) and r' is randomly taken, we can say that power of g in both are indistinguishable. Hence, T_{sig} and $\widetilde{T}_{sig}$ are indistinguishable.

Besides, the indistinguishability of $\widetilde{\tau}_u^{\Psi_f}$, $\widetilde{\tau}_s^{\Psi_f}$ with respect to $\tau_s^{\Psi_f}$, $\tau_u^{\Psi_f}$ respectively follows from the pseudo-randomness of F.

4.2 Deletion Support

Ψ_f can be extended to deletion support by duplicating it. Together with Ψ_f for addition, a duplicate Ψ_f' can be kept for deleted files. During search, the auditor verifies both separately. The client gets result from both Ψ_f and Ψ_f', accepts only if both are verified and gets the final result calculating the difference.

5   Comparison with Existing Schemes

We have compared our verifiable DSSE scheme Ψ_f with verifiable dynamic schemes by Yoneyama and Kimura [23], Bost and Fouque [3], Miao et al. [14], Zhu et al. [26] and Jiang et al. [9]. The comparison is shown in Table 2. From the table, it can be observed that Ψ_f is very efficient with respect to low resource owner. Extra computation needed by the owner, to verify the search, is only $|R_w|$ multiplication which very less from the others. The owner also does not require any extra storage than the built in forward secure DSSE scheme.

Table 2. Comparison of verifiable dynamic SSE schemes

Scheme name	Forward privacy	Public verifia-bility	Extra Storage		Extra Computation			Extra Communication	
			Owner	Cloud	Owner	Cloud	Auditor	Owner	Auditor
Yoneyama and Kimura [23]	✓	✗	$O(|W|)$	$O(|W|log|\mathcal{DB}|)$	$O(|R_w|)$	$O(|R_w|)$	–	$O(1)$	–
Bost and Fouque [3]	✗	✗	$O(|W|)$	$O(|W|)$	$O(|R_w|)$	$O(1)$	–	$O(1)$	–
Miao et al. [14]	✗	✓	$O(|W|)$	$O(N+|W|)$	$O(|R_w|)$	$O(|R_w|)$	–	$O(1)$	–
Zhu et al. [26]	✗	✗	$O(1)$	$O(1)$	$O(|R_w|)$	$O(|R_w|+N)$	–	$O(|R_w|)$	–
Jiang et al. [9]	✗	✓	$O(1)$	$O(|W|)$	$O(\log|W|)$	$O(|R_w|+N)$	–	$O(1)$	–
Ψ_f	✓	✓	$O(1)$	$O(N)$	$O(|R_w|)$	$O(|R_w|)$	$O(1)$	$O(1)$	$O(1)$

Where N is the #keyword-doc pairs. Here extra storage is calculated over all storage, extra communication and computation are for a single search.

6 Conclusion

Throughout, we have seen that we have successfully presented a publicly verifiable dynamic SSE scheme which is are simple and easy to integrate. Moreover, the VDSSE scheme achieves forward secrecy. In the scheme, we have achieved our target to make efficient for low-resource owner. Due to low computational and communication cost of the owner, we do need an auditor. The presence of the auditor, who verifies the search result, reduces workload of the owner.

Our proposed scheme is only for single keyword search queries. There are many other complex queries too. As a future work, one can design complex queried verifiable DSSE scheme. On the other hand, while designing, keeping them forward secret is also a challenging direction of research.

References

1. Azraoui, M., Elkhiyaoui, K., Önen, M., Molva, R.: Publicly verifiable conjunctive keyword search in outsourced databases. In: 2015 IEEE Conference on Communications and Network Security, CNS 2015, Florence, Italy, 28–30 September 2015, pp. 619–627 (2015)
2. Bost, R.: $\sum o\varphi o\varsigma$: forward secure searchable encryption. In: Proceedings of the 2016 ACM SIGSAC Conference on Computer and Communications Security, Vienna, Austria, 24–28 October 2016, pp. 1143–1154 (2016)
3. Bost, R., Fouque, P., Pointcheval, D.: Verifiable dynamic symmetric searchable encryption: optimality and forward security. IACR Cryptol. ePrint Arch. **2016**, 62 (2016)
4. Bost, R., Minaud, B., Ohrimenko, O.: Forward and backward private searchable encryption from constrained cryptographic primitives. In: Proceedings of the 2017 ACM SIGSAC Conference on Computer and Communications Security, CCS 2017, Dallas, TX, USA, 30 October–03 November 2017, pp. 1465–1482 (2017)
5. Chai, Q., Gong, G.: Verifiable symmetric searchable encryption for semi-honest-but-curious cloud servers. In: Proceedings of IEEE International Conference on Communications, ICC 2012, Ottawa, ON, Canada, 10–15 June 2012, pp. 917–922 (2012)
6. Chase, M., Kamara, S.: Structured encryption and controlled disclosure. In: Abe, M. (ed.) ASIACRYPT 2010. LNCS, vol. 6477, pp. 577–594. Springer, Heidelberg (2010). https://doi.org/10.1007/978-3-642-17373-8_33
7. Cheng, R., Yan, J., Guan, C., Zhang, F., Ren, K.: Verifiable searchable symmetric encryption from indistinguishability obfuscation. In: Proceedings of the 10th ACM Symposium on Information, Computer and Communications Security, ASIA CCS 2015, Singapore, 14–17 April 2015, pp. 621–626 (2015)
8. Curtmola, R., Garay, J.A., Kamara, S., Ostrovsky, R.: Searchable symmetric encryption: improved definitions and efficient constructions. In: Proceedings of the 13th ACM Conference on Computer and Communications Security, CCS 2006, Alexandria, VA, USA, 30 October–3 November 2006, pp. 79–88 (2006)

9. Jiang, S., Zhu, X., Guo, L., Liu, J.: Publicly verifiable boolean query over outsourced encrypted data. In: 2015 IEEE Global Communications Conference, GLOBECOM 2015, San Diego, CA, USA, 6–10 December 2015, pp. 1–6 (2015)

10. Kamara, S., Papamanthou, C., Roeder, T.: Dynamic searchable symmetric encryption. In: The ACM Conference on Computer and Communications Security, CCS 2012, Raleigh, NC, USA, 16–18 October 2012, pp. 965–976 (2012)

11. Li, Y., Zhou, F., Qin, Y., Lin, M., Xu, Z.: Integrity-verifiable conjunctive keyword searchable encryption in cloud storage. Int. J. Inf. Sec. **17**(5), 549–568 (2018)

12. van Liesdonk, P., Sedghi, S., Doumen, J., Hartel, P., Jonker, W.: Computationally efficient searchable symmetric encryption. In: Jonker, W., Petković, M. (eds.) SDM 2010. LNCS, vol. 6358, pp. 87–100. Springer, Heidelberg (2010). https://doi.org/10.1007/978-3-642-15546-8_7

13. Liu, Z., Li, T., Li, P., Jia, C., Li, J.: Verifiable searchable encryption with aggregate keys for data sharing system. Future Gener. Comp. Syst. **78**, 778–788 (2018)

14. Miao, M., Wang, J., Wen, S., Ma, J.: Publicly verifiable database scheme with efficient keyword search. Inf. Sci. **475**, 18–28 (2019)

15. Miao, Y., Ma, J., Wei, F., Liu, Z., Wang, X.A., Lu, C.: VCSE: verifiable conjunctive keywords search over encrypted data without secure-channel. Peer-to-Peer Netw. Appl. **10**(4), 995–1007 (2017)

16. Ogata, W., Kurosawa, K.: Efficient no-dictionary verifiable searchable symmetric encryption. In: Kiayias, A. (ed.) FC 2017. LNCS, vol. 10322, pp. 498–516. Springer, Cham (2017). https://doi.org/10.1007/978-3-319-70972-7_28

17. Sardar, L., Ruj, S.: The secure link prediction problem. Adv. Math. Commun. **13**(4), 733–757 (2019)

18. Soleimanian, A., Khazaei, S.: Publicly verifiable searchable symmetric encryption based on efficient cryptographic components. Des. Codes Crypt. **87**(1), 123–147 (2019)

19. Sun, S., et al.: Practical backward-secure searchable encryption from symmetric puncturable encryption. In: Proceedings of the 2018 ACM SIGSAC Conference on Computer and Communications Security, CCS 2018, Toronto, ON, Canada, 15–19 October 2018, pp. 763–780 (2018)

20. Sun, W., Liu, X., Lou, W., Hou, Y.T., Li, H.: Catch you if you lie to me: efficient verifiable conjunctive keyword search over large dynamic encrypted cloud data. In: 2015 IEEE Conference on Computer Communications, INFOCOM 2015, Kowloon, Hong Kong, 26 April–1 May 2015, pp. 2110–2118 (2015)

21. Wang, J., Chen, X., Sun, S.-F., Liu, J.K., Au, M.H., Zhan, Z.-H.: Towards efficient verifiable conjunctive keyword search for large encrypted database. In: Lopez, J., Zhou, J., Soriano, M. (eds.) ESORICS 2018. LNCS, vol. 11099, pp. 83–100. Springer, Cham (2018). https://doi.org/10.1007/978-3-319-98989-1_5

22. Xu, C., Zhang, C., Xu, J.: vChain: enabling verifiable boolean range queries over blockchain databases. CoRR abs/1812.02386 (2018)

23. Yoneyama, K., Kimura, S.: Verifiable and forward secure dynamic searchable symmetric encryption with storage efficiency. In: Qing, S., Mitchell, C., Chen, L., Liu, D. (eds.) ICICS 2017. LNCS, vol. 10631, pp. 489–501. Springer, Cham (2018). https://doi.org/10.1007/978-3-319-89500-0_42

24. Zhang, R., Xue, R., Yu, T., Liu, L.: PVSAE: a public verifiable searchable encryption service framework for outsourced encrypted data. In: IEEE International Conference on Web Services, ICWS 2016, San Francisco, CA, USA, 27 June–2 July 2016, pp. 428–435 (2016)

25. Zhang, Y., Katz, J., Papamanthou, C.: All your queries are belong to us: the power of file-injection attacks on searchable encryption. In: 25th USENIX Security Symposium, USENIX Security 16, Austin, TX, USA, 10–12 August 2016, pp. 707–720 (2016)
26. Zhu, X., Liu, Q., Wang, G.: A novel verifiable and dynamic fuzzy keyword search scheme over encrypted data in cloud computing. In: 2016 IEEE Trustcom/BigDataSE/ISPA, Tianjin, China, 23–26 August 2016, pp. 845–851 (2016)

A Hidden Markov Model-Based Method for Virtual Machine Anomaly Detection

Chaochen Shi[1($\boxtimes$)] and Jiangshan Yu[2]

[1] China Mobile IoT Ltd., Chongqing, China
2011212793@bupt.edu.cn
[2] Monash University, Melbourne, Australia
jiangshan.yu@monash.edu

Abstract. The normal operation of virtual machine is a necessity for supporting cloud service. Motivated by the great desire of automated abmornal operation detection, this paper proposes a Hidden Markov Model-based method to conduct anomaly detection of virtual machine. This model can depict normal outline base of virtual machine operation and detect system outliers through calculating non-match rate. Through verifying the method in a real distributed environment, experiment results indicate that this method has 1.1%–4.9% better detection accuracy compared with two leading benchmarks with a much better efficiency.

Keywords: Hidden Markov Model · Virtual machine · Anomaly detection · Cloud computing

1 Introduction

Cloud computing uses virtualization technology to achieve abstract processing and dynamic allocation of computing resources. However, as the scale of cloud-service continues to expand, the current virtualization environment encounters many hidden security dangers, such as virtual machine sprawl and hardware performance bottle-neck [1]. All of them lead to the failure rate of cloud environment staying at a high level. Anomaly detection strategy can check the abnormal behavior of the system in time and notify the administrator to take actions to keep the virtual machine running properly. Thus, to improve the security of cloud-computing system, it is of vital significance to conduct anomaly detection for virtual machine.

The Hidden Markov Model (HMM) [2] has been well applied in the fields of genetic analysis and natural language processing, but it has not been applied in virtual machine anomaly detection. Because the sample space of virtual machine in cloud environment is large and contains various running parameters, the data stream is a complex time-varying discrete time series. The HMM is a powerful statistical tool for describing such discrete-time data samples, which can better represent the running state of the virtual machine, so the established model is

© Springer Nature Switzerland AG 2019
R. Steinfeld and T. H. Yuen (Eds.): ProvSec 2019, LNCS 11821, pp. 372–380, 2019.
https://doi.org/10.1007/978-3-030-31919-9_24

more representative and accurate than traditional models. In addition, it only needs a small amount of data in normal state to build a nearly complete feature database by HMM; the feature library established by HMM method is small, so the system exceptions can be detected more quickly; higher mismatching rate between normal and abnormal states can be obtained by using HMM method, so as to distinguish normal and abnormal states more efficiently.

Considering advantages mentioned above, this paper presents a HMM-based virtual machine anomaly detection method. This method aims to use the HMM to distinguish between normal and abnormal virtual machine running states and to train and test in a real cloud environment. The basic idea is: building up corresponding Hidden Markov prediction model and collecting the externally observable performance data of virtual machine to train HMM. When virtual machine is operating, deploy the trained HMM to detect the operating system by collecting data in real time. This method can give full play to the advantages of HMM, achieving rapid and accurate detection of virtual machine anomalies without long-time model training.

The rest of this paper is constructed as follows. Section 2 introduces the related work. Section 3 illustrates the modelling and training methods of HMM. Section 4 gives the detection strategy based on the trained model. Evaluation methods and experiment results are given in Sect. 5. Finally, the conclusion and further study are provided in Sect. 6.

2   Related Work

Related research in the area of anomaly detection methods can be categorized into two main areas as follows:

The first strategy is based on the clustering algorithm. Smith et al. [3] used Self-Organization Maps (SOM) and other clustering algorithms to realize data cluster, then determined the outliers through calculating the distances from test data to their nearest centers of clusters. However, if outliers are many enough to form individual clusters, clustering algorithm is difficult to detect this kind of outliers.

The second strategy is based on the nearest neighbors. Breunig et al. [4] proposed a nearest neighbor-based anomaly detection algorithm LOF (Local Outlier Factor). This algorithm puts forward the "local outlier" concept. When conducting anomaly decision towards any target in the data concentration, it only considers the local spatial region of the target. Compared with traditional algorithm detection, this algorithm has higher accuracy when the sample data is not evenly distributed.

There are some other anomaly detection methods that could be used as the basis of further study, such as algorithms based on neural network [5] and Bayesian network [6]. In general, clustering and nearest neighbor algorithms have disadvantages of high randomness and instability when processing mixed data in virtual machine environment. Classifiers like SVM need massive labeled data. In summary, methods with high accuracy, small feature library and short detection period are rare. In this paper, we introduce HMM-based anomaly detection method to fill the gap in the literature of cloud scenarios.

3 Formal Model

Hidden Markov Model is a dual random process and composed of two aspects; one is implicit Markov chain that describes state transition, the other is common random process that describes the corresponding relationship between states and observed event sequence. Supposing the observed sequence of this model is $O = \{O_1, O_2, \ldots, O_T\}$, the HMM system can be described by a quintuplet $\lambda = \{N, M, \pi, A, B\}$. The notations used in the scheme are summarized in Table 1, where the probability of an event A is written as $P(A)$.

Table 1. Notations used in the scheme

N	The number of states, the set of states is $S = \{S_1, S_2, \ldots, S_N\}$
M	The number of observations, the set of observations is $V = \{V_1, V_2, \ldots, V_M\}$
A	The transition probability matrix between hidden states q, $A = \{a_{ij}\}, a_{ij} = P(q_{t+1} = S_j \mid q_t = S_i), 1 \leq i, j \leq N$
B	The probability matrix of observable states, $B = \{b_{jk}\}, b_{jk} = P(O_t = V_k \mid q_t = S_j), 1 \leq k \leq M$
π	An initial probability distribution over states, $\pi = \{\pi_i\}, \pi_i = P(q_1 = i), 1 \leq i \leq N$

To build up a Hidden Markov Model, firstly, the state sets and monitor sets of the model should be decided. Other three parameters, π, A, B, can either be set artificially or be acquired with samples. According to the definition of HMM, they should satisfy the following relation:

$$\sum_{i=1}^{N} \pi_i = \sum_{j=1}^{N} a_{ij} = \sum_{k=1}^{M} b_{jk} = 1 \tag{1}$$

For virtual machine, property indexes during system operation can be divided into a time-varying discrete-time data sequence after sampling. The Hidden Markov Model is a powerful statistical tool for describing discrete-time data sequence. It has the ability of processing non-linear time-varying signal, so it can be applied to describe the statistical law existing between the property index and operation state of virtual machine. As stated above, the Hidden Markov Model is a dual random process. The application of it here corresponds with two sequences, one is hidden sequence of the internal operation state of virtual machine, the other is observable virtual machine property index sequence. The application of HMM in anomaly detection can be transformed into two main procedures:

(1) The training model enables it to depict the normal operation outline of virtual machine;

(2) The under-detection property index sequence of virtual machine is transmitted into the model after completion of training. If it does not fit in with the normal out-line, the system is abnormal.

This paper deploys the state set S to represent the state space of the system. Due to the complexity of computer system [1], the definition of virtual machine operation states is difficult to be generalized in a concrete way, so here the state is comprehended as an abstract concept. In this paper, the state set S is set to be $S = \{0, 1\}$, 0 represents normal state while 1 represents abnormal state. The state amounts N is 2.The monitor set V in this paper is a property index set of virtual machines.

In this paper, we choose Baum-Welch algorithm [7] to gradually learn three parameters π, A, B of model λ from the training sample X. It belongs to a normal EM iterative method. Repeating E-procedure and M-procedure until values of π_i, a_{ij}, b_{jk} satisfy the convergence condition, and thus acquiring the trained Hidden Markov Model.

4 Detection Strategy

The principle of detection is based on the conclusion that the normal behavior pattern of virtual machine is consistent, and the exception will only cause the drastic change of behavior pattern in a local range [9]. That is to say, the normal state transition vector is stable, and the state transition vector obtained during normal operation of the system should belong to the normal outline base. Once it is found that the state transition vector is not in the normal outline base, it indicates an exception. This section introduces the method of establishing normal outline base and the corresponding anomaly detection method.

4.1 Acquiring the Best Transition Sequence

The hidden state sequence of the model can reflect the system operation situation more stable than the observable sequence. After the model training, state sequence of normal operation is able to be input to the model and its corresponding best state transition sequence would be acquired. The corresponding model decoding problem can be solved by Viterbi algorithm [8]:

step 1: Setting the hidden system state q_t to be S_j at the t moment, hidden state path $Q = (q_1, q_2, \ldots, q_t)\,(q_{t-1} = S_i, q_t = S_j)$. Viterbi variable $\delta_t(i)$ is the maximum probability of observable sequence $O = (O_1, O_2, \ldots, O_t)$. Thus,

$$\delta_t(i) = \max_{1 \leq j \leq N} [\delta_{t-1}(j) \cdot a_{ji}] \cdot b_{ik_t}, (2 \leq t \leq T; 1 \leq i \leq N) \qquad (2)$$

Setting $\varphi_t(i)$ to be the precedent state of current hidden state q_t on the state path of maximum probability, thus,

$$\varphi_t(i) = \arg \max_{1 \leq j \leq N} [\delta_{t-1}(j) \cdot a_{ji}], (2 \leq t \leq T; 1 \leq i \leq N) \tag{3}$$

step 2: Deploying Viterbi algorithm to acquire the biggest final state $q_T{}^*$:

$$q_T{}^* = \arg \max_{1 \leq j \leq N} [\delta_T(i)] \tag{4}$$

step 3: Each hidden state $q_t{}^*$ can be acquired through backtracking of state sequence path:

$$q_t{}^* = \varphi_{t+1}(j)(q_{t+1}{}^*), t = (T-1, T-2, \ldots, 1) \tag{5}$$

4.2   Setting up Normal Outline Base

The application of the method in Sect. 4.1 brings about virtual machine state transition sequence $Q = (q_1, q_2, \ldots, q_T)$ which corresponds to virtual machine property index sequence $O = (O_1, O_2, \ldots, O_T)$. O_i represents the i property index vector in chronological arrangement, $o_i \in \{V_1, V_2, \ldots, V_M\}$; q_i represents the i state in chronological arrangement, $q_i \in \{S_1, S_2, \ldots, S_N\}$. The size of sliding window is x. When the sliding window slides the sequence Q successively, a normal state transition vector e can be acquired each time a state slides. Similarly, the sliding window slides all the sequences and the normal state transition vector set $E' \in \{e_1, e_2, \ldots, e_{r-x+1}\}$ can be acquired, among them, $e_i = (q_i, q_{i+1}, \ldots, q_{i+x-1})$. After taking out the same normal state transition vectors in E', the else constitute the normal outline base E of the system.

4.3   Detection Method

The detection principle bases on such a conclusion: the normal property indexes of virtual machine have significant consistency, outliers usually cause property indexes to change dramatically within a mere local range [9]. That is, the acquired state transition vector e should belong to normal outline base during the normal operation of virtual machine. Once state transition vectors that appear intensively and are outside the normal outline base are discovered, virtual machine is found abnormal.

To verify in the real case, within the period of virtual machine being monitored, the sampled property parameter sequence of the system is $O^* = (o_1, o_2, \ldots, o_s)$. Through the sliding window method mentioned in section B, state transition vector set $E^* = (e_1, e_2, \ldots, e_{s-x+1})$ is acquired, among them $e_i = (q_i, q_{i+1}, \ldots, q_{i+x-1})$, $q_i \in \{S_1, S_2, \ldots, S_N\}$. Because normal outline base has included all the normal state transition vectors, what we need to do is finding out whether E contains a matching vector of e_i. There are many methods for matching, this paper deploys the most common matching method, complete matching, to search for the totally same state transition vector in normal outline base. If the matching fails, e_i is a mismatching state transition vector. Supposing the amount of mismatching state transition vectors is l, the mismatching rate of the normal state transition sequence is:

$$\eta = \frac{l}{s - x + 1} \times 100\% \tag{6}$$

η can well reflect outliers of virtual machine, the lower the η is, the more normal the performance of virtual machine is. The threshold of η can be set flexibly to adjust the sensitivity of anomaly detection in reality (0.1 in this paper). The framework of the algorithm is shown as Algorithm 1:

Algorithm 1. Framework of anomaly detection for virtual machine.

---

input: The sampled system property parameter sequence, O^*; A sliding window of size k; The normal outline base, E; The threshold of anomaly judgement θ;

output: The result of anomaly detection, F (normal or abnormal);

1: Initializing $N = 0$, $l = 0$, $F = normal$. Inputting O^* into trained Hidden Markov Model as observed sequence and getting the state transition sequence Q^* with Viterbi algorithm;

2: Dividing Q^* with the sliding window, getting the state transition vector set E^*;

3: Take a vector e_i from E^*, finding the matching vector in E. If it is not found, go to step 4; If all the vectors in E^* are taken, **return** F;

4: $l = l + 1$, calculating η. If $\eta \geq \theta$, $F = abnormal$, **return** F; If not, go to step 3.

---

5   Experiment Environment and Results

5.1   Experiment Environment

This experiment bases on cluster built up by five servers, including one control node and four computing nodes. Computing nodes belong to the same local area network and have same soft hardware, they can be regarded as isomorphic nodes. The experiment deploys open-source OpenStack Juno to set up a virtual machine cluster. Each computing node is arranged three virtual machines and installed CentOS 7.4-version operating system. Libxenstat, libvirt and other tools collect the system property index vectors of the detected target (virtual machine) during the experiment. In addition, Detection Virtual Machine is solely arranged. DVM is a dedicated virtual machine for anomaly detection, it is equipped with corresponding anomaly detection programs and used as an anomaly detection node. Resources of DVM can be configured dynamically according to the load size of detection tasks (the scale of detected target).In this experimental environment, we collected 20 consecutive hours of normal operation data of virtual machines as model training samples.

Virtual machines in the cloud environment suffer various types of failures, which can be divided into system failures and network failures. Among system failures, memory faults and CPU faults are the most common and the most representative. For example, memory leak causes a waste of system memory, which slows down the running speed of programs and even lead to the crash of the cloud system; CPU hog causes processes to be unresponsive and accelerates chip aging. Among the network failures, network hog caused by excess HTTP requests are prone to occur in the cloud environment with high data traffic, resulting in increased network resource occupancy, congestion or outage of network services. This paper deploys the subjective injecting fault method to simulate abnormalities of virtual machine. Three types of representative faults mentioned above are injected by Sysbench standard testingprogram, the total number of injected faults is 50.

5.2   Experiment Results

To verify the validity of HMM-based method in this paper, two typical anomaly detection methods SOM-based and LOF were compared in the same experiment environment and acquired corresponding experiment result as Tables 2, 3 and 4.

Table 2. The detection result with memory fault injection

Method	Number of detected anomalies	Number of faults	Precision	Recall Rate	F-measure	Average time cost (s)
HMM-based	50	48	96.0%	96.0%	96.0%	0.21
SOM-based	52	46	92.4%	90.7%	91.5%	0.31
LOF	54	49	93.6%	88.9%	91.1%	0.23

Table 3. The detection result with CPU fault injection

Method	Number of detected anomalies	Number of faults	Precision	Recall Rate	F-measure	Average time cost (s)
HMM-based	51	47	94.1%	92.2%	93.1%	0.27
SOM-based	52	46	90.5%	93.6%	92.0%	0.41
LOF	54	49	89.2%	94.9%	91.9%	0.30

Table 4. The detection result with network I/O fault injection

Method	Number of detected anomalies	Number of faults	Precision	Recall Rate	F-measure	Average time cost (s)
HMM-based	49	45	90.1%	89.6%	89.8%	0.28
SOM-based	50	47	87.7%	84.0%	85.8%	0.46
LOF	53	46	91.3%	87.3%	89.3%	0.33

Tables 2, 3 and 4 represent the performance of three anomaly detection methods with three kinds of fault injection. From the tables we can see the HMM-based method in this paper performs better in all three situations. The F measure of HMM-based model keeps the highest in all three cases. It also has faster detecting speed and 1.1%-4.9% better detection accuracy compared with two benchmarks. The reason is that the collected property indexes well describe these fault situations. Even the training samples are not sufficient to train a perfect HMM, the F-measure can still remain at a high level. By contrast, the performance of SOM-based and LOF method is limited by the high dimensional data or insufficient training data. In addition, the detection time cost of HMM-based method is relatively low for the simple matching method. Therefore, this HMM-based method has certain universality in the virtual machine environment.

6 Conclusion and Further Study

According to common regularity indicated by system parameters when virtual machine is operating normally, this paper proposes a method for virtual machine anomaly detection via Hidden Markov Model as well as experiments this method in the real virtual machine operation environment through the means of fault injection. Experiment results shows that compared with traditional LOF and SOM-based algorithm, method in this paper has better performance, less time cost and better accuracy in virtual machine anomaly detection.

There is practical significance in studying and developing HMM-based anomaly detection systems. Furthermore, there are still some details to be explored. For example, how to effectively locate the source of exceptions? And how to predict possible system failures before it happened? In a future study, we intend to apply our method to other kinds of virtual machine systems, such as EVM [10] in Ethereum system.

References

1. Goldberg, R.P.: Survey of virtual machine research. Computer **7**, 34–45 (1974)
2. Rabiner, L.R.: A tutorial on Hidden Markov models and selected applications in speech recognition, **77**(2), 257–286 (1989)
3. Smith, R., Bivens, A., Embrechts, M., Palagiri, C., Szymanski, B.: Clustering approaches for anomaly based intrusion detection. In: Proceedings of Intelligent Engineering Systems Through Artificial Neural Networks, pp. 579–584 (2002)
4. Breunig, M.M., Kriegel, H.-P., Ng, R.T., Sander, J.: LOF: identifying density-based local outliers. In: ACM Sigmod Record, pp. 93–104. ACM
5. Sani, Y., Mohamedou, A., Ali, K., Farjamfar, A., Azman, M., Shamsuddin, S.: An overview of neural networks use in anomaly intrusion detection systems. In: 2009 IEEE Student Conference on Research and Development (SCOReD), pp. 89–92. IEEE (2009)
6. Tylman, W.: Anomaly-based intrusion detection using Bayesian networks. In: Third International Conference on Dependability of Computer Systems, DepCos-RELCOMEX 2008, pp. 211–218. IEEE (2008)

7. Welch, L.R.: Hidden Markov models and the Baum-Welch algorithm. IEEE Inf. Theory Soc. Newsl. **53**, 10–13 (2003)
8. Forney, G.D.: The viterbi algorithm. Proc. IEEE **61**, 268–278 (1973)
9. Chandola, V., Banerjee, A., Kumar, V.: Anomaly detection: a survey. ACM Comput. Surv. (CSUR) **41**, 15 (2009)
10. Hirai, Y.: Defining the Ethereum virtual machine for interactive theorem provers. In: Brenner, M., et al. (eds.) FC 2017. LNCS, vol. 10323, pp. 520–535. Springer, Cham (2017). https://doi.org/10.1007/978-3-319-70278-0_33

Author Index

Printed in the United States
By Bookmasters